CONTEMPORARY PUBLIC SPEAKING

SECOND EDITION

CONTEMPORARY PUBLIC SPEAKING

SECOND EDITION

Courtland L. Bovée

C. Allen Paul Distinguished Chair
Grossmont College

CONSULTING EDITORS

JoAnn Edwards
University of Mississippi

Jon A. Hess
University of Missouri, Columbia

Cynthia Irizarry
Stetson University

Shannon McCraw
Southeastern Oklahoma State University

Timothy P. Meyer
University of Wisconsin, Green Bay

Louis J. Rosso
Winthrop University

Collegiate Press

Collegiate Press
San Diego, California

This book was published in its first edition by Harcourt Brace & Company
under the title of *Excellence in Public Speaking*.

Publisher: Christopher Stanford
Executive Editor: Steven Barta
Senior Developmental Editor: Jackie Estrada
Interior Design: John Odam
Cover Design: John Odam

Credits and acknowledgments can be found beginning on page 483,
which constitutes a continuation of this copyright page.

Library of Congress Control Number: 2002117128

ISBN: 0-939693-60-7

Printed in the Republic of China

10 9 8 7 6 5 4 3 2 1

Contents

C H A P T E R   O N E

INTRODUCING PUBLIC SPEAKING

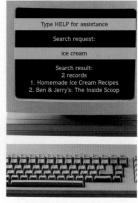

C H A P T E R   T W O

OVERCOMING ANXIETY AND GIVING YOUR FIRST SPEECH

C H A P T E R   T H R E E

FREE SPEECH AND ETHICAL RESPONSIBILITIES

Special Features

C H A P T E R   F O U R

IMPROVING YOUR LISTENING SKILLS

Part Two Preparing the Speech

C H A P T E R   F I V E

DEVELOPING YOUR TOPIC, PURPOSE, AND CENTRAL IDEA

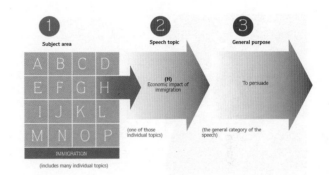

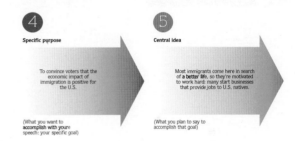

C H A P T E R   S I X

ANALYZING YOUR AUDIENCE

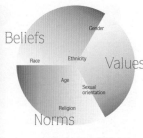

C H A P T E R   S E V E N

SUPPORTING YOUR SPEECH

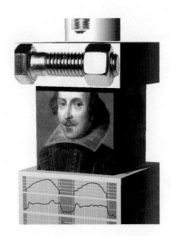

Special Features

GATHERING YOUR SUPPORT MATERIALS

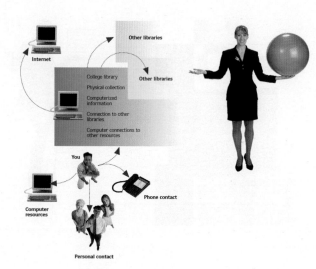

Part Three Organizing the Speech

C H A P T E R   N I N E
ORGANIZING YOUR SPEECH

Special Features

 Organizing a Speech: Do's and Taboos of
     Addressing International Audiences 192

 What You Don't Say May Be Used Against
     You 201

C H A P T E R   T E N

INTRODUCING AND CONCLUDING YOUR SPEECH

C H A P T E R   E L E V E N

OUTLINING YOUR SPEECH

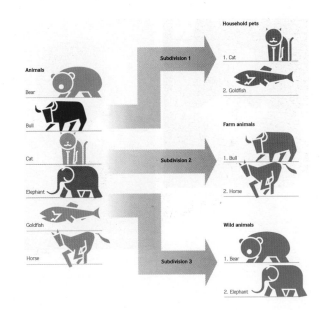

Special Features

Part Four **Presenting the Speech**

C H A P T E R   T W E L V E
WORDING YOUR SPEECH

C H A P T E R   T H I R T E E N

USING VISUAL AIDS

Special Features

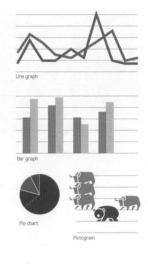

Line graph

Bar graph

Pie chart

Pictogram

C H A P T E R   F O U R T E E N

REHEARSING AND DELIVERING YOUR SPEECH

CHAPTER FIFTEEN
SPEAKING TO INFORM

Special Features

 How to Paint Powerful Word Pictures that
    Bring Your Speeches Vividly to Life 325

 Cause and Effect: Can You Support Your
    Claims? 333

C H A P T E R   S I X T E E N

SPEAKING TO PERSUADE

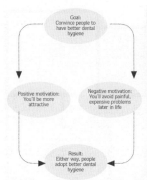

Special Features

Beliefs, Attitudes, and Values: Why You Should Analyze These Hidden Audience Attributes 352

How to Minimize the Agony of Negative Audience Reaction 359

C H A P T E R S E V E N T E E N

DEVELOPING PERSUASIVE ARGUMENTS

Special Features

CHAPTER NINETEEN
SPEAKING IN SMALL GROUPS

B A C K   M A T T E R

APPENDIXES, CREDITS, AND INDEX

Preface

One voice can make a difference—and so can one book. Our goal in developing *Contemporary Public Speaking* has been to help students gain the skills and the confidence to prepare and deliver speeches that will make a difference in their communities, their careers, and their personal lives. To become more effective communicators (and more effective listeners), students need classroom instruction, independent study of chapter concepts, and practice (in planning, delivering, and analyzing speeches). Our text is specifically designed to facilitate that learning process.

The number one problem faced by most students taking a public speaking course is speech anxiety. Although no text can substitute for the experience of addressing an audience, *Contemporary Public Speaking* devotes an entire chapter (Chapter 2) to reassuring students that nerves are normal. This text helps students transform anxiety into excitement as they prepare for their first speech. In addition, a series of "Overcoming Speech Anxiety" boxes are strategically placed throughout the text, providing practical ideas that help students at all skill levels develop more confidence in their ability to speak to an audience.

Of course, understanding theory is important, and students need to see concrete examples of how concepts are actually applied. This text helps students learn by example as they study the sample excerpts, outlines, and complete speeches that appear in every chapter. Most of our examples are drawn from actual classroom speeches. In many chapters, students can study the contrast between poor and improved examples, as well as compare their own work to the models in the text. These concrete examples not only reinforce the underlying principle but make the vital connection between theory and practice.

The ethical and social responsibilities of speakers are no less important today than they were in the days of the great Greek and Roman orators. A full chapter (Chapter 3) guides students through a careful examination of the individual rights, social responsibilities, and the ethical obligations of contemporary public speakers. In addition, "Focusing on Ethics" boxes are positioned throughout the text, highlighting specific ethical dilemmas. Moreover, examples and exercises have been integrated into the text of individual chapters to call students' attention to important ethical issues.

Sensitivity to cultural diversity is an ongoing theme in *Contemporary Public Speaking*. This text respects students of all backgrounds and promotes respect for diversity in both speakers and audience members. Starting in Chapter 1, students learn strategies for addressing culturally diverse audiences. Coverage of intercultural issues continues throughout the book in examples and illustrations, as well as in "Speaking Across Cultures" boxes placed in carefully selected chapters.

The study of public speaking has been supported through the years by voluminous research. In preparing *Contemporary Public Speaking* , we sought to ensure the book's scholarly integrity by consulting thousands of sources, including academic, consumer, trade, and professional journals and publications. This solid foundation of research ensures that the text reflects current thinking, as well as giving students a thorough grounding in classical theories.

Public speaking is as much an art as a science; to be able to inform, persuade, or entertain an audience, students need to do more than simply read a text. That's why we designed this book to work in conjunction with classroom instruction and practice. With *Contemporary Public Speaking* students can learn the underlying principles, understand how and why these principles are applied, and use these principles as they polish their skills. Ultimately, being able to speak and listen more effectively will help students make a difference in the world around them.

SOLID CONTENT BRINGS PUBLIC SPEAKING INTO THE TWENTY-FIRST CENTURY

The dynamic field of public speaking continues to evolve as technological advances, cultural trends, and other factors influence the way people research, draft, and deliver speeches. *Contemporary Public Speaking* includes all the traditional fundamentals as well as the hottest issues in public speaking today. This comprehensive coverage provides students with the tools they need to analyze and apply public speaking principles.

Explores Major Public Speaking Themes

A series of thirty-eight boxed special features offer insights into key themes:

- *Speaking Across Cultures* provides practical ideas about addressing culturally diverse audiences.
- *Developing Your Creativity* shows how to apply creative thinking in public speaking situations.
- *Improving Your Critical Thinking* helps students develop their ability to analyze and evaluate issues.

- *Overcoming Speech Anxiety* reinforces attitudes and practices that reduce nervousness.
- *Focusing on Ethics* discusses the complex ethical dilemmas that challenge public speakers.

Designated with an icon, each of these boxes is strategically placed throughout the book.

Emphasizes Ethical Speaking

This text encourages students to develop high ethical standards by helping them explore the ethical issues and responsibilities that challenge today's speakers. *Contemporary Public Speaking* draws a clear distinction between ethical dilemmas and ethical lapses, helping students understand the difference between unresolved ethical questions and behavior that is simply unethical. The book covers ethics in three ways: in a full chapter (Chapter 3), in numerous theme boxes, and in examples and exercises in selected chapters.

Demonstrates Public Speaking Throughout the World

Because today's student's—tomorrow's communicators— interact with people from many countries at school, at work, and in the community, *Contemporary Public Speaking* demonstrates the use of public speaking throughout the world. So that students can learn from speakers in other countries as well as make themselves better understood in international settings, our text includes advice and outstanding examples from an array of countries, including China, Russia, Mexico, Japan, South Africa, Nigeria, Israel, India, The Netherlands, Sweden, and the United Kingdom.

Offers Expert Advice on Common Challenges

Many students have difficulty using humor in speeches, understanding diverse audiences, applying critical and creative thinking, reducing speech anxiety, tackling ethical issues, and handling conflicts in group meetings. Unique to this book are seven "Ask an Expert" features in which acknowledged academic specialists answer common student questions. Each feature closes with a discussion question and an application question to help students think about and apply what they've learned.

Integrates Technological Applications

To help students understand, apply, and adapt to the technological tools of communication, we have integrated public speaking technology throughout the text. This book introduces students to the specific technological developments that have an impact on all aspects of public speaking—from using the Internet and computer databases during research, to using computer software for outlines and drafts, to using computerized graphics during delivery.

Motivates Student with Accessible Content

The readability level of this text makes learning easy. The conversational style and careful attention to clarity make the text highly readable, lively, and interesting. This approachable style and reading level encourages students to move through the text painlessly, helping them gain the skills they need to become proficient public speakers.

Features Real-World Public Speaking

In textual examples and throughout the photo program, this text provides insights and advice on the art of public speaking from a wide range of individuals. Students learn not only from prominent speakers such as Colin Powell and Sandra Day O'Connor but also from their peers—other public speaking students whose speeches and ideas are quoted in the text.

Promotes Learning with a Unique Design and Exhibit Program

Because of the pervasive influence of television and film, students are conditioned to being visually stimulated while they learn. The design and illustrations in *Contemporary Public Speaking* have been developed for more than just artistic reasons. Based on extensive research, the state-of-

the-art design and the extensive photo and illustration program invite students to delve into content. Also, the design eases reading, reinforces learning, and increases comprehension.

EFFECTIVE PEDAGOGY ENHANCES STUDENT LEARNING

To complement the comprehensive content, *Contemporary Public Speaking* includes reliable learning tools that encourage skill building and enhance student understanding. Many of these pedagogical elements are unique to this text and were specially designed to support an integrated learning program for public speaking.

Instructs Students Using a Step-by-Step Presentation

Because students are guided through the public speaking process one step at a time, they can more easily understand and master the principles and skills necessary to achieve excellent results. Starting with an overview of the foundations of public speaking and proceeding through preparing, organizing, and presenting the speech, this text offers practical treatment of every topic. Tips and techniques, checklists, annotated speeches, individual and group end-of-chapter exercises, and informative photos and illustrations all contribute to the practicality of the text.

Includes Helpful Checklists

Numerous checklists throughout the book assist students in organizing their thinking, making decisions, expressing their thoughts logically, and checking their work. These checklists are located as close as possible to the related discussions. They provide useful guidelines without limiting student creativity, and they are handy for stimulating recall of effective speaking techniques.

Presents Sample Speeches and Outlines for Analysis

A variety of full-length speeches, excerpts, and outlines invite students to analyze principles in action. By reading the commentary and comparing the examples with the concepts covered in each chapter, students become more knowledge-able about the practical aspects of developing an effective speech.

Suggests Both Individual and Group Exercises

To give instructors maximum flexibility in making assignments to students, each chapter includes a variety of "Sharpen Your Skills" exercises. Some are geared to individual work; others are intended for group work.

Stimulates Critical Thinking with Thoughtful Questions

Students are challenged to improve their critical thinking skills as they answer the seven "Apply Critical Thinking" questions at the end of each chapter. In addition, "Improving Your Critical Thinking" boxes positioned throughout the text develop evaluation and analysis skills.

Offers Practical Tips for Success

Every chapter includes three or more brief "Success Tips" that highlight and reinforce important techniques for public speaking excellence.

Begins Each Chapter with Learning Objectives

At the beginning of each chapter, a concise list of goals tells students what they will be able to achieve by reading the chapter and completing the exercises. These objectives provide structure for the learning process, encourage students to expand their knowledge of the material, and serve as a measure of learning progress.

Ends Each Chapter with a Summary

End-of-chapter summaries complement the learning objectives by presenting a succinct wrap-up of each chapter's material. After reading the summaries, students are better able to comprehend the chapter concepts and applications.

Defines Key Terms

The first time an important term is introduced in the text, it is shown in boldface type, followed by its definition. At the end of that chapter, students will see every key term listed, followed by the page number where it is defined. This handy reference allows students to quickly check any definition.

EXEMPLARY SPEECHES PERMEATE THE TEXT

Because students learn by example, we have chosen only top-quality, exceptional speeches that demonstrate creativity in public speaking. Every speech and excerpt has been carefully selected to augment chapter content and show how key concepts are applied. Some of these speeches are taken from professional speakers; others are taken from students speaking on a wide variety of topics. By showcasing creative, thought-provoking examples of key concepts, we aim to encourage students to stretch their imaginations as they develop their speaking and listening abilities.

A number of chapters include annotated speeches that identify the elements of effective speeches. Full-length examples of informative, persuasive, and special occasion speeches include insightful analyses, helping students learn how to apply the same principles to their own speeches. In addition, commentaries linked to extended examples (such as a sample introduction, sample conclusion, sample planning outline, and sample speaking outline) highlight specific elements for special attention.

SOUND ORGANIZATION SUPPORTS LEARNING

Instructors and students alike will appreciate the logical yet adaptable organization of topics in this text. Beginning with an overview of the fundamentals of public speaking, the book progresses through parts that guide students through the steps in preparing, organizing, and presenting a speech. The final part includes advanced topics that are generally covered later in the course, after students have gained some experience with the basics.

Although many instructors are quite comfortable with this sequence, those who favor another approach can easily change the order of chapters to suit their needs, because each chapter's topic coverage is carefully designed to stand on its own.

Part I, "The Foundations of Public Speaking," introduces the basic elements of public speaking. In Chapter 1, students learn about the value and evolution of public speaking, the communication process, the effect of cultural diversity, and the elements that contribute to public speaking excellence. Chapter 2 helps students understand and cope with speech anxiety so that they can gain confidence in their public speaking abilities. The chapter leads students through the preparation and delivery of their first speech, and includes a sample speech of self-introduction. Chapter 3 discusses the social and ethical responsibilities of speakers, analyzes the effects and limits of free speech, and presents guidelines for ethical speaking. Chapter 4 examines the listening process and offers strategies for effective listening and speech evaluation.

Part II, "Preparing the Speech," shows how to begin the process of planning a speech. In Chapter 5, students learn how to identify a topic, define the purpose, and refine the central idea. Chapter 6 covers audience analysis, including the internal, social, and situational factors that influence audience reaction and suggestions for adapting to an audience. Chapter 7 shows how speakers can use a variety of materials to support their ideas. Chapter 8 shows how to gather support materials by drawing on personal experience, using libraries and other resources (including the Internet), and conducting interviews.

Part III, "Organizing the Speech," helps students put ideas into a logical structure. Chapter 9 demonstrates how to develop, organize, and connect the ideas in a speech. Chapter 10 explains how to plan an effective introduction and conclusion, and it includes a sample introduction and conclusion. Chapter 11 shows how to develop and use a planning outline and a speaking outline, and it includes a sample planning outline and a sample speaking outline.

Part IV, "Presenting the Speech," covers wording, visual aids, rehearsal, and delivery. In Chapter 12, students learn how to choose words that are effective, vivid, and appropriate. Chapter 13 examines the selection, preparation, and use of visual aids. Chapter 14 offers a practical guide to using voice and body language when rehearsing and then delivering speeches.

Part V, "Varieties of Public Speaking," focuses on various public speaking situations. Chapter 15 examines the development of informative speeches and includes a sample informative speech. In Chapter 16, students learn about persuasive messages and goals, motivating audiences, and managing listener response. In Chapter 17, students learn how to organize points and how to choose the appeal during the development of a persuasive argument. Chapter 18 is devoted to speaking on the job, speaking at special events, and making impromptu speeches. Chapter 19 explores the dynamics and challenges of speaking in small groups.

Appendix A suggests a number of lively, creative topics that students may want to consider for classroom speeches. Appendix B includes a variety of highly effective speeches for study, analysis, and inspiration.

RESOURCE MATERIALS SUPPORT THE TEXT

The resource materials for this textbook are specially designed to simplify the task of teaching and learning.

The comprehensive instructor's manual written by Kimberly Batty-Herbert at Clovis Community College includes course syllabi, speech evaluation forms, and more than 900 test questions.

A video features student speeches of varying quality.

ACKNOWLEDGMENTS

We are grateful to the following manuscript reviewers who made valuable suggestions and constructive comments: James Wolford, Joliet Junior College; Deborah Smith-Howell, University of Nebraska-Omaha; Mary Haslerud Opp, University of North Dakota; Bill Loftus, Austin Community College; Gary Eckles, Thomas

Nelson Community College; Kimberly Batty-Herbert, Clovis Community College; Bill Poschman, Diablo Valley College; Connie Morris, Wichita State University; James Di Sanza, Idaho State University; Laurence Hosman, University of Southern Mississippi; Katherine Thompson, University of Hawaii; Marion Couvillion, Mississippi State University; Carl Burghardt, Colorado State University; Julie James, Grand Rapids Community College; Ralph Thompson, Cornell University; Clark Olson, Arizona State University; Jacquelyn Buckrop, Ball State University; Kellie Roberts, University of Florida; and Jill Voran, Anne Arundel Community College.

We also feel it is important to acknowledge and thank the National Communication Association, an organization whose meetings and publications provide a valuable forum for the exchange of ideas and for professional growth.

Special thanks to Thomas G. Endres, University of St. Thomas, for his valuable contributions; to Terry Anderson for her outstanding ability that helped assure this project of clarity and completeness; and to Jackie Estrada for her dedication and expertise. Finally, we thank designer John Odam, art consultant Normad McLeod, and photo researcher Susan Holtz for their superb work.

Chapter One

INTRODUCING PUBLIC SPEAKING

LEARNING OBJECTIVES

After studying this chapter, you will be able to

1. Discuss how public speaking can be helpful in your personal and professional lives.

2. Trace the development of public speaking traditions in Western civilization.

3. Describe the three conversational skills and the four public speaking skills you use when addressing an audience.

4. Define communication, and differentiate between verbal and nonverbal communication.

5. Outline the communication process.

6. Define cultural diversity and examine its influence on public speaking.

7. Identify the seven ways public speakers work toward audience understanding.

PUBLIC SPEAKING AND YOU

Can one voice make a difference? The answer is definitely *yes,* as Martha Rhodes will tell you. During a public meeting with government and railroad representatives, Rhodes spoke out against a fare hike planned for the commuter railroad that serves her home in Danbury, Connecticut. "We are faced with less than optimum service on the Danbury line," she told the officials, "and yet we pay the most." Rhodes argued that since Danbury commuters weren't being served as frequently as commuters in other towns, they shouldn't have to pay the fare increase. Government officials were swayed by her words, and they decided to leave Danbury fares alone—even as other fares went up.[1]

College student Ricardo Gonzalez also knows that one voice can make a difference. Gonzalez wanted his school to become more active in recycling paper. He investigated paper use on campus and then presented the results to faculty groups and administration officials. He talked about how many trees, how much water, and how much electricity would have been saved if the college had recycled paper during the previous year. He also talked about specific actions the administration might take, such as buying only recycled paper. Persuaded by Gonzalez's presentation, several faculty groups backed his recommendations.[2]

Because of Martha Rhodes, thousands of commuters saved money on railroad tickets, and because of Ricardo Gonzalez, a college saved trees, water, and electricity. The voices of Martha Rhodes and Ricardo Gonzalez made a difference, and so can yours—whether you're for or against an issue in your school, your community, your company, or your country. Many situations—some extraordinary, some everyday—call for individuals to speak in front of others (see Exhibit 1.1).

The Many Voices of Public Speaking

If you think about why someone might address a group of people, you'll probably come up with numerous examples. Here are a few of the many voices of public speaking:

- Politicians speaking to voters
- Instructors speaking to students
- Managers speaking to employees
- Religious leaders speaking to congregations
- Coaches speaking to athletes
- Red Cross volunteers speaking to blood donors
- Citizens speaking to government officials

Sometimes these speakers are trying to achieve personal goals; other times, they're working toward career or public service goals. Whatever their objectives, all these people are engaging in **public speaking**, the process of addressing an audience effectively. Public speaking is a *process* because it involves much more than simply talking to a group. Before delivering a speech, you find out about your audience, select your topic and purpose, research the facts, organize your material, plan what you'll say, and rehearse your presentation. Only then are you prepared to address your audience.

EXHIBIT 1.1
Use Public Speaking to Make a Difference
No matter what personal or professional goals you set, you can use public speaking to make a difference.

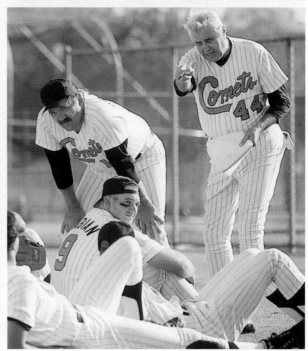

As you move through the process of public speaking, you develop a variety of skills that you can use to achieve both career and personal goals. You practice thinking clearly and logically, which helps you work through problems at work, at school, and at home. You learn about your audience, which gives you insight into how other people think and feel—an important element in building good relationships on and off the job. You gather facts and figures for a speech, which sharpens your research skills and improves your ability to find, analyze, evaluate, and use information.

In addition, you plan and deliver your speech, which gives you valuable experience in using words and actions to inform and persuade. Finally, you become a better listener, which helps you figure out what people are actually saying, allows you to examine their arguments critically, and ultimately helps you become an even better speaker. In short, as you perfect your public speaking skills, you'll become a better communicator, which can help you succeed, no matter what your goals.[3]

Most people use public speaking in work-related situations. You can also use public speaking skills to get the job or promotion you want, work well with others, build your own business, build a network of business and social contacts, and get work done properly. In fact, employers report that communication skills—both speaking and listening—are the most important factors in helping college graduates get jobs.[4]

Public speaking is also important in school. The ability to express yourself effectively in the classroom can lead to better grades. In addition, your own pride and self-confidence will grow as you learn how to express yourself—and as you discover that others not only understand what you say but are moved by it. Once you master public speaking, your voice *will* make a difference.

The Public Speaking Tradition

As you learn how to speak in public, you're continuing a tradition that, for Western civilization, began in antiquity. *Rhetoric,* the art of influencing an audience through words, was championed before 500 B.C. by Corax and Tisias, teacher and student on the island of Sicily. Both were concerned with the true meanings of words, and they acted as advisors to citizens who represented themselves in court and needed persuasive words to influence the court's decisions.[5] The work of Corax and Tisias led to the early Greek tradition of public speaking.

Early Greek Tradition

Starting in 481 B.C., the public speaking tradition in ancient Greece was shaped by *sophists,* philosophers who taught methods of thinking and persuasive speaking. Protagoras of Abdera, known as the "father of debate," required his students to speak first in favor of one position and then in favor of the opposing position so that they would understand the reasoning on both sides of an issue.[6] Gorgias of Leontini studied how language expresses what human senses perceive; he taught the use of rhythm, rhyme, parallel structure, and other techniques for polishing the spoken word.[7]

This rich sophist tradition was continued by Isocrates, the "father of eloquence," who insisted that students learn about a variety of subjects to be able to form political, social, and ethical judgments that would help them become good citizens as well as eloquent speakers.[8] The statesman Demosthenes wasn't a sophist, but his speeches were renowned throughout Athens, and he influenced generations of public speakers.[9]

One of the most famous philosophers and writers in ancient Greece was Plato, who founded the Academy in Athens. A student of Socrates, Plato stressed the *dialectic,* a structured question-and-answer process used to search for truth (see Exhibit 1.2). Many of Plato's writings took the form of dialogues, conversations between characters who debated issues such as the nature of knowledge and the immortality of the soul.[10]

Another major influence on the public speaking tradition in Greece was Aristotle, who studied at Plato's Academy. He disagreed with some of Plato's concepts and later opened his own school in Athens, where he studied and

EXHIBIT 1.2
Socrates and the Dialectic
Plato (right), wrote about how his teacher, Socrates (left), used the dialectic, which had a great influence on the Greek tradition of public speaking.

taught about knowledge based on scientific principles. He wrote about the relationship of perception, opinion, and thought and saw logic as a prerequisite to learning any subject. Aristotle was the first to systematically describe the methods and uses of the dialectic.[11]

Early Roman Tradition

The Greek tradition of public speaking was continued by the Romans in the second century B.C. Orator and statesman Marcus Tullius Cicero fused rhetoric and philosophy in his writings about public speaking. Like Socrates, Cicero believed that people need a well-rounded education to be able to speak persuasively. He also devised a structured process for analyzing issues. When preparing a speech, he started by thinking about his audience's interests, and he used humor, questions, and other techniques to make his points.[12]

In the first century A.D., Marcus Fabius Quintilianus upheld the Roman tradition of public speaking, despite increasing government limitations on speech to suppress political turmoil. He developed a series of questions to spark creative and critical thinking about an issue. He also wrote about using gestures to invoke emotion in the audience and to enhance the speaker's words. In Quintilianus's view, a great orator had to be moral and ethical as well as eloquent.[13]

Later Traditions

Aspects of the Greek and Roman traditions of public speaking continued to influence speakers in the centuries that followed. During the middle ages and into the modern era, religious leaders regularly spoke before groups of believers and nonbelievers. Over the centuries, speakers such as Muhammad, Martin Luther, and John Calvin helped shape religious, social, and political events that have reverberated through history.

Just as it did in ancient Greece and Rome, public speaking supported patriotic movements in many nations during the eighteenth and nineteenth centuries. The power of the spoken word in U.S. history can be seen in the conclusion of Patrick Henry's stirring 1775 speech: "I know not what course others may take, but as for me—give me liberty or give me death."

The power of public speaking is also evident in President Abraham Lincoln's Gettysburg Address of 1863. The occasion of Lincoln's brief speech was the dedication of a cemetery on the site of one of the Civil War's most significant battles. During that same dedication, another speech was delivered, a two-hour address by noted orator Edward Everett. At the time, Everett's speech (not Lincoln's) made front-page news, but Lincoln's stirring words are the ones we've remembered through generations.[14]

In the twentieth century, speakers such as President John F. Kennedy and Dr. Martin Luther King Jr. continued the public speaking tradition in the United States. In his 1961 inaugural address, President Kennedy called on "my fellow

Americans" to become active in the affairs of the country, ushering in a new era of service to the nation. In 1963 Dr. King's "I Have a Dream" speech served as an inspiring call to peace, freedom, and equality for African Americans.[15]

The tradition of public speaking lives on. Community and business leaders such as Jesse Jackson, Gloria Steinem, and Bill Gates use public speaking to inform, persuade, and motivate audiences here and abroad. Political leaders such as Nelson Mandela of South Africa and Vaclev Havel of the Czech Republic use public speaking to promote freedom and cooperation among the peoples in their countries and around the world.

Although the basic skills have changed little since ancient times, styles in public speaking have changed during the past century. A popular pastime in the nineteenth century was **declamation,** the recitation of a classic speech. Early in this century, the focus changed to **elocution,** the control of voice and gesture for emphasis in public speaking. Today, the emphasis is on **extemporaneous speaking,** giving a speech that has been planned in advance but is delivered spontaneously.

Your Public Speaking Skills

Few people today are as renowned for their public speaking skills as Lincoln or King. Most are ordinary people who use public speaking to inform or persuade others. Like you, they've had to learn certain skills to communicate with groups of people. You already use several of those skills in everyday conversation. However, since public speaking isn't exactly like conversation, you'll need some additional skills when communicating with many people at one time.

Communicating One to One

When you have a conversation with another person (or even with several people), you do three things that you would also do in public speaking. First, you organize your thoughts into a logical

Success Tip

In extemporaneous speaking, you plan the points you want to make and the order in which to make them, but you don't memorize the exact words. Instead, you talk spontaneously and make adjustments based on audience feedback.

sequence. Each separate thought builds on the one before it and is linked to the one after, providing an overall structure for your message. This organization allows your listeners to follow what you're saying. Just as you organize your message in conversation, you organize your message in public speaking.

Second, you adapt what you're saying to your audience. By your choice of words and sentences, by the speed of your speech, and by the language you use, you adapt your message to the people you're addressing. For example, the words you choose when speaking with a child aren't the same words you would choose when speaking with an adult. Just as you adapt your message in conversation, you adapt your message in public speaking.

Third, you refine what you're saying in response to the reaction of your audience. Say the person you're talking with has a puzzled look. Instead of continuing your thought, you would probably stop, possibly ask what needs clarification, and then find other words to get your message across. The skill of refining your message according to your audience's reaction is as essential in public speaking as it is in good conversation.

Communicating with Many

Although conversation and public speaking have three skills in common, public speaking requires four additional skills. First is the ability to set a formal purpose. You may have a general reason for starting or continuing a conversation, but every public speaking occasion revolves around some definite goal. Your purpose may be to persuade a group to vote for a particular candidate, or it may be to explain how to invest wisely. Whatever the purpose, you begin by determining why you are addressing your audience.

The second skill needed for public speaking is the ability to fit your message into a formal structure. Imagine that you've been asked to convince a large group of college-bound high

OVERCOMING YOUR SPEECH ANXIETY

NERVOUSNESS IS NORMAL: HOW TO BEAT THE BUTTERFLIES

What do Barbra Streisand, Willard Scott, Sidney Poitier, and Liza Minnelli have in common? All are professional performers, and all admit to being nervous about public speaking. If the pros can feel fear, it's no wonder beginners are sometimes scared speechless. In fact, survey after survey has confirmed that public speaking is the number one fear in the United States, so if you're anxious about stepping in front of an audience, you're not alone.

Nervousness might make your hands tremble, your knees knock, your mouth feel dry, or your stomach churn. As bad as these symptoms can be, bear in mind that nerves are a good indicator of your concern for the occasion, the topic, and the audience. If you didn't care, you wouldn't be anxious. A speaker who cares is more likely to seek out every method of communicating with the audience.

Remember also that you'll feel a little less nervous with every speech. Once you see how the audience responds to your first speech, you'll realize that you did better than you feared you would. Audience members can't see the butterflies fluttering; they're too busy paying attention and responding to your ideas. People in the audience want you to succeed; they're interested in learning from you or being inspired by your words, not in straining to hear the sound of your knees knocking together.

You can harness your nerves by focusing on what you want to accomplish. In the words of actress Carol Channing, "I don't call it nervousness—I prefer to call it concentration." Like Channing, you can concentrate your efforts on making that all-important connection with your audience. But don't make the

mistake of expecting perfection. Put that nervous energy into planning, preparing, and practicing, and you'll be better equipped to face your audience, the first time and every time. Look for more tips on overcoming anxiety in Chapter 2.

One way to overcome nervousness is to practice your speech in front of a mirror.

school students to apply to your college. If you were in conversation with a few students, you could take 40 minutes (or however long you needed) to persuade them. However, you have been allotted only 30 minutes to address this large group, so you'll need to structure your message more formally, tailoring it to the time you have and the points you want to make.

The third skill is the ability to use language suitable for the audience and the occasion. You might use slang or sloppy grammar in conversation, but more formal language is needed when you speak in front of a group. For public speaking, use polished, respect-ful, even inspiring language that's appropriate to the audience and the situation.

The fourth skill is the ability to use an effective method of delivery. You can deliver your message in a spontaneous, casual way during a conversation, but delivering your message in a public speech requires more poise and control, a more polished approach. During a conversation, you might use a soft voice or wave to a passerby, but not if you were speak-

ing to a large audience. Instead, you would use your voice and gestures to deliver your message confidently and convincingly. Also remember that you're closer to your audience during a conversa-tion than you are during a speech. Successful public speakers enunciate distinctly, make their voices audible to everyone, and use deliberate gestures to enhance their meaning.

Becoming an effective public speaker means adding these four skills to the three skills you've gained from years of making conversation (see Exhibit 1.3). Studying and practicing public speaking concepts will help you master these skills and communicate better in any situation, whether with one person or many. You can begin by looking at how communication actually works.

HOW COMMUNICATION WORKS

Whether you're having a conversation with a friend or speaking to a room filled with hundreds of strangers, you get your point across through **communication**, exchanging information and sharing meaning.[16] In exchanging ideas, you can use verbal and nonverbal communication. **Verbal communication** is the use of language, such as the words in a speech, to exchange information. In contrast, **nonverbal communication** is the use of body language, voice qualities, and other methods that don't involve words to exchange information.

The communication process shows how people participate in sharing the meaning of their ideas verbally and nonverbally. In the course of this process, (1) the speaker has an idea, (2) the idea becomes a message, (3) the message is sent through a medium, (4) the audience receives the message and uncovers the meaning, and (5) the audience sends messages, in the form of feedback, to the speaker. This process is affected by interference and context.

What makes communication a process is the simultaneous, ongoing interaction of the speaker and the audience (see Exhibit 1.4). The speaker both sends and receives messages throughout the speech, just as audience members both send and receive messages throughout the speech. In essence, the speaker is also an audience, even as members of the audience are also speakers. This continuing exchange shapes the meaning of the messages that speaker and audience members share.[17]

The Source

The **source** is the origin of the information that will be communicated. As the source, the speaker's perceptions shape any information to be expressed. Because no two people experience the world in exactly the same way, every speaker has a unique view of the world, so the information each person conveys is also unique.

Imagine you're walking in the park with a friend. Even though you're walking side by side, each of you has slightly different impressions of the park, depending on what you pay attention to and how you interpret what your senses tell you. Noticing a cool breeze and a bubbling brook, you conclude that the park is a good place to escape from the outside world. Noticing graffiti and the sound of a lawn mower, your friend concludes that the park offers no escape from the outside world. Because each of you has filtered out some elements and focused on others, you have come to

EXHIBIT 1.3
Public Speaking Builds on Conversation Skills

EVERYDAY CONVERSATION + FORMALIZATION = PUBLIC SPEAKING
Involving
1. Organizing ideas
2. Adapting to audience
3. Refining based on feedback

Of
1. Purpose
2. Structure
3. Language
4. Delivery

EXHIBIT 1.4

The Transactional Communication Process
When you address an audience, you're the source in the transactional communication process, which involves a source, messages, a medium, an audience, and mutual feedback. Your speech can be interrupted by interference, and it is influenced by context.

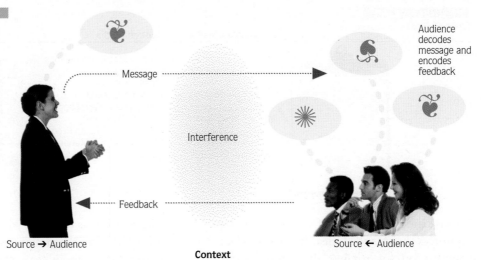

Message

Interference

Audience decodes message and encodes feedback

Feedback

Source → Audience

Source ← Audience

Context

different conclusions about the park, and any information the two of you express about the park will differ as well.

If you're giving a speech, you're the source of the information, so your perceptions shape the ideas you convey. You decide what to include and what to exclude, what is important and what is not. You make assumptions about cause and effect or about the problem and the solution. Once you transform your assumptions, impressions, and thoughts into an idea to be communicated, you're ready to create a message.

The Message

Your **message** is the idea you want to communicate to the audience. Your idea may be anything, from "I have a dream" to "Give me liberty or give me death." To convey the message during a speech, you **encode** the idea by translating it into symbols—words and actions—that your audience can understand.[18] The symbols may include specific words, a particular tone of voice, certain hand gestures, and appropriate facial expressions that emphasize what you want to say.

Just as no two people have an identical view of the world, no two people encode a message in quite the same way. What's important is that

Success Tip

Match your media to the complexity of your message. In a public speaking situation, you can transmit the meaning of a complex message through a combination of words, tone of voice, and body language, all of which help the audience interpret your meaning.

you encode your message in a way that allows your audience to grasp your meaning. When you prepare and deliver a speech, you use a combination of verbal and nonverbal communication to help the audience comprehend what you intend to say. However, if your words and your body language conflict, an audience is more likely to believe your body language and thus may receive a message you didn't intend to send. To avoid confusion, effective speakers carefully coordinate their words and behavior.

The Medium

To get a message across, you send it through a **medium,** the form the message will take to be transferred to the audience (see Exhibit 1.5). Written media include letters, memos, contracts, reports, books, newspapers, magazines, fax messages, and computer messages, among others. Spoken media include face-to-face conversations, telephone conversations, small meetings, academic lectures, seminars, workshops, training programs, television and radio programs, videotaped presentations, and speeches, among others.

Media that allow the speaker to use both verbal and nonverbal signals are well suited to complex messages,

9

EXHIBIT 1.5
Types of Media

Written Media	Spoken Media
Letters	Face-to-Face Conversations
Memos	Telephone Conversations
Contracts	Small Meetings
Reports	Academic Lectures
Books	Seminars and Workshops
Newspapers	Training Programs
Magazines	Television and Radio Programs
Fax Messages	Videotaped Presentations
Computer Messages	Speeches

because the combination of signals carries and reinforces the intended idea. In a face-to-face conversation, for instance, the reinforcement of visual, vocal, and verbal signals leaves less room for misinterpretation. On the other hand, a simple, routine message can be effectively transmitted through words only, as in a memo or letter. [19]

The Audience

Your **audience** is the person or group of people who receive your message. As a speaker, you may have an audience of one or one hundred, depending on the situation. Regardless of audience size, communication won't occur unless the audience actually receives and understands your message. To do this, audience members must **decode** or interpret the symbols you have used to convey the meaning of your message.

In the same way that you as the speaker shape and filter the message being sent, audience members arrive at the meaning of the message through their own perceptions of the world. Backgrounds, experiences, assumptions, and values differ from person to person, so each audience member is likely to interpret the verbal and nonverbal components of your message in a slightly different way. In particular, differences such as age, gender, language, and culture can strongly influence an individual's perception. Because of these differences, not everyone in the audience will receive the precise meaning you intended.

How can you reduce the potential for misinterpretation when you're speaking to an audience?

The best way is to use a "you" orientation, which means keeping the audience's needs and interests in mind throughout every stage of the public speaking process. As explained later in this chapter, the "you" orientation goes beyond merely selecting the right words; it extends to topic selection, speech organization, delivery, and everything else you do as you plan, rehearse, and give a speech.

Feedback

Once audience members have received and decoded your message, they react by sending **feedback**, a response to the speaker's message. Verbal feedback in the form of questions or statements (during or after your speech) can help you determine whether the audience understands your meaning. However, the audience may not be able to give verbal feedback if you are in the middle of your talk. Then you have to look for nonverbal feedback such as facial expressions, head movements, body position, and other signals. One person may look puzzled about your message; another may gasp in astonishment; a third may nod in approval. These nonverbal signs convey the audience's message to you, giving you some sense of whether the audience has received your intended meaning—and letting you know when you need to refine your message, if the meaning hasn't been properly understood.

In turn, you offer feedback to indicate that you have received and understood the messages sent by people in the audience. Most often, your feedback will take the form of adjustments to what you say and how you say it. Sometimes your feedback may be in the form of a message that explicitly addresses ideas you've received from audience members. Imagine that you see many surprised faces in the audience when you talk about a dramatic rise in temperature, from −4 to 45 degrees Fahrenheit, in a two-minute period in Spearfish, South Dakota.[20] Reacting to the nonverbal signal sent by the surprised looks, you send a new message, saying, "That's right, the temperature rose an astounding 49 degrees in just 120 seconds." In this way, you let the audience know that you received their messages and that they heard you correctly. You also reinforce the idea you want to send, which gives you another opportunity to share the meaning with your audience.

Interference

While you're speaking and receiving messages, you may have a problem with **interference** (also known as *noise*), any impediment that prevents the successful transmission of a message. A crackling microphone connection, a rumbling air conditioner, and a clanging fire alarm are examples of external interference that can block you or your audience from receiving messages. Experienced speakers generally check the location where they will be speaking and eliminate any external interference before they begin to speak.

In addition to watching for external interference, you have to be alert for internal interference, physical and emotional distractions that can arise in audience members and speakers alike. Hunger pangs, family worries, and anger are examples of internal interference that can distract you or someone in the audience and prevent successful communication. Strongly disagreeing with the speaker's or audience's point of view can be another source of an internal interference. Although you can try to be aware of and avoid internal distractions of your own, you can't check your audience's internal state in the same way you can check the physical surroundings before you speak. Even so, an effective speaker can find a way of holding the audience's attention, regardless of interference.

Context

Communication is affected by the context in which a speaker and audience exchange ideas. Both time and place can exert influence. Do you know students who are too sleepy to pay attention to what an instructor says in an early morning class? Or students who tune out when they're sitting in a large lecture hall? Do you think you could convince school officials to buy a $100,000 computer system in a ten-minute speech given in the boardroom? In a two-hour speech given at poolside? In such cases, the time and setting contribute to the context that influences the audience's receptivity.

Excellent public speakers adapt their messages (and their forms of delivery) to the occasion (see

Checklist for Identifying Interference

1. Examine conditions inside the speech location (such as poor lighting and inadequate amplification) that might prevent successful transmission of your message.
2. Look at conditions outside the area (such as honking horns and flashing lights) that might prevent successful transmission.
3. Check for audience problems (such as drowsiness, stress, or emotion) that might prevent successful transmission.
4. Monitor external speaker problems (such as stuttering, appearance, or body language) that might prevent successful transmission.
5. Scrutinize internal speaker problems (such as anger or extreme nervousness) that might get in the way of encoding or decoding.

Exhibit 1.6). The speech that Martha Rhodes gave when opposing the railroad fare hike wasn't the same as the speech that Ricardo Gonzalez gave when advocating paper recycling. Different occasions and different audiences generally call for different speeches and different approaches.

Communication in Action

The speaker, message, medium, audience, feedback, interference, and context each play an important role in the communication process. Now it's time to put these elements together. The best way to understand the communication process is to examine it in relation to an actual speech.

Diana Bock (*speaker*) gave a speech (*medium*) before an audience a few years ago. The occasion was the National Speakers Association annual meeting in Palm Desert, California (*context*), and she was addressing 400 professional speakers from all over the United States (*audience*).

Bock talked about the importance of facing the inner fears that everyone has (*message*). To illustrate, she told the story of how her friend's family had escaped from war-torn Laos by crossing a raging river to reach Thailand. She described how one of the boats flipped, dumping many of the family's belongings into the water and nearly drowning one of the children. Eventually, the entire family arrived safely in Richmond, California.

At times, Bock's voice was unsteady, and the audience had some difficulty hearing her (*interference*). Once or twice she was overcome by nervousness and forgot what she was going to say next. Still she continued, linking the concept of facing fears to the dangers—and triumphs—that the Laotian family experienced in crossing the

river. Throughout the speech, audience members used body language to send the message that they were listening intently and understanding her ideas (*feedback*). Bock received those messages and responded with her own messages, adjusting her voice and words to make her meaning clear. She finished by saying, "and by speaking before you here today, I'm crossing my own river," and everyone in the audience jumped up and clapped thunderously (*feedback*). Such a positive response would be encouraging for any speaker, but the message was especially satisfying for Bock, who was only 11 years old when she made that speech.[21]

HOW CULTURAL DIVERSITY AFFECTS PUBLIC SPEAKING

Excellent public speaking requires a sensitivity to the audience's **cultural diversity**, the mix of people from various national, ethnic, racial, and religious backgrounds. The United States has always been a culturally diverse nation, more of a *smorgasbord* than a *melting pot* of peoples. Recent immigration has brought families from Europe, Latin America, Canada, and Asia, each group with its own language and traditions. Today, one out of every seven people in the United States speaks a language other than English at home.[22]

At the same time, more people of every age and background are crossing national borders to live, work, study, and vacation. The result is a patchwork world of cultures, stitched together by technologies such as the

EXHIBIT 1.6
Adjusting to the Context
Excellent public speakers think about the context of their speeches and adjust their messages and their forms of delivery to the occasion.

Public Speaking Can Bridge Cultural Differences
As president and chief executive officer of the NAACP, Kweisi Mfume uses public speaking as a bridge to connect people of diverse racial and cultural backgrounds.

information superhighway, fax machines, television, and jet planes. This means more languages, more cultures, and more diversity in every country and every audience.

Public speaking can help you bridge the gap between these diverse cultures (see Exhibit 1.7). After all, the world seems smaller and the distances between countries (and individuals) seems shorter when you're able to communicate thoughts and feelings. However, when you're speaking to a culturally diverse audience, you'll want to pay special attention to the way you communicate.

Using Appropriate Communication

To get your meaning across in today's culturally diverse world, you need to think about the way your audience is likely to perceive the language and nonverbal signals you use. Although millions of people the world over use English as a second language, not everyone will understand your slang, your idioms, or your humor. Any regional accent in your speech is also likely to be a hindrance. What's more, the words you use may not have the same meaning in another culture. For example, a U.S. speaker who talks about putting napkins on the table will get puzzled looks from an audience in Britain, where the word *napkin* means *diaper*.

Remember, too, that the meaning of body language can vary from one culture to another. When people in the United States and Canada want to signal *no,* they shake their heads back and forth. But people in Bulgaria nod up and down; people in Japan move their right hands; and

people in Sicily raise their chins. So depending on the cultural diversity of your audience, you'll want to think carefully about any facial expressions, hand movements, and other nonverbal signals you use. This shows respect and consideration for your audience—and it helps your audience understand exactly what you want to convey.

Respecting Cultural Differences

Too often, cultural pride creates **ethnocentrism,** the tendency to see other cultures as inferior when compared with your group's standards, behaviors, and customs. People in every culture feel that their ways are the right ways, but ethnocentrism can increase the possibility that your words and actions will be misunderstood. That's why the most important tool you can use to overcome communication barriers is an open mind.

As you research and analyze your audience in the course of preparing a speech, think about the differences that can affect the way you share meaning. Even though you may not completely understand or agree with aspects of your audience's culture, knowing about the differences between your culture and your audience's culture can help you plan what you'll say and how you'll say it. Showing respect for cultural differences is part of a strong "you" orientation, and it helps build rapport with your audience, adding to your credibility. Look for more information on dealing with cultural diversity in Chapter 6 and in the "Speaking Across Cultures" features throughout this book.

WHAT MAKES AN EXCELLENT PUBLIC SPEAKER

No matter what kind of audiences they are addressing, all speakers hope for—and look for—some indication that their messages have been understood and have touched the audience. Excellent public speakers achieve audience understanding through (1) a strong "you" orientation, (2) critical and creative thinking, (3) active listening, (4) good topic selection, (5) effective use of verbal and nonverbal communication, (6) proper preparation and practice, and (7) an awareness of legal and ethical issues in public speaking.

Strong "You" Orientation

As mentioned earlier, the "you" orientation means keeping your audience's needs and interests in mind throughout the public speaking process. You can't inform or persuade people unless you know what they think about, care about, and dream about. Learn all you can about your audience by asking questions such as these:

- What does this audience want or expect?
- What topics or examples interest this audience?
- How is this audience likely to react to my topic and examples?
- What verbal and nonverbal signals are meaningful to this audience?

For example, you can see how the closing words of the late Israeli Prime Minister Yitzhak Rabin's speech (given during the signing of a peace treaty with Jordan) revealed his "you" orientation:

As dawn broke this morning and a new day began, new life came into the world—babies were born in Jerusalem. Babies were born in Amman. But this morning is different. To the mother of the Jordanian newborn—a blessed day to you. To the mother of the Israeli newborn—a blessed day to you. The peace that was born today gives us all the hope that the children born

today will never know war between us—and their mothers will know no sorrow. Allow me to end by the simple words: Shalom, Salaam, Peace.[23]

By discussing the benefits of peace in terms that listeners could appreciate, Rabin demonstrated his understanding of their hopes and dreams. In the same way, you can use the "you" orientation to step into your audience's shoes and see what motivates them and how to involve them in your speech. Even if you're speaking to a group you've addressed before, you need to analyze your audience again, because their needs or interests may have changed since your last speech. Audience analysis, which makes the "you" orientation work, is explored further in Chapter 6.

Critical and Creative Thinking

In the course of putting together a speech, you'll have to select a topic, gather facts and figures, draw conclusions about what you find, decide whether your conclusions make sense, plan what you're going to say, and then plan how to say it. Two types of thinking can be valuable throughout this process. **Critical thinking** is the process of evaluating evidence, assumptions, and ideas on the basis of context, sound reasoning, and logic. Critical thinking skills include the abilities to make comparisons, to theorize, to classify, to analyze, to question, to summarize, to collect and organize data, and to make reasoned decisions.[24]

For example, when Pulitzer Prize–winning author David McCullough spoke on arts and U.S. public policy, he used critical thinking to draw conclusions about the amount of money spent on libraries: "How do we spend our money? For all public libraries nationwide: $4.3 billion a year, which is considerably less than we spend on potato chips or sneakers. Less than we spend on our lawns or for cellular phones. Last year, we spent $7.5 billion on our lawns, $9 billion on cellular phones." McCullough compared the cost of maintaining

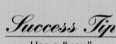

Success Tip

Use a "you" orientation to keep your audience's needs, interests, and aspirations in mind as you plan, prepare, and deliver your speech.

Ask an Expert

Frank E. X. Dance
John Evans Professor of Human Communication Studies
University of Denver

Q: How does critical thinking really affect my public speaking? How can I sharpen my thinking skills?

A: When we give a public speech, we set out to tell people what we are thinking. To support our ideas, we try to give evidence that is acceptable and convincing to others who have not had our personal experiences. As we try to move our thoughts from inside ourselves to outside ourselves, we use words. These words not only reveal what we think but also shape our thoughts. To succeed, we must critically analyze our thoughts and our evidence.

One sure way to advance your ability to think critically is to make it a practice to question your own beliefs by expressing those beliefs aloud, even if only to yourself. When you hear yourself expressing your thoughts out loud, you have an opportunity to evaluate your thinking. Do you have reflexive dislikes for some kinds of people (thin people, heavy people, children, old people)? While driving or walking alone, give yourself a speech expressing your dislike and explaining it with as much supporting data as possible. Are you dead certain about something (right to life, voting a certain political party)? State your position out loud, either to yourself or to someone else—providing a clear exposition of your idea along with whatever supporting material you can muster. How much sense are you making? Keep sharpening your ideas by sharpening your ability to express those ideas. Critical thought is created and expressed in precise language with adequate support.

1. As a speaker, can you apply your critical thinking skills to areas other than beliefs and evidence? What about as an audience member?
2. The next time a classmate presents a speech, listen carefully for solid, objective evidence that supports the speaker's viewpoint. Is the support material specific, complete, and credible? How might this speaker better support his or her position?

libraries with the cost of other items. This allowed him to show how little was being spent on libraries, bringing the figure into perspective for his audience.

Experts say that you may have difficulty thinking critically about a particular topic if you have too little information about it. Similarly, you may not be able to think critically when you have too little experience or familiarity with the topic.[25] So the first step is to find out as much as you can about your speech topic. Then you're in a better position to use your critical thinking skills to examine what you've uncovered, determine its accuracy and its significance, and draw conclusions. Such skills can be applied to any public speaking situation and to any work, school, or home situation (see "Ask an Expert").

Excellent public speakers also need to unlock their minds in order to develop new ideas (new messages, new topics) and to express these ideas with flair. **Creative thinking** is a mix of flexible thinking and restructured understanding that enables people to generate new ideas.[26] Whereas critical thinking helps you look under the surface to evaluate ideas, creative thinking helps you look at ideas in new and original ways.

You can apply creative thinking when choosing your topic, finding and expressing the details that support your ideas, selecting the words you use, creating the visual aids that illustrate your ideas, and polishing your style of delivery. Creative thinking can also help you bring your topic to life. Consider how Glen Martin, a speech student at William Jewell College in Missouri, described the 135,000 or more guns carried by students in U.S. schools: "there are more guns in our nation's schools, every day, than were on the battlefield at Gettysburg. Every day." Creative thinking helped Martin turn a boring statistic into a vivid image that would stay with his audience.[27]

Active Listening

Most people don't listen actively. Research shows that people remember roughly half of a message right after they hear it. Eight hours later, the amount they retain has dropped to about 35 percent; two months later, they can recall only 25 percent of what they heard.[28] Active listening is paying close attention to what you hear, working hard to understand it, reacting to it, and remembering it.

Excellent public speakers don't just talk—they listen actively. They concentrate on what they hear, they wait to make judgments until they've heard all the speaker has to say, they pick out the key points, and they apply critical thinking to evaluate the message. Active listening requires effort. Use your active listening skills before, during, and after you address an audience.

Before a speech, active listening helps you disregard interference and focus on what other people tell you as you gather information or learn about your audience's needs. When you're in front of an audience, active listening helps you decode the audience's encoded messages, telling you whether your meaning has been received as you intended. After a speech, active listening helps you understand audience questions and comments that reinforce, challenge, or expand the ideas you conveyed.

Good Topic Selection

Selecting a topic is a basic but crucial part of public speaking. In some cases, you'll be assigned a specific topic; in others, you'll have the freedom to select your own topic. You'll learn more about topic selection in Chapter 5, but here are five questions you can ask to help you choose a good topic:

1. *What are the needs and interests of my audience?* Using the "you" orientation helps you focus on what your audience needs or wants to hear about. When Michael Salem was invited to tell a Massachusetts college class about his experiences as a prisoner of war in Europe during World War II, he discovered that many students couldn't "relate" to what happened decades ago on another continent. He decided that his audience needed to hear about the human side of war, especially what happens to captured soldiers.[29]

2. *What is the occasion for my speech?* The topic a valedictorian chooses for a graduation speech won't be the same as the topic a scientist chooses for a speech during a conference. Thinking about the occasion can point you in the general direction of an appropriate topic.

3. *How long will I speak?* When you decide on a topic, you need to be sure that you can cover the important points in the time you have. You might be able to explain a complex topic such as genetic engineering in a 60-minute speech, but it's unlikely you could do more than define the term if you had only three minutes. Be sure your topic matches the time you have.

4. *What topic is important to me?* You'll speak with more enthusiasm and conviction when you choose a topic that is important to you. What's more, you can get so wrapped up in a topic you believe in that you won't get sidetracked by speech anxiety. Think back to Diana Bock, the 11-year-old California girl who spoke about facing her fears. Because she believed in her topic, she didn't let nervousness get in the way of conveying her message.

5. *What do I know about the topic?* Most of the time, you'll want to speak about a topic you're familiar with. Because you know something about the topic, you'll have a head start in researching facts and figures to support what you want to say. Even when you're assigned a topic for a speech, you can often think of an angle that puts your knowledge and background to work.

Effective Use of Verbal and Nonverbal Communication

Throughout history, excellent public speakers have found they could captivate, inspire, and challenge their audiences through the effective use of both words and body language. As you plan a speech, don't worry about using fancy words or stilted phrases. Simply concentrate on using language that expresses precisely what you want to convey. Words that are specific, clear, and descriptive can make the difference between understanding and misinterpretation. Words that

EXHIBIT 1.8
Conducting Research Via Computer
As you prepare your speech, you can find facts and figures for your speech by using your school or public library's computer system to identify research sources.

> Type HELP for assistance
>
> Search request:
>
> ice cream
>
> Search result:
> 2 records
> 1. Homemade Ice Cream Recipes
> 2. Ben & Jerry's: The Inside Scoop

are lively and vivid can bring your speech to life for the audience.

Use only as many words as you need, and make each word count. This was the principle behind the Gettysburg Address. President Lincoln used fewer than 300 words to call for "a new birth of freedom." Although his topic was broad and his message important, Lincoln deliberately limited his speech. Using simple language and a logical flow of ideas, he was able to involve his audience and leave a lasting impression of the significance of the event. [30]

Nonverbal communication is just as important as verbal communication. Your gestures, tone of voice, posture, facial expressions, and other nonverbal signals can add subtle nuances of meaning or emphasis to the words you choose. From the first moment you appear in front of your audience, you're communicating nonverbally. How would you expect your audience to react if you were wearing a Greenpeace T-shirt while presenting a speech about eliminating the Environmental Protection Agency? The contrast between what you're wearing and what you're saying would probably confuse and distract your listeners.

As you plan the words you'll say, you'll also want to plan the nonverbal signals you use to support your message. In addition to your overall appearance, pay close attention to the way you walk and stand and how you use your hands, arms, facial expressions, and voice. In simple terms, it's not only *what* you say, but also *how* you say it, that can make communication successful.

Proper Preparation and Practice

Everything a speaker does before stepping in front of an audience is preparation. Proper preparation is important because it reflects a strong "you" orientation. As former chairman of NYNEX (now Verizon), William C. Ferguson asked, "Why should I sit there and listen to somebody who didn't think enough of the audience to prepare?"[31] Don't wait until the night before your speech to start preparing. The earlier you decide on a topic, the earlier you can begin researching facts and figures, outlining your speech, and creating visual aids (see Exhibit 1.8). When you're thoroughly prepared, you'll have a better command of your material, your actual presentation will be more effective, and your self-assurance will help you overcome any nervous feelings.[32]

As a business owner and best-selling author, Harvey Mackay believes in preparation. When asked to address 300 businesspeople in Moscow, he took more than 200 hours of language instruction so that he could give the first eight minutes of his speech in Russian. His preparation paid off. Says Mackay, "You should have seen their faces when the American business speaker stood up and spoke to them in their own language!"[33]

However, preparation isn't enough. The key to public speaking excellence is practice: Practice saying the words and practice using the gestures that enhance those words. Don't memorize, but practice delivering your speech out loud, over and over, until the words are so familiar that they flow easily. Rehearsal is discussed in more detail in Chapter 14.

An Awareness of Legal and Ethical Issues

Public speaking carries some significant legal and ethical responsibilities. However, these responsibilities also present opportunities to be a better speaker. Making sound legal and ethical choices increases your effectiveness as a speaker because it increases your credibility with the audience. If people trust you, they're more likely to accept your message. You'll learn more about legal and ethical questions (and their impact on your credibility) in Chapter 3, but here's a quick overview to help you recognize the important issues.

Laws affect public speaking in two basic ways: protecting people and organizations and protecting the work of other speakers and writers. A key issue in protecting other people is freedom of speech. This issue requires a delicate balance between the rights of the speaker to express his or her opinions on one side and the rights of people and organizations to be protected from dangerous or harmful speech on the other side. Societies have been struggling with the freedom of speech issue for as long as people have been speaking in public, and the issue remains both complex and controversial.

The key issue in protecting the work of other writers and speakers is **plagiarism**, which is taking someone else's ideas or words and presenting them as your own. Plagiarism is not the simple, black-and-white issue it might appear to be. At one extreme, plagiarism is a legal issue when a person profits from someone else's legally protected words and ideas. In most cases, however, plagiarism is not so clear-cut, and it becomes a question of ethical choices. As you'll see in Chapter 3, speakers can engage in varying degrees of plagiarism, all of which are unethical, but some of which are easier to slip into than others. Even speakers who would never dream of stealing someone else's words and ideas can cross the ethical boundary into plagiarism through careless research, for instance.

In your role as a public speaker, you need to be aware of a variety of other ethical issues, which range from the goals and consequences of your speeches to the way you present information. Also, as you learn more about ethical speaking, pay close attention to the public speaking you hear from politicians, talk show hosts, and others with access to the media. Not everything you hear on the airwaves today fits the traditional notion of ethical speech. One of the most important choices you'll have to make as a speaker is whether you'll follow the crowd or make your own ethical decisions.

WRITING RESPONSIBLY: STEERING CLEAR OF PLAGIARISM

The difference between echoing someone else's words and stealing them outright can be serious. Just ask Joseph R. Biden, Jr., senator from Delaware. During his campaign for the 1988 presidential nomination, Senator Biden made speeches using phrases and concepts that had originated with Robert Kennedy, Hubert Humphrey, and British politician Neil Kinnock. The problem was that he failed to credit his sources. Close examination of his speeches revealed the plagiarism, and Biden was forced to end his presidential bid.

How can you avoid plagiarism? Here are five methods you can use:

1. Consult a variety of sources, use critical thinking to analyze what you learn, and draw your own conclusions. Don't rely on the ideas and findings of only one source.
2. Use your own words and sentence structure rather than imitating those of others. No matter how much you admire someone else's language, you need to find new ways of creating the desired tone or mood.
3. Let your audience know when your speech incorporates the unique ideas of others. You can give proper credit by referring to your source during the speech, using phrases such as "According to [name]. . ."
4. Mention your sources when you quote passages from interviews, speeches, books, articles, or other materials. To do this, say "In the words of . . ." or "As [article's author] says in the April edition of [magazine] . . ." or similar phrases.
5. When you paraphrase from a source, be sure to add your own interpretation, and restate the conclusion in your own words, giving credit where it's due.

Remember that the audience can't consult footnotes during a speech, so it's up to you to paraphrase as well as to offer proper credit.

Be careful not to plagiarize someone else's unique ideas, words, or conclusions when you research and prepare your speech.

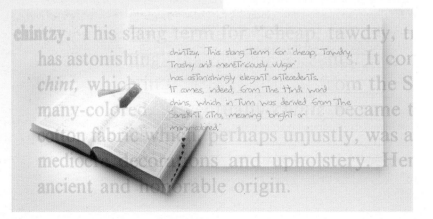

SUMMARY

Excellent public speakers know how to use their voices to make a difference. Public speaking is the process of addressing an audience effectively. As you move through each step in the process of public speaking, you become a better communicator and develop a variety of skills that can be used to achieve both career and personal goals.

The public speaking tradition in Western civilization began in antiquity. The work of Corax and Tisias led to the early Greek tradition of public speaking, which was shaped by the sophists as well as by Plato and Aristotle. Building on Greek traditions, orators such as Cicero and Quintilianus advanced the early Roman tradition of public speaking. In the centuries that followed, public speaking supported both religious and political movements around the world. Since the nineteenth century, public speaking styles have shifted from declamation and elocution to extemporaneous speaking.

Three conversational skills can be applied to public speaking: (1) organizing your thoughts into a logical sequence, (2) adapting what you say to your audience, and (3) refining what you say depending on the audience's response. In addition, you need four more skills for effective public speaking: (1) setting a formal purpose, (2) fitting your message into a formal structure, (3) using language appropriate to the audience and the occasion, and (4) using an effective delivery method.

Communication is the process of exchanging information and sharing meaning. Verbal communication is the use of language to exchange information. Nonverbal communication is the use of body language, voice qualities, and other methods that don't involve words to exchange information.

The communication process shows how people participate in sharing the meaning of their ideas verbally and nonverbally. In the course of this process, the speaker encodes the message for transmission to the audience through a medium. The audience is the person or people who receive the message and decode its meaning and offer feedback. Communication can be distorted by interference, any impediment that prevents the successful transmission of the message. Communication is also affected by the context in which a speech is presented. In the communication process, the speaker and the audience simultaneously interact by sending and receiving messages.

Cultural diversity is the mix of people from various national, ethnic, racial, and religious backgrounds. Audiences are more diverse than ever before, differing in both language and culture. Paying attention to appropriate verbal and nonverbal signals, and avoiding ethnocentrism, can help speakers bridge the gap between people of various cultures. Excellent public speakers achieve audience understanding with (1) a strong "you" orientation, (2) critical and creative thinking, (3) active listening, (4) good topic selection, (5) effective use of verbal and nonverbal communication, (6) proper preparation and practice, and (7) an awareness of legal and ethical issues in public speaking.

KEY TERMS

audience (10)
communication (8)
creative thinking (15)
critical thinking (14)
cultural diversity (12)
declamation (6)
decode (10)
elocution (6)
encode (9)
ethnocentrism (13)
extemporaneous speaking (6)
feedback (10)
interference (11)
medium (9)
message (9)
nonverbal communication (8)
plagiarism (18)
public speaking (2)
source (8)
verbal communication (8)

APPLY CRITICAL THINKING

1. Should today's public speaking students study and practice principles of declamation or elocution? Defend your answer.

2. Think of a public speaker you particularly admire. How does this speaker demonstrate a strong "you" orientation?

3. What interference might you encounter as a kindergarten teacher talking to your students about how to cross the street safely?

4. Why do you think audiences tend to believe nonverbal cues rather than verbal cues when the two conflict?

5. Do you agree with Isocrates that learning about a variety of subjects can help you become a better citizen as well as an eloquent speaker? Explain your answer.

6. What are at least two ways an audience can determine whether a speaker is using active listening skills?

7. Should public speeches of the U.S. government be restricted in any way? What if a speech advocates breaking the law or violently overthrowing the government?

SHARPEN YOUR SKILLS

Individual Exercises

1. Find a newspaper or magazine article that describes a public speaking situation. Examples include an author addressing fans gathered at a book signing and a government official addressing a group of citizens.

    a. What is the speaker's goal? How do you know?

    b. Why is the speaker's topic interesting to the audience?

    c. How did the speaker display a "you" orientation toward the audience?

2. Attend a talk by an expert (such as a gardening specialist) or another speaker.

    a. Was the speaker's language suited to the audience and the occasion? Give an example to support your answer.

    b. What was the speaker's message? Did the speaker convey the same message through verbal and nonverbal signals? If not, how did the signals conflict? How did the conflict affect the audience?

    c. How did the audience communicate with the speaker during this speech? Did the speaker make any adjustments in response?

3. Watch a televised speech by a politician or another public speaker.

    a. Who is the audience for this speech? How do you know?

    b. How can this speaker know that the audience has received and understood the message?

    c. What interference might prevent successful communication?

4. Do you have the three conversational skills and four public speaking skills needed to address an audience? Write a brief (one- to two-page) report on the strength of your skills. Be sure to identify the skills you want to improve and those you are strongest in.

Group Exercises

5. Working with two or three classmates, select a common communication situation.

    a. Identify the speaker, message, medium, and audience.

    b. Draw a diagram of the elements in this communication situation, labeling each element.

    c. Show any potential interference. Be prepared to present your group's diagram to the class.

6. With another student, attend a meeting of your school's student government. Answer the following questions separately, and then compare your answers:

    a. Which speakers showed the strongest "you" orientation?

    b. Which speakers displayed the most effective use of language? Which made the most effective use of nonverbal signals? Cite examples.

    c. Did any speaker appear particularly well prepared or rehearsed? Did this affect your reaction to that speaker? In what way?

    d. How did the speakers show that they were actively listening to each other's messages and to the audience's messages?

7. Pair up with a classmate and list six phrases a speaker might use to describe your speech classroom. Which of these phrases would be understood by someone who has never been inside the classroom? Which would be understood by someone whose native language isn't English? What phrases would you suggest a speaker use to help a culturally diverse audience understand a spoken description of your classroom?

8. With another student, select and analyze a speech from the Appendix. How did the speaker demonstrate the use of critical thinking? Of creative thinking? Cite examples. As members of the audience, how would you be likely to react to these examples? Explain your answer.

OVERCOMING ANXIETY AND GIVING YOUR FIRST SPEECH

LEARNING OBJECTIVES
After studying this chapter, you will be able to

1. Identify ten techniques that can help you build confidence as a public speaker.

2. Differentiate between a speech's general and specific purpose.

3. Define the central idea of a speech.

4. Explain how to analyze the audience for your first speech.

5. Discuss how the major points and supporting material relate to the central idea.

6. Describe the functions of the three main sections of a speech.

7. Explain the reasons for practicing before delivering a speech.

BUILDING CONFIDENCE AS AN EXCELLENT PUBLIC SPEAKER

Can you imagine Darth Vader or the Lion King being afraid? James Earl Jones, whose voice gave life to both characters, wasn't always a confident public speaker. As a teenager, he dreaded speaking to audiences because of his stutter. Jones conquered his fear (by reciting poetry aloud) and went on to become an accomplished actor.[1]

If you're nervous about facing an audience, you're not alone. Even speakers with years of experience feel some anxiety about getting up in front of an audience. The good news is that you can do something about your nerves. Taking this course in public speaking and learning the basic principles is an important first step.[2] Once you recognize that nerves are normal, you're ready to apply effective fear-busting techniques that will help build your confidence as a public speaker.

Feeling Nervous Is Normal

Not everyone feels nervous about public speaking, but you know when *you* feel nervous. Perhaps your hands or legs shake, your mouth feels dry, your heart pounds, or your voice squeaks. For some people, even the thought of talking in front of a group can start the butterflies fluttering. You may be nervous about public speaking, but you may not know that a nervous feeling is common and that it tends to follow a predictable pattern.

Studies show that the pattern starts when you feel your level of anxiety rising in anticipation of

a speech (see Exhibit 2.1). As you might expect, anxiety peaks when you actually stand in front of your audience and start to speak. Slowly your nerves settle down, and by the end of your speech, your anxiety is at or below the level you felt before you started to speak.[3]

What are speakers afraid of? Some are afraid they won't measure up to the audience's expectations. Others fear that they'll look foolish. When he was a graduate student facing an oral exam at Pennsylvania State University, Tim Hopf worried that "these people are going to see me as incompetent and stupid."[4] Speakers also fret that they won't be able to finish without fainting or forgetting what they planned to say.

At one time or another, nearly everyone who faces a group—large or small—feels such fears. Singer Barbra Streisand, Rev. Billy Graham, and actor James Earl Jones are just a few of the well-known people who confess that they've felt nervous about public speaking. Of course, if you've ever seen Streisand, Graham, or Jones in action, you may find this hard to believe. After all, no one in the audience can see their nervousness. And when you get up to speak, your audience isn't likely to notice your anxiety, either.[5]

Even if you can't make nervous feelings disappear entirely, you can learn to cope with your anxiety. Actually, accomplished public speakers worry most when they don't feel anything before a speech. Centuries ago, the great Roman orator Cicero suggested that excellent public speaking is characterized by some degree of nervousness.[6]

Nervousness shows that you care about the audience, the speech topic, and the occasion. It

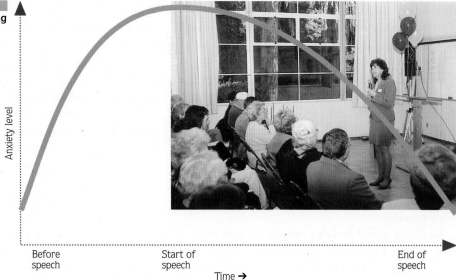

EXHIBIT 2.1
Anxiety About Public Speaking
Research indicates that anxiety peaks by the time a speaker launches into a speech, then drops slowly and steadily as the speech continues.

Anxiety level

Before speech   Start of speech   End of speech

Time ➔

also shows that you're excited about what you're doing. If your palms get wet or your mouth goes dry, don't think of nerves, think of excitement. Excitement can give you the energy you need to pep up your planning, preparation, and performance. It works for the pros, and it can work for you too.

Developing Confidence in Your Public Speaking Skills

Whether you're new to public speaking or practicing to improve your skills, you can reduce speech anxiety by changing what you do, how you feel, and how you think.[7] To harness nervous energy and become a more confident speaker, try these techniques: (1) concentrating on your message, (2) preparing your introduction and conclusion, (3) planning and practicing your speech, (4) talking with individuals, (5) thinking positive, (6) visualizing success, (7) being yourself, (8) projecting confidence, (9) reducing tension, and (10) looking for speaking opportunities.

Concentrate on Your Message
What happens when someone tells you not to think about the word *hippopotamus?* You immedi-

> *Success Tip*
> Use, don't lose, your nervous energy. By minimizing your nervousness and transforming it into excitement, you can give your speech a lively sparkle that the audience will enjoy.

ately find the word fixed in your mind, of course. The same principle applies to speech anxiety. The more you try to ignore your nervousness, the larger it looms. So instead of trying to forget your fears, change your focus.

Think about the ideas you want to convey. Dottie Walters, who gives speeches and writes books about public speaking, banishes her fear by imagining that her audience is hungry and that she has food for them: "I visualize that everyone is holding out empty bowls, like the orphans did in *Oliver,* and I have exactly what they want."[8] Like Walters, you can take your mind off your nerves by concentrating on the food for thought you're offering your audience, especially your introduction and your major points. In just a moment or two, you'll be so absorbed in your message that you'll forget all about any shaking or quivering.

Prepare Your Introduction and Conclusion
Even when you concentrate on your message, you may feel a bit more tense as you start and end your speech. After all, the introduction and conclusion are your first and last chance to make an impression on your audience. Being

thoroughly prepared for these critical moments can make a big difference in how you feel when you step in front of an audience.

First, get your speech off to a good start by thinking carefully about how you can present your topic and establish a link with your audience at the start of your speech. Once you've decided how you'll begin, go through your introduction again and again. This will fix the ideas and the order in your mind so you can face your listeners with assurance. After a strong start, you'll be in a better position to concentrate on the major points of your message.

Similarly, you'll want to prepare an effective conclusion. This is your final opportunity to get your points across. That's why you'll want to take time to plan how you will close your speech. Then you can practice the conclusion out loud until you're thoroughly familiar with it. When you know your conclusion well, you'll feel a surge of confidence as you reach the end of your speech.

Plan and Practice

Giving a speech is much like taking a test. When you've studied beforehand, you feel more at ease and ready to do your best. Similarly, speakers are less nervous when they know their speech topics and have prepared in advance.[9] Plan what you want to say and how you want to say it. Then rehearse over and over until you can speak calmly, naturally, and convincingly. Planning and practicing will boost your confidence and keep those butterflies under control.

Sometimes speakers are so nervous that they rush to get through their speeches. If you find yourself speaking too quickly, practicing will help you regain control. As you rehearse, you'll learn how to slow down and where to insert pauses to emphasize major points. By the time you actually talk to your audience, you'll be speaking at a more natural rate.

If possible, rehearse your speech under the same conditions as when you will be giving it. Go to the room where you'll speak, and position yourself in front of where the audience will be. Bring along any notes and visual aids you plan to use, and give your speech as though the audience were present. To make the rehearsal even more realistic, wear the same clothing and accessories you will wear on the day of the speech. This practice session is the time to find out if your clothing isn't comfortable or your jewelry jangles. You'll feel better prepared and more in control after you've practiced your speech in this way.

Talk with Individuals

If the thought of facing an audience gets your knees knocking, remember that an audience is nothing more than a group of individuals.

Checklist for Managing Speech Anxiety

1. Concentrate on your message, not on your nervous feelings.
2. Prepare your introduction and conclusion so that you're thoroughly familiar with the beginning and ending of your speech.
3. Plan and practice your speech so that you can speak calmly, naturally, and convincingly.
4. Talk with individuals, not a faceless, anonymous audience.
5. Think positive by replacing negative thoughts with positive ones.
6. Visualize success, seeing yourself as a confident, skillful speaker.
7. Be yourself, using natural phrases, gestures, and movements.
8. Project confidence to convince your audience and yourself that you are confident.
9. Reduce tension through steady breathing, pausing to relax, and using controlled movements.
10. Look for speaking opportunities in class, on campus, in your community, and on the job.

They're not faceless or nameless. Like you, each is an individual, and each wants to hear what you have to say. This helps you maintain your "you" orientation. Thinking of individuals reinforces the importance of considering your audience's needs and interests when you plan and give a speech.

So pick out a few individuals, make eye contact, and talk to them. As you talk, watch your audience for indications that your message is getting across. Public speaking is less frightening when you think of communicating with individuals rather than performing for an anonymous crowd.

Think Positive

Many times, our deepest fears about public speaking are exaggerated and irrational. These fears can take up energy that would be better applied to planning and giving a good speech. Imagine how tightrope walkers might manage fear of falling. They replace negative thoughts about falling with positive thoughts about remaining steady on their feet. Like a tightrope walker, you can replace negative thoughts with positive thoughts. The power of positive thinking can reduce your anxiety and help you feel confident about addressing an audience.[10]

Start by looking at your negative thoughts. You may want to write each on an index card so you can examine it more objectively. Consider how each thought keeps you from doing your best. Be especially alert for negative thoughts such as *I'll never be able to get through my introduction,* which are clearly unrealistic once you stop to examine them.

Then turn the index cards over and write a positive thought to counteract every negative thought. As you did with your negative thoughts, take a close look at each positive thought to be sure that it's realistic. A positive statement such as *I can deliver a perfect introduction* is likely to make you more nervous. On the other hand, a more realistic thought such as *I can deliver an introduction that will capture the audience's attention* gives you a specific positive image to think about as you prepare your next speech. Reviewing these positive thoughts can help you develop a more positive attitude about your abilities.[11]

Visualize Success

Once you're able to replace negative thoughts with positive thoughts, you're ready to take the next step and visualize public speaking success. Athletes have long known what communication research confirms about the visualizing process. Seeing yourself successful in a stressful situation puts you in the right frame of mind for actually achieving success. Just do it: Picture yourself as a skillful speaker.

You can reduce your anxiety by using visualization as a script for public speaking success.[12] In the words of Tim Hopf, the former grad student turned associate professor of communication at Washington State University, "I realized that my script was a negative script, and I was the only one who could rewrite it."[13] Like Hopf, you can challenge yourself to visualize a positive script for successful public speaking.

In your mind's eye, you walk confidently to the front of the room. You're fully prepared and ready to communicate with your audience. Everyone in the audience is engrossed in what you have to say, and they react positively to your speech. Visualizing success as you plan your speech can pave the way for excellence during the actual delivery.

Be Yourself

Trying to be perfect, or trying to be just like a speaker that you admire, can put a strain on anybody. It can also put a damper on your speech. As radio and television personality Charles Osgood says, "If you try to be what you are not, you probably won't get away with it."[14] As you take this course, you'll be exploring the kind of speaker you want to be (see Exhibit 2.2).

So be yourself: let your personality come through with a speaking style that's comfortable for you. Use phrases, gestures, and movements that come naturally to you. In the process, you'll release nervous energy and demonstrate your excitement about the topic.

Project Confidence

When you're in front of an audience, no one but you knows—or cares—whether your mouth is dry or your legs feel weak. The audience is more

EXHIBIT 2.2
Self-Test for Speakers

Part of being yourself is understanding your individual speaking style. Place a check mark on the continuum between each of the following public speaking characteristics to show where you see your style. Remember that this self-test has no right or wrong answers, because a style that's effective for one person may not work for another.

serious .... humorous	
informal .... formal	
direct .... storytelling	
slow-paced .... fast-paced	
logical .... emotional	

As you look over your answers, think about how you can put your style to work in front of an audience. For example, if humor comes naturally to you, you'll feel more comfortable telling humorous anecdotes. But don't play only to your strengths. Work on your style so that you can develop the flexibility to be effective in a broad range of speaking situations.

interested in your message, so use every action to demonstrate that you have something vital to say. "The important thing is to stand up and say what's on your mind in a confident way," advises John W. Amerman, chairman of Mattel toys.[15]

Just act confident, and you'll convince your audience that you *are* confident. Move to your place with confidence, look at your audience without wavering, and start your speech in a firm, clear voice. Once you get in the habit of projecting confidence, you'll feel more self-assured without any special effort.

Reduce Tension

You'll appear more confident if you reduce the physical tension that grips your body just before you start a speech. Although a little tension goes a long way toward giving your speech a lively quality, too much can make you seem wooden or disorganized. Your goal is to bring tension down to a manageable level.

Start by taking several slow, deep breaths to calm yourself. As you walk to face your audience, keep your breathing steady. Then, before you launch into your introduction, pause for a moment to get your nerves under control. This pause will also signal your audience to settle down. Look around, pick out a few friendly faces, and let yourself relax as you begin to talk. The tension

will drain away as you become absorbed in communicating your message and in reaching the audience.

Another way to reduce tension is through controlled physical movements during your speech. As long as your movements are natural and appropriate, feel free to emphasize some points by gesturing. When you ask for questions from the audience, you might want to take a step or two closer to your listeners. Even the smallest movement can let some of the tension out of your body. The key is to keep your movements under control, so they enhance your message while serving as an outlet for a bit of your nervous energy.

Look for Speaking Opportunities

Practice really does make perfect. As the famous essayist Ralph Waldo Emerson observed, "All the great speakers were bad speakers at first."[16] Public speaking is just like any other skill: The more you speak, the better you get, and the more confident you feel.

This class is a good start on the road to excellent public speaking. During the course, you'll gain experience using a variety of public speaking techniques. At the same time, you'll learn where you're strong and where you need improvement. Keep practicing, and you'll come closer and closer

OVERCOMING YOUR SPEECH ANXIETY

WHAT YOU SHOULD KNOW ABOUT BREATHING THAT WILL HELP CALM YOUR NERVES

When you're getting ready to speak in public, you can get tripped up by breathing problems. Some people get so nervous that they hold their breath or take shallow breaths. Try these breathing tips to calm your nerves, slow your racing heartbeat, and gain the energy you need for a lively speech.

- *Feel your breathing.* Put a hand on your diaphragm, above your waist at the point where your ribs separate. Feel the diaphragm expand and contract as you breathe in through your nose and out through your mouth. If your diaphragm doesn't move, slow down and breathe deeper and more deliberately.
- *Breathe deeply.* Inhale as you count to five, feeling your diaphragm expand. Hold for two counts and then exhale as you count to five again, feeling your diaphragm contract. Repeat several times during the day and just before you get up to speak. You'll feel more refreshed, calmer, and ready to meet your audience.
    - *Practice breathing.* Make deep breathing part of your daily routine. The relaxed feeling you get as you slow your racing heart is what you're aiming for during a speech. With a bit of practice, you'll be able to bring your nerves under control during stressful speaking situations.

Remember that breathing is highly individual. As you learn to pace yourself, you'll find out how often you need to stop for a breath.

Practice breathing with a hand on your diaphragm to learn how to slow down and pace yourself.

to your goal of public speaking excellence.

To get more practice polishing your skills, seek out other speaking opportunities on your campus, in your community, and on the job. In the classroom or during meetings on campus, just asking a question or offering a comment can be a good way to gain speaking experience. In your community, you can practice by giving short talks (about your hobby or another topic) to local school, civic, or religious groups. On the job, speak up during a group discussion or volunteer to give a presentation to your managers or coworkers. You can learn something from every speaking experience, and as your speaking abilities grow, you'll bring those nervous feelings under control.

PREPARING YOUR FIRST SPEECH

Now it's time to get on your feet in front of the class and apply the confidence-building techniques you've just learned. Your instructor might ask you to give a speech of self-introduction, in which you tell the audience about yourself. This is often the first speech you're asked to prepare for your speech class. Through a self-introduction speech, you help your classmates get to know you better by sharing your ideas, feelings, and opinions. In turn, you find out more about the other students by listening to their speeches. In addition to practicing your public speaking skills, you'll learn enough about the classroom audience to help you select appropriate topics for speeches you make later in the course.

EXHIBIT 2.3
Overview of the Public Speaking Process

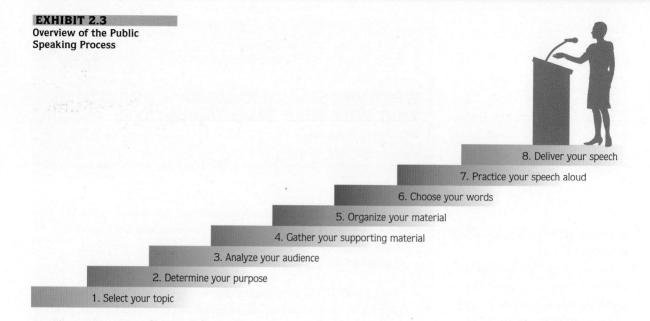

8. Deliver your speech

7. Practice your speech aloud

6. Choose your words

5. Organize your material

4. Gather your supporting material

3. Analyze your audience

2. Determine your purpose

1. Select your topic

No matter what kind of first speech your instructor assigns, you'll need an overview of the public speaking process to get started. The rest of this chapter serves as an introduction to the main steps in public speaking, which will be discussed in more detail during later chapters. In the course of planning your speech, you'll select your topic, determine your purpose, and analyze your audience (see Exhibit 2.3). Next, you'll gather your material, organize it, and choose your words. Finally, you'll practice your speech aloud and then deliver it to the class.

Select Your Speech Topic

As you saw in Chapter 1, excellent speakers choose a topic by considering the audience's needs and interests, the occasion for the speech, the length of the speech, the personal importance of the topic, and the speaker's knowledge of the topic. Even if you're assigned a topic, these factors will shape your approach to it. If you haven't been assigned a topic, you can choose one by thinking about your everyday life, school or work experiences, news headlines, or any of a number of other sources. You can also check Appendix A for topic ideas.

You're likely to speak more effectively if you choose a topic that you care about and know something about. However, be careful to give your speech focus by narrowing the subject to a particular topic that meets both your audience's needs and your time constraints. A *subject area* such as the Internet is too broad for one speech. You'll have difficulty saying anything meaningful in the few minutes allotted for your speech if your subject covers a lot of ground.

In contrast, a *speech topic* is a particular concept or issue within a subject area. If your subject is the Internet, you might choose a topic such as choosing browser software or safeguarding personal privacy. By clearly defining your topic, you'll waste less time preparing your speech. You'll also help your audience focus on the important points you make.

For example, when Professor D. Stanley Eitzen of Colorado State University addressed a seminar on "Sport and American Values," he knew that his audience didn't have time to hear about every sport, even if he could talk about them all. Professor Eitzen narrowed the subject of his speech to the ethics of winning at any cost. This focus allowed his audience to follow his argument from beginning to end.[17]

What topic should you choose? For a first speech, you may want to think about any expertise you can share with your audience. Perhaps

EXHIBIT 2.4

Selecting a Specific Topic for a Speech of Self-Introduction

In a speech of self-introduction, you can show the audience who you are and what you care about by discussing your hobbies and interests, significant childhood experiences, or your personal or professional goals.

you can explain how to do something: how to photograph animals, how to build a bluebird house, how to bake bread. For example, Heather Mannion, who enjoyed games, created a classroom speech on the subject of Scrabble. She planned to discuss one specific topic: how to create short, high-scoring words. Setting boundaries for her topic helped Mannion reduce the amount of preparation needed for the speech. It also helped keep her listeners focused throughout the speech.

If you're giving a speech of self-introduction, the subject is *you*. Of course, you can't tell an audience all about yourself in a brief classroom speech. Instead of trying to cover everything, narrow your focus to one specific aspect of your life that the audience will find interesting. Then, as you plan your speech, think about how you can move beyond the bare facts to give your audience clues about who you are, what you think is important, and how you react to the world. Picking out just the right topic may take a bit of time and effort, but it can be a fun and interesting process as well (see Exhibit 2.4):

- *Talk about your personal or professional goals.* What do you want out of life, school, or work? During her speech of self-introduction, Kimiko Yamagishi explained why she planned to become an advocate for consumer rights when

she returned to Japan. "Japan doesn't have the kind of consumer protection laws that Americans take for granted," she said. "That's why my goal is to help make business and government in Japan more responsive to the voice of the consumer."

- *Talk about an experience that changed your life.* How has your life been influenced by an unusual or unique experience? Hiker Joe DeSousa discussed a near-disaster that taught him the importance of survival planning. Stranded without food or water on a chilly mountain peak one fall evening, he had to find his way down using the light of his wristwatch. "I was lucky," DeSousa said. "Now I keep a small survival kit in my car and in my backpack, so I'm ready for anything."

- *Talk about someone who means a lot to you.* Has a family member, friend, or hero made a difference to you? Wally Andrews told about becoming a volunteer because of the example set by his uncle, who teaches printing skills at a nearby prison: "My uncle doesn't just talk about helping other people—he does something about it. Like my Uncle Ted, I want to be part of the solution, not part of the problem."

- *Talk about your work, a hobby, or a favorite activity.* What satisfaction, frustration, or excitement do you get from a job, hobby, or sport? Amanda Mastrio told her class about the

DEVELOPING YOUR CREATIVITY

INSPIRATION, PERSPIRATION, DESPERATION? A SECRET TO FINDING TOPICS FAST!

If coming up with a speaking topic is a problem for you, try *divergent thinking*, a type of thinking that takes the mind in many different directions. When you use divergent thinking, you assume that every problem has more than one right answer and you deliberately try to think of as many options as possible. In contrast, most people solve everyday problems by trying immediately to reduce the number of solutions and quickly finding the best one. This approach can lead you to rule out other potentially good topic ideas too early in the process.

By using divergent thinking to come up with a speech topic, you move beyond a few obvious choices to come up with a much wider variety of possibilities, some familiar and some entirely new to you. Set your imagination free to identify topics when you're watching a sports event, reading the want ads, taking a family trip, listening to someone talk, reading about history, or listening to music. Turn every idea around in your mind, thinking about it from another angle or even considering its opposite. Some ideas may make sense, some may not, but don't eliminate any until you've explored as many possibilities as you can think of.

At this point, you can apply critical thinking skills to narrow the choices through logic and analysis. Put aside topics that have no meaning for you or your audience, and discard topics that are inappropriate for the occasion.

Look at the topics that remain and determine which can be explored in the time you have for your speech. By applying both creativity and critical thinking, you can explore many possibilities and then select just one with the knowledge that among the others are good speech topics waiting for another audience or occasion.

Divergent thinking can help you come up with a creative new topic for a speech.

rewards of learning Russian. "I've come to realize that language represents a different way of looking at the world," she said. "Every time I learn a new word, I feel I'm that much closer to understanding the way Russian people think."

In the sample speech shown at the end of this chapter, the speaker talks about how she learned an important lesson from a sailing adventure. In the process of describing the incident, the speaker reveals a lot about herself: she is devoted to sailing, she first sailed when she was 12, she had no formal training before she set sail, and she's proven to herself that her instincts can get her through tough situations. Like this student, you can choose the topic for a speech of self-introduction to give your audience a brief glimpse of your inner self.

Determine Your Purpose

In addition to selecting a specific speech topic, you'll want to determine your purpose before you begin to prepare a speech. The purpose guides you in conducting research, organizing your points, and planning what you'll say in your speech. Start by defining your general purpose and then focus on your specific purpose in addressing the audience. After that you're ready to express the central idea of your speech. (You can read more about determining your purpose in Chapter 5.)

Your General Purpose

The **general purpose** is the overall reason, in general terms, for your speech. Depending on the occasion and the audience, your speech may fall into one of three general-purpose categories.

- *To inform.* When you speak to inform, your purpose is to share your knowledge of a topic with your audience. For example, in his award-winning student speech "Superbugs: Scourge of the Post-Antibiotic Era," Andy Wood of Berry College in Georgia wanted to inform the audience about the dangers of overusing antibiotics to combat disease. He cited a number of startling statistics and anecdotes to describe the problem and then explained how individuals can guard against overusing antibiotics.[18]

- *To persuade.* When you speak to persuade, your purpose is to influence the audience's attitudes, beliefs, or actions. During the seminar on "Sport and American Values," Professor Eitzen's general purpose in speaking about the ethics of sports competition was to persuade his audience to alter their attitudes about emphasizing winning.

- *To motivate or entertain.* When you speak to motivate, your purpose is to inspire your audience; when you speak to entertain, your purpose is to amuse your audience. Speeches to motivate or entertain are often given during special occasions. For example, after Dr. Robert E. McAffee was elected president of the American Medical Association, he gave a speech to motivate the members. He talked about pushing boldly into the endless frontier of medicine and told the doctors that their actions would make a real difference to the patients and to the world.[19]

Your Specific Purpose

In contrast to the general purpose, which is quite broad, your specific purpose is much narrower, because it is intended to show where your speech is headed. Your **specific purpose** indicates exactly what you want the audience to know, do, or feel as a result of your speech. This is the actual goal you set for your speech, defining what you want to accomplish (see Exhibit 2.5). One way to think about your specific purpose is to see how it ties together your topic, your general purpose, and what you want to share with your audience. The stronger the ties, the stronger the basis for your speech.

When Nancy Letourneau of Kansas State University prepared a persuasive speech about the problems caused by faulty credit reports, she wanted to convince students to check their credit files regularly. Her speech linked the topic (the problems caused by faulty credit reports) and the general purpose (to persuade) to what she wanted to accomplish (give students a reason to check and correct their credit files).[20]

Your Central Idea

Although your specific purpose shows where your speech is headed, it doesn't describe what you will say. The actual content of your speech is contained in your **central idea**, a concise statement of the single compelling idea around which your speech will be built. An appropriate central idea will guide you through researching your topic, organizing your materials, and preparing what you will say during the speech. No matter how long or complex you expect your speech to be, your central idea summarizes your message in a single sentence. If you have difficulty with your central idea, you may be trying to tackle too much in your speech.

Nancy Letourneau's specific purpose was to persuade audience members to watch out for errors on their credit reports. In contrast, her central idea summarized what she actually would say during her speech: Credit reporting agencies sometimes make mistakes that can cost unsuspecting consumers time, money, even a job.

Everything Letourneau said during her speech related to the central idea. She talked about how a credit bureau had mistakenly reported that thousands of people in a Vermont town were deadbeats, how the credit report on one St. Louis couple erroneously reported that they had gone bankrupt, and how current laws and regulations don't hold credit bureaus accountable for their errors. Each of these thoughts is connected to the central idea, painting a vivid word picture of the problems caused by faulty credit reports. This central idea supported Letourneau's specific purpose, to persuade listeners to check the accuracy of their credit files.

Analyze Your Audience

At this point, you've determined where you want your speech to go (your specific purpose) and what you want to say (your central idea). But you can't chart your course without taking the time to find out about your audience. After all, how can you try to influence the attitudes or behaviors of audience members without understanding who they are, what they care about, and how they think or act? The audience is truly the center of the public speaking process.

One way to analyze your audience is according to personal factors such as age, gender, education,

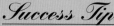

Success Tip

Build your entire speech around the specific purpose and the central idea. Once you know precisely what you want to achieve and what you want to say, you can gather your support materials and then organize your major points into a sequence that makes sense.

and occupation. These factors offer clues to audience interests. A second way to analyze the audience is according to psychological factors such as needs and motives, attitudes, values, and lifestyles. Such subjective factors offer clues to what audience members consider important and why they act as they do. A third way to analyze your audience is according to social factors such as group membership or cultural, racial, and ethnic identification. In particular, cultural differences between speaker and audience can complicate the communication process.

When you're speaking to a culturally diverse audience, be especially sensitive to differences in assumptions, beliefs, attitudes toward time, language, nonverbal signals, humor, and style of expression. Of course, these differences aren't right or wrong, nor are they good or bad. They simply shape how people think of themselves and how they react to the world around them, including public speakers and their messages. Excellent public speakers not only recognize and respect cultural differences, they search for common points of understanding to bridge the gaps between cultures.

In addition, your connection with the audience can be affected by the speaking situation. Analyze the situation by examining how much time is available for your speech, the time of day, week, or year, and the physical surroundings in which you'll address the audience. Also look at the reason you've been invited to speak and how your speech fits with any others being presented. For example, when Robert D. Haas, chief executive officer of Levi Strauss, made a speech titled "Ethics—A Global Business Challenge" in front of a group of business leaders in New York, he started his speech by referring to the speaking situation:

We are meeting at a time when it seems that in every facet of contemporary life, people are placing self-interest ahead of

Checklist for Communicating with a Culturally Diverse Audience

1. Identify any cultural differences (such as language or nonverbal signals).
2. Use simple phrases and sentences to express complex thoughts clearly without sounding condescending.
3. Repeat or summarize major points when appropriate to help the audience understand and remember your central idea.
4. Consider using visual aids (such as handouts or a poster) to help the audience better grasp your meaning.
5. Come to the point slowly if your research or experience indicates that your audience's culture is oriented toward a less direct approach.
6. Use body language and facial expressions carefully and appropriately.
7. Consider using an interpreter to translate your speech for the audience.
8. Look for audience signals (such as facial expressions and other nonverbal cues) to see whether your message is being received.

---

ethical values. Pick up almost any day's edition of the *New York Times,* and accounts of faltering ethical standards are chronicled in virtually every section of the paper. For purposes of my comments today, however, I want to focus on the business pages, since business and ethics is what we're here to talk about.[21]

Haas's introduction was brief, only three sentences long. Still, he was able to explain why he was addressing the audience, link his speech with the location where he was speaking, and show how his comments fit with the purpose of the meeting. By making these connections, Haas demonstrated his understanding of the occasion and of his audience's background and interests.

Gather Your Material

With your central idea in mind, you're ready to find the supporting material that will give that idea credibility and help you achieve your specific purpose. Some information may come from your personal experience, some from outside sources. Look for concrete, accurate details that will help you inform, persuade, motivate, or entertain your audience and, at the same time, bring you closer to the goal expressed in your specific purpose. Through research, you can find supporting material such as facts and figures, examples,

stories, or quotations that will prove your point and bring your ideas to life. Think, too, about personal experiences that can be used to illustrate your ideas in a more sincere and individual way.

Conduct Research

Even speakers who are experts in their fields generally conduct research to uncover details that support their central ideas. Like these experts, you'll want to find evidence to back up your statements and opinions. You can gather material from a variety of sources (see Exhibit 2.6).

- *Library sources.* The first stop for speakers in search of supporting material is generally the library. Check reference books, magazines, newspapers, journals, government publications, and online computer databases.
- *Interviews.* Think about who has knowledge of your topic. You might talk with specialists, people who've solved certain problems, government officials, or others.
- *Observations.* Sometimes you can gather the details you need simply by watching. Look for evidence by observing people, events, or processes that relate to your central idea.
- *Surveys.* To gather statistics about your topic, you might survey a group of people by telephone, by mail, or in person. Even an informal survey can be helpful. Surveying your

EXHIBIT 2.6
Sources of Supporting Material

Library sources	Interviews	Observations

Surveys	Other sources

classmates about some aspect of your topic can prove helpful, too.

• *Other sources.* You can collect additional facts and figures from websites and from printed materials distributed by companies, nonprofit organizations, government agencies, and so forth.

Because their time and money are both limited, student speakers don't choose surveys and observations as often as other research sources. Still, interviews and library sources can provide a vast amount of compelling evidence. When Andy Wood was researching the consequences of overusing antibiotics, he checked newspapers, magazines, and medical journals. He found many

statistics and examples of individual incidents in *Harvard Health Letter, Newsweek,* and other publications. Wood also interviewed the head of the Centers for Disease Control—and he learned a startling fact: The agency tracks problems in only 160 hospitals across the country. So the CDC has no way of knowing whether patients in other hospitals are responding to antibiotic treatments.[22]

As you conduct your research, keep careful records of your sources and the supporting material you turn up. You will be able to tell your audience where you got your information, and you'll be able to double-check your facts later, if necessary. You'll also be using your notes as you develop the major points that support your central idea.

Develop Your Major Points

Now that you have a lot of material about your topic, it's time to go back to your specific purpose and central idea for help in selecting your major points. Start by reviewing your research notes. What did you find out that will support your central idea and help you achieve the goal of your speech?

As you pick out your major points, keep your time limit in mind. If you try to make too many points in a short speech, you won't be able to develop each fully. You may also find yourself rushing through your speech if you have too many points to cover. By confining yourself to only the major points, you help your audience follow what you're trying to say.

For example, Robert A. Plane, president of Wells College in Aurora, New York, had only a few minutes in which to address the Women's Leadership Institute at Wells. His central idea was that society can be improved by encouraging shared values such as honesty. His specific purpose was to persuade audience members to help improve society by practicing honesty and instilling its value in others. As important as his topic was, Plane covered only three major points in his short speech: (1) societies are held together by shared values, (2) honesty forms the cornerstone of an ethical society, and (3) honesty can be both taught and learned.[23]

Once you've identified your major points, put them into a logical order, such as chronologically, cause and effect, topic, and so on (see Chapter 9 for details on how to organize your points). Next, break each major point into its essential subpoints and add supporting facts, figures, and other details as evidence. Because of the limited time he had, Plane provided only one or two items as supporting material for each major point. But the supporting material he used was effective. For example, he used an expert's quote to support his second major point:

The noted American educator Robert Maynard Hutchins spoke simply and eloquently on this complex subject when he said, "Any system of education that is without values is a contradiction in terms, a system that seeks bad values is bad. A system that denies the existence of values denies the possibility of education."[24]

These words were more powerful because Plane attributed them to Hutchins. In doing so, he added the weight of a respected expert to his argument. Audience members could evaluate both the supporting quote and its source as they digested Plane's second major point.

Apply Creative and Critical Thinking

You'll be looking for a variety of supporting details in the course of researching your topic. This is an opportunity to use both creative and critical thinking (see Exhibit 2.7). You'll want your speech to include a range of concrete, lively evidence that will be appealing to your audience, which requires creative thinking. At the same time, you'll want your points to build to a compelling conclusion in support of your central idea, which requires critical thinking.

First think creatively about research sources. Where can you find the most interesting and powerful details to support your main points? As you gather research materials, use critical thinking to assess their accuracy and timeliness. Also be sure you have enough data on which to base your case. Then continue your analysis by comparing and interpreting facts and figures so that you can draw conclusions.

Now step back and look at what you've got. How can creativity bring your points to life? Would a colorfully worded expert's opinion or an unusual anecdote capture the audience's attention? How can you engage your audience's senses? Even the most technical topic will benefit from a touch of originality, as Randall L. Tobias knows well. Tobias is vice chairman of AT&T, and when he

> *Success Tip*
>
> Match the number of major points to the length of your speech. This gives you time to fully develop each point and show how it connects to the central idea without rushing through your speech.

EXHIBIT 2.7
Applying Creative and Critical Thinking to Research
In the course of gathering supporting materials, you'll want to apply both creative and critical thinking. Creative thinking is helpful for generating ideas about research sources. Once you have a number of ideas, you can use critical thinking to eliminate inappropriate sources and focus on relevant ones.

Central idea: Television exerts a powerful influence on young children

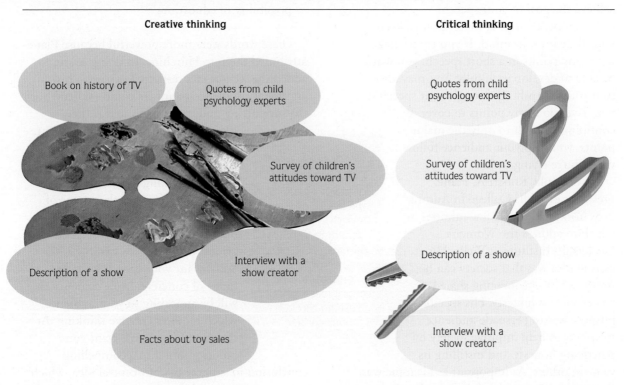

Creative thinking

- Book on history of TV
- Quotes from child psychology experts
- Survey of children's attitudes toward TV
- Description of a show
- Interview with a show creator
- Facts about toy sales

Critical thinking

- Quotes from child psychology experts
- Survey of children's attitudes toward TV
- Description of a show
- Interview with a show creator

spoke to students at the University of West Virginia in Morgantown, he appealed to his audience's senses as he described the progress of computer technology:

> The number of components on a chip has been doubling every 18 months, without a substantial cost increase. To put that into perspective, if we had had similar gains in automotive technology, today you could buy a Lexus for about $2. It would travel at the speed of sound and go 600 miles on a thimble of gas. It would be only three inches long . . . but easy to parallel park![25]

Tobias helped audience members envision the fast pace of progress in information technology by translating it into images they could see as he talked. He also added a humorous reference to parallel parking, which drove home the point by making it more concrete and linking it to a nearly universal experience. Even students without a technical background would be able to follow this example and understand how it supports the central idea in Tobias's informative speech, which is that rapid progress in technology will change how people work and relax in the coming years.

Of course, you have an ethical obligation to your audience to be both fair and accurate when you discuss facts and figures related to your topic. At the very least, you can't earn your audience's respect if you tell only half the story. However, if you use critical thinking to

EXHIBIT 2.8
The Organization of a Speech

General Purpose: A statement of the overall reason for your speech: to inform, to persuade, or to motivate or entertain.

Specific Purpose: A statement of exactly what you want the audience to know, do, or feel as a result of your speech.

Central Idea: A statement of the single compelling idea around which your speech is built.

INTRODUCTION
The first section of the speech, in which you greet your audience, capture audience attention, stir interest, explain what you will talk about, and preview your major points.

BODY
The middle part of the speech, in which you develop your major points and present supporting details that relate to your specific purpose.

CONCLUSION
The end of the speech, in which you let the audience know that the speech is over, summarize and reinforce your major points, and motivate the audience to act.

present a balanced treatment of the topic, your audience will be more willing to trust you.

For example, when AT&T's Tobias stated that "technology touches on some of society's deepest hopes and fears," he was acknowledging that people have a love-hate relationship with technology. In addition, even though he noted that some of the advances he was describing might seem improbable now, he reminded the audience that portable phones and fax machines didn't seem feasible just 15 years ago. This even-handed treatment showed Tobias's knowledge of his topic and thus encouraged his audience to believe what he said.

Organize Your Material

At this point, you've sifted through your research, separated the major points, and applied critical and creative thinking to make the supporting details meaningful. Now you're ready to organize your material and give your speech a definite shape. No matter what your topic, you'll divide your speech into three main sections: the introduction, the body, and the conclusion (see Exhibit 2.8).

Introduction

The **introduction** is the first section of the speech. You begin by greeting your audience and "telling them what you're going to tell them." A good introduction serves as a concise preview of the speech. It briefly explains what you plan to talk about and lays the foundation for the major points you will make. Although your introduction is the first part of your speech, you can't plan its

contents until you've determined the major points you'll make in the body of the speech.

First impressions count, so use your introduction to capture the audience's attention and to stir interest in your topic. This is where your creativity can work wonders. Consider this slightly mysterious introduction to "Faceless Enemies," a speech by Donald McPartland of Emerson College in Boston:

They wait patiently beneath the surface of the earth, virtually undetectable. They sit motionless in utter silence for years at a time, yet in an instant can claim the life of any living being that crosses their path. They received almost no media attention, and yet they number over 100 million and can be found in every corner of the globe.[26]

McPartland used suspense to build interest in a speech topic that most people wouldn't ordinarily think fascinating: the problem of military land mines. Once the first paragraph had his audience hooked, McPartland's next two paragraphs unveiled the topic and previewed the major points.

Body

After your introduction previews the speech for audience members, they're ready to follow what you say in the **body**, the middle section of the speech. This is where you develop your major points and present supporting information. Even though the body is the longest part of the speech, don't load it with too many points. Stick to a few major points and organize them to build toward a logical conclusion. So that your speech will flow smoothly, use transitions to connect one major point to the next.

Depending on your research, time, and topic, you may be able to vary your supporting evidence by including a few carefully selected examples, quotes from experts, and stories as well as statistics and facts. This variety helps you flesh out your speech, making it more than a skeleton of major points held together by impersonal facts and figures. Heather Larson, a student at Northern State University in South Dakota, mixed quotes from experts, government statistics, health facts, and real-life examples in her speech "Stemming the Tide," about the problems of breast cancer. Here is one paragraph from the body of her speech:

"It's about time," says National Breast Cancer Coalition President Frances M. Visco, "that we stopped pointing the finger at women, [saying] that it's their fault they have breast cancer." Some recent theories back this position, suggesting chemicals in the environment may be partially at fault. A research team led by Frank Falck, Jr. at the University of Michigan has linked human breast cancer to DDT, DDE and PCBs. They found significantly higher levels of these in cancerous tissues of test subjects. Ana Soto, a cell biologist at the Tufts University School of Medicine, believes that many currently used pesticides masquerade as estrogen when absorbed into the body.[27]

By quoting Frances Visco, Larson brought a knowledgeable observer's words into the speech. Then she followed the quote with ideas drawn from researchers at two respected universities. Using this approach, Larson turned what could have sounded like a clinical recitation into an engaging and memorable talk about preventing breast cancer.

Of course, the points you make in the body of a speech of self-introduction will be more personal. Develop your points using both personal experiences and examples that help you build a closer relationship with your audience. By sharing information about what you've seen, heard, or done, you show your human side, proving that you're someone your audience can identify with and learn from. However, beware of rambling stories that let your audience's attention drift during the body of the speech. Keep your stories short and lively, and help the audience see how they support your major points and central idea.

Conclusion

The **conclusion** is the end of the speech. In this section, you "tell them what you told them." Your conclusion lets the audience know that the speech is over, summarizes and reinforces what you've presented, and motivates the audience to act. Just as your introduction leads artfully into your major points, your conclusion leads gracefully out of them, bringing the speech full circle. In the words of William Safire, a celebrated journalist and accomplished speaker, "What every audience needs . . . is a sense of completion; what the speaker needs is a way out on a high note."[28]

A well-planned conclusion can leave a lasting impression on your audience. Consider Nelson Mandela's uplifting conclusion in a speech to the nation made shortly after he was elected president of South Africa:

We must therefore act together as an united people, for national reconciliation, for nation building, for the birth of a new world. Let there be justice for all. Let there be peace for all. Let there be work, bread, water and salt for all. Let each know that for each the body, the mind and the soul have been freed to fulfill themselves. Never, never and never again shall it be that this beautiful land will again experience the oppression of one by another and suffer the indignity of being the skunk of the world. The sun shall never set on so glorious a human achievement! Let freedom reign. God bless Africa![29]

Mandela's conclusion brought his speech to a rousing climax. As he reminded audience members of the central idea (protecting freedom and peace in a newly united land), he also motivated them to act (to build a united nation with equality for all). An excellent public speaker, Mandela made every word count.

Choose Your Words Carefully

When you're in front of an audience, your words can carry considerable weight. When you give a speech to inform, people can learn from you. When you give a speech to persuade, people may change their behaviors or attitudes because of you. When you give a speech to motivate, people can be inspired by you. But only if you choose your words carefully (see Exhibit 2.9).

Be specific: Use words that clarify rather than confuse your meaning. Your audience will develop mental images as you talk, so the more concrete your descriptions, the better. If you want to say that you "moved" away from something that frightened you, you could substitute a more active word, such as "jumped" or "ran." Either word would leave little doubt about what you did and give the audience a clearer picture of your reaction.

At the same time, be yourself. Choose words that sound natural rather than stilted or artificial.

Be exciting: Bring your major points to life by using vivid language that's appropriate to the audience and the situation. When veteran magazine editor Fran Carpentier speaks to groups of aspiring editors, she pays special attention to the two or three nuggets of information she wants to leave with her audience. One piece of advice she offers is that "A good editor is like a good thief. An editor should sneak into a story and get out without anybody knowing." Long after the rest of the speech has faded from memory, this kernel of advice will linger on because of its wording.[30]

Be respectful: Choose words that don't hurt, embarrass, or offend your listeners. Be careful about what you say and how you say it. This sign of respect will support your credibility with your audience.

Practice Your Speech Aloud

Research confirms that the more time you spend practicing, the better your speech is likely to be.[31] Practicing aloud also helps you control your nervousness. What's more, it can give you a sense of what works in your speech and what doesn't.

> *Success Tip*
>
> When you plan your speech, choose words that will help you communicate with your audience and accomplish your specific purpose. Use words that are specific, exciting, natural, and respectful.

EXHIBIT 2.9
Using Specific Words to Clarify Meaning

SPEAKER SAYS:	AUDIENCE GETS A MENTAL PICTURE OF:
"I have a new pet."	parakeet, rabbit, fish, turtle, cat, dog
"I have a new dog."	great dane
"I have a new little dog."	chihuahua
"I have a new toy poodle."	black toy poodle
"I have a new white toy poodle."	white toy poodle

Ask an Expert

Arden K. Watson
Associate Professor of Speech Communication, Pennsylvania State University

Q: I've been advised to turn my public speaking anxiety into positive energy, but that's easier said than done. Do you have any suggestions?

A: If you fear speaking, you're in good company. In a survey published in *The Book of Lists*, several thousand people in the United States identified public speaking as their greatest fear. However, as difficult as it may seem, you can control this fear by following this simple method:

In your own words, make a list of statements that describe each of your fears: (1) the *behavior* that will show you have this fear, (2) the *effect* this fear and its behavior will have, and (3) the *action* you can take to change the behavior and get rid of the fear. By making your list, you're isolating the problem causing your fear so that you can do something to change that problem and reduce or eliminate the fear caused by it.

Your fears will probably fall into one of three categories: poor preparation, physical responses, or fear of failing yourself or your audience.

Preparation Fears

Do you fear that your speech won't be interesting?
The *behavior* you identify for the fear is (1) I'll choose a boring topic. The *effect* will be (2) people won't like what I have to say. To change this behavior and control your fear, the *action* for you to take is (3) BE THE EXPERT. You can know more about your topic than anyone else—what it looks like, feels like, sounds like. You can research it, interview others about it, experience it. Through good preparation, you can know your topic so well that you can talk all day about it and make it interesting to anyone.

Do you fear that you'll make a fool of yourself?
(1) I'll forget what I'm going to say (behavior), so (2) the audience will be confused (effect). When preparing your speech, (3) STRUCTURE THE CONTENT FOR EASY RECALL (action). A strong and logical structure keeps you from forgetting and helps your audience follow what you say. Plan your major points around a structure suitable for your topic, such as a story, time, a comparison, a list, a problem and its solution, classification, or cause and effect.

Do you fear that the audience won't like you?
(1) I'll start the speech in a way the audience dislikes (behavior), so (2) they'll think everything I have to say is boring (effect). When preparing your speech (3) CONSTRUCT A MEMORABLE INTRODUCTION AND CONCLUSION (action). You capture and hold audience attention in the first 30 seconds or not at all. So be ready to start off with a quotation or something funny, exciting, or surprising. Then in your conclusion, tie your speech together with the same meaningful idea.

Physical Response Fears

Do you fear looking silly when you give your speech?
(1) I'll stand stiff as a board (behavior), so (2) the audience will know how nervous I am (effect). To change this physical response, (3) CREATE INTERACTION WITH YOUR AUDIENCE (action). Use your anxiety to energize your delivery. Move a bit, make comfortable gestures, and look audience members in the eye. Try to be natural when you gesture, and avoid movement that is meaningless.

Do you fear looking at the audience?
(1) I'll look over their heads at the back wall (behavior), so (2) my listeners will get the feeling I don't care about them or what they think (effect). When giving your speech, (3) TALK WITH YOUR AUDIENCE NOT AT THEM (action). Imagine a two-way conversation with each person there. Watch your listeners' eyes, and note their expressions. Adjust to their reactions—return their smiles and head nods, speed up or slow down if needed. Talk just as you would talk with your best friend.

Are you afraid you won't be able to talk with expression?
(1) I'll stutter and stammer (behavior), so (2) the audience will think I'm unsure of my information and myself (effect). When giving your speech, (3) SLOW DOWN, PAUSE, AND PHRASE FOR IMPACT (action). Emphasize certain phrases for effect. By pausing after delivering the phrase, you allow your audience to grasp the idea behind it. Also, by pausing silently, you eliminate "uhs" and "ahs" while your mind is searching for the next idea. You'll actually appear more sure of your information by pausing to think about it.

Fears of Failing (Yourself or Your Audience)

Do you fear you won't be as good as you would like to be?
(1) I'll leave out parts of my speech or act nervous (behavior), so (2) I won't get a good grade (effect). Before giving your speech, (3) MAKE THE SPEECH YOUR OWN (action). Practice, practice, practice. Listen to yourself on a tape recorder. Have yourself videotaped and look for strengths and weaknesses. Practice out loud until you're in control, until you feel you've mastered the speech and it's yours. If you like your speech, your audience will like it, and you'll get a good grade.

Do you dread giving the speech?
(1) I'll look scared (behavior), so (2) the audience will sense my nervousness and will snicker and make fun of me (effect). When giving your speech, (3) ACT CONFIDENT (action), even if you feel otherwise. Listeners want you to succeed, and they can't see what's happening inside you. Don't apologize for anything. If you make a mistake, don't start over; just keep going.

Do you fear not knowing what to do at the conclusion?
(1) I'll say something silly like "That's it, I'm done" (behavior), so (2) I'll feel dumb, and the audience will feel embarrassed for me (effect). When you reach the conclusion of your speech, (3) END THE SPEECH EFFECTIVELY (action). As already mentioned, plan your conclusion carefully, and practice it out loud. Your final impression is very important. Deliver the conclusion just as you planned it, maintain eye contact for just a moment, and then move confidently back to your seat. Then enjoy the applause—your moment in the spotlight!

1. Does the behavior-effect-action structure described here contradict this chapter's advice to "think positive"? How can you combine the two approaches to more effectively overcome any anxiety you might feel?
2. Using the behavior-effect-action structure, list one of your fears and show how you plan to counter it in your next speech. After your speech, evaluate the effectiveness of the action you planned. What action, if any, would you take if you felt this fear again?

EXHIBIT 2.10
Launching into a Speech
As you stand in front of your audience and get ready to start your speech, take a deep breath, smile, and make eye contact with audience members for a moment or two. This brief pause will give you time to settle your nerves while alerting the audience that you are about to begin.

It's also a good opportunity to pace yourself and make sure that you can finish (without rushing) within the time you're allowed.

As you practice, think about your central idea, your major points, and what you want to accomplish. Think, too, of the relationship you want to build with the audience using both words and body language. Show the audience that you care about your topic by putting feeling into your voice and using gestures when appropriate to convey your ideas (but not so much that you distract your audience).

If possible, rehearse in front of friends or family so that you can practice projecting your voice and making eye contact. Instead of memorizing every word, give your speech over and over until the words are familiar enough to flow naturally. Concentrate on communicating your meaning rather than on using the same words every time you practice the speech. If you plan to use drawings, charts, slides, or other visual aids, practice with them, too. Only after practicing

will you be ready to deliver your speech.

Deliver Your Speech

This is it: you're about to face the audience and present your first speech (see Exhibit 2.10). Think back to those tension-busting tips and breathe deeply as you walk confidently to address your audience. Smile naturally, making eye contact with individuals as you look around the audience. Before you begin to speak, pause to get a grip on your nerves and to give the audience a moment to settle down. Then launch into your introduction.

As you move from the introduction to the body and the conclusion, stay alert to your audience's reaction. Depending on audience feedback, you may want to adjust your timing or your words during the speech. As time goes on and you have more opportunities to address audiences, you'll get better at adapting your speech to your audience. Right now, your goal is to complete your first speech and learn from the experience so that you can improve your public speaking skills.

SAMPLE SPEECH OF INTRODUCTION

The following sample speech provides a twist on the usual speech of introduction. The speaker is not actually introducing another person or herself. Rather, she is telling a story about herself. This speech provides a good example of how telling a personal story can help a speaker feel more at ease giving his or her first speech.

(1) Eleanor Forseby McMahon. That is not my name. It is the name of my best friend, who is thirteen feet long, weighs nearly half a ton, and is scratched and dented. Ellie is a sailboat. Learning to sail her involved much more than simply acquiring a new skill. She taught me the most important lesson in my life: how to trust in myself, no matter what the odds. This is how it happened.

(2) My father bought Ellie the summer I turned twelve. The boat was not for me, but for my sixteen-year-old twin sisters. They took sailing lessons from a cute college student who kept their interest level high, although he made slow progress in actually teaching them to sail. I begged to go along during the lessons, but the twins complained the boat was too small for four people.

I stayed on the shore, my eyes glued to the small craft. Stuck on land, I imagined myself in my sisters' place. I dreamed of being a great sailor. And every day, my dreams grew bigger.

In exchange for taking down the sails and cleaning out the boat after each of my sisters' outings, I was given permission to sit in the empty, tied-up craft. I still had not had a lesson, but I had no trouble imagining what I wasn't experiencing. More than ever, I wanted to be out on the water, skimming over the tops of waves, squinting in the sunshine.

One day, temptation overcame me. I had no high opinion of my sisters' talents, and I was sure that all my careful watching from the shore would equal what they had learned out on the water. I ran to the boathouse and grabbed the oars, sails, and life preserver.

(3) Back at the dock, I raised the small jib sail halfway, as I had seen my sisters do, and readied the boat for departure. I slowly made my way out into the calm harbor water, where the boat rocked and heaved as I struggled to get the main sail up. Even now, I'm not sure how I managed it. But there I was, sailing!

Commentary

(1) In the introduction, the speaker captures attention, stirs interest, builds rapport with her listeners, and explains what the speech will be about.

(2) In the body of her speech, the speaker takes her listeners back in time to a dramatic event that changed her life.

(3) Note how the speaker uses specific, natural, vivid language to describe what happened.

At first, it seemed heavenly. Then reality set in. I was out in the middle of the harbor, and I was only *pretending* to know how to sail. Visions of disaster quickly replaced my dreams of glory. I decided to go back, and that's when the real trouble began.

The boat seemed to have a mind of her own. It took all my strength to keep her pointed back toward the dock. As I approached the narrow channel that led to our slip, I lost control. The boat swung round sideways and bobbed crazily. A cabin cruiser swept by me, its owner in a rage. "Girlie!" he bellowed. "Get control of that boat or get it out of the water!" I didn't know what to do. I just gave up. I sat motionless on the deck, frozen with fear.

Suddenly, Ellie took over. She lurched and practically threw me out of the boat. As I fought to keep from going overboard, I realized that the water was where I belonged. I jumped out, grabbed the bowline in one hand, and began to swim, towing Ellie toward the dock. She was so heavy! After only a moment or two, I was ready to give up. It was too much. I couldn't do it.

Again, Ellie took charge. This time she raised herself high in the water, knocking the bowline up against my face. Of course! If I put the line in my mouth, and clamped my teeth hard around it, I would have the use of both my arms as well as my legs. Now I made steady progress toward the dock. Ellie seemed to grow lighter and lighter, the nearer we came to the slip. As the water slapped her hull, it sounded like she was singing to me, "Yes, you can. Yes, you can."

(4) Nearly eight years and hundreds of hours of sailing have passed since the day I towed Ellie in. I still haven't become the great sailor of my dreams, but I am good enough to win races sometimes. Sailing Ellie remains my favorite pastime, and the lesson she taught me is still fresh in my mind: I am capable of doing whatever needs to be done.

(4) In the conclusion, the speaker brings her listeners back to the present day, signals that the speech is over, summarizes what she has said, and restates what she learned from her experience.

SUMMARY

Even experienced public speakers feel nervous about facing an audience. Nervousness shows that you care about the audience, the topic, and the occasion. In addition to taking this course, you can build your confidence as a public speaker by (1) concentrating on your message, (2) preparing your introduction and conclusion, (3) planning and practicing your speech, (4) talking with individuals, (5) thinking positive, (6) visualizing success, (7) being yourself, (8) projecting confidence, (9) reducing tension, and (10) looking for speaking opportunities.

When you select a topic, start by considering the audience's needs and interests, the occasion for the speech, the length of the speech, the personal importance of the topic, and your knowledge of the topic. Then narrow the subject to focus on a particular topic that meets both your audience's needs and your time constraints.

The general purpose is the overall reason, in general terms, for your speech: to inform, to persuade, and to motivate or entertain. In contrast, the specific purpose indicates exactly what you want the audience to know, do, or feel as a result of your speech. The central idea is a concise statement of the single compelling idea around which your speech will be built.

The audience is the center of the public speaking process. One way to analyze your audience is according to personal factors such as age, gender, education, and occupation. A second way to analyze the audience is according to psychological factors such as needs, motives, attitudes, values, and lifestyles. A third way to analyze your audience is according to social factors such as group membership or cultural, racial, and ethnic identification.

You can bring your central idea to life and give it credibility by finding supporting materials such as facts, figures, quotes, examples, and stories. Select a few major points from these supporting materials to help you build a case for your central idea and, at the same time, move you closer to the goal of your speech. Use critical and creative thinking when selecting and organizing your supporting materials and major points.

Speeches have three main sections. The first is the introduction, in which you greet your audience, preview your speech, and capture your audience's attention and interest. The middle section is the body, in which you develop your major points and present supporting details in subpoints. The last section is the conclusion, in which you signal that the speech is over, summarize and reinforce your message, and motivate the audience to act.

Practicing your speech aloud helps you feel less nervous. It also gives you a chance to see what works and what doesn't and to check your speech's length. Finally, practice is an opportunity to become familiar with the words so that they flow naturally. This sets the stage for your delivery, when you actually face the audience and give the speech.

KEY TERMS

body (40)
central idea (33)
conclusion (40)
general purpose (33)
introduction (39)
specific purpose (33)

APPLY CRITICAL THINKING

1. Which symptoms of nervousness might be apparent to someone who is watching a speaker carefully? Have you seen a professional speaker show any of these telltale signs? What aspect of the occasion, audience, or topic might have contributed to that speaker's anxiety?
2. Do you need to analyze your audience if you're planning a speech of self-introduction? Why or why not?
3. Think about the most persuasive public speaker you've seen in action. How did his or her supporting material provide convincing evidence for the speech's major points? How did the speaker's use of words make the speech more persuasive?
4. Which is the most important section of a speech: the introduction, body, or conclusion? Why?
5. Do you agree with William Safire that every speech should send the speaker out on a high note? Explain your answer.
6. What ethical issues might be raised by the use of some types of vivid language (such as insulting slang words) in a speech of self-introduction? Be specific.
7. How does delivering a speech resemble a performance? How does it differ from a performance?

SHARPEN YOUR SKILLS

Individual Exercises

1. Plan and write a speech of self-introduction to present to your class.

a. List two or three points about your audience that you want to keep in mind.

b. Narrow your topic and write down your general purpose, your specific purpose, and your central idea.

c. Gather supporting material, if needed, and list your major points.

d. Draft your speech, practice it aloud, and then deliver it.

e. Were you nervous? Write a paragraph about how you plan to build your confidence as an excellent public speaker.

2. List at least four opportunities for public speaking on your campus and in your community.

a. Next to each one (1) describe, in general terms, the audience you would expect to be addressing, and (2) identify an appropriate general purpose for your speech.

b. Choose one of these opportunities and draft a one-page letter volunteering to speak.

c. Describe the specific purpose and central idea you would use in the speech you would give.

3. Of all the public speakers you've seen, who do you think is the most skillful? List two specific reasons why this speaker is a good model for you to follow when developing confidence in your public speaking.

4. Read one of the speeches in the appendix, and choose two related facts or figures cited by the speaker.

a. How would you use critical thinking to analyze this evidence?

b. How would you use creative thinking to bring the evidence to life or to make it more concrete for the audience?

Group Exercises

5. Working with a classmate, analyze one of the speeches in the appendix.

a. What is the general purpose? The specific purpose?

b. What is the central idea? Express it in one sentence.

c. What major points does the speaker use to support the central idea? List them.

d. How does the speaker use critical thinking or creative thinking in this speech? Cite at least one example.

6. Working with your classmate, analyze the organization of the speech you selected for #5.

a. Where does the introduction end and the body begin? How does the introduction relate to the speaker's specific purpose? To the central idea?

b. What portion of the speech represents the body? How are the major points presented in the body? Is the order important? Why?

c. Where does the conclusion begin? How does the conclusion relate to the specific purpose? To the central idea?

d. What words does the speaker use to signal transitions from introduction to body, from one major point to the next, and from body to conclusion?

e. After reading this speech, what action do you feel motivated to take or what position have you been persuaded to adopt? Does your classmate feel the same way? Do you think either of you would feel differently if you saw and heard the speech being delivered? Why?

FREE SPEECH AND ETHICAL RESPONSIBILITIES

LEARNING OBJECTIVES

After studying this chapter, you will be able to

1. Define defamation and distinguish between slander and libel.

2. Differentiate ethics and values.

3. Explain the effect that values have on ethics.

4. List seven steps speakers can take to help ensure ethical communication.

5. Discuss the impact of ethical credibility on a speaker's effectiveness.

6. Enumerate the three stages of credibility.

7. Describe the listener's ethical responsibilities for successful speeches.

IS CIVILIZED SPEECH NOTHING BUT A QUAINT MEMORY?

If you read this chapter and then turn on a television or radio, you're going to detect a rather startling discrepancy. This chapter essentially offers ethical guidelines for civilized, constructive public speaking. However, all around you you'll hear instance after instance of uncivilized, rude, counterproductive speech—at all levels of speaking, from the most powerful officials in our national government to the people who call in to local talk radio shows. Insults, rumors, character assassinations, foul language, shouting, and sexist and racist language seem to rule the public airwaves today. Negative "attack" ads and speeches seem to have all but replaced calm, reasoned discussion of important issues in our political campaigns. Members of Congress openly insult each other during House and Senate speeches.

Compare this distressing state of affairs with the guidelines established by George Washington 200 years ago when he wrote "Rules of Civility." His set of 160 rules (more than a fifth of which deal with public speaking) might sound hopelessly quaint in today's world of "shock jock" radio. A few examples: "Speak not injurious words neither in jest nor earnest. Scoff at none although they give occasion. Let your conversation be without malice or envy. And in all causes of passion admit reason to govern."[1] Even though his contemporaries didn't always follow his suggestions, it's safe to assume that our first president would be downright appalled by the state of public speaking today.

Given the wide gap between the uncivilized speech you hear around you and the guidelines for civilized speech presented in this chapter, you as a speaker have a choice to make—and it isn't an easy one. Negative campaigns and other examples of uncivilized public speaking are gaining ground for the simple reason that they are often effective. Trying to make ethical choices may at times isolate you as others drown out your voice of reason. However, one of the most important assets you'll ever have, in both your personal and professional lives, is your reputation. When you speak ethically, you enhance that reputation. You make a powerful statement to the audience about who you are as a human being. Ethical speaking can dramatically enhance your **ethos**, or character, so that you will be perceived by your audience as credible.[2] Public speaking offers an opportunity to build a reputation for honesty and integrity.

No matter how difficult civilized speech may become, remember that you always have a choice. The high road may be hard to travel, but it is never closed. To travel that road successfully, you first need to be aware of some legal issues that affect public speaking. You need to understand how to strike a balance between a concern for the rights of others and your individual rights as a public speaker.

INDIVIDUAL RIGHTS AND SOCIAL RESPONSIBILITY

Public speaking can be a powerful instrument for change—both positive change and negative change. That power is what leads society to attach responsibilities to public speech. Some of these responsibilities are expressed in legal terms, and others are considered ethical issues. This section provides a brief overview of key legal points related to public speaking.

Protecting Governments and the Public

Societies and governments have wrestled with legal concerns in public speaking for as long as people have been speaking in public. In the United States, freedom of speech was first addressed in 1791 with the Bill of Rights. The First Amendment to the Constitution states that "Congress shall make no law abridging the freedom of speech, or of the press." However, freedom of speech isn't such a simple issue. Only seven years after passing the Bill of Rights, Congress passed the Alien and Sedition Acts of 1798, which tried to restrict public speeches opposing the government. However, following an outcry from officials who questioned the constitutionality of restricting public criticism, the law was allowed to expire.[3]

A little more than a century later, public criticism of the government caused a great deal of concern during World War I. The Espionage Act of 1917 prohibited people from saying or doing anything to damage military morale or to interfere with recruiting or drafting soldiers. In upholding the constitutionality of the Espionage Act, the U.S. Supreme Court said that the government could restrict speeches that pose a "clear and present danger" to the country or the public. It was in this case that Justice Oliver Wendell Holmes delivered the opinion that freedom of speech does not allow a person to falsely shout "Fire!" in a crowded theater and thereby cause a dangerous panic that could endanger the safety of people in the theater. This example is frequently repeated when people discuss how much freedom public speakers should have.[4]

In 1925 a public speaker was arrested in New York for advocating the violent overthrow of government, and the ensuing court case imposed further restrictions on the idea of clear and present danger by establishing tests to determine whether a speech could *eventually* lead to public harm. In other words, for a speech to pose a clear and present danger, it wouldn't have to cause any sort of trouble *directly*, as long as it had a *tendency* to cause trouble for the government or the public.[5]

Congress and the Supreme Court modified "clear and present danger" again in the 1940s with the idea of "clear and probable danger." This idea tries to balance the gravity of the supposed harm with the probability that such harm might actually take place.[6] In fact, balance has been the common theme running through discussions of free speech, from our country's earliest times right up to the present day. For example, the U.S. Supreme Court addressed a controversial free speech issue in 1989 when it defended the individual's right to burn the U.S. flag for political protest purposes as a speech act protected by the First Amendment.

Clearly, it's difficult to balance the rights of government and the public to be protected versus the individual's right to speak freely. We acknowledge the importance of free expression in maintaining a democracy, but at the same time, we realize what a powerful instrument public speaking can be, so we also recognize that restraint is necessary from time to time (see Exhibit 3.1).

Freedom of speech varies widely from country to country. Recognizing the potential power of free and open discussion, totalitarian governments tend to restrict both individual expression and freedom of the press. For example, the People's Republic of China lived up to its reputation as one of the most restrictive governments when it hosted the United Nations Fourth World Conference on Women in 1995. Any visiting groups likely to stage public protests over China's human rights policies were restricted to using an athletic field that was an hour away from the capital city of Beijing. Chinese citizens were not allowed to witness any of the protests, and government security officials issued rules stating that protest speeches and signs must "not infringe on the sovereignty of the host country and should not slander or attack leaders of the host country."

EXHIBIT 3.1
Restrictions on Free Expression
Although these New Yorkers protesting education funding cuts enjoy the right to free speech, they must abide by other constraints, such as not inciting riots.

Protecting Individual Rights

As a public speaker, you must comply with laws that protect the rights of individuals. Interestingly, how you perceive the individual rights of others may vary depending on several things: your gender, age, education level, and political orientation. For instance, as educational level increases, support for freedom of expression tends to increase; but, getting older tends to be associated with less support for individual rights to free speech. Also, support for freedom of expression is higher at the left side of the political spectrum than the right. So it's important as a public speaker to think about your own attitudes toward the rights of others and what would happen if you were to abuse those rights.[7]

Calling someone a cheat or a thief can bring charges of **defamation** (or making a statement that falsely or unjustifiably hurts a person's reputation). Spoken defamation is **slander**; written defamation is **libel**. You can avoid charges of defamation in several ways: [8]

- *If you disagree with someone, be careful to attack the idea, not the individual.* Rock musician and hunting enthusiast Ted Nugent appeared on a radio talk show in Detroit to defend hunters against charges of animal cruelty leveled by Heidi Prescott, the director of the Fund for Animals. Instead of addressing Prescott's ideas, however, Nugent attacked her character and her morals with a variety of insults not printable in a textbook. Prescott sued both Nugent and the radio station for defamation and won a $125,000 settlement.[9]

- *Don't let anger or revenge influence what you say.* The controversy between hunters and animal rights activists is just one of many public issues that stir strong passions on both sides. Let passion motivate and inspire your speeches, but don't let it take over. Nugent's radio outburst was a classic example of passion overruling civilized, reasonable discussion, and he paid a steep price for his indiscretion.

- *Check your facts and be sure that your message is accurate.* Spreading false and damaging information about a person or a group can leave you open to charges of defamation, even if you think your information is accurate. You're responsible for the content of your speeches, so if you have any doubts about the accuracy of your sources, double-check them with additional research. Be aware that even jokes can be interpreted as defamation.

- *Don't use abusive language that might be interpreted as slanderous.* You can say someone has his or her facts wrong, that he or she has reached an incorrect conclusion, or that a speaker isn't telling the public the whole story. If you go beyond this and call the person dishonest, stupid, evil, or anything else of that nature, you're entering potential defamation territory. Let your facts and logical reasoning speak for themselves.

Protecting the Work of Other Writers and Speakers

A third important legal matter in public speaking is the protection of existing books, articles, speeches, songs, and other original works. This complex field of law is known as **intellectual property,** or the ownership of intangible property created by an individual or a group. The class of property discussed here is called "intellectual" because its value lies in the ideas and the creativity it represents, not in the physical form it might take. For instance, if you steal a book from a library, you're stealing a piece of tangible property. If you steal an *idea* from a book, you're stealing intellectual property.

As discussed in Chapter 1, taking someone else's ideas or their presentation of those ideas in words is known as plagiarism. Plagiarism remains a troublesome point in public speaking (and other communication endeavors), partly because it is so hard to define precisely.[10] If you were to take a chapter from this book and include it word-for-word in a book of your own, the case for accusing you of plagiarism would be clear. But what if you took some of the ideas and presented them in a unique way? What if you borrowed just some of the words? Because plagiarism is so hard to define precisely, it is both a legal issue and an ethical issue. The most extreme cases, such as stealing an entire chapter, are clearly illegal, but what about the murkier cases of borrowing ideas? In both written and spoken communication, most scholars agree that it's important to understand what plagiarism is and why ethical questions about it aren't clear-cut.[11] You'll read more about plagiarism in the following section on ethics.

ETHICAL ISSUES IN PUBLIC SPEAKING

A variety of laws attempt to define freedom of speech, defamation, and plagiarism. These laws can help to some extent in preparing and presenting your speeches. However, they don't address all of the choices you'll have to make as a public speaker about what's right and wrong to say or do. You won't be able to count on black-and-white laws all the time. There may be times when you'll have to choose between society's written and unwritten standards for public speech and your own personal standards. Those personal standards represent your *ethics*, your own internal sense of the right and wrong thing to do as a public speaker. Consider the following ethical dilemmas. In situations such as these, your ethical decisions will determine how you'll use the power of public speaking to influence or inform others.[12]

- In a political campaign, you've discovered some ethically negative information about one of your opponents. Should you withhold the information, knowing that it doesn't directly affect the person's ability to do the job? Or should you tell the public, knowing that negative news about your opponent will probably help your campaign?
- A national retail chain wants to open a new store in your small town. You don't want the increased traffic the store will bring, but you know a lot of your neighbors would benefit from the jobs the store would create. Given an opportunity to speak on the issue at a town hall meeting, what would you say?
- Your next presentation in public speaking class is due soon and you know you need to perform well. The grade on this speech could really affect your final grade in the class. Unfortunately, you don't have time to research and plan an original speech as thoroughly as you'd like. However, you could use information and a speech outline from another presentation you gave in another class. Would that be the ethical thing to do?

EXHIBIT 3.2

Examples of Values and Ethical Decisions
Values represent what you hold to be important in life. On
the basis of what you value, you make ethical decisions
about what you say or do.

VALUES (judgments of worth or importance)	ETHICAL DECISIONS (good/bad or right/wrong)
Respect for individuals	Listen to opinions open-mindedly
Success and achievement	Work hard and climb the corporate ladder
Freedom of expression	Allow others to have their say
Belief in progress	Support economic growth

A single course in public speaking can't establish a complete ethical foundation for you that will act as a base for every choice you'll ever have to make as a speaker. Experts in communication continue to discuss this challenge and search for such an all-encompassing speech ethic.[13] But the course you're now taking should make one point clear, no matter where you stand on the issue of speech ethics. The ethical choices you make in your role as a public speaker are an extension of the choices you make in your life overall. If you try to live your life according to your personal beliefs about what is right and wrong, that approach will help ensure ethical decision making in your speeches, too.

Ethics and Values

The term *ethics* can be applied in several ways. However, in the most general sense, **ethics** is a branch of philosophy that explores what constitutes "good" (or "right") and what constitutes "bad" (or "wrong") and how people can decide whether a particular decision or activity is good or bad. More specific ethical systems can be found in particular religions (such as Christian or Islamic ethics) and professions (such as medical ethics). In fact, emergency room doctors can find themselves in an ethical conflict with people whose religious beliefs discourage medical intervention.

Our ethical decisions are determined to a large degree by our **values**, judgments about the relative

worth or importance we place on various behaviors.[14] We all have certain values as individuals. For example, choosing to devote 80 hours a week to your business or your career (instead of balancing your time between work, family, and social interests) reflects a value judgment you've made about the importance of work or of material success. In addition, we accept values as part of our membership in various groups. Religions, countries, and cultures all have values they expect their members to share. In the United States, for instance, values often include respect for individuals, emphasis on success and achievement, freedom of expression, and belief in progress (see Exhibit 3.2).[15]

Of course, in a country as diverse as the United States, you can't expect everyone to have the same values—which can lead to conflicts and disagreements over ethical decisions. Freedom of expression is a good example. People in the United States treasure their freedom of speech; nevertheless, they can become uncomfortable when they don't like what someone else is saying. What if a leader of the Ku Klux Klan (or another group often associated with negative views) were planning to deliver a speech in your town? Would you respect this person's right to present his or her opinions, even though you find them deeply offensive?

Put yourself in the shoes of James Cameron, an African American and noted historian of racial violence, who has studied and experienced hateful

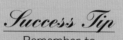

Success Tip
Remember to consider your audience's values when preparing a speech; they may differ considerably from your own and have a significant impact on your speaking success.

speech all his life. In 1930 he narrowly escaped a Klan lynch mob that murdered two of his friends.[16] If you were Cameron, listening to Klan members scream racial slurs and threats at a 1995 rally in Wisconsin, would you respect the Klan's right to freedom of speech? Events such as Klan rallies bring our value choices into sharp focus because they force us to pin specific decisions on such vague phrases as "freedom of expression." In the case of the Klan rally, it might be hard to say, "I disagree with what you have to say but I respect your right to say it!"

Just as you are aware of the shared values of the social and cultural groups to which you belong, you should keep in mind the ethical perspectives of the world around you. While it is true that your own conscience must ultimately guide your choices in life, your public presentations should reflect an awareness of generally held ethical beliefs. Granted, gray areas abound and will continue to be debated by communication experts. But for greater success in public speech, you'll win over more audiences by respecting the ethical consensus than by striking off on your own. Following are a few accepted guidelines for ethical speech that you may find helpful.

Guidelines for Ethical Presentations

Because excellent public speakers can make a difference when they inform, persuade, or inspire, speaking carries important responsibilities in any situation. Public speaking can make a positive difference if you follow these guidelines for ethical communication.

Analyze Your Goals and the Potential Consequences of Your Speech

One of the most important ethical decisions you can face when preparing a speech relates to the goals of your speech. Simply put, are you working toward a goal that is compatible with your personal values and ethical choices? Many of your classroom and career speeches won't have profound ethical implications, of course. If you're talking about car repair, vacation opportunities, or your company's investment in a new technology, you're not likely to face ethical dilemmas. How-

ever, some of the speeches you'll make, even in the classroom, can affect the behaviors and attitudes of your fellow classmates—and the better you become as a speaker, the more influence you will have.

When you plan a speech, you need to examine the ethics of both the message and its consequences. Imagine that you're attending a local political meeting, and you hear your neighbor Alice Washburn make the following speech:

Friends, you and I have a lot in common. We work hard, follow the rules, and try to do the best for our families. But lately I have to wonder just what all this hard work is leading up to. How many times in the last year have you read about some bureaucrat in Washington spending your hard-earned tax dollars on some frivolous special-interest program? How much of your money is shipped overseas to help other countries, when we don't even help all our own people here at home? How much of it is just wasted by bungling government agencies? Are you tired of government officials living off fat pensions when you're not sure where next month's rent is coming from? Have you had enough?

Well, I've been struggling with this issue for quite some time now, and I've decided I've had enough. More than enough. I tried to play fair, but the system isn't playing fair with me or my family. It's time to take action, to send a message that we won't stand for it anymore. And I plan to hit those bureaucrats right where it hurts—in the wallet. They won't stop wasting my money, so I'm going to stop giving it to them. Yes, you heard me right. From this day on, I refuse to hand over my hard-earned money to a bunch of wasteful freeloaders. I sent the final tax payment of my life to the government on April 15th of this year. I will not pay my taxes again until the system is free of waste and corruption.

I realize this is a serious step to take, my friends, but we have a serious problem. It doesn't seem to matter who we send to Washington, the mess and the fraud and the waste just keep getting worse. I've agonized over my decision, and I firmly believe it is the right and moral thing to do. What's the point of working so hard for our children's futures if the government is just going to steal it away from them? Let's stand together on this, just as the founders of this great nation stood together to throw off the shackles of their financial oppressors.

Ignoring the issue of whether Washburn's initial decision to stop paying taxes is ethical, would this speech be considered ethical by most people? After all, she didn't explicitly tell anybody to do anything illegal or unethical; she simply explained why she was taking a particular course of action. But what if a number of people in the audience were already leaning in her direction, and the speech convinced them to join her? What if they respect her because of her position as a visible political figure—a position that in their minds gives her **credibility**, or makes her seem worthy of their belief and trust? And what if these people follow her lead and wind up in jail for tax evasion? What about the effect this could have on their lives and careers, not to mention the effect it could have on their families? Washburn didn't force anybody to evade taxes, but a case could certainly be made that her speech could have played an important role in the actions of these people. How ethical does her speech seem now? As a speaker, you must be prepared to accept responsibility for any action the audience takes based on your speech.

Prepare Thoroughly
Do more than just collect data; understand what the information means. Understand how each piece of data connects with the other points you plan to make, and know what each point implies. For a speech on AIDS, it might be tempting to criticize the government for not spending enough on research to find a cure, but is that the only side of the story? What about personal responsibility for avoiding new cases? What about those research efforts working toward cures for cancer, heart disease, and other common killers? Be honest about your facts and figures, your conclusions,

and your position. It's not enough to avoid untrue, incomplete, unproved, or irrelevant evidence; be sure to support your position without misrepresenting or distorting your evidence. Tell the truth about how old your evidence is, and say whether newer evidence supports your conclusions.

Of course, accuracy and truthfulness by themselves do not ensure an ethical presentation. You must also be concerned with how to present your information so that audience members will understand it. Avoid trying to impress or confuse your listeners with big words or convoluted logic. Define your terms whenever your audience is likely to be unfamiliar with words you use. And be careful to choose the best words to express what you really want to say. Here are some things to consider when choosing words:

- Avoid using words that are demeaning to gender, sexual orientation, race, religion, or ethnic group. Some people complain that speakers today carry "political correctness" to extremes, but in public speaking, it's generally better to err on the side of caution.
- Recognize the various ways people can interpret the same words. What does the phrase "freedom of choice" mean to you? What about "right to life"? Depending on the ethical position you've chosen to take on abortion, these phrases can mean very different things, even though they both focus on the issue of abortion. In fact, the labels chosen by the two sides in the abortion controversy reflect ethical decisions about someone's individual rights—those of the mother or those of the child.
- Be aware that a slight change in wording can make a huge change in the emotional impact of a phrase, changing the whole tone. When describing someone's blond hair, for example, the words *bleached*, *light*, and *flaxen* might bring to mind the same color, but the attitude or emotion implied by each of the three words might change from negative to neutral to positive.

FOCUSING ON ETHICS

IS IT EVER OK TO LIE?

One of the toughest issues in the study of ethics—and in the study of ethical speaking—is whether an acceptable end justifies an unacceptable means. An example of this is distorting the truth to persuade an audience to accept a position that may be absolutely right and honorable. Say you deliver a speech to persuade your classmates to donate food to a local food bank. Your speech turns out to be successful because you tell your listeners that children are starving to death right in our own backyards, even though children aren't actually starving to *death*. On the one hand, you accomplish the worthy goal of increasing reserves at the food bank. On the other hand, you do it by lying. Or say you make a speech in which you overstate the risks of cholesterol in an attempt to get people to modify their diets. This action would be good for them, but have you acted unethically by lying to them?

Deciding whether these noble ends justify questionable means is an ethical choice you'll have to make as a speaker. However, you also need to consider a larger question here, which is the effect that such tactics might have on the integrity of the speaker-audience relationship (not to mention your own credibility). Can these "noble lies" harm the communication process we human beings rely on? Dag Hammarskjold, former secretary general of the United Nations, expressed his concern for ethical communication when he said that respect for truthful language is essential to society's growth and well-being. He also asserted that misusing language betrays a lack of respect for your audience. It seems reasonable to conclude from this that Hammarskjold would not agree with a speaker's choice to distort the truth—even for noble ends—because doing so is harmful to society overall.

Another way to view this dilemma is to define the central component of ethical communication as fostering choice making. In other words, it's your job as a speaker to let your audience know what choices are available and to help them make good choices. Given this definition, even "helpful" lies are unethical communication because they fail to give your audience correct and complete information on which to base good choices. You are denying them the opportunity to make a fully informed choice. You are also implying that you do not respect or trust your audience to make good choices for themselves. Think how you would feel in your audience's situation. Would you want someone to withhold information from you "for your own good," or would you feel they were not treating you as a responsible adult?

Consider these two additional perspectives next time the opportunity arises to pursue honorable goals with dishonorable tactics.

Would you ever consider unethical speech in pursuit of a worthy goal?

Be Yourself

It's true that people are more persuaded by someone they perceive as being similar to themselves.[17] But don't pretend to be someone you're not. Avoid the temptation to act, dress, or speak like someone very different from the real you. Similarly, don't feign a dedication to or interest in your topic; such behavior is unethical.

Be sure to let the audience know your feelings about your topic (unless your speech is strictly informative, such as reporting the news). Your audience needs to understand your motivation in order to make an informed decision. Approaching your presentation with a hidden agenda is unethical, and it may backfire on you. What if you give

a speech at a school board meeting, urging the school district to expand classroom space in the interest of better education, when your real motive is based on the fact that your family is in the construction business and you'd like to bid on the school's expansion project? People are likely to pick up on your feelings, even if you try to mask them, and your effectiveness as a speaker will suffer.

Present All Relevant Information

Even if you have some information that doesn't support your message, you have a responsibility to your audience to present everything that is relevant. In other words, do your best to avoid withholding information. For example, if you ever have the chance to speak with a film critic, ask about reviewer quotes in movie ads. Most critics have stories of how an ad managed to withhold information and twist their words to mean something different from what was intended. If a critic wrote, "I had a blast counting up all the tired clichés and editing mistakes in this spectacular mistake of a movie," those words might turn into "I had a blast watching this spectacular movie." This case is an extreme example of withholding (and actually distorting) information, but make sure you don't fall into this trap. Include opposing views in your speech, and don't be tempted to ignore or falsify them. In fact, bringing up opposing views and then explaining why your view is better can make your speech even more effective because you're addressing important questions that audience members may be asking themselves as you speak.

Try not to withhold information from an audience by disguising the complexity of an issue. For example, don't propose simple solutions for difficult problems. During campaigns, some politicians offer easy answers to complex questions, hoping to attract votes. Crime, unemployment, and taxes are three complicated issues that politicians tend to oversimplify in speeches when elections draw near.

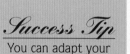

Success Tip
You can adapt your message and your delivery to your audience without changing who you are or what you stand for.

Also, don't withhold information by telling your audience what you think they want to hear (rather than telling them what you believe they should hear). Being the bearer of bad news is no fun, but ethical speakers present the facts even when such facts are unpopular with the audience. Of course, you can present negative information in as positive a light as possible, as long as you don't distort the truth.

Be aware that in some cases, withholding or distorting information in a public speech can bring serious *legal* consequences, in addition to reflecting negatively on your ethics. For example, investors in public corporations have on occasion sued various company executives for failing to disclose important information about the company's financial prospects.

Document Your Sources Carefully

One of the most troublesome issues you'll face as a speaker is plagiarism, which the first section in this chapter defined as taking someone else's words or ideas and passing them off as your own. Since you probably wouldn't consider engaging in plagiarism under any circumstances, you might wonder why this issue is considered such a problem. The trouble comes from the ease with which we can use other people's ideas and words, often without even thinking about it. Even though there are degrees of plagiarism, from blatant to subtle, they are all unethical, and the most extreme forms are illegal. But by understanding the various degrees of plagiarism, you can consciously avoid all of them. Here's a list of a few types of plagiarism that ethical speakers avoid:[18]

- *Repeating word for word what someone else has said or written, without giving credit.* This is the most obvious and blatant form of plagiarism. If you use someone else's words, give the original writer or speaker credit. Quoting someone verbatim is perfectly ethical, as long as you acknowledge that you're repeating what that person has said or written. It is also unacceptable to use someone else's paraphrased interpretation of an original source, unless you give credit.

- *Borrowing a series of phrases spiced with only a few words of your own.* This form of plagiarism involves "gluing" together other people's phrases with a few connecting words of your own. It's a little less blatant than copying one source verbatim, but it's plagiarism nonetheless. Say that you found the following statements in two pieces of research:

> Graham stressed the importance of considering both the quantitative and qualitative aspects of a potential investment.[19]

> Graham, generally, had misgivings about the emphasis placed on qualitative factors.[20]

And say you borrowed the essence of both to construct a new phrase: "Graham stressed the importance of both quantitative and qualitative aspects of a potential investment, but he had misgivings about the emphasis placed on qualitative factors." This sentence doesn't appear in either source, so it's not stolen in that sense, but all you really did was drop a few words and add a couple more. This is simply borrowing from two sources instead of one, and both sources should be acknowledged.

- *Paraphrasing a source's words too closely.* More than a few students have attempted to use original material by changing just enough words to make it look like their own work. What if you started with this original material:

> Graham stressed the importance of considering both the quantitative and qualitative aspects of a potential investment.

And say you changed it to the following:

> Graham emphasized how important it is to consider both quantitative and qualitative aspects of an investment.

Are these now "your" words? The answer is no, because the sentence is basically intact, with only a couple of minor variations in wording.

- *Piecing together multiple sources and presenting the result as your own thinking.* This form of plagiarism can trip up speakers who would never dream of stealing someone else's words. You may have heard the cliché "Stealing from one source is plagiarism; stealing from many sources is research." Well, that cliché is wrong: Stealing from many sources is stealing, not research. The difference is simple when you ask yourself this question: Did I add anything to this material through my own interpretation, analysis, or synthesis? If you did, then it's perfectly acceptable to present your work as original, while giving credit to the sources you analyzed. If you did not add any new information and simply connected enough bits and pieces to create a speech, then all you've done is report on what other people have said, and you must give them the credit.

The seriousness of plagiarism comes to light when you view it for what it is: stealing, plain and simple. Earlier in the chapter, you read about intellectual property rights, the ownership of ideas. An idea or a particular expression of an idea can be every bit as valuable as a diamond ring or a sports car, and you probably wouldn't consider stealing either of those items. Moreover, plagiarizing shows serious contempt for your audience, because it involves not only stealing but also lying to your listeners. Plagiarizing also demonstrates a lack of confidence in your own ability to communicate effectively with your audience.

Finally, if the ethical and legal issues surrounding plagiarism aren't a powerful enough deterrent, consider the risks. Chances are good that your fellow students have seen some of the same research material, and chances are extremely good that your instructor has seen the material. He or she has probably heard quite a number of speeches on related topics. In other words, people are likely to recognize plagiarized material, and they'll think less of you for using it.

Plagiarism really doesn't make sense when you consider how easy it is to avoid. First, start your research early and be thorough. That way, you'll have plenty of material to synthesize, and you'll avoid a last-minute rush that could tempt you into leaning too heavily on one or more sources. Second, give credit to any source from whom you've borrowed words, phrases, thoughts, or organizational structures. These citations can enhance your credibility and they're easy to work into the flow of your speech:

> In an interview in the December 1995 issue of *Tennis* magazine, Croatian tennis star Goran Ivanisevic mentioned that a visit to a hospital in his war-torn country convinced him to start a foundation to help children hurt by the war.[21]

> In her book *Becoming a Writer*, Dorothea Brande put it this way: "The best books emerge from the strongest convictions—and for confirmation, see any bookshelf."

The first example reports the essence of what Ivanisevic said; the second is a direct quote. In

IMPROVING YOUR CRITICAL THINKING

SOLVING THE PROBLEM OF USING SOURCE MATERIALS: WHICH OF THESE FOUR ACTIONS WOULD YOU CHOOSE?

Paraphrasing presents a challenge for some people because they're not quite sure where the line exists between paraphrasing a source and plagiarizing it. In addition, some people have trouble paraphrasing their sources accurately. You can solve these problems by recognizing that for every piece of research material you use in a speech, you must choose among four actions. The first two of these actions are ethical; the last two are not:

- *Quote the source exactly.* This action is straightforward. Take care to report exactly what your source says, and be sure to name the source accurately, too.
- *Paraphrase the source in your own words.* Paraphrasing is the process of conveying another person's ideas and opinions in your own words. To paraphrase effectively, make sure the material is actually in your own words, and be careful to credit the source, of course.
- *Make a superficial attempt to paraphrase, without really doing so.* To avoid this unacceptable paraphrasing, take care to actually rewrite the information in your own words. Don't simply rearrange your source's original words or replace just a few words to make the material look different.
- *Distort the source's meaning or intent.* Avoid the unethical choice of intentionally distorting your source's material to better fit your speech. Be sure you don't drop or ignore information that doesn't support your case, and don't take information out of context.

Here's a brief example to help illustrate the differences:

Accurate quotation: According to Christine Kinealy, "No one knows precisely how many people died in Ireland's Great Famine of 1845–52, but in a population of more than eight million people, the death count reached at least one million."

Acceptable paraphrase: Although no one knows for sure, Christine Kinealy estimated that one million of Ireland's eight million people died in the Great Famine of 1845–52.

Unacceptable paraphrase: We don't really know how many people died in Ireland's Great Famine of 1845–52, but in a population of more than eight million people, the toll was at least one million.

Distortion: Author Christine Kinealy says that no one knows how many people died in Ireland's Great Famine of 1845–52.

The first and second examples represent an ethical use of a source. The third is an unacceptable paraphrase, first, because only a few words were changed from the author's original statement and, second, because the material was presented without credit. The fourth statement is also unacceptable because it distorts the meaning. Yes, it's true that no one knows *precisely* how many people died, but the author does offer an estimate. The difference between "nobody knows" and "nobody knows, but at least a million" is significant.

EXHIBIT 3.3

Manipulating Audiences
Television evangelist Jim Bakker admitted to abusing his power of speech when he solicited funds for religious purposes and then used some of that money for personal reasons.

addition to supporting your credibility, the need to provide citations will keep you from quoting or paraphrasing too many sources in a speech. Doing so would make you sound as though you were reading a bibliography rather than delivering a speech. Remember, the audience wants to hear what you have to say, not what your sources said.

Avoid Coercion and Manipulation

Coercion is forcing people to act in a particular way when they don't want to but fear some form of reprisal from you. In his search for Communists during the Cold War of the early 1950s, Senator Joseph McCarthy used coercion to force people to inform on their friends and relatives. People were afraid that if they didn't cooperate, they would be accused of being Communists themselves, losing their jobs and reputations. Today, if you're in a position of power, you need to avoid even the appearance of coercing your audience members.

Manipulation is an attempt to manage people's emotions and actions in a devious or deceitful way. An example would be exploiting the basic instinct most people have to help others. It's fine to persuade people to do things that are good for them or good for others. However, manipulating people is unethical, regardless of whether you're doing it for good reasons or bad. Political ads often border on manipulation, charging that an opponent's programs will end medical coverage or decrease Social Security benefits to the elderly. Some television evangelists have been guilty of manipulation over the last few years. They asked people to send in money to further religious

activities, but they used large portions of that money to increase their own financial worth (see Exhibit 3.3). (This does not mean that all television evangelists are unethical, only that some have behaved unethically by manipulating their audiences.) Think back to our earlier discussion of the relationship of values to ethical choices and behaviors. The manipulative evangelists apparently value material success more than respect for individuals. Based on those values, the evangelists appear to have chosen manipulative communication to take advantage of the rights of others. The people listening to them and sending in money have been deprived of information on which they could base well-informed choices.

As you can see, ethical speaking is a complex issue that is full of details you need to remember every time you plan and deliver a speech. However, even though ethics can be complex, you can reduce your worry by developing ethical habits as a speaker. These habits will help you make ethical choices, and they'll help you avoid unintentional ethical problems. In summary, ethical habits can apply to four aspects of planning and delivering speeches:[22]

- *The habit of researching topics thoroughly.* Willingly search out information that both supports and refutes your point of view. Acknowledge the complexity of an issue, and avoid presenting simple solutions. [23]
- *The habit of working toward fairness and justice.* Present information accurately and fairly for maximum understanding. It is not enough merely to be accurate; you must also present

information so that the audience can understand it.

- *The habit of acknowledging private motivations.* Be aware of your personal biases, and let the audience know about them whenever those biases might influence what you have to say. Don't approach an issue with hidden agendas. Let the audience know what motivates your interest in a topic.
- *The habit of respecting dissenting opinions.* Look at opposing viewpoints as a way of generating new ideas and arriving at good decisions. Communicate your respect for differences in opinions openly to the audience. Acknowledge that there are a variety of ways of looking at any topic.

Ethics and Credibility

Your credibility determines the degree to which an audience believes in you and is one of the most important assets a public speaker can possess. In the fourth century, B.C., the Greek philosopher Aristotle referred to this essential speaker credibility as *ethos*. Four hundred years later, the Roman writer Quintilianus said that to possess ethos a speaker needs to be a good person speaking well. He was saying that for you to be perceived as credible by the audience, listeners need to think of you as a good person, competent and trustworthy. To put it another way, if you communicate ethically, you will possess ethos or credibility.[24]

As a speaker, your credibility is based on the audience's perception of your reputation and character—if they believe you're acting ethically, they are more likely to perceive you as competent and believable. Although you can achieve your objective by being unethical, such behavior can backfire on you. If your audience (or your speech professor) finds out that you've been unethical, they'll suspect everything you've said or will say. Besides, developing and delivering a successful speech and staying on the ethical high road are admirable accomplishments in and of themselves. You owe it to your audience and to yourself to do it right.

The ethical decisions you make as a speaker help you build credibility with an audience in three phases (see Exhibit 3.4):[25]

1. *Initial credibility.* Your initial credibility is based on what the audience knows (or does not know) about you before hearing you speak. Your reputation precedes you. If listeners have heard or read that you are competent or expert on the topic being presented and that you are trustworthy and ethical, they will be more likely to believe you and accept what you say. If they know that you have behaved unethically in the past, your initial credibility will be low. If members of your audience know nothing about you, your initial credibility will be based on their first impression of you.

2. *Derived credibility.* You develop derived credibility as your audience listens to you speak. Based on what you say and how you behave, audience members change their preconceptions about you. If your listeners believe you are being honest and acting in their best interest, your derived credibility improves, so audience members are more likely to accept what you say and to act on your recommendations.

3. *Lasting credibility.* Your lasting credibility is the long-term impression you leave behind—what happens after listeners go home and think about what you said. As they receive more information about what you told them, they will judge you

---

EXHIBIT 3.4

Building Credibility as a Speaker
Your initial credibility is the reputation that you bring with you before the speech starts. You build derived credibility during your speech, and your lasting credibility is the perception your audience takes away with them. As you build a reputation for credible speaking, your initial credibility will rise.

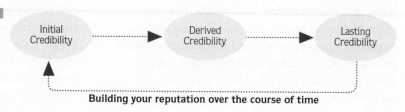

Building your reputation over the course of time

Ask an Expert

Stephen W. Littlejohn
Adjunct Professor of Communication and Journalism, University of New Mexico, and Senior Consultant, Public Dialogue Consortium

Q: If I'm promoting a controversial position in a persuasive speech, what steps can I take to avoid ethical lapses?

A: When you believe strongly in a certain position, especially a controversial one, you may feel compelled to prevail at all costs, focusing on your own opinion and forgetting about your audience. What can you do to avoid this tendency? I think ethical behavior is mostly a matter of attitude, and you can work on shifting your attitude in three ways.

First, instead of *demanding* that others accept your position, try *inviting* them to do so. You don't have to agree with other people to respect them and accept that they, too, have good reasons for what they believe. At the same time, you have your reasons, and in a speech you're essentially inviting your audience to consider your point of view.

Second, try to move from a closed position to an open one. When you try to manipulate people, withhold information, and distort facts, you reveal your closed attitude. Be willing to listen to other ideas as well as promote your own. Create a speaking environment that's like a dialogue, a give and take, a safe setting in which the audience might explore a point of view different from their own.

Third, share the responsibility for the outcome of your speech. Speakers often take full responsibility for the outcome of a speech, giving no credence to the decision-making abilities of the audience. This attitude breeds unethical behavior by pressuring the speaker to make sure that the audience complies. If you let the audience share responsibility for a satisfactory outcome, then you must be willing to be honest and provide complete information so that audience members can make up their own minds.

1. Is a "you" orientation appropriate for a persuasive speech in which you take a strong stand on a controversial topic? How does the concept of shared responsibility for a speech's outcome relate to the "you" orientation?
2. During a classroom persuasive speech, listen carefully as your classmate takes a position with which you disagree. Does the speaker demand or invite you to accept the other position? How does the speaker create an open environment of give and take?

and your speech in light of the new evidence. You may initially win over the audience with a glib tongue and personal charm, but over the long term, your credibility will determine whether an audience will act on what you say. If it becomes obvious that you used unethical tactics, your credibility will suffer. The audience will not be likely to follow your recommended actions or to believe you in the future.

Without a doubt, telling the truth enhances your credibility, your reputation, and your effectiveness as a speaker. As you develop a reputation for being honest and forthright, people will come to trust you and act on what you say. You'll find it easier to persuade people because they'll be inclined to believe you. And on a practical level, being truthful is ultimately easier on you. Alexander Pope once advised that telling one lie can multiply your work because you have to "invent 20 more to maintain that one."[26] Many situation comedy plots are based on a little white lie that becomes more and more complicated as the teller either forgets or embellishes the original story. Telling the truth lets you relax and move on, without fear of contradicting yourself later. Any way you look at it, you will reap the rewards of ethical speaking throughout your career and your life in general.

THE LISTENER'S ETHICAL RESPONSIBILITIES

Ethical responsibilities don't stop with the speaker. As a listener you also have a responsibility to behave ethically. Think of public speaking as a loop that includes speaker and listener; it isn't simply a one-way path from the speaker to the listener. In other words, as a member of the audience, you share the responsibility for a successful speech. To that end, you

EXHIBIT 3.5
The Listener's Responsibility
Occasionally the content of Danny Glover's speeches about AIDS upsets some people, but audiences have a responsibility to at least listen to what he has to say.

have an ethical responsibility to listen to a speaker with an open mind. Most of us like to think we have open minds, but in fact we all perceive the world through various filters. These filters are shaped by our experiences (both as adults and as children), our values and ethics, our goals and ambitions, and even our moods during any particular speech. Once we recognize the existence of these filters, we can take steps to keep them from distorting a speaker's message.[27] For example, if you believe the government has the obligation to provide every citizen with basic medical care, you might interpret a speech on health insurance differently than someone who views medical coverage as an individual responsibility.

Of course, keeping an open mind doesn't mean that you have to agree with what the speaker has to say. Just don't let your filters and biases keep you from hearing the message. Don't be afraid to listen to and reasonably evaluate an opposing viewpoint (see Exhibit 3.5). The worst that can happen is that you may change your point of view, or you may be convinced more than ever that your original position is correct. Either way, you come away better informed on the issue.

Be sure you listen not only to *what* the speaker is saying but also to *how* he or she says it. The emotional content of a speech may be as important as the factual content. What motivates the speaker? What is his or her interest in the topic?

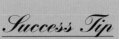

Success Tip
When listening to controversial speeches, try not to formulate arguments in your head until the speaker has finished. It's difficult to pay full attention if you're busy creating your own counter-message.

Does the speaker have obvious biases on the issue? A person who has experienced homelessness, for example, has an emotional and psychological perspective on the problem that other people don't have.

Also try to listen to the details of the message regardless of your personal reaction to the speaker. Maybe you feel the person speaking is inappropriately dressed, perhaps you have trouble understanding his or her accent, or you might think the speaker is too young (or too old) to have valid opinions on the issue. Don't let any of these reactions color your opinion of what is being said. Allow yourself to learn more and thus make better choices and decisions.

Finally, do your best to give the speaker appropriate feedback. Don't pretend to understand something that confuses you. The person speaking cannot judge the effectiveness of a presentation unless the audience gives accurate feedback. Audience members may nod knowingly or refrain from asking questions because they think everyone else understands and they don't want to appear uninformed. Chances are that if you're confused, at least one other person is confused, too. The speaker and every member of the audience (including you) will be better served if you admit you don't understand and ask for clarification. One question may be all that is needed to open up a constructive conversation between the speaker and the audience.

SUMMARY

Public speaking is such a potentially powerful force that governments have attached legal responsibilities to it and societies have attached ethical responsibilities. Your legal responsibilities include the protection of both society as a whole and individual members of society. While protecting your right to free speech in general, laws prevent you from saying things that could cause physical or financial injury to other people. You're also not allowed to defame or injure the reputations of other people through slanderous speech.

Ethical concerns in public speaking involve issues that aren't necessarily addressed by laws but are judged to be good and bad by society as a whole. The ethical choices you make and the things you say are influenced by your values, which are judgments about the relative worth of objects, behaviors, or concepts. Valuing individual freedom, for example, could lead you to say something about government that someone who values social harmony might never say.

To help you address the many complex details of public speaking ethics, you can follow seven common-sense guidelines. First, analyze your goals and the potential consequences of your speech before you prepare it. Many people would argue that you are responsible for the results brought about by your speeches. Second, prepare thoroughly to help avoid the temptation of copying source material and to give yourself more time to explore all sides of an issue. Third, be yourself; don't pretend to be someone you're not just to get the audience on your side. Fourth, present relevant information, even if it doesn't support your message. You have a responsibility to explore dissenting opinions. Fifth, be careful to document your sources. Sixth, avoid coercing or manipulating people through intimidation or emotional trickery. Seventh, help yourself in all of these areas by developing ethical habits as a speaker: the habit of researching topics thoroughly, the habit of working toward fairness and justice, the habit of acknowledging private motivations, and the habit of respecting dissenting opinions.

Ethics also play an important role in credibility, which is one of the most important assets you have as a speaker. The more ethical you are, the more your listeners are likely to accept you as a credible speaker, so they'll be more inclined to believe what you have to say.

Finally, the responsibility for successful and ethical communication is shared by speaker and audience. As listeners, we must all do our part to make a speech a success. An important step in this effort is realizing that we all have biases and diverse experiences that filter our perception of the world. These filters affect how we listen and what we hear, so understanding what they are is an important part of training ourselves to listen effectively and responsibly. In addition, ethical listeners focus on the emotional content of a speech, ignore personal reactions to the speaker that might bias their interpretation of the message, and give timely and accurate feedback to help speakers.

KEY TERMS

coercion (61)
credibility (56)
defamation (52)
ethics (54)
ethos (50)
intellectual property (53)
libel (52)
manipulation (61)
slander (52)
values (54)

APPLY CRITICAL THINKING

1. Does your college or university have an "anti-hate" policy prohibiting certain kinds of language directed at ethnic minorities or other groups? Do you think such policies are an unfair restraint on a student's right to freedom of expression?

2. If someone (say, a political opponent) is dishonest and you can prove it, should you be able to call that person dishonest in public? What's your opinion?

3. Good speakers adapt their messages and their styles to their audiences. Does this conflict with the ethical guidelines in this chapter about being yourself and avoiding manipulation? Why or why not?

4. One of the defining issues of a culture is its values. Since the United States is a multicultural society, you might encounter audiences with values very different from yours. How would you handle speaking to those audiences?

5. What would you do if during your research you were to uncover some opposing information that is stronger than the information supporting your case?

6. Would you ever again believe anything from a speaker who was caught giving an unethical speech? Why or why not?

7. Do you agree with the statements in the chapter that listeners share the responsibility for successful speeches? After all, listeners are just sitting there; isn't it the speaker's job to get the message across? Support or refute this point of view.

SHARPEN YOUR SKILLS

Individual Exercises

1. Listen to (or read excerpts from) speeches presented by two opponents in a political campaign. Since the opponents are likely to take opposite sides of a given issue, try to detect any unethical use of information in an attempt to persuade the voting public to think one way or the other.

2. Find a speech or speech excerpt that strongly attacks a public figure. Why wouldn't the speaker be considered guilty of slander? (You may need to research the laws of defamation as they pertain to public figures.)

3. Find a speech by a well-known public figure, either notably popular or unpopular. Examine how the speaker, in that speech, enhances his or her ethos/credibility. How is competence/expertise demonstrated? How is trustworthiness/integrity communicated?

4. Using the speech of the well-known public figure, determine the speaker's values, as presented in the speech. What does the speaker hold to be of worth or important, and what ethical choices are supported as a result of those values?

Group Exercises

5. In a group of four to six students, split into opposing sides of a current public issue, such as immigration reform. With both sides using the latest government statistics on immigration (or your chosen issue), see whether both sides can use some of these statistics to advantage without committing any ethical violations.

6. In a group of four to six students, individually develop your personal list of values, five or six things you think are really important in life. Compare your lists and try to merge and combine things so you have one common set of values. Then identify at least two ethical choices or decisions a speaker might make, based on those values.

IMPROVING YOUR LISTENING SKILLS

LEARNING OBJECTIVES

After studying this chapter, you will be able to

1. Differentiate between hearing and listening.

2. Explain the benefits of effective listening.

3. Identify four types of listening.

4. List and describe the five factors of listening.

5. Discuss six strategies you can use to improve your listening skills.

6. Explain how internal filters influence listening.

7. Describe how to evaluate a speech.

IMPORTANCE OF EFFECTIVE LISTENING

What does effective listening have to do with excellent public speaking? As author Susan Faludi found out, the two go hand in hand. Writing about women's issues, Faludi had a lot of experience putting words on paper, but she was less sure of her ability to convey her ideas when speaking to a large audience. Then she was invited to speak at the Smithsonian Institution in Washington, D.C., on the topic of "The Status of American Women." Nervously, she approached the microphone and prepared to speak. Here's what happened next:

> I cleared my throat and, to my shock, a hush fell over the room. People were listening—with an intensity that strangely emboldened me. It was as if their attentive silence allowed me to make contact with my own muffled self. I began to speak. A stinging point induced a ripple of agreement. I told a joke and they laughed. My voice got surer, my delivery rising. A charge passed between me and the audience, uniting and igniting us both.[1]

Without effective listening on the part of both Faludi and her listeners, this speech would have been less successful. Faludi would have been unable to recognize and interpret the initial silence and then the ripple of agreement and laughter that greeted her words (see Exhibit 4.1).

She was also alert to nonverbal signs, such as smiling faces, that reinforced the meaning of what she heard. By paying attention with both her ears and her eyes, she was able to determine that the audience was not only listening to what she said but also understood and agreed with her ideas. This audience feedback strengthened Faludi's confidence, freeing her to communicate even more enthusiastically.

As you can see from Faludi's experience, listening links the speaker and the audience in the communication process. Communication occurs only when the audience listens to a speaker's message, and the speaker listens for audience feedback. Listening paves the way for the exchange of ideas. What's more, listening helps forge a closer relationship between the speaker and the audience, as it did for Faludi and her audience. Listening is a key skill for both the speaker and the audience, a skill that you can apply as a student or teacher, a customer or businessperson, a voter or politician.

Even in ancient times, listening was recognized as an important skill. As the Roman philosopher Epictetus observed nearly two thousand years ago, "Nature has given us one tongue, but two ears, that we may hear from others twice as much as we speak."[2] Good listening can help you absorb and retain more information in the classroom, as well as develop critical thinking skills to examine the information. Studies show that college students spend more time listening than they do reading, writing, or speaking. So effective listening can lead to more effective learning—and higher grades.[3]

Listening is also critical in today's high-speed information age. Thanks to advanced technology,

EXHIBIT 4.1
Listening Is the Connection
Listening is the vital connection between the speaker and the audience: By paying attention to verbal and noverbal signs, you can determine how your audience is receiving and interpreting your message. The concerned looks on these parents' faces show that they understand this school administrator's message about the need to temporarily close the local elementary school so that asbestos can be safely removed.

people can ask for and receive information in an instant. Only by listening carefully can you respond well in such a pressured climate.

In the business world, listening can mean the difference between profit and loss. Employees in North America spend about 60 percent of their workday listening; executives spend an average of 57 percent of the day listening. Small wonder that listening problems on the job can be costly: If each U.S. worker were to make just one $10 mistake as a result of poor listening, the combined cost would exceed a billion dollars. That's why many corporations offer listening training to their managers and employees.[4]

In a world filled with sounds—spoken words as well as music and plain old noise—being a good listener means more than merely hearing. You hear when your ears receive the sound waves that surround you and transmit those sounds to your brain. Because hearing is a *physiological* process, all you need is a set of properly functioning ears, and you're ready to hear. You don't have to do anything; you can be passive, and you'll hear the sounds anyway.

In contrast, listening is an active process, as much *mental* as it is physiological. Unlike hearing, listening requires that you put your mind and body on alert. When you're actively listening, you're paying close attention to the sounds you hear so that you can interpret, remember, and evaluate what you've heard and be prepared to react appropriately. As a speaker who actively listens, you're ready to react to audience feedback; as an audience member, you're able to receive and understand a speaker's message (see Exhibit 4.2).

Benefits of Effective Listening

As a speaker, you need effective listening skills throughout the public speaking process. Before a speech, listening helps you develop a clearer picture of your audience's needs and interests so that you can express your ideas in an appropriate way.[5] During a speech, listening is the key to gaining feedback so that you can determine whether the audience is receiving and correctly interpreting what you say. After a speech, listening allows you to focus on your audience's thoughts, questions, and concerns so that you can respond.

As an audience member, listening helps you take in the speaker's ideas and then analyze and evaluate their meaning. You can learn about a wide range of topics by listening to speakers who come from all walks of life. Effective listening helps you follow the speaker's reasoning and identify any inaccuracies or unethical techniques. What's more, listening prepares you to act on the basis of the information you gain from a speech. In addition, listening to a number of speakers can help you figure out which public speaking techniques work best so that you can sharpen your own skills.

Whether you're in front of the audience or in it, listening has one more key benefit: It creates a respectful, caring atmosphere in which people are encouraged to share their thoughts and feelings. In such a climate, speakers and audiences can safely explore topics that touch both the heart and the mind. Reporter Brenda Ueland, a confidant of the celebrated poet Carl Sandburg, recognized this power of listening:

EXHIBIT 4.2

Self-Test for Listeners
Are you a good listener? Rate yourself on each of the following aspects of listening. Then compare the results with the scoring guidelines at the end.

Listening Aspect	Almost Always	Usually	Sometimes	Seldom	Almost Never
1. I am able to become interested in the speaker's topic.					
2. I am able to adapt to the speaker's appearance and delivery.					
3. I am able to overcome or adjust to distractions during a speech.					
4. I am able to listen for concepts and major points.					
5. I am able to avoid pretending to listen.					
6. I am able to listen without judging or refuting the speaker's message.					
7. I am able to focus on speech content even when the material is difficult.					

Scoring: Give yourself 10 points for every "almost always" answer, 8 points for "usually," 6 points for "sometimes," 4 points for "seldom," and 2 points for "almost never." If your total score is 60 points or above, congratulations—you have excellent listening skills. If your total score is 45–60, you have generally good listening skills. If your total score is below 45, you need to improve your listening skills overall; repeat this test after listening to your classmates' first speeches, and then determine which aspects of listening require your special attention.

When we are listened to, it creates us, makes us unfold and expand. Ideas actually begin to grow within us and come to life . . . When we listen to people there is an alternating current, and this recharges us so that we never get tired of each other.[6]

Ueland's words echo how Susan Faludi felt when she addressed her audience at the Smithsonian Institution. Listening completes the circuit of ideas passed between speaker and audience, uniting them in the excitement of exchanging ideas. When you get up to speak, you want an audience that displays its respect and care by actively listening. In turn, you can show other speakers the same respect and caring by actively listening when

you're in the audience. Then, like Ueland and Faludi, you'll experience the exhilaration of successful communication—whether you're in the audience or addressing one (see Exhibit 4.3).

Types of Listening

Just as you can classify types of speeches according to general purpose, you can classify types of listening according to purpose. The purpose of **content listening**, also known as *comprehensive listening,* is to understand the speaker's message. When you use content listening, you concentrate on the meaning of the information that the speaker is offering.

Although you use content listening when listening to any speech, it's

> **Success Tip**
>
> Use effective listening to tune into your audience's interests before you give a speech, detect audience feedback during a speech, and focus on the audience's questions and concerns at the end of a speech.

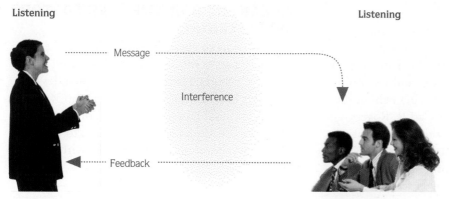

Listening

Message

Interference

Feedback

Listening

EXHIBIT 4.3
Listening Enables the Communication Process
Through the continuous use of listening, your audience receives your message and you, as the speaker, receive your audience's feedback, which facilitates the communication process.

especially important with an informative speech such as "BioSteel" by Eileen Monaghan, which is contained in Appendix B. If you were in the audience for this speech, you would use content listening to pay closer attention to the facts, figures, and examples so that you could better understand the topic. On the other hand, if you were the speaker, you would be using content listening to determine the meaning of any audience questions and comments.

The purpose of **critical listening** is both to understand and to evaluate the meaning of a speaker's message. You weigh what the speaker is saying; discriminate among facts, opinions, and assumptions; and ask questions to confirm your evaluation.[7] Of course, critical thinking is part of critical listening, because you use critical thinking to examine the speaker's major points and challenge the speaker's reasoning. With critical listening, you detect any weak links in the speaker's logic, and you mark statements that are vague, misleading, overblown, or unsupported (see Exhibit 4.4).

Critical listening is applicable to every listening situation, but it's particularly helpful when you're listening to a persuasive speech such as "Genetic Patents" by Elizabeth Storey, which is in Appendix B. Sitting in the audience while Kern argued against the lure of credit cards, you would use critical listening to sift the ideas and the evidence, and then to form your own conclusions, which may or may not be the same as the speaker's conclusions. When you're the speaker, you use critical listening to weigh whatever facts and arguments audience members

EXHIBIT 4.4
Critical Listening
Critical listening is especially important in situations where the speaker is trying to persuade the audience to act in a certain way. In a courtroom situation, where a lawyer tries to persuade the jury of the defendant's innocence on a particular charge, it is up to the jury to use critical thinking to weigh the evidence and the arguments the lawyer offers.

offer in response to your speech.

With content and critical listening, you're concentrating on the speaker's information. However, the purpose of **empathic listening** is to understand the speaker's feelings and viewpoint. The purpose is to perceive what lies behind the speaker's words. Psychologist Carl R. Rogers called this understanding *with* a person, not *about* the person. "This means seeing the express idea and attitude from the other person's point of view," he said, "sensing how it feels to the person, achieving his or her frame of reference about the subject being discussed."[8]

With empathic listening, you don't have to agree with what the speaker says; you simply have to accept that this is the speaker's viewpoint.[9] To develop your empathic listening skills, mentally ask yourself these questions as a speaker talks:

What is the speaker trying to tell me?
What does the message mean to him or her?
How does the speaker see this situation?
What is the speaker feeling right now?[10]

Empathic listening is appropriate in situations where the speaker needs a supportive audience. Guidance counselors use empathic listening when they meet with students, as do health care professionals working with patients and parents talking with children. On a personal level, empathic listening can help you understand the thoughts and feelings of a friend who wants to talk about an upsetting incident.

The purpose of the fourth type of listening, **appreciative listening**, is to enjoy the speaker's presentation. Audiences use appreciative listening when they listen to an entertaining speech. The point of such speeches is not to persuade, communicate vital information, or arouse sympathy; rather, it's to make listeners feel good. In addition, you're applying appreciative listening when you admire a speaker's choice of powerful words, enjoy the speaker's style of presentation, or take pleasure in the speaker's vivid language.[11]

SPEAKERS AND THE FIVE FACTORS OF LISTENING

How do you go about listening? As noted earlier, listening means more than simply hearing someone else's words. Listening actually includes five factors: (1) attending, (2) interpreting, (3) remembering, (4) evaluating, and (5) responding (see Exhibit 4.5). Each factor contributes to your ability to communicate successfully with another person.

Attending

One factor that affects listening is **attending**, focusing on selected sounds out of the many that the ears receive. Your ears can pick up a mind-boggling number of sounds from your environment: Conversations, vehicles, equipment, and many other sounds compete for your attention. By attending, you actively select one or more of these sounds to concentrate on.

From the speaker's viewpoint, you may think that audience members who look directly at you are attending to your words. But you can't assume they're listening: Many have learned how to politely fake attention. Look for signs that your audience is actually attending to your speech. Look at facial expressions, watch for people nodding as you talk, and see whether people lean forward in their seats. If your audience doesn't seem to be with you, try varying the speed at which you speak, asking for audience participation, changing your tone of voice, or adding a vivid example to grab attention.[12]

Your audience may need a minute or more to settle down and concentrate at the beginning of your speech. Because they're not ready to attend to your speech, audience members may miss part of your introduction. That's why, early in the speech, you'll need an effective attention-getting hook and a compelling explanation of what listeners can expect to get out of your message.[13]

Consider how student speaker Amy Stewart of Western Kentucky University used her introduction as a hook during a speech on campus crime:

Christina Powell, University of Florida in Gainesville, freshman . . . Jeanne Ann

EXHIBIT 4.5
Factors in Listening

Attending helps you actively focus only on certain sounds.

Interpreting involves assigning meaning to sounds and words you hear.

Remembering helps you recall what a speaker has said.

Evaluating what you hear helps you weigh the speaker's thoughts and evidence.

How you are Responding shows the speaker how you're reacting to the message.

Cleary, Lehigh University, sophomore . . . Nathan Butler, UCLA, senior . . . Adam White, NYU, junior . . . Jessica Brown, Ohio University, sophomore. What do these five students have in common? They all held aspirations of success that began with their college career—and ended with a disastrous nightmare. All were victims of the ultimate university crime—murder.[14]

Stewart gave her audience time to settle down by naming not one or two but five students. The contrast between the students' "aspirations of success" and the "disastrous nightmare" was vividly drawn to grab listeners' attention. Stewart built suspense by not revealing the topic of her speech, campus crime, until her fourth sentence. By that time, audience members were likely to be actively attending to her words and ready to hear what caused the nightmare she mentioned.

Interpreting

Another factor affecting listening is **interpreting**, assigning meaning to sounds such as a speaker's words. When you hear words, you may not automatically know how to interpret them because meaning isn't inherent in the words. Meaning is determined by the people using the words, not by the words themselves. So the speaker may use a word to mean one thing, but you may interpret that word to mean something entirely different. If a speaker and an audience don't share the same language, education, background, or experiences, the possibilities for misunderstanding are greatly increased.

Even if you start by attending to the speaker and interpreting the words, you may miss some of the speech. After all, people can listen at a rate of 500 to 600 words per minute, even though the average speaker talks at a rate of only 125 to 150 words per minute.[15] In the gap between what the speaker says and what you're able to hear, you and other members of the audience may find your attention wandering and may lose track of the speaker's meaning. Instead, use the extra time to review what the speaker has said, recall the purpose and the major points, test the speaker's logic, and see whether the ideas fit with your own knowledge and experience.[16]

As a speaker, you can help your audience absorb your meaning. Remember, no two listeners are the same: People grasp meaning at differing rates and in differing ways. To accommodate these differences, you can vary your pace and pepper your speech with facts, figures, examples, and other evidence that keeps listeners thinking about your meaning.

Amy Stewart used several kinds of supporting materials as evidence in her speech on campus crime. She first cited statistics showing that violent crime on campus is rising. Next she offered a quote from a professor of criminal justice about reporting campus crime. Then she described two incidents of crime that could have been avoided. Finally, she returned to statistics and then offered a list of recommendations to prevent crime in the dormitory. Such a variety of evidence helped reinforce the meaning of Stewart's message and, at the same time, gave listeners a lot to think about.

Remembering

A third factor affecting listening is *remembering*, the ability to recall what a speaker has said. Can you remember what a speaker said four minutes ago? Four days ago? Four years ago? Of course, remembering something you've just heard is easier than remembering something you heard in the distant past. However, you can improve your ability to retain the information you hear (and help audience members to retain what you tell them) by using memory-building techniques to fix important points in your mind.

One commonly used technique is to construct a word or sentence from the first letters of a list of items you or your audience members need to remember (see Exhibit 4.6). For example, you might use the word HOMES to represent the five Great Lakes (Huron, Ontario, Michigan, Erie, and Superior). If you want the audience to remember the musical lines on the treble clef (E, G, B, D, F), you might offer the sentence "Every good boy does fine."

SPEAKING ACROSS CULTURES

CROSSING CULTURES WITHOUT CROSSING SIGNALS: SEVEN SKILLFUL WAYS TO BRIDGE THE GAP

No matter where or when you speak, chances are good that your audience will include people from a number of cultures as well as people who are less than fluent in your language. Recognizing these differences is the first step to successful communication across cultures. Here are some additional steps you can take to help your audience keep up with what you're saying and understand the meaning of your words.

- *Speak clearly.* Pronounce your words carefully, slowing down slightly to give your audience time to register and absorb the names of people, places, and companies. Rephrase important points so the audience has several opportunities to catch your meaning.
- *Explain more fully.* Add a few words or a sentence to expand on important points. This gives audience members more background to consider when they're grappling with unfamiliar words or phrases.
- *Speak realistically.* Exaggerations can confuse listeners from other cultures, who may be accustomed to more realistic language. Similarly, steer clear of sarcasm, jokes, and idioms, because they can obscure rather than clarify your message.
- *Reinforce verbal messages with nonverbal cues.* Use facial expressions and other nonverbal signals to help convey your meaning. However, avoid gestures and other nonverbal cues that may be misunderstood or considered inappropriate in other cultures.
- *Use appropriate visual aids.* Help your audience absorb statistics and key facts by summarizing them on charts, slides, or other visual aids.
- *Check for feedback.* Watch for puzzled, blank, or unchanging expressions that can indicate confusion or misunderstanding. Recognize that nodding may be a polite way of showing that your words have been heard—but not necessarily understood.

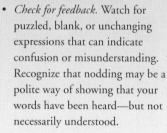

To avoid confusing listeners from other cultures, avoid idioms and overdramatic language.

EXHIBIT 4.6

Memory Aids for Listeners

Memory aids help listeners remember what speakers say. Here, one listener has created a phrase from the initials of Babe Ruth and Willie Mays, while the other has formed a mental image of a baseball next to a candy bar (representing Babe Ruth) and a maze (representing Willie Mays).

Another memory-building technique is to link a vivid mental image with an important idea or a name the speaker mentions. Every time you think of the image, you recall the associated idea. For example, if a speaker on nutrition says that women need 1500 milligrams of calcium every day, you might picture a woman drinking from a bottle of milk labeled "1500." When you want to remember what the speaker said, think back to your mental picture of the woman drinking the milk from the numbered bottle. This image will provide you with the clues you need to recall the idea.

Also, as a member of the audience, you can remember more of what you hear by reviewing it right after the speaker's words reach you. Silently repeat key words, and categorize or label the material to help fix it in your mind. To test your understanding and establish the ideas more firmly in your memory, think about how the speaker's ideas relate to each other. In addition, you'll remember more if you put the information to use as soon as possible, before it can slip away. Another way to strengthen your memory (especially if you expect to need the material in the future) is to take notes; note taking is discussed later in the chapter.[17]

As a speaker, you can help your audience remember major points by using charts and other visual aids when appropriate. You can also preview your ideas in the introduction, link your major points to your

central idea in the body of the speech, and then summarize your major points in the conclusion. Such repetition gives audience members several opportunities to fix your ideas in their minds. Mark Sanborn, a professional speaker and leadership-training expert, calls this the PIP technique (note his use of a memory aid to help you remember this technique). First he explains the premise (P) of a major point he's trying to make; next, he illustrates (I) it with quotes or other evidence; then, he summarizes the point (P) to emphasize it one more time.[18]

Amy Stewart helped her audience remember her major points by outlining in the introduction what she planned to say:

There is a problem of university crimes that needs to be addressed. I will do so today by first examining the increase in crimes on college campuses, next the reasons these crimes are so prevalent, and finally, ways in which we can protect ourselves against these types of offenses.[19]

After she cited and analyzed statistics illustrating her first point, the increase in college crime, she summarized that discussion and previewed the second major point, the significance of the crime trend nationwide. After supporting her second major point, she recapped that discussion and prepared the audience for the third major point, tips for preventing

Success Tip

Help your audience remember your message by previewing your ideas in the introduction, showing the link between your major points in the body of the speech, and summarizing your major points in the conclusion.

crime. Stewart concluded her speech by reciting the list of murdered students one more time and warning the audience, "We can't afford to ignore this very serious and sometimes deadly problem of crimes against college students."

Evaluating

A fourth factor affecting listening is *evaluating*, applying critical thinking skills to weigh the speaker's points and evidence. Even if you're not aware of evaluating the information you receive from a speaker, that's what you're doing when you ask yourself questions about the speech:

- Does the information sound complete, accurate, and truthful?
- Are the sources of the supporting material reliable?
- Is the speaker presenting opinions or assumptions as facts?
- Is the speaker's logic sound?
- How does the information fit with my experience and knowledge?

Audience members who heard Amy Stewart's speech on campus crime would probably think carefully about her sources of information, which included a well-respected education journal, a national news magazine, and a professor of criminal justice. The audience would also weigh Stewart's assertion that off-campus apartments are "not only unsafe but unkempt as well." In addition, the audience would consider the value of the crime prevention tips Stewart provided, choosing to remember only the pertinent ones.

Responding

The fifth factor affecting listening is *responding*, reacting once you've evaluated the speaker's message. Your response starts internally. You may accept or reject what you've heard, agree or disagree with the speaker, empathize with the speaker, or react in some other fashion. You can give the speaker feedback about your internal response in four ways: by saying something, by using nonverbal cues (such as clapping or frowning), by using both verbal and nonverbal cues, or

by remaining silent. In fact, silence can be a powerful form of feedback: Audiences use silence when members are angry at the speaker's words, sympathetic with the speaker's position, or indifferent to the speaker's ideas.[20]

As an audience member, you can use any of the four responses to show speakers how you think or feel about their ideas. In turn, your reaction helps the speaker determine whether the message is getting through and often where you stand on the issues or ideas being presented. As a speaker, you're using your listening skills to detect such feedback so that you can make any needed adjustments to your speech delivery, organization, and so on. Even if you don't hear a verbal reaction, you're likely to spot subtle nonverbal clues (such as fidgeting or smiling) that indicate the audience's response. And when you practice interpreting the audience's verbal and nonverbal cues, you get better at it and become more confident in your listening skills.[21]

STRATEGIES FOR EFFECTIVE LISTENING

Understanding the five factors that affect listening is the first step toward sharpening your listening skills. The next step is to overcome the barriers to effective listening. Any one of the barriers shown in Exhibit 4.7 can derail your listening effort. Without effective listening, you may not be able to get back on track to absorb and respond to the speaker's message.

To gain the benefits of effective listening, you can improve your listening skills with six strategies: (1) improving concentration, (2) focusing on verbal and nonverbal cues, (3) withholding judgment, (4) managing personal reactions, (5) taking notes, and (6) sharing responsibility for successful communication. By practicing these strategies inside and outside the classroom, you'll soon find that good listening becomes a habit rather than an effort.

Improve Your Concentration

Noise, both physical and mental, is always lurking in the background, ready to disturb your listening if you let it. Physical distractions such as mechani-

EXHIBIT 4.7

Barriers to Effective Listening
Every listener faces a series of obstacles that can potentially block the path to effective listening:

Noise Physical distractions such as sirens and mental distractions such as personal worries can interfere with your ability to listen.

Lack of concentration If you daydream or let your mind wander off to follow a thought suggested by the speaker, you're apt to miss some or all of the message.

Snap judgments
When you jump to conclusions before the end of the speech, you close your mind to any additional points or evidence that the speaker may offer.

Personal reactions What you think and feel about the speaker's topic, words, delivery, appearance, race, religion, and beliefs can divert your attention and derail your listening.

Internal focus When you think about how you would refute the speaker, or when you disregard the speaker's points because you don't agree, you shift your concentration from the speaker to yourself.

Focusing on facts If you listen only for facts, you may miss the speaker's ideas or, just as bad, overload your memory with many individual bits of information that obscure the overall message.

cal sounds, odors, lights, and outside voices can draw your attention away from the speaker. Similarly, mental distractions such as time pressures, anger, and sadness can keep you from giving the speaker your full attention. What's more, you're probably not used to concentrating for long periods because nearly every important speech made today is systematically reduced to *sound bites,* the brief speech excerpts broadcast on television or radio.[22]

Your first strategy for effective listening, then, is to make a conscious effort to improve your concentration. Start by sharpening your focus even before the listener gets up to speak. Think about the occasion, the audience, and the speaker's background, credentials, and topic. This prepares you for the speech. Resist the temptation to tune out if you fear the topic will be too complex or challenging, which causes problems for many listeners.[23]

As the speaker launches into the introduction, stay alert so that you can identify the specific purpose and central idea. Continue to follow along with the speaker, reviewing the major

points, testing the reasoning, examining the organization, anticipating what the speaker might say, and seeing how the speaker's words fit with your expectations and experience.[24] At the same time, stay on guard so that you can refocus your attention on the speech if your thoughts quietly wander away.

This strategy works well because it takes advantage of the fact that we can listen with much greater speed than we can speak, a difference that works against untrained listeners. In the words of Ralph G. Nichols, a pioneer in listening research, "Not capitalizing on thought speed is our greatest single listening handicap."[25] Building concentration through this strategy may take effort at first, but if you practice regularly, it will soon come naturally.

Focus on Verbal and Nonverbal Cues

Only part of the meaning of a speaker's message is communicated verbally; the rest is communicated nonverbally, through body language and tone of voice (see Exhibit 4.8). Therefore, you're likely to miss vital information about the speaker's meaning if you listen with your ears alone. Instead, train

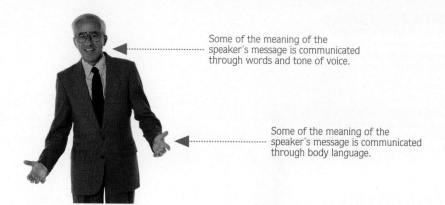

EXHIBIT 4.8
Communicating Meaning Verbally and Nonverbally

Some of the meaning of the speaker's message is communicated through words and tone of voice.

Some of the meaning of the speaker's message is communicated through body language.

yourself to get as much information as possible from the speaker by using your eyes as well as your ears.[26]

Compare the words you hear with the signals you get from the speaker's face, posture, gestures, and tone of voice. Ask yourself whether the nonverbal cues reinforce or contradict the verbal cues. You may find mismatches such as the contrast between a speaker's sympathetic words and her clenched fists or the contrast between a speaker's broad smile and his angry language. When you think about these contrasts in the context of the occasion and purpose for the speech, what do they tell you?

Of course, you can get more mileage from this strategy by using it when you're the speaker. Remember that the audience will be listening not just to what you say but how you say it. So as you stand in front of your audience, focus on your body language as well as your words. "To an overwhelming degree, *you* are your message." says Patricia Ward Brash, director of communications for Miller Brewing and an experienced public speaker.[27]

Withhold Your Judgment

Maybe you don't want to hear yet another speech on a certain topic, or you think you know what the speaker is going to say before the speech even begins. Maybe you don't agree with the first words out of the speaker's mouth, or you decide you're for or against the speaker's position before the speech is over. By rushing to make a judgment, you show disrespect for the speaker and deprive yourself of a chance to learn something new.

To be fair to the speaker, take the ethical high road and listen to the entire speech before passing judgment. For all you know, the speaker may have some startling new theory or example that can put the topic in an entirely new light. You'll never find out if you close your mind before the speaker finishes. So instead of jumping to conclusions, work especially hard on using your critical thinking skills to test the speaker's ideas.

Compare your conclusions to the speaker's conclusions. You don't have to agree or disagree at this point; you simply want to keep an open mind until the speech is complete. See whether the speaker's points and evidence support his or her conclusions. Also decide whether each new point meshes with previous points. Try to see where the speaker's argument is going and mentally challenge the reasoning. By the end of the speech, you'll have everything you need to come to an informed decision about whether the speaker's conclusions make sense or not. In the process, you may pick up some new ideas or facts that you didn't have before.

Manage Your Personal Reactions

Another strategy for effective listening is to practice managing your personal reactions. Although you may not be aware of it, your ability to listen is influenced by internal **filters**, emotions or attitudes that can distort messages or block all or part of them from entering your mind. In the same way a paper filter keeps coffee grounds from slipping into the coffee pot, your internal filters screen the messages that you receive.[28]

If you once had a painful experience with a topic, for example, you might unknowingly tune out

"After a brief period in prison . . ."

"Prison" can be a trigger word for some people. How would you react to a speaker who introduced himself this way?

"After a brief stint in the Peace Corps . . ."

Would you react the same way to a speaker who introduced himself as having been in the Peace Corps?

EXHIBIT 4.9
Appearances Can Deceive
As you listen to a speaker, examine your personal reactions to appearance as well as language and speaking style so you can learn to focus on the message itself.

anything to do with that topic in the future. Similarly, if you've taken a liking to a certain person or topic, your reactions are likely to be colored by those feelings. Think about what happens when you hear a **trigger word,** a word that arouses a strong positive or negative response in you. When someone older says, "You're just a child," how do you react? The trigger word *child* may make you angry, causing you to misinterpret—or disregard—anything else the speaker says. Addressing a group of fourth-year college students as *seniors* would probably evoke a positive or neutral reaction, whereas using the same term to address a group of newly retired employees could possibly trigger negative feelings toward everything else you have to say.

Everybody has personal reactions that interfere with the ability to listen objectively. As religious philosopher Jiddu Krishnamurti observes,

To be able to listen, one must abandon or put aside all prejudices, preformulations, and daily activities. We are screened with prejudices, whether religious or spiritual, psychological, or with our daily worries, desires, and fears. And with those as a screen, we listen.[29]

Take your first step toward managing personal reactions by identifying what sets you off. Do certain people, styles of clothing, regional accents,

hairstyles, words, topics, or examples arouse strong negative or positive reactions? As you listen to a speaker, be alert to what you're feeling and thinking. When you feel a response, pick out what triggered it. Once you know what causes you to react, you're in a better position to control the reaction so that you can listen with an open mind (see Exhibit 4.9). Then you can move beyond the speaker's race, gender, age, speech pattern, trigger words, and topic and be able to interpret, evaluate, and respond to the message itself.

Take Notes

Remembering what the speaker said is an important part of the listening process. But what exactly do you want to remember? If you listen only for facts and figures, that's all you'll get out of the speech, and that's not enough. Listening primarily for facts actually poses a barrier to effective listening.[30] You miss the big picture when you're listening just for the tiny details.

Instead, train yourself to listen for the central idea and the major points as well as the facts and figures that the speaker offers as evidence. Also, identify the overall structure that the speaker is using to build a case for the central idea. Then you can see how each piece of the puzzle—each major point and each scrap of evidence—fits into the overall picture.

Once you know what you want to remember, the next step is to boost your ability to retain the information so that you can recall it later. That's

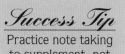

Success Tip
Practice note taking to supplement, not substitute for, your understanding of a speaker's message. Use the key-word outline system to capture the speaker's major points and indicate how they relate.

where taking notes comes in. If you take notes while the speaker is talking, you'll have a record of the major points, the main evidence, and the structure used in the speech. You can review this record again and again, any time you want to refresh your memory.

Note taking can enhance your ability to learn in the classroom, on the job, or in any situation where you need to understand and retain information provided by a speaker. By taking notes during a speech or lecture, rereading them later, and rewriting them in a format that clarifies the connections between major points, you can create a meaningful summary for study and review. This process helps you focus on the essence of the speaker's message both during and after the speech.

One of the most commonly used methods of taking notes is the **key-word outline,** a short outline that summarizes the content of the speech and the sequence of the major points in only a few words. You're not trying to write down everything the speaker says, and you're not concentrating on just the facts and figures. Instead, you're writing down a handful of words about each major point and each important piece of supporting evidence.

Imagine that you're in the audience when Alison

IMPROVING YOUR CRITICAL THINKING

MIXED MESSAGES: THE RESPONSIBILITIES AND PERILS OF NOTE TAKING

The question of whether to take notes may not seem much of a dilemma. After all, how can you remember what the instructor says if you don't write it down? This is sound logic, because experts estimate that as much as 87 percent of the information coming to the brain is gathered by the eyes. You therefore improve the odds of retaining information simply by seeing it in writing. In addition, when you know you'll be relying on your notes, you're apt to pay more attention to the speaker and to do more to analyze and evaluate the message. Also, notes are almost a necessity when you want to review the material later or study for a test.

However, note taking may not make sense in every situation. If you don't have to be able to recall the information days, weeks, or months later, you may do better by listening carefully without taking notes. And if you're one of those people who can remember details well without notes, don't bother. Also, if you try to record everything you hear rather than concentrating on the meaning of the words, your note taking will slow you down. You won't have time to understand or evaluate what the speaker says because you'll be so busy writing it all down. In the rush, parts of the message can easily get mangled or lost.

In the end, only you can decide whether you need to take notes during a speech. But if you do decide to take notes, remember: notes are no substitute for paying attention to the meaning of the speaker's words.

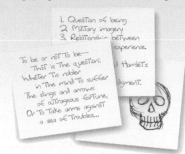

People who need to review the speaker's ideas at a later date often take notes during a speech. Note taking is highly personal: What works for one person may not work for another, so experiment and use the system that works best for you.

Shapiro, president of the Television Action Committee, delivers a speech titled "Television After 9/11: Transformation from Tragedy." Shapiro's central idea is that television underwent sudden changes in programming after the shock and horror of the terrorist attacks on the Pentagon and World Trade Center on September 11, 2001:

What did audiences want after hours spent staring at news footage of the collapsing towers? They did not want the violence, cynicism, sick jokes, or meaningless trivia common in the '90s. As the country came together in a groundswell of sympathy, compassion, and generosity, network programmers scrambled to supply the nobler values audiences demanded.

They downplayed the greedy antics of "reality TV" shows. They produced special fundraisers for the victims' families. They paid tribute to heroes who emerged among firefighters, police officers, and ordinary citizens. Snide talk show hosts such as David Letterman shed tears on air, as did New York Mayor Rudi Guiliani, veteran newscaster Dan Rather, and even the President of the United States.

As you listen to this part of the speech, you might take notes like these:

Programming after 9/11 tragedy
    Audiences demand less violence,
        sick humor, trivia
    Programmers supply nobler values
        Fundraisers
        Special tributes

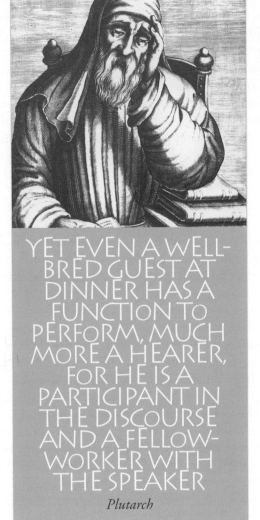

YET EVEN A WELL-BRED GUEST AT DINNER HAS A FUNCTION TO PERFORM, MUCH MORE A HEARER, FOR HE IS A PARTICIPANT IN THE DISCOURSE AND A FELLOW-WORKER WITH THE SPEAKER

Plutarch

EXHIBIT 4.10
The Shared Responsibility for Communication
Plutarch, a first-century Greek writer, recognized that both speaker and audience share responsibility for successful communication. Just as speakers are responsible for sending messages, listeners are responsible for paying attention to the speaker's message and for responding.

On-air emotional displays

This key-word outline uses just 21 words to summarize Shapiro's 116 words. All you need are a few words to jog your memory so that you can recall the major points long after the speech. You'll also be able to remember the evidence that Shapiro offered to demonstrate how programmers quickly adapted to changing audience demands. What's more, you'll be able to analyze the speech's organization and see whether the points do, in fact, come together to support the central idea. Another benefit: You'll get better at organizing your thoughts for speeches you prepare.

Share the Responsibility for Successful Communication

The process of communication isn't complete without both a speaker and an audience. Speakers can send messages, but if listeners don't do their part by listening and providing feedback, the process isn't complete. The Greek biographer Plutarch recognized this and offered the following advice to listeners (see Exhibit 4.10):

There are others who think that the speaker has a function to perform, and the hearer none. They think it only right that the speaker shall come with his discourse carefully thought out and prepared while they, without consideration or thought of their obligations, rush in and take their seats exactly as though they had come to dinner, to have a good time while others toil. And yet even a well-bred guest at dinner has a function to perform, much more a hearer, for he is a participant in the discourse and a fellow-worker with the speaker.[32]

According to Plutarch, listeners (whom he calls "hearers") can't simply sit back while the speaker talks. Quite the reverse: listeners are responsible for actively participating in the communication process. This point was made clear for freelance writer Joanne Sherman when she was interviewed on a television show. The interviewer had prepared a series of questions for the half-hour show. As he asked them, one after another, he didn't listen to Sherman but instead looked ahead to review the next question. When the questions ran out ten minutes before the end of the show, the interviewer had no idea what else to ask because he hadn't heard any of Sherman's replies.

Sherman quickly jumped in, asking herself a question and proceeding to answer it. Forced to concentrate on what his guest was saying, the interviewer soon picked up enough information to ask one follow-up question and then another, until the interview was over. Writing about the incident later, Sherman observed, "When I watched a tape of the program it was obvious that the last 10 minutes, while the interviewer was actively involved and participating, was by far the most interesting segment of the interview. . . . What did I learn from that experience? Basically, that to communicate effectively, one must listen as well as speak."[33]

FORMAL SPEECH EVALUATION

Every speech you hear—as well as every speech you give—offers an opportunity to improve both your listening and your public speaking skills. As you listen, you can apply the strategies for effec-

tive listening to sharpen your ability to attend to the message, understand it, remember the major points, evaluate what you've heard, and be able to respond appropriately. Similarly, you can apply critical thinking to make formal evaluations of the speeches and the public speaking skills of other speakers. Such structured evaluations produce helpful feedback for speakers, and they give you a chance to learn from other speakers' experiences. You can learn even more when your speeches are formally evaluated by others.

Learning from Formal Speech Evaluations

When you're in front of an audience, you search for verbal and nonverbal cues that tell you whether your message is getting through. However, when you're practicing the public speaking concepts you learn in class, you need additional feedback to gauge your progress. You can't ordinarily get this kind of detailed feedback from an audience. That's where a structured speech evaluation comes in.

Formal speech evaluations are designed to offer **constructive criticism**, criticism that is helpful and supportive, not stinging or hurtful. Research shows that the most useful evaluations are presented in impersonal terms and yet point out specific areas for improvement.[34] With the feedback from a structured speech evaluation, you can confirm your mastery of some skills and pinpoint other skills you need to practice.

Look at classroom speech evaluations as road signs marking the path to becoming a better public speaker. Positive feedback is always welcome, of course. Speakers need to know what they're doing well so that they can keep doing it and feel good about their progress. At the same time, speakers can learn a lot from evenhanded evaluations that tell them which of their public speaking skills seem to be less effective. Evaluators will also be sharpening their listening skills as they pay close attention to classmates' speeches so that they can give them useful feedback on evaluation forms.

Conducting Formal Speech Evaluations

When you conduct a formal speech evaluation, you study both the content of the speech and the speaker's delivery. Even though you may come away with an overall impression of the speech and the speaker, that speaker can't put your comments to use unless your feedback is specific. Depending on whether the speech is to inform, persuade, motivate, or entertain, the exact areas that your instructor asks you to observe and critique may differ. Nonetheless, every speech, regardless of purpose, can be evaluated according to six factors:

- *Topic and purpose.* Consider how the topic and purpose relate to the audience and the occasion.
- *Central idea, major points, and supporting material.* Look at the way the speaker presents the central idea and builds a foundation for it.
- *Speech organization.* Evaluate the speech's introduction, body, and conclusion, and the transitions linking the points and sections.
- *Language.* Examine the effectiveness of the speaker's language.
- *Delivery.* Evaluate the way the speaker delivers the speech.
- *Ethics.* Check for the use of ethical and unethical techniques.

In the course of conducting a formal speech evaluation, you'll apply content listening as well as critical listening. Content listening will help you answer questions about the ideas and information contained in the speech. Critical listening will help you analyze and weigh the evidence and logic used in a speech. By using both, you'll not only hone your listening skills but also help yourself and your fellow students become better public speakers.

Checklist for Evaluating a Speech

1. Topic and Purpose
   a. Speaker's topic is appropriate for the audience.
   b. Speaker's topic is appropriate for the occasion.
   c. Speaker's topic fits the time allotted for the speech.
   d. Speaker's specific purpose is clear.
   e. Speaker's specific purpose is appropriate for the audience.
2. Central Idea, Major Points, and Supporting Material
   a. The central idea is clear.
   b. The major points are clear.
   c. The major points support the central idea.
   d. The supporting material is appropriate.
   e. The supporting material is convincing.
   f. The supporting material is varied.
3. Speech Organization
   a. The introduction captures attention, previews the topic, and introduces the major points.
   b. The major points are presented in a logical sequence.
   c. Transitions are used to effectively connect the major points.
   d. The conclusion summarizes and reinforces the major points and motivates the audience to act.

4. Language
   a. The language is appropriate for the audience.
   b. The language is appropriate for the occasion.
   c. The language is concrete.
   d. The language is vivid.
5. Delivery
   a. The speaker's nonverbal cues reinforce the words.
   b. The speaker's nonverbal cues stimulate and maintain interest.
   c. The speaker uses effective eye contact, gestures, and body movement.
   d. The speaker speaks at an appropriate speed.
   e. The speaker's voice varies in tone and volume.
   f. The speaker seems enthusiastic.
   g. The speaker seems poised.
   h. The speaker seems prepared.
   i. The speaker finishes within the time limit.
6. Ethics
   a. The speaker credits sources when appropriate.
   b. The speaker mentions several options for the audience to consider, rather than focusing on only one.
   c. The speaker's information is accurate and truthful.
   d. The speaker earns the audience's trust.

SUMMARY

Listening is the link that connects the speaker and the audience in the communication process. Hearing is a physiological process in which our ears receive sound waves and transmit them to our brain. Listening is both a mental and a physiological process, because it requires that we actively pay attention to sounds; interpret, remember, and evaluate the meaning; and then respond.

Effective listening benefits both speakers and audience members. By listening before the speech, the speaker can pick up the audience's needs and interests; by listening during the speech, the speaker can obtain feedback; and by listening after the speech, the speaker can focus on audience questions and concerns. Audience members benefit from listening because they can absorb, analyze, and evaluate the speaker's meaning; learn from speakers; follow the speaker's reasoning and be ready to respond; and learn how to improve their own public speaking skills. For the audience as well as the speaker, listening creates an atmosphere in which people are encouraged to share their thoughts and feelings.

The four types of listening are content, critical, empathic, and appreciative listening. Content listening helps you understand the speaker's message. Critical listening helps you both understand and evaluate the meaning of the message. Empathic listening helps you understand the speaker's feelings and viewpoint. Appreciative listening helps you enjoy the speaker's message and delivery. The five factors of listening are (1) attending, (2) interpreting, (3) remembering, (4) evaluating, and (5) responding.

You can improve your listening skills through six strategies. First, make a conscious effort to improve your concentration. Second, get as much information as possible from the speaker by using your eyes as well as your ears to pick up verbal and nonverbal cues. Third, listen to the entire speech before you pass judgment. Fourth, manage your personal reactions so that your internal filters (emotions and attitudes) don't distort or block the speaker's message. Fifth, listen for more than facts and figures, and take notes so that you can remember what the speaker says. Sixth, share responsibility for the communication process by actively participating as a listener.

Formal speech evaluations offer constructive criticism of topic and purpose, central idea, major points, supporting materials, speech organization, language, delivery, and ethics. Content and critical listening are the types of listening involved in speech evaluation.

KEY TERMS

appreciative listening (72)
attending (72)
constructive criticism (82)
content listening (70)
critical listening (71)
empathic listening (72)
filters (78)
interpreting (73)
key-word outline (80)
trigger word (79)

APPLY CRITICAL THINKING

1. What place does content listening have in a speech to motivate?
2. If listeners can understand words more quickly than speakers can say them, should speakers be encouraged to speed up their delivery? Explain your answer.
3. Why do listeners have to evaluate as well as interpret what they hear?
4. What can you, as a speaker, do to determine the reason for an audience's silence during your speech?
5. What risks do you see in relying on information from sound bites to make up your mind about a political issue or candidate?
6. In what situations outside the classroom do you ordinarily take notes while listening to a speaker? Discuss why you take notes and how you use your notes in these situations.
7. When you evaluate a persuasive speech, what questions would you add to this chapter's Checklist for Evaluating a Speech?

SHARPEN YOUR SKILLS

Individual Exercises

1. Attend a speech on or off campus, or watch a speaker on television. Write down any nonverbal cues you notice, and indicate how these cues relate to the verbal message. What did you learn from facial expressions, tone of voice, gestures, and other body language? Was the nonverbal message consistent with the verbal message? Draft a one-page letter to the speaker, explaining your findings and offering advice about effective nonverbal cues, if needed. Submit the letter to your instructor.

2. Identify a situation in which content listening is especially important, and list two reasons for its importance. Do the same for critical listening, empathic listening, and appreciative listening. Do you see any overlap in the situations or the reasons? Prepare a two-minute presentation to the class summarizing your ideas and conclusions.

3. Listen to a political speech in person, on television, on audiotape or videotape, or on the radio. Use the keyword outline method to take notes during the speech.

   a. How many major points did you identify? List them.

   b. What supporting evidence, if any, did you write down? Why? How does this evidence relate to the major points?

   c. Write a one-page summary of this speech. Include the specific purpose and the central idea as well as the major points.

4. Select one of the speeches in the Appendix.

   a. After you read the introduction, stop and determine your personal reaction to the topic. Why do you feel this way?

   b. Before you continue reading, write down the conclusion you would reach about the central idea right now, if you read no further.

   c. Finish reading the speech. At this point, is your conclusion the same as the one you reached before reading the body and conclusion of the speech? Has your personal reaction to the topic changed? Explain.

Group Exercises

5. Team up with a classmate for this exercise.

   a. Working separately, list five trigger words that cause you to react emotionally, and note next to each the reaction it triggers. Now think of a word or phrase you can substitute for each that would *not* trigger an emotional response.

   b. Compare your list with that of your classmate. What similarities and differences do you see? What are the implications for speakers?

6. Attend a speech (or watch a speech on television) with two other students. As you listen, think about the elements used to evaluate a speaker and speech. Then evaluate the speech, following the guidelines in the Checklist for Evaluating a Speech. Compare your evaluation with those of the other students. What areas did you agree or disagree about? As a group, discuss this comparison and write a one-page report summarizing the results of your discussion.

DEVELOPING YOUR TOPIC, PURPOSE, AND CENTRAL IDEA

LEARNING OBJECTIVES

After studying this chapter, you will be able to

1. Identify the steps for developing a clear idea for your speech.

2. Define the process of brainstorming and explain how it can help generate speech topics.

3. Explain why it's usually necessary to narrow your topic before you start to write your speech.

4. Distinguish subject areas from speech topics.

5. Define the three general purposes you can have in a speech.

6. Distinguish a specific purpose from a central idea.

7. List the features of a strong central idea.

EVERY GREAT SPEECH STARTS WITH A CLEAR, CONCISE IDEA

Have you ever jumped into your car and just started driving with no idea of where you were going? You drive for five or six minutes, and wherever you end up, that's where you are. Probably not, but many novice speakers do just that with their speeches. They focus on filling up their five or six minutes, without a plan for telling their audiences anything specific. In the end, the experience is unsatisfying for everyone—for the listeners (who must sit through a speech without learning or enjoying anything) and for the speaker (who doesn't develop any speaking skills and who probably gets a low grade as well). Effective speakers never leave their audiences to ask themselves, "What was that all about?"[1] By setting clear goals for every speech, you'll find this course much more fulfilling.

Starting with a clear idea of your goal does more than help make a great speech. It reduces the amount of research and preparation you need to do. You won't be wasting time and energy on material that gets cut at the last minute, so you can focus your limited planning and practicing time on the issues that are central to your speech. Plus, a clear goal can help you gain confidence so that you're not so nervous. Knowing you have a clear purpose and a well planned message means you won't have to fumble

Success Tip

The most effective speeches are found at the intersection of four forces: your knowledge, the audience's knowledge, your interests, and the audience's interests.

for thoughts or words. To develop a clear idea for your speech, follow three steps: identify your topic, define your purpose, and refine your central idea (see Exhibit 5.1).

STEP 1: IDENTIFY YOUR TOPIC

After you graduate and begin speaking in professional and social situations, the topics you'll address will often be chosen for you or restricted to a narrow subject area. A local civic organization might ask you to speak at a luncheon and explain your company's line of business. As a medical professional, you might speak at a conference dedicated to the health problems of newborn babies. The financial services firm you work for might ask you to talk to groups of investors about saving for retirement. Whatever your situation, you probably won't have to worry about finding a topic—the topic will usually find you. (Keep in mind, though, that even in those cases where a topic is assigned, you still need to pay attention to defining your purpose and refining your central idea.)

However, the circumstances in your public speaking class could be different. Your instructor may assign general categories and leave it up to you to find your own topic. This freedom can make the process more challenging at times, but it does offer some advantages. First, you won't get stuck talking about something that doesn't

EXHIBIT 5.1

Developing a Clear Idea for Your Speech
Here are the steps to take to come up with a clear and concise idea for your speech. This chapter covers each stage of the process: (1) identify your topic, (2) define your purpose, and (3) refine your central idea.

Identify your topic

Brainstorm and then research ideas	My cousin was a crime victim	Identified through brainstorming
Narrow your topic	I've found some frightening statistics about crime rates	Comes from research
	Crime against travelers	Crime in general is too much to cover in a short speech

Define your purpose

| Define your general purpose | To inform | Your options: to inform, to persuade, to entertain or motivate |
| Make your purpose specific | I want people to recognize the risks of being victimized in hotel rooms and know how to protect themselves | You've chosen to speak about one narrow aspect of your topic (crimes against travelers in hotels) |

Refine your central idea

| Summarize your message, and then sharpen your focus if necessary | Because hotel guests are victimized more often than people realize, all travelers should be aware of the steps they can take to defend themselves (keeping your door locked, not letting on which room you're in, not letting unexpected visitors into your room) | You've identified your topic and you're ready to move on |

Ready to begin gathering support and organizing material

Ask an Expert

Craig Johnson
Associate Professor of Communication, George Fox College

Q: I've never felt very creative; is there something I can do to improve my creativity when it comes to developing speeches?

A: You may not feel creative, but don't underestimate your creative talents. If you've ever resolved a conflict, written a term paper, or started a new dating relationship, you've exercised your creative thinking abilities. These same skills can be applied to developing speeches.

Creative thinking is sometimes referred to as divergent thinking because it requires looking at a problem from a number of different perspectives and generating a variety of solutions. Preparation is the key to creative success. First, acquire the necessary raw materials (ideas, information, strategies) through study and practice. To generate a creative speech, research your subject and set aside plenty of time for planning and rehearsing.

Creative problem-solving techniques can help you customize your speech. Select a topic through *associative listing*. That is, record your general topic at the top of a page and then generate a list of subtopics related to that subject. Choose one of these subtopics as the focus for your presentation. Next, organize your major points by clustering. Write the topic you selected earlier in the center of a clean sheet of paper and circle it. Record related words radiating out of your topic. Each new word should be circled and connected by a line to the previous circle. Start again at your topic word, and go in a different direction when you have an unrelated thought. The visual pattern that emerges out of your cluster will reveal which concepts belong together. The result will be a creative picture of your speech and a preliminary organization for it.

1. Speakers can use associative listing to spark creativity in a variety of ways. How can you use associative listing to find just the right title for your speech?
2. Before your next speech, use the clustering technique to record and link words that relate to your topic. Continue until you have refined the links to reveal a logical connection and smooth flow for the ideas. How does this help you plan the structure of your speech?

interest you personally. Second, you can be your own best source of information; some of the best student speeches stem from personal experience.

Mild panic is a common reaction when students face the task of selecting a speech topic. Don't worry; this chapter gives you the skills you need to find lots of interesting topics. What do other students talk about? Look at the winning speeches in the annual contest sponsored by the Interstate Oratorical Association and you'll discover a huge variety of topics, ranging from the AIDS drug AZT to the financial and political struggles faced by zoos around the world. Here are some of the subjects entered in a recent contest: Brazilian death squads, sleep deprivation, failures of school lunch programs, government regulation of higher education, the environmental hazards of dry cleaning, jury trials, false memory syndrome, hepatitis, airline accidents, drive-by shootings, and energy-generating algae.[2] The number of potential topics is limitless.

Because you have so many topics to choose from, start looking immediately. With false starts and dead ends, topic selection can be a slow part of the speech process, so the sooner you start, the less likely you are to be scrambling the night before your speech is due. Moreover, as soon as you've identified a potential topic, your mind will automatically begin generating ideas that will make your speech easier to write and more effective when you deliver it.[3] So how do you find topics that mean something to you? The two main methods are brainstorming and research.

Brainstorming Ideas

Where do ideas come from, anyway? The human mind is a marvelous and mysterious piece of machinery with an ability to recognize potential links or connections between separate ideas. Albert Einstein used to play around with collections of ideas, looking for new connections. He called this sort of thinking "combinatory play."[4]

EXHIBIT 5.2

What Comes to Mind from Everyday Scenes?
Simply standing on the sidewalk and looking around for a few minutes can generate dozens of potential speech topics. How many topics come to mind when you look at a scene like this? Overcrowding, crime, good neighbors, the stimulating rush of city life, regulation of small businesses, pollution, customer service in retail stores, the risks of being a bus driver—you can generate a long list of possibilities.

Once you get rolling with brainstorming, you're likely to generate a large number of potential topics. Of course, you may need a few tricks to get the process started. You might try reminding yourself of issues that are important to you. If you're stuck for starting ideas, ask yourself the following questions:[7]

- What have I heard on the news lately that upset me?
- What have I read recently that made me angry, sad, concerned, happy, or excited?
- What successes or accomplishments have I heard or read about that motivated me to excel in my own life?
- What's the last debate, argument, or stimulating discussion I had with friends?
- What do I usually disagree—or agree—with my parents about?
- What movies have I seen that moved me emotionally?

You can use the same approach. Start with practically anything—an object, a person, a place on the globe, a point in time, whatever comes to mind first—and then turn your brain loose. It will jump from idea to idea, a process called **free association**.[5]

Look at the street scene pictured in Exhibit 5.2. Pick a person or a building. What comes to mind? Are there any connections between the people and the buildings? A single scene like this has enough material to generate dozens of potential topics. All you need to do is sit back and take notes. When you use free association to come up with ideas (topics for your speech), it's called **brainstorming**.[6]

Success Tip
Your brain needs lots of raw material if you expect to be able to use free association and brainstorming. The French writer Stendahl once said that he required "three to four cubic feet of ideas every day."

The answers to these questions might be good topics in and of themselves. They might also spark a brainstorming session that leads to the idea you eventually use.

Another good way to start the brainstorming process is to make a personal inventory of your skills, experiences, favorite books, vacation places, favorite holidays, college courses, and so forth. Some of the best speeches are drawn from or inspired by students' own life experiences and knowledge. This kind of speech is also easier to develop because you know what you're talking about, and it can be presented more confidently and often more effectively. Exhibit 5.3 shows a way to arrange personal experiences that may uncover interesting speech possibilities. As you define and describe the experience using the categories shown in the exhibit, you think about lessons you learned, emotions you felt, friends you made, and other elements that will help you build a powerful speech.

Researching Ideas

When you use brainstorming, you look inside your own head and heart for ideas and inspiration. When you use research, you look at external sources for ideas and inspiration. Your research doesn't have to be rigorous or formal—you can even flip through the pages of a dictionary and look at the guide words to search for ideas.

Visit the library and poke around areas that interest you. If you like science and technology, for instance, new developments in these fields often make

DEVELOPING YOUR CREATIVITY

MIND MAPPING: AN INGENIOUS TECHNIQUE FOR FINDING A GREAT TOPIC

Free association, brainstorming, and other methods of generating ideas can be tremendously helpful, but they are limited in one important respect: They all follow the normal *linear* nature of spoken or written language. You start with Idea A, which prompts Idea B, which prompts Idea C, and so on. What if Idea A is also connected to C and D and M? What if a connection between Ideas A and B represents another idea? Topic areas don't always follow the straightforward, linear flow of our language.

Learning specialist Tony Buzan coined the term *mind-mapping* (professors Joseph Novak and Robert Gowin called it *concept mapping* in their research) to explore ideas that may be related in *nonlinear* ways. Ray Harlan, a trainer and professional speaker, uses mind-mapping in the example shown here. The topic is "Improving Employee Performance on the Job." Start with "Improve performance," then begin writing down all the topics that might be related to it.

The next step is to expand each idea and search for other connections. In the second map shown here, "Supervision" is expanded and connected to other ideas. All of these connections represent potential ideas. You see that a speech on the vague topic of improved performance could be narrowed to a speech about better hiring practices or about the need for better training. In this sense, mind-mapping not only helps generate ideas you may not have considered but also helps you focus and narrow your topic by bringing more specific issues (better hiring, for instance) to the surface.

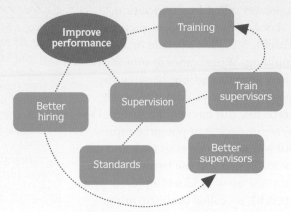

EXHIBIT 5.3

Arranging Personal Experiences to Uncover Topics

Using a chart such as this one, you can develop a speech topic from a personal experience. First, think of some experience you've had that impressed you somehow. Second, modify the categories as needed to fit your own experiences. As you progress from left to right, you can build a story around the experience—What did you learn? Who was affected, and how? Could it happen again?

The experience: _____

What kind of experience was it?	Where did it happen?	Who else was involved?	When did it happen?
Embarrassing	At home	Strangers	In high school
Funny	At work	Teachers	In college
Happy	At school	Family	
Uncomfortable	In a car	Friends	
Educational	On an airplane		
Dangerous	In a store		
Interesting			
Sad			
Exciting			
Surprising			

interesting and informative speeches. Some developments even raise thought-provoking ethical or political questions. Magazines such as *Discover, National Geographic, Natural History, Wired, Popular Science,* and *Scientific American* are all good places to look for ideas on science and technology.[8] No matter what your field of interest, from agriculture to zodiacs, you'll find periodicals (magazines and other publications) that can help you get ideas for speech topics. Browsing through your library may be surprisingly rewarding. It can stimulate your thought processes by helping you find a topic and gather support materials for later use in the speech itself.

In addition to browsing through printed materials, be sure to take advantage of all the computerized information you may have available. CD-ROM encyclopedias can be great sources of ideas, since they make it so easy to jump from entry to entry. Microsoft Encarta is one of the leading products in this field. Encarta lets you poke around in several ways, using subject categories, historical dates, place names, or simply combinations of words. Say you dive into the category selector and choose "performing arts." From the list of subcategories, you choose "theater." Encarta informs you that it has 341 articles on the subject of theater, covering actors, playwrights, and other related topics. You scroll through the list until you see John Wilkes Booth, the actor who assassinated Abraham Lincoln. While you read this tragic story, you start to wonder about presidential assassinations in general.

EXHIBIT 5.4

Subject Areas of Interest Today
Thinking about a career as a public speaker? What subject areas are in demand today? A survey of meeting planners (who organize events and invite professional speakers) uncovered the subject areas that interest today's audiences. Business and management issues led the list of subjects requested of speakers, something to keep in mind if you'd like to make a living as a speaker. Top speakers earn tremendous fees, too. For instance, former President Bill Clinton gets $110,000 per speech, Suzanne Sommers makes $20,000, and Tom Brokaw earns $75,000.

Top 10 Requested Subject Areas	Percentage
1. Business and the economy	42.2
2. Management development & communication	38.8
3. New technologies	33.3
4. Legislative issues	32.1
5. Self-development or motivation	26.6
6. Future projections	21.5
7. New products & services	16.5
8. Legal issues	16.0
9. National affairs (politics)	13.1
10. National affairs (policies)	11.8

Clinton $110,000

Sommers $20,000

Brokaw $75,000

Moving to Encarta's word finder, you ask to see a display of all articles that contain the words "assassination" and "president." This produces a list of 159 articles, one of which is on the U.S. Central Intelligence Agency (CIA). Reading this article, you learn that investigations into the CIA's activities have uncovered illegal spying activities on U.S. citizens and assassination attempts in other countries.[9] You start to wonder whether we even need an agency such as the CIA, now that the Soviet KGB is just a shadow of the threat it once was. There you are: You have an interesting, important topic (and one that's a long way from your original choice of performing arts).

Using research to identify a topic may seem awfully similar to free association. In fact, you're combining research with free association; you just have additional resources at your fingertips to stimulate new ideas. New information technologies make this process much easier and more enjoyable.

Narrowing Your Topic

One of the most valuable things you can learn from this chapter is the difference between *subject areas* and *speech topics*. A **subject area** is a broad category of knowledge, skills, information, or other ideas (see Exhibit 5.4). Such areas include numerous subcategories. The world economy, baseball, the U.S. presidency, and cooking are all subject areas, and they all have one thing in common: they're too big for any single speech. If you set out to give a five-minute speech on baseball, you won't succeed because you can't convey anything meaningful about this huge subject in such a short time period.

The secret is to narrow your subject area to a **speech topic**, which is a single concept, issue, or block of information within a subject area. The subject area of baseball contains dozens of speech topics, including the economics of multimillion-dollar major league salaries, the community benefits of minor league baseball, and injuries in Little League games. In fact, each of these can be narrowed even further. For the topic of injuries in the Little League, you might focus on the dangers of unsafe batting helmets or the risks of letting young pitchers throw curve balls before their muscles are fully developed.

Why Should You Narrow Your Topic?

Beyond the obvious limitation of fitting your speech within your assigned time limit, narrowing your topic is important for several other reasons:

1. *It increases your chances of success.* Read the following two examples:
   a. Geraniums are available in pink, blue, and violet.
   b. Lobelia, or *lobeliaceae* if you prefer the Latin names, are available in a variety of sizes, colors, and blooming seasons, from the late spring red *cardinalis* to the summer-blooming purple *gerardii* to the blue *siphiliticia*, a stately favorite in the late summer garden.

Without looking back, can you remember which colors geraniums are available in? Which colors are lobelia available in? Chances are you remember the colors of geraniums because that message is focused on a single issue; however, the second message contains a lot of information unrelated to color. Now apply this notion of simplicity to your entire speech. The tighter your message, the better your chances of success. In fact, a number of research experiments have proven that simplicity and focus are important to successful communication. These experiments found that there is a limited capacity for using any channel of communication. As a result, speech performance suffers when listeners are confronted with too much information (or information that is presented in a cumbersome manner). The more focused, simple, and narrow your speech is, the more likely the audience will understand it.[10]

2. *It reduces your preparation work.* We've all fallen into the trap of rushing into a project such as a term paper, furiously gathering research and cranking out paragraphs before stopping to think through what we need to write about. The result can be a lot of wasted time and energy. The same thing can happen when preparing a speech. You'll gather more information than you need and waste time analyzing and synthesizing material you never use. So make it easy for yourself and start with a narrowly and clearly defined topic.

3. *It helps the audience stay focused.* You probably already know that listening to speeches can be hard work. Your mind wanders, people and noises around the room distract you, the speaker's message prompts you to think about things unrelated to the speech, and so on. Even if a speech is well crafted, well delivered, relevant, and interesting, it's still hard to pay attention all the way through. The reason for

Checklist for Identifying Potential Speech Topics

1. Start thinking about topics immediately; identifying a topic may take a lot more time than you think, so the sooner you identify a topic, the more time you'll have left to develop it.
2. Write down any idea or topic that occurs to you so that you won't forget about it.
3. Take notes when you're doing other things, such as exercising or watching TV; good ideas can come when you least expect them.
4. Fill your head with ideas—read, talk with people, watch the news; the more ideas floating around in your head, the better chance you'll have of identifying a good topic.
5. Stop, look, and listen; the world is full of interesting and controversial topics.
6. Search for inspiration in the library, on the Internet, and from other information sources.

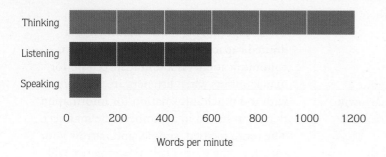

Thinking

Listening

Speaking

Words per minute

EXHIBIT 5.5
How Fast Can You Think? Listen? Speak?
Your audience can listen several times faster than you can talk—and think seven or eight times faster. In a five-minute speech, for instance, you might be able to say 625–750 words, while the people sitting there can think at a rate of about 4000 words. To keep the minds of your listeners from wandering, you need to narrow and focus your speech as much as possible; the more focused your topic, the better your chances of keeping your audience's attention.

this difficulty has to do with the power of the human brain. Most people talk at around 125–150 words per minute (anything faster would be too fast for public speaking). However, most people can listen at three or four times that rate, and they can think at seven or eight times that rate (see Exhibit 5.5).[11] Even when a listener is paying attention, his or her brain has lots of extra power sitting there idle, just itching for other things to think about. As a speaker, you can't talk fast enough to occupy all this brain power, but you can get your fair share of it by focusing your audience with a narrow topic. When you speak on a precise, well-defined topic, your listeners are more likely to follow along. If you start to wander or cover too much subject area, you won't even get the attention you "deserve" because your listeners' minds may wander off and never come back. Their bodies may wander off, too, as President Bill Clinton discovered during his State of the Union address one year. Several members of Congress got so restless during the rambling 80-minute speech that they actually walked out.[12] Failing to narrow the topic sufficiently is a mistake made by speakers at all experience levels. Speakers who try to cover too much material may also be tempted to rush through the speech and fail to develop the specific purpose adequately.

Consider two example topics. The first has been narrowed sufficiently for a typical classroom speech, but the second has not:

(a) The benefits of wearing a helmet when riding a bicycle
(b) Bicycle safety concerns

To give a speech on the first topic, you can talk about the danger of head injuries and how helmets protect the cyclist's head. A few good examples of riders who did and didn't wear helmets will round out your persuasive message. In contrast, the second topic requires you to address a wide range of issues, from weather and traffic to dogs and tire blowouts. You couldn't possibly cover all of these subjects in a single five- or six-minute speech.

How Can You Narrow Your Topic?
When it comes to judging whether a topic is narrow enough for a given speech assignment, your ability will increase as you prepare and give more speeches. In the meantime, you can follow some general guidelines that will help. Ask yourself the following questions:

• *What does your particular audience need or want to hear about this topic?* The people in your audience will require varying depth and detail from your speech, thereby determining whether you need to narrow or fine-tune your topic.[13] Consider a topic such as funding for public universities. A speech to the state legislature might include the details of funding and taxation. However, a speech to a group of parents or students might simply highlight the need for more money and call on the audience to contact the legislature.

EXHIBIT 5.6

Estimating the Length of Your Speech

With the numbers in this table, you can figure out your approximate speaking rate. You'll need a watch or clock with a second hand and something 500 words long. (The first five paragraphs of the section titled "Your General Purpose" comprise about 500 words—from the sentence beginning "Most speeches fall . . ." to the first paragraph of the first speech excerpt, at the phrase "A similar occurrence was reported . . .") Time yourself as you read the 500-word section, then find the number in the top line of the table that's closest to your measured time. The second line will then tell you your approximate reading rate, and the line below that will tell you how many words you can expect to cover in a five-minute speech.

Reading time in minutes	2:30	3:00	3:30	4:00	4:30	5:00	5:30	6:00	6:30	7:00	7:30	8:00
Speaking rate in words per minute	200	167	143	125	111	100	91	83	77	71	67	63
Words in a five-minute speech	1000	833	714	625	556	500	455	417	385	357	333	313
Equivalent pages of double-spaced type	4	$3\frac{1}{3}$	3	$2\frac{1}{2}$	$2\frac{1}{4}$	2	$1\frac{3}{4}$	$1\frac{2}{3}$	$1\frac{1}{2}$	$1\frac{1}{2}$	$1\frac{1}{3}$	$1\frac{1}{4}$

- *What level of explanation does your audience need?* Whether your audience is made up of classmates, potential clients, or city dignitaries, every audience has a collective ego. Just as you would resent someone talking down to you about something you're already familiar with, so your audience will resent you for insulting their intelligence. You probably wouldn't speak to a meeting of journalists about hot news issues of the day; they consider such a topic their area of expertise and don't need you explaining the news to them. Similarly, you wouldn't presume that a roomful of men would want to hear only about "men's" topics or that a roomful of women would be interested only in "women's" topics.[14] Removing potentially insulting issues from your speech is often a good way to narrow your topic. Be sure the topic and your coverage of it are both appropriate for the audience and the occasion.
- *How much background, description, and evidence will you need?* If you were speaking to a group of homeowners about a new fast-food restaurant planned for their neighborhood, you wouldn't need to explain what a fast-food restaurant is or what it does. However, if you were discussing a semiconductor fabrication plant or a veneer mill, you would probably have to spend time explaining what these facilities are all about before you get down to the business at hand.
- *How much time do you have?* To estimate the actual length of your speech in words, look at Exhibit 5.6. Figure that most people deliver around 125 words a minute (up to 150 words or so a minute if you are a naturally quick talker). So for a five-minute speech, assume you'll have time to speak roughly 625 words. To get an idea of how much you can cover, compare this with papers you've recently written; 625 words isn't that much once you get into a topic. (It's less than one-tenth the length of this chapter, for example.)

Following these guidelines for narrowing your speech topic will help you in two ways: You'll end up covering less information but covering it more effectively, and you'll get more in tune with your audience.

STEP 2: DEFINE YOUR PURPOSE

Now that you have a good idea of what your topic is, it's time to clarify *why* you're going to talk about it. In other words, what do you hope to accomplish by making this speech? Sure, getting a good grade and getting through the public speaking course are your immediate goals, but think about speaking in a larger sense, after college. Your ability to accomplish a desired purpose in a speech might mean making a sale, winning elected office, keeping a toxic waste facility out of your neighborhood, winning acceptance of a new medical treatment, or advancing in your career. No matter what the situation, all successful speeches are built around a well-defined purpose. If you aren't clear about what your purpose is, you won't be able to achieve it.

Note that steps 1 and 2 don't necessarily happen in the order discussed here. You may define your purpose first, then select and narrow your topic. (In your public speaking class, you're typically assigned a general purpose, then you go off and select a topic.) In other cases, you may arrive at both the topic and the purpose simultaneously. The important point to remember is that you need to take both steps, regardless of order.

Your General Purpose

Most speeches fall into one of three **general purpose** categories: *to inform, to persuade,* or *to motivate or entertain.* The primary goal of an **informative speech** is to convey information, whether it's news about changes in the tax laws or instructions on installing kitchen cabinets. The primary goal of a **persuasive speech** is to change the attitudes or behaviors of your audience. The primary goal of a **motivational or entertainment speech** is to make people feel happy, energized, or empowered. (Most of the speeches in a beginning speech course will be either to inform or to persuade.)

It's important to understand that few speeches qualify as purely informative or purely persuasive. In an informative speech, for instance, you won't

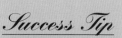

Success Tip

One of the most powerful words in informative speeches is *how.* Most people want to know how to perform better, how to look better, how to be wealthy. Tell them how, and they'll pay close attention to your speech.

get your point across unless the audience is persuaded that you know what you're talking about and that your sources of information are reliable. Similarly, you probably won't persuade people to donate money to a charity unless you inform them about what the charity does. A persuasive speech requires more than a passion for a cause or a topic; you'll need lots of supporting information and detail to make your case effectively. When Jaime José Serra Puche, Mexico's Secretary of Commerce and Industrial Promotion, delivered a speech promoting the benefits of the North American Free Trade Agreement (NAFTA), he set the stage by first discussing five elements required for international competitiveness. He then told the audience that he would attempt to prove that those elements "will be brought about by NAFTA as an instrument to the region."[15] In other words, he first *informed* the audience about the foundations of international competitiveness, then *persuaded* the audience that NAFTA would help lay those foundations.

The following speech excerpts illustrate these points further. Both address the issues of crime and personal safety, but the first is more informational, whereas the second is more persuasive. (By the way, both are recent award winners in a collegiate speaking competition.)

The first excerpt conveys disturbing information about the high rates of theft and personal attacks against hotel guests. The two paragraphs quoted here follow the introductory paragraph and provide several examples of hotel security breakdowns.

Hotel security is quickly becoming an issue impossible to dismiss. With the increase in reported cases, it is obvious that these are not isolated incidents. According to *USA Today,* the hotel industry doesn't keep track of hotel crimes. Former Director of the National Crime Prevention Institute, Richard Mellard, says that hotel crimes are cloaked in silence. The transient population doesn't report them, and the local police are ignorant of at least 60 percent of actual crimes—crimes like the one that involved world famous Brazilian jazz guitarist Joao Bosco and his wife, Angela. As recently reported in the *San Francisco Chronicle,* the two returned to their St. Francis hotel room in San Francisco to find their safe empty and all of their belongings missing. Apparently, the intruder had managed to obtain a key to the room after convincing hotel security that he was Bosco. A similar occurrence was reported in the *Los Angeles Times.* A New Jersey surgeon and his family returned to their Ritz-Carlton hotel room to find it had been broken into. The estimated total loss was in excess of $200,000, including their return plane tickets home. After the robbery was reported, several hours passed before hotel security called to say that they were not responsible for room safes.

Far more disturbing cases were reported on ABC's "20/20." A man claiming to be hotel maintenance gained access to guest rooms on two separate occasions, both times brutally raping the women inside the rooms. Another woman fooled by the hotel maintenance scam was robbed and left with a shattered cheekbone. That same broadcast goes on to give the ordeal of Stacy Cason and her parents. Cason's father was attacked by an intruder while Cason desperately

dialed the front desk but got no answer. The front desk closed at 10:30. Finally, Cason got through to the local 911 operator but not before her father was stabbed several times. Cason's father survived the attack but Cason and her father blame the premature death of her mother on the trauma of the ordeal. [16]

The rest of the speech addresses statistics for the hotel industry, the factors behind weak hotel security, and the steps people can take to protect themselves. One of the goals of this speech is to persuade people to be more careful in hotels, but the primary goal is to inform listeners and raise their awareness of the safety issue in general. Compare this excerpt with the following excerpt from a speech on stalking laws. Again, the paragraphs quoted here come after the introductory section.

Whether it's because of poor laws, unsympathetic police officers, or victims who won't help themselves, these laws are not the solution they were intended to be. To better protect ourselves, we need to advocate better laws and learn how to protect ourselves.

As advocates, we must let our state legislators know there is a viable option available. Recently, the National Criminal Justice Association released a model anti-stalking law. Written in cooperation with such groups as the ACLU, the American Bar

Checklist for Reviewing Your Specific Purpose Statement

1. Include three issues: your general purpose, your audience, and the specific goals you want to achieve.
2. Define your specific goals in terms of modifying audience knowledge, attitudes, beliefs, or behaviors.
3. Make sure your goal is relevant and meaningful to your audience—or that you can make it relevant and meaningful with your speech.

4. If you have trouble writing the specific purpose statement, or if it becomes longer than an average sentence, consider the fact that something is probably wrong with your purpose.
5. If you have to abandon an idea at this stage and start over, consider it good news; you've saved yourself a lot of time and frustration.

Association, and the U.S. Department of Justice, this law is designed to withstand court challenges and provide early intervention, strong protective measures, tougher penalties, and specialized training for police so they can treat victims with the respect they deserve.

Until a better law is in place, be aware of the protection you currently have. Consult your state's revised code available at any local library. Be aware of what the law can and cannot do if you should need help.

Meanwhile, make sure your state's local law enforcement agencies know your state has a stalking law. When I called the county prosecutor recently, the legal assistant I spoke to was not aware our state had enacted a stalking law.[17]

This speech encourages people to protect themselves, but its major thrust is to convince the audience of the inadequacy of most stalking laws and to persuade people to take action to solve the problem. Note how this speech also conveys information to get the main point across.

FOCUSING ON ETHICS

IS YOUR PURPOSE ETHICAL? ASK YOURSELF THESE QUESTIONS TO AVOID COMMON SPEAKING BLUNDERS

Even in the confines of a classroom, public speaking carries with it a tremendous ethical responsibility. The ramifications can be great, for you and for perhaps thousands or even millions of other people. Speeches can help feed the hungry, get great leaders elected, and build businesses that create jobs; they can also start wars, mislead investors and voters, and change the course of history in unexpected ways. Before you move forward with a specific purpose, make sure you're standing on solid ethical ground. Common sense and thoughtfulness will help you avoid most problems. Here are some specific questions to ask:

- Have you represented your sources fairly? Be careful not to use selected pieces of data from a source if treating them separately changes their meaning or interpretation. For great examples of what not to do, look at the reviewer quotes in almost any movie advertisement. Some movie advertisers don't hesitate to take a positive-sounding word out of the context of a lukewarm or even negative review.
- Have you considered opposing viewpoints? Should you explain those viewpoints in your speech? Presenting one side of an issue as if it's the only viewpoint can mislead the audience in an unethical way.
- What biases do you have that might creep into your speech? These aren't necessarily negative biases, as in racism or sexism. Innocent and even admirable biases, such as allegiance to your family, company, or country, can influence your thinking and lead to biased purposes.
- Have you considered the potential consequences of your speech? What are you asking your audience to do? What will happen if people leave the room and actually do what you've encouraged them to do?

Remember that emotions— both positive and negative— are contagious. Before you stir a crowd to action with your passionate speech, consider the potential consequences of your efforts.

Beyond the general purposes of informing or persuading, every speech you create needs a precise goal. After you've chosen (or been assigned) a general purpose, you're ready to define a *specific purpose* for your speech. It's your job to narrow the general purpose to a specific purpose that answers these questions: "Why am I giving this speech?" and "What will it accomplish?"

Your Specific Purpose

The **specific purpose** of your speech is whatever you want your audience to know, do, or feel as a result of your speech. The statement of your specific purpose covers three issues: (1) your general purpose; (2) your audience; and (3) the specific knowledge, attitude, belief, or behavior you want to result. The specific purpose is phrased as an infinitive statement describing the response you hope for from the audience (*to inform my audience about . . . , to persuade my audience that . . . ,* and so on). Here are ten strong statements of specific purpose:

- To inform my classmates about the benefits of investing in stocks (knowledge)
- To inform this gathering of reporters of my company's plans to build a new factory (knowledge)
- To inform my classmates about the new computer tools available to help in job searches (knowledge)
- To inform my classmates about the discoveries I helped make on an expedition to Antarctica last summer (knowledge)
- To persuade my classmates to write letters to the college president protesting the proposed cuts in the communication department's budget (behavior)
- To persuade my neighborhood association to welcome a family of immigrants (attitude or behavior)
- To convince my classmates that participating in next week's protest rally would be a waste of time (behavior)
- To persuade our North American distributors to accept 10 percent increases in their sales goals for the next quarter (behavior)
- To motivate this group of graduates to take control of their careers (attitude or behavior)
- To inspire my youth organization to appreciate the goodness they can find all around them (attitude)

You can see how each statement contains the three elements of general purpose, audience, and precise goal. It's particularly important to include the audience in your specific purpose because the exact goals can change dramatically from one audience to another—even for the same topic. You would probably need certain information to talk to your classmates about stock investments and entirely different information to talk to a group of high-school students or retired military personnel about similar stock investments.

Here are several things to keep in mind as you craft your specific purpose statement. First, start with one of the three infinitive phrases, *to inform, to persuade* (or *to convince*), or *to motivate* (or *to inspire*), then write a full statement that includes all three of the essential elements. Avoid using a fragment (such as "Ideas on investing") or a question (such as "What should the CIA be doing today?"). Neither of these statements adequately defines your purpose and direction. Second, save your figurative, fiery, passionate language for the speech itself; keep your purpose statement calm and concrete so that your goal remains clear. Third, if you find your specific purpose statement running long, your purpose probably isn't narrow enough, or your goal isn't defined clearly enough. Purpose statements rarely need to be longer than the ten examples just listed.

Don't be discouraged if you get to this point in the process and discover that your original plans for a speech are falling apart because you can't pin down a reasonable goal or because you can't narrow the topic enough to fit your time limit. One of the benefits of this planning is rooting out weak or bulky ideas before you get to the time-consuming tasks of research and preparation. It's far better to find out now that an idea won't work. When you're sure you have a clear and workable specific purpose, the next step is to decide what you'll say to accomplish that purpose. The purpose, the response you hope for from the audience, is converted into a central idea that you'll actually say out loud to the audience. The central idea usually is phrased as a simple declarative sentence that restates the specific purpose clearly for the audience.

STEP 3: REFINE YOUR CENTRAL IDEA

The first two steps in developing your topic haven't really addressed the content of your speech. You've considered the subject area and the goals you want to accomplish, but you haven't yet thought about what you're actually going to say. The third step in developing your topic is refining your central idea. The **central idea** (also called the *thesis statement,* the *theme,* or the *major thought*), is a one-sentence summary of what you plan to say.

How a Central Idea Differs from a Purpose

Your specific purpose defines what you want to accomplish with a speech; your central idea summarizes what you're going to say. The central idea doesn't *describe* what you're going to say—it actually *is* what you're going to say.

Take a look at the flow of ideas shown in Exhibit 5.7. In addition to being a good review of everything covered in this chapter, the diagram highlights the difference between a purpose and a central idea. The goal of the speech in the diagram is to convince voters that immigration has a positive economic effect on the U.S. economy, but simply saying that would be a weak speech. However, if you say something like the text shown in block 5, you'll accomplish the purpose stated in block 4. The difference between your central idea and your specific purpose is the difference be-tween a *means* and an *end.* Your central idea is your means to accomplish your end, or your specific purpose.

Features of a Strong Central Idea

A strong central idea has the same general features as a good purpose statement, only it summarizes

content, not goals. Make sure your central idea meets the following criteria:

- *Does it focus on your audience?* Successful speeches always consider the audience and what these people need or want to hear.
- *Is it phrased as a complete sentence?* Using a complete sentence helps ensure that you've fully developed your idea. Also, avoid phrasing your central idea as a question. A declarative sentence (see the following examples) makes it much easier to summarize the content of your speech.
- *Is your central idea clear?* Unclear language is usually a symptom of unclear thinking; if you're having trouble summarizing your content, you probably haven't conquered the topic yet. Clarify your idea before moving ahead.
- *Is it limited to a single idea?* One of the biggest challenges in speech writing is to focus on a single idea. It's tempting to cover too much, particularly if you have a rich topic with lots of issues.

Here's an example of a weak central idea state-ment, followed by some suggestions for making it stronger.

Subject area: Health
Speech topic: Healthier living
General purpose: To persuade
Specific purpose: To convince my classmates to adopt healthier lifestyles.
Central idea: Healthy lifestyles involve many components, including body weight, physical stamina, energy and enthusiasm, physical flexibil-ity and agility (which are required to succeed not only in sports but in many jobs and leisure pur-suits), as well as emotional well-being and personal happiness. Pursuing good physical and emotional health requires lifelong commitments and a well-conceived plan for addressing each area.

How did that central idea strike you? If it seemed huge and poorly focused, you grasped what is wrong with it. The problem doesn't start with the central idea, however. The problem starts with the speech topic, which is way too vague and broad

EXHIBIT 5.7
Five Key Concepts in Selecting a Topic and Purpose
This diagram helps you distinguish five key concepts: the subject area, your speech topic, your general purpose, your specific purpose, and your central idea.

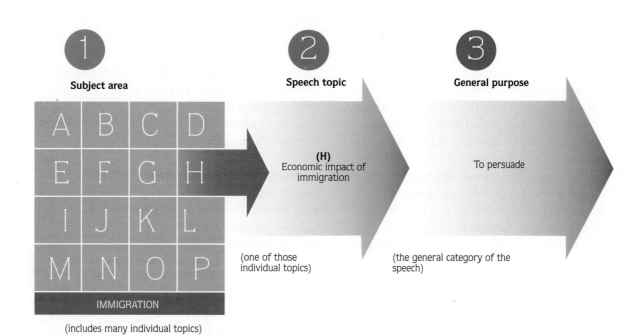

1 Subject area

A	B	C	D
E	F	G	H
I	J	K	L
M	N	O	P

IMMIGRATION

(includes many individual topics)

2 Speech topic

(H)
Economic impact of immigration

(one of those individual topics)

3 General purpose

To persuade

(the general category of the speech)

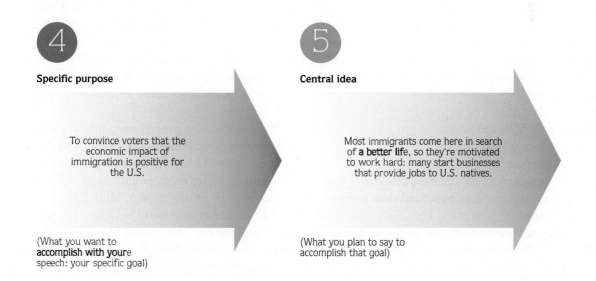

4 Specific purpose

To convince voters that the economic impact of immigration is positive for the U.S.

(What you want to **accomplish with your** speech: your specific goal)

5 Central idea

Most immigrants come here in search of **a better life**, so they're motivated to work hard: many start businesses that provide jobs to U.S. natives.

(What you plan to say to accomplish that goal)

for any speech. A much narrower topic is an important first step:

Subject area: Physical health
Speech topic: Losing weight
General purpose: To persuade
Specific purpose: To convince my classmates to get off the couch, get some exercise, and stop eating and partying so much.
Central idea: You'll feel better, look better, and live longer if you start taking better care of your body.

This version narrows the speech to a manageable body of information, but it introduces an entirely new problem. Chances are low that every student in the class is inactive, overweight, and in poor health. A few are probably in poor shape, but many might be in adequate shape, and a few are probably in terrific shape. Some may even be on athletic teams. The central idea as presented here could offend people who are already in adequate or great shape. People don't like to be lectured about flaws they do have, and they certainly don't relish being lectured about flaws they don't have or about mistakes they didn't make.

The key to this problem is audience analysis. If you're addressing a group of people who came to hear you talk about improving weight loss, such a speech would be appropriate. But for a diverse group such as the typical college class, your central idea will miss the mark with a significant portion of the audience. You'll be much more successful if you choose an angle that will be relevant to all or most of your audience. Consider the following speech plan:

Subject area: Physical health
Speech topic: Weight control
General purpose: To persuade
Specific purpose: To convince my classmates that lifestyle changes are more beneficial than traditional dieting.
Central idea: Permanently changing your eating and exercise habits is a better strategy for controlling weight than dieting fads.

This central idea avoids the problem of the first attempt (which would have covered too much information) and the problem of the second attempt (which could have offended many in the audience). Learning about dieting might interest people who are in poor shape, as well as people who are in adequate shape (whether they want to stay that way or improve) and people who are in top shape and want to stay at that level. You aren't insulting anyone or telling them to change habits they don't even have.

Another example is an informative speech on local attractions, and it should help clarify the notion of the central idea and its relationship to your specific purpose. The first example is how not to develop the central idea. Right after you read the example, see if you can figure out what's wrong with it, before reading on.

Subject area: Local amusements
Speech topic: Interesting places to visit in the local metropolitan area
General purpose: To inform
Specific purpose: To inform my audience about local places they might want to visit with friends or family.
Central idea: This area has dozens of interesting places to visit. For the technically minded, there's the Pacific Science Center, the Museum of Flight, and the Museum of Science and Industry. For sports fans, we have professional football, soccer, hockey, baseball, and basketball, as well as dozens of other sports and amateur teams. Nature lovers will enjoy the Woodland Park Zoo. If you need to entertain children, Wild Waves and the Discovery Zone offer many entertaining options.

This central idea tries to accomplish way too much for a typical classroom speech. You can find entire books written about interesting places to see in all major metropolitan areas. And what about sites for music, theater, hiking, boating, and all the other interesting activities people might engage in? This central idea tries to do too much and ends up doing it poorly. The solution is to narrow the topic dramatically:

Checklist for Reviewing Your Central Idea

1. Make sure the audience will benefit by what you're planning to say.
2. Limit yourself to a single, distinct idea.
3. Describe your central idea in one sentence and no more.
4. Make sure you write your central idea in a complete, declarative sentence—not in question form.

5. Use clear, simple wording—if you can't write a clear central idea, you're not ready to move ahead.
6. Pay attention to the words and phrases in the central idea. It sets an emotional tone for your speech and helps determine the reaction you'll get from the audience.

Subject area: Local musical venues
Speech topic: Good places to enjoy live jazz in the local metropolitan area
General purpose: To inform
Specific purpose: To inform my audience about local places that showcase jazz music.
Central idea: Local jazz fans can enjoy music in concert halls, in formal dinner clubs that feature jazz music, and in relaxed tavern settings.

This speech picks a much narrower topic and is therefore able to cover the chosen topic adequately. If your central idea starts to feel like a paragraph, this is a sure sign that you need to tighten your focus.

How to Use Your Central Idea

Your central idea represents an important turning point in the development of your speech. Up to this point, you've been planning, searching, questioning, and generally trying to figure out what your speech is going to be about. With a central idea in hand, you're ready to proceed. The next nine chapters will carry you through preparing, organizing, and presenting your speech. Along with your specific purpose, your central idea will be the guiding force at every step. The processes of generating, selecting, organizing, and presenting ideas are all based on the purpose and central idea. Here are some of the ways you'll be using your central idea:

- When you analyze your audience (Chapter 6), you'll do so based on your central idea. You should ask yourself what you need to know about the audience in light of the main points stated in the central idea.
- As you define (Chapter 7) and collect material (Chapter 8) for your supporting points, the central idea will guide your decisions and choices of what to include and what to leave out.
- As you organize your material, define your introduction and your conclusion, and outline your speech (Chapters 9–11), your efforts will focus on getting your central idea across to your audience.
- Finally, as you select the words you'll use (Chapter 12), select visual supporting materials (Chapter 13), and then rehearse and deliver your speech (Chapter 14), you'll project that central idea with confidence and success.

SUMMARY

Planning your speech involves three steps: identifying your speech topic, defining your purpose, and refining your central idea. To identify your topic, start with a subject area, a broad category of knowledge, skills, or other type of information. Next, narrow that area to a speech topic, a single issue or idea within a subject area. You can use brainstorming and research to find topic ideas. When you use brainstorming, you use free association to explore a wide variety of ideas and connections between ideas. Research makes use of external sources such as talking to others, browsing in the library, and exploring computerized databases.

Most of the topics you'll come up with will need to be narrowed even further because they will simply be too broad and rich for the few minutes you'll have for your speech. Also, narrowing your topic increases your chances of success by reducing your preparation time and helping your audience stay focused. You may have to subdivide a subject area several times to identify a topic that is narrow enough for a speech.

To define your purpose, start with a general purpose (to inform, to persuade, or to motivate or entertain). Informative speeches try to convey information, persuasive speeches try to

change the attitudes or behaviors of an audience, and motivational or entertainment speeches try to make people feel happy, energized, or empowered. Once you have a general purpose, you can define your specific purpose, the goal you want to accomplish with your speech. Your specific purpose, phrased as an infinitive statement, summarizes the response you hope for from the audience. Together with the central idea, it will guide the rest of the speech process.

Finally, you're ready to refine your central idea, the concise summary of what you plan to say in your speech. The specific purpose (which defines the goal of your speech) differs from the central idea (which summarizes what you actually plan to say). A strong central idea offers something to the audience; is phrased as a complete sentence (reflecting a well-developed idea); is clear and unambiguous; and is limited to a single, distinct idea.

KEY TERMS

brainstorming (91)
central idea (102)
free association (91)
general purpose (98)
informative speech (98)
motivational or entertainment speech (98)
persuasive speech (98)
specific purpose (101)
speech topic (94)
subject area (94)

APPLY CRITICAL THINKING

1. Would the Gulf War be a general subject area or a specific topic? Why or why not?
2. Would the economic effects of the Federal Reserve Board's interest rate hikes be a workable specific topic for a four-minute speech? Why or why not?
3. Is the president's annual State of the Union address an informative speech or a persuasive speech? Explain your answer.
4. Is "Telling my classmates about the time I was mistakenly arrested in Texas" a good statement of specific purpose? Why or why not? If not, can you improve it?
5. What does it mean to say that your central idea is a means to an end?
6. Why shouldn't your central idea statement be a complete outline of your speech?
7. If you're struggling with your central idea and running out of time before a speech is due, should you forge ahead with what you have? Why or why not?

SHARPEN YOUR SKILLS

Individual Exercises

1. Listen to a political leader's speech on television (C-SPAN airs congressional speeches frequently).

a. What subject area(s) might this topic fit into?

b. How would you define the speech topic?

c. Is the speaker staying within the confines of a single speech topic?

d. What do you think the speaker's specific purpose was?

2. How many speech topics can you identify in the overall subject area of "computers in education"?

3. Which of the following statements of specific purpose are informative and which are persuasive? Explain your answers. (Note that the wording of some statements differs slightly from the examples you read in the chapter.)

a. To describe for my history class the events and forces that sparked World War I.

b. To convince people to wear their seatbelts while driving.

c. To explain to drivers how seatbelts can reduce injuries in accidents.

d. To outline the reasons people should lower the fat content in their daily diets.

e. To refute the points made by a consumer advocate during a TV show last week.

4. Reread the statements of purpose in Question 3. Do all these statements contain the three elements of a good purpose statement? If not, which ones need correcting? What would you do to fix them?

5. Consider the last movie you saw. Did it have an identifiable central idea? Would you be able to build a speech around this central idea? Why or why not?

6. When you plan your first speech, narrow your topic and develop the statement of specific purpose, then try this technique to develop a central idea that should express and connect the important points of your speech:

a. List approximately ten points you want to make in the speech. Of course, ten points are too many for a short speech, but by brainstorming many ideas, you're less likely to overlook any important ones.

b. Categorize points that seem to relate to one another, eliminating unimportant ideas and narrowing the ten down to between two and five.

c. Compose a single sentence that states and relates these points to each other.

The result should be a well-crafted central idea for your speech.

Group Exercises

7. With a few classmates, brainstorm ideas to explain the low voter turnout for presidential elections. Use the mind-mapping technique if you find it helpful. As a group, choose the single most important explanation from the ideas you uncover.

8. With three or four classmates, make a list of speech topics that you would consider inappropriate for a public speaking class. (Use brainstorming if you want.) Would any of these be appropriate in another public speaking situation?

9. This exercise requires two separate teams. Pick one of the following four topics (both teams pick the same topic), and use it to conduct separate brainstorming sessions. The teams should not communicate while brainstorming. At the end of a specified amount of time (say five minutes),

compare notes on your brainstorming results. Did the two teams arrive at similar subtopics?

a. Food poisoning

b. Overcrowding

c. Relaxation

d. Dancing

10. With five other students, create two teams of three. Debate if and when it might be ethical to develop a specific purpose and central idea for a speech that does any of the following:

a. Conceals some sources of information from the audience

b. Doesn't consider opposing viewpoints

c. Is biased toward the speaker's views

d. Ignores the consequences of the speech

Chapter Six

ANALYZING YOUR AUDIENCE

LEARNING OBJECTIVES

After studying this chapter, you will be able to

1. Explain why understanding your audience is a key part of successful speaking.

2. Define egocentrism and explain its role in audience reactions.

3. List four personal influences on audience behavior.

4. List three psychological influences on audience behavior.

5. Explain how cultural, racial, and ethnic factors can affect audience reactions.

6. Describe the elements of a speaking situation that you need to consider when planning a speech.

7. Describe the three phases of adapting to your audience.

WHY IT'S IMPORTANT TO UNDERSTAND YOUR AUDIENCE

This book focuses mainly on you and what you do before and during your speeches. However, this chapter focuses on all those other people involved in the process: your audience. **Audience analysis** is the task of understanding enough about the members of your audience to predict how they'll react to what you're planning to say and how you're planning to say it. This analysis helps you know how to adapt your speech to be as successful as possible. Thorough audience analysis is one of the most important steps in preparing a speech—and the primary reason why speeches fail is a lack of audience analysis.[1]

You might visualize your public speaking goal as moving your audience from one place to another. Before your speech, people are sitting in one location, and your goal is to get them to move to another location. So if your goal is to move them to a particular spot in the room, you need to know where they are to start with. That's the purpose of analyzing your audience. If you know about your audience's knowledge, attitudes, and behaviors beforehand, and if you know how you'd like your audience's knowledge, attitudes, or behaviors to change (which is the purpose of your speech, as discussed in Chapter 5), you'll have a better idea of what to say to make those changes happen (see Exhibit 6.1). Every audience is unique, of course. Sometimes you'll talk to a group of people who share the same basic thoughts and opinions regarding your speech topic. Other times, your audience will be more intellectually diverse, with some people more inclined, and others less inclined, to agree with you.

Keep in mind that the primary reason for learning about your audience is so that you can adapt to their needs and expectations. Such adaptation falls into three categories: (1) *planned adaptation* is based on the research you do about your audience and the situation, (2) *emergency adaptation* results when you discover right before your speech that your audience or your speaking situation isn't what you expected, and (3) *reactive adaptation* occurs during your speech in response to feedback from the audience. Most of this chapter covers planned adaptation, since that's where you'll need to spend most of your time and energy. Guidelines for emergency and reactive adaptation are presented later in the chapter. Planned adaptation begins with your understanding of just how your audience is likely to respond to you and your speech.

HOW YOUR AUDIENCE WILL REACT TO YOU

Although you might have formed the impression that audiences are basically hostile and uncaring, this perception is generally wrong. Perhaps the most important thing to remember about audiences is that most people who listen to your speeches *want* you to succeed. This is true for two reasons. First, with a successful speech, the audience goes home having learned something of value. Who wants to waste time sitting through a bad speech? Second, in most cases, most people find it

EXHIBIT 6.1

Why You Need to Understand Your Audience

To take the audience where you want them to go, it helps to know where they're coming from. The four groups represented here are at various "distances" from where you want them to be. The people who understand you but don't agree with you will probably be the most difficult to move.

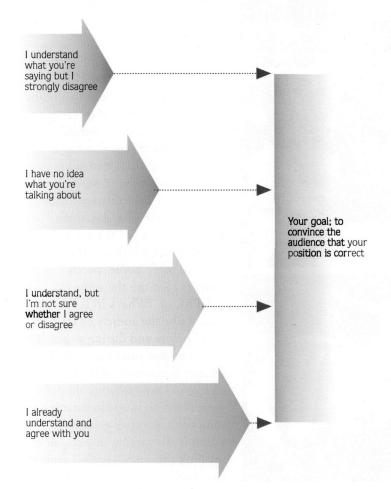

I understand what you're saying but I strongly disagree

I have no idea what you're talking about

I understand, but I'm not sure **whether** I agree or disagree

I already understand and agree with you

Your goal; to convince the audience that your position is correct

Remember, even though the audience may want you to succeed, the responsibility for success is overwhelmingly yours. (Of course, the audience still has a responsibility to listen actively and ethically.) No matter how good your material or how many times you've practiced, you won't succeed if you don't connect with your audience. Fortunately, connecting isn't all that hard, once you understand what listeners are like. The groups of people who make up speech audiences tend to follow several unwritten rules of conduct:[2]

- *Audiences start out cool and neutral, not warm and comforting.* Unless you're a celebrity your audience already loves, you'll face people who are willing to give you a chance to win their hearts but who won't give that affection automatically.
- *Audiences expect you to be the initiator.* It's your show when you step up on the stage, and people in your audience will sit back and wait for you to take charge. They'll settle into the tone you set, whether it's relaxed and friendly or serious and businesslike.
- *People in the audience don't usually want to be part of the show.* How many times have you seen a speaker ask for volunteers and have dozens of people rush to the stage? Probably never. The audience doesn't come to participate, and

embarrassing to sit through a speech that's failing. (Protesters at a political rally might take pleasure in a speaker's on-stage troubles, but this is one of the few public speaking situations in which some members of the audience might be predisposed to be hostile toward the speaker.) Unless you've given the audience a strong reason to dislike you, they'll be pulling for you. Of course, the audience's reasons for wanting you to succeed are largely selfish—they want something from you.

EXHIBIT 6.2
What Kind of Message Are You Sending the Audience?
You send subtle signals to your audience with your dress, posture, facial expression, and other conscious or unconscious actions and decisions; make sure you're sending the message you want to send!

asking them to help or singling them out with questions can generate some unpleasant responses, anything from avoiding your gaze to becoming downright hostile.

In addition, audiences will react to your attitude and behavior during your speech. Things you may not even think about can increase or decrease your effectiveness as a speaker. Noted speech trainer Ron Hoff cautions speakers not to underestimate an audience's sensitivity. They'll pick up on your emotional signals and respond in kind (see Exhibit 6.2). If you start out on a slow, negative note, you'll set the tone for your entire speech. Audiences can sense how you feel about yourself and your material. If you come across with confidence, they'll have more confidence in you. On the other hand, if you feel helpless or defeated, they'll pick up those emotions, too. Audiences can tell such things as whether you're reciting a memorized speech, whether you're bluffing your way through material you don't understand, and whether you're trying to give them a sales pitch.[3]

Keep these points in mind as you study the factors involved in audience analysis. Perhaps the most important of these is recognizing *audience egocentricity*.

Egocentric Factors

Have you ever walked into a room where someone was about to give a speech and said to yourself, "Boy, I hope this person has a swell time up there and talks about whatever he or she feels is important"? Probably not. Your thoughts were probably more along the lines of "What can I get from this speech that will be of value to *me?*" Some speech trainers even use the acronym WIIFM, or "What's In It For Me," to describe the audience's state of mind before and during a speech.[4]

It's not that you or any other listener is unusually selfish. We'd all like to know whether the time we're about to invest in listening to someone's speech is going to be worth it. To varying degrees, all of us think the world revolves around us, which means that all of us can be egocentric. Communication professor Frank Dance describes a process people go through as they grow. He describes the infant as **egocentric**, only perceiving things from his or her own point of view. As people mature, they become less egocentric and develop the ability to see different points of view expressed by other people. Decentering, described earlier as the ability to understand the views of others, plays a key role in Dance's maturation model. According to Dance, decentering involves assessing and

Checklist for Winning Over an Audience

1. Prepare with care so that the audience members will know you take their time seriously.
2. Give the audience a reason to be interested early in the speech.
3. Support your ideas so that people don't think you're just spouting opinions.
4. Show how your message affects the people in your audience; show why it's important to them.

5. Use positive, appealing images to convey the benefits of your idea or message.
6. Involve listeners, even if you only ask them to consider your ideas.
7. If appropriate, ask the audience to take action.

appreciating the experiences of others. This ability is vital to public speaking because it enables you to understand the mental viewpoint of others. The speaker who can decenter engages in good audience analysis and prepares and presents his or her speech with the audience's viewpoints in mind.[5]

Although an egocentric person can be tiresome on a daily basis, you'll do best to assume that everyone in your audience is egocentric, at least as far as your speech is concerned. If you approach your task with the idea that these people care mostly about themselves, you'll prepare and present a more satisfying (and therefore more successful) speech. A key part of connecting with the egocentric listener is **relevance**, the degree to which the audience finds your message personally meaningful and important. If you've selected (or been given) a speech topic that is relevant to start with, you've already won this battle. And you can always use audience analysis to figure out ways to make your topic relevant.

Three other sets of factors influence how people are likely to respond to your speech: objective *personal* factors such as age and gender, subjective *psychological* factors such as attitudes

Success Tip

Norman Vincent Peale, one of the most successful public speakers in history, recognized the importance of adapting to your audience, even if you give the same basic speech over and over again. As he put it, "I give the same mashed potatoes for each speech; I just change the gravy."

and values, and *social* factors such as group membership and culture. Ultimately, of course, all reactions are personal, but dividing them into these three categories makes it easier to understand the specific issues.

Personal Factors

Knowing who your listeners are can help you predict how they'll respond to your speech—and how you may need to adapt your speech to their needs and expectations. Collections of objective, personal characteristics such as age and income are called **demographics.** Demographic factors of interest to a public speaker include age, gender, household type, education, occupation, and income. (Officially, race and ethnicity are also considered demographic factors, but they're addressed in a later section on culture.)

Age

The age of your audience can provide some helpful clues about attitudes, subject awareness, and interests and concerns. For instance, 73 percent of people in the United States over the age of 50 say that religion is very important in their lives, compared to only 38 percent of people between the ages of 18 and 29.[6] Compared with older adults, nearly twice as many young adults consider themselves physically attractive.[7] The majority of young adults accept or approve of interracial marriages and premarital sex, while the majority of older adults frown on both.[8] Also, younger people tend to be more open to new ideas and more vulnerable to persuasion than older people are, although this is a broad generalization that doesn't always hold true.[9]

The word *Vietnam* probably conjures up one meaning for a person of 50 and quite a different meaning for a person of 25. Similarly, the 25-year-old is probably thinking about career planning, whereas the 50-year-old is probably thinking about retirement planning. Someone starting college at 48 views education differently than someone starting at 18. In addition, young adults and older people probably have different views of couples living together. The things we know about and care about are affected by how old we are and by what was going on in the world during various stages of our lives (see Exhibit 6.3). So age can be an important factor when you use jokes, make references to popular culture or historical events, or make assumptions about how your audience will respond to a particular issue. If you have classmates of varying ages, you may already have experienced the influence of this personal factor.

However, making assumptions based on age can also get you into trouble. Not all retired people want a quiet, retiring lifestyle—and they might resent a speaker who makes that assumption. Not all young people are familiar with the newest popular music, nor are all young people politically liberal. Not all middle-aged parents like to spend their free time riding around suburbia on lawn mowers. In general, though, you'll be safe making assumptions about (a) the basic concerns people have at various ages (whether it's finances, health, or something else) and (b) the key historical events that all people of a given age lived through. Wars, political scandals, and natural disasters help shape the perceptions and attitudes of those people who live through them.

Gender

Assumptions and preconceptions based on gender are powerful forces that shape our reactions to the world and our relationships with each other.[10] By the time children are four or five years old, they've already developed clear ideas of roles that seem appropriate for women versus those that seem appropriate for men. They also begin to act out these gender roles by this age.[11] In other words, members of your audience have been living with their notions about gender most of their lives.

Gender issues continue to get even experienced speakers into trouble, whether it's someone referring to a group of women as "girls" or "you guys" or someone assuming all men feel the same way about raising families and pursuing careers. Whatever the particular mistakes, they all stem from the same type of flawed thinking: making generalizations about a diverse group of people. In addition to caring about the feelings of the people in your audience, you'll want to avoid gender-based mistakes for a selfish reason: Many listeners are so offended by an inappropriate reference that they tune out the rest of your speech.

Moreover, making a gender-based mistake signals many listeners that you're out of touch or behind the times, which can influence whether they accept the rest of your message—even if that message has nothing to do with gender issues. You could be talking about leading-edge techniques in microsurgery, but if you refer to surgical nurses as the "girls" or the "gals" in the operating room, many in the audience will be wondering about your gender bias rather than about the techniques you're describing. You can avoid offending men and women in nearly all cases by following two simple rules: (1) make no gender-based assumptions about anyone, and (2) treat everyone's personal choices with respect.

Household Type

There was a time in our nation's history when people automatically assumed that everybody grew up in a household where Dad went off to work and Mom stayed home to raise the two or

EXHIBIT 6.3

Defining Events in the Lives of Your Audience

The age of your listeners can influence their response to your speech; trends and events such as the Great Depression, the Vietnam conflict, and the AIDS epidemic have affected various generations in different ways. Listed here are the ages that various people would have been during a number of significant events in this century. For example, people born in 1920 faced World War II during the prime of their youth. Thirty years later, people born in 1950 faced the Vietnam war during their teens and twenties. Another 60 years later, both wars were ancient history to people born in 1980.

	Born in 1920	Born in 1930	Born in 1940	Born in 1950	Born in 1960	Born in 1970	Born in 1980
The Great Depression: Unemployment in the U.S. hits 32 percent by 1932	12	2	—	—	—	—	—
World War II: 292,000 Americans killed; Nazis kill 6 million Jews and 7 million others (ended in 1945)	25	15	5	—	—	—	—
McCarthy hearings:Senator Joseph McCarthy creates national hysteria by claiming that Communists have infiltrated the U.S. government; this "witch hunt" ruins the careers and lives of thousands of people (ended in 1954)	34	24	14	4	—	—	—
JFK: President Kennedy assassinated (1963)	43	33	23	13	3	—	—
Space travel: First astronauts reach the moon (1969)	49	39	29	19	9	—	—
Vietnam war: 76,000 Americans killed; sometimes violent protests across the United States (ended in 1975)	55	45	35	25	15	5	—
Environment: Becomes a mainstream concern, punctuated by worst oil spill to date and near-meltdown at Three Mile Island (1979)	59	49	39	29	19	9	—
Personal computers: 3 million IBM PCs sold in 1984	64	54	44	34	24	14	4
Fall of the Soviet Union and other Communist governments: Ends the Cold War but unleashes new hostilities in several countries (1991)	71	61	51	41	31	21	11
AIDS crisis: The disease strikes 3 million people worldwide by 1994	74	64	54	44	34	24	14

three kids. Some people still make that assumption, but it was never a terribly accurate picture of life in the United States, and it's even less true now than it was back then. Be sure your speeches make no reference to any sort of family life that applies to only a few members of your audience. For example, consider these statistics illustrating the changing nature of U.S. households: a quarter of all U.S. households are people living alone, and step-families were the most common U.S. household type in 2002.[12] If you ask your audience members to recall the good old days of childhood when Dad came home from the office and the family gathered around to eat Mom's home-cooked meal, you're going to miss the mark with many people—and possibly offend others.

Education, Occupation, and Income

The personal factors of education, occupation, and income are often related, but even taken individually, they can tell you a lot about an audience. The implications for your speech can be obvious in some cases and not-so-obvious in others. For instance, when addressing a group of investment bankers, you can assume that most of them understand a wide variety of financial and business concepts. They also probably keep up on current political and social trends and events, since those things affect the banking business. When Douglas Hurd, the British foreign secretary (equivalent to the U.S. secretary of state), addressed a group of bankers in London, he was able to launch right into topics such as overseas investment and the European single-currency debate without explanation.[13]

However, if Hurd had been talking to a group of students, artists, or doctors, he could not have made the same assumptions. Since the people in these other groups don't normally wrestle with international finance issues in the course of their daily work, he would probably have spent less time talking about specific details and more time explaining basic concepts. Similarly, political leaders are great models when it comes to adapting speeches to various audiences; you can be sure that each speech is carefully adapted to the concerns of the people in that particular audience.

When you're analyzing your audience, the information you obtain can help you better understand the people you'll be addressing, but be careful. Regarding the factors of education, occupation, and income, consider the following:

- *Education can give you clues about your audience's awareness of different subjects.* Education exposes people to a variety of ideas and vocabulary. By the time they get through high school and college, for instance, people have been exposed to major figures in literature and major events in history. So if you know that most of your audience members are college graduates, you should be able to quote Hemingway without explaining who he was. Of course, if you're addressing people with similar educational backgrounds, such as groups of psychology or

---

Checklist for Analyzing an Audience

1. Know how many people will attend.
2. Know whether this is a formal group gathering.
3. Know the gender ratio.
4. Know the average age.
5. Know what occupations are represented.
6. Know the audience's average socioeconomic status.
7. Know what religions are represented.
8. Know what cultural or ethnic groups are represented.
9. Know how much your audience knows about your topic.
10. Know how much your audience cares about your topic.

engineering majors, you can also make some assumptions about what these people know.

- *Don't equate education with intelligence.* Being uninformed is vastly different from being unintelligent. Just because someone has been to college doesn't mean that he or she is smart enough to comprehend complex topics. Conversely, some very bright people never attended college, and others didn't bother to graduate, for any number of reasons.

- *The connection between income and occupation is not always as obvious as you might think.* If you're addressing a gathering of medical doctors and a gathering of people who own dry cleaning shops, you can assume that the doctors all have impressive incomes and the dry cleaners have more modest incomes, right? Wrong! You can't make this assumption. Your doctors might be university researchers or small-town family practitioners, groups whose salaries tend be lower than those of other doctors. The audience of dry cleaners, on the other hand, may include at least a few wealthy entrepreneurs.

- *Education, occupation, and income can open— and close—an audience's eyes.* At first glance, it might seem reasonable to assume that highly educated, well-paid professionals have "seen more of the world" or generally experienced more than other people. In one sense, this assumption is true. People who can afford it are more likely to know what it's like to stay in a grand hotel or how it feels to choose from a wide variety of investment options. On the other hand, those people who fit the popular stereotype of success in the United States may know very little about important issues in the lives of millions of people, such as the struggle faced by lower- and middle-income parents in finding safe, affordable day care or the aesthetic pride a carpenter feels after installing a beautiful set of kitchen cabinets. Life encompasses a lot more than material success, so don't assume that "successful" people have a more complete picture of contemporary life.

If you're fortunate enough to have even basic data about your audience, you'll be well on your way to understanding them better. In some cases, the personal factors discussed so far are things you can research beforehand or make educated guesses about. In other cases, though, the best you can do is be aware of potential issues to minimize personal offense and maximize your speaking effectiveness. For instance, you might be able to learn beforehand that your audience will be middle-aged people interested in retirement planning. Those two simple facts can be of tremendous help in shaping your speech. On the other hand, you may never know what percentage of your audience grew up in single-family homes or how many have attended college. However, just knowing that such issues exist will help you avoid embarrassing mistakes.

Psychological Factors

Personal factors describe the objective information you can learn about people. In addition, audience members are influenced by a variety of psychological factors. Collections of subjective, qualitative characteristics such as emotional needs and attitudes about current events are called **psychographics.** Three major categories of psychographics are needs and motives, attitudes, and values and lifestyles.

Needs and Motives

We are all driven by **needs,** which are the gaps we perceive between where we are (or what we have) and where we'd like to be (or what we'd like to have). Some needs are fairly straightforward, such as the need for food when you're hungry or the need for shoes to protect your feet. Needs create **motives,** which are the forces that guide our behavior toward satisfying those needs. In other words, people are motivated to satisfy their unmet needs.

Needs range from the very basic requirements for food and shelter to psychological needs that determine how we feel about ourselves. You may have heard of Maslow's hierarchy of needs, which can be represented as a ladder or pyramid, with the basic physical needs at the bottom and self-actualization needs at the top (see Exhibit 6.4). Self-actualization is a rare state, according to

EXHIBIT 6.4
The Wide Range of Human Needs

Psychologist Abraham Maslow proposed a hierarchy to show the levels and variety of human needs. This model is probably oversimplified, but it reminds us of how complex human needs are.

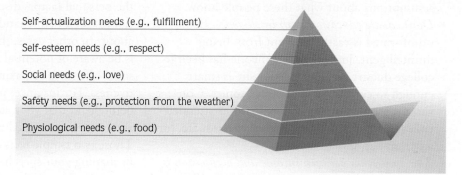

Self-actualization needs (e.g., fulfillment)

Self-esteem needs (e.g., respect)

Social needs (e.g., love)

Safety needs (e.g., protection from the weather)

Physiological needs (e.g., food)

Maslow; he estimated that fewer than 1 percent of the world's population could be considered self-actualized, and most of these people are more than 60 years old.[14] Although Maslow's model has been criticized as being too rigid and simplistic, it is a good reminder of the complex variety of human needs.

As a speaker, one of your goals is to satisfy the needs of the people in your audience. When listeners get ready to hear you speak, they'll be asking "What's in it for me?" and this question is driven by their needs. If you're speaking to your class about recreational opportunities in the area, listeners will want to know whether your ideas match their needs for excitement, relaxation, or socialization, for instance. However, in a speech about career planning, your audience will be driven by financial security concerns, self-esteem, and other, more serious needs.

When you're planning your speech, try to anticipate how audience needs will relate to your message. A lot of this will simply be common sense. Your classmates may need to relax, but they don't need information about $20,000 luxury cruises. Such information wouldn't be relevant to most people living on a typical student's income. You'll recall that relevancy is one of the keys to satisfying an egocentric audience.

Attitudes

An **attitude** is a person's enduring positive or negative inclination toward something (a city, another person, an idea, a food, and so on).[15] Take special note of the word *enduring* in this definition; attitudes aren't something that people like to give up. In fact, they're liable to hold a particular attitude long after the reasons for forming that attitude are gone. You may detest spinach because your parents forced you to eat it years ago, and yet if you tasted spinach now, as an adult, you might very well enjoy it.

It's difficult to imagine a speech in which you won't have to confront attitudes of some kind. While speaking to your class, for instance, your classmates in the audience will have a variety of attitudes concerning you, your topic, your presentation style, the instructor, the conditions in the room—and those are just the obvious issues. One person might accept your message immediately, whereas the next person may think you're preaching and reject it. Some may come ready to listen and learn; others will refuse even to pay attention.

Attitude is a complex factor, but you can simplify it by concentrating on three issues whenever you plan a speech. First, is the audience's position with respect to you and your message likely to be positive, neutral, or negative? If you're trying to convince a group of gun owners that banning certain types of guns is a good idea, it's safe to assume that many members of the audience will start in a negative position. You may need to build a careful, logical, step-by-step argument to get them to reconsider. On the other hand, if your speech is about what a bad idea such bans are, that same audience might be on your side before you even begin speaking. A long and relentlessly logical presentation would seem downright silly in this case.

EXHIBIT 6.5
Focusing in on Your Audience's Attitude Through Interest and Position
Here are strategies to consider for six different combinations of audience interest and position.

	Low interest	High interest
Positive position	Audience members are pleasant but lethargic, convinced but unmoving. Talk to them about value; express results and benefits with emotion. Make action easy and immediate.	Audience members are sold, so don't bother with elaborate proofs or motivation. Go light on information and heavy on catchy themes, color, and emotion. Move them toward specific action.
Neutral position	Get audience members to listen. Here's the place for a punchy dog-and-pony show delivered with spirit. Get audience members into your topic quickly—either mentally or physically. Get on their wavelength and keep them tuned in. Then convert them.	Prove your case clearly and thoroughly. Show benefits and make sure your facts are well supported. Be prepared to discuss all options and defend your views. Stress logic over emotion.
Negative position	Find out why audience members are so hostile and what you can do to rectify the situation (or at least to show you're aware of where they're coming from). Try a challenge, an unusual approach, or self-effacing humor to lighten the mood and perhaps get them to listen.	Approach carefully. Set modest objectives. Look for common concerns or opinions. Show that you understand and respect your audience's position. Stay cool and firm but don't be arrogant.

Second is your audience's interest level. How much does your audience care? Some people may think that a proposed tax on gasoline is a bad idea, but since it's only two cents per gallon, they may not really care that much. In this case, you would need to arouse your audience's interest before they'll even consider your point of view. These first two attitude issues, position and interest, can give you helpful ideas for framing your basic speech strategy (see Exhibit 6.5).

Third, how committed are audience members to a particular attitude? Some people may have just slipped into an attitude without thinking too much about it. By getting them to stop and think, you might easily get them to change their attitude. Other people may have grown up thinking things should be a certain way, and no matter how much evidence you show them to the contrary, they're not going to change their minds. People who have cast their attitudes in concrete are said to have **dogmatic opinions.** Be realistic; your chances of changing someone's dogmatic opinions (particularly in a single

speech) are slim to none. Remember the notion of *enduring* inclinations. Think of attitudes as giant sailing ships at sea: they can't change directions very quickly, and it's just about impossible to get one to stop and back up. In many cases, you won't achieve the goal of changing an audience's attitudes, but you might at least get them to reconsider their own opinions. Attitude change is easiest when it comes in small doses that allow people to adjust comfortably.

Values and Lifestyles
How people live their lives and what they consider important can affect how they will respond to your speech. A person's **values** reflect the principles and qualities that she or he believes to be important. Personal freedom, social responsibility, and family harmony are all examples of personal values. Values differ from person to person and from culture to culture.

Values affect a person's **lifestyle,** the combination of interests, activities, likes, dislikes, and other personal behaviors that shape a person's life. If you value hard work and material success, your lifestyle is likely to be rather different from someone who values leisure time with friends and family. Of course, some aspects of lifestyle are controversial and can upset audiences if you're not careful. Sexual preferences and opinions of unmarried couples living together are two good

EXHIBIT 6.6
Grouping People by Values and Lifestyles
The Values and Life-Styles model, called VALS II for short, is a way of grouping people according to their orientation toward life and the resources they have at their disposal.

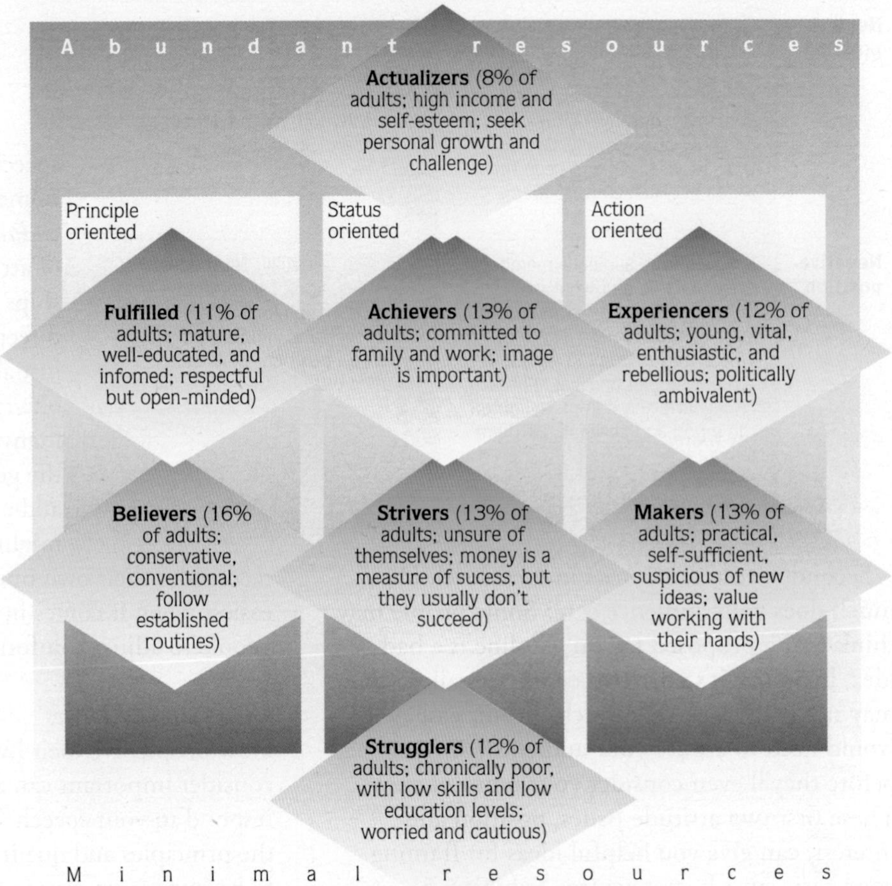

Abundant resources

Actualizers (8% of adults; high income and self-esteem; seek personal growth and challenge)

Principle oriented | Status oriented | Action oriented

Fulfilled (11% of adults; mature, well-educated, and infomed; respectful but open-minded)

Achievers (13% of adults; committed to family and work; image is important)

Experiencers (12% of adults; young, vital, enthusiastic, and rebellious; politically ambivalent)

Believers (16% of adults; conservative, conventional; follow established routines)

Strivers (13% of adults; unsure of themselves; money is a measure of sucess, but they usually don't succeed)

Makers (13% of adults; practical, self-sufficient, suspicious of new ideas; value working with their hands)

Strugglers (12% of adults; chronically poor, with low skills and low education levels; worried and cautious)

Minimal resources

examples. Something that might seem perfectly acceptable to some listeners may anger others—and cause them to adopt a hostile attitude toward you and your speech.

Values and lifestyles receive a great deal of attention from people who specialize in psychographic measurements. Much of their effort is directed toward identifying people who have similar values and lifestyles and then understanding how they differ from other groups of people. One well-known model is called Values and Lifestyles (VALS). The VALS II version groups people into eight categories on the basis of resources and orientation (see Exhibit 6.6). If you're status-oriented and have enjoyed some material success in your life, VALS II would call you an Achiever. In contrast, if you are driven more by action than status, you'd be called an Experiencer.

Social Factors
Demographic and psychographic research focuses on individuals and how their personal and

psychological makeup might affect their response to speeches and other forms of input. The third class of influencing factors deals with how people are affected by other people. These associations with other people take two forms: (1) groups we choose to join, such as professional associations and religious organizations, and (2) groups we are typically born into or grow up in—cultures, races, and ethnic groups. (Although you can choose to "join" a culture, it's not the same kind of decision as choosing to join a computer club.)

Group Affiliation

The groups that people belong to can give you some valuable clues about what they'll expect from a speech and how they'll react to it. In many cases, this is rather obvious. If you're a lawyer addressing a gathering of doctors on the subject of malpractice, the audience members might expect you to help them deal with the costs of medical malpractice insurance. However, if you were talking to a group of consumers, they might expect you to have sympathy for *their* side of the issue, which is protecting themselves from medical mistakes.

In your classroom speeches, you can work with a couple of obvious group affiliations. Even though your class-mates have chosen to go to school at this institution and are all members of this public speaking class, they probably represent a diverse mix of academic and professional interests, including business, the sciences, art, and education. If you're giving a speech on contemporary art, for instance, your class audience might include people who know more about the subject than you do, people who know nothing about art, and a wide mix of people in between. In contrast, if you're asked to speak to a group of business majors about career develop-ment, their affiliation with the business department will help you understand their concerns and interests. You can safely assume that they all want a career in business, they care about business, and they know something about business.

Depending on the topic and the situation, practically anything you can learn about your audience's group affiliations can help you prepare. Religions, professions, athletics, hobbies, civic organizations, and political parties are just a few of the affiliations that can provide you with clues. Think about *why* audience members might have joined such groups, and you'll understand them a little better. If you're asked to give a luncheon speech to the Lions Club, you'll know that your

> ### Success Tip
>
> Where you are can affect the kinds of questions you're asked after a speech. For instance, Swedish audiences tend to ask theoretical questions to search for implications, German audiences often ask highly technical questions, U.S. audiences usually ask practical questions, and French audiences rarely ask questions at all.

listeners volunteer their time to help people in the community, and you'll know you won't have to sell these people on the idea of helping others.

Cultural, Racial, and Ethnic Identification

Group affiliations involving culture, race, and ethnicity, are a bit more complicated. Also, these affiliations are extremely important in a multicultural society such as the United States. Look around the world, and you'll realize that the United States is one of the most successful experiments in multiple cultures living within the same borders. The key reason for this success is the effort people make to understand and accept others with different cultural backgrounds. However, beyond our personal and civic responsibili-ties to get along with each other, today's audiences simply demand that speakers be sensitive to cultural richness and differences. As with the gender issues discussed earlier in the chapter, exhibiting a lack of cultural awareness can doom the most carefully prepared speech. Even if your speech has nothing to do with culture or race, if you unintentionally offend people in your audience, they're not likely to pay attention to or accept your message.

Chapter 1 defines cultural diversity (the mix of people from various national, ethnic, racial, and religious backgrounds) and ethnocentrism (the tendency to view other cultures as inferior to one's own). Now it's time to explore the issue of culture in more depth. **Culture** is a collection of beliefs, values, and norms that influence or dictate the behavior of a relatively large group of people.[16] You already know what *beliefs* and *values* are; **norms** are models or patterns that people in a given culture expect each other to follow. In other words, culture sets guidelines for people to follow in terms of what they

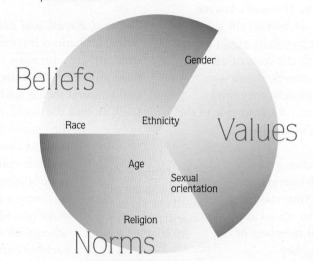

EXHIBIT 6.7
The Components of Culture
Every culture is structured around beliefs, values, and norms and includes a variety of social and personal factors.

should believe, what they should value or consider important, and how they should behave (see Exhibit 6.7).

Race and ethnic identity are two issues closely related to culture. **Race** is a physical identifier, meaning that people of the same race have fairly similar physical features such as skin color. **Ethnic identity** is a broader term that signifies a group of people who may be united by race, religion, geography (nationality), or culture. When referring to skin color, for example, the terms black and white are race distinctions. The term *African American* is an ethnic or cultural distinction. The genetic feature of darker skin is one component of being African American, but the concept includes a larger set of cultural and geographic factors as well. The same idea is behind terms such as *European American* and *Asian American*. The terms *Hispanic* or *Hispanic American* can be confusing labels because they really denote only a link to the Spanish language and a link (sometimes quite distant) to Spain. Some people consider *Latino* to be a more appropriate cultural identifier. However, all of these labels describe groups of related but sometimes rather different cultures. For example, many cultures are included under the umbrella term *Hispanic American* or *Latino.* More specific terms such as *Cuban American* and *Mexican American* help identify unique cultures in this broader group.

Culture is a powerful force in all our lives, even if we don't stop to consider how it affects us. For instance, people expect you to come to class fully clothed, recently bathed, ready to converse in English, and relatively well-behaved and respectful. However, unlike students in some countries, you're not expected to sit perfectly quiet and accept anything your instructor says or does to you. In fact, a healthy skepticism about knowledge and authority is one of the defining aspects of U.S. culture. People in the United States do show respect for teachers, government officials, and others in positions of leadership and influence, but they tend not to give blind (or quiet!) devotion. In contrast, Japanese students are expected to show respect for their teachers by sitting quietly and accepting what the teacher or professor has to say.[17] Of course, U.S. culture doesn't grant you "permission" to just open your mouth and argue at random. You're expected to have a rational argument with logical support for your contrary position and to continue showing respect for your teacher while offering a different opinion.

As a speaker, you need to be aware of cultural issues because they determine how your audiences will react to you and your message, and because they help you adapt your speech to your audience. Unfortunately for everyone who speaks in public, culture is not a simple issue. You won't find a

Ask an Expert

Teresa A. Nance
*Associate Professor, Communication Arts Department,
Villanova University, Villanova, Pennsylvania*

Q: The number of cultural concerns a speaker must consider seems overwhelming. How can I avoid offending a multicultural audience if I don't know everything about the various cultures?

A: Embedded in your question is an earnest desire to attend to the cultural sensibilities of all the people who compose your audience. This is a good attitude that will help you understand your audience's needs and concerns and will enable you to use your speeches to address those issues.

Several realizations will help you here. The first is that all audiences are diverse—not just audiences labeled *multicultural*. Recognizing and addressing the commonalities and differences of the people who compose your audience is part of the art and challenge of public speaking.

The second realization is that there are civilities to which speakers generally adhere. These civilities include avoiding any language that disparages or demeans another person; approaching issues of difference with sensitivity, openness, and flexibility; and always recognizing that cultural differences are an inevitable and valuable part of all human interaction.

The third realization is that *difference* is only a problem when it's based on fear and suspicion. Even though it's impossible to know and remember everything about every culture, it isn't impossible to respect the simple fact that all people are entitled to be treated with dignity and respect.

As a speaker, approach an audience with a sincere desire to create shared understanding. Then even if you inadvertently say the wrong thing or gesture incorrectly, you will have established with your audience the kind of relationship that will allow you to correct your mistake, move forward, and work toward achieving your communication goals.

1. When analyzing your audience, how might you identify the similarities as well as the differences among the people making up that culturally diverse audience? Why are these similarities important for you to note as you prepare and present your speech?
2. Before your next classroom speech, think carefully about the students who make up your audience. What cultural differences can you detect that you should consider as you plan your speech? Afterward, evaluate your effectiveness in adapting to these cultural differences. What would you do differently next time? Why?

concise set of rules that will get you through every speech safely and successfully. Even the most experienced professional speakers occasionally stumble into cultural mistakes. However, by following these general guidelines, you can communicate with success in most multicultural situations:

- *Don't be afraid to ask questions.* There are two kinds of ignorant people: those who blunder ahead still not knowing what they should know, and those who stop to ask questions so that they don't have be ignorant anymore. If you're not sure about a cultural issue, just ask somebody who belongs to that culture. Honest, sincere questions will gain you a lot more respect than taking your chances. In fact, most people will be flattered by your interest in them and their culture.
- *Avoid culturally sensitive issues whenever possible.* If a particular issue has the potential to touch a cultural nerve in some or all of the members of your audience and it's not really crucial for your speech, why take the risk? Don't invite trouble when you don't need to. If an amusing anecdote involving your live-in boyfriend isn't a key part of your message, leave it out; unmarried living arrangements aren't viewed the same by all cultures.
- *Don't assume anything about your audience.* Just because you grew up in a culture where multiple generations of a family live under the same roof, don't assume that's the case everywhere. What might be viewed as natural family harmony by one culture could be viewed as financial necessity by another.
- *Be sensitive to cultural differences in nonverbal communication.* For example, pay attention to your use of gestures and slang language. Phrases and hand signals you may have been using for years might mean something entirely different to other people. The "OK" sign people in the

EXHIBIT 6.8
One Culture's Habits Are Another Culture's Mistakes
The meaning and appropriateness of gestures and other aspects of nonverbal communication can vary widely from culture to culture.

United States make by touching their thumb and index finger together in a circle is insulting in some cultures and obscene in others (see Exhibit 6.8).

- *If you'll be addressing a distinct cultural group, try to learn something of that culture.* A little effort can go a long way toward helping you avoid the most alarming and embarrassing errors. If you're planning to speak in another country, for instance, spend a few hours with a good guidebook to acquaint yourself with the country's customs and cultural norms. You obviously can't learn everything you'd like to know about another culture, but you can hit the high points. Just knowing that your audience in a particular culture is uncomfortable with overly friendly

Success Tip

It's important to be yourself in intercultural speaking situations, but you still need to communicate respect for your audience and avoid offending or confusing them.

speakers who share intimate personal information or with chatty speakers who feel the need to talk constantly might mean the difference between a satisfactory speech and a disaster. Also, if you can find a subtle way to communicate that you're trying to understand the culture and to avoid offending your audience, people are likely to appreciate your efforts and be more forgiving if you do make mistakes. During a speech in France, for instance, you might casually mention some interesting fact you ran across in one of the books on French culture you were reading in preparation for your speech.

Although it's important to adapt to an audience's cultural expectations, don't try to be

Checklist for Analyzing a Speaking Situation

1. Know how much time you've been given.
2. Know whether you're constrained by other speakers or other events either before or after your scheduled time slot.
3. Know how early you should arrive in order to make sure everything is in place.
4. Know who's in charge of the situation and whether you can get more information from this person.
5. Know the seating arrangement and how far away the audience will be.
6. Know whether you'll have to use a microphone.
7. Know the occasion—whether it's a special holiday or celebration, for example.

SPEAKING ACROSS CULTURES

How to Enhance Your Ability to Connect with Intercultural Audiences

Although speakers can stumble into dozens of major and minor cultural potholes in the course of their speaking careers, this complex challenge can be greatly simplified with a few commonsense guidelines:

- *Stay up to date with trends and terms.* You don't hear informed people use terms such as *cripple, Negro,* or *retarded* anymore. If someone does use one of these terms, the audience will assume (rightly so) that the speaker is out of touch. This isn't an exact science, of course. Some people say *black* and some say *African American,* and many people aren't sure whether to say *person with disabilities, physically challenged person,* or perhaps *differently abled person.* As long as you're using a term that is in general current use, you'll be safe with all reasonable audiences. And by trying to use the right term, you'll communicate an earnest respect for all audience members.
- *Don't add irrelevant identifiers and associations.* Does it matter that the environmental scientist you quote in a speech is a woman, has a physical disability, or is Arab American? In nearly all cases, the answer is no. Unless your speech is about job discrimination in the environmental control industry, for instance, this sort of extra information is totally unnecessary. You're not quoting the person because she's a woman, you're quoting her because she's a technical expert. Focus on the relevant qualifications and skip everything else. Don't say anything like, "One woman from the Centers For Disease Control testified that the chemical had serious health risks." Instead, say simply "A scientist from . . ."
- *Avoid stereotypes.* Once this becomes a habit, you'll hardly even think about it, but it may take some work in the beginning. Even well-intentioned people have developed some stereotyped perceptions of others over the course of their lives. Using these stereotypes can insult others unknowingly. Whether it's assuming that African Americans are all good at sports or that "housewives" all wear aprons and bake cookies (or even that they are women), the root problem is generalizing limited and faulty perceptions of a few people to an entire race, gender, or other large group. Of course, you'll want to avoid stereotypes regardless of whether or not your audience is multicultural.

The richly diverse experiences of an intercultural audience provide an extra challenge for speakers.

somebody you're not. If you're a naturally lively speaker, don't force yourself to be calm and emotionless for a Japanese audience just because you've heard that Japanese speakers are typically less demonstrative than speakers in the United States. You'll come across just as you'll feel—unnatural.[18]

How to Analyze a Speaking Situation

By now you might be feeling rather overwhelmed by everything there is to know about an audience. You'll be pleased to learn that analyzing your speaking situation is much easier—just three major issues to worry about: time, the physical surroundings, and the context of your speech.

Time

You consider time in three ways. First, and perhaps most obvious, most speeches are prepared with a fixed amount of time in mind. One of the fastest ways to alienate an audience is to run past your allotted time, particularly if you're one of a number of

speakers that day. Practice your speech at a reasonable speaking speed to make sure you can finish in your allotted time. It's always a good idea to identify a section you can drop or condense if you get into time trouble.

Second, think about the time of day you'll be speaking. Audiences behave differently in the early morning, just before lunch, just after lunch, in the late afternoon, and in the evening. Most people hit their peak around midmorning, so that's a good time for serious subjects. On the other hand, many people start to lag intellectually and emotionally anytime past mid-afternoon, when thoughts start turning toward the drive home, what to make for dinner, or which party to attend that night. During afternoon speeches, you may need to work harder to arouse people's interest and keep their attention.[19]

Third, how does your speech fit in with the larger sequence of events? If you're scheduled to deliver the toast at a wedding banquet, you know that your speech will follow the ceremony, which may be religious or secular, grand or modest, and so on. If you're the last speaker scheduled during a class period or during an industry seminar, you may have to cut your time short so that the entire group can stay on schedule. Any time you're one of a number of speakers scheduled to talk, voluntarily taking less time than you're scheduled for

(and making a comment about it in passing) is often a great way to score points with an audience. Scheduling a speech as part of a sequence of events usually isn't a major concern. However, if it might affect your speech, consider it carefully.

Physical Surroundings

Light, color, and even furnishings can affect the way your audience responds to a speech. Lower lighting levels tend to make people relax, but really dim lighting forces people to spend more mental and physical energy just to see clearly, so they have less energy available to pay attention to you and process your information. You don't often have control over the speaking environment, but when you do, try to make sure the audience will be comfortable enough to focus on you, but not so comfortable that they fall asleep.

Your classroom may not be the plushest place around, but at least the environment is predictable. If you're going to be speaking outside, at a rally, or in any other situation that's likely to be crowded and noisy, think about the best way to succeed. If you're going to be competing with lots of distractions, keep your speech short and simple, and be ready to talk forcefully and dramatically if the situation requires it. If you need to out-shout passing traffic, make sure you'll have a bullhorn or an amplification system (see Exhibit 6.9). Whatever the situation, remember to check it out early, if possible. Look over every aspect of the physical environment, considering things such as where you'll stand and how you'll move around, where the audience will be relative to you, and where you'll put your notes and any visual aids. If possible, practice in the actual speaking location. Eliminating surprises will help you avoid problems before they occur and will boost your speaking confidence.

Context

Why are all these people gathered to hear you speak? Did they come to hear you specifically, or are you just one of a panel of speakers? Perhaps most important, are audience members here voluntarily? People who go out of their way to hear you talk are usually on your side already (except those who want to hear you because they want to challenge you). On the other hand, people who have to hear you because you're part of the program are going to greet you from a neutral position at best.

In the classroom situation, your captive audience could probably think of a long list of things they'd rather be doing than sitting in a hard chair listening to their classmates' speeches. Consequently, you need to get these people on your side. Your personal style and your message are the tools at your disposal. If the audience is bored to start with, and you shuffle up to the front of the room looking like you would rather be someplace else, you're signaling your audience that what you have to say isn't going to be useful or important.

Two more key issues to analyze in any speaking situation are the degree of formality and the degree of control you have over the situation. Will people be on their best behavior in a formal social setting, or will they have their feet up on the tables while they pass coffee and doughnuts around the room? Should you expect, and do you have control over, interruptions and questions? Thinking about such issues beforehand can help you prepare your material—and prepare yourself psychologically. For classroom speeches, you'll know much of this information simply by observing what happens in the room. For other speeches,

however, you may have to ask the person in charge of the event to characterize the situation for you.

Finally, think about anything else regarding the speaking situation that might affect the audience's response to your speech. Every speech presents *rhetorical exigencies*, factors that shape or influence what you should say and how you should say it. When Lyndon Johnson was sworn in as U.S. president shortly after the assassination of John F. Kennedy, the rhetorical exigencies in his speaking situation included not only a sense of public shock and grief, but also fear. Johnson needed to offer assurances to the nation and to the world that he would take over and that the country would move ahead. This is an extreme example, to be sure, but it illustrates how speeches need to conform to the situation in which they are given.[20]

HOW TO ADAPT TO YOUR AUDIENCE AND THE SPEAKING SITUATION

The bulk of this chapter has been devoted to planned adaptation—learning about your audience and the speaking situation, then adapting your speech to those people and conditions. This section discusses more immediate types of adaptation: making adjustments right before your speech and during your speech.

Adapting Before Your Speech

You've researched your material thoroughly and practiced so many times that you're as smooth as a well-oiled machine. You've visualized just how the audience will look and how satisfied they'll be when you deliver your message. Everything is ready for a great speech. When you arrive, the audience is twice as large (or twice as small) as you thought it would be. For some reason, people are expecting another speaker. The microphone won't work, the temperature in the room is at least 95 degrees, and you lost half your notes. Your hair is standing straight up and won't lie down. Help!

How well you handle these minor emergencies can be as important as all the research and planning you've done to create your speech. Panic is a natural response when things go wrong, but panic only makes the situation worse. Remember what you learned early in the chapter: audiences are sympathetic. When things go wrong before or during a speech—and something is bound to go wrong at some point in your speaking career—the audience will support you if you try to make things right again. Tell yourself to stay calm and think your way through the situation.

Jan Broenink is a technical specialist employed by the big electronics firm Hewlett-Packard. Based in Amsterdam, he spends much of his time speaking to customers across Europe. Arriving at his hotel the night before an important seminar in Hamburg, Germany, Broenink realized that the dozens of full-color overhead transparencies he needed were sitting on his desk back in Amsterdam. His audience was expecting a professional-looking presentation; in fact, they'd paid a lot of money to listen to him.

Someone less prepared and less creative might have panicked. However, Broenink arose early the next morning and did two things: (1) he called home and coaxed a colleague to drive down and bring the color transparencies to him, and (2) he borrowed a computer to print out some simple black-and-white transparencies from an emergency floppy disk he was carrying. At the beginning of the presentation, he announced good-naturedly that he was missing all his nice visuals, but that he had some backups and would make do with what he had. By joking about it and moving ahead with confidence, he sent a subtle message to the audience that if he could survive without the fancy color graphics, so could they. Fortunately, he knew his material well and wound up impressing the audience not only with his knowledge of the subject but with his ability to respond to a difficult situation. By lunchtime, when his color transparencies arrived, Broenink had already won over the audience with his knowledge and manner. Thanks to his preparation and some adaptive problem solving (and

the high speeds allowed on the German Autobahn!), his presentation was a great success.[21]

You may get tired of hearing this advice, but its importance can't be overstated: Thorough preparation is critical. The better prepared you are, the better you'll be able to handle emergencies. In fact, it's a good idea to think through things that might go wrong and devise responses beforehand. What will you do if the bulb in the overhead projector burns out and you can't show the wonderful diagram you've created? Do you know your subject well enough to explain it to the audience anyway? Will there be a flip chart or chalkboard to use as a backup, on which you can quickly sketch the diagram? What if the start of your speech is delayed, and you need to chop it down from six minutes to three? Will you know what to leave out and still get the main points across? What if you're talking about a deadly serious subject, and the speaker before you gives a funny speech that leaves the audience in stitches? Of course, you can drive yourself crazy with worry if you go overboard with this. Just consider the few things that could conceivably go wrong and figure out potential responses in case they do.

Adapting During Your Speech

Even when you have all your materials and everything is in place, it's important to keep a close eye on the audience once you get started. How are they reacting? Audiences are good at sending clues, from rolling their eyes and talking with their neighbors to taking careful notes and watching you intently (see Exhibit 6.10). If things aren't going well, stop for a second and consider how you might adjust. If you see puzzled looks, for instance, you might need to back up and explain a difficult point in a different way. If people are starting to fidget, they might be bored, and you might consider skipping certain details or making some other adjustment.[22]

How can you pick up on audience signals? The first step is to dispel some illusions you may have

> *Success Tip*
>
> After you've prepared your speech, consider things that might go wrong, such as a mechanical visual aid not working or some of the audience being unable to see your charts clearly. Devise a backup plan to cover these potential glitches.

EXHIBIT 6.10
Are They Listening?
Judging from the audience's reactions, this speaker is doing a great job of keeping the audience's attention and interest.

about audience behavior. Kittie Watson and Larry Barker, two specialists in listening and other aspects of audience behavior, have identified several false assumptions that speakers often make about their audiences. Don't fall prey to these illusions and you'll be in a better position to respond to your audience:[23]

- *Misconception #1: If people are watching you, they must be listening to you.* As a student, you probably know it's not too hard to fake attention. You can watch your instructor move around the room, smile whenever you make eye contact, and still not pay attention to a single word that's being said. People in your audiences can do the same thing, so don't assume that just because they're watching, they're listening. See whether they're nodding their heads, leaning forward, and matching your facial expressions; then you'll know they're listening.

- *Misconception #2: When you start talking, people start listening.* In the moments leading up to your speech, you're thinking about what you're going to say, so your mind is already on the topic. That's not the case with your audience. They've been thinking about a thousand other things, and their minds will take a few moments to get into your topic. If you jump right into an important point, some people will miss it.

Instead, start off with a quick story, an enlightening example, or something else to pull everybody in. Then hit them with the heavy information.

- *Misconception #3: People keep listening as long as you're talking.* Most audience members tune in and out and back in during the course of a speech. By using a variety of supporting elements, changing the pitch and volume of your voice, mentioning people by name, and asking questions for the audience to think about, you can keep more people engaged more of the time.

- *Misconception #4: All audience members process information in the same way.* While giving a speech filled with statistics and technical details, you might see some people eating it up and others sliding into a daze—even if they're all interested in the topic. The reason is that various people have different information-processing preferences. People with strong technical backgrounds are used to processing lots of facts and figures. Graphs and technical diagrams are second nature to these people. They usually know how to construct the big picture if you show them all the pieces. In contrast, other people may want the big picture first, without all the details. If you know which type of people will be in your audience, you'll

THE BEST-KEPT SECRET FOR REDUCING YOUR PUBLIC SPEAKING WORRIES

Talking to strangers sometimes generates anxiety, even if you're just asking someone on the street for directions. You want to be understood, and you want to get the information you may need, but you probably don't want to come across as pushy, ignorant, or foolish. Much of the stress in these situations comes from the fact that you don't know much about the person you're having a conversation with. You don't know what that person knows or cares about, and you don't know what phrases or gestures might be somehow offensive. Just think how much easier it is to talk to a close friend than to a total stranger!

Now carry this thought over to the process of analyzing a speech audience. The more you know about them, the less anxious you'll be. That's one of the beauties of thorough audience analysis—not only will you be better prepared to develop and present a successful speech, you'll feel more confident because it won't seem like you're talking to total strangers.

Audience analysis can reduce your anxiety in two ways. First, if you know what the audience wants to hear, you can develop a speech around those expectations, knowing that it stands a good chance of being successful. Second, the feeling of telling people something they're glad to hear is one of the best emotions you can experience as a speaker. When you see people grab a pencil to write down something you just said or nudge a neighbor to say "I told you so," the feeling is tremendously satisfying.

Knowing what is important to your audience and delivering a message they care about is a great way to reduce the anxiety of speaking in public.

have the luxury of being able to adjust what you have to say. If not, you may have to look for signs of confusion or boredom during the speech and make adjustments as you speak. If you're loading the audience up with details and notice that people look confused, for instance, you might want to step back and put all the facts and figures into a larger context that these holistic thinkers can grasp more easily.

Making real-time adjustments takes some practice and enough presence of mind (1) to sense that adjustments are required and (2) to think your way through the problem. Once again, solid preparation will save the day for you. If you know your material thoroughly, you'll have both the flexibility and the confidence you need to stop, think, and adjust. On the other hand, if your knowledge of the subject is limited to the several minutes of words you've prepared and memorized, you'll be stuck with what you brought, so to speak. Watch how good teachers adapt during lectures. They don't have to stick to a prepared script, regardless of how well it's going. They can expand on some points, gloss over other points, back up and repeat, and make other adjustments as needed. You know how frustrating it can be to listen to a lecture that isn't hitting the mark while the teacher just plows ahead anyway. Don't do the same thing to your audiences.

Two-Choice Questions

(can be yes or no questions, but they don't have to be)

Do you think tests are an effective way of measuring student progress?

Do you prefer essay questions or objective tests?

Open-Ended Questions

(require the person to respond in his or her own words)

How would you rate the governor's performance so far this term?

How would you change this course if you were the teacher?

Multiple-Choice Questions

(limit the person's options and let you summarize results more easily than open-ended questions)

What are your plans after receiving your bachelor's degree?

a. Pursue a master's degree
b. Travel/vacation
c. Find a job
d. I haven't decided yet

EXHIBIT 6.11
Basic Survey Questions

Here are the three basic types of questions you can ask in a simple survey. Survey research is a fairly involved subject, so consult a reference book on research methods if you need more information.

HOW TO LEARN MORE ABOUT AUDIENCES AND SITUATIONS

Obviously, the more you know about your audience and your speaking situation, the better you'll be able to prepare. Here are four steps you can take to learn more:

1. *Stop and think.* You can often reach logical conclusions about audiences and situations just by mulling them over in your mind. What does this group of people care about? What do they have in common? Why are they coming to this speech? How much are they likely to know or care about your topic?

2. *Interview someone from your audience or someone who knows your audience.* In many professional speaking engagements, you'll be asked to talk to an audience gathered for a dinner, a conference, or some other reason. The person who invited you to speak probably knows his or her fellow audience members well, so arrange a phone call or in-person interview to learn more. It's particularly important to ask about the room, the sound system, the expected size of the audience, and who's speaking before and after you. Also, another speaker who has already addressed the same audience might be willing to help as well.

3. *Survey your audience or people who are similar to members of your audience.* This technique is useful when you have access to the audience beforehand. For a classroom speech, for instance, you may have a chance to poll your classmates to find out how much they know or what they believe about the topic you're planning to cover (see Exhibit 6.11).

4. *Conduct some library research.* Chapter 8 is full of guidelines for researching your speech topic, and you can apply many of these techniques to researching your audience as well. Some of the statistical reference guides described in Chapter 8, for instance, can give you data about household types, race, ages, occupations, and many other factors. Of course, these don't apply specifically to your audience, but you can often use these general figures to give you a better idea of what your audience will be like. For example, even simple facts can give you insight into an audience, such as knowing that only about one-third of U.S. residents under age 35 own their own home (versus two-thirds of the people over 35).[24]

You'll never know as much as you'd probably like to know about your audience, but you can discover many important points through some fairly simple research. Give yourself enough time during the preparation stage to ask questions and learn as much as you can.

SUMMARY

Understanding your audience is a critical part of successful speaking. Because your speech is really a mechanism for changing your audience's beliefs, opinions, or behaviors, you need to know what those beliefs, opinions, and behaviors are before you can effectively change them.

All audiences are self-centered to a degree, a quality known as egocentrism, which is simply basic human nature. Decentering is the ability to understand others' viewpoints. If people are going to listen to you, they want to know how they will benefit from the experience. Developing a successful speech means creating a listening experience that meets the needs of your audience.

Audience reactions are shaped by personal factors, including age, gender, household type, education, occupation, and income. This information can help you predict what an audience knows about and cares about, as well as how they might react to you and your speech.

Also influencing audience reactions are psychological factors: needs and motives, attitudes, and values and lifestyles. Most people act in ways that promise to meet their personal needs, whether it's a need for shoes or love or self-esteem. Those needs provide the motives that drive their behavior. Audience attitudes about you, your topic, and lots of other things not even related to your speech can influence how they respond to you. The audience might start out with a positive attitude about your topic, a negative attitude, or a neutral attitude. Some people cling to some attitudes so tightly that a simple speech won't get them to change, but in most cases, reasonable people are at

least willing to listen to a different point of view.

When you're planning a speech, try to confirm three things about the situation. First, how much time will you have, and what time of day will you be speaking? Second, what will the physical surroundings be like, and will you have any control over them? Third, what is the overall nature of the occasion? In other words, why will the audience be there?

Cultural, racial, and ethnic factors can affect audience reactions because they help set expectations for beliefs and behaviors. If your speech topic, your language, or other aspects of your presentation conflict with the cultural expectations of your audience, you'll run into resistance from audience members.

The three phases of adapting to your audience are the planned adaptation you make during your research and preparation, the emergency adaptation you make if you discover something is amiss right before you deliver your speech, and the reactive adaptation you make in response to audience feedback during your speech.

KEY TERMS

attitude (118)
audience analysis (110)
culture (121)
demographics (113)
dogmatic opinions (119)
egocentric (112)
ethnic identity (122)
lifestyle (119)
motives (117)
needs (117)
norms (121)
psychographics (117)
race (122)
relevance (113)
values (119)

APPLY CRITICAL THINKING

1. Should you always cater to your audience's egocentrism? Why or why not?

2. What factors might keep you from decentering, even if you know it's a good idea? What might you do about this?

3. Whose opinion would be harder to change: someone who has never considered your topic and has no feelings or beliefs about it, or someone who knows the topic well and disagrees with you? Explain your answer.

4. To what degree are your own values influenced by your parents or other adults you were close to while you were growing up? Do you hold the same opinions as your parents on major issues?

5. In general, people with more education have been exposed to a broader range of ideas and opinions. Would this make it easier or harder to convince them of your position. Why?

6. Can such factors as religious beliefs and political convictions color an audience's attitude about such "impersonal" subjects such as economics or technology? Explain your answer.

7. Why would it matter who comes before you and after you in a program of speeches?

SHARPEN YOUR SKILLS

Individual Exercises

1. What assumptions can you make about your classmates based on their estimated ages? Are most of them your age, or are some more than a few years older or younger? How might such differences affect the assumptions you've just identified?

2. Assume that you're going to give a speech to your class in favor of a particular political candidate in some forthcoming election. What should you find out about your classmates before delivering this speech in order to make it as effective as possible?

3. How could you get your hands on the information you identified in the previous question?

4. Keep a role-playing journal over the course of several days. In this journal, you'll assume the role of another person who is very different from you. Assume you are that person by decentering and thinking about things from that person's viewpoint.[25]

Group Exercises

5. In a team with three other students, choose one of the following questions. First, each of you records how you personally feel about the issue. Second, split up and poll 20 or 30 students on campus about how they feel. Now compare the results of your quick and rather unscientific poll with your own opinion. Do you find yourself agreeing or disagreeing with the majority opinion? Is this result a surprise?

   a. Would government registration of handguns violate gun owners' constitutional rights?

   b. Should people be required to pass a test concerning basic governmental issues before they are allowed to vote?

   c. Should parents who pay to send their children to private schools still be required to pay taxes that support public schools?

   d. Should the United States have an open immigration policy, in which anyone who wants to move here can do so?

6. In a group of four to six students, find an issue on which there is some disagreement. Make it an important issue on which people are likely to have strong opinions. Give yourselves a designated period of time, such as 30 minutes, and let the group members try to change each other's minds. Do you find this to be easy or difficult? If anyone was successful, was it because of a logical appeal or an emotional appeal? How might you apply what you've learned in this exercise to your speeches?

SUPPORTING YOUR SPEECH

LEARNING OBJECTIVES

After studying this chapter, you will be able to

1. Explain why support is essential to effective public speaking.

2. Define analogies and describe how they can help support to your speeches.

3. Explain how narratives can improve your speeches.

4. Define testimony and explain its role in supporting your speeches.

5. List the potential ethical problems with testimony and quotations.

6. Describe the two basic types of statistics.

7. Identify at least three ways to ensure accurate use and interpretation of statistics.

EVEN GREAT IDEAS NEED SUPPORT

"Why?"

"Because I said so, that's why!"

How many times did you hear *that* when you were growing up? Even if the adult who was saying it was right, you wanted reasons, evidence, and explanations. Your speech audiences are just as demanding as you were back then. They're not going to sit back and accept whatever you have to say. They, too, want reasons, evidence, and explanations. This chapter describes the major supporting elements you can use in your speeches. (Chapter 8 helps you find those materials.)

Support material can help you

- *attract and maintain interest* (with narratives and anecdotes)
- *clarify your meaning* (with definitions, examples, and analogies)
- *prove your points* (with facts and statistics)
- *control controversy* (with testimony and quotations)

You'll keep audiences riveted if you use your imagination to mix different types of support into your speech. For example, you might balance hard-hitting figures with more gentle illustration or narration, or offset a brief reference to authority with detailed description. You could use a single, compelling fact or a whole pile of statistical data. The only limits are the thoroughness of your research and your own creative and critical thinking (see Exhibit 7.1). Compare two possible ways you could introduce the problem of drunk driving:

a. I walk down the hallway and pass that door a dozen times a day. But where I used to hear laughter, music, and the other sounds of a happy, lively ten-year-old girl, I now hear nothing. There is nothing to hear, for there is no girl. My little sister Marie died six months ago, another senseless victim of yet another drunk driver.

b. Maybe we should rename our highways "dieways." The Centers for Disease Control report that last year more than 17,000 people died in alcohol-related traffic accidents.[1]

Success Tip

Combine different types of supporting elements to increase your chances of reaching everyone in the audience.

The two approaches do an effective job of highlighting a problem, but each does its job in a unique way. The first approach uses an *example;* in this case, it's a powerful, emotional, and very personal example. The second approach relies on a *fact* to make the point. Although both approaches effectively introduce the central idea, each one lacks something, too. The example of Marie doesn't tell the audience just how widespread the problem is. On the other hand, the statistics in the second example don't grip the audience with the emotional power of the first. Numbers can't personalize a tragedy in the

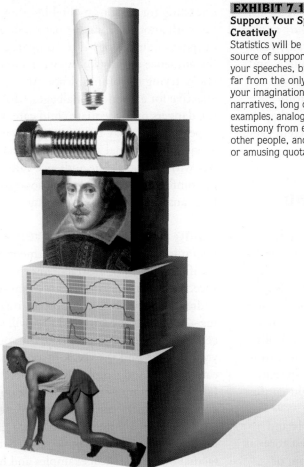

EXHIBIT 7.1
Support Your Speeches Creatively
Statistics will be a major source of support for many of your speeches, but they are far from the only choices. Use your imagination: Try narratives, long or short examples, analogies, testimony from experts or other people, and interesting or amusing quotations.

same way. So effective speakers often combine supporting elements for maximum impact.

The rest of this chapter explores the five categories of support materials you can use to be successful: definitions, examples and analogies; narratives; testimony and quotations; and statistics and other facts.

No matter what kind of support you select for each speech, keep several points in mind as you collect your material:

- *Make sure your support materials are meaningful to the audience and appropriate in the context of your speech.* Prepare your speech with your audience in mind. Presenting a collection of scientific data might be perfect for a gathering of technical specialists but totally inappropriate for a group of reporters or homeowners.

- *Make sure your support materials are significant.* Divide your support materials into two piles: things that you truly need to support your central idea and things that are just interesting or entertaining. Then discard the second pile. That sort of support will just clutter up your speech.

- *Use clear and concrete support materials.* Poorly handled evidence can work against you by confusing or distracting the audience.

- *Use a variety of support materials.* Nobody wants to listen to five minutes of statistics or a long string of examples. Noted researcher and professor Frank Dance suggests a ratio of 30 percent objective support (facts, statistics, etc.) and 70 percent subjective support (narratives, examples, etc.). Audiences are more likely to remember well-crafted stories than strings of facts and figures.[2]

- *Use only those supporting materials that relate to and support your central idea.* Each bit of information should prove a point, clarify an idea, add color, or somehow make your message more memorable to your audience.

- *Mix in some humor to emphasize support materials when it's appropriate.* Yes, humor can provide powerful support for your speeches. However, it can also work against you. You'll find more

information about using humor in Chapter 13.
- *Choose appropriate techniques to integrate various types of support into your speech.* Generally, you'll (a) convey the material, (b) cite the source, and (c) explain its relevance. But you'll need to handle quotations a little differently from statistics, for example. Throughout this chapter, you'll find tips for integrating the different types of support effectively.

DEFINITIONS, EXAMPLES, AND ANALOGIES

Perhaps the simplest form of support is a **definition**. For example, let's say you're giving a speech about the ethics of cloning. You'll need to clarify whether by "cloning" you mean cloning cells at the embryonic level, now common in the development of new pharmaceuticals, or whether you're talking about the far more difficult and ethically challenging task of cloning an identical twin from an adult mammal. At the outset of your speech, you'll want to define any terms that might confuse or mislead your audience.

Examples and analogies, used with style and imagination, can be among your strongest tools as a speaker. An **example** is one item, person, or event that is representative of a group or type. A cloudy, rainy day is a good example of weather in the Pacific Northwest. However, the huge cloud of smoke and ash from the eruption of Mount St. Helens is a bad example of the area's weather because it doesn't occur often—it isn't representative. An **analogy** is a way of making a point about one thing (or person) by highlighting its similarities with another thing (or person or event). The purpose of an analogy is to compare something the audience already knows with a new concept you're trying to communicate. Analogies are effective for audiences of all ages.[3] To emphasize the dangers of inadequate child care, for instance, a speaker might say that starting life without adequate emotional support is like starting your day without food. The audience can relate the discomfort caused by a lack of food to the discomfort caused by a lack of nurturing.

Using Examples Effectively

Examples can help prove a statement or opinion, clarify a difficult or abstract concept, and make a speech more interesting and relevant to your audience. They can be humorous, tragic, uplifting—whatever you can find that will support your central idea and be appropriate for your audience, your subject, and the speaking occasion. Examples can be short and simple or long and complex (although examples that are long enough to be considered stories are usually called *narratives* and are covered in another section). Two decisions you need to make about examples are whether to use factual or hypothetical examples and how many examples to use.

Choosing Between Factual and Hypothetical Examples

One great feature of examples is that you can make them up if you need to. No, you can't just create evidence to suit your needs, but you can

---

Checklist for Selecting Support Elements

1. Make sure your supporting materials will mean something to the audience.
2. Don't waste your time or the audience's with insignificant support.
3. Be clear and concise.
4. Mix it up; vary the types of support you use.
5. Balance the use of subjective, personal information with objective, factual information.
6. Be sure all your supporting material serves a purpose in the speech and helps support your central idea.
7. Use humor when it will help the speech along (but only when it will help).

build **hypothetical examples**, which haven't actually taken place but could conceivably happen. **Factual examples**, on the other hand, are based on real facts. If you're trying to make the point that most cities were started next to major rivers, for instance, you could say that Washington, D.C., is on the Potomac River, or that Paris is on the River Seine.

Most of the time, you'll want to use factual examples because they provide concrete evidence to support your central idea. Hypothetical examples have two main purposes. The first is to help the audience visualize something in the future. The second is to draw audience members into your speech by encouraging them to imagine themselves doing or experiencing something. Of course, you need to point out that you're taking your audience on an imaginary journey by using such phrases as "Imagine you are . . ." or "What if you could . . ."[4]

These imaginary journeys can be something realistic, such as "Imagine you're walking home and a suspicious character starts following you . . ." or something more fanciful, such as "What if you could ride a red blood cell as it flows through a cancer patient's veins . . ." You have to be careful with these farfetched examples, of course. You don't want your audience to react by thinking, "Yeah, right; like that could really happen." You want them to suspend disbelief long enough to join you on this imaginary journey. When done well, these hypothetical examples can be extremely effective ways to draw your audience into your subject.

Choosing the Right Number of Examples

Have you ever had to stop someone's long-winded, repetitive discourse to say, "All right already; I get the point!"? You don't want your audience to get that same feeling by bombarding them with one example after another. Using too many examples dilutes a speech and makes it meander. One or two pithy, relevant examples can do the work of a half-dozen weaker examples.

Combining one strong example with broad-

Success Tip

As a general rule of thumb, the longer your examples, the fewer you should use. Don't try to string together complicated examples.

based statistics is a powerful way to make a point. The example helps "put a face" on the numbers, and the statistics convince your audience that this isn't just one isolated case. Jill Catherine Dineen gave a speech describing the extent of financial aid fraud and default involving trade schools. She started her speech with a highly personal example of a young woman who responded to a recruiting pitch for a trade school that went bankrupt, leaving her owing a huge debt. Clearly, one shaky school caused some trouble for this one woman, but how widespread is this problem? Dineen answered that question immediately by pointing out that the 900,000 trade school students (who make up just 6 percent of all college students) account for 50 percent of all student loan troubles.[5] It was a great combination of personalizing with an example and then supporting with a statistic.

Although you will usually avoid long lists of examples, you'll find occasions when several short examples repeated in quick succession can create a great effect. To introduce the problem of senior citizens being defrauded by dishonest investment schemes, you could say something like this:

Angela Barros lost $54,000. Charles Shue, $42,000. The Grants from Ft. Lauderdale lost $86,000. And Al Shosack was the biggest loser of them all: He lost his entire life savings of $214,000.

Your audience would quickly get the point that some people, presumably a lot of people, are losing a lot of money. This approach works only when the examples don't need much explanation, however. In her speech on student loans, Dineen might have considered using four or five short examples of troubled student loans to create the impression that the country was facing a serious problem. In her case, however, each example would probably have taken too long to explain, so one strong example was a better choice.

If you do decide to pile on the examples, watch

EXHIBIT 7.2
**Help Your Audience
Visualize with
Analogies**
When an analogy works,
the audience can see a
point of similarity
between the old concept
they are familiar with
and the new concept
you're trying to describe
or explain.

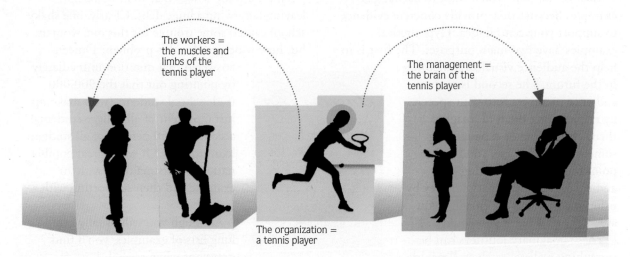

The workers =
the muscles and
limbs of the
tennis player

The management =
the brain of the
tennis player

The organization =
a tennis player

out for the possibility of misleading your audience. You are creating the illusion of a statistic when you do this, and you have an ethical responsibility not to mislead. Say you could string together six quick examples of slow-moving farm equipment causing traffic accidents. List these accidents in your speech, and you're likely to create the impression that farm equipment on highways is a major safety hazard. But what if it's not? What if there are only eight or ten instances a year of these accidents? Make sure your examples are truly representative of what you're trying to illustrate.

Using Analogies Effectively

Analogies can help communicate difficult and new ideas by referencing things the audience already understands. However, be sure to avoid using analogies that are inappropriate, distracting, or not easily understood. The key to a successful analogy is to make sure that the basic structure of

the two things being compared is the same. You might compare a well-run company with a talented tennis player, for instance. The top management in the company prepares the work force (through training), points the way, then gets out of the way to let people do their job. The mind of a tennis player prepares the body (through practice), points the way by setting up good strategies, then gets out of the way to let the body do its job (the brain has to step aside and let the body work instinctively).

As you can see in Exhibit 7.2, the company and the tennis player have the same basic structure in this context. Moreover, the nature of the two activities is the same: a continuing cycle of planning, doing, assessing performance, modifying plans, then trying again, day after day. This analogy could work in either direction, actually. As a tennis pro, you could tell a group of businesspeople that playing tennis is like managing a company, something they're all familiar with. As a business consultant, you could tell management trainees that running a company is like playing tennis and then explain about the mind preparing and leading the body, and so on. Anybody who's even vaguely familiar with tennis should be able to follow your analogy.

A poor analogy, on the other hand, doesn't help the audience grasp the essential idea you're trying to illustrate. You couldn't very well say that running a company is like working on a jigsaw puzzle—finding the right pieces and making sure to put them in the right places. The jigsaw puzzle may be like hiring the right people for the right jobs, but it doesn't illustrate anything about planning or leadership. The action comes to a screeching halt once all the pieces are in place, which is the exact opposite of what running a company is like. If you tried using the puzzle analogy in a speech, you'd probably leave some audience members wondering how jigsaw puzzles relate to leadership and other audience members convinced that leadership is just about finding the right people.

You can choose from two kinds of analogies. When you compare two things that are basically the same (such as two songs, two politicians, or two countries), you're using a **literal analogy**. When a political candidate compares her record with John F. Kennedy's, for instance, she's using a literal analogy to persuade voters that she fits the perception people already have of Kennedy.

The tennis player analogy, on the other hand, is a **figurative analogy**, in which you compare two things that are fundamentally different but have some kind of similar structure or flow. When the late Israeli Prime Minister Yitzhak Rabin described the "walls of hostility" built up along the River Jordan, which separates Israel from Jordan, he wasn't talking about actual walls.[6] He was referring to the years of conflict and mistrust between these two countries. But you can see the essential similarity between a wall of concrete and a wall of hostility: both prevent people from passing back and forth, both are barriers that must be knocked down if people are to move freely from one side to the other.

Should you use a literal analogy or a figurative analogy? You'll have to decide in each case, based on the information you're trying to convey, the speaking occasion, and your audience's background. In a general sense, literal analogies are going to be safer, with fewer chances of miscommunication, since you're talking about two of the same things. On the other hand, figurative analogies can give you more options because you don't have to find another person, item, or situation that's the same as the one you're trying to describe. Also, figurative analogies give you more room for creative expression. Of course, they also present more opportunities for running off course. If you have any doubts as to whether a figurative analogy will work, go for a literal analogy instead.

Checklist for Selecting Successful Analogies

1. Make sure the structure of the two objects or concepts being compared is the same, even if they are fundamentally different.
2. Make sure audience members are in fact familiar with the old concept before comparing it to the new concept; don't leave people with two unfamiliar concepts.
3. Use literal analogies only between two objects or concepts that are of the same basic type.
4. Use figurative analogies when comparing two objects or concepts that are fundamentally different.
5. Make sure the familiar concept is easy to understand; you don't want audience members to be stuck on the old idea when you're trying to get them to think about the new one.

NARRATIVES

A **narrative** in public speaking is a short story, usually a very short story, that helps you make a point. In a sense, narratives are extended examples and can be either factual or hypothetical. Case studies are narratives, but so are children's stories. Think back to the stories and fables you read or listened to as a child. In the tale of the tortoise and the hare, the slow but persistent tortoise outruns the fast but overconfident and inconsistent hare. This narrative illustrates the point of sticking to a task. Think back to the stories that were told and retold in your family as you grew up. Family stories, or narratives about family members, are so important that they act as a cohesive element in holding families together. In a similar way, many religions rely on narratives, or stories, to convey messages.[7]

Narratives perform much the same function as examples. They can add color, support, and interest by involving your listeners in a miniature story, complete with plot, characters, and climax. As public speaking coach Kenneth Wydro put it, "One story that interprets and focuses all the facts can make more impact than one hundred pages of statistics."[8]

However, few things will lose an audience more quickly than a story that doesn't fit. When you get to the narrative part of your speech, avoid creating the impression that you're going to put your speech on hold for a few minutes while you tell an interesting or amusing story. Be sure your narratives blend smoothly. The speech flows from start to finish, including the narrative as one of many elements.

Of all the supporting elements in this chapter, narratives might be the ones that you need to select and use with the greatest care. They consume precious time and even more precious audience attention, so if they fail, they tend to fail in a big way. Follow these guidelines to make sure your narratives succeed:

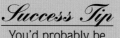

Success Tip

You'd probably be amazed by how many children's stories and fables you can still remember after all these years. These narratives stay with you because they were relevant and meaningful.

- Select narratives carefully and don't try to force a story that doesn't fit or isn't relevant.
- Keep them as short as possible while still getting the effect you need; a narrative should be an element in your speech, not your entire speech (at least not in the vast majority of speeches you'll give).
- Use narratives sparingly; you don't want to sound like you're just repeating other people's words; the audience came to hear you and your ideas.
- Use real **dialogue,** the spoken words of characters in the story, whenever possible; if it supports the point you're trying to make, dialogue can be lively and effective.
- Make sure the detour you're asking your audience to take is worth the trip; if a quick example or some other form of support will do the job more effectively than a narrative, go with the shorter option.

Perhaps most important, keep in mind that you're telling a story, not reciting a list of facts. Get personal. Put some feeling into it. You can hook the audience with emotion, then back it up with facts. If you can develop, structure, and tell a story effectively, the telling of it will fuel your speech with engaging energy.[9]

Kenneth Wydro suggests five elements of effective storytelling:[10]

1. Set the story in a specific time, place, and situation and make sure the characters have a goal in mind.
2. Make something happen in the story; as the narrative moves from start to finish, something about the characters or the world around them should change.
3. Show the main character(s) learning or seeing something at the end of the story; this conclusion helps your audience learn or see something.
4. Create a picture in the audience's mind by using visual words and images.
5. Get off to a strong start to catch the audience's

interest right away. For good examples of a strong start, check out most of the articles in a well-written newspaper; the first sentence will catch your attention and make you want to read on.

Here's an example of a short narrative used effectively in a speech on the risks of deceptive medical claims:

Recently, the maker of a children's cough syrup began to claim its drug to be "prescribed by Dr. Mom." Ad campaigns like this sell the idea that drug companies care about our health, not our money. Kathy Tobin believed that promise. She took a drug called Ritodrine when her unborn daughter's life was at risk. But, according to the *New England Journal of Medicine*, Ritodrine did nothing to help her baby and, in fact, caused Kathy's heart to shut down. Her daughter survived, but Kathy required an emergency heart transplant. She soon learned that the drug's manufacturer, Astra Pharmaceuticals, discovered Ritodrine's side effects in safety tests—but never told the FDA. She learned that Dr. Mom may be hazardous to her health, and she's not the only one.

In testimony before the House Subcommittee on Health, consumer advocate Sydney Wolfe said that falsified drug testing data kills over a thousand people a year.[11]

You can see how some introductory comments set the stage for the story, then the speech makes a smooth transition once the story is finished. This narrative is only five sentences long, but the same approach will work well with much longer examples, too.

TESTIMONY AND QUOTATIONS

This category of support involves using other people's words to make your speeches more interesting and more effective. Other people's

words fall into two categories. **Testimony** is a form of opinion, personal experience, or interpretation of facts and statistics. You use testimony to make your case because the other person's words will hold a lot of weight with your audience. In many cases, you'll want to use testimony to "deliver" other forms of supporting evidence, such as using a statement from a medical expert that includes a health care statistic. The other category is **quotations,** in which you use someone else's words because they help move your speech along in some fashion.

Testimony and quotations sound similar (and much of the testimony you use will be in the form of direct quotations from experts and other people). However, the key difference between the two is your purpose in using them. With testimony, you're interested in the *information* that the other person's words convey. With a quotation, you're interested in the *actual words themselves.* Two examples will help you see the difference:

Testimony: Dr. Charles Hinshaw, former president of the American Academy of Environmental Medicine, believes that the oil field fires are indeed the cause of Gulf War Syndrome.[12]

Quotation: As Mark Twain said, "History doesn't repeat itself. But it does rhyme."

In the first case, Jerri Gillean wanted to bolster her argument about Gulf War Syndrome, so she used testimony from a medical expert. In the second case, Twain's insightful quotation is a great lead-in to a discussion of how we can find repeatable patterns in history but shouldn't expect tomorrow to be exactly like yesterday. Twain's words are much more concise than the sentence you've just read, which tries to describe what he was saying. Such conciseness is the essence of a great quote.

Using Testimony Effectively

Most of the testimony you use will probably come from experts in specific subject areas, but not all of it. You can choose from three types of testi-

EXHIBIT 7.3

Expert Testimony or Celebrity Limelight?
When actress Meryl Streep testified at a Senate hearing on the use of pesticides on fruit and their effect on children, her celebrity status no doubt helped raise awareness of the issue. However, it's not likely that she would be considered a scientific expert on the subject.

mony. **Expert testimony** is just what it sounds like, testimony from people your audience will recognize as experts or from people you can convincingly present as experts. Few, if any, of the people in Jerri Gillean's audience knew who Dr. Hinshaw was, but by including his *qualifications,* she was able to present him as an expert.

Prestige testimony relies more on the status or prominence of the person giving the testimony. A good example would be the celebrity endorser in a television commercial. The idea is the same: You want to "borrow" some of that person's positive image for your speech. You might quote a popular actor or actress on the subject of drug abuse or AIDS prevention. Even though you could find hundreds of people who have more "expertise" in these subjects, the celebrity's public image is what you're using here (see Exhibit 7.3).

The third type of testimony comes from people who are neither experts nor celebrities but who have experienced something important or who have something interesting to say (including you, if you have experience in the subject). This is called **lay testimony,** or *peer testimony.* Use lay testimony carefully; it's advantage is the perspective of people who are close to the action, so to speak. Your great grandmother may have witnessed changing attitudes about family life in her 95 years of living. She hasn't studied and analyzed the issue in the same way that an academic expert would, but she's been there. You can see and hear

lay testimony all the time in the news media. The classic "person on the street" interviews are considered lay testimony.

Keep several points in mind when you use any of the three types of testimony:

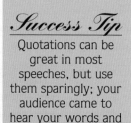

Success Tip
Quotations can be great in most speeches, but use them sparingly; your audience came to hear your words and ideas.

- *The different types of testimony work best in particular situations.* Expert testimony is best for factual support. Prestige and lay testimony often work best as introductions, transitions, and conclusions.
- *You don't have to use the source's exact words.* In some cases, you'll find it hard to work the source's words into the flow of your speech. You don't have to. If it makes your speech smoother, **paraphrase** the material by keeping its essential meaning but putting it into your own words. (When you use the source's words exactly, it's called using a text **verbatim.**)
- *Using testimony carries ethical responsibilities.* First, if you paraphrase, you must present the source's meaning without changing it to fit your speech. Second, understand the biases and motivations of people whose words or ideas you plan to use. You don't want to discover that you've made yourself a conduit for an idea or position that you don't really agree with. Third, make sure your testimony is representative. If 80 percent of schoolteachers believe something is true, don't try to portray the beliefs of all teachers by quoting one of the 20 percent who says it isn't true.

Using Quotations Effectively

When using quotations, you want to use them in the most valuable way possible to enhance your speech. Remember, you want to include quotations when someone else's words can make a point better than you can. The following guidelines will help you make the most of quotations:[13]

- *Don't build a speech out of quotations.* The audience didn't come to hear you recite a bunch of other people's words; they want to hear yours. Use quotations to embellish and highlight, not as the substance of your speech. In general, plan on no more than one good quote for every five or six minutes of speaking time.
- *Keep quotations short.* With long, complex quotes, the audience may stop paying attention to you and start paying attention to whomever you're quoting, as if you were simply reading from the source's own writings. Keep it short and get back to your message.
- *Make sure the connection is obvious.* The last thing you want to do is confuse the audience. If you have to explain why you're using the quote, don't use it.
- *Don't use a quote that you're not comfortable with.* If you can't pronounce the source's name, or if the quote contains foreign words you can't pronounce correctly or ideas you don't really grasp, you'll end up looking more than a little foolish in front of the audience.
- *Use some variety and be creative.* Shakespeare, Churchill, Lincoln, and other famous people have been quoted thousands and thousands of times. Don't fill up a speech with nothing but standard quotes from the heavyweights. Quote your mother, a scientist, a politician, or a comedian, perhaps. Famous quotes got that way by being used over and over again, so your audience is likely to groan if you try to present a famous quote ("A penny saved is a penny earned" or "All's well that ends well") as something you just discovered.
- *Collect quotes.* Scribble them in a notebook or keep them in a simple database on your computer. As you create your own stockpile of quotations, you'll be able to drop them into your speeches without having to dig through the library looking for them.
- *Take advantage of published collections of quotations.* Some categorize quotes by subject area; some specialize in inspirational, humorous, or other categories of quotes.
- *When you give your speech, watch how you introduce the quote.* Sometimes it's better to launch right into a quote, rather than announcing to the audience that you're about to share a quotation.

STATISTICS AND OTHER FACTUAL SUPPORT

Facts and figures are the workhorses of your support materials. The vast majority of your speeches will use them as evidence to help support your central idea. Unfortunately, even though facts and figures are plentiful and powerful, they are not necessarily simple. To use them effectively and ethically, you first have to understand them.

Checklist for Jazzing Up Your Speech with Quotations

1. Use quotes to supplement your own thoughts and words, not to replace them.
2. Use short quotations.
3. Make sure the quote fits your speech.
4. Make sure you're comfortable with the meaning and pronunciation.
5. Don't use the same standard quotes that people have been using for years; find some new and fresh ideas.
6. Build your own collection of quotes so that you'll have plenty to choose from.
7. Refer to published collections of quotes.
8. Introduce each quote effectively.

EXHIBIT 7.4
Drawing Conclusions with Inferential Statistics
Opinion polls are a common use of inferential statistics. Pollsters can ask a fairly small number of people which candidate they plan to vote for or what they think of a new law and then project those answers onto the entire population of the country.

Poll Reveals 69% of Smokers Favor Law Prohibiting Workplace Tobacco

87% of Internet Users Against Laws Curbing Content

37% Against Capturing Whales for Aquariums

...urvey Shows 73% of Voters Against Repeal of Helmet Law

Understanding Facts and Statistics

The distinction between *facts* and *statistics* can become blurred in everyday usage, but these two terms mean different things. **Facts** are individual pieces of data that you can verify in some direct way. The U.S. Congress is an elected body. Your Uncle Bill works for IBM. Franklin D. Roosevelt was president of the United States. **Statistics,** on the other hand, are numerical summaries, conclusions, or estimates about figures groups of data. (These data might represent people, ideas, companies, countries, or any other entity.)

Statistics fall into two basic categories. **Descriptive statistics,** as you can guess from the name, describe groups of people, items, ideas, and so on. They are summary statistics. They help us make sense of a great mass of data. Saying that NBA player Shaquille O'Neal averaged 20.1 points per game last season is a lot easier to grasp than a long list of how many points he scored in each of 70 or 80 games. **Inferential statistics,** on the other hand, draw conclusions ("inferences") or make estimates based on a sample or part of an entire group. What is learned or known about a sample of a group is inferred to be true of the entire group. When you hear that 45 percent of the country plans to vote for a certain candidate, this information doesn't mean that somebody asked every registered voter in the country. Instead, somebody asked a **sample,** or representative portion, of that group and then applied the results to the entire group (see Exhibit 7.4).

Here's an example to help you keep the two

types of statistics clear in your mind. Count the number of redheads sitting in your class today. Say it's 5 out of 25 students, or 20 percent of the class. This is a descriptive statistic; you're summarizing some data associated with this group, but you haven't made any conclusions or estimates. However, if you then conclude that redheads make up 20 percent of the entire student body, based on the sample you took in your classroom, you're using inferential statistics. You're making a conclusion based on part of the data.

The two types of statistics are similar in many respects. Both can lend authenticity to the statements you make in a speech. Also, both can be misused in a variety of ways, such as using only those statistics that support your central idea and ignoring those that don't, or using statistics out of context and assigning them a meaning they don't really have.

At the same time, the key difference between the two types of statistics is the way they are created. Unlike descriptive statistics, inferential statistics are derived numbers, so the process

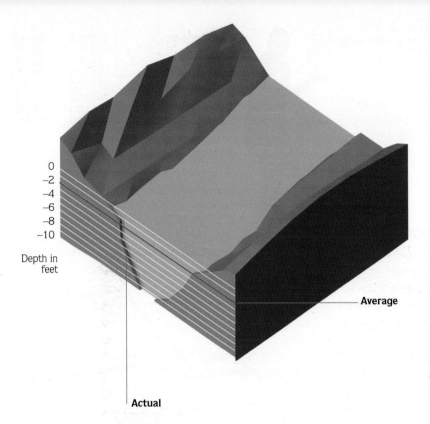

0
−2
−4
−6
−8
−10

Depth in feet

Average

Actual

EXHIBIT 7.5
Walking Across a River That's Two Feet Deep (on Average)
Would you try to walk across this river if someone told you it was two feet deep? Sure, it averages two feet, but about halfway across, you'll encounter a rather unpleasant surprise. Keep this in mind as you start using averages and other statistical measures in your speeches.

Understand What the Numbers Mean

What's average? People tend to use this term to characterize a group of figures, but it is only one of several terms that can help you understand what's going on with a group of figures. The technical term for **average** is **mean**, and you figure it out by adding up all the figures and dividing by the number of figures in the group. The mean of 12, 10, and 8 is 10 (30 3).

But what does an average really tell you? You've probably heard the old joke about trying to walk across a river that has an average depth of two feet. The problem, of course, is that the river is only a couple of inches deep at its edge but perhaps ten feet deep in the middle. An average or mean hides this critical information (see Exhibit 7.5). Some other pieces of information about the river would give you more insight, including minimum depth, maximum depth, and the range of values between minimum and maximum (particularly important when you're about to wade in!). Such terms help you present statistical information more realistically.

Another key term is **median,** the number that splits a group in half—half the numbers are smaller than the median, and half of them are higher. The median gives you a better idea of how the numbers in the group are spread out, or *distributed*. If the mean average and the median aren't close together, this tells you that some large

used to create them affects their accuracy and reliability. With descriptive statistics, ten people could count the number of redheads in your classroom, and all would arrive at the same answer. However, with inferential statistics, ten people could use sampling to estimate the number of redheads among the entire student body and arrive at ten different answers. One person might count the number of people walking past the library and see how many redheads were in the group. Another person might sample classes in the engineering school. They might come up with answers that are close, but they probably won't come up with answers that are exactly the same.

Using Facts and Statistics Effectively and Ethically

Statistical accuracy may seem a little scary, but a few simple concepts will go a long way toward helping you use statistics better. This section will help you understand what various statistical measures mean and how to use them effectively and responsibly in your speeches.

EXHIBIT 7.6

Which Is the More Lucrative Career?
Say you're advising a group of high school students on lucrative career options. Career A seems the profitable choice, since the average salary is $80,000, compared to the $46,000 average for Career B. However, the picture changes when you look at the median figures. Half the people in Career A make less than $60,000. The $80,000 mean is mainly the result of a few employees pulling the average up. So even though the average salary in Career B is lower, it seems less risky.

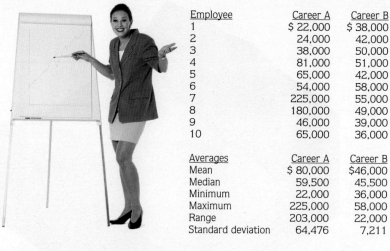

Employee	Career A	Career B
1	$ 22,000	$ 38,000
2	24,000	42,000
3	38,000	50,000
4	81,000	51,000
5	65,000	42,000
6	54,000	58,000
7	225,000	55,000
8	180,000	49,000
9	46,000	39,000
10	65,000	36,000

Averages	Career A	Career B
Mean	$ 80,000	$46,000
Median	59,500	45,500
Minimum	22,000	36,000
Maximum	225,000	58,000
Range	203,000	22,000
Standard deviation	64,476	7,211

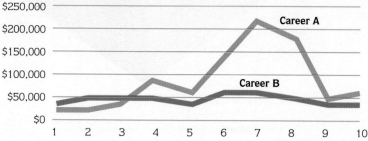

or small numbers are skewing your average. Look at the two sets of salary figures in Exhibit 7.6. Any time the mean and median figures are spread apart, as they are for Career A, you can suspect that some unusual data points are pulling the average up or down. Another term that can help paint a clearer picture of distribution is the **mode**, which is the number that occurs most often in a group.

The statistical term for the variations you see in the two groups of figures in Exhibit 7.6 is the **standard deviation**, a measure of how close a group of data points are to the average. The large value of $64,476 shown for Career A tells you that salaries cover a wide range. On the other hand, the standard deviation for Career B is only $7,211, meaning that the salaries are much closer to the average.

Why should you care about these statistical details? If you had convinced a group of high schoolers to pursue Career A by telling them the average salary is $80,000, what happens when several of them find out they're going to earn much, much less? You would have misinformed and misled them by failing to explain what the numbers really meant.

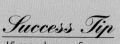

Success Tip

If members of your audience leave your speech remembering only one fact, what do you want it to be? Keep this question in mind, and it will keep you from overloading your audience with unimportant numbers.

Don't Overload Your Audience with Numbers
Numbers can make your speech much more effective, but more is not necessarily better. If you start to drone on with number after number after number, you'll lose the audience. Remember that you're using statistics to support your central idea; statistics themselves are not the primary message. The key to giving a good speech is to use just enough statistics to make your case, not to tell the audience everything you know about a subject.[14]

How many statistics are enough, then? Like other aspects of planning a speech, it depends on your goal and your central idea. If you stay focused on the goal, it'll be easier to separate the support points you need from those you don't. One helpful planning technique is to ask yourself, "If my audience leaves with just one or two numbers in mind (an optimistic goal at best), what should those numbers be?" This will help you concentrate on the most important statistics and drop the others.

Help Your Audience Interpret Your Facts and Statistics

Many listeners aren't sure how to interpret basic statistical concepts, such as the difference between a mean and a median. It's your job to help them understand. Not only will this satisfy the audience, it will help you meet your speech goals and appear more credible. Here are some guidelines:[15]

- *Don't show more detail than is really needed.* For a speech about the cost of living, does your audience really need to know that the average U.S. household spends exactly $2,136 per year on groceries?[16] Probably not. $2,100 or $2,000 would be fine for your purposes, and both are easier for your audience to absorb.
- *Identify the source and explain any biases the audience might not be aware of.* Not only is this good practice in general, but it helps your audience interpret and understand the data. Knowing that a piece of information about pollution came from the Environmental Protection Agency, the Sierra Club, or the National Association of Manufacturers can clarify what the figure really means.
- *Explain what statistics mean.* What does it mean to say that the average renter in this country pays nearly as much for shelter (mortgage or rent, taxes, and upkeep) as the average homeowner? You could simply mention the two numbers, about $4,100 for renters and $4,700 for homeowners. But these numbers represent something that affects the lives of millions of people. Help your audience explore the meaning of these statistics—that renters are spending huge amounts of money but not building any equity, that more people could buy houses if they could get over the downpayment hurdle, and so on. Make the numbers come alive by explaining their signficance.
- *Be consistent.* Don't confuse the audience by mixing different types of statistics. One student speaker tried to highlight the problem of

people who don't show up for jury duty by using no-show rates from three cities across the country. The first city said that only 50 percent of the people called actually appear, the second said that 44 percent fail to appear, and the third said that 13 percent show up.[17] These numbers might seem like a dramatic pattern: 50 to 44 to 13. But the numbers aren't measuring the same thing: the first and third numbers are measures of how many *do* appear, but the second is a measure of how many *don't* appear. The speaker should have said that the three cities reported either (1) that 50, 56, and 13 percent do appear or (2) that 50, 44, and 87 percent don't appear.

- *Make sure percentages are clear.* In a speech about teenage suicide, a student speaker pointed out that 85 percent of people aged 15 to 18 consider committing suicide and that of those 85 percent, 50 percent of them will attempt suicide, and 32 percent will succeed.[18] The speaker helped the audience understand that half of all teens who consider suicide go on to attempt it, but what about those who succeed? Is it 32 percent of the 50 percent, or 32 percent of the 85 percent? The problem here is that the point of comparison changed with every new statistic. Had the speaker listed the percentage of all teens who (A) consider, (B) attempt, and (C) succeed at suicide, rather than layering percentages on top of percentages, the point would have been clearer (see Exhibit 7.7). The technique the speaker used can be helpful in some cases, but it's easy to mishandle and should probably be avoided.

Beware of Inaccurate or Misleading Numbers

Inaccurate and misleading numbers are addressed together because they have the same effect: The audience gets bad information. Either the numbers themselves are faulty, or the way they are presented results in faulty conclusions.

Before discussing intentional errors, however, it's important to realize that all inferential statistics are imprecise, at least to a degree. Fortunately, the error doesn't usually matter. Statisticians deal with several sources of potential error, anything from the size of the group being sampled to the number of people who refuse to participate in the process.

EXHIBIT 7.7

Are You Confusing Your Audience by Using Layered Percentages?

When you layer percentages, the final number can be hard for the audience to grasp because it's several steps removed from where you started. The left side of this diagram shows layering, starting with 50 percent of all students, then 50 percent of that group, then 60 percent of *that* group. The right side of this diagram shows that the final figure is really just 15 percent of all students. (*Note:* The numbers here were made up for the purposes of illustration.)

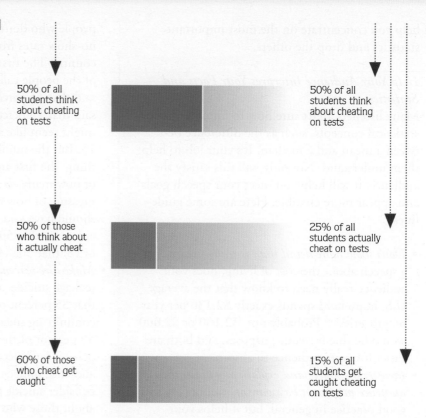

50% of all students think about cheating on tests

50% of those who think about it actually cheat

60% of those who cheat get caught

50% of all students think about cheating on tests

25% of all students actually cheat on tests

15% of all students get caught cheating on tests

So when the evening news reports a statistic along with a **margin of error**, this figure describes the potential error resulting from the size of the sample. The statistic might be "65 percent, with a margin of error of 4 points" (or 4 percent)—which means the real number might be anywhere from 61 to 69 percent. In simple terms, the more people (or items) included in a sample, the smaller the margin of error. For instance, with a sample of 625 people, your margin of error might be 4 percent, but it drops to 1 percent if you sample 10,000 people.[19]

As another example, say that a poll shows one candidate leading the other by 2 percent (51 percent to 49 percent). If the margin of error is 4 percent, one candidate may have anywhere from 47 to 55 percent of the voters, and the other may have 45 to 53. In other words, the political race is too close to call because the margin of error is bigger than the difference between the two statistics. Even though the potential for error in inferential statistics is more complicated than suggested here, you can see two basic issues to consider: (1) the smaller the sample, the less confidence you can have in the numbers, and (2) comparing two statistics can be difficult.

To avoid inaccurate and misleading numbers, be sure the numbers you're using make sense. Remember the speech about teenage suicides? In it the speaker said that over 3,000 teenagers die

annually from suicide. To see whether that number makes sense, you can work backward through the chain of percentages (85 percent of teens think about it; of those 50 percent try it; of those 32 percent succeed). This should tell you how many teenagers between 15 and 18 years old there are in the United States. Using the speaker's percentages, you discover that there are roughly 22,000 people between the ages of 15 and 18 in the United States. Does that number seem right? Actually, it isn't even close. According to statistics from the U.S. Bureau of the Census, the right number is about 13,500,000, and the number of teen suicides is closer to 1,500. In this case, the speaker got both the percentages and the number of teen suicides wrong. This example was chosen not to pick on any individual student but to emphasize how easily bad numbers can slip past all of us—this was an award-winning speech in a national competition.[20]

Problems with accuracy and misdirection (intentional or unintentional) fall into several categories:[21]

EXHIBIT 7.8
You Can't Just Ignore Data That Don't Fit

Is milk good for you? Is milk bad for you? You could make either case sound reasonable by grabbing selected pieces of information from this nutrition label. Yes, the vitamins are good, and the protein is good. Yes, the cholesterol and saturated fats are bad. As a speaker, you have a responsibility to your audience to present the whole picture, good points and bad. Remember that ethical communication means sharing enough information with the audience so they can make informed decisions and choices for themselves.

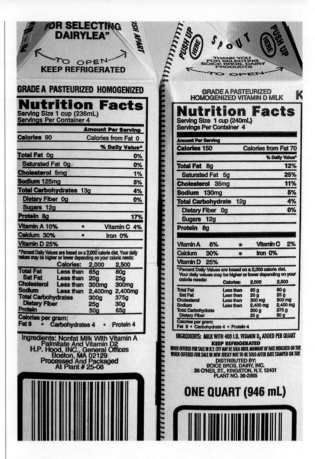

- *Selective reporting.* In a speech about good eating habits, you could mention that milk is a healthful food because it offers calcium and other essential minerals and nutrients. In a speech about bad eating habits, you could mention that milk is an unhealthful food because it contains cholesterol and animal fat. Which statement is right? They both are, and ignoring either side of this issue would mislead your audience. It's tempting to ignore contrary evidence when you're trying to persuade an audience, but you have an ethical responsibility to at least understand the evidence and its impact on your argument (see Exhibit 7.8).

- *Statistics based on faulty data or flawed analysis.* It's amazing how numbers can sometimes become "real" without any true foundation to support them. For years, the news media have been promoting the idea of a 500-channel cable television. You would think a well-planned effort to deliver 500-channel systems would be underway. Not at all; the 500 figure was somebody's guess about how many channels an advanced system could carry. Systems may eventually have 100, 300, or 800 channels— who knows? Such bits of flawed information circulate all over the world because people repeat statistics that are bad to start with or because they misuse and misinterpret good statistics. Don't add to the confusion.

- *Statistics with different bases of comparison.* You've probably heard an older relative say something along the lines of, "You youngsters have it so easy today—when I was your age, I worked for two dollars a day." Well, that may in fact be true, but you can't compare a dollar today with a dollar from 20 or 30 or 50 years ago. A dollar today won't buy anywhere near what a dollar would buy in years gone by (but people earn much higher salaries than they did 50 years ago, too). Inflation keeps changing the basis of comparison.

- *Misleading conclusions that result from statistical groupings.* Grouping people or things and computing averages can mislead the audience if the people or things inside the group vary widely (see Exhibit 7.9). For instance, while researching a speech on rising medical costs, you might learn that medical doctors in the United States earn an average (mean) salary of roughly $165,000. However, a closer look at that number uncovers some interesting details. General practitioners (such as your regular family doctor) generally earn about $103,000 ($62,000 less than the average), and surgeons generally earn $236,000 ($71,000 more than the average).[22] Clearly, lumping all doctors in one group can mislead your audience, as you saw in the discussion of data distribution. Moreover, the salaries within each category vary widely, too. Family doctors in rural areas, for example, may earn less than those in well-off urban and suburban areas. Similarly, a handful of high-salary specialty surgeons could be skewing the surgeon category's average upward. For instance, surgeons who make more than $1 million a year are not unheard of. If you had just three of these million-dollar earners in a group of 20 surgeons, the other 17 could each earn just one-tenth as much ($100,000), and you'd still hit the average of $236,000.

Also, you may run across conflicting statistics in your research from time to time. If this happens, look for additional sources that you can cross-check, and try to find out why two sources provide different answers to the same question. Whatever you do, don't average them or ignore any of the data.

FOCUSING ON ETHICS

BE CAREFUL! YOUR NUMBERS MAY BE BIASED

Most of us like numbers. We may not all like math, but we like numbers. They give us a sense of security. You like knowing that you have exactly $105.56 in your checking account, or at least you prefer having an exact number to having no idea at all of how much money is there. You like knowing that 25 people are going to come to your party (not 5 or 150) so that you can plan appropriately. Numbers seem precise, trustworthy, and most of all *true*. Unfortunately, we are tricked by biased numbers all the time. Sometimes people try to mislead us; other times, numbers trick us without any human intervention.

Numbers can be biased by the people who create them and by the people who use them. When you gather statistics for a speech, you're going to run across some that have opinions attached. This is one of the most subtle ways to intentionally or unintentionally mislead an audience, so make sure you are not misled by your sources and that you don't mislead your audience. Consider these four statements:

1. Engineers outnumber architects by more than 12 to 1.
2. No wonder this country has problems; we have more lawyers (753,000) than college professors and instructors (737,000).
3. The number of computer specialists nearly tripled from 1993 to 2003.
4. The prices we consumers are forced to pay for U.S. products have to cover the salaries of 14 million managers, administrators, and others who don't do any actual productive work.

In Average Lifetime Americans See 345 Movies in Theaters

90% Chance You'll Regain Your Weight After Dieting

Risk of Death from Asteroid is 1 in 6,000

Only 1 in 20 Calls to 911 Are True Emergencies

Foreign Travelers Prefer Honolulu over Las Vegas by 2 to 1

Which ones are true? Actually, the numbers are correct in each case, but notice how items 2 and 4 say more than simply reporting numbers. They are using numbers to convey value judgments and opinions. This can be a great way to make a point, particularly in a persuasive speech, but be careful: You don't want to influence your audience in ways that are unintentional or unethical.

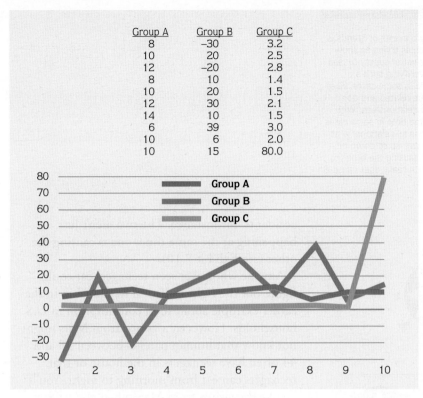

Group A	Group B	Group C
8	–30	3.2
10	20	2.5
12	–20	2.8
8	10	1.4
10	20	1.5
12	30	2.1
14	10	1.5
6	39	3.0
10	6	2.0
10	15	80.0

EXHIBIT 7.9
The Details Hiding Behind Averages
These three groups of numbers don't seem to have much in common, do they? Group A is fairly consistent, Group B jumps all over the place, and Group C contains nine very small numbers and one very big number. The groups may look quite different, but they have exactly the same average (10). In other words, if the only information you give your audience about these numbers is the average values, you might be hiding some important details.

Don't Imply Relationships That May Not Exist

Don't fall into the trap of assuming that you know how statistics are related. For example, a table of government statistics relates how much U.S. households spend on food, and it shows that food spending peaks when the head of the household is in the age bracket between 35 and 44 years old. Households in this group spend roughly twice as much as households headed by 25-year-olds or 75-year-olds.[23] Can you conclude that people between the ages of 35 and 44 eat more than younger or older people? That's what the data seem to indicate, right? Of course, a big part of the answer is that most of these high-consumption households contain those big eaters known as teenagers. In other words, there is no direct relationship between the head of household's age and the amount the household spends on food. The key variable is missing from this table—the number and age of other people living in the house.

Sets of data can be related at three different levels. The first level is called **coincidence**, in which two data sets seem to be related somehow but really aren't. The fact that ten guys in your public speaking class are named Phil is a coincidence; there is no connection whatsoever between first names and class choices or section assignments. The second level is **correlation**, in which two or more sets behave in similar ways at the same time, but not because one causes the other.

Checklist for Avoiding Flawed Statistics

1. Be sure the numbers you're using make sense.
2. Avoid selecting only those statistics that support your case while ignoring those that don't.
3. Avoid repeating statistics that are based on bad data (although it's impossible to know in many cases).
4. Avoid comparing statistics that have different bases.
5. Avoid using group statistics that hide important differences among subgroups.

EXHIBIT 7.10
Are They Really Related?

Trying to show the relationship between two events or trends is a common challenge in public speaking, such as trying to show that the release of a toxic chemical into the water supply caused an increase in a certain disease. However, verifying such a relationship can be difficult, even impossible in some cases. Keep in mind the three levels at which data can be related and don't jump to conclusions about cause-and-effect relationships. With coincidence, A and B may happen at the same time in some cases but at different times in other cases. There is no relationship at all. With correlation, A and B happen (or move up or down or whatever) together, but not because one is causing the other to do so. With a cause-and-effect relationship, A really does cause B to happen.

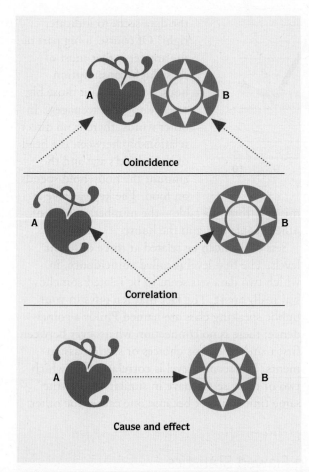

Attendance at baseball games may increase as temperatures start to increase in spring, but weather doesn't *cause* baseball. The two are related to a third variable (season), but not to each other. The third level is **cause and effect**, in which changes in one set of data actually do cause changes in the other set. An increase in snowfall might cause an increase in traffic

accidents, for instance. The two aren't just happening at the same time; one is causing the other (see Exhibit 7.10).

Anyone who's ever seen teenagers eat could figure out the right statistical relationship in the earlier example about food consumption in U.S. households. However, a visitor from Mars might not know that human parents between 35 and 44 often have teenagers in the house or that teenagers can eat from morning to night. You'll be like the visitor from Mars when you venture into unfamiliar subject areas. You'll uncover statistical links that seem to make perfect sense but only because you aren't aware of everything that's going on. It's your responsibility as a speaker to make sure you're not implying cause-and-effect relationships where they don't exist.

Unfortunately, these relationships aren't always this simple because the relationships between data aren't always clear. You won't always be able to tell whether the relationship is cause and effect, correlation, or simply coincidence. People trying to influence public opinion take advantage of this confusion all the time. A classic example is the voter poll taken during a presidential election campaign that asks whether you're better off now than you were four years ago. The implication, of course, is that the person who's been running the country for the last four years has done a good job or a bad job (depending on who's asking the question).

Next time you hear this question, ask yourself this: "What possible connection is there between my personal situation and the president's job performance over the last four years?" If you

IMPROVING YOUR CRITICAL THINKING

DO YOUR SPEECHES PASS THE LOGIC TEST?

Play in the snow without a jacket, and you'll catch a cold. Run outside on a cold morning with your hair still wet from the shower, and you'll catch a cold. We've all heard variations of these warnings, but there is no actual medical evidence to suggest that exposure to lower temperatures increases your chances of catching the common cold. Nevertheless, millions of parents continue to pass these warnings on to their children, who pass them on to their children, and on and on.

Think about it for a minute. If being in cold temperatures leads to catching a cold, people who live in icy climates would have colds all winter long, whereas people who live in mild climates would never or rarely catch colds, right? Plus, you wouldn't get colds in the spring, summer, or autumn, right? Wrong. With just a little logic, you can see that the "catch a cold" warnings are not true.

How many times have you heard people tell you to bundle up so you won't catch a cold, when medical science has known for a long time that viruses, not temperature, cause the common cold?

Most cases of the common cold are caused by one of more than 200 viruses. Although people get more colds in the winter, there is no identifiable link with temperature. Perhaps we're just indoors more with the windows closed, breathing each other's air and coming into physical contact more often. So why do so many of us continue to believe something that is so easy to disprove? Because we don't stop to think. We believe things we see or hear without stopping to ask ourselves, "Does this really make sense?"

Don't fall into this trap when you're gathering support materials for your speech. Examine your claims and statistics to see whether they pass even the simplest tests of logic. If something doesn't make sense, don't use it.

things get murky. Say you lost your job last year because your company went out of business. Was this the president's fault? Perhaps if he led the country down some perilous economic path and your company folded because the economy collapsed, you could say so. But what if your bosses mismanaged the company or aggressive competitors did a better job of satisfying customers? Any one of dozens of causes may have produced the effect of your losing your job.

If you can't be sure of a statistical relationship, be very careful about how you present the data to your audience. Even mentioning two facts or conclusions in the same speech is enough to cause many listeners to draw some sort of connection, even if you don't. If you aren't sure of the relationship, tell your

were hit by a bus or won the lottery, your situation would have changed dramatically—and the president would have had absolutely nothing to do with it. In between these two extremes is where

audience not to assume any relationship. If you demonstrate a sincere desire not to misuse statistical data but to use it as ethically as possible, you'll impress the audience with your integrity.

SAMPLE SPEECH

Soft Landings, Gentle Breezes:
The Lure of Hot-Air Ballooning

(1) The French writer and philosopher Michel de Montaigne once said, "It's the journey that counts, not the arrival." Thousands of hot-air balloonists agree, and every night around sunset, they take off in flying contraptions you and I might consider untrustworthy—little more than a silken bag of air, described by some as "an upside down Christmas ornament" or "a kitchen stove with a garbage bag suspended over it."

(2) In the United States alone, 2,000 licensed sport balloonists find balloon flight one of the most peaceful ways to travel. Frank Reed owns Sunset Balloon Flights in Southern California and has been taking people up in balloons for more than 15 years. He says, "When I take off, I don't know exactly where I'm going to land; that's part of the romance and adventure of it."

It's fairly easy to enjoy that romance and adventure for yourself. But before I tell you how and where you can try ballooning, let me tell you how it started.

(3) Two French brothers, Jacques and Joseph Montgolfier, invented the hot-air balloon more than 200 years ago. They started by warming the air inside a paper bag and letting it float to the ceiling. They thought that if they could just make a bag big enough, they might be able to send a human being into the sky—something that had never been done before.

(4) By September of 1783, King Louis XVI, Marie Antoinette, and a crowd of onlookers watched the Montgolfier brothers coax a sheep, a rooster, and a duck into a basket beneath a 41-foot paper-and-fabric balloon in the garden at Versailles. The brothers then lit a wood fire in a brazier strapped inside the basket. The crowd cheered as it lifted off, rising 1700 feet, sailing two miles in eight minutes, and landing safely in a nearby forest. Success!

(5) Two months later, in November, the Montgolfier brothers put a soldier and a scientist into a basket beneath an elaborately decorated, blue-and-gold balloon. After drifting over Paris for 25 minutes, the two passengers landed five and a half miles away—the first humans to conquer the skies! But by December, another pair of brothers launched the first hydrogen-filled balloon, and hot-air ballooning was already on its way out.

(6) The Montgolfier balloons did have some flaws. During landings, the basket often tipped over so that the fire in the brazier ignited the paper balloon—with disastrous results. Also, the brothers added manure to their fires, thinking the foul smell was a gas that helped produce lift. They were wrong, of course, but the odor could be why hot air soon fell out of favor with balloonists.

(7) Not until the 1960s did an engineer named Ed Yost use liquid propane stored in small fuel tanks to produce a flame that heated the balloon—no manure required! For the bag, called the "envelope," he used nylon or polyester, coated with polyurethane for durability—and the modern sport balloon was born! Its popularity has spread like airborne spores across North America, Europe, Africa, Australia—anywhere smooth terrain, gentle winds, and mild weather combine to make balloonists feel welcome. The Balloon Federation of America counts its international membership at 4,000 and growing.

(8) That means there are plenty of places to try ballooning, but you may have the same questions I did: (1) How do I know it is safe? and (2) How much does it cost?

(9) Let me reassure you on the first count. Some commercial balloons are as tall as a 9-story building and hold up to 10 passengers. Others are about half as high, around 40 feet, and hold only three passengers. Most still use wicker baskets, called gondolas, because wicker "gives" a bit during rough landings. Strong cables

Commentary

This creative speech was presented using slides of balloons in flight as visual aids. The speaker also used many other techniques of support to communicate substantial amounts of what could be dry information in this informative speech.

(1) The speaker assumes that her listeners have not experienced hot-air ballooning, so she prepares them for the information she will convey. Her opening quote expresses the attitude or state of mind that's part of the appeal of hot-air ballooning, and her quoted analogies underline her point that hot-air balloons appear to be flimsy contraptions—drawing support from her listeners as outside, "skeptical" observers.

(2) With the stage creatively set, the statistic in the first sentence now carries added meaning: not just "2,000 balloonists," but 2,000 brave individuals so enamored of "the journey" that they're willing to fly in these flimsy contraptions. The speaker then establishes the credibility of her expert, whose words support the enthusiasm of the opening quotation.

(3) Now that her audience is intrigued, the speaker can take time to introduce historical facts, but she makes them interesting by relating them in narrative form.

(4) The speaker integrates dates and flight statistics with the narrative in a lively and creative way, making them more meaningful and easier for the audience to interpret.

(5) Reciting too many historical dates can numb listeners, who probably won't retain this information anyway. Here the speaker puts the date in context ("two months later") to convey the speed with which the inventors moved toward their achievement.

(6) The speaker uses examples to explain why hot-air balloons lost favor. She's able to inject light humor throughout the speech because it works well with the subject matter.

(7) Again, the date is given in a context that gives it added meaning. In the last two sentences, the speaker introduces her point about the growth of the sport by using a colorful analogy, then backing it up with a supporting statistic from a reputable source.

(8) By introducing the two questions in this transition paragraph, the speaker can follow up with a factual passage that conveys information in a meaningful context. She lays the groundwork for supplying facts that demonstrate the safety of hot-air ballooning, slowly shifting her own and her listeners' perspective from the skepticism of the speech's opening.

(9) The speaker combines straight figures with analogies and comparisons to make this factual paragraph easier to comprehend.

attach the gondola to the balloon. Only a few instruments are needed, plus a two-way radio and a vent lever for quick deflation.

(10) Hot-air balloons function so simply, they can be launched in about 15 minutes. Stretch it out on the ground, inspect it carefully, and then fire up a portable blower that pushes cold air inside the envelope. Start warming that air, and the balloon pops upright. Then keep warming the air until it's hotter than the surrounding atmosphere, and the gondola slowly lifts off the ground. The crew lets go and you're off!

(11) The first thing you notice is the quiet. No wind blows against you because you're moving with it. And the view is unsurpassed: 360 degrees of earth and sky. Periodically your pilot breaks the awesome silence with a sharp, hissing pull on the overhead blast valve, which shoots a long flame up toward the hollow center of the balloon.

(12) Because she can't steer the balloon like a car or an airplane, your pilot changes altitude to find a wind going her way. She maintains the envelope temperature to stay level, warms it to rise, and lets it cool to fall. Meanwhile, she's keeping in touch with your "chase" crew, who are speeding along back roads with your picnic, trying to second-guess your landing site.

(13) Most balloon injuries, and a few fatalities, have occurred when balloons struck power lines or when passengers bounced out of the gondola during rough landings. Frank Reed advises you to choose a pilot who knows the area well and to hold on tight during landings. He also reminds you that, statistically, the greatest danger is probably the drive home after your champagne picnic.

(14) Okay, it sounds safe—but how much does it cost? That depends on you. Commercial balloon operators usually charge $100 to $150 for a one- or two-hour champagne flight. Some companies will let you earn free flight time by crewing a few launches.

(15) If cost isn't an issue, several international companies offer deluxe ballooning vacations over France, England, Australia, the Swiss Alps—even the African veldt. The views of castles, mountains, and elephants are said to be breathtaking, and so is the price—from $2,000 to $8,000 per person.

(16) Or for about the cost of a new sports car ($10,000–$50,000), you can buy your own balloon. If you fly about 50 hours a year—the national average, according to *The Ultimate Adventure Sourcebook*—your annual operating costs should run between $4,000 and $5,000.

(17) Even if you don't want to fly, you can enjoy a balloon fiesta. Imagine watching 650 rainbow-colored balloons lift off at sunrise in a simultaneous "mass ascension." It happens every October at the Albuquerque, New Mexico, International Balloon Fiesta, one of the world's largest.

(18) For some brave souls, the ultimate balloon adventure is offered by a company in Los Angeles, called "Cowabungee." Licensed balloonists will gladly take you up and toss you overboard for a hundred-foot free-fall on a bungee harness. You'll make 75-foot yo-yo bounces for a few minutes before they set you back down. I believe they ask you to pay up front, and the cost is about $99. That includes a videotape, in case you don't want to try it again.

(19) Which brings me to the Balloonist's Prayer. I'd like to leave you with these words, traditionally recited at the end of your flight, with champagne glasses held high: "May the winds welcome you with softness; May the sun bless you with his warm hands; May you fly so high and so well that God joins you in laughter and sets you gently back in the loving arms of Mother Earth. Soft landings, gentle breezes throughout life!"

And don't forget your camera!

(10) Now the speaker shifts from simply relating facts about modern balloons to engaging her audience in another narrative. This time, by implication, the listener plays the leading role in the story.

(11) Imagine how dull this material might have been if not related in narrative form. The speaker has used her creativity to put her audience right in the middle of the action, so that every fact comes alive with purpose and meaning.

(12) Once again the speaker uses a subtle shift in perspective to educate her listeners: by using the feminine pronoun when talking about the balloon pilot, she tells her audience, without making a direct statement, that women pilots are as common as men among balloonists.

(13) A widely recognized statistic (supported by the already-established expert and conveyed without numbers) bolsters the speaker's point that ballooning is at least as safe as driving—if not safer.

(14) Throughout the next few paragraphs, the speaker must convey facts and numbers in an interesting way. To add interest and significance, she takes a light approach, playing her figures against one another and against her listeners' attitudes toward fun, sport, and money.

(15) Note the contrast between the breathtaking view and the cost.

(16) The speaker balances facts and sources with a descriptive analogy.

(17) An example demonstrates why watching a ballooning fiesta could be fun.

(18) Subtle humor and narrative technique put the listener in the action once again, but the speaker is still conveying useful information.

(19) The lengthy quotation provides a good balance with the previous paragraph, bringing the audience back to the peaceful, light mood of the speech's opening, emphasizing again the appeal of hot-air ballooning, which has been built gradually throughout this creative informative speech.

SUMMARY

Supporting your ideas is essential to your speech because it gives your audience a reason to believe the things you say. When audience members have fewer doubts, they are more likely to change their beliefs, attitudes, or actions, and your speech will be more likely to accomplish your goals. The main types of support are examples and analogies, narratives, testimony and quotations, and statistics and facts.

You can use analogies to help your audience understand new ideas by comparing the new idea with a concept they already understand. Literal analogies are comparisons between two things or concepts that are the same: two people, two cities, two situations, and so forth. Figurative analogies are comparisons between two things or concepts that are fundamentally different but that have some structure or process in common.

Narratives can improve speeches because most people like listening to a well-told story. Even if the narrative takes only half a dozen sentences, your audience will pay attention to see what happened to your character(s). As long as the narrative flows well with your speech and supports your central idea, it can be an effective way to communicate.

Both quotations and testimony involve someone else's statements. With testimony, you're interested in information. The three types of testimony are expert, prestige, and lay or peer. With quotations, you're interested in the actual words another person wrote or said. Testimony does carry some ethical responsibilities. If you paraphrase someone else's words, you have a responsibility to convey the essence of their thoughts and opinions accurately.

You also need to understand the biases and motivations of your sources because these may influence the accuracy or appropriateness of the information you'll be using in your speech. In addition, your audience will often give expert testimony the same weight as statistical evidence, so you need to make sure that the testimony you use is truly representative. Don't use an opinion from the minority to represent the opinion of the majority.

You'll run across two kinds of statistics when you're researching support materials. Descriptive statistics make data easier to understand by summarizing and analyzing masses of facts. Inferential statistics help you draw conclusions or make estimates about a group of things by taking a look at a portion, or sample, of the things in that group. Opinion polls are a common application of inferential statistics.

As a speaker, it's your job to use statistics accurately and responsibly. Guidelines to help you are (1) make sure you understand what the numbers really mean before you use them, (2) don't overload your audience with numbers, (3) help your audience interpret the numbers you use in your speech, and (4) watch out for statistics that come from biased sources or that were compiled inaccurately.

KEY TERMS

analogy (138)
average (147)
cause and effect (153)
coincidence (153)
correlation (153)
descriptive statistics (146)
dialogue (142)
example (138)
expert testimony (143)
facts (145)
factual examples (138)
figurative analogy (141)
hypothetical examples (138)
inferential statistics (146)
lay testimony (144)
literal analogy (141)
margin of error (149)
mean (147)
median (147)
mode (147)
narrative (141)
paraphrase (144)
prestige testimony (143)
quotations (143)
sample (146)
standard deviation (148)
statistics (145)
support materials (137)
testimony (143)
verbatim (144)

APPLY CRITICAL THINKING

1. If you were preparing a presentation on the side effects of a new drug, would you use the same type and amount of support when addressing doctors as when addressing patients? Why or why not?

2. In the mayor's election, the two candidates used statistics to support their positions on crime in the city. However, one said crime had gone up, and the other said crime had gone down. Speculate on how both might have used statistics to "prove" opposing positions.

3. Decide whether the following phrase is a factual or a hypothetical example, and explain: "Suppose you had met the president when you visited Washington, D.C., last month."

4. If the mean IQ of freshmen has a standard deviation of 25 points, and the mean IQ of sophomores has a standard deviation of 20 points, which group tends to be closer to the mean?

5. Would you recommend a figurative analogy or a literal analogy for a speech to young children about the dangers of drug abuse? Why?

6. Could a narrative that involved something from your high school days possibly backfire in a speech to your current college classmates? Explain your answer.

7. Would testimony from a singer on the subject of cultural censorship be expert testimony or prestige testimony? Why?

SHARPEN YOUR SKILLS

Individual Exercises

1. Listen to a political speech or debate on radio or television. How many kinds of support does the speaker use for the point(s) being made? Is the support convincing?

2. Find the most persuasive piece of support you can for one of the following propositions:

    a. Quality of life is better today than it was 30 years ago.

    b. U.S. cars are every bit as good as Japanese cars.

    c. Going to college is a good idea.

3. Find an example of an inferential statistic and a descriptive statistic. Which one do you find most believable? Why?

4. Create a figurative analogy and a literal analogy for one of the following (you can pick different items for the two analogies):

    a. The feeling of relief when a migraine headache disappears

    b. Falling in love

    c. Buying a car

    d. Sending electronic mail to people you've never met in person

5. Develop a short narrative on one of the following topics:

    a. A lesson you learned about the value of hard work

    b. A discovery you made about how wonderful people can be

    c. A discovery you made that damaged your faith in your fellow human beings

6. Develop a short personal narrative to complete one of the following sentences:

    a. An important communication event that changed my life occurred when . . .

    b. I learned the meaning of "best friend" when . . .

    c. A funny thing happened to me on my way to . . .

Group Exercises

7. Have four or five students listen to the same speech or read the same newspaper editorial and discuss whether the supporting material provided by the speaker or writer was sufficiently persuasive.

8. For this exercise, you need two teams, each with three or four students. Assign one team to gather evidence supporting the idea that pollution is getting worse every year, and the other team to gather evidence supporting the position that pollution is getting better every year. Once you've collected your evidence, take turns presenting your supporting materials to the class, and see which team is most convincing.

9. With three other students, do the research needed to create a profile of the "average" U.S. citizen, using income, family status, education, and any other variable you can find. Now check yourselves against this average. How many of you feel close to this average? How does it feel now when people talk about the average citizen?

10. With three or four other students, choose a process, such as driving a car, planning a speech, or something else that you can all agree on. Each student must think of an analogy to help explain this process to someone who's never done it before. Finally, compare your analogies. Which is most effective? Why?

GATHERING YOUR SUPPORT MATERIALS

LEARNING OBJECTIVES

After studying this chapter, you will be able to

1. List the general steps to follow for researching any speech topic.

2. Explain the pros and cons of using your own personal experience as a source for speeches.

3. Plan and conduct a successful personal interview.

4. Identify the four major categories of research materials available in libraries.

5. List the five types of reference books you can use for research.

6. Differentiate the four classes of periodicals.

7. Describe the two major online research options besides libraries.

FINDING MATERIALS TO SUPPORT YOUR SPEECH

*Y*ou have a great idea for a speech, you understand your audience, and you know how to use support materials. Now you just have to find those materials. That may seem like a formidable task to you right now. However, if you approach research in the right way, you'll prepare an effective speech and polish some skills that will be valuable to you in many different courses. The purpose of this chapter is to help you locate whatever materials you need to support your speech.

Conducting research is like being on a treasure hunt. Of course, you'll rarely find a pot of gold just waiting for you to pick up. In other words, you probably won't find a nice, complete package of information sitting on a library shelf with your name on it. Sometimes you can be that lucky, but most of the time your clues will lead you to a pile of disorganized information that you'll have to sort through and summarize. It would be nice to look in the card catalog under "Five-minute persuasive speeches" and find everything you need, but unfortunately that doesn't happen.

Another point to keep in mind is that different subjects have varying levels and kinds of research materials available. One subject might be covered primarily in high-level academic journals, whereas another might be covered only in popular magazines or books. Good advice bears repeating: Start early so that you have plenty of time to find the materials required. Don't expect to log onto the Internet the night before a speech is due and find everything you need.

Before exploring the main sources of support material, consider the following general process you can follow to conduct your research. Not all speeches will require every step, but you can usually follow this basic approach (see Exhibit 8.1):

1. *Start with a clearly identified speech topic.* Be sure to follow the advice in Chapter 5 about selecting and narrowing your speech topic. By starting with a clear and narrow topic, you're sure not to waste time.
2. *Don't start in the library.* You probably chose your topic because it interests you, and you probably know something about it already. Start by writing down everything you know about your topic.[1] This list may spark some ideas about where to find other materials.
3. *Try to find a quick overview of the subject.* Imagine that the information you'll need is all in a dark room. You can stumble around and pick up one thing at time, or you can turn on the light and see where everything is. A subject overview from an encyclopedia or other reference can be that light. It might save you a lot of time stumbling around in the dark.
4. *Don't be afraid to ask a librarian for help.* A few minutes of guidance can save you hours of lost time and lots of frustration. However, it's important to ask for help with as much focus as possible, describing your topic and specific purpose clearly to the librarian.
5. *Order materials that need to be gathered from other locations.* Even the biggest and best funded

EXHIBIT 8.1
Finding Materials to Support Your Speech
Following a logical process for doing your research will save both time and effort.

The research steps are as follows:

1 Start with a clearly identified speech topic.

2 Don't start in the library.

3 Try to find a quick overview of the subject.

4 Don't be afraid to ask a librarian for help.

5 Order materials that need to be gathered from other locations.

6 Devise a plan to collect data that aren't available anywhere else.

7 Consult reference books.

8 Find articles that cover your topic.

9 Identify books that cover your topic.

10 Use other research materials as needed.

college library may not have the one piece of information you badly need for a speech. You might need to ask your library to borrow a source from another library, or you may need to order information from a company or a government agency. Try to identify these external sources as early as possible to increase your chances of receiving them in time.

6. *Devise a plan to collect data that aren't available anywhere else.* As you'll see in this chapter, there is more to conducting research than digging through books and magazines. In some cases, you'll want to hit the streets and get the data yourself, through interviews perhaps. Collecting this sort of information can also take time, so start early.

7. *Consult reference books.* The category of "reference books" includes some you're familiar with, such as encyclopedias and dictionaries, and many specialized volumes you may use once in your life. Some references (encyclopedias in particular) may provide the quick overview you need to get started. Others offer more detailed information but require you to have some idea of what you're looking for.

8. *Find articles that cover your topic.* Thousands of magazine, journal, and newspaper articles are published every year. You'll rely on these resources for two key reasons: to get information that's up to date (and not yet found in books) and to get information that probably won't ever be found in books (such as stories about everyday people and minor news events).

9. *Identify books that cover your topic.* Nonreference books make up most of every library's collection. Use the card catalog to identify the shelf location of books on your

EXHIBIT 8.2
Using Different Kinds of Sources
All magazines and journals are not created equal. Here are the types of articles you can expect to find in a popular magazine, a more literate current affairs magazine, and an academic journal.

FATAL PURSUIT

Behind a zany Mountain Dew ad lies the sad saga of the death of pro skydiver Rob Harris

LETTER FROM PYONGYANG

IN THE LAND OF THE DEAR LEADER

North Korea's grand situation begins to unravel
By Orville Schell

JOURNAL OF SECOND LANGUAGE WRITING, 4 (3), 253-272 (1995)

The Use of Metadiscourse in Good and Poor ESL Essays

Puangpen Intaraprawat
Margaret S. Steffensen
Illinois State University

subject, and then browse around this part of the collection to see what's available. Keep in mind that these books weren't written to give readers quick access to topics, so consulting them will usually be more time-consuming than consulting reference books or periodicals.

10. *Use other research materials as needed.*
Don't forget to consult such materials as maps, brochures, reports, government documents, the Internet, and electronic resources of various sorts. As the least-organized resources, these materials can be the hardest to use.

Once you've collected your materials, it's a good idea to organize them before digging into them. Say you're researching the subject of depression and find four articles: One is in the *Journal of Applied Psychology*, one is in *The Atlantic*, one is in *Newsweek*, and the fourth is in your local newspaper. Should you read all of these from front to back? Probably not, at least not to begin with. Start with the sources that are likely to be easy, short, and general; then work your way up to the more involved, specialized sources (see Exhibit

Success Tip
It may be beyond your budget now, but when you're on the job, consider the services of an *information broker* or *freelance researcher*. These specialists know how to locate the hard-to-find information you may need for a speech.

8.2). In this example, the newspaper article is easy to read and probably presents current information on the subject, but not in any depth. As a news magazine, *Newsweek* probably covers trends and notable recent events, possibly with some background on the subject. As a popular but fairly intellectual magazine, *The Atlantic* provides in-depth coverage. In fact, the article might be five or ten times longer than the *Newsweek* article. Skim it first to see whether it really covers the subject you're interested in. The article in the *Journal of Applied Psychology* was written for experienced specialists in a particular field, and unless you're a psychology major, you might get very little from it. You may be able to dig out some research conclusions or other bits, but that might be about all you find.

The key to conducting research is putting your efforts into those areas that will be the most profitable. Once you have clearly identified your speech topic and specific purpose, you'll want to conduct your research wisely. So before exploring the wide variety of printed and electronic research materials available, take a moment to look at one of the best resources around, and one that is available only to you: yourself.

DRAWING FROM PERSONAL EXPERIENCE

For some speeches, your own experiences and knowledge will be the primary source of material. Even if you don't think you've led an interesting or exciting life so far, you still have quite a storehouse of information, emotions, and moral lessons. Even if you've built your speech around other sources, your own experiences can add personal interest and insights. In fact, many experienced speakers keep files of material that they can quickly assemble into speeches, and these files contain everything from magazine articles to personal memories.[2]

Chances are you picked a speech topic that you knew something about or at least cared about, so start with an inventory of what you already know. A good way to jog your memory is to mull over the major events in your life:

- *Successes.* Success can be something as enjoyable as winning the state basketball championship (and learning about teamwork or leadership) or as dramatic as working your way out of dire financial straits (and learning more about government assistance, the causes of unemployment, or the value of true friendship).
- *Failures.* We've all failed at something in our lives. Did you learn anything from the failure, either about yourself or the world around you?
- *Losses.* Unfortunately, loss is as much a part of life as success and happiness. And like failure, loss can be a very instructive experience. For instance, losing a parent or someone else you love may have given you the opportunity to think about what it means to be part of a family.
- *Emergencies.* From taking a ride in an ambulance to helping rescue your neighbors from a flood, emergencies offer both opportunities and motivations to learn more about a huge variety of topics. If you had experienced a flood disaster, for example, you might have learned more about a variety of topics: the difficulty of forecasting the weather, the risks of channeling rivers, or the complexities of flood insurance and government regulations.
- *Adventures.* Like emergencies, dramatic or interesting adventures no doubt left you with information and emotions as well. Whether the adventure took place in some exotic location across the world or while using the Internet in your dorm room, it can provide both the spark of interest and the supporting detail you need to carry a speech.

Using personal experience as research materials for a speech has both advantages and disadvantages. On the positive side, it infuses your speech

---

Checklist for Using Your Own Experience for Supporting Materials

1. Track personal, academic, or professional successes.
2. Reflect on a personal, academic, or professional failure.
3. Recall the loss of someone or something that meant a lot to you.
4. Look back at an emergency situation that taught you something about yourself or the systems available to support people.
5. Recollect an interesting or exciting adventure.

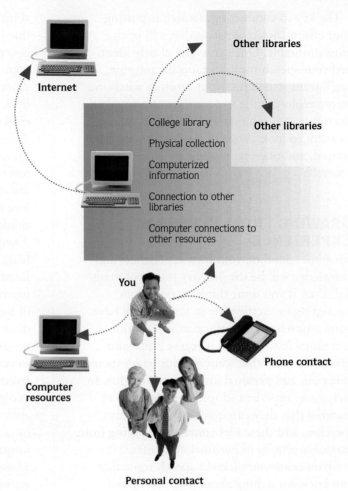

EXHIBIT 8.3
Using Today's Research Tools
To get the most from your research, take advantage of all the resources at your disposal.

Internet

Other libraries

College library
Physical collection
Computerized information
Connection to other libraries
Computer connections to other resources

Other libraries

You

Phone contact

Computer resources

Personal contact

with human interest and emotion that you can't get from library research. Personal experience can bring a speech to life and make it more interesting. This can also help you relax because it's easier to be confident when talking about a subject you know so well. It also gives you (and your audience) access to a pool of information that may not be available from any other source. On the negative side, personal experience may not present a complete or unbiased picture of a subject area—which simply means that you should try to balance your experience with some objective, external materials.

USING LIBRARIES AND OTHER INFORMATION RESOURCES

"Library research" used to be a fairly simple concept. You went into the actual library and flipped through the card catalog to find books and scoured the periodicals indexes to find magazine and journal articles. It's not that simple anymore, but you can often find a lot more information in a lot less time using today's information tools (see Exhibit 8.3).

Before entering the library, be aware of the most important resource there: the librarians. They spend their days managing information and helping people find materials, and they know how to get the information you need. Visit the reference desk, where the staff is trained in research techniques. Try to be as specific as possible when requesting help (which should be easy if you did a

good job narrowing your speech topic and determining a specific purpose). Also, try to visit during the day, when most of the experienced reference librarians will be at work.[3]

You're probably already familiar with the basic tool for finding things in the library, the card catalog. Most college and university libraries now have online catalogs, but you may have to use the card catalog if you're at a smaller school or if your library hasn't been able to computerize all its records (this is sometimes the case with older books). If you need help using either type of catalog, the library staff will be happy to help.

If you haven't already done so, this is a good time to take an orientation tour of the library, a workshop on research, or one of the other learning opportunities that practically all college and

EXHIBIT 8.4
Multidimensional Answers from a Multimedia Encyclopedia
Computer-based and online encyclopedias can provide audio tracks, video clips, and animation to enhance the presentation of information.

university libraries offer. Ask to see a copy of *The American Library Association Guide to Information Access*. This book provides both a general guide to library resources and detailed instructions on conducting research in 26 topic areas, from agriculture to writing. It also provides a good overview of electronic research tools, from online catalogs to the Internet.[4] If you understand the library and its resources, you'll spend less time researching your speeches and more time developing better speeches.

Reference Books

Reference books are designed to provide quick access to specific pieces of information, whether you need the definition of a word, an overview of a subject, or a single fact. Some references try to cover the entire field of human knowledge and accomplishment; others are much narrower. Here's a look at the major works you're likely to find in your library.[5]

Encyclopedias and Dictionaries

Since elementary school, you've used encyclopedias for research. They can still help you, mostly because they provide an overview of a subject area. You'll find cross references, suggestions

Success Tip
Develop a healthy skepticism about everything you uncover in research. Don't put yourself in the position of passing faulty data on to your audience.

for additional reading, and even the names of experts in a particular field. Encyclopedias fall into four categories:

- *Multiple-volume printed encyclopedias.* The biggest names in this category are *The New Encyclopaedia Britannica* and the *Encyclopedia Americana*. Several printed encyclopedias now offer indexes on CD-ROM to speed the search process.
- *Single-volume printed encyclopedias.* These are of less value for your research because they offer much less information, but they can provide quick introductions to subject areas. The best known are *The Columbia Encyclopedia* and *The Random House Encyclopedia*.
- *CD-ROM and online encyclopedias.* Two of the best known in this group are *Microsoft Encarta* and *Compton's Multimedia Encyclopedia*. Compared to printed encyclopedias, electronic encyclopedias make it easier to trace specific topics, although they're not always as easy to flip through at random. Also, CD-ROM encyclopedias often provide sound, video, and animation (see Exhibit 8.4). Websites for Encyclopedia.com, Encyclopædia Britannica, and Columbia Encyclopedia also give you access to online encyclopedias.
- *Specialized encyclopedias.* You can find multiple- and single-volume encyclopedias that cover particular subject areas, including art, philosophy, religion, sociology, technology, and ethnic

studies. Expect these to be more in-depth and more difficult to read in many cases.

You may not think about consulting a dictionary while preparing a speech, but it can be a useful resource in some cases. Specialized dictionaries that cover technical and professional fields can help you understand the terminology in the subject area you've chosen. To explore the history of a particular word, which can help you put a subject in both historical and social context, consult the mammoth *Oxford English Dictionary (OED).* The *OED* is available in print (20 volumes or the compact two-volume edition) and on CD-ROM.

Directories

You've been using the most important directory of all for years: the telephone book. More than 14,000 directories of various kinds are published in the United States, covering everything from accountants to zoos. Some of these are telephone directories, of course, but many include membership information for all kinds of special interest groups. No matter what speech topic you come up with, chances are that an association of some kind is fighting for it, fighting against it, making money on it, or just enjoying it as a hobby. The *Encyclopedia of Associations* can put you in touch with groups that might be happy to provide information for your speeches.

Biographical References

If you need to know more about a famous (or at least important) person for your speech, the information might be found in one of the many biographical references available in printed form, on CD-ROM, and online. Start with *Who's Who in America* and *Who's Who in the World,* which are available separately as printed volumes and together on a CD-ROM called the *Complete Marquis Who's Who Plus.* The *Who's Who* directories contain brief descriptions of the backgrounds and accomplishments of tens of thousands of notable (and still living) people. If the person you're interested in is deceased, try *Who Was Who in America.*

If you need more information on a historical figure, try the *Dictionary of American Biography.* It offers detailed biographies of roughly 18,000 people who died before 1971. You might also try one of the biographical indexes; these don't contain the information, but they can tell you where to find it. *Biography Index* and *Current Biography* are two notable sources.[6] Of course, if the person is truly famous or important, entire books have probably been written about his or her life.

Almanacs and Statistical Sources

Almanacs are collections of various statistics and other facts. You can quickly find information about countries, politics, the labor force, natural accidents, and so on. Whenever you're looking for a specific figure about almost any subject, consider starting with an almanac. Even if it doesn't give you the answer, you'll spend no more than a few minutes looking. The *Information Please Almanac,* the *World Almanac and Book of Facts,* and the *Universal Almanac* are the best known.

Do you need to know the average wind speed in New Orleans or the amount of aid the U.S. government gave the government of Portugal last year? Both numbers are available in the *Statistical Abstract of the United States,* published annually by the U.S. Department of Commerce. This mind-boggling collection can be extremely useful for backing up your speeches with statistics about life, work, and government in the United States. Whether you're interested in population patterns, health issues, business, crime, or the environment, you'll find more than 1,400 tables of statistics. The *Statistical Abstract* is one of several statistical handbooks that provide a mass of details about every aspect of the contemporary world. Many are also now available on CD-ROM.[7]

Quotation Books

Every library has a selection of quotation books that you can search by topic to find witty or insightful quotes from political leaders, writers, artists, and other famous people. The best known of these books is *Bartlett's Familiar Quotations.*

The tens of thousands of quotes in Bartlett's range from ancient Egypt, the Bible, and Confucius to people from the present day. The *Oxford Dictionary of Quotations* is another key source of quotes. Your library may also offer references that specialize in quotations from women, people from particular religious groups, and people from particular ethnic groups.

Don't limit your quotation search to serious, academic books. You can find some great material for introductions, transitions, and conclusions in the growing number of popular books that cover quotations, slip-ups, and other linguistic tidbits. For instance, if you wanted to talk about how things change (or don't change) over time, you might pick the worn out cliché that thousands of speakers have used: "The more things change, the more they stay the same." It might do the job, but it's been used too many times. Instead, try this amusing slip-up from former President Gerald Ford: "Things are more like they are now than they have ever been."[8] If you're comfortable using humor and the context is appropriate, such an alternative phrase would be much fresher. Here are a few of the off-beat reference books that offer interesting quotes:

- *The 776 Stupidest Things Ever Said*, by Ross and Kathryn Petras. (This is the source of the Ford quote.)
- *Rotten Reviews: A Literary Companion,* by Bill Henderson. (Example: "He is like a man trying to run in a dozen directions at once, succeeding thereby merely in standing still and making a lot of noise."—V. S. Pritchett, in a review of John Dos Passos's novel *The 42nd Parallel.*)
- *The Curmudgeon's Garden of Love*, by Jon Winokur. (Example: "If love is the answer, could you rephrase the question?"—Lily Tomlin.)
- *The 637 Best Things Anybody Ever Said*, by Robert Byrne. (Example: "Humankind cannot bear very much reality."—T. S. Eliot.)
- *The Guinness Book of Poisonous Quotes,* by Colin Jarman. (Example: "Like most poets, preachers and metaphysicians, he burst into conclusions at a spark of evidence."—Henry Seidel Canby referring to Ralph Waldo Emerson.)
- *The Dark Side: Thoughts on the Futility of Life from the Ancient Greeks to the Present,* by Alan R. Pratt. (Example: "There is no moral precept that does not have something inconvenient about it."—Denis Diderot.)

These volumes may be easier to find in a retail bookstore; they may not be available in your library. However, you can see from even this short list how much spice you can add to your speeches with amusing or thought-provoking quotes. With a little imagination, you can work these gems into a variety of speaking situations. The point here is, don't settle for the tried and true; don't use a quotation the audience has heard a thousand times before.[9]

Newspapers and Periodicals

Newspapers provide a good look at daily life—the flow of politics, crime, trends, fashion, and the

---

Checklist for Identifying Reference Books

1. Start with encyclopedias and dictionaries to get an overview of your topic.
2. Consult directories to learn where to find the information you need.
3. Check biographical references for information about famous people.
4. Use almanacs and statistical sources to get information about countries, politics, the labor force, and so on.
5. Refer to books of quotations for witty or insightful quotes.

thousands of major and minor events that mold every society. Today's news becomes tomorrow's historical records. Libraries carry only limited back issues of newspapers, for two reasons: Bulky newspapers quickly eat up storage space, and the acid in the paper causes it to decay rather quickly. However, you can access newspapers in three other ways: on microfilm, through online and CD-ROM full-text services, and through online and CD-ROM indexes. You've probably searched newspapers on microfilm for other research projects. The electronic full-text options give you access to the articles and editorials in as many as 50 or more newspapers, depending on the services your library subscribes to. The indexes let you search for key words, but they don't give you access to the actual text of the articles. For that, you need to go back either to microfilm or to a full-text source.[10]

Regular publications that aren't considered newspapers are called **periodicals.** Most periodicals fall into one of four categories: popular magazines, trade journals, business magazines, and academic journals:

- **Popular magazines** are all those publications that aren't intended for business, professional, or academic use. This group includes thousands of titles, from *People* to *Rolling Stone* to *Newsweek*. Some cover the news, and some cover particular activities or lifestyles.
- **Trade journals** cover particular professions, industries, and occupations, providing news and other information about specific jobs and industries. You might be surprised at the range of periodicals in this category, which includes such specialized journals as *Honey Producer Magazine, Police Chief, American Papermaker,* and *Heavy Duty Trucking.*
- **Business magazines** differ from specialized trade journals in that they appeal to all major industries and professions. They cover management, marketing, consumer trends, international

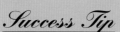

Success Tip

If your classroom is equipped with a VCR and TV, consider using a camcorder (you can rent one for a day) to collect evidence for your speech. Audiences can get a lot more excited when they see your evidence, rather than just hear you describe it. Don't turn your speech into a video presentation, however. Use the video to support your speech.

competition, government taxation and regulation, business and the environment, and other issues of concern to people involved in any aspect of business.

- **Academic journals** are the communication channels for professional researchers and educators. You probably won't benefit from them for most of your speech research. This group includes such diverse choices as *The Journal of Object-Oriented Programming, The Journal of Applied Communication Research,* and *Administrative Law Review.* They are intended to advance the state of knowledge in a particular field, not to provide the general public with information. Don't exclude them from your research, of course, but don't count on them to provide the bulk of your support materials.

Your library probably carries back issues of several hundred or more periodicals, plus a variety of tools for finding articles of interest from all four types. *The Readers' Guide to Periodical Literature* is the one you're probably most familiar with from high school and other college courses. It is available in both printed and CD-ROM formats. Other indexes, some specializing in particular subject areas, are available online and on CD-ROM. The library's online catalog may also have a periodicals index. The new *Cumulative Contents Index* provides indexing of more than 3,000 academic journals dating back to the nineteenth century.[11]

Government Documents and Agencies

By one estimate, 700,000 government employees in this country specialize in collecting and distributing information.[12] As you can imagine, those folks can generate quite a few publications every year, and their government documents can be a gold mine of support materials for your speeches. The process of getting your hands on this information can be slow and frustrating, but it does give you a way to find information not available anywhere else.

EXHIBIT 8.5
Visiting a Home Page
A unique feature of the University of Washington's website is a constantly changing view of the campus, accompanied by updated weather reports on the Seattle area.

Much of the information published by the government is distributed to the 1,400 **depository libraries** around the United States. These are public and institutional libraries selected to receive some or all of the materials in the depository program. (Check with your librarian for more information.)

Several indexes are available to help you find government documents. The Government Printing Office publishes the *Monthly Catalog of United States Government Publications*, and several companies make this information available on CD-ROM and online, as well.[13]

You've probably heard of journalists using the Freedom of Information Act (FOIA) to pry information loose from some government agencies. The agencies are required to provide the information requested but they are allowed to delete portions that the government deems too sensitive for reasons of national security or someone else's privacy. You, too, can use the FOIA to request information of interest, but it can take much more time than you have available to prepare for a speech. Taking a year or more to fill an FOIA request is not unheard of. However, it doesn't hurt to make a few phone calls to see what you might be able to get. Government agencies have an FOIA officer you can talk to about your request.[14] Check with your library's government document specialist for more information.

FINDING INFORMATION ON THE INTERNET

The **Internet**, the worldwide collection of computer networks, can be everything from a priceless resource to a frustrating waste of time. For a particular speech, you may find exactly what you're looking for in a matter of minutes, or you may find nothing of value. Research is like that, particularly on the Internet.

The most widely used part of the Internet is the World Wide Web, which enables users to search for, display, and save multimedia resources such as graphics, text, audio, and video files. A wide variety of organizations make information about themselves available to the public via the web. This information can range from a company's products and its background to the research projects underway at a large university. For instance, in a matter of minutes, you can read about new music CDs that Sony is about to release and then jump over and read about the engineering projects underway at a university halfway around the world. The information available at these websites is as diverse as the organizations that create it. Some of this information is promotional, some is educational, and some is simply entertaining. The University of Washington, for example, provides an online photograph, taken outside on campus every five minutes, so that you can see for yourself whether Seattle's climate really lives up to its gloomy reputation[15] (see Exhibit 8.5). Of course, if you want to do something useful, zip over to the university's online catalog and search for supporting materials for your speech.

Your college or university probably offers seminars or self-study information to help you navigate the Internet and find information of value. The library probably has an expert in online research who can point you in the right direction. Just like using a traditional library, the more you know about getting information from the Internet, the more efficient and effective your research will be.

Your most important tool in doing Internet research is the **search engine** (see Exhibit 8.6). Yahoo!, Google, AltaVista, Excite, Hotbot, Lycos, and Ask Jeeves are examples of search engines. Type in what you want to look for, and they search their indexes of pages and give you the results. Because the various search engines use different types of indexing, it is a good idea to use two or three search engines to find what you are looking for. The web is expanding rapidly, and new pages are being created all the time.

When using a search engines, it's tempting just to type in whatever you're looking for and see what pops up. However, it's wise to stop and ask yourself several questions before you begin your search:

- What organizations would have information on my topic?
- What keywords should I use in my search? What synonyms, variant spellings, or equivalent terms could I use?
- What related ideas or topics do I want to eliminate from my search?

When you use a keyword for your search, narrow it down as much as possible so you don't get hundreds of thousands of hits. Also, think about exactly what you're looking for. For example, suppose you want information about saddles. If you go to Google and type in "saddles," you'll get approximately 392,000 hits, including a site that sells motorcycle seats, hundreds of reference to the movie *Blazing Saddles,* an Arizona bed and breakfast called Boots and Saddles, and

the Australian Stock Saddle Company site, among others. Be sure to look at how many hits you get so you don't waste your time wading through useless information.

Most search engines offer tips on how to search. If you're looking for a phrase, type it in quotes so you'll get the whole phrase, not just separate instances of each word. If you try your Google search again and type in "English saddles"—being sure to put the phrase in quotation marks—you narrow the hits down to 7,510—still too many. On the other hand, if you don't put the phrase in quotation marks, you're going to get everything you got the first time, plus innumerable sites containing the word *English*.

You can use **Boolean operators** (named after George Boole, a 19th-century English mathematician and logician) to narrow and refine your search. The Boolean operators are AND, NOT, and OR. Some search engines use + and – instead of AND and NOT. So, for example, you could search for "saddles NOT motorcycles" or "saddles AND English" to narrow your search.

Another way to search is by subject. When you search by subject, you begin with a broad general area and narrow it down gradually to approach what you are looking for. Peer-reviewed subject directories contain links selected by subject experts. Some sites to begin your subject search include the University of California at Santa Barbara (www.library.ucsb.edu), Academic Info (www.academicinfo.net), Librarians' Index to the Internet (www.lii.org), and the Internet Public Library (www.ipl.org). Many other sites, including Yahoo!, Hotbot, and Ask Jeeves, also offer subject searches.

A **metasearch engine** is a search engine that performs a search using a number of search engines simultaneously, speeding up the process and increasing your chances of finding what you need. Examples of metasearch engines are Dogpile.com, Ixquick.com, MetaCrawler.com, Vivismo.com, and Teoma.com.

When you find an interesting page, you're very likely to find **hyperlinks**—links to other pages on the same or related subject. Hypertext links can

EXHIBIT 8.6

Using a Search Engine

Lynette Anderson needs information about intercultural communication in Afghanistan and logs on to Google, one of the most popular search engines on the Internet (www.google.com). She enters her search terms in the search window. A list of categories, all related to intercultural communication in Afghanistan, appears. Lynette can scan the results and click on "Advanced Search" above the search window that will allow her to narrow her search terms.

lead you far afield from your original page. Before you stray too far, *bookmark* any useful sites that you think you might want to come back to. Microscoft Explorer calls this feature "Favorites."

In addition to using search engines, you can use many other sources, such as virtual libraries and commercial databases, where you have a better chance of finding the specific information you need. Examples of virtual libraries are Bartleby.com, the Internet Public Library (www.ipl.org), and Britannica.com. Bartleby offers free access to full-text versions of literature, reference books, and poetry. Britannica has some free elements, but access to the entire encyclopedia is fee-based.

Your library may offer reference resources that you can access either from the library or from your own computer using a password. Some of these might be fee-based services that you can access without charge through the library.

More than 5,000 **commercial databases**, collections of information that you can access by computer, are available today. Some of these hold electronic versions of newspapers, periodicals, and other documents. Others provide data and information not available anywhere else. You can view commercial systems on three levels:

- *Systems designed for scholars and professional users.* These are the systems that the online researchers in your library use. The best known include LexisNexis (services that cover news, politics, and legal matters) and Dialog (a "gateway" to more than 450 databases that together contain several hundred million records). All of these systems have two things in common: They require special training, and they can be expensive. If you ask a librarian to conduct a search, be prepared to spend some time narrowing your topic; you may also have to pay part of the costs.
- *Systems designed for students and other users.* Several companies have been working to put

databases into the hands of people who need information but who don't have the time or money to use the professional systems. E-library (www.elibrary.com) and xrefer (www.xrefer.com) give you access to some of the most popular databases for a flat monthly fee.
- *Online systems aimed at consumers.* The major consumer systems include America Online and MSN. They offer access to some databases and other online reference information. As you might expect, these systems focus on information of interest to consumers and the general public.

For general research, you can find a number of reference sources free on the Internet. Do you need to check the spelling or definition of a word but don't want to drag out your printed Webster's? Go to Merriam-Webster Online (www.m-w.com). Need a synonym? Check out *Roget's Thesaurus* at Bartleby.com, where you can also find *Gray's Anatomy* and the complete *Columbia Encyclopedia.*

For business information, you'll probably start with the website of the particular company or organization you're interested in. Just about every major company and most small ones these days feel compelled to have an Internet presence. That presence may or may not be useful to you. Smaller companies, in particular, may have a website that is out of date, neglected, or not very informative. Still, it's worth looking. And the best sites are chock-full of information. Don't forget to check out nonprofit organizations if they are relevant to your subject.

News sources are plentiful on the web. Examples are The New York Times, Los Angeles Times, CNN, NPR, and MSNBC. See also www.newspapers.com for an index to smaller, local newspapers. This site will link you to newspapers throughout the United States and around the world. College newspapers are also indexed.

For health and medical information, you might want to start with WebMD, which is geared to

Success Tip
Avoiding plagiarism starts with good note taking. Keep your words and ideas separate from the words and ideas of your sources, and be sure to record the information you need to give your sources credit.

consumers. At the U.S. National Library of Medicine (www.nlm.nih.gov), you can search the vast medical literature.

Government sources abound on the Internet. You can isit the White House (www.whitehouse.gov), FedStats (www.fedstats.gov), the Census Bureau (www.census.gov), the Securities and Exchange Commission (www.sec.gov), the Library of Congress (www.loc.gov), and the National Archives (www.archives.gov), as well as state and local governments. Using EDGAR (Electronic Data Gathering, Analysis, and Retrieval), which is part of the SEC site, you can find the information that publicly held companies are required to file with the SEC, such as the compensation paid to high-level officers.

The Internet can be a goldmine when it comes to research. You can find people all over the world who know all kinds of things about every subject imaginable. Many will take the time to answer questions or engage in electronic discussions with you. Something about being online seems to bring out the best in many people; they'll go to great lengths to help others who are looking for information.

You can search for people who you think might have the information you need by using Yahoo People Search or AnyWho.

Along with its benefits, the Internet has its drawbacks: For one thing, information is amazingly easy to copy and distribute. Rumors and wild ideas can spread all over the world in a matter of hours, as people read and forward things they see on their computers. Myths and urban legends take on a life of their own. There are several sites where you can check out the validity of urban legends: www.snopes.com is a good place to start.

Second, unlike regular journalism, in which editors and fact checkers usually verify and approve everything writers put down on paper, many websites do not have these checks and balances. In addition, any information posted to a discussion group must be taken with a grain of salt. Discussion groups are free-for-alls in which anybody can say just about anything. Some groups monitor quality and content, but many

don't. Don't accept anything off these groups as gospel until you verify it.

For all information that you find on the Internet, ask yourself the following questions:

- Who is the author of the document? What is the author's affiliation? What are his or her qualifications or academic degrees? Is there a link to more information or a way to contact the author? Does the author have conventionally published material on this topic?
- Who sponsors the website? Is this person or organization reputable?
- Is the information current? Is a date given? Do the links work? Broken links indicate poor maintenance of a site.
- Does the content appear to be reliable and accurate? Be cautious and skeptical. If in doubt, verify it by using other sources. Doing so will help you discover which Internet sources are credible and which are not.

Finally, just as you would when doing research in the library, it is important to document your Internet sources and give credit where credit is due. Keep a record of the sites you've visited and found useful. When you retype a URL for later reference, proofread it carefully. It's best to cut and paste if possible so you don't introduce typos. With care and caution, you will reap fruitful results from your research on the Internet.

RECORDING AND USING YOUR RESEARCH

Finding all this information is just the first step, of course. Now it's time to start using what you've found. You begin with effective note taking. By taking down complete notes, you'll capture the information you need and avoid backtracking to look up something you forgot. Be sure to record bibliographic information (so that you can cite the source accurately in your speech), some indication of the subject, and whether the information is a direct quote, a paraphrase of someone else's idea, or an idea of your own.

The system that most students use (and many instructors recommend) is to take notes on three-

EXHIBIT 8.7

Sample Note Card
Whether you use a computer or note cards, taking clear, complete notes about each source is an important step in the research process.

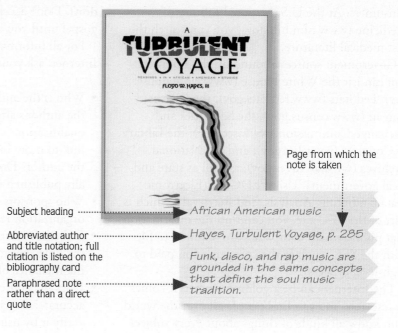

Page from which the note is taken

Subject heading ············· → *African American music*

Abbreviated author ············· → *Hayes, Turbulent Voyage, p. 285*
and title notation; full
citation is listed on the
bibliography card

Paraphrased note ············· → *Funk, disco, and rap music are*
rather than a direct *grounded in the same concepts*
quote *that define the soul music*
tradition.

by-five-inch index cards, with one thought, quote, or other piece of information per card (see Exhibit 8.7). This system has several advantages: Cards are easy to use, easy to carry around, and easy to sort and rearrange.

The card system works, without question. You won't go wrong with it. Up until very recently, people generally agreed that taking notes on a computer was slower and more cumbersome than taking them on index cards. Computers simply didn't have the tools to make this task easy, and they tended to get in the way more than they helped. However, advances in software are beginning to change this picture. Here are several ways that computers can help you capture and organize research information:

• *Organizing and outlining.* If you've used the outlining capability in a good word processor, you already know how helpful these can be. You can quickly move headings and blocks of information—about as easily as you can shuffle a deck of index cards. And outliners have a major advantage over index cards in that they let you select the amount of information you want to see at any given time. Sometimes it's hard to see where the big picture is if you have 30 or 40 pieces of detailed information lying on the table. Outliners let you collapse or expand your outline, showing as many levels as you

want. This can be a great help when you're trying to organize the flow of your speech (see Exhibit 8.8).

• *Searching.* Now where was that quote about water pollution? If you have more than a few dozen cards, which is easy to do, finding a specific piece of information can be time-consuming. With the notes in your computer, you simply use the "find" function to locate the information. It's faster, and there's much less chance of missing whatever information you're looking for.

• *Linking.* This is not a feature found in the typical word processor, but software packages such as Info Select make it easy to weave "threads" through your research materials. For instance, for some research on water pollution, information-management software could highlight for you all the research notes that involve government regulation. If you had organized your notes by problems and solutions, in chronological order, or from general concepts to specific details, these bits of information about regulation were probably spread throughout your outline. By reminding you of such links, the software helps you remain clear and

EXHIBIT 8.8
Using Computer Tools to Outline Speeches
The outline feature in a good word processor can help you organize and manage the information you plan to include in your speech. For example, by allowing you to move back and forth between a larger picture and the finer details, an outliner helps you develop a speech that is coherent and cohesive.

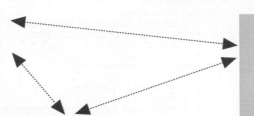

I. Introduction: Get Their Attention

II. Highlight the Problem

III. Propose a Solution

I. Introduction: Get Their Attention
  A. Much of the Food You'll Eat Today Has Chemicals in It
  B. Many Chemicals Are in the Food Chain
  C. Producers Don't Always Have to Say What's in the Food

II. Highlight the Problem
  A. Many Chemical Treatments Are Carcinogenic
  B. Many People Have Allergies to Chemicals

III. Propose a Solution
  A. Part 1: Educate Yourself
  B. Part 2: Raise Your Voice

I. Introduction: Get Their Attention
  A. Much of the Food You'll Eat Today Has Chemicals in It
    1. Average person in U.S. consumes 5 pounds of food additives each year
    2. Other examples
  B. Many Chemicals Are in the Food Chain
    1. DDT outlawed in 1972 but still found in sea creatures
    2. Other examples
  C. Producers Don't Always Have to Say What's in the Food
    1. Milk from cows doctored with Bovine Growth Hormone doesn't have to be labeled as such
    2. Other examples
    3. Other examples

II. Highlight the Problem
  A. Many Chemical Treatments Are Carcinogenic
    1. Common fungicides
    2. Common herbicides
    3. Common insecticides
  B. Many People Have Allergies to Chemicals
    1. MSG
    2. Other examples

III. Propose a Solution
  A. Part 1: Educate Yourself
    1. Learn more about additives and treatments
    2. Read labels when you shop
  B. Part 2: Raise Your Voice
    1. Write to government officials
    2. Talk to your grocer
    3. Whenever possible, don't buy chemically treated or altered products

---

consistent with all the themes and subthemes in your speech.

You may find that a combination of index cards (to capture information while you're reading it) and computer software (to manage the information once you've captured it) is the best solution. Whichever method you choose, be sure to record all the facts you need to responsibly credit the source. Not only is this an ethical responsibility, but it can save you plenty of time later if you need to go back and check facts or quotes.

INTERVIEWING TO COLLECT PERSONAL TESTIMONY

One of the most useful but frequently overlooked sources of supporting materials is the personal interview. Interviews can provide information that has some of the advantages of personal experience (because the process can be highly personal and engaging), and they can provide unique information not available through any other source. In addition, the information you collect can provide expertise and insights that are outside the realm of your own experience.

EXHIBIT 8.9

The Interviewing Process
A successful interview requires careful planning and organization to make sure you get the information you really need.

1. Contact people to interview.
   - Introduce yourself and your purpose.
   - Arrange a time and place.
   - Decide whether to use a tape recorder and get the subject's permission.
2. Plan the interview.
   - Think about the sequence of your questions.
   - Choose the most important questions.
   - Plan smart questions.
   - Plan neutral questions that are easy to understand.
3. Conduct the interview.
   - Dress appropriately.
   - Arrive a few minutes early.
   - Be respectful and polite.
   - Be ready to ask new questions in response to the answers you get.
   - Thank the subject.
4. Use the information wisely.
   - Review notes as soon as possible after the interview.
   - Organize the results, looking for important themes or information.

Getting answers straight from an expert on a subject can be a great way to collect materials for your speech. Of course, you don't necessarily have to interview "experts" in the usual sense of the word. People who have survived a dramatic event such as an airline crash can provide powerful testimony without being experts in airline safety. They are experts in the experience they lived through.

You may have two notions of interviews. The first may come from any job interviews you've had. The object of these interviews is to exchange information with employers to see whether you and a company are right for each other. The second notion may come from all the talk shows you've seen on television. The object of these interviews is to entertain the television audience.

Neither of these interviews is the type of interview you'll conduct when researching your speech. You're not evaluating the person you're interviewing (except to establish his or her expertise and credibility); you're after the information this person can offer. You don't have to entertain anyone, either. If you need "dull" information, then by all means ask the questions that will get those dull answers. The goal is information; that's what research

interviews are all about (see Exhibit 8.9).

Before you decide to do an interview, ask yourself two questions. First, is an interview really the best way to get the information you need? Interviews are time-consuming, both for you and for the **interview subject**, the person you plan to interview. Respect the time of the people you might interview by not asking for information that you could quickly find in the library.

Second, what will happen if you can't arrange the interview or if the interview doesn't provide you the right information? You don't want your entire speech hinging on one interview that may or may not take place. The subject might get sick, might change his or her mind about sitting down with you, or might not provide the quality or quantity of information you'd hoped for. You can see that, like everything else in developing a speech, the sooner you start, the less likely you'll be to wind up short of information right before your speech is due. If you decide that an interview is a good source of support material, then preparation is the most important key to its success.[16]

Contacting People to Interview

Once you've decided to go ahead with a personal interview, the next step is identifying the best person to interview. In some cases, this is a simple question. You already know the person, or you know who he or she is. In other cases, you'll need to do some preliminary research to find the right person or persons. Say you're doing a speech on campus crime, and you need to know just how widespread the problem really is. Who might have the answer? The head of campus security, dorm counselors, the local police, a rape crisis hotline, the school newspaper, and a victim's support group might all have a perspective. So might a professor in the sociology department or someone from a fraternity or sorority that sponsors a nighttime walk-home program. Use your imagination.

With the right person in your sights, follow these steps to set up the interview:

1. *Introduce yourself and your purpose.* You'll have to judge for yourself the best way to approach a potential interview subject, whether by phone, in person, by mail, by fax, or by e-mail. It's hardest to be ignored when you show up in person, but just walking into someone's office, job site, or home is not always appropriate. The person is likely to wonder, "Who is this student and why should I take time out of my busy schedule for an interview?" Be prepared with a quick and clear introduction of who you are, what you're trying to find out, and why this subject is the right person for the interview. Appealing to your subject's ego won't hurt; people like to know that others value their opinions. It's also important to show respect and to show that you're prepared and won't waste valuable time.[17] On the other hand, most successful people are busy, and they're looking for reasons not to allow one more interruption, so make sure you have a good "sales pitch" ready. Don't give them an easy way to decline to your request, such as asking "Is this a bad time to talk?" Instead, apologize for interrupting and ask if you might have a moment of his or her time, now or in the near future.

2. *Arrange a time and place.* You probably won't have a chance to interview the person when you introduce yourself; you'll have to arrange a time and a place for the interview. Try to be flexible—this person is giving you valuable time.

Suggest how much time you think the interview will take, but be prepared to accept less.

3. *Decide whether to use a tape recorder and get the subject's permission.* A tape recorder is generally a good idea if the questions you plan to ask and the likely answers might be complex or if you'll be looking for direct quotations from your subject. You won't have to spend your time furiously writing notes, and you won't have to wonder later whether you got the words and facts just right. On the other hand, some interview subjects will clam up in the presence of a tape recorder. Always ask for permission to bring a tape recorder, and ask again when you're setting up the interview. Don't try to sneak it in, and don't surprise the subject by asking for permission when you arrive. You might put the subject on the spot and create a situation that's embarrassing for both of you.

As soon as you've arranged the interview, get started on the questions. You may need extra time to mull over possible topics to bring up, and you may even need to do some other research before the interview.

Planning the Interview

You get only one chance to conduct the interview, so solid preparation is essential. The secret is to develop an efficient set of effective questions. Being *efficient* means you get as much information as you can in as little time as possible. Being *effective* means you get the right kind of information to build your speech. While preparing your questions, keep these two cautions in mind. First, the kind of answer you get will be influenced, to some extent, by how you ask the question. Second, the subject's cultural and language background can affect both how your questions will be perceived and how they'll be answered. Race, gender, age, educational level, and social status are all potential factors of influence. Know your subject before you start writing questions.[18]

Pretend you're planning an interview about pollution control with the plant manager of a nearby factory. Follow these guidelines, and you'll come up with a great set of questions:

EXHIBIT 8.10

Planning Your Interview Questions
When you first brainstorm a list of questions, you might end up with something like the left column shown here. Items aren't necessarily in any sensible order, some of them might be less important than others, and some (such as #1) might be viewed as antagonistic by your subject. The right column shows the result of some editing—getting rid of contentious and less important questions and putting the remaining questions in a logical sequence.

1. ~~Why isn't the city doing anything about traffic congestion?~~
2. What is the city doing about traffic?
3. How can individuals help?
4. What are employers doing to help?
5. Is the federal government helping to finance solutions?
6. What have traffic engineers concluded about the problem?
7. Why is traffic such a problem now?
8. How does the situation compare with traffic 10 years ago?
9. How does our city's traffic compare with other cities of similar size?
10. ~~Why don't we have more commuter trains like European cities have?~~

1. Why is traffic such a problem now?
2. How does the situation compare with traffic 10 years ago?
3. What have traffic engineers concluded about the problem?
4. How does our city's traffic compare with other cities of similar size?
5. What is the city doing about traffic?
6. How can individuals help?
7. What are employers doing to help?
8. Is the federal government helping to finance solutions?

- *Think about the sequence.* Arrange your questions in a way that helps uncover layers of information or that helps the subject tell you a complete story. Does the topic you're covering have an inherent order to it? In other words, does it make sense to go in chronological order, from general to specific, or from problems to solutions? Consider possible answers to each question and how those answers might affect the flow of the interview (see Exhibit 8.10).

- *Rate your questions and highlight the ones you really need answers to.* Chances are that some of your questions will be more important than others. Make sure you've identified the important ones before you head into the interview. If you start to run out of time during the interview, you may have to skip less important questions.

- *Ask smart questions.* Someone once said: "There is no such thing as a dumb question." That person was wrong. If you ask a question that your subject perceives to be less than intelligent, the interview could go downhill in a hurry. What do you think would happen if you asked the plant manager whether she cares about the environment, whether she thinks pollution control is important, or whether you might see a copy of the company's strategic plans?

- *Ask neutral questions that are easy to understand.* *Neutral* means three things: First, you don't want to lay a trap for the subject that will make him or her appear foolish or heartless if the answer isn't just "right." Second, you don't want to lead the subject to the answer. Third, you don't want to put the subject on the defensive unless it's unavoidable. *Easy to understand* means that the person can easily grasp what you're saying. The topic and the answer may be complicated, but the questions shouldn't be.

Consider these examples:

EXAMPLE 1
Question to be asked of your local mayor
"Wouldn't you agree that the city should be doing more to provide shelters for the homeless people, many of whom are forced to sleep outside because the city government is not meeting their needs?"
What's wrong with the question?
This question misses on all three points of neutrality.

It's a **loaded question.** You're "setting up" the mayor if he or she doesn't answer in the "correct" way. If the respondent doesn't respond in exactly the way you'd like, you'll make the person appear not to care about the problems of homeless people.

It's a **leading question**; you're leading the subject to a particular answer that you've built into the question (that the city should build more shelters). Maybe the solution isn't more shelters. Maybe the city should reduce taxes to entice more businesses to provide employment in the city. Whatever the solution, by trying to lead the answer, you force the subject to start by disagreeing with you if he or she wants to provide a different answer.

It's a **hostile question** that immediately puts the subject on the defensive. You're basically telling the mayor that he or she is failing professionally. The "answer" you'll get is likely to be motivated more by the mayor's emotional need to defend his or her job record than by the desire to provide you with helpful information.

How to fix it
Rephrase the question to make it neutral:

"What steps is the city taking to address the needs of the homeless?"

"Do you think that building more shelters is the right approach to meeting the needs of the homeless?"

Both of these alternatives will give the subject the chance to answer calmly and objectively.

EXAMPLE 2
Question to be asked of your local mayor
"The person you've put in charge of helping the homeless was convicted of embezzling money from the city and was just released from prison. Are you comfortable with this decision?"
What's wrong with the question?
Depending on the circumstances, this might be a time to be more aggressive. After all, the mayor hired a convicted criminal to be in charge of an important city function. Plus, you've asked a simple yes-or-no question when what you really want is more information on why the mayor made this decision.
How to fix it
Get to the heart of the matter: "Why did you hire someone who is a convicted criminal for such an important position in city government?" This is an aggressive question, but it's not out of line.

EXAMPLE 3
Question to be asked of your college's director of admissions
"A recent article in the *Wall Street Journal* said that some colleges lie about their acceptance rates and the average SAT scores of their incoming freshmen in order to get better rankings in the

Checklist for Asking Effective Interview Questions

1. Ask questions in an order that helps your subject tell you a complete story.
2. Ask intelligent questions that show you've done your homework.
3. Avoid asking leading questions in which the answer is already built into the question.
4. Avoid asking loaded questions that will inflict a value judgment on the subject, depending on how he or she answers.

5. Avoid asking hostile questions that will prompt people to defend themselves rather than provide the information you want.
6. Ask questions that are easy to understand—avoiding double negatives, complicated sentences, unfamiliar vocabulary, and other potentially confusing elements.
7. Avoid two-part questions, which may be confusing or lead to contradictory answers.

annual college guidebooks published by various magazines and that the magazines continue to publish the numbers knowing that they are not always true; do you think this is ethical?"[19]

What's wrong with the question?
It's unclear just which ethical problem you're referring to, the fact that some colleges fudge the numbers or that magazines continue to publish fraudulent data. This is a double-barreled question, or two questions in one.

How to fix it
Break it into two questions:

"A recent article in the *Wall Street Journal* said that some colleges lie about their acceptance rates and the average SAT scores of their incoming freshmen in order to get better rankings in the annual college guidebooks published by various magazines; do you think this practice is ethical?"

"And do you consider it ethical for the magazines to continue publishing the figures when they know some are fraudulent?"

This organization will help the admissions director give you a clear and complete answer to both of your questions.

EXAMPLE 4
Question to be asked of the chairman of a legislative committee
"I don't think your committee's plan to redefine local voting districts is fair."

What's wrong with the question?
It is not a question. It's a statement of your own personal opinion, and your goal in the interview isn't to share your opinions.

How to fix it
Phrase it as a question and remove the bias: "Your committee's redistricting plan favors several incumbents by putting more supporters in each of their districts. Can you explain why you think this is fair?" You've highlighted the problem with facts (rather than just saying it's not fair), and you've given the subject a real question to answer.

Edit your questions as needed to make them neutral and easy to understand. Then practice

them several times to make sure you can say them smoothly. Now you're ready for the interview. Gather the tools you'll need, including extra pens and paper. Does this advice sound obvious? Perhaps, but you'll feel foolish if you get to the interview and have to borrow something to write with. It just doesn't look professional. Also, make sure you have enough blank tape and fresh batteries for your tape recorder (if you've been given permission to use one). You'll have to decide whether to bring a laptop computer if you have one. Typing your notes directly into your word processor will save you time later, but typing during an interview might bother your subject. Don't even think about bringing a computer if you can't use it quickly and smoothly. In general, try to get by with a pen and a tape recorder; they're less trouble and less likely to get in the way of a useful conversation.

Conducting the Interview

Your physical appearance, particularly the initial impression you make, can affect the quality of information you get during an interview. Appropriate dress and respectful behavior are extremely important.[20] If you show up at an executive's office dressed like you're heading for the beach, don't expect to be treated as a serious professional. On the other hand, you wouldn't want to show up at a ranch or landfill wearing an expensive suit, either. Choose clothes that fit the situation. If you're in doubt, err on the side of being too formal.

Arrive at the interview location several minutes early to make sure you're ready when the subject is. If you're kept waiting for a few minutes, keep your cool. The person is probably busy and trying to get to you as soon as possible. Be prepared for some small talk when you meet a subject for the first time. You may not be particularly interested in the weather or how well the school did in the basketball tournament, but a few moments of small talk help you and the subject feel at ease with each other. If you hit the person with a tough question as soon as you sit down, he or she might immediately become defensive.

Remember that you're a guest during the interview. Respect the subject's time. Use the listening skills you've learned in this course. Take good notes, even if you've been given permission to tape-record. Seeing you actually write down things they say is enough to make most interview subjects think carefully about what they're telling you. Don't feel bashful about asking the person to pause for a moment while you catch up with your notes or about asking for something to be repeated or clarified. After all, the whole reason you're here is to collect this information.

Be polite, even if you feel passionately about the topic and the subject is saying things you disagree with. Don't argue. This isn't a debate or a contest. You've asked the person to provide information or opinions, and that's what he or she is doing.

You may find that you need to adapt your questions as you move through the interview. The subject may answer two questions at once, and you'll sound silly asking a question the person has already answered. Also, an answer might spark a new line of questioning. If the information would help your speech, by all means ad lib some questions on the spot. You may get better quotes by asking follow-up questions during the actual conversation.[21]

Some people have a tendency to wander when they're answering questions, so you may find yourself in the potentially uncomfortable positioning of needing to pull the interview back on track. You'll need tact and judgment to do this smoothly. If the person is telling an amusing story, and it seems like it might last only a minute or two, let him or her go with it. Losing a small amount of your available time is worth avoiding a potentially embarrassing moment. However, if the person is really wandering off track, you may have to be more direct. Don't say that *you* have limited time. Tell your subject that you want to make the best use of *his* or *her* time. It accomplishes the same goal, but it's a lot more tactful.

When you've covered your questions or run out of time, leave a favorable lasting impression by making a graceful exit.[22] Thank the subject for his or her time and emphasize how much the information will help you create a great speech. You might also ask whether you can follow up with a quick visit or phone call if you later find you need to clarify something. Many interview subjects will make this offer on their own, in fact. They want to make sure you understand what they said and that you've interpreted them correctly.

Using the Interview Information

Try to review your notes as soon as possible after the interview. You probably won't have captured every detail in your notes, and going over them while the interview is still fresh in your memory will help you fill in the details. If you made a tape recording, *transcribe* it (which means to take down word for word what the person said) or take notes from the tape in the same basic way you take notes while listening to someone in person. The advantage of the tape, of course, is that you can rewind and replay whenever you need to.

Checklist for Conducting a Successful Interview

1. Make sure your physical appearance is appropriate for the situation; if you show up in a business office with ripped-up clothes and lots of body piercing, you probably won't receive much respect.
2. If you're not sure how to dress, go more formal just to be on the safe side; as the guest, it's better to communicate respect by putting some effort into how you look.
3. Arrive early to make sure you're ready to start on time.
4. Have patience if you have to wait.
5. Start with some small talk to build rapport.
6. Don't take a tape recorder unless you have previously asked for permission to bring it.
7. Make sure you get the information you need, without being rude or pushy.
8. Be polite, even if you don't agree with something the subject says.

SPICE UP YOUR SPEECHES WITH THIS RECIPE FOR SUCCESS

Speech coach Lani Arredondo uses an effective figurative analogy when teaching people how to find the right support materials for their speeches. It's like making a stew, she says. The meat and potatoes of your speech "stew" are the major supporting points. They are the foundation of your message, but they may not be the most exciting things the audience has ever heard. With your core message in place, spice it up with some carefully selected extras—quotes, jokes, unusual facts, amazing stories, and so forth.

Like cooking spices, these "flavor enhancers" for your speech need to pass several tests:

- *Are they interesting?* Interest is the primary reason you use spices in cooking, too—to raise the presentation above the ordinary, to make a dish richer and perhaps a little more complicated without making it confusing. Find some extra bits of intellectual or emotional spice that arouse the audience's curiosity, make them think, or challenge their favorite assumptions and beliefs.
- *Are they invigorating?* Spices can stimulate the audience and add strength to your message.
- *Are they inspiring?* Can you add something that will lift the audience's spirits, give them hope, or encourage them to excel?
- *Are they in good taste?* If you've ever experimented with spices in cooking, you know how easy it can be to create something truly unappetizing. You'll often find spicy speech materials that are tempting to throw in but that really don't belong there.

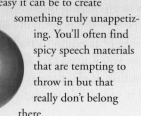
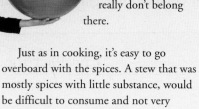

One way to spice up a speech is to use an eye-catching prop.

Just as in cooking, it's easy to go overboard with the spices. A stew that was mostly spices with little substance, would be difficult to consume and not very satisfying. The same holds true for a speech. Remember that spice is an enhancer, something that makes the main body of your speech more interesting and enjoyable.

Your notes, whether from the interview or the tape, will probably be a disorganized pile of quotes, statistics, phrases, key words, and other bits and pieces of information. Taking notes during an interview isn't like taking notes from a book; you can't think through each point carefully before you write it down. The first step is to organize all the facts and thoughts so that you can see what you have. Look for important themes, helpful facts or statistics, and direct quotes that might make your speech more compelling.

Keep in mind that interviews don't necessarily have to take place in person. As more and more people get connected online, e-mail interviews are becoming more common. Many interviewers and subjects like this approach.[23] Perhaps one of the biggest advantages is that e-mail gives subjects a chance to think through their responses thoroughly, rather than rushing to fit the time constraints of an in-person interview.

SUMMARY

When you need to gather materials to support a speech, you'll follow some or all of the following steps: (1) start with a clearly identified speech topic and specific purpose, (2) ask a librarian for help, (3) try to find a quick overview of the subject, (4) order materials that need to be gathered from other locations, (5) devise a plan to collect data that aren't available anywhere else, (6) locate reference books that might help, (7) find newspaper and periodical articles that cover your topic, (8) identify nonreference books that cover your topic, and (9) use other research materials as needed, such as maps and catalogs. You may not need all of these steps for every speech, but this is the general process.

You can be your own best resource for many speeches, using your experience and knowledge to support your central idea. Personal experience has both advantages and disadvantages when it comes to supporting a speech. While it does infuse your speech with interest and emotion and give you access to information that may not be available anywhere else, it may not present a complete or unbiased picture of a subject area.

Your college or university library holds four major categories of research materials that'll help with your speech preparation: reference books, newspapers and periodicals, nonreference books, and an all-purpose category that covers everything from maps to government reports. The five types of reference books you can use for research are encyclopedias and dictionaries, directories, biographical references, almanacs and statistical sources, and books of quotations. The four types of periodicals are popular magazines, trade journals, business magazines, and academic journals. Each has a specific goal for its own readers, and you can get different kinds of information from periodicals in each category.

Your research doesn't have to be limited to physical materials sitting in the library. If you have access to the Internet, you can tap into its vast resources to search other libraries' card catalogs, find information about research projects underway all over the world, and communicate with a variety of people who might be able to help you. A second alternative is to use one of the many commercial database services. Your library probably has access to at least one of these, or you might want to subscribe to one on your own.

Planning is the key to a successful research interview. Start with two questions: whether an interview is the best way to get the information you need, and what alternatives you'll have if the interview you need turns out to be impossible to get. Once you decide that an interview is the right way to go, your first step is to contact likely subjects, people who will have something valuable to say to you. Setting up the interview involves introducing yourself and your purpose, arranging a time and place, and getting the subject's permission to bring a tape recorder if you decide to use one. Planning for the interview itself means creating a list of questions that get the information you need in as little time as possible. Secrets here include developing neutral questions that are easy to ask and to understand and respecting cultural and language differences. Conducting the interview calls for respect, politeness, and courtesy while keeping an eye on your goal. At times, you may need to gently redirect the subject's thoughts to get the information you came for. The final step is to make effective use of the information you've collected. One of the most important points is to go over your notes as soon as possible after the interview, before you forget details.

KEY TERMS

academic journals (170)

almanacs (168)

Boolean operations (172)

business magazines (170)

commercial databases (174)

depository libraries (171)

hostile question (181)

hyperlinks (174)

Internet (171)

interview subject (178)

leading question (181)

loaded question (181)

metasearch engine (172)

periodicals (170)

popular magazines (170)

search engine (172)

trade journals (170)

websites (171)

APPLY CRITICAL THINKING

1. Is using your own experience for support materials a legitimate form of research or not? Why?

2. How can you address the question of bias when using your own knowledge and experience?

3. Is bias necessarily wrong or undesirable? Explain your answer.

4. Is an encyclopedia a good research tool for your speeches? Why or why not?

5. Why are regular, nonreference books in a library a less attractive research source in many cases?

6. How can you avoid accidental plagiarism when doing research for a speech?

7. Will the Internet and other computer tools eventually replace traditional libraries? Why or why not?

SHARPEN YOUR SKILLS

Individual Exercises

1. List five things you've learned about college life so far that you could use as supporting evidence in a speech to high school seniors.

2. Find evidence to support or refute the claim that air pollution is a significant threat to the ozone layer.

3. Some states use primaries to select presidential candidates; others use party caucuses. See whether you can find out which method political experts think is best for the country.

4. Find a humorous quotation that you could use to introduce the subject of planning for the future. It can be about successful planning, unsuccessful planning, or even the futility of planning.

Group Exercises

5. This exercise involves competitive research between two teams of students. Assemble a team of two, three, or four students (more than that may be difficult to coordinate) and challenge another team. Pick one of the following topics, follow the research guidelines presented in this chapter to develop a research plan, do the research, and write a one-paragraph summary of what you find. Which team found the most convincing evidence?

a. What are the political and economic forces that caused World War I?

b. What progress has been made toward curing cancer?

c. Do college students receive a better education now than they did 100 years ago?

d. Are the most expensive colleges worth the price?

6. In this exercise, one student plays the role of an expert in college admissions policy, and another plays the role of a student interviewing the expert. Three other students will critique the performance of the student interviewer. Afterward, the three critics should prepare constructive, specific comments that the interviewer can use to improve his or her questions and interviewing technique. If time permits, rotate roles so that some or all of the students on the team get to play the role of interviewer. (You may change the topic from college admissions to anything the student playing the expert is familiar with.)

Chapter Nine

ORGANIZING YOUR SPEECH

LEARNING OBJECTIVES

After studying this chapter, you will be able to

1. Discuss how the structure of a speech guides both the audience and the speaker.

2. Define a major point, and discuss how to determine which points to include in a speech.

3. Identify six methods of organizing your major points.

4. Discuss how to use and organize subpoints.

5. Describe how to integrate support material into your speech.

6. Discuss the use of transitions, signposts, internal previews, and internal summaries.

7. Explain how internal previews and summaries help your audience.

EXHIBIT 9.1

When you organize your speech, you fit your ideas into the structural framework of an introduction, a body, and a conclusion.

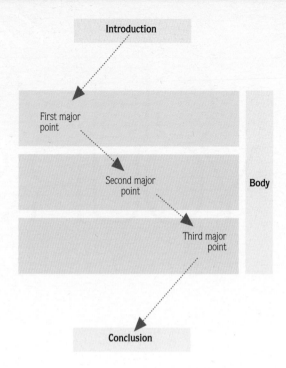

STRUCTURE WHAT YOU HAVE TO SAY

At this point in the public speaking process, you've laid the foundation for your speech by selecting a topic and a purpose and by identifying your central idea. You've also researched your topic and gathered support materials, which serve as the building blocks of your speech. Now you're ready to put those building blocks together in a structure that will convey the central idea of your speech and lead the audience to your conclusion.

When you consider what a structure does for a speech, you might want to think of a house. A well-constructed house stands on its own because it's more than a pile of bricks, boards, and nails put together haphazardly. Similarly, a good speech is more than a jumble of ideas, facts, and figures. As a public speaker, you're like an expert carpenter. It's your job to organize your support materials and ideas into some kind of structure that has definite shape and dimensions and that can stand on its own (see Exhibit 9.1).

A speech has three main parts. In the introduction, you briefly preview what you will talk about. In the body, you develop your major points and cite support materials to make your case. And in the conclusion, you briefly summarize and reinforce what you've said.

The structure of your particular speech depends on how you arrange your ideas within these three parts. First you structure the body, as discussed in this chapter. Once you've decided exactly what

you're going to say and how you're going to say it, you organize the introduction and the conclusion, as discussed in Chapter 10. Remember, your ideas will hold together only if the structure of your speech is sound. A sound structure will guide both you and your audience through all the points you want to make, one at a time and in a meaningful sequence.

Guide Your Audience and Yourself

To see how organization guides an audience through a speech, imagine you're listening to a speaker who simply reels off a list of facts. As fact follows fact, you become increasingly confused about where the speech is going. How can you make sense of these facts unless the speaker arranges them in a meaningful order and shows how one relates to the next? Even though the speaker may be leading up to an important point, you can't follow the reasoning, let alone agree with the conclusion. Soon your mind starts to wander. You don't care how knowledgeable the speaker is; you only care that you can't understand what the speech is all about.

Although this example is certainly extreme, it shows why you need to carefully structure your

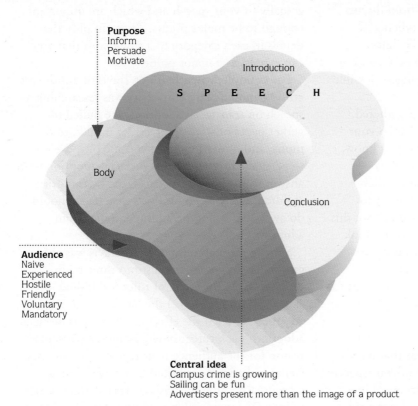

EXHIBIT 9.2
Shaping Your Speech
Your specific purpose, central idea,
and audience all affect the shape
and structure of your speech.

Purpose
Inform
Persuade
Motivate

Introduction

S P E E C H

Body

Conclusion

Audience
Naive
Experienced
Hostile
Friendly
Voluntary
Mandatory

Central idea
Campus crime is growing
Sailing can be fun
Advertisers present more than the image of a product

speech so that you can guide the audience through your message. Speech organization reflects your "you" orientation, the ability to focus on your audience's needs and interests as you plan and deliver your speech. By giving coherence and direction to an otherwise random set of ideas, you help your audience stay with you, point by point, until you arrive at your conclusion. A well-structured speech lets audience members know that you're not wasting their time. They'll also know that you're prepared, which adds to your credibility. What's more, audience members will be able to understand, absorb, and retain your message more effectively.[1]

The process of organizing your speech can help you, as a speaker, gain more skill in applying both critical and creative thinking skills. You'll use critical thinking to analyze the relationships among your ideas and to develop a meaningful progression from one point to the next. Then you'll use creative thinking to find the words that will help your audience follow your train of thought and pick out your most important points.

As a bonus, preparing your speech so well beforehand will make you more confident and able to speak more fluently during your presentation.[2]

Regardless of length, every speech needs a structure to guide the audience and the speaker. In a short speech, you have only a few minutes to get your message across, so you can't afford to drift aimlessly from one idea to the next. You have to organize your thoughts so that you come to the point quickly and leave the audience with a lasting memory of your message. In a long speech, you risk losing your audience's attention if your ideas are out of sequence or fail to build to a logical conclusion. Your audience must be with you every step of the way for you to achieve your purpose in speaking.

Remember Your Purpose, Central Idea, and Audience Analysis

As you think about the sequence in which you'll present your points, review your specific purpose and your central idea. Think, too, about what you've learned by analyzing your audience. Ask yourself what your audience will think and feel about your central idea and supporting materials. These elements determine how you will structure your speech (see Exhibit 9.2).

Imagine, for example, that you want to persuade your classmates to vote for mandatory fingerprinting of all college students as part of a crime-control program. You know, from discussions with your friends, that your audience is likely to be against fingerprinting. Therefore, you'll want to think carefully about how you can organize your ideas to build the strongest possible case.

First, review all the research you've gathered. Think about how these materials relate to your purpose and central idea and to what you know about your audience. Ask yourself whether anything you turned up during your research would cause you to change what you want to accomplish or what you want to convey. If so, this is the time to make necessary revisions and look for any additional research you may need. Now you're ready to go through the research more carefully to pick out the major points you want to make during the body of your speech.

Select Your Major Points

A **major point** is one of the key ideas that builds toward your central idea. The body of your speech is actually a series of major points arranged in a meaningful sequence. Each major point is a single idea that is connected to—but doesn't duplicate—the ideas expressed in your other major points. By adding one major point to another, you build a powerful, cohesive case to show why your audience should accept your central idea.

How do you know which point is major and which isn't? You can find the answer as you sort and group the details you've researched, searching for ideas that directly relate to your purpose and central idea. As you sort, watch for natural categories that emerge from the research, such as three causes of a particular problem or four uses for recycled newspapers. Also watch for ideas that are repeatedly emphasized in your research. Both can lead you to major points that will help your listeners understand your central idea.

Next, divide and group your materials into categories, avoiding overlap between categories. Think about how to group your materials so the audience understands the distinctions between categories. Then examine your categories and relate them to your purpose, central idea, and audience. This way, you can see which categories

actually fit your speech and which are important enough to be major points. Then simplify the details in each category to a single idea that you can express as a major point.

For example, when Jennifer Travis of Southwestern Oklahoma State University was researching a speech on transracial adoption, she pulled together pages of statistics, facts, examples, testimony, and quotations. Her specific purpose was to persuade listeners that transracial adoption is an answer to the adoption crisis faced by minority children. Her central idea was that states should do away with rules forbidding families from adopting children of another race.

Sorting through her research, Travis was able to group her support materials into three main categories: (1) the effect of rules forbidding transracial adoption, (2) the barriers to transracial adoption, and (3) the effect of allowing transracial adoption. Each category represented a particular reason for the audience to accept the premise that transracial adoption should be allowed. These categories became the basis of Travis's three major points: (1) many children waiting for adoption are shuffled around in long-term foster care, (2) laws and policies forbidding transracial adoption don't represent the best interests of the children, and (3) transracial adoption benefits the children, the families, and society as a whole.[3]

Like Jennifer Travis, you'll want to look for more than one major point to support your central idea. One point is not compelling enough to build a strong case for your central idea. It's also not enough to fill the body of your speech, which accounts for roughly three-quarters of your talk (see Exhibit 9.3).[4]

So what number is the right number of major points? Travis selected three major points for her speech, but the number varies. Sometimes you'll need only two major points; occasionally you'll need as many as five. However, if you present too many points, you'll confuse your audience and reduce the impact of each point. You'll give your audience so much to think about that no one will be able to remember all your points.

Just as you narrowed your topic so that you could cover it in the time allotted, you'll want to

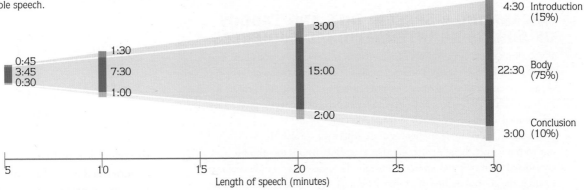

EXHIBIT 9.3

Distributing Your Time During a Speech
Your conclusion is shorter than your introduction, and both your introduction and conclusion together should be no more than a quarter of your whole speech.

4:30 Introduction (15%)

3:00

1:30

0:45
3:45
0:30

7:30

15:00

22:30 Body (75%)

1:00

2:00

Conclusion
3:00 (10%)

Length of speech (minutes)

narrow your supporting material by including only the most important points. Also, review your audience analysis to see which points listeners might already be aware of and to determine what's appropriate for the occasion. No matter how many points you decide on, leave time for statistics, quotations, and other support materials that both bring your speech alive and corroborate your major points.

PUT YOUR POINTS IN ORDER

After you've selected the major points for your speech, you're ready to arrange them in an appropriate order. The order you choose depends on your topic, your purpose and central idea, and your audience's needs and interests. Your goal is to help listeners follow your ideas and your reasoning all the way to your conclusion.

You can organize your major points in many ways. Six of the more common are according to (1) time, (2) cause and effect, (3) importance, (4) problem and solution, (5) space, and (6) topic. Some of these organizational methods are better for informative speaking and some are better for persuasive speaking, as discussed in more detail in Chapters 15 and 17. As you put your points in order, consider any cultural differences that might

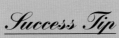

Success Tip

The way you organize your major points depends on your topic, your purpose and central idea, and your audience's needs and interests. Select the method that best helps listeners follow your ideas and your logic.

affect your audience's perceptions of the speech organization. Maintaining a "you" orientation will help you settle on the appropriate organization for your speech and audience.[5]

Organizing by Time

When you organize your points in order of time, you arrange them according to when they occurred. This helps the audience track the timing and sequence of each point. Arranging points by time is an effective organizational method for a speech describing a series of events or the steps in a process.

Most of the time you'll start with the oldest points and work your way forward in time until you reach the most recent point. That's the organizational method Alison Shapiro, president of the Television Action Committee, used in a speech to inform, titled "Television After 9/11: Transformation from Tragedy." By first describing the development of television, Shapiro laid the groundwork for her ideas about the transformation of the medium after a national tragedy. Here's the structure of her speech:

Specific Purpose
To inform my audience of the developments that

ORGANIZING A SPEECH: DO'S AND TABOOS OF ADRESSING INTERNATIONAL AUDIENCES

If you think that a straight line is the only way to get from major point A to major point B, think again. Public speakers in the United States are taught to organize their ideas so that they can move directly from one point to the next in linear fashion. However, audiences in other parts of the world prefer a less streamlined approach to speech organization.

In Japan, for example, audiences don't expect the speaker to come right out with one specific point after another. A speaker who is too blunt is considered aggressive and impolite. Instead, the speaker uses subtle language to circle the general outline of a topic. Although U.S. audiences might find this a roundabout route, Japanese audiences understand how to interpret the speaker's hints and follow the points being made.

Similarly, speakers in China offer clues before they make their major points. The clues provide some background details to prepare the audience for each point. Based on the context of the speaker's words, the audience can figure out exactly where the speech is going.

Hindi speakers also use nonlinear speech organization, mixing many ideas within each major point. As confusing as this might seem to audiences of other cultures, Indian audiences are aware that a speaker will branch off and then return to the major point. Hindi speakers aren't illogical or disorganized; they're simply following the conventions of their culture.

For speakers who plan to address audiences in other cultures, the message is clear: don't assume that your speech should move straight from one point to the next. Take time to research the culture of your audience members. Only then can you organize your speech to fit their needs and expectations.

When addressing people from another culture, stay alert to your audience's preferences for indirect organization of speech ideas.

have transformed television in the 21st century.
Central Idea
Television has grown through revolution, expansion, and sudden transformation.

Major Point 1: From the 1950s to the 1970s, the television industry experienced a revolution, with more programming and innovations such as color increasing viewer interest.
Major Point 2: In the 1980s and 1990s, viewers' options expanded with new technologies, from cable and satellite innovations to widespread use of VCRs and DVD players.
Major Point 3: In 2001, the September 11 terrorist attacks caused viewers to demand more noble values in television programming, and networks responded.

This speech starts with the earliest point and moves forward chronologically to reach the final point. Organizing according to time helps the audience follow the sequence of events leading from the early days of television to the sudden change that affected television programming in late 2001 and 2002. Note how the final point completes Shapiro's central idea, that television growth was spurred by revolution, expansion, and sudden transformation (see Exhibit 9.4).

At times, you may want to emphasize the historical roots of your topic. To do this, you can

EXHIBIT 9.4

Organizing Major Points in Order of Time

Alison Shapiro of the Television Action Committee arranged her major points in order of time to help the audience appreciate the historical context of changes in television programming. Her speech painted a word picture of television history spanning the 1950s (the Milton Berle era), the 1960s (*Laugh-In*), the 1970s (*M*A*S*H*), the technological expansions of the 1980s and 1990s, and the sudden demand for nobler programming values after the September 11, 2001, terrorist attacks on the Pentagon and World Trade Center.

begin with the most recent points and work backward. Although infrequently used, this reverse chronological order is a way of giving the audience a familiar starting point from which to journey back in time.

Organizing by Cause and Effect

Organizing your major points according to cause and effect is a good way to demonstrate how one event or situation results from another. Using this method of organization, your speech will have two major points, one representing cause and the other representing effect. You can either trace the cause that led up to a particular effect or work backward from the result to examine the cause. Which approach you use depends on what you want to emphasize. For example, to demonstrate how certain events contributed to a particular situation, you would begin by describing the effect in one major point. Then you would discuss the cause in another major point:

Specific Purpose
To inform my audience of the cause of a growing threat to U.S. public health.
Central Idea
A growing crisis threatening public health in the United States is being caused by children and adults not being vaccinated on time.

Major Point 1: An increasing number of children and adults are becoming seriously ill or dying of diseases that can be prevented by timely vaccinations.
Major Point 2: Children and adults aren't being immunized at the right time against measles, polio, mumps, rubella, diphtheria, and pertussis.[7]

In this speech, your introduction will lay the foundation for the cause-and-effect organization of the speech. The first major point in the body covers the nature and scope of the public health crisis, which is the effect. To support this point, you would include statistics and other evidence. Then the second major point in the body examines the cause of the crisis, again supported

by facts, figures, and other relevant information from your research. Your conclusion recaps how the causes led up to the effect, reemphasizing the causes you want the audience to understand and remember.

On the other hand, to focus more on the situation that results from certain events, you can structure your two major points to emphasize the effect. So if you want your audience to understand what a lack of jurors is doing to the U.S. legal system, you start with the cause and then explore the effect:

Specific Purpose
To inform my audience about the effect of people failing to show up for jury duty.
Central Idea
The lack of jurors is resulting in costly, unproductive delays throughout the U.S. legal system.

Major Point 1: The legal right to a speedy trial before peers is being threatened by a lack of jurors.
Major Point 2: The costs of court and jail mount up unproductively when trials are delayed for lack of jurors.[8]

In this case, you're structuring the body of your speech to help your audience look beyond the causes to the effects of people not showing up for jury duty. Your first major point will explain the causes of the problem. Your second major point will explain the effect that a lack of jurors is having. Then your conclusion will show how the cause and effect comes together (see Exhibit 9.5).

Organizing by Importance

When some of your major points are more important than others, you can help your audience distinguish among them by arranging them in order of importance. To inject drama into your speech and build to a climax that ends your speech on a powerful note, you may want to save the most important point for the end.[9] Suppose you were giving a speech about where charities get their contributions. You

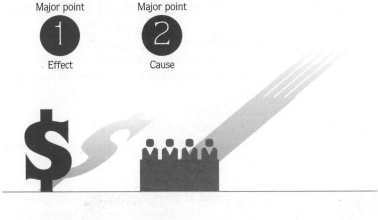

EXHIBIT 9.5
Using Cause and Effect to Organize Major Points
When you want to emphasize the cause of a problem, you can begin the body of your speech with the major point that describes the effect, then go on to the major point that explains the cause. In this case, the effect of the problem, such as higher costs for the judicial system, is presented first, followed by the cause of the problem, a lack of jurors. On the other hand, when you want to emphasize the effect, you'll reverse the major points, discussing the cause before presenting the effect.

Here, you've organized your four major points in ascending order of importance, from least to most important. This helps the audience see the significance of each point in the context of the points before and after. It also encourages listeners to anticipate the most important source of donations, which is your final point.

On the other hand, you may want to start off with the most critical point and then, after stressing its importance, continue with your points in descending order of importance. That was the approach Winston Lord used when he addressed a Los Angeles audience about "Changing Our Ways: America and the New World." As chairman of the National Commission on America and the New World (sponsored by the Carnegie Endowment for International Peace), he helped create a report about how the United States fits in a world being transformed by political and economic changes. By putting his major points in order of importance, Lord called attention to the most vital findings in the report:

could heighten listeners' interest by building up to the single most important source of contributions:

Specific Purpose
To inform my audience of the sources of charitable contributions.
Central Idea
Charities get donations from four sources, but one is by far the most important source.

Major Point 1: Although corporations annually donate more than $5 billion to U.S. charities, they're the least important group of contributors.
Major Point 2: Nonprofit foundations donate $10 billion annually to U.S. charities.
Major Point 3: Bequests also provide nearly $10 billion to U.S. charities every year.
Major Point 4: Individuals are the single most important source of contributions for U.S. charities, donating more than $110 billion annually.[10]

Specific Purpose
To inform the audience of the findings in the commission's report about the role of the United States in today's fast-changing world.
Central Idea
The United States must change to position itself for improved economic prosperity, a safer world, and

more effective global competition and collaboration.

Major Point 1: The country's top priority should be domestic renewal, in the form of a strengthened economy, better education, and better quality of life.
Major Point 2: The second priority should be building and maintaining strong coalitions with other nations to tackle international issues such as armed conflicts, trade agreements, and environmental problems.
Major Point 3: Other specific goals for U.S. foreign policy include environmental initiatives, defense, and human rights.[11]

The way Lord organized his points left readers with little doubt about what he considered the most important ideas in his speech. He alerted the audience to the relative importance of major points by introducing one as "our highest priority" and another as "a second theme." Then he reaffirmed their importance by telling listeners to keep both points in mind as he discussed the specific goals suggested in the report.

Organizing by Problem and Solution

To show your audience how to solve a problem, you establish two major points representing the problem and its solution. This organizational method is well suited to persuasive speeches in which you demonstrate why your solution to the problem is the best. It's also appropriate for informative speeches in which you emphasize the seriousness of the problem and present a possible solution.

Merie Witt of McLennan College in Texas used the problem-solution organization in her speech titled "Outpatient Surgery Centers." Her first major point described the safety problems of nonhospital surgery clinics, where patients don't stay overnight following medical procedures. Her second major point offered some possible solu-

tions. Here's how Witt arranged her major points:

Specific Purpose
To persuade my audience to push for solutions to the serious safety problems of outpatient surgery clinics.
Central Idea
Solutions exist to the life-threatening problem of inadequate medical care in some outpatient surgery clinics.

Major Point 1: Poor regulations, inadequate training, and conflicting financial interests all contribute to the problem of poor health care at outpatient surgery clinics.
Major Point 2: The audience should pursue governmental, medical, and individual solutions to the problem.[12]

Witt offered narratives, quotations, statistics, and other support materials to develop her first major point. Once she had shown the severity of the problem, she spurred her audience on to take action to solve the problem. By discussing solutions after the problem, she helped her audience focus on what can be done, rather than on all the things wrong with the system.

Sometimes you'll want to emphasize the seriousness of a problem. Then you'll devote most of your time to aspects of the problem and spend less time on the solution. Of course, you'll mention both problem and solution in your introduction and your conclusion. When Jeffrey D. Greene of Austin Peay State University in Tennessee spoke on "The Poisoned Fields" (about the problem of green tobacco sickness), he chose this approach:

Specific Purpose
To persuade my audience that green tobacco sickness is a serious problem that needs to be addressed.
Central Idea
Green tobacco sickness is a serious problem that endangers the health of tobacco workers, although it

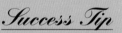

Success Tip
You can organize your major points according to problem and solution when you want to persuade listeners to accept your solution. You can also use this organization to inform listeners about a serious problem and its potential solution.

EXHIBIT 9.6

Organizing to Focus on the Seriousness of the Problem
Jeffrey Greene's speech, "The Poisoned Fields," used the problem-solution organizational method to explore the issue of green tobacco sickness. He devoted most of the body of his speech to the severity of the problem; he offered potential solutions and ideas for audience action after exploring the problem in detail.

can be solved by better education and stricter government regulations.

Major Point 1: Green tobacco sickness is a sometimes life-threatening illness, caused by contact with dissolved nicotine from wet tobacco leaves, that affects 30,000 workers every year.
Major Point 2: To solve the problem, inform workers about the dangers of green tobacco sickness and urge government regulators to strengthen safety standards for workers.[13]

Greene used most of the body of his speech to explore aspects of the problem, which he presented in his first major point (see Exhibit 9.6). Once he had presented several subpoints to show his audience the severity of the problem, he devoted his second major point to show suggested solutions. Finally, in his conclusion, Greene asked audience members to take action by contacting their federal legislators about green tobacco sickness.

Organizing by Space

When you arrange your major points according to spaces, you help the audience understand where each is located in a directional pattern. The directional pattern may be left to right, top to bottom, front to back, north to south, inside to outside, or some other meaningful order. By starting at one location and progressing in order through each point until you arrive at the final location in the pattern, you'll help your audience follow the entire sequence.

Consider how one student speaker arranged the major points of a speech about sightseeing in Japan:

Specific Purpose
To inform my audience about historic sites to visit in central Kyoto, Japan.
Central Idea
Tourists can visit three major historic sites that form an inverted triangle around Karasuma-dori Avenue in Kyoto, Japan.

Major Point 1: The Imperial Palace, former home of two emperors, is on the northern end of Karasuma-dori Avenue, at one corner of the triangle's base.
Major Point 2: Nijojo Castle, which housed the powerful Tokugawa shoguns on their visits to Kyoto, is located southwest of the Imperial Palace, in the opposite corner of the triangle's base.
Major Point 3: Higashi-Honganji Temple, the largest wood structure in Japan, is at the southern end of Karasuma-dori Avenue, at the bottommost tip of the inverted triangle.

The audience follows the speaker on a sightseeing trip that begins in the north and ends in the south of Karasuma-dori Avenue. However, the three sites aren't in a straight line. That's why the speaker adds a word picture of an inverted triangle to enhance the description of the spatial relationship among the three points.

Another student described how the masts on an eighteenth-century battleship were designed. Each major point described one of the ship's masts. The major points were organized according to the location of each mast at the front, back, or middle of the ship. Here's how the speech was put together:

Specific Purpose
To inform my audience about the design of the masts on an eighteenth-century battleship.
Central Idea
Each of the masts on an eighteenth-century battleship was designed to help the ship maneuver in the water.

Major Point 1: The foremast, located in the front of the battleship, held the fore topgallant at the top, the fore topsail below that, and the foresail at the base.
Major Point 2: The main mast, located in the middle of the ship, held the main topgallant sail at the top, the main topsail below that, and the mainsail at the base.
Major Point 3: The mizzen mast, located in the back of the ship, held the mizzen topgallant sail at the top, the mizzen topsail below that, and the spanker sail at the base.

Organizing major points according to space helped listeners envision the location of each mast. Note that each mast held more than one sail. So that listeners could follow the description more clearly, the speaker referred to the sails on each mast by their position at the top, middle, or base. This is an example of using space to organize subpoints.

Organizing by Topic

At times, you will be able to divide your overall topic into parts, making each part a major point. When you use this approach, you organize your major points according to topic. To do this, break your overall topic into smaller divisions or categories, known as *subtopics*. Each subtopic will be one of your major points.

For example, if you were planning a speech about the books of the Bible, you might divide the overall topic into two subtopics, the Old Testament and the New Testament. You would make each of these subtopics a major point. Similarly, if you were going to speak about the armed forces, you could divide your topic into five subtopics: Army, Navy, Air Force, Coast Guard, and Marines. Each is a branch of the U.S. armed services, and each can be presented as a major point.

Here's how Alfred Mutual of Whitworth College in Washington arranged his major points according to topic when he prepared his award-winning speech on Amnesty International:

Specific Purpose
To inform my audience of the functions of Amnesty International.
Central Idea
Amnesty International is a global organization that successfully fights for human rights for oppressed people.

Major Point 1: The organization's first main function is to end cruel, inhuman, and degrading treatment of political prisoners.
Major Point 2: The second major function is to secure the release of prisoners of conscience, people imprisoned because of their beliefs, race, gender, ethnic origin, language, or religion.[14]

As you can see, Mutual broke his overall topic into two subtopics, (1) fighting for political prisoners and (2) fighting for prisoners of conscience. Each subtopic corresponded to a function of Amnesty International. These two subtopics, which together form the organization's reason for being, became his major points. If Amnesty International had more than two main functions, Mutual would have presented more than two major points. However, if the number of functions was five or more, he could avoid confusing his audience by grouping the functions into a few logical categories.

DEVELOP AND SUPPORT YOUR POINTS

Once you've selected your major points and organized them into a structure for your speech, you can begin to put some meat on the bones of these

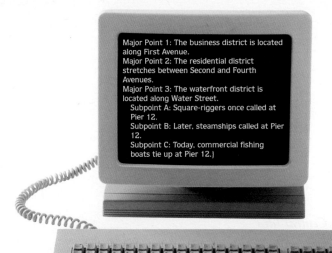

Major Point 1: The business district is located along First Avenue.
Major Point 2: The residential district stretches between Second and Fourth Avenues.
Major Point 3: The waterfront district is located along Water Street.
  Subpoint A: Square-riggers once called at Pier 12.
  Subpoint B: Later, steamships called at Pier 12.
  Subpoint C: Today, commercial fishing boats tie up at Pier 12.)

EXHIBIT 9.7
Organizing Subpoints
The subpoints in your speech can be organized as appropriate, regardless of the way your major points are organized. For example, in a speech about development in a northeastern city, the major points are presented according to space, and the subpoints are presented according to time.

points. Until now, you've been working with a skeletal description of each major point. The next step is to develop each point more fully. To do this, subdivide complex major points to bring out important details. Then add support materials that give listeners concrete reasons to understand or accept each major point.

Subdivide Complex Major Points

Although you want to express only one idea in each of your major points, some ideas may be quite complex. To develop each point more fully so that the audience can understand and absorb it, you can break it into its component parts, or **subpoints**. Each subpoint has a direct, specific relation to its major point, which you can make clear by the organizational method you choose for your subpoints. You don't have to use the same organizational method for all subpoints that you do for all major points. If appropriate, you can use one method to organize your major points and another to organize the subpoints under any one major point.

When speech student Merie Witt organized her speech about outpatient surgery clinics, she subdivided her

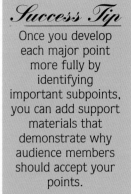

Success Tip
Once you develop each major point more fully by identifying important subpoints, you can add support materials that demonstrate why audience members should accept your points.

final major point into four subpoints, each corresponding to a possible solution:

Major Point 2: The audience should pursue governmental, medical, and individual solutions to the problem.
  Subpoint 1: Enact legislation to deal with the high cost of immunization.
  Subpoint 2: Enact legislation to make immunization mandatory for people of all ages in every state.
  Subpoint 3: Develop a computerized national registry to remind people when immunizations are due and to identify people who haven't acted to vaccinate themselves or their children.
  Subpoint 4: Protect yourself by supporting legislative actions and by getting or updating your vaccinations.[15]

Even though Witt organized her major points in order of problem and solution, that approach wasn't appropriate for the subpoints, because every subpoint was a kind of solution (see Exhibit 9.7). Instead, she arranged the four subpoints in order of topics. This helped the audience distinguish among the various solutions.

Add Support Material

After you divide complex major points into subpoints, you're ready to integrate the support materials that prove each point. Look through your research notes again. Pick out the most effective statistics, facts, quotations, and other items that relate to each major point. Then put them together to lead your audience to your conclusion. In outline form, the pattern of major points and support material in the body of your speech will look like this:

I. Major Point
   A. Support Material
   B. Support Material
   C. Support Material
II. Major Point
   A. Support Material
   B. Support Material
III. Major Point
   A. Support Material
   B. Support Material
   C. Support Material

For example, when baseball player Steve Sax addressed the Annual Awards Banquet of the Sacramento County Sheriff's Department in California, his general purpose was to motivate the police officers in the audience. Sax presented and supported three major points leading to his specific purpose and central idea. He organized his major points by topic, showing what law enforcement officers need in order to do their jobs more effectively.

Specific Purpose
To show officers that their efforts are appreciated and deserve to be backed by additional support and tools.

Central Idea
Police officers need support and the proper tools to continue making California's communities safer for everyone.

I. **Major Point:** To do their jobs, law enforcement officers need more support from the criminal justice system.
   A. **Support material:** Some 93 percent of prisoners are either violent or repeat offenders.
   B. **Support material:** Convicted felons spend little time in prison.
   C. **Support material:** Most convicted killers spend less than 10 years in prison.
II. **Major Point:** To do their jobs, law enforcement officers need the proper tools.
   A. **Support material:** "Three Strikes, You're Out" makes a difference.
   B. **Support material:** Government officials are starting to provide tools such as tougher laws, more prisons, and more resources for the police.
III. **Major Point:** Law enforcement officers are doing their jobs even without the support and the tools they need.
   A. **Support material:** Police officers being honored during this banquet have risked their lives to protect citizens.
   B. **Support material:** These courageous acts reflect well on everyone in the sheriff's department.[16]

Sax presented three major points to lead listeners to his central idea. He also included at least two

WHAT YOU DON'T SAY MAY BE USED AGAINST YOU

One of the stickiest ethical questions public speakers face is deciding how to handle research that contradicts or casts doubt on major points. Should you tell your audience? If so, how?

If you conceal negative support material, you're being disrespectful to your audience by assuming that listeners can't weigh the evidence and follow your reasoning to your conclusion. Withholding negative material can also break the bond of trust you've worked so hard to establish with your audience, which damages your credibility as a fair and honest speaker.

In the interest of respect, fairness, and balance, you can do only one thing with unfavorable evidence: disclose it. State that you're going to present both sides of the issue, but be careful not to distort or misrepresent the negative material. Instead, say what you've uncovered, discuss the implications, and explain how the material fits with your other points. Then listeners will be properly equipped to evaluate all your points and materials.

For example, when William J. Madia of the Battelle Institute addressed students at Ohio State University on the topic of assessing the risk in environmental problems, he knew that evidence existed for and against his position. His central idea was that U.S. policy makers must weigh the tradeoffs between spending to solve environmental problems and spending to solve other problems. Instead of ignoring opposing arguments, Madia introduced them and went on to carefully explain why each was unconvincing.

When he discussed the controversy over fluoride in drinking water, he first mentioned a study linking high doses of fluoride to bone cancer in laboratory animals. Having acknowledged this potential danger, he presented the results of additional studies that showed no link between fluoride and cancer. Then he reminded the audience of the health benefits of fluoride. By balancing his presentation with both favorable and unfavorable evidence, Madia actually helped the audience appreciate the significance of his arguments. He also won the trust of the audience and proved his credibility. By disclosing material that contradicts your purpose, you'll do the same.

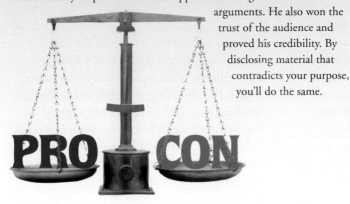

types of support material for each point. Taken together, the pattern of major points and support materials strengthened the message that Sax wanted to convey to his audience.

As you integrate your support material with the corresponding major points, don't separate the support materials from the identification of your sources. You'll want to cite your sources when you present the support material during your speech. You can expect your audience to evaluate your sources as well as your major points and your support materials, especially if you're tackling a controversial or technical topic.

Balance Your Points

Plan carefully to balance the amount of time you spend on each major point and its associated support material. You don't have to give each point equal time, but strive for a balance that won't short-change any vital point or overemphasize one point at the expense of others.

How much time and how many support materials do you need for each major point? The answer depends, in part, on your topic,

EXHIBIT 9.8
Breathing Life into Major Points
This docent in the San Francisco Mission District uses both narratives and quotations to maintain audience interest and enliven talks about the history, architecture, and inhabitants of the buildings she describes.

your purpose, and the knowledge that you and your audience have of the topic. Major points and support materials related to highly technical topics can rarely be explained in a few seconds. On the other hand, you'll usually spend less time and need fewer support materials for most points when your purpose is to entertain. Also, when both you and your audience are familiar with the topic, you may be able to make your points with fewer support materials.

In addition, ask these questions about your major points:

Is the point controversial? Add support material such as facts, statistics, and testimony to show that the point isn't just an unsubstantiated opinion. Use enough evidence to convince your audience that the point makes sense.

Is the point abstract or complicated? Spend some time clarifying the idea and offering support materials that can help the audience grasp your meaning. Analogies, testimony, and examples (which take more time to relate than facts and statistics) can be especially useful when you want to make an abstract point more concrete.

Is the point far from your listeners' daily lives or experience? If you believe your audience will have difficulty relating to the point you're making, include narratives, examples, and quotations to bring your point to life (see Exhibit 9.8). Using these support materials, you can dramatize the point and add human interest.

Consider how Philip M. Burgess, president of the Center for the New West, made and sup-

ported a major point during a commencement address at the University of Toledo in Ohio. Trying to motivate graduates to move into the working world with a positive attitude, he wanted to counteract the misconception that the Midwest is in decline because manufacturing is going away. Burgess spent more time on this point than on almost any other because he thought that the audience would doubt that manufacturing was still going strong in the Great Lakes area. He elaborated on that point using a narrative as well as facts, statistics, and comparisons.

One way he proved his point was by relating his personal experience of traveling through the area and marveling at the strength of Xerox, Kodak, and other manufacturers. This reminded students that such manufacturing giants were still located there. The second way he proved his point was by showing how the economy of the Midwest states compared with the economy of major industrial nations:

If you add up the wealth of the seven Great Lakes states, their GDP totals $1.6 trillion. That makes this Great Lakes region the *third largest nation in the world*— smaller than the U.S. and only slightly smaller than Japan but larger than Germany, France, and Britain. This region is an economic powerhouse and its manufacturing prowess is a major reason.[17]

Like Burgess, you'll want to take into account your audience, your topic, and your purpose as you balance your points. Regardless of how much time and how much support material your points require, make sure that each point builds on the one before and links with the next. With the correct balance, you'll be able to fully develop your topic and major points and successfully build a structure that solidly supports your central idea.

CONNECT YOUR POINTS

Now you're ready to assemble your collection of major points, subpoints, and support materials into a cohesive body for your speech. As the speaker, you understand how your major points and support materials fit together—but your audience doesn't. You can use four tools to connect your points and help your audience follow the direction of your ideas: transitions, signposts, internal previews, and internal summaries. Think of your major points as the cars in a train, and the subpoints as the freight and baggage in each car. Transitions, signposts, internal previews, and internal summaries act as the couplings linking your major points and keeping your speech on track.

Transitions

Transitions are words, phrases, or sentences that show how each point relates to the one before and the one after. You can use transitions to signal the audience that you're ending one idea and moving on to the next. By guiding listeners smoothly from point to point, you keep them focused on where you've been, where you are, and where you're going.

Think about the underlined transitions that follow: <u>For example,</u> look at how this sentence begins. *For example* is a common transition that alerts the audience to movement from a point to a piece of evidence that supports the point. <u>Similarly,</u> the word *similarly* alerts the audience that you're going to offer a second piece of evidence or a second major point much like the first. Both transitions serve as a bridge between

one point and the next so that the audience can follow along easily.

Here's how Sue Weber, a student at Moorhead State University in Minnesota, used transitions to guide her audience through an informative speech about the need for more widespread and comprehensive emergency training. Her central idea was that people should be prepared to act in a life-threatening emergency. In the body of her speech, she used transitions to link the need for training in life-supporting first aid to other steps people take to stay healthy:

> Americans are trying to eat healthier, exercise more, and smoke less, all in an effort to reduce our risks of heart disease. <u>In a similar vein,</u> we should learn life-supporting first aid in order to lower the risk for tragedy.[18]

Weber used the transition *in a similar vein* as a bridge connecting the two ideas. This phrase alerted the audience that the second idea had a direct connection to the first. Elsewhere in the body, she used a sentence to signal a transition between a subpoint about CPR and additional subpoints covering other life-saving techniques:

> While it is a vital skill, it is only one of many tools used in the process of saving lives.

This transition began with the word *while,* signaling that Weber was going to build on the idea she made in her previous subpoint. The rest of her transition helped the audience get ready to hear about other tools that can be used in addition to CPR to save lives. In this way, Weber was able to show her audience how the ideas in this major point were linked.

When you're moving from the body to the conclusion of your speech, you can signal the audience using transitions such as *finally* and *to summarize.* Although many speakers use *in conclusion* as the transition to the conclusion of a

Success Tip

Use transitions, signposts, internal previews, and internal summaries to link your major points and support materials and to signal the audience that you're moving into or out of an idea.

speech, you may want to choose a less clichéd phrase. However, once you signal that your speech is coming to an end, your audience will be expecting to listen for just a few minutes more. That's why you'll want to use these transitions only when you're actually concluding your speech (see Exhibit 9.9).[19]

Signposts

Signposts are words or phrases that help your listeners follow the order of the major points or subpoints as you speak. Often, signposts are numerical words or phrases, such as *First* or *the first problem*. You can also use signposts such as *the final problem* to signal the end of a series of points. Each time your listeners hear a signpost, they are reminded of where you are in your speech. They're also prompted to relate the next point in the series to the points you made earlier.

Carol J. Walker, a speech student at Grossmont College in California, effectively used signposts in her speech, "Zoos and Aquariums: Are They an Endangered Species?" Walker's signposts skillfully marked the path from one point to the next so that listeners could follow the linkage between her two major points.

In the body of her speech, she said she would present two myths surrounding the initiative to do away with zoological institutions. To introduce the first myth, she said: "One reason given for the elimination of zoos and aquariums is that they are consumers of wildlife." Her transition told listeners that this idea was the first of two. Once Walker had developed her first major point, she alerted the audience that she was moving on to the second point: "Another myth that is circulating is the myth that long-term captive animals should be released." This transition marked the second (and last) of the two myths.[20]

Internal Previews

An **internal preview** is a transition statement that alerts the audience to what comes next. More than just a word or phrase, an internal preview in the body of the speech serves as a detailed signpost indicating the direction your speech is about to take. You can use internal previews to prepare the audience for your next point or to signal that you're planning to make several connected points in the next section of your speech.

For example, Carol Walker used an internal preview to ease her audience into a new section of the body of her speech on aquariums and zoos:

> There are certainly many compelling reasons to eradicate zoos and aquariums. However, many of these reasons are based on myth, misunderstanding, and misinformation.[21]

Note how Walker's internal preview gave audience members a general idea of what they would hear next. In addition, the internal preview signaled the audience that she would both present reasons and show how they were invalid. Without this kind of guidance, listeners could easily become confused about why Walker was introducing a reason for eliminating zoos and aquariums and then, in the next breath, arguing against that reason.

When you're moving from the introduction of your speech into your body, an internal preview can help your audience recognize the transition to the new section. When Edward E. Crutchfield, Jr., chairman of First Union Corporation, addressed a banking conference in Atlanta, he used an internal preview to let his audience know what to expect in the body of his lengthy speech on changes in the banking industry:

> First, I'll comment on today's headlines, including the news that Congress finally seems ready to deal with interstate banking. Then, I'll look "over the hill" a few years, and focus on the banking industry's move into new markets and products. Finally, I'll touch on the risk raised by these moves and what we must do as an industry to deal with that risk.[22]

As you can see, Crutchfield's internal preview laid out a clear road map for the audience. He briefly touched on the major points he planned to make and the order in which he would make

EXHIBIT 9.9

Transitions and Signposts to Guide Your Audience
Speeches include numerous transitions and signposts between components, all of which overlap and reinforce each other.

Introduction: _____
_____
_____
_____

Major point: _____
_____
_____
_____
_____
_____
_____

Major point: _____
_____
_____

Major point: _____
_____
_____
_____

Subpoint _____
_____

Subpoint _____
_____

Subpoint _____

Major point: _____
_____
_____
_____
_____

Conclusion: _____
_____
_____
_____
_____
_____
_____

Signaling the beginning of a point
First ... Second ... Third ...
One argument ...
One reason ...

Shifting time or perspective

Afterward ...	Meanwhile ...	Previously ...
Later ...	Next ...	Subsequently ...
In the future ...	Now ...	Then ...
In the past ...	Soon ...	Until now ...

Signaling the beginning of a point

Moving to a contrasting viewpoint

Although ...	However ...	On the other hand ...
But ...	In contrast ...	Still ...
Conversely ...	Nevertheless ...	Yet ...

Signaling the beginning of a point

Linking one point to another

Also ...	In addition ...	Moreover ...
Another ...	In the same way ...	Not only ... but also
Besides ...	Likewise ...	Similarly ...

Signaling the beginning of evidence

Tying two major points into a conclusion

Therefore ...	Thus ...	As a result ...

Moving from body to conclusion

Finally ...	In conclusion ...	To summarize ...

them. By letting the audience know ahead of time the direction his speech would take, he helped them follow both the points and the logic used to connect those points.

Later in his speech, Crutchfield included single-sentence internal previews to introduce each of the three specific points. Like Carol Walker, he used these briefer internal previews to tell the audience what to expect in a certain part of the speech. As a result, his listeners were ready for the information they would hear—and were likely to remember it better, as well.

Internal Summaries

An **internal summary** is a transition statement that reminds the audience of what was covered in the previous section or point. In the same way that an internal preview sets the stage for what the audience will hear next, an internal summary repeats (in condensed form) what the audience heard in the previous section or point. This repetition gives your listeners another opportunity to grasp and remember your idea.

Consider how Devall L. Patrick, U.S. assistant attorney general for civil rights, used an internal summary during a recent speech about civil rights. He described the three principles that guide the work of his department. Then he condensed and restated his point this way:

> It is our faith in affirming these principles—of equality, opportunity and fair play—that makes us Americans.[23]

In this one-sentence internal summary, Patrick signaled that he was coming to the end of a major point. He also reminded the audience, one last time, of the three principles he had stressed during that point. After fixing those principles in his listeners' minds, Patrick moved on to make another point.

You can also combine an internal summary with an internal preview. This gives the audience a chance to reflect on the point you're leaving and then get ready for the point you're going to make next. Carol Walker used such a combination transition when she moved from one major point to another in her speech about zoos and aquariums:

> Now that we have examined a couple of the myths surrounding zoos and aquariums, let's look at some of the benefits that may be derived from them.[24]

Notice how Walker used only a few words to restate what her previous two points had been about. Because she had used an internal preview earlier in the speech to prepare the audience for the discussion of the myths, her internal summary gave the audience a sense of closure. Then she used a second internal preview to help the audience follow a shift away from myths toward benefits of zoos and aquariums.

After Walker talked about the benefits, she again combined an internal summary with an internal preview to let her audience know that she was moving from one point to another:

> So far, we have considered some myths and also we have analyzed some benefits that can be derived from zoos and aquariums. Now the question to ask is, "What exactly can I do?"[25]

The first sentence, an internal summary, reminded the audience of both the previous points. The second, an internal preview, led the audience directly into the section to follow. Because of internal summaries, internal previews, transitions, and signposts, the audience was always able to determine where Walker was in her speech, what she had already covered, and where she was going.

SUMMARY

The structure of a speech guides the audience and the speaker through all the points, from the introduction through the body and the conclusion. A well organized speech tells the audience that the speaker is well prepared and helps the audience understand, absorb, and retain the message. In the course of organizing the speech, the speaker gains skill in applying both critical and creative thinking skills.

A major point is one of the key ideas that builds toward and supports the central idea of the speech. One way to determine the major points to include in your speech is to see which are stressed in your research. Another way is to group your research into natural categories, then see how each category relates to your purpose, central idea, and audience analysis. Choose the most relevant, important categories, and simplify each to a single idea that becomes a major point.

You can organize your major points in one of six ways: according to (1) time, (2) cause and effect, (3) importance, (4) problem and solution, (5) space, and (6) topic. To develop a complex major point more fully, break it into its component parts, known as subpoints. Each subpoint should have a direct, specific relation to its major point. Regardless of the pattern you choose for your major points, you can arrange the subpoints using any appropriate organizational method.

Once you've selected your major points, look through your research and pick out the support materials that relate to each major point. Then create a pattern of major points and support materials to lead your audience through the body of your speech to your conclusion. Be ready to cite the sources of any narratives, quotations, statistics, and other materials you present to support each major point.

A transition is a word, phrase, or sentence that shows how each point relates to the one before and the one after. Speakers use transitions to indicate that they're ending one idea and moving to the next so that the audience can follow along. A signpost is a word or phrase that helps listeners follow the order of the major points in the speech. An internal preview is a transition statement that alerts the audience to what comes next. This prepares the audience for the next point or the next section of the speech. An internal summary is a transition statement that reminds the audience of what the speaker covered in the previous section or point. This restatement helps listeners understand and remember the point that was just made.

KEY TERMS

internal preview (204)
internal summary (206)
major point (190)
signposts (204)
subpoints (199)
transitions (203)

APPLY CRITICAL THINKING

1. What is the maximum number of major points you think can be effectively covered in a single speech? The maximum number of subpoints under a single major point? Explain your answers.
2. What organizational method would you use for the major points in a speech about each of the following topics? Why?
   a. Progress in finding a cure for cancer
   b. Four uses for recycled plastics
   c. The layout of your college campus
   d. Why talk shows should be taken off the air
3. Would you expect to integrate many support materials or just a few into a speech to immigrants about restricting the number of immigrants allowed to enter the United States? How about into a speech to college freshmen about keeping tuition affordable for all students? Explain your answers.
4. Why do you think the body usually accounts for 75 percent of the speech?
5. How does the speaker benefit from organizing a speech about sightseeing spots in Montreal by space? How does the audience benefit from this approach? What other pattern could be used for organizing the sightseeing attractions?

6. Should an internal preview always be balanced with an internal summary? If you decide to use internal previews and internal summaries, should they be linked to every major point?

7. Would you use internal previews and internal summaries in a five-minute speech? In a three-minute speech? Explain your answer.

SHARPEN YOUR SKILLS

Individual Exercises

1. Analyze the major points and organizational method used in one of the speeches in the appendix.

a. How many major points can you find? Would the speech be just as effective without one of these points? Which?

b. Which organizational method does the speaker use to organize the major points? How does this organizational method help the audience follow the speaker's ideas?

c. Could the speaker have used another organizational method? Which one(s) would you suggest? Why?

2. Prepare for an informative speech based on personal experience.

a. Identify your topic, central idea, and specific purpose.

b. List two or more major points.

c. Suggest two ways of putting these points in order. What are the pros and cons of each? Which do you think would be most helpful to the audience? Why?

3. Working with a speech from the appendix (or another speech), analyze how the speaker divided the major points into subpoints and balanced the major points.

a. List the major points, and under each, list its subpoints, if any. How does each subpoint support its major point?

b. Does the speaker use the same number of subpoints and the same amount of support material for each major point? What can you conclude from the way the speaker balances the major points and the support materials?

4. Sharpen your knowledge and use of transitions, signposts, internal previews, and internal summaries.

a. Think of three transitions or signposts not listed in Exhibit 9.9. Indicate what each would signal to an audience.

b. Choose a speech from the appendix. Pick out the transitions, signposts, internal previews, and internal summaries. Indicate what each is intended to signal to the audience.

c. Suggest a substitute for one transition, one signpost, one internal preview, and one internal summary identified in (b). How do your substitutes help the audience follow the speaker's train of thought?

Group Exercises

5. Pair up with a classmate. Exchange information about the general and specific purpose, central idea, and support materials for the next speech each of you will make.

a. What major points do you suggest your classmate select for the upcoming speech?

b. Which organizational method would you suggest for these major points? Why?

c. Write an internal preview and summary to be used before and after each major point.

d. Review each other's work. How can you improve on suggestions from your classmate?

6. Working with another student, analyze a problem-solution speech from the appendix or another source.

a. Does the speaker emphasize the seriousness of the problem or the possible solution? How do you know?

b. Does the speaker include any negative support material? How is it handled? If you were in the audience, would you accept the speaker's conclusion? Would your classmate? Why?

Chapter Ten

INTRODUCING AND CONCLUDING YOUR SPEECH

LEARNING OBJECTIVES

After studying this chapter, you will be able to

1. Describe what a speech introduction should accomplish.

2. List eight techniques you can use for an introduction.

3. Explain rhetorical questions and discuss their use.

4. Discuss the use of humor in an introduction, and indicate four possible problems with humor.

5. State the functions of a speech conclusion.

6. List seven techniques you can use for a conclusion.

7. Discuss how to choose among the various introduction and conclusion techniques.

PLANNING YOUR INTRODUCTION

First impressions count—and you can never take them back.[1] As soon as you start to speak, your audience begins weighing your words and actions and deciding whether to continue listening to your speech. In the first few minutes, you demonstrate why the audience should listen to you, believe what you say, and remember your message, and these minutes are among the most critical of your speech. In fact, you may have only a few seconds to prove yourself, because some listeners form judgments more quickly than others.[2]

The introduction is your first and best chance to show that you're not going to waste your audience's time. Prepare a strong introduction, and you'll be rewarded with more than your audience's interest—you'll also gain an extra measure of self-confidence as you watch your listeners become involved in what you're saying. Even though you already know you've done a good job analyzing your audience, selecting and researching your topic, and organizing your major points, your listeners don't know what you've been doing behind the scenes. So with your first words, it's up to you to show the result of all your planning and preparation.

Introduction Functions

A strong introduction performs four functions. First, it captures your audience's attention and builds interest in you and your speech. Second, it establishes your credibility and helps you build rapport with your listeners. Third, it identifies your topic, telling the audience what you plan to talk about. Fourth, it previews your major points, preparing the audience for the transition into the body of your speech. The following sections look at each of these four functions in more detail (see Exhibit 10.1).

Capture Attention and Build Interest

Distracted by external or internal interference, even the best listeners may let their minds wander if a speech doesn't immediately arouse their interest. To win out over interference, your introduction has to hook your audience and quickly. Moreover, once you've grabbed your audience's attention, you have to hold it by building interest in your message.

Consider how Rebecca Witte, a student at the University of Missouri in St. Louis, introduced a speech to a college audience:

> I am a seven letter word. I destroy friends, families, neighborhoods and schools. I am the biggest killer among teenagers today. I am not alcohol. I am not cocaine. I am suicide.[3]

Witte's introduction aroused curiosity and encouraged listeners to stay tuned for the answer. Then, to keep listeners involved, Witte cited a few surprising statistics and went on to pose two thought-provoking questions:

> Why is it then that the high schools aren't doing anything? Why is it that high schools do not have mandatory suicide prevention

EXHIBIT 10.1
Using An Introduction
The first words from a speaker's mouth accomplish four important functions: Capture audience attention and build interest, establish credibility and build rapport, introduce the topic, and preview the speech's major points.

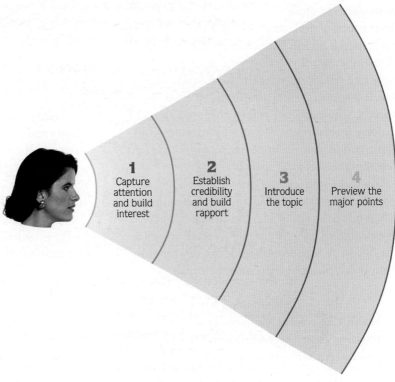

1 Capture attention and build interest

2 Establish credibility and build rapport

3 Introduce the topic

4 Preview the major points

programs as a part of their everyday curriculum? Those are very good questions and that is why I am here today.[4]

Initially, Witte's introduction intrigued her listeners and therefore captured their attention for a minute or two. But Witte had to do more to keep her audience interested after the first few sentences. By quoting statistics and asking questions, she gave her audience solid reasons for staying interested.

Establish Credibility and Build Rapport

Why should the audience listen to you? Your introduction answers that question by establishing your credibility and building rapport. You want listeners to see you as qualified to tackle your topic, either because of your extensive research or your personal or professional experience. When audience members believe that you know what you're talking about, they'll listen more closely and take your message more seriously. In this way, you build a strong connection—a *rapport*—that puts you on good terms with your listeners.

Establishing your credibility means walking a fine line. On the one hand, you want to show your competence; on the other hand, you don't want to seem boastful. So aim for middle ground: matter-of-factly describe your qualifications and link them to your topic and central idea. When

John F. Ferguson, a minister, spoke during a Veterans' Day assembly at a high school in Kirkland, Washington, he stated his credentials during his introduction:

> We have come together to honor the military service of American men and women, particularly those who participated in the war in Vietnam. I'm one of those people. I served in the United States Marine Corps in Vietnam in 1967 and 1968. I was a member of the 15th Marine Counter-intelligence Team, operating just below the Demilitarized Zone. Our team was a part of small unit combat and intelligence operations, now known as the Phoenix Program.[5]

Ferguson let his audience know that he was personally involved in the war. He didn't brag or boast; he simply explained what his wartime role was. His experience was directly relevant to the topic of war veterans and to the purpose of the school's assembly, to honor veterans, so he seemed more credible to the audience.

Introduce the Topic

Your introduction also has to present the topic of your speech and indicate why it's important. Remember, until you start your speech, you're the only one who knows exactly what you're going to say. If you don't reveal your topic early in your speech, your audience will be confused and will quickly lose interest. So plan to introduce your topic and explain its importance within the first few sentences of your speech.

You can come straight out with the topic in your first sentence, as Murray Weidenbaum did when he spoke about U.S. health care policy. Weidenbaum, who is director of the Center for the Study of American Business at Washington University, plunged right into the topic:

> The time is ripe for taking a new look at health-care reform. Conventional approaches have bogged down in the legislative process. A fresh start is necessary.[6]

Weidenbaum's audience was knowledgeable about the topic, so they needed little background to orient themselves. That's why the speaker was able to get down to business right away. A brief comment on the problems of dealing with health-care reform through conventional approaches was all he needed to show the importance of the topic.

Of course, not every speaker will want to be as direct. Sometimes a less direct introduction is more effective, especially for certain persuasive speeches. As you saw earlier in Rebecca Witte's introduction to a speech on teen suicide, a bit of suspense goes a long way in capturing attention. However, Witte didn't let the audience's anticipation build for too long; she was careful to tie her first sentences to the topic of her speech within a short time.

Preview Your Major Points

You'll also use your introduction to preview the major points you plan to make in the body of your speech. Knowing the topic is not enough; your listeners need some advance warning of what you're going to say about the topic. Then they'll have a better sense of the organization of your speech and be prepared to listen for each point during the body of your speech.

The preview of major points often comes near the end of your introduction, after you've grabbed your audience's attention, built interest in the topic, revealed your topic, and established your credibility. In your preview, touch lightly on your points and the order in which you plan to present them. At the end of your preview, lead your audience smoothly into the body of your speech, where you make and support each major point in turn (see Exhibit 10.2).

For example, Merie Witt of McLennan College in Texas ended her introduction to a speech titled "Outpatient Surgery Centers" with this preview:

> For the next few minutes, I'm going to discuss a trend in medical care—outpatient clinics—that has compromised our safety. First, I'll give you a diagnosis of the problem. Next, we'll examine the symptoms, or why these outpatient clinics suffer from inadequacies; and finally, I'll offer you a prescription for recovery.[7]

Note how Witt restated her topic before mentioning her three major points. This preview reminded audience members of the topic and tied it to the sequence of points the speaker would make in her speech. Note also how Witt used words such as *diagnosis, symptoms,* and *prescription,* to call attention to the content of each major point and show how they fit together.

Effective Introduction Techniques

The introduction to your speech will span only a few sentences or, for a longer speech, a few paragraphs. How can you effectively capture attention, present your topic, establish credibility, and preview your major points in just a few minutes? Try one of these eight tried-and-true techniques: (1) using a startling statement, (2) asking a question, (3) telling a story, (4) using a quote, (5) using suspense, (6) talking about personal experience, (7) referring to the audience, or (8) using humor. Not every one of these techniques is appropriate for every speech or

EXHIBIT 10.2

Using Introductions to Make a Strong Start

Anthony Robbins, a well-known motivational speaker, used this introduction to draw his audience into a speech about the power of words and to preview what he planned to say: "Words. They've been used to make us laugh and cry. They can wound or heal. They offer us hope or devastation. With words we can make our noblest intentions felt and our deepest desires known."

occasion. However, among these eight techniques, you're sure to find at least one that will work well for your next speech.

Using a Startling Statement

If you want your audience to snap to attention immediately, start your introduction with a startling statement. You might describe an extremely unusual situation, reveal a shocking statistic, or vividly portray an alarming problem. Not only will listeners sit up and take notice, they'll also listen carefully to find out more about what you just said and why you said it.

For example, when student Heather Larson of Northern State University in South Dakota wrote her speech "Stemming the Tide," she used a series of startling statements to draw her audience instantly into her message:

> Every eleven minutes one American dies from this killer. That is twice as many as will be murdered in crimes of homicide. It took eight years of Vietnam to exceed the 46,000 that will die this year. Three times as many Americans have died of this disease in the last decade than the 133,000 who died of AIDS. This disease will cost you and me and other Americans over $6 billion in medical costs and lost productivity this year alone, not to mention the human losses we will suffer. This tide awash on our shores may

well directly touch each and every one of us in this room. I speak of breast cancer.[8]

Larson didn't rely only on shocking facts and figures to grab her audience's attention. A few sentences later, she reminded the audience that men, too, can suffer from breast cancer. Then she disclosed that the previous president of the university had recently died from the disease. Larson's startling comments weren't so strong that they were offensive or intimidated her listeners. Instead, her introduction gave audience members something to think about as they continued listening to her speech.

Asking a Question

You can get listeners involved in your introduction by asking a question that leads into your central idea. A **rhetorical question** is one that is asked for effect rather than to elicit an answer. Inviting your audience to actually answer a question you pose can be disruptive. However, when you ask a rhetorical question, you're inviting audience members to answer silently and then continue thinking about the question throughout your speech.[9]

For example, Heidi L. Wadeson, a student at University of Mary in North Dakota, posed two rhetorical questions in this introduction to her speech:

See this dollar bill? What can it do for you? You can invest it, save it to buy something more expensive, or you can just spend it, although there isn't much to buy for a dollar these days. Kids, on the other hand, would take this dollar and be able to spend it on something that they would be satisfied with, even if what they were spending it on could kill them. This dollar bill can buy kids a high that's cheap, available, and legal to purchase.[10]

Clearly, Wadeson didn't want her listeners to actually respond. What she wanted was to get them thinking about her topic, the dangers of inhaling solvents and aerosols. Just as Wadeson didn't leave her audience hanging with unanswered questions, you'll want to answer any questions you pose. Otherwise, your audience will feel cheated and will focus on your unanswered questions rather than your message.

Telling a Story

Everybody likes a good story, so long as it relates to the topic at hand. Stories can be effective in leading off any kind of speech. When you use a good story to bring your topic alive in dramatic or human terms, you'll engage your audience from the first sentence on.

Gretchen Richter of Cornell College in Iowa used this story to introduce her speech, "Health Care Combat Zones:"

California emergency room nurse Tim Dufelmeier became a hero—not because of his successful efforts to save a patient, but because of his valiant rescue of an emergency room physician. A disgruntled patient had lunged at three ER physicians without warning, wounding two slightly and shooting one point-blank in the head and chest. Dufelmeier charged past the gunman, grabbed the doctor and rushed him to emergency life-saving surgery.[11]

If Richter had simply quoted statistics about violence in hospitals and emergency rooms, the audience might have seen the problem as remote or abstract. Instead, Richter's story put a human face on the problem she wanted to expose. And the twist of the nurse's heroism in ending a patient's shooting spree and saving a doctor's life added to the drama of her introduction.

Using a Quotation

Another way to draw listeners into your speech is by offering an appropriate quotation. Look for a vivid, succinct quotation that will interest the audience and, at the same time, allow you to build on the credibility of the source. You can quote (or paraphrase) the words of a famous author, politician, or anybody else who has something significant to say about your topic (see Exhibit 10.3).

Consider how John J. McGrath, director of marketing and management communications for Argonne National Laboratory, used a quotation to start his recent speech, "Sell Your CEO! Winning the Corporate-Image Battle":

"There are many excellent speakers in the United States. There also are many business executives. Apparently, the policy is not to intermingle the two." Those are the words of Norman Augustine, chairman and CEO of Martin Marietta Corporation. I've known Norm Augustine for more than a decade. He is the rarest of creatures—an American chief executive who speaks common English, and speaks it well . . . even in public.[12]

Notice how McGrath cited the source of the quotation he used. He then drew a contrast between Augustine and the business executives mentioned in the quotation. Later in the introduction, McGrath stated his central idea: that a chief executive officer must have good communication skills. Seen in the light of that central idea,

> ### Success Tip
>
> Plan your introduction carefully. It has a big job to do: attracting attention and arousing interest in your topic, building your credibility, presenting your topic, and previewing your major points.

EXHIBIT 10.3
Create Interest with Quotations
To find an appropriate story or quotation to introduce your speech, check one of these books, which are generally available in local libraries.

the quotation that McGrath chose is fitting and ironic.

Using Suspense

People are curious, and audiences are no exception. You can play on this curiosity by using suspense in the opening moments of your speech. If you don't reveal the topic or the point of your opening right away, audience members will wonder where you're taking them. They'll be hooked, and they'll listen carefully if you skillfully draw a connection between your opening and your central idea within a minute or two.

Earlier, you saw how Rebecca Witte used suspense to introduce a speech on teenage suicide and how Heather Larson used it to open a speech on breast cancer. Jenean Johnson of Sheridan College in Wyoming also used suspense, but in a slightly different way. Here's her attention-getting introduction to a speech about drug-resistant bacterial infections:

> For a moment I'd like you to visualize this scene: A vast hospital ward with row upon row of cots, each occupied by an individual dying of tuberculosis. The patients are coughing, wheezing, gasping for air, begging

that the doctors do something for them. But they can't. The physicians stand helplessly by, unable to render any assistance. They are baffled by the disease and unable to treat it with any of their medicines or medical knowledge. Does this scene sound like a military hospital during the Civil War or a tuberculosis ward in the 1800s? It is not. It is a New York prison in the 1990s.[13]

Johnson's introduction was suspenseful because her audience had no idea where or when the scene might have taken place. As a result, listeners would be surprised to learn that tuberculosis and other diseases once thought to be virtually wiped out are back today, in force. And they would continue to listen as Johnson moved into the body of her speech, explaining how and why this situation developed and then suggesting solutions.

Talking About Personal Experience

A good way to introduce your topic and simultaneously build your credibility is by sharing your personal experience. This adds human interest, shows why the topic is important to you, and gives the audience a compelling reason to believe what you say. Be sure to relate your personal experience to the broader topic and to the audience's interests so that listeners can see how the topic touches them (see Exhibit 10.4).

Consider how Chris Fleming, a student at Western Kentucky University, introduced a speech about car insurance:

Starting from Personal Experience
By linking the introduction of the topic to your personal experiences, you can add human interest while showing how and why your topic is meaningful in your life.

Part of every teenager's great "American Dream" is to some day get a driver's license, and more important . . . to own some wheels. Since there are nine children in my family, to realize my dream, I knew that I would have to earn the money for a car. The day finally arrived when I could go to our local car dealer with checkbook in hand. I found a six-year-old candy apple red Mustang that was well within my price range. My dream was shattered when I discovered that I would have to pay more for insurance coverage than my car would be worth on the resale market. I know that sounds unreal . . . but it's true. I am in a high risk category because I am male, unmarried, and under 25 and attend college in a designated high premium area.[14]

Fleming's opening gave his audience some insight into his background. In addition, he encouraged the audience to identify with his experience by starting with a reference to "every teenager's great 'American Dream.'" By the time Fleming finished his introduction, his listeners understood how and why high car insurance premiums could be a problem for them.

Referring to the Audience
Few motivations are as powerful as self-interest. Listeners always want to know, "What's in it for me?" When you refer to your listeners in your introduction and show them how your message relates directly to them, you heighten their interest in your speech. Your audience analysis will help you find ways of linking your introduction to your listeners' interests. And using the word *you* makes your introduction even more personal.

For example, one student used the following introduction to open his informational speech about conversing on the Internet:

You know what it's like at the end of the day. You drag yourself home from your last class or after-school job, feeling tired and hungry. Sometimes you want to party, but you don't have the energy. However, if you have a computer, you can have an adventure without leaving home. All you have to do is make yourself a sandwich, sit down in front of the screen, and fire up your modem for a night of chat on the Internet.

This speaker involved his listeners by crafting an introduction that reflected their daily lives. Then he helped them envision the contrast between going out after a tiring day and going out on the

Internet. Once he had the audience hooked on the convenience of cyberspace conversation, he moved into the body of his speech to talk about the Internet in more detail.

Using Humor

One popular way to break the ice and build rapport with your audience at the start of a speech is to use humor in your introduction. By linking humor to the topic of your talk, you'll give your audience a reason to smile and a way to remember your message. Once you and your listeners share a laugh, you're both more relaxed and ready to think about your major points. In fact, sharing a joke has been identified as one of the best devices for establishing rapport with an international audience.[15]

You might tell a joke, relate a funny story, or offer a witty quote that you immediately connect with your message. Avoid stale stories that your audience has heard before; look for a fresh angle or insight to bring your material alive. Also avoid vulgar, sexist, and racist humor. Your audience doesn't expect you to be a stand-up comedian, so just be yourself when you use humor.

For example, Neil A. Armstrong, the first person to set foot on the moon, rarely talks in public about his achievements. That's one reason he drew laughter from an audience of dignitaries when he started a speech commemorating the twenty-fifth anniversary of his historic moon walk this way:

FOUR KEYS TO SPONTANEOUS HUMOR THAT WILL HAVE YOUR AUDIENCE LAUGHING

"Have you heard the one about . . .?" You have. And your listeners have, too. So treat your audience to something special in your next speech: Use spontaneous humor. The point of spontaneous humor is to make your audience feel that you crafted a funny remark on the spot for their unique interests or situation. Here are four keys to spontaneous humor:

- *Prepare to be spontaneous.* Prepare by collecting funny experiences, witty remarks from printed sources, and comments you overhear. Then you'll have a stock to choose from when something happens unexpectedly. You'll also be able to find the right remark to match the needs and interests of your audience.
- *Observe and comment.* Be observant before and during your speech, and weave your observations into a funny comment. You might talk about the facility where you're speaking, the way the audience is huddled in the back of the room, or something else that makes the audience laugh without maliciousness.

Like Jerry Seinfeld, you will feel more comfortable with spontaneous humor if you are properly prepared.

- *Dare to be spontaneous.* Once you've prepared possible quips and observed your audience, you have to take the next step and risk being funny. You'll need some courage, but your audience will make it seem worthwhile when they laugh appreciatively.
- *Practice being spontaneous.* Your humor will come more naturally as you practice and become more comfortable with this skill. You'll be able to find your audience's funny bone more often, and your audience will enjoy humor tailored just for them.

Wilbur Wright once noted that the only bird that could talk was the parrot, and he didn't fly very well. So I'll be brief.[16]

Armstrong's audience could appreciate the significance of a one-time astronaut quoting the words of a pioneer in air flight. Further, the quotation poked fun at Armstrong's well-known reluctance to talk in public about his accomplishments. This gentle humor put Armstrong's audience into a receptive frame of mind for the rest of his remarks.

Of course, humor isn't always appropriate, and it can backfire if you're not careful. First, not everyone has the same tastes or comes from the same cultural background, so what's funny to one person may be offensive to another. Second, if your humor falls flat, your audience may lose interest in the rest of your speech, and you may lose some of your momentum. Third, reserve your humor for lighthearted topics or occasions, not serious ones. Finally, using sidesplitting humor risks putting the focus on your jokes, not your message. So think carefully before using humor, and show the audience how your humor relates to your message.[17]

Analysis of an Introduction

You have a lot riding on your introduction. You have to capture attention and build interest, establish credibility and build rapport, introduce your topic, and preview your major points. How, exactly, does an introduction accomplish all these things?

The best way to understand how an introduction works is to analyze one, paragraph by paragraph. The following introduction was used in a student's classroom speech. By reading through the introduction and the commentary on the side, you'll get a better idea of how the speaker put the theory of introduction into practice.

Can you answer this riddle? "The Tooth Fairy, Santa Claus, the Easter Bunny, the

Perfect Man, and the Perfect Woman were all in a room together. The light suddenly went out. Who changed the bulb?" The correct answer? The Perfect Woman, of course. All the others are fictitious characters. Unlike these fictitious characters, the Perfect Woman shapes the standards used to judge *real* women in our society—our mothers, our sisters, our girlfriends, and ourselves. Moreover, even though these fictitious characters can't change light bulbs, their traits are well-established and unchanging. Santa Claus is always fat, bearded, and jolly; the Easter Bunny is always white, fluffy, and generous. But the characteristics of the Perfect Woman are harder to pin down.

The speaker attracts audience attention by starting with a question that leads into a riddle. Her humorous punch line and follow-up analysis introduce the topic and build interest. She demonstrates the importance of the topic by relating the Perfect Woman to the women in the audience as well as listeners' mothers, sisters, and girlfriends.

We're all familiar with the Virginia Slims version of the Perfect Woman, who replaced her rigid and frigid tendencies with a carefree and independent spirit. But how many of us have noticed that, having "Come a long way," the Perfect Woman now appears to be beating a hasty retreat? Nearly 80 percent of real women in the United States are part of the labor force. Yet, according to today's advertis-

Checklist for Planning a Speech Introduction

1. Start with confidence.
2. Protect and respect your audience.
3. Use creativity when developing your introduction.
4. Relate your introduction to your message.
5. Be realistic about what your speech will cover.
6. Avoid apologizing or offering excuses.
7. Avoid insulting, endangering, or offending your audience.
8. Avoid using hackneyed material.
9. Avoid starting with an irrelevant opening.
10. Avoid promising what your speech won't deliver.

EXHIBIT 10.5
Using a Conclusion
With a conclusion the speaker reinforces the central idea, provides closure for the speech, and motivates the audience to take action.

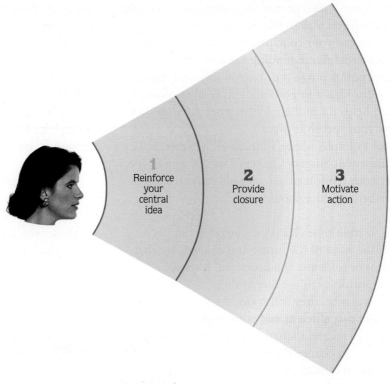

1 Reinforce your central idea

2 Provide closure

3 Motivate action

ing, the Perfect Woman now prefers the kitchen table to the conference table.

Next, the speaker presents more information about the topic. She invites listeners to think about the contradiction in women's roles, which she illustrates by citing a well-known advertising campaign and a startling statistic.

Are advertisers engineering this latest change? They're sending us the message that their products are essential to the Perfect Woman. But they're really selling more than the products themselves: They're selling an image that is far removed from real women. To see just how advertisers are influencing the Perfect Woman image, I analyzed hundreds of recent ads directed toward women. Let's take a closer look at the portrayal of women in ads for bread machines, convection ovens, pressure cookers, and wide-body refrigerators.

Now the speaker presents her central idea: that advertisers are molding perceptions of the Perfect Woman. She establishes credibility by mentioning that she analyzed hundreds of ads. Finally, she previews the points she will make about product advertising and alerts her audience that she is moving into the body of the speech.

PLANNING YOUR CONCLUSION

Just as your introduction helps you make a good first impression, your conclusion helps you make a final, lasting impression. By the time you reach your conclusion, you've spent considerable time and effort building up to and supporting your central idea. Now you've reached the climax of your speech, where everything you've said before comes together. Think of your conclusion as your last opportunity to influence the audience's view of your ideas and yourself.

Conclusion Functions

A powerful conclusion performs three functions. First, it reinforces your central idea and shows how your major points fit together. Second, it provides closure by signaling the end of the speech. Third, it motivates your audience to take action based on your message (see Exhibit 10.5).

Reinforce Your Central Idea

Throughout your speech, you've been presenting major points and support material to convince your audience of the soundness of your central idea. Some audience members may have lost sight of the central idea to which your points relate. You can use your conclusion to put these points into a structure, reminding the audience how your major points prove your central idea and stressing why this idea is important. This final reinforcement helps the audience remember your message after your speech is over.[18]

For example, Merie Witt closed her speech, "Outpatient Surgery Centers," with a conclusion that both reinforced her central idea and showed why her audience should care:

> It should be clear that outpatient surgery is the wave of the future and chances are that you or someone you know will have the opportunity to use one of these clinics. At first glance, they will seem like the most cost efficient and convenient way to go and they may be, but there is a chance that you could come in contact with an underregulated clinic or an unethical physician. Please remember the safety tips I have offered and push for stronger legislation. After all, the point is to walk out of these clinics in better shape than you came in.[19]

Notice Witt restated her central idea that solutions exist to the problems of inadequate medical care in certain outpatient clinics. She reminded listeners that, according to her major points, they or someone they know might find similar problems. After urging the audience to pursue solutions by following safety tips and supporting legislative action, Witt reinforced her message one last time, pointing out that clinics should cure people, not put them in danger.

Provide Closure

A good conclusion also provides **closure,** giving the audience a sense of completion. Without closure, listeners may feel confused and dissatisfied at the end of a speech. In fact, if you end too

abruptly, your audience may not realize that you're finishing your speech. So use your conclusion to signal that you're ready to close your speech. This prepares your audience to listen carefully for your final words.

Earlier, you saw how John Ferguson introduced his speech to high school students during a Veteran's Day assembly. Now look at the way Ferguson concluded that speech:

> Let me leave you with an idea. If you truly desire to honor Vietnam veterans, don't stop with this assembly. Seek out those who served (perhaps your father, mother, uncle, aunt, teacher, or neighbor). Thank them for their service. Ask them to share their feelings and memories. That will bring them real honor, because in so doing you are telling them you understand and value their experiences and contribution. Again, from my heart, I thank you for the privilege of speaking to you this morning.[20]

The first sentence of Ferguson's conclusion warned the audience that his speech was winding down. His next few sentences asked the audience to take action, something else a conclusion accomplishes. The last sentence signaled that he was finished speaking. In this way, Ferguson avoided an abrupt ending to the speech, and he left his audience with a sense of closure.

Motivate Action

John Ferguson's conclusion did more than alert listeners that his speech would soon be over. It also mentioned what he wanted his audience to do. Every persuasive speech concludes by stirring the audience to action. But informative, entertaining, and motivational speeches can also lay the groundwork for action by shedding new light on an issue, by leaving the listener with a lasting memory, or by changing the listener's feelings about a subject or issue.

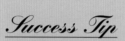

Success Tip

Craft your conclusion with care. In those few moments, you have one final chance to make a lasting impression on your audience. Make it as strong and as memorable as you can.

TURNING OFF BEFORE YOUR AUDIENCE TUNES OUT

Even experienced public speakers don't always know when to stop talking. For many listeners, President Clinton's 1995 State of the Union address was memorable not for the message but for its ear-numbing 80-minute length. And he's not the only politician partial to marathon speeches. On the other side of the aisle, some Republicans' speeches haven't always been concise, either. So how does a speaker decide when to conclude a speech?

Take a tip from Calvin Coolidge: "Never rise to speak 'til you have something to say; and when you've said it, cease." As far as your audience is concerned, less is more. Keep their needs and interests in mind as you plan your conclusion. No matter how brilliant your speech, your listeners can't possibly remember everything you say. Therefore, once you've made your major points, don't prolong your speech; use one of the conclusion techniques to wrap things up gracefully and succinctly, and step off the stage.

Learn to trust your audience's reaction. As you move through the body of your speech, look for signs that the audience is following along. If you see a number of people dozing, whispering, checking the time, shifting restlessly, snoring, or sneaking out, you'll want to make a quick transition to your conclusion (the shortest component of your speech) and finish up. Make your last few moments strong and memorable so that the audience will remember what you said, not how long you spoke.

In short, be brief.

For example, when Michael Tanner, director of health and welfare studies at the Cato Institute, spoke on the subject of health care reform, he discussed various proposals being considered by Congress. Then he concluded his informative speech by calling for a particular action:

> The debate in Congress can seem very confusing. But when you break it down to basics, it is a simple question. Will we take all the money, all the power, and all the decision-making that is in the health care system today, and turn it over to the government? Or will we take that same money, that same power, that same decision-making, and turn it over to individual consumers and patients? That is what this debate is all about. The decision is yours.[21]

Tanner's conclusion reinforced his central idea that a free-market system of health care works best. It also provided closure, reducing the body of the speech to two contrasting positions. His final sentence called on audience members to take action by making a decision about how they wanted health care reform to proceed.

Effective Conclusion Techniques

You can develop an effective, memorable conclusion by applying one of these seven common techniques: (1) using a summary, (2) telling a story, (3) using an inspirational appeal or challenge, (4) using a quotation, (5) referring to the introduction, (6) asking a question, or (7) appealing to action. Many of these techniques echo those used in introductions. If you use the same technique for your conclusion as for your introduction, your speech will seem balanced and symmetrical. However, you can also be quite effective if you open with one technique and close with another. Of course, as with introduction techniques, not every conclusion technique is right for every speech or occasion.

Using a Summary

When you use a summary to end your speech, you help your audience remember your major points and central idea by quickly reviewing them one final time. This is a straightforward technique that can be used to close any type of speech, keeping your audience's attention focused, until the last moment, on the issues you want to emphasize.

When Andrea Owens of Berry College in Georgia gave a speech about the role of Occupational Safety and Health Administration (OSHA) in protecting employees from unsafe work conditions, she first described several problems that the government agency wasn't adequately addressing. She used the term *Industrial Darwinism* to emphasize the problems employees faced in surviving the hazardous, junglelike conditions of some industrial plants. After describing some inadequate solutions that had been tried, she urged her listeners to speak out in favor of more effective solutions. Her conclusion summarized what she had said in the body of her speech:

> Today, we've examined the declining situation of OSHA by first reviewing the nature of the problem, citing specific reasons for these problems, and finally examining some ineffective solutions to discover the significant role we [can] play in effecting change. In a nation such as ours, the idea of Industrial Darwinism is regrettable, even shameful. We need to reject the notion that the laws of the jungle are fit for the American workplace. Realizing the significant impact that are our voices can have, we must speak out against the valuing of corporate profits over human lives.[22]

Owens alerted her listeners that she had completed the body of her speech by using the words "Today, we've examined . . ." Then she related the summary of her major points to the action she wanted the audience to take as a result of her speech: to speak out for better worker safety. This final sentence brought the topic to closure by showing how listeners could play a role in preventing more injuries.

Telling a Story

A story makes an effective conclusion because it helps your listeners remember what your speech was about. This is a less direct technique than the summary, but it works well when you can connect a vivid or dramatic story with your central idea or topic. When audience members recall the story, they'll also remember your message.

Philip M. Burgess, president of the Center for the New West, concluded his commencement address to graduates of the University of Toledo in Ohio with a story. He spoke about Roger Bannister, the first person to run a mile in less than four minutes. After Bannister's 1954 achievement, runner after runner followed in Bannister's footsteps (see Exhibit 10.6). Here's how Burgess tied this story to his central idea:

> Runners and coaches now believed in their objective. They now believed in themselves and gained confidence in their new methods of preparation and training. Armed with the knowledge that it could be done, they simply went out and did it— again . . . and again . . . and again— improving with each passing year. So that's my message to you today. Defend your legacy of freedom. Believe in our society and its capacity to provide new opportunities for those willing to take risks and accommodate change. But most of all, believe in yourself. Have confidence in your preparation and training. And then, go out there and do it—again . . . and again . . . and again—improving with each passing year.[23]

Burgess painted a memorable and inspiring word image of Roger Bannister breaking the four-minute mile. Then he linked the story to

EXHIBIT 10.6

Using a Conclusion to Summarize Your Speech

Telling a dramatic and exciting story can be a good conclusion to a speech. When Philip Burgess talked about Roger Bannister's record-breaking performance, he inspired his audience to have confidence in themselves, to apply self-discipline, and to be willing to smash barriers—just as Olympic athletes Jesse Owens and Gail Deaver smashed barriers and set new records.

Jesse Owens, 1936 Berlin Olympics, 200m dash, 20.7 seconds record

Gail Deaver, 1992 Olympics, 100m high hurdles, 12.8 seconds

the message he wanted his audience to remember: believe in yourself and in your preparation and training. This way, the audience would recall both the story and the underlying message.

Using an Inspirational Appeal or Challenge

You can stir your audience to action by offering an inspirational appeal or challenge to close your speech. With an inspiring, climactic conclusion, you'll leave your listeners with an uplifting feeling. You'll also leave them with a strong sense of commitment to a particular course of action.

For example, James B. Hayes, publisher emeritus of *Fortune* magazine, closed a speech about the growing problems of child neglect and called for the help of all Americans by using this inspiring appeal to his audience:

Many years ago, Sir Edward Grey likened America to a gigantic boiler. "Once the fire is ignited under it, there is no limit to the

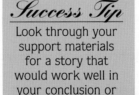

Success Tip

Look through your support materials for a story that would work well in your conclusion or your introduction. A good story can bring your topic to life and help your audience remember your message.

power it can generate." The time has come for us to light that fire! Our children need your help to light the fire under America. Won't you please join with us to save the dream for the children of America? Thank you.[24]

The inspiring words that Hayes used were more effective than simply ending with a plea such as, "Won't you help our children?" Instead, he offered the quote from Sir Edward Grey, once Great Britain's foreign minister. Then he brought the speech to a climax by calling on the audience to light the fire and save the dream for all children (see Exhibit 10.7).

Using a Quotation

You can also conclude your speech with a quotation that's appropriate for your central idea or topic. You can quote directly or you can paraphrase if you don't want to include the entire quotation. In all cases, be sure to show your audience how the quotation or the

EXHIBIT 10.7
Issuing an Inspirational Appeal or Challenge
An inspirational appeal is a good way to end an emotionally
charged speech, such as this one to striking Alitalia airline
employees. By building to a strong and inspiring climax, the
speaker seeks to encourage listeners to remain committed to the
strike.

person being quoted relates to your message.

Consider how Meryl Irwin, a student at
Concordia College in Minnesota, used a quotation to close her speech about the need for
specialized emergency medical care for children:

> You now know that children need special-
> ized emergency care, and that the present
> system isn't giving it to them. Through the
> solutions I presented, we can do our part to
> make sure that the children we care about
> don't become just additional testimonials for
> reform. I'd like to leave you with the words of
> Dr. Richard Flyer as a reminder of why
> action is needed now. Dr. Flyer says, "The
> worst part about it is, after it's all over, a child
> is dead. And the parents come up and thank
> the doctor. They say, 'We know you did
> everything you could.' My head is exploding,
> because I know, too often, it's not true."[25]

Irwin's specific purpose was to persuade her
audience to contact their state legislators and urge
passage of legislation to establish training and
funding for emergency medical care for children.
The quotation from Dr. Flyer, a pediatrician who
was mentioned earlier in the speech, added
credibility to this message. Now the audience
could see that Irwin's drive for action had support
from a respectable outside source with firsthand
knowledge of the issue.

Referring to the Introduction
Another way to close your speech is by referring to
your introduction in your conclusion. This
technique brings your listeners full circle, ending
your speech where you began. In the process,
you show your listeners how the major points
you made in the body of your speech connect
with what you said in your introduction.

You have already seen how student Gretchen
Richter used a story to introduce her speech,
"Health Care Combat Zones." Now look at how
she referred to her introduction during her
conclusion:

> Tim Dufelmeier's heroic act in the
> California emergency room produced some
> healthy outcomes. All three wounded
> physicians will make full recoveries.
> Security in the emergency room has been
> upgraded by installing a wall of bullet
> proof glass and card-key systems to restrict
> access. Assault in the medical arena is
> something we all need to combat. After all,
> the only thrills we need in the hospital are
> the life-saving efforts of our doctors and
> nurses.[26]

Richter's concluding remarks fleshed out the
aftermath of the opening story by describing
how the facility took steps to combat crime in
the emergency room. By repeating the phrase
"life-saving" in both the introduction and the
conclusion, she also reinforced the vital importance of the topic. This gave her audience a
compelling reason to remember her words.

Asking a Question
Just as you can ask a question to arouse your

EXHIBIT 10.8
Using an Appeal to Action
A speaker who wants audience members to do something specific, such as walk a picket line, can issue an appeal to action in the conclusion of the speech. To motivate audience members, such a conclusion should clarify the reasons for taking the action as well as the expected results.

listeners' curiosity at the start of your speech, you can leave your audience with a question at the end of speech. This is a common way to end a persuasive speech, but it can be equally effective for informative, entertaining, or motivational speeches. By using a question in a persuasive speech, you help prod your audience to take action. In contrast, when you pose a question in other kinds of speeches, you give listeners food for thought.

For example, Norm Bertasavage used a rhetorical question to conclude a speech to a local American Legion post. His speech commemorated the fiftieth anniversary of D-Day in World War II, the day that the Allied forces invaded Normandy to battle Hitler's forces. He ended this way:

> That day was a day of reckoning. It was a day when the bill came due. It was the day the price was paid for past failures. As we call to mind today those who paid that price on that day, we must ask ourselves one question. If we again let freedom and liberty slip through our fingers, who will come to pay the price to restore democracy and Western civilization? Remember this.[27]

Even though he framed his question rhetorically, Bertasavage knew that many listeners would think of their friends, relatives, and colleagues who had been wounded or killed in battle. To these listeners, the question was real because it called to mind the price—in human terms—of fighting for freedom and liberty. His audience was likely to remember such a powerful question even if they forgot Bertasavage's other words.

Appealing to Action

Many speakers end persuasive speeches by issuing an appeal to action. You can use this technique to conclude any type of speech in which you ask your audience to do something (see Exhibit 10.8). No matter what kind of action you're urging, be sure to let the audience know what they should do—and why.

Maria Lucia R. Anton, a student at the University of Guam, concluded her speech titled "Sexual Assault Policy a Must" by urging her audience of students and teachers from around the United States to take action:

> You and I can actively assist in this task and can make a giant contribution to move it forward. On my campus students have not only voiced their concerns but we have also started a petition demanding that the university formulate a sexual assault policy. The bottom line is, we need to prevent sexual assault on campus. The key to prevention is a sexual assault policy. If you don't have a policy, then you need to petition your administration to have one. I know I won't stop my advocacy until I see a policy on my campus.[28]

Note how Anton specified the actions she wanted her listeners to take. Then she linked these actions to the goal of preventing sexual assaults on campus. Listeners came away from Anton's speech understanding not only what they could do to stop assaults, but how they could do it.

Analysis of a Conclusion

The conclusion is your final opportunity to reach the audience with your message. To see how an effective conclusion works, look at the following conclusion used in a classroom speech. (Earlier, you saw how this student introduced the same speech.) As you read this conclusion and the related commentary, think about how the words and the structure reinforce the speaker's central idea, provide closure for the audience, and motivate action:

> We've seen how manufacturers of bread machines, convection ovens, pressure cookers, and wide-body refrigerators are portraying their products as essential for today's Perfect Woman. We've also seen how these manufacturers are trying to sell us much more than specific products. They are pushing a carefully constructed image of womanhood. Thanks to her decision to buy their products, the Perfect Woman is able to execute her many homebound responsibilities flawlessly. Perfection, the ads suggest, is just a purchase away.

The speaker closes her speech with a brief but effective summary. By reviewing her major points and support materials, the speaker reminds the audience of how these points lead to the central idea:

> But as we have also seen, no amount of purchasing will close the gap between the Perfect Woman and *real* women living in the real world. Rather than finding fault with our mothers, our sisters, our girlfriends, or ourselves, we need to be more critical of the ideal images we allow to shape our standards. I hope that the next time you watch a television commercial or read a magazine advertisement, you'll notice the image that is

being promoted along with the product for sale. Remember: You can buy one without the other.

In her final sentences, the speaker provides closure and motivates action. Note how she signals the audience that the speech is ending by referring to "the next time . . ." She asks listeners to take action by critically examining advertising and distinguishing between real women and the image of the Perfect Woman.

CHOOSING INTRODUCTION AND CONCLUSION TECHNIQUES

Given the importance of your introduction and conclusion and the variety of techniques available to you, how do you decide which to use in your speech? The answer depends on five elements: your audience, the occasion for your speech, the purpose of your speech, your time constraints, and your personal preferences.

Think first about what your analysis revealed about your audience's needs, interests, and expectations. Which technique will best show your audience that you understand them and have something to say that will benefit them? Which is most likely to give your audience a compelling reason to pay attention to and remember your message? The most arresting opening or inspiring closing in the world won't be effective if it isn't meaningful to your audience.

Next, consider why you're speaking to this audience at this time. What is the occasion for your speech? How can you set an appropriate tone for your message through your introduction and conclusion? Does the situation call for a solemn or light approach? How can your introduction and conclusion help you achieve your general purpose and your specific purpose on this occasion? For example, humor may be a good way of reaching out to your audience during an entertaining or motivational speech, but it may be out of bounds for a persuasive or informational speech on a solemn occasion.

The length of your speech also has a bearing on the techniques you choose. If you have only a few minutes to speak, you won't have time to get your major points across if you start or end with a long, involved story or quote. Of course, if you're speaking for a longer period, you might want to warm up your audience (and yourself) with a paragraph-length introduction of a story, humorous anecdote, suspenseful opening, or personal experience. If you have enough time, you may want to conclude your speech by referring to your introduction, quoting at length, or issuing a rousing appeal to action that requires more than a word or two.

In the end, personal preference determines the kind of introduction and conclusion you choose. If you're not comfortable talking about a personal experience or telling a funny story, use another technique. Remember, the introduction is your audience's first glimpse of you as a public speaker, just as the conclusion is your audience's final glimpse of you. So choose techniques that show off what you do best.

At times, you may want to mix techniques, starting with one technique (such as a startling statement) and then using another (such as a personal experience) before you launch into the body of your speech. You can also put two conclusion techniques together to form a powerful ending. Whatever you decide, you'll feel less anxious and more confident if you're comfortable with the way you start and end your speech. Then you'll be able to concentrate on getting your message across to your audience.

SUMMARY

A speech introduction performs four functions. It captures audience attention and builds interest in your speech. It also establishes credibility and builds rapport between you and your audience. It introduces your topic, and finally, it previews your major points. You can use any of eight techniques for an introduction: (1) a startling statement, (2) a question, (3) a story, (4) a quote, (5) suspense, (6) personal experience, (7) some reference to the audience, or (8) humor.

A rhetorical question is asked for effect rather than to elicit an answer from the audience. Such a question works well in introductions and conclusions. Use this technique when you want your audience to answer silently and think about your question while you speak or after you've finished.

Using humor in your introduction can help you break the ice and build rapport with your audience at the start of a speech. It can also relax you and your listeners and help your listeners remember your message. In a humorous introduction, you might tell a joke, relate a funny story, or offer a witty quote that is connected with your message. Four possible problems with humor are (1) not everyone laughs at the same thing, (2) humor that doesn't go over well can cause your audience to lose interest and cause you to lose your momentum, (3) humor isn't appropriate for every topic or occasion, and (4) too much humor can take the spotlight off your message.

A speech conclusion performs three functions. First, the conclusion reinforces your central idea and shows how your major points fit together. Second, it provides closure. And third, it motivates the audience to take action. Seven techniques for concluding a speech are (1) using a summary, (2) telling a story, (3) using an inspirational appeal or challenge, (4) using a quotation, (5) referring to the introduction, (6) asking a question, or (7) appealing to action.

The choice of which technique to use in your introduction and conclusion depends on five elements: your audience, the occasion for your speech, the purpose of your speech, your time constraints, and your personal preferences. You can also mix techniques in your introduction and your conclusion. Once you have a strong opening and strong closing, you can feel confident and concentrate on getting your message across to your audience.

KEY TERMS

closure (220)
rhetorical question (213)

APPLY CRITICAL THINKING

1. Can you go too far when opening your speech with a startling statement? What should you consider when using this technique?
2. When you're not an expert on your speech topic, how can you use your introduction to establish your credibility?
3. List three occasions or topics that are inappropriate for a humorous introduction. What introduction techniques would be appropriate for each? Why?
4. To avoid plagiarism, what guidelines would you suggest for using a quotation in an introduction or conclusion?
5. Why are some of the introduction techniques not suitable for conclusions? Explain.
6. After reading the checklist on planning an introduction, what would you suggest speakers avoid when planning conclusions?
7. How might a speaker's introduction or conclusion show disrespect for the audience?

SHARPEN YOUR SKILLS

Individual Exercises

1. Listen to a speaker on campus, on radio, or on television.

   a. Identify the technique the speaker used to introduce the speech. Why do you think this technique was appropriate for the audience, the topic, or the occasion?

   b. Identify the technique the speaker used to conclude the speech. How did this conclusion provide closure for the audience? How did it reinforce the central idea?

2. Analyze the conclusion of a persuasive or motivational speech selected from the appendix or from another source. What action did the speaker want the audience to take? How did the conclusion encourage the audience to take that action? If you had been in the audience, would you have been persuaded to take action? Why? Write a one- to two-page paper summarizing your answer.

3. Read through the speeches in the appendix to find an example of a rhetorical question used in an introduction and an example of one used in a conclusion. How do you know that each question is rhetorical? How does the speaker relate each question to the topic, the central idea, and the audience's interests? Prepare a two-minute talk to your class to report your findings.

4. Which of the introduction techniques would you use to open a speech on one of the topics in the appendix or one of the following topics? Defend your answers.

   a. An informational speech about the problems of a vegetarian diet

   b. A persuasive speech about joining one of the armed forces

   c. An entertaining speech about a trip to Disney World

   d. A motivational speech about competing in the Olympic Games

Group Exercises

5. With two other students, select a speech from the appendix and analyze its introduction.

   a. Which technique did the speaker use to open the speech? Did this technique work? Why?

   b. Working separately, write a new introduction for this speech using another of the techniques in this chapter.

   c. Exchange your work with your teammates and discuss the appeal of each introduction. As a group, compare your introductions with the speaker's actual introduction, and decide which is most effective.

6. Work with two other students to analyze the conclusion of the speech you selected for exercise 5.

   a. Which technique did the speaker use to close the speech? Do you think this technique was effective? Explain your answer.

   b. Working separately, write a new conclusion for this speech, using another of the techniques in this chapter.

   c. Exchange your work with your teammates and discuss the appeal of each conclusion. As a group, compare your conclusions with the speaker's actual conclusion, and decide which is most effective.

Chapter Eleven

OUTLINING YOUR SPEECH

LEARNING OBJECTIVES
After studying this chapter, you will be able to

1. Differentiate between the planning outline and the speaking outline.

2. Explain how numbering and indentation clarify the relationships among all points in an outline.

3. Discuss how to use parallel form in a speech outline.

4. Describe the format of a planning outline.

5. Discuss what goes into a bibliography.

6. Identify the three types of titles you can use for your speeches.

7. Explain how to develop a speaking outline from a planning outline.

Using an Outline as a Blueprint for a Speech
Congresswoman Loretta Sanchez of Orange County, California, works on the outline for each speech well in advance so she can be sure she has covered all the points she wants to make.

USING SPEECH OUTLINES

As a public speaker, you have a lot in common with an architect. Just as an architect must design a blueprint for a building, a public speaker must develop an outline for a speech. Without an outline, you have only the building blocks of your speech and no way to put them together. Your outline helps you determine how to fit your major points and support materials together and how to connect one part of the speech to the next. In short, before you can prepare and then deliver your speech, you need an outline.

As you prepare your outline, you can try out various structures for your speech before choosing the most effective. You can test your reasoning to be sure it's sound, and check whether you need more support for a particular point. You can also lay out your ideas to form a smooth, cohesive flow from the introduction through the body to the conclusion. In effect, your outline becomes your blueprint for giving a well-organized speech that fits the audience, the occasion, and the purpose (see Exhibit 11.1).

In the course of getting ready for a speech, you'll actually develop two types of outlines. The first is the planning outline, which is quite detailed. The second is the speaking outline, which guides you through the actual speech.

The Planning Outline

As the term suggests, the **planning outline** is a detailed outline you develop in the course of preparing for your speech. At this point, you may not know exactly what you want to say in your introduction, body, and conclusion. You may not even have a specific order in mind for the ideas in each part of your speech.

Preparing a planning outline gives you the opportunity to put all your points on paper and look for the best order in which to present them. Because the planning outline is not your final outline, you can change it as you refine your ideas and your structure. In fact, trial and error is part of the process. You may draft two or three planning outlines as you experiment with ways of organizing your ideas to achieve your specific purpose.

Although developing a planning outline takes some time, it's the key to extemporaneous speaking. Your goal is to deliver a well-planned, well-rehearsed speech with spontaneity. Once you've done your homework and drafted a detailed planning outline, you'll feel properly prepared. Your audience will certainly appreciate the difference, as playwright Lillian Hellman did when she commented, "I like people who refuse to speak until they are ready to speak."[1] Once your planning outline is ready, your next step is to reduce it to a speaking outline.

The Speaking Outline

The **speaking outline** is a brief outline you develop as a guide for practicing and delivering your speech. The purpose is to prompt your memory about what you plan to say and in what order so that you can choose words that sound natural rather than scripted. You put less detail into your speaking outline than you have in your

EXHIBIT 11.2

Let Your Computer Help You Outline

A personal computer can help you prepare and refine your planning outline quickly and conveniently. With a few keystrokes and the click of a mouse, you can

- Compose and change your points and subpoints
- Rearrange your points and subpoints to find the best organization
- Add and eliminate subpoints where needed
- Reword points to reflect parallel form
- Set tabs for proper indentation

Once you're satisfied with the way your planning outline looks, simply send it to the printer. Then you've got an easy-to-read outline that you can change any time you wish.

planning outline because you're only using the speaking outline as a memory aid.

You don't read from your speaking outline so much as you check it periodically to jog your memory and keep your place as you address your audience (or as you rehearse your speech). With practice, excellent public speakers become accustomed to using the speaking outline as a springboard. The speaking outline allows speakers to concentrate on their ideas and on their audiences, rather than be bound to the exact words in a script. Jerry L. Stead, chief executive officer of Square D Company, is one of many executives who use speaking outlines when they stand in front of employees or other audiences. "I don't read speeches," says Stead. "I write an outline in bullet form and speak from that."[2]

Compared with your planning outline, your speaking outline is skeletal. It omits all the elements you won't mention to your audience, such as statements of general purpose and specific purpose. At the same time, it includes additional elements, such as cues to guide you through a smooth delivery. Although the speaking outline is shorter than the planning outline, it's structured around the same framework, as discussed in the next section.

DEVELOPING AN OUTLINE

Both the planning outline and the speaking outline follow the standard outlining format. In this format, each point and subpoint is identified through a specific numbering system. When you subdivide points, you create two or more

subpoints that are indented below the point they support. Finally, you use parallel form for each point and capitalize the first word of each. The format is the same whether you draft your outline by hand, on a typewriter, or on a personal computer (see Exhibit 11.2).

Outline Numbering

The most commonly used method of numbering points in an outline is the alphanumeric system. You use Roman numerals to identify your major points in order. Then you label the subpoints (which may be support materials) under each major point according to a consistent pattern of letters and numbers, as in this example:

I. First major point
   A. Subpoint of major point I
   B. Subpoint of major point I
      1. Subpoint of subpoint B
      2. Subpoint of subpoint B
         a. Subpoint of subpoint 2
         b. Subpoint of subpoint 2
      3. Subpoint of subpoint B
II. Second major point
   A. Subpoint of major point II
      1. Subpoint of subpoint A
      2. Subpoint of subpoint A
   B. Subpoint of major point II
   C. Subpoint of major point II

With this numbering system, you can see the correct position of points that belong on the same level. You can also see where to position the subpoints that support each major point or subpoint. In addition, you can visually examine what you've identified as major points and determine whether they're important enough to be major points. You can be sure you've covered all the component points of your topic, and you can review the logic of how you've arranged your ideas. Finally, you can determine whether you have enough or too many subpoints for each major point.

Outline Indentation

As you study the alphanumeric numbering system of the outline, you see that subpoints are indented below the points they support. This format gives you a visual indication of the relationships among all points. The most important and broadest are the major points, which appear to the left of the least important and most specific, the subpoints. By scanning the way points are indented in your outline, you can see how each relates to the one above and below.

The most important points, your major points, appear farthest left. These are labeled with Roman numerals. Align the periods after each Roman numeral, and line up the first word of each major point. Here's an example:

   I. First major point
  II. Second major point
 III. Third major point

Next, position the subpoints under each major point by indenting them to the right. Align each with the first word of the point it supports, as in this example:

 I. First major point
   A. Subpoint of major point I
   B. Subpoint of major point I
   C. Subpoint of major point I
 II. Second major point
   A. Subpoint of major point II
   B. Subpoint of major point II

Continue in this manner, indenting subpoints of subpoints to the right. Be sure that all subpoints on the same level belong to and support the level above. This way, you use the indentation pattern in your outline to structure your points logically so that they progress in order from the general, important points (located farther left) to the narrow, specific support points (located farther right).

Outline Subdivisions

Just as you can't divide a pie into fewer than two pieces, you can't divide a major point or a subpoint into fewer than two subpoints. This means that you will have at least two subpoints if you decide to divide any of your points. In other words, if you create subpoint A, you also need to create a subpoint B (and possibly C and D); if you create subpoint 1, you also need to create a subpoint 2 (see Exhibit 11.3).

Now look at the ideas in each of the major points and subpoints you selected and developed when you began organizing your speech. As you fit these points into your outline, make sure that each point contains only one idea. Linking two ideas in one point can confuse your listeners. It can also cause you to mix subpoints out of sequence or in an illogical way, which weakens your reasoning. Consider the subdivisions in these two outline excerpts:

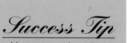

Success Tip

Use your planning outline's numbering system and indentation to put your points in proper sequence and reveal the relationship among them. When you transfer your points to your speaking outline, you can follow the numbering and the indentation to stay on track as you speak.

POOR	IMPROVED
I. The U.S. flag gains a star for every state that joins the union.	I. The U.S. flag gains a star for every state that joins the union.
A. The 49th star was added in 1959 for Alaska.	A. The 49th star was added in 1959 for Alaska.
B. The 50th star was added in 1960 for Hawaii.	B. The 50th star was added in 1960 for Hawaii.
C. Until 1818, the flag gained both a star and a stripe for each new state.	II. Until 1818, the flag gained both a star and a stripe for each new state.

EXHIBIT 11.3

Subdividing Ideas

When subdividing a group of items, be sure your subdivisions account for all items. For example, if you tried to subdivide this group of animals into (1) household pets and (2) zoo animals, you might have trouble placing the bull and the horse. Or if you tried to divide it into mammals and fish, the fish category would have only one item.

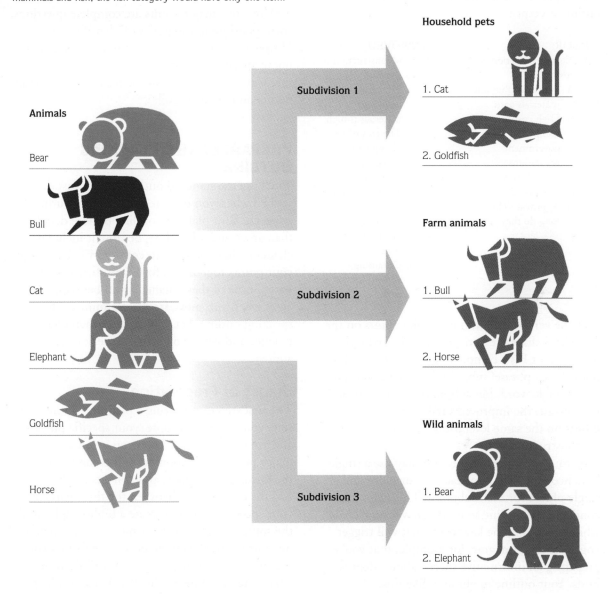

In the poor outline, two important ideas are mingled under major point I. In the improved outline, the two main ideas are separated and shown as major point I and major point II. The corresponding evidence below major point I supports only that point, so the audience can follow the speaker's reasoning.

Parallel Form

Help your audience understand and compare points on the same level by using **parallel form**, expressing ideas in the same grammatical pattern. If you state major point I as a complete sentence, also state major point II as a complete sentence; if you express subpoint A as a question, express subpoints B and C as questions; and if you use a phrase as a point, use a phrase for every other point on the same level. For consistency, capitalize the first word of each point in your outline.

Compare the wording in the following two outline excerpts:

POOR	IMPROVED
I. New construction is costly.	I. New construction is costly
A. What do labor and materials cost?	A. The cost of skilled labor and materials is high
B. High cost of complying with government regulations	B. The cost of complying with government regulations is high
II. Time problems	II. New construction is time-consuming
A. Blueprints	A. Preparing blueprints takes time
B. Approvals: How long do they take?	B. Obtaining approvals takes time

In the version at left, none of the points on the same level share the same grammatical patterns. Major point I is a complete sentence, but major point II is a phrase; subpoint A under major point II is a single word, but subpoint B is a question. In contrast, the improved version expresses all points on the same level using the same grammatical construction.

In your speaking outline, you may use a single sentence or question for each major point and a single phrase for each subpoint. This helps condense the outline so it takes fewer note cards, while preserving the key words that will trigger your memory. Imagine, for example, that you're preparing an informative speech about identifying birds. Your outline might look like this:

I. What shape is the bird's bill?
  A. Small and thin
  B. Plump and short
  C. Long and knifelike
  D. Hooked
II. What shape is the bird's tail?
  A. Forked

  B. Squared-off
  C. Notched
  D. Rounded
  E. Pointed

Here, your major points are complete questions, corresponding to categories of identifying marks. However, your subpoints are phrases, corresponding to specific markings to watch for. This mixture is fine, as long as you use parallel form for all points on the same level.

PREPARING THE PLANNING OUTLINE

You'll use the standard outline format just described when you prepare the planning outline for a speech. Your planning outline is more detailed than any standard outline, because it includes elements that you need to consider when you put your points together to form a unified speech. Later, some of these elements will be stripped away when you move from a planning outline to a speaking outline that you can use when you practice and when you actually speak to your audience.

Stages of Preparation

The first step in preparing a planning outline is to state your general purpose, your specific purpose, and your central idea. Then you organize your major points and subpoints and go on to identify the introduction, body, and conclusion. Next, you add the connections between the three parts of your speech. Then you create a bibliography to list the sources of your support materials. (Depending on your instructor's preferences, the format you use for your planning outline may differ from what's presented here.) Finally, choose a title if you need one.

State Your Purpose and Central Idea

Keep your general purpose, specific purpose, and central idea firmly in mind by writing them at the top of your planning outline. This is more than an exercise. Remember, you want to build all the major points, subpoints, and support materials

Checklist for Preparing a Planning Outline

1. At the top of your planning outline, position a statement of general purpose, a statement of specific purpose, and a statement of central idea.
2. Arrange major points and subpoints in the standard outline format, and separate them into an introduction, a body, and a conclusion.
3. Position the transitions, internal previews, and internal summaries where they will help the movement from one part of your speech to the next.
4. Position the bibliography of sources at the end of the outline.
5. Show the title (if needed) at the top of the outline.

into a unified speech that accomplishes your purpose and conveys your central idea.

So as you develop your outline, you'll want to check frequently to be sure that the points, organization, connections, and title relate to your purpose and your central idea. Of course, you won't directly state these three elements when you address your audience, but they will be embedded in the words and the structure of your speech. That's why they appear in the planning outline.

Organize Your Major Points and Subpoints

Your major points and subpoints (which include your support materials) are the building blocks of your speech. Now is the time to arrange them in your planning outline and test the strength of your speech structure. First, express each major point as a single, complete sentence. That helps you keep track of one specific idea you want to convey in each point. If you use short phrases instead of sentences, you may not be able to see exactly what each major point represents, so you may not be able to spot omissions, duplications, or unsupported ideas. Later on, after you're satisfied with the organization, you may want to condense lower-level subpoints into phrases that will jog your memory.

Next, look at the order in which you've organized your major points and subpoints. Check to make sure that the organizational method makes sense with regard to your central idea and the content of each point. Also be sure that the organizational method helps the audience follow your reasoning.

Finally, look at the overall picture. Do your points and subpoints come together to convey the central idea and accomplish your specific purpose? Does the overall organization of the points make sense to you? Do you think it will make sense to your audience? This is the time to make any changes that will make your speech more cohesive and logical. Move points around, add or delete points, or change the organizational method as needed. You may even have to revise your central idea on the basis of what you learn by putting your major points and subpoints together. Do it now, while your speech is still in the planning stages.

Identify Your Introduction, Body, and Conclusion

Now you're ready to divide your speech into three parts. Start by laying out the body. Number each major point with a Roman numeral, and continue using the alphanumeric system to label each subpoint in turn. Indent as you move from a broader point to a more specific supporting point.

Once you've completed the body, you can lay out the points in your introduction and your conclusion. State the points in your introduction and conclusion in full sentences, and then put them into outline form. Work on each part separately, starting with the Roman numeral I for your first major point in the introduction and your first major point in the conclusion. Thus, you'll have three points labeled with a Roman numeral I: one point in the introduction, one in the body, and one in the conclusion.

In terms of your outline, each part of the speech is a distinctly separate unit. That's why you begin the alphanumeric system over for each part. Before you show how these parts are connected, check again that the points in your introduction and conclusion relate directly to your central idea and specific purpose. Make any changes before proceeding.

Show Your Connections

Once you've identified your introduction, body, and conclusion, you can add the connections that link the three parts. Write out, in sentence form, the transitions you plan to use to move from one part to the next, and to use signposts where appropriate. Remember to include additional transitions between major points in the body of your speech. Also, compose any internal previews and internal summaries you need to guide the audience smoothly through the speech.

For the purposes of your planning outline, mark all transitions clearly. These aren't points or subpoints, so don't label them using the alphanumeric system you used in your outline. Instead, position each on a separate line between the two sections it will connect. Put each transition in parentheses to make it stand out.

Now that you've added the transitions, step back and look at how well they connect the various parts of your speech. Do your transitions signal the audience about your movement from one part of the speech to the next? Do they help the audience follow your train of thought and remember your ideas? If necessary, rework your transitions until they enhance the flow of your speech.

Show Your Sources

The final section of your planning outline is your **bibliography,** a listing of the sources you used when gathering the support materials for your speech. Show the books, magazine articles, newspaper articles, interviews, government documents, and commercial database sources from which you drew information. Depending on your instructor's requirements, you may list only the sources for the

support material you actually cited in your speech, or you may list all the sources you consulted as you planned your speech.

For each entry, indicate the author and the title of the work, the publisher or the periodical, and the date. Include page numbers in newspaper and periodical entries, but not in book entries. Alphabetize your listing according to authors' last names. Bibliographies can be prepared using a variety of formats. Your instructor will indicate the bibliographic format to use in your planning outline. A typical bibliography might look like this:

Cunningham, Helen, and Greene, Brenda. *The Business Style Handbook.* New York: McGraw-Hill, 2002.
Martin, Paul R. *Wall Street Journal Guide to Business Style.* New York: Simon & Schuster, 2003.
McMillan, Iris P. *A Guide to Style.* New York: Loganfield Publishers, 2000.
Wilkinson, Cy. "In Search of Business Style," *New Orleans City Business,* 15 August 2002, 4.
Yu, Larry. "Blending Cultural Business Styles," *MIT Sloan Management Review,* 44 (Fall 2002), 12.

Note how each entry in this bibliography is easy to read and follows a consistent format. The author is always mentioned before the title and the publisher or periodical. Also, book titles and the names of periodicals are underlined or italic. Whatever system you use to format your bibliography, be sure to include all the details that identify your various sources.

Choose a Title

If you have a title for your speech, position it at the top of your planning outline (see Exhibit 11.4). Not every speech needs or has a title. As comedian Steve Allen notes, "We may be sure that at the top of the envelope on which he wrote his now-famous speech, Abraham Lincoln did not write the words 'The Gettysburg

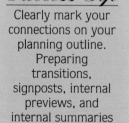

Success Tip

Clearly mark your connections on your planning outline. Preparing transitions, signposts, internal previews, and internal summaries in advance helps smooth the movement from one part of your speech to the next.

EXHIBIT 11.4
Overview of Planning Outline
Your planning outline has five major
sections: (1) title (if necessary),
purpose, and central idea; (2)
introduction; (3) body, (4) conclusion,
and (5) bibliography.

TITLE (if needed)

General purpose: _____
Specific purpose: _____
Central idea: _____

INTRODUCTION
 I. _____
 II. _____

(transition)

BODY
 I. _____
   A. _____
   B. _____
   C. _____

(transition)

 II. _____
   A. _____
   B. _____
   C. _____

(transition)

 III. _____
   A. _____
   B. _____
   C. _____

(transition)

CONCLUSION
 I. _____
 II. _____

BIBLIOGRAPHY

Address.'"[3] Lincoln's speech gained that title later, when people began to talk about what he said at Gettysburg. Like Lincoln, you may not have a reason to title your speech. So unless your instructor asks for a title, you'll probably leave your classroom speeches untitled.

However, speech titles can be useful in some situations. If your speech will be publicized ahead of time or introduced by someone else, a good title can help. Announcing an interesting title in advance of your speech can help you gain attention and draw an audience. This is especially important when listeners have a choice about whether or not to attend your talk. When used on a published speech, a title attracts readers and lets them know something about the speech they're about to read. At the same time, don't promise something your speech can't deliver, and be careful not to mislead your audience about the content of your speech. Be sure your title actually relates to what you plan to say in your speech.

You can use one of three types of titles. A *descriptive title* describes exactly what the speech will be about. In contrast, a *creative title* is less straightforward, using more imaginative wording to capture audience interest. The *question title* takes the form of a question and can be both descriptive and creative. To see how titles work, consider the following examples:[4]

Descriptive title: *Toward A Cure for AIDS*
(A speech to a college class about progress in curing AIDS and alternative treatments)
Creative title: *From the Lone Ranger to Power Rangers* (A speech to businesspeople about changes in caring for and educating children)
Question title: *Schools: Learning Zone or Battle Zone?* (A speech to a college class about violence in schools)

A good title can make the difference between an audience of attentive listeners and an empty room. Executive speech coach Thomas Leech tells of reading about an upcoming speech titled "Penal Reform and Rehabilitation." That title didn't strike him as a crowd-puller, so he came up with another. His recommended title described the content of the same speech, yet it had a punch that the original lacked: "Ex-Cons—Recyclable or Lost Causes?"[5] Which title would prompt you to join the audience for this speech?

Analysis of a Planning Outline

To see how the various parts of a planning outline come together, take a close look at the following sample. Note how this speaker used the standard outline format, where he put his transitions, and how he arranged the points in each of the three parts of his speech. As you read through the outline and the commentary, think about how this outline would help you prepare to give this speech in class (see Exhibit 11.5).

DEVELOPING YOUR CREATIVITY

FROM THE ORDINARY TO THE EXTRAORDINARY: HOW TO CHOOSE A GREAT TITLE FOR YOUR SPEECH

How do you come up with a title that's catchy, informative, and intriguing all at the same time? Experimenting with various titles can really stretch your creativity as you think about your topic, your central idea, your points, and your audience. Once you have a number of options, how do you put aside those that are merely ordinary and choose the one that's truly great?

Lilly Walters, an internationally known speaker, has some suggestions. Here are questions she recommends that speakers ask to measure their titles:

- Does the title stress what the audience will gain from listening (rather than what the speech will cover)?
- Does the title reflect the purpose of the speech?
- Does the title reflect the audience's concerns or interests?
- Does the title reflect the content of the speech?
- Does the title suggest action? Drama? Mystery?
- Does the title stimulate the imagination?
- Does the title sound catchy enough to be remembered after the speech is over?

The answers to these questions will help you differentiate between a good title and a great title. As Walters points out, "People judge a book by its cover, and they'll judge your presentation by its title." So make sure that your title—the cover of your book—makes your audience want to come, listen, and remember.

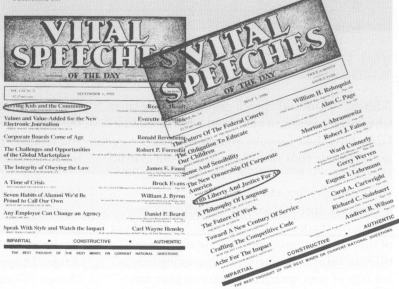

EXHIBIT 11.5

Paris Lodgings
Mentioning landmarks such as the Church of the Sacred Heart is a good way to spark audience interest in a speech about a budget tour of Paris.

PARIS ON A BUDGET

General purpose: To inform
Specific purpose: To inform my audience about how to stay in Paris on a limited budget.
Central idea: When visiting Paris, you can save money on accommodations by thinking creatively.

INTRODUCTION

I. Walking along the cobblestone banks of the Seine, wandering through the rose-colored aisles of the Church of the Sacred Heart, lingering over coffee at a sidewalk café—these are all part of a dream vacation in Paris.

II. Although Paris is a dream destination, paying for a hotel room can be a nightmare.
   A. The U.S. dollar has been falling against the euro, so the dollar buys less today than when I visited Paris last month.
   B. You may pay as much as 15 percent more than I paid if you visit Paris now, which means that a 150-euro hotel room now costs $145 instead of $130.

III. Still, a stay in Paris doesn't have to break the bank.
   A. Cheaper hotels are one alternative you might explore.
   B. However, research for my recent trip to Paris uncovered a variety of cost-effective, creative alternatives to hotels.

IV. You can save money by trying, in ascending order of cost, a home exchange, camping, student hostels, rooms in private homes, and furnished rentals.

(Transition: To get you started on a Paris vacation that won't break the bank, let's look first at the least expensive of these options.)

BODY

I. You can enjoy a native's Paris digs by trading your stateside home or apartment at no cost.
   A. Home-exchange organizations publish annual directories that list possible exchanges, including details about each home or apartment.
   B. Agreements for actual exchange are made by the two parties involved, not the organization.
   C. You can contact organizations such as
      1. Intervac U.S./International Home Exchange in San Francisco
      2. Vacation Exchange Club in Key West, Florida
      3. Loan-a-Home in Mount Vernon, New York

Once you have listed your general purpose, specific purpose, and central idea at the top, you can check how the major points and subpoints in your outline fit with what you want to accomplish in your speech.

Set the introduction apart from the rest of your speech by labeling it in the outline.

By describing three distinctly Parisian experiences, the speaker attracts the audience's attention.

The speaker arouses interest by mentioning problems that could prevent listeners from fulfilling the dream of visiting Paris.

Here, the speaker introduces the topic and establishes credibility by mentioning his recent trip and research on the topic.

This internal preview prepares the audience for the five options that represent the major points in the speech. It also reveals that the speaker will discuss the options in order of cost, from the least costly to the most costly.

Identify transitions so they stand out, but don't include them as part of the alphanumeric numbering system in the outline.

Set the body apart from the rest of your speech by labeling it in the outline.

Major points are expressed in full sentences.

The speaker is organizing the major points from cheapest to most expensive option.

Transitions guide listeners from one major point to the next.

Each subpoint covers a single idea.

(Transition: The next cheapest lodging is an alternative you might not have thought would be available in Paris.)

II. This second option, camping in the Bois de Boulogne, means spending a little more money to enjoy the outdoors and meet campers from all over France.
   A. Rates are $15 a night for a two-person tent.
   B. The campground is open year-round.
   C. The campground accepts no advance reservations.
   D. For information, contact Les Campings du Bois de Boulogne in Paris.

(Transition: As students, you have access to several slightly more expensive alternatives.)

III. This third option, for students only, is to bunk in dormitories, residence halls, or hostels and meet other students from around the world.
   A. Accommodations are basic, not fancy.
      1. Remember to bring linens or you'll have to rent them on-site.
      2. Be prepared for long lines for showers.
      3. Find out if you have to obey curfews.
      4. You may find arrangements restrictive.
         a. Need cash to pay, not credit cards.
         b. May require minimum/maximum stay.
         c. Need proof you're a full-time student.
   B. If you're interested in student accommodations, here are several contacts in Paris.
      1. Accueil des Jeunes en France
      2. French Youth Hostels Association
      3. UCRIF

(Transition: Another creative form of lodging will introduce you to the real Parisian lifestyle.)

IV. This fourth option, renting rooms in private homes, is more costly still, but you'll get a taste of living as Parisians do.
   A. Many hosts are eager to help their visitors.
      1. Tips about local sights
      2. Suggestions for restaurants
      3. Information about local transportation
      4. Useful French phrases
   B. For a room in a private home, contact either of two Paris agencies.
      1. Accueil France Lodge
      2. Bed & Breakfast = Connexion +
   C. Home stays with Parisian families can be arranged through two U.S. agencies.
      1. Servas in New York City
      2. The Friendship Force in Atlanta

(Transition: The final alternative is most appropriate if you're traveling with a group or a family.)

V. This fifth and most expensive option is staying in a furnished rental with all the convenience of home, including cooking facilities.

You can use full sentences or memory-jogging phrases for subpoints at lower levels; major points and higher-level subpoints require full sentences.
Notice how the speaker cites specific support material in the subpoints.

The speaker carefully subdivides major point III into two subpoints. In turn, each subpoint is further subdivided.

When supporting materials are cited, they are indented below the point they support.

Here, as in other subpoints, the speaker presents specific and interesting ideas to keep the audience involved throughout the speech.

The speaker's use of signposts reminds his listeners of where he is in the speech. In this way, he helps the audience follow his ideas and relate each successive point to the one before.

A. Starting at $125, such homelike rentals are still a bargain over hotels.
B. Two New York City companies handle rentals in Paris.
    1. At Home Abroad
    2. Villas and Apartments Abroad
C. In Paris, the best agency is Rothray.

(Transition: Each of these creative, less-expensive alternatives to getting a hotel room has its own charms.)

CONCLUSION

  I. By investigating creative alternatives such as home exchange, camping, student hostels, rooms in private homes, and furnished rentals, you can take your dream trip to Paris and still save money on lodging.

  II. To help you plan your dream trip, I have a list of all organizations I mentioned, along with addresses and phone numbers.

 III. Now that you know how to find lodgings in Paris that won't break the bank, I urge you to plan your trip soon—<u>Bon Voyage!</u>

BIBLIOGRAPHY

"Best Travel Deals," *Consumer Reports Travel Letter,* January 2002.
Europe's Great Itineraries. New York: Fodor's Travel Publications, 2003.
Fun in Europe: A Travel Guide for Grown-Ups. New York: iUniverse, 2002.
Grimes, Nikki. *On the Road to Paris.* New York: Penguin Putnam, 2003.
Townsend, Sue. *France.* Oxford, England: Heinemann Library, 2002.

The transition shows how the speaker plans to move from the body to the conclusion.

Set the conclusion apart from the rest of your speech by labeling it in the outline.

The speaker uses a straightforward summary to review the major points one last time, reinforcing the central idea.

So that listeners won't be tempted to read through the list of organizations during the speech, the speaker distributes it at the end.

The speaker's final words provide closure, recommend action, and send the audience off on a high note.

This bibliography includes only the sources that were used to research the points in the speech.

PREPARING THE SPEAKING OUTLINE

As you saw earlier, the speaking outline is the one you use when you rehearse and deliver your speech. It's less detailed than your planning outline, so it will only jog your memory, not supply the exact words for your speech. As a result, your wording is likely to vary a bit every time you rehearse. But as you practice, you'll soon become so comfortable with the content of your speech that you'll be able to convey your ideas in a consistent yet lively and natural way.

John C. Canepa, chief executive officer of Old Kent Financial Corporation, knows how valuable a speaking outline can be. In the course of preparing for a 30-minute speech, he first develops a detailed planning outline of 12 to 14 pages. Next, he condenses the planning outline to a more manageable eight-page outline. Finally, the day before the speech, he cuts the eight-page outline to a single-page speaking outline that he can carry to the podium.[6]

Stages of Preparation

Like John Canepa, you're going to pack a lot of detail into your original planning outline. So as you create your speaking outline, you cut the elements that don't belong in your actual speech, being careful to maintain the outline format. Then you condense your points and add delivery cues. Once you've transferred your speaking outline to note cards or a single sheet of paper, you can use it during rehearsal and, ultimately, in front of your audience. Don't rush this process; a solid speaking outline can help you improve your delivery.[7]

Follow the Planning Outline

You want your speaking outline to be as short as possible, freeing you to make eye contact with your audience. Still, you want to use the standard outline format, because it helps you see at a glance where you are in your speech and how each part and point relates to the one before and after. So follow the same format as you used for your planning outline, but first strip away anything that you don't plan to say to your audience. If you developed your planning outline on a computer, you can easily convert it to a speaking outline. Save a second copy of the original outline and then start stripping away the elements you don't need in your speaking outline.

Remove your statements of general purpose, specific purpose, and central idea, all of which are implicit in the points you'll make during your speech. Also remove your bibliography, although you may want to have it handy in case someone asks a question about a source. At this point, you're left with the introduction, body, and conclusion of your speech, plus your transitions.

Condense Points to Key Words

As a listener, you can create a brief key word outline to capture and retain the important ideas from a speaker's presentation. Use the same process to create a short but effective speaking outline. Shorten the points and the transitions in your planning outline by condensing each into a few key words. Be careful to choose words that will prompt you to remember what each point is about so that you can talk fluently when you face your audience.

Remember, shorter is better, because your speaking outline is intended as a reminder, not a script. All you want to do is quickly pick up a few words that trigger your memory of what you planned to say so that you can return your attention to your audience. You can't interact with your listeners when you're reading a lengthy section from your speaking outline. That's why you reduce the complete sentences in your planning outline to key words in your speaking outline.

For example, here's how you might condense two major points in the outline for a speech about identifying birds:

COMPLETE SENTENCE
 I. What shape is the bird's bill?
 II. What shape is the bird's tail?

Success Tip

Refer to your speaking notes when you need to refresh your memory about a point or about where you are in the order of points. Be sure your notes are large enough and clear enough to be read at a glance.

KEY WORDS
 I. Bill shape?
 II. Tail shape?

The brief phrase "bill shape?" is all you really need to remind you of the first major point. Similarly, "tail shape?" helps you remember your second major point. At first, you may be concerned about being able to make the leap from the two words in your outline to a complete sentence you compose as you speak. This fear will fade as you practice with your speaking outline and become more familiar with every point you plan to make. By the time you stand in front of your audience, you'll be accustomed to seeing a phrase and recalling the idea it stands for.

However, you may not want to condense everything you plan to say. To avoid stumbling over statistics, quotations, and other specifics, you may want to write these out in your speaking outline. You may also want to write complete sentences for critical points in your introduction or your conclusion so that you won't be afraid of forgetting what to say. Use your judgment, and aim for the shortest outline you can comfortably use.

Add Delivery Cues

Your speaking outline is a handy guide to delivering your speech. During rehearsals, note the places in the outline where you plan to enhance your meaning by pausing, speaking more slowly, raising your voice, using visual aids, and so on. If you choose, you can underline a few specific words you want to emphasize or use colored ink to highlight your cues (see Exhibit 11.6).

Although delivery cues are helpful, avoid cluttering your outline by marking every little movement you might make. Just show the most important cues. As you continue practicing your speech, you may decide to change, delete, or add delivery cues. Simply mark the changes on your speaking outline and then transfer them to your final version. Then you'll be better prepared to plunge into your delivery.

EXHIBIT 11.6
Adding Delivery Cues
Once you have drafted your speaking outline, you can write in delivery cues as reminders to add special emphasis during selected parts of the speech.

Eye Contact !!

Slow Down

Firm Voice

INTRODUCTION

I. Cobblestone banks of Seine, rose-colored aisles of the Church of the Sacred Heart, sidewalk cafe—dream vacation in Paris.

Pauses

II. Paris is dream destination, paying for hotel can be nightmare.

   A. U.S. dollar falling against euro.

   B. Pay 15% more (150-euro hotel $145 not $130).

III. Stay in Paris doesn't have to break bank.

   A. Cheaper hotels one alternative.

   B. Research for recent trip uncovered cost-effective, creative alternatives.

IV. Save money by trying, in ascending order of cost: home exchange, camping, student hostels, rooms in private homes, furnished rentals.

Arrange Your Notes

You'll probably redo the speaking outline and put it into final form after you decide on all your points, transitions, and delivery cues. Make sure your final version is legible and accessible so that you can refer to it as you speak. If you prefer, you can type or hand-print the speaking outline in large, clear letters on one side of a single sheet of paper. If you're using a computer, you can select a larger type size for your outline. Use wide margins, and leave room between points for changes or notes. This arrangement works best when you

OVERCOMING YOUR SPEECH ANXIETY

KEEPING DETAILS AT YOUR FINGERTIPS: A POWERFUL WAY TO GAIN CONFIDENCE

Who can recite the sizes of the world's four oceans? If you were making a speech about oceans, this question would be frighteningly real. During your speech, you don't want to worry about getting the statistics, quotations, examples, and testimony right. To avoid panic, you can write the details on your note cards, and refer to the cards while you speak.

In most cases, you need only a word or two (such as *Pacific*) and a number (*64 million*) for each statistic. You may want to include longer phrases or complete sentences to ensure the accuracy of any quotations, examples, or testimony you plan to mention. But be brief: Include only those phrases or sentences that you can't afford to get wrong. Otherwise, you'll wind up with a fistful of cards, which can be unwieldy.

Even though you'll be speaking with a few notes in your hand, don't fret about hiding them. As long as you peek at them instead of reading them, you won't distract your audience. In fact, you may actually boost your credibility by letting the audience see that you're checking your notes to get the details right.

The next time you prepare a speech with statistics, give yourself confidence by jotting the details on note cards. By keeping the details at your fingertips, you'll be able to say that the Pacific Ocean covers 64 million square miles, the Atlantic Ocean covers nearly 32 million square miles, the Indian Ocean covers just over 25 million square miles, and the Arctic Ocean covers more than 5 million square miles. And you'll do it with confidence.

can rest the paper on a lectern during your speech. Then your hands will be free to gesture or point to visual aids, and the audience won't be distracted by your shuffling note cards or turning pages.

However, when you're speaking without a lectern, you may want to arrange your outline on note cards. Cards are smaller and less noticeable than a sheet of paper, and they slip easily into a pocket or envelope. What's more, cards don't rustle, so they won't distract your audience.

Type or print your outline in large letters on one side of a few 3 x 5, 4 x 6, or 5 x 8 cards. Then number the cards so that you can keep them in order. One way to arrange your notes is to fit your introduction on one card, your body on a second, and your conclusion a third. If you've reduced your points to only a few key words, each part will fit on a card. Then, as you finish one part of the speech, you simply flip to the next card and go on.

Analysis of a Speaking Outline

The following example of a speaking outline was developed from the planning

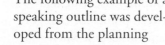

outline that appears earlier in this chapter. Be alert to the differences as you examine this outline and read the accompanying commentary. Also, think about how this outline would help you rehearse and deliver this speech to your class.

Eye Contact *!!*

Slow Down

Firm Voice

INTRODUCTION

   I. Cobblestone banks of Seine, rose-colored aisles of the Church of the Sacred Heart, sidewalk cafe—dream vacation in Paris.

—Pause—

  II. Paris is dream destination, paying for hotel can be nightmare.
     A. U.S. dollar falling against euro.
     B. Pay 15% more (150-euro hotel $145 not $130).
 III. Stay in Paris doesn't have to break bank.
     A. Cheaper hotels one alternative.
     B. Research for recent trip uncovered cost-effective, creative alternatives.
 IV. Save money by trying, in ascending order of cost: home exchange, camping, student hostels, rooms in private homes, furnished rentals.

(First look at least expensive of options.)

—Pause—

BODY

   I. Trade stateside home or apartment at no cost.
     A. Organizations publish directories of listings.
     B. Agreements between two parties.
     C. Contact
        1. Intervac U.S./International Home Exchange (San Francisco)
        2. Vacation Exchange Club (Key West, FL)
        3. Loan-a-Home (Mount Vernon, NY)

(Next cheapest, surprising alternative in Paris)

  II. Camp in Bois de Boulogne to meet French campers.
     A. $15 two-person tent.
     B. Open year-round.
     C. No advance reservations.
     D. Les Campings du Bois de Boulogne in Paris.

(Students access other alternatives)

 III. Student dorms, residence halls, hostels to meet world.
     A. Not fancy.
        1. Bring linens or rent.
        2. Long shower lines.

The speaker uses these delivery cues as a reminder to look at audience members and to speak slowly and distinctly.

Here the speaker includes a reminder to pause momentarily before continuing with the introduction.

Including specific facts and figures is a way to guard against forgetting something important.

Notice how the speaker condenses the transition into a few key words.

The speaker pauses to signal the movement into the body of the speech.

Label the body in the speaking outline as well as in the planning outline.

The major points and subpoints are organized and indented as in the planning outline. This helps speakers keep their place.

Carefully chosen key words prompt the speaker to talk about each point. The exact words the speaker chooses will vary in rehearsal and in delivery.

3. May be curfews.
4. Restrictive arrangements.
   a. Need cash, no credit cards.
   b. May want minimum/maximum stay.
   c. Need student proof.
B. Contacts in Paris
  1. Accueil des Jeunes en France
  2. French Youth Hostels Association
  3. UCRIF

(Another creative form, introduce to real Parisian lifestyle)

IV. Rent rooms in homes to taste Parisian living.
  A. Hosts eager to help.
   1. Sights.
   2. Restaurants.
   3. Local transportation.
   4. French phrases.
  B. Rooms in homes, Paris agencies.
   1. Accueil France Lodge.
   2. Bed & Breakfast = Connexion +
  C. Home stays with Parisian families, U.S. agencies.
   1. Servas, New York City
   2. The Friendship Force, Atlanta

(Final alternative appropriate for group or family)

V. For families, furnished rentals with cooking facilities.
  A. $125 beats hotel prices.
  B. New York City companies handle rentals.
   1. At Home Abroad
   2. Villas and Apartments Abroad
  C. Best in Paris, Rothray.

(Each creative choice has own charms.)

—Pause—

CONCLUSION

I. Investigate home exchange, camping, hostels, private rooms, rentals to take dream trip and save.
II. List of organizations, addresses, phones.
III. Plan your trip—<u>Bon Voyage</u>

The speaker writes out the full names of contact organizations to avoid stumbling over these during delivery.

As before, the speaker uses key words for the transition to the conclusion.

Help the audience make the shift from the body to the conclusion by pausing before the first point in the conclusion.

Label the conclusion in your speaking outline, as you did in your planning outline.

The speaker underlines the final words as a reminder to stress them during delivery.

SUMMARY

As a public speaker, you'll use two types of outlines. The planning outline is a detailed outline that you develop as you prepare for your speech. In contrast, the speaking outline is a brief outline that you prepare as a guide for practicing and delivering your speech.

Both outlines follow the standard outlining format. You use the alphanumeric system to number your points. First, you label your major points with Roman numerals, then you label your subpoints according to a consistent pattern of letters and numbers. This numbering system shows which points are on the same level and which points support more major points. Indentation visually indicates how points in your outline are related. Major points, the most important and most general, appear to the left; less important, more specific subpoints are indented, appearing farther to the right.

When you use parallel form in a speech outline, you express all the ideas on the same level by using the same grammatical pattern. This means that all your major points—which are labeled with a Roman numeral—will be a complete sentence or a question. Similarly, all subpoints on the same level will share the same grammatical pattern.

A planning outline includes a statement of the general purpose; a statement of the specific purpose; a statement of the central idea; major points and subpoints arranged in an introduction, a body, and a conclusion; connections between parts, such as transitions, internal previews, and internal summaries; a bibliography; and a title, if needed.

A bibliography is a listing of the sources you used when gathering the support materials for your speech. It includes the books, magazine articles, newspaper articles, interviews, government documents, and commercial database sources from which you drew your information. Be sure to use a clear, consistent format to state the details of the sources you consulted.

You can choose any of three types of titles for a speech. A descriptive title describes what the speech will be about. A creative title uses more imaginative wording to capture audience interest. A question title is phrased as a question and can be both descriptive and creative.

To develop a speaking outline from a planning outline, you first eliminate elements that you won't state in your speech, including the general purpose, the specific purpose, and the central idea. Next, you condense your points from complete sentences to key word phrases. Finally, you add delivery cues and, if desired, transfer your speaking outline to note cards or to a single sheet of paper for use during rehearsal and delivery.

KEY TERMS

bibliography (238)
parallel form (235)
planning outline (232)
speaking outline (232)

APPLY CRITICAL THINKING

1. Some speakers prepare a planning outline, write out their speeches, and then condense them into a speaking outline. What are the advantages and disadvantages of this method?

2. Why would you give a classroom speech a title?

3. If one subpoint in an outline is too few, how many are too many? How can you fit a large number of subpoints into your outline?

4. Some speakers draft the ideas in their speaking outlines in bullet form, without numbering points or subpoints. Can this be as effective as the alphanumeric system?

5. Speakers can either write their speaking outlines on a single sheet of paper or on a series of notecards. What are the advantages and disadvantages of the two methods? Which do you prefer and why?

6. Imagine you're planning a speech that will persuade students to support special fees to fund the building of a new athletic center. Suggest a descriptive title, a creative title, and a question title for this speech. Which would be most effective in drawing an audience? Why?

7. Following the rules of parallel form, revise the following major points for a planning outline:

I. Project Mercury was the first U.S. effort to send astronauts into space.

II. Longer missions during Gemini program.

III. Apollo—astronauts on moon.

IV. Space shuttle program deploys satellites and conducts space experiments.

SHARPEN YOUR SKILLS

Individual Exercises

1. Select a speech from the appendix, and prepare a planning outline from it.

a. Identify the central idea and specific purpose.

b. Indicate the introduction, body, and conclusion, as well as the major points and subpoints.

c. Show the transitions between each part of the speech.

d. Can you improve the flow or logic of the speech by rearranging the outline in any way?

e. Suggest an alternative title, and indicate why you think it's effective.

2. Look again at the planning outline you prepared in exercise 1.

a. How would you modify this outline to develop a speaking outline?

b. What delivery cues would you add?

c. What elements would you write out in your speaking outline if you were delivering this speech?

3. Working from the support material you've gathered for an upcoming speech, draft a planning outline with a bibliography. Depending on your instructor's preferences, choose a title, and explain the reason for your choice.

4. Use the planning outline you prepared in exercise 3 as the basis for a speaking outline for your speech. What delivery cues are appropriate for this speech?

Group Exercises

5. With a classmate, observe how a speaker (in person, on videotape, or on television) uses notes during a speech.

a. Did the speaker seem to be reading from the notes? Was the delivery smooth?

b. Did the speaker use notes only at certain times, such as during the introduction or conclusion or when referring to specific support material?

c. What suggestions can you offer to help this speaker use notes more effectively?

6. Team up with another student and exchange planning outlines for a future speech.

a. Check the numbering, indentation, subdivisions, and parallel format.

b. Are the relationships among points in the body clear? Is the sequence of points logical? Can you suggest any improvements?

c. Review the introduction and the conclusion. How do they relate to the points made in the body?

d. Where are connections used? Do you think additional transitions, signposts, internal previews, or internal summaries might be helpful? Suggest specific improvements.

e. If you were going to use this planning outline as the basis for a speaking outline, where would you add delivery cues? What cues are appropriate for this speech and audience?

f. If the speech has a title, how does it arouse interest or reveal the topic? What alternatives can you suggest?

Chapter Twelve

WORDING YOUR SPEECH

LEARNING OBJECTIVES

After studying this chapter, you will be able to

1. List three ways that the words in your speech can touch your audience.

2. Clarify the difference between spoken language and written language.

3. Discuss the importance of using familiar wording that is concrete, precise, accurate, unbiased, and concise.

4. Differentiate between metaphors and similes, and describe their use in public speaking.

5. Identify four techniques you can use to create rhythm in a speech.

6. Explain why wording in a speech should be appropriate for the audience, the topic, the occasion, and the speaker.

7. Discuss how you can use humor in a speech.

THE POWER OF SPOKEN WORDS

When you speak to inform, persuade, motivate, or entertain, your choice of words can make the difference between audience apathy and audience action. This is true whether you're speaking to a club, a class, or a business audience. To achieve your goal and touch your audience, you need to know how to harness the power of spoken words.

Imagine two candidates running for local office. One promises to "improve the employment picture," and the other promises to "make employment skyrocket." Both phrases share the same meaning, yet each one projects an image that affects how people think and feel about the candidate's message. Of course, words can't change what happens to employment, but they can change an audience's view of it. In turn, this view affects listeners' attitudes toward each candidate and ultimately influences how listeners will vote.

"A choice of words is a choice of worlds," observes C. Ray Penn, professor of communication at Radford University.[1] By carefully choosing your words, you can convey nuances of meaning that clarify your message to your audience (see Exhibit 12.1). The world you describe with your words might be what once was, what is, or what is to come. But just any words simply won't do. Only the specific words that are right for your message, your audience, your topic, and the occasion will bring your chosen world to life.

When selecting your words, consider both the denotative meaning and the connotative meaning.

The **denotative meaning** is what the word means literally. This is the objective meaning you would find if you checked the dictionary. In contrast, the **connotative meaning** is the word's subjective meaning. The connotative meaning covers the feelings you associate with that word. For example, the denotative meaning of *home* is the place where someone lives. However, the word can have a wide range of connotative meanings. One person may associate *home* with security; another may associate it with love; a third, with fear. Because your words have the potential to stir up powerful emotions and associations, you'll want to consider both the denotative and the connotative meanings of the words you choose.

Spoken words can touch your audience in three important ways. First, words can help you create a powerful mental image (such as employment skyrocketing) that will live on after your speech is over. Second, the words you speak can influence your audience's feelings and attitudes. Third, they can inspire your listeners to take a specific action.

Creating Mental Images

Just as skilled painters use color and brushstrokes to convey their impressions of a subject, you can use words to create vivid mental images of your ideas. With words, you can share your view of the world and introduce listeners to worlds they've never known. Of course, you're doing more than drawing the outline of an idea: you're also adding color and emphasis to help your audience understand, remember, and react to your message.

For example, consider Jerry Davis's speech to employees at Network Equipment Technologies

EXHIBIT 12.1

Choosing the Right Words

Reverend Jesse Jackson uses vivid wording in his speeches to influence his audience's feelings and attitudes and to inspire his listeners to take action.

"In urban cities in Connecticut, for example, about $6,000 per year is spent to educate a child; in West Hartford, about $13,000 per year is spent to educate a child. And after 12 years, one child goes to Yale, and the other child goes to jail. When we're willing to spend more money to jail inner-city youth than to educate them, it's a shameful condition . . ."

(N.E.T.) in Redwood City, California. As vice president of worldwide client support, Davis and his staff have the responsibility of solving any problems customers may have with N.E.T. products. The goal of his speech was to encourage better product design to avoid as many customer problems as possible. During his speech, Davis told the true story of a wing-walker who fell off a biplane in flight. The man hung by a lifeline as the pilot flew low over the airport in search of help. Thinking fast, the ground crew drove a pickup truck along the runway beneath the dangling man. Then they reached up and cut the lifeline, which released the wing-walker safely into the pickup truck.

Davis's words helped his audience envision the danger and thrill of this dramatic rescue. Then he brought listeners back to the problems at hand: "N.E.T. does an Olympic job of bailing us out of problems after they occur. But we don't do a good enough job on the front end. I can't buy enough pickup trucks to keep solving these problems." The mental imagery fit N.E.T.'s situation so perfectly that employees talked about wing-walkers and pickup trucks for weeks after Davis's speech.[2]

Often, the images that an audience develops during a speech are colored by the speaker's passion for the topic. This is a particular danger with controversial topics such as abortion and gun control, where both sides can use powerful language to support their cases and devalue other arguments. It's also a concern when you're addressing any topic that arouses strong feelings in your listeners. So when you speak, bear in mind

your ethical responsibilities to provide honest, accurate, well-reasoned information that will support your central idea without distorting or hiding points from the other side. You can stay on the ethical high road by avoiding the use of words to create images that hide information or distort the truth.

Influencing Feelings and Attitudes

As a public speaker, you can influence the feelings and attitudes of your audience with your words. You may move your listeners to tears, anger, or joy; you may move them to like, dislike, accept, or reject something. How the audience reacts depends on the specific words you select. That's why wording your speech is such an important part of the public speaking process.

For example, Ryan Ries of North Dakota State University carefully planned the language in his speech "An Ominous Warning" to arouse feelings of alarm in his audience. In his introduction, Ries told his listeners:

Lead has not only found its way into our country's drinking water, it is also contaminating our air, soil, and homes. This lead poses a deadly threat to American children and yet our government is doing very little about this menacing metal, even failing to adequately warn us about its dangers.[3]

Ries's words left no room for doubt about lead's effects. He described it as "contaminating" and posing "a deadly threat." He called it a "menacing metal" and mentioned its "dangers." These words

EXHIBIT 12.2

Using Language to Inspire Action
Police officers who address elementary school students in the D.A.R.E. antidrug program use no-nonsense wording to motivate youngsters to stay away from illegal drugs.

were calculated to make listeners feel strongly about banning lead and warning people of its hazards.

Inspiring Action

Your words can also inspire people to take action. In an informative speech, you may ask people to take actions such as to remember your ideas or follow your advice. In a persuasive speech, you may ask them to vote for a particular candidate or bill, buy or boycott a certain product, or take other actions. Influencing feelings and attitudes is a prerequisite to inspiring action. But before listeners can be moved to action, they'll want to know exactly what they should do and why they should do it.

For example, when Ben Smith, a student at Ohio State University, spoke on daytime use of car headlights, he started by presenting evidence that poor visibility contributes to traffic accidents and deaths. Then he discussed the drop in accidents in Canada, Finland, and Sweden thanks to laws requiring daytime use of headlights. Once he'd given his audience reasons for feeling strongly about using headlights during the day, Smith asked listeners to do two things: He urged them to write their legislators in support of a law mandating headlight use day and night, and he encouraged a more personal action:

> It seems so simple. One flick of the wrist and you can possibly save your life as well as 15,000 other lives and 36,000 injuries each year. The next time you step into your car, turn on your low beam headlights.[4]

By linking his call to action with life-saving benefits, Smith gave his audience a compelling reason to follow through and act. He also announced that the action was simple, and he reinforced its simplicity with the words "one flick of the wrist." Like Smith, if you choose your words carefully, you can inspire your listeners to take a particular action (see Exhibit 12.2).

Tapping the Power of Spoken Words

What you say during your speech to create mental images, influence feelings and attitudes, and inspire action is not what you'd write to accomplish the same things. In fact, spoken language differs from written language in several ways.[5] First, speeches use less formal language than written communication. When you address an audience, your words and phrases are usually shorter, simpler, and more varied than those you'd write. You may sometimes speak in sentence fragments or use slang that would be inappropriate in written messages. These work well in public speaking, because they give your speech a natural, conversational tone.[6]

Speeches are intended for the ear, not the eye, as President John F. Kennedy was well aware. He judged his speeches not by the way they looked on paper but by the way they sounded when he read them aloud. The hallmark of Kennedy's speeches was plain and unpretentious wording, as well as elements of rhythm that were pleasing to the ear but that would seem out of place in written form.[7]

Second, speeches contain more repetition than written communication. Readers can review a written passage if they don't understand or remember its content; listeners must rely only on what they hear, one word at a time. By making a point in several ways during your speech, you can help your listeners understand and remember what you've said.[8] In contrast, readers would quickly grow tired of repetition in written communication.

Third, spoken language allows personal interaction between speaker and audience. Your spoken words bring you closer to your audience than words on paper; your speech can communicate your personality in a way that wouldn't be as effective in a written message. Consider the introduction that Pamela Kay Epp, a student at the University of Nebraska, used in a speech about food packaging:

> In a recent investigation of my waste-basket, I discovered an empty yogurt container, a cup of microwavable Cheez Whiz, a handy pack of Teddy Grahams, a V-8 sip box and a single-serving package of raisins. It appears that I, like many Americans, have fallen into the ocean of garbage created in our society by convenience foods and their plastic packaging.[9]

Such a personal introduction would be out of place in a written document such as a letter to a legislator or a report to an employer. Here, however, spoken language reveals Epp's personality and interests. It also helps her build rapport with a college audience that can identify with her snacking habits.

Speaking instead of writing not only brings you closer to your audience, it also allows you immediate feedback about your ideas. You can make changes on the spot in reaction to such feedback. This personal interaction, which is impossible with written communication, is a key element in public speaking.

EFFECTIVE WORDING IN SPEECHES

Every word you choose and every phrase you use in a speech has the potential to clarify or obscure your message. As discussed in Chapter 1, communication doesn't occur unless the speaker encodes

a message and the audience decodes the message. With the right words, you can encode your message and express your ideas more effectively. Just as important, the right words can help your audience decode and understand your intended meaning.

Your challenge is to choose the wording that is most effective for you as a speaker, for the message you want to convey, for the occasion, and for the audience you are addressing. To do this, you'll want to make sure your wording is familiar, concrete, precise, accurate, unbiased, and concise. The next sections look at each of these elements in more detail.

Using Familiar Wording

Audiences react most favorably to words that they know. When you express yourself in simple language, you help your listeners understand and relate to your message. Even though you may be tempted to use more elaborate language to discuss a particular topic or to impress a specific audience, you'll do better to use simple language (see Exhibit 12.3). Not only will you avoid the embarrassment of mispronouncing or misusing a fancy word, you'll also leave less room for misunderstanding.

In general, you'll want to follow the advice of George Orwell, author of *1984* and *Animal Farm*: never use a long word where a short one will do.[10] Also, be alert for jargon or technical words that may creep into your speeches. If you think that even a few listeners may be unfamiliar with these words, you'll want to either define your terms as you use them or substitute everyday words that mean the same thing. Consider, for example, how listeners would react if you included the following passage in a speech:[11]

> Preservation of one percent of a dollar is analogous to acquisition of a similar aggregate through the application of remunerative exertion.

What is the message buried deep in these fancy phrases? Put yourself in your audience's place, and see whether you can puzzle out the meaning. Give

EXHIBIT 12.3

Quiz Yourself: Using Familiar Language
Choose a familiar word or phrase from Column B to replace each of the longer, more stilted-sounding words in Column A. You can check your answers at the bottom.

Column A	Column B
1. abbreviate	A. keep
2. ascertain	B. home
3. commence	C. meet
4. diminutive	D. possible
5. duplicate	E. begin
6. edifice	F. end
7. elucidate	G. shorten
8. encounter	H. cut out
9. endeavor	I. copy
10. eradicate	J. clarify
11. feasible	K. try
12. observe	L. building
13. residence	M. find out
14. retain	N. watch
15. terminate	O. little

Answers: 1-G, 2-M, 3-E, 4-O, 5-I, 6-L, 7-J, 8-C, 9-K, 10-H, 11-D, 12-N, 13-B, 14-A, 15-F.

up? Here's the same message, expressed in simple, familiar language:

A penny saved is a penny earned.

As you plan what you'll say in your next speech, take the time to choose words that your audience will know and understand. Wherever possible, replace overblown, pretentious wording with simpler, more commonplace substitutes. This way, your words won't get in the way of what you want to say. At the same time, beware of clichés, which are so familiar that they're boring. A better approach is to use familiar wording in a fresh way. Just a little twist in wording can capture your audience's imagination and make your point that much more memorable.

Using Concrete Wording

To be sure that your audience receives the message you want to send, you'll want to use concrete rather than abstract words. A concrete word refers to something specific that your audience can visualize, such as an object, a person, or a place. In contrast, an abstract word is more general and describes something less able to be visualized, such as a category of objects, a type of person, a kind of place, or an idea.

Apple is a concrete word. You can, however, include an apple within a larger category that is described by the more abstract word *fruit*. The word *food* is even more abstract than

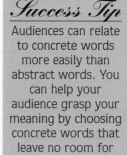

Success Tip

Audiences can relate to concrete words more easily than abstract words. You can help your audience grasp your meaning by choosing concrete words that leave no room for misinterpretation.

fruit, because it describes a broader category than fruits or apples. Similarly, *catcher* is a concrete word, but it can also be included in a larger category that is described by the more abstract word *baseball player*. More abstract still is *athlete,* a word that describes many kinds of sports participants. And the word *athletics* is even more abstract, because it refers to sports in general (see Exhibit 12.4).

The more concrete your words, the more specific the word picture you can paint for your audience. If your words are too abstract, you may inadvertently leave room for misinterpretation. So help your audience zero in on your exact meaning by choosing concrete words that convey specifically what you want to say.

For example, consider the concrete wording used by Michael Riley, a student at Creighton University in Nebraska. In his award-winning speech, "There's No Place Like Home," Riley's specific purpose was to inform his audience about the problems faced by homeless children. Here's an excerpt from his first major point:

All across this nation, there are children who have no address, receive no mail, attend no school,

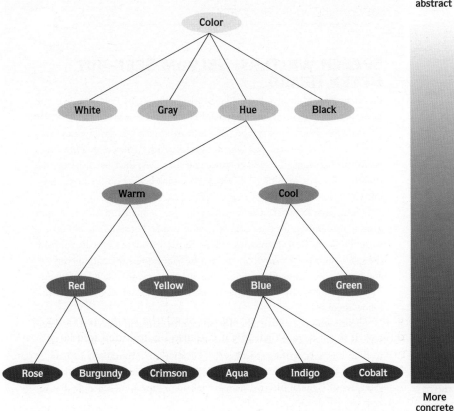

More abstract

More concrete

EXHIBIT 12.4

Word Choice: Stay Low on the Hierarchy

Abstract words can be viewed as larger, more general categories that contain the smaller, more concrete words. The closer you are to the bottom of the hierarchy, the closer you are to actual experience, to the real things that people know about.

of each point. Then you can step back and look at the words from your audience's point of view, asking:

• What nuance of meaning does each word or phrase carry?
• What emotions might listeners associate with each word or phrase?

and have no access to showers, bathrooms, or laundry facilities.[12]

Riley could have simply used the abstract label *homeless* and left his audience to imagine the circumstances of children in such situations. Instead, he cast the situation in more personal terms by using concrete wording that spelled out exactly what homeless children miss. By being so specific, Riley was able to help his listeners appreciate and sympathize with the problems that homeless children face every day.

Using Precise Wording

To help your audience understand the exact meaning you intend to convey, you'll want to choose words that are precise. This is an ongoing process that starts when you first determine the points you want to make. As you plan your speech, you can jot down several words or phrases that you might use to communicate the meaning

The first question helps you think about the various shades of meaning that words can have. To see how this works, look at the subtle difference in meaning between *high costs* and *soaring costs*. In both cases, the audience will understand that a lot of money is involved, but when they hear *soaring costs,* they're likely to think that costs are rising rapidly. That's the exact meaning that Darwin R. Peterson, a student at the University of Alaska in Anchorage, wanted his audience to take away when he used *soaring costs* to describe what was happening to U.S. health care in his speech "National Health Care in the United States."[13]

The second question helps you consider the feelings that listeners may associate with the words you use. For example, Patricia A. Cirucci of West Chester University in Pennsylvania used the word *epidemic* several times in a student speech about preventing skin cancer. An epidemic can be both serious and alarming, and

Cirucci expected that her listeners would pay attention to her suggestions about how to avoid becoming part of the epidemic. Here's how she used the word in the introduction of her speech:

> In order to shed some light on why we should stay in the shade, it's important, first to wake up to the alarm over skin cancer, then to pay attention to who's at risk, and finally to declare our own war on this undeclared epidemic. Because unlike most epidemics, this one doesn't depend on the discovery of a vaccine or miracle drug to put an end to it. In this epidemic, it is common sense that will save lives.[14]

In her speech, Cirucci might have referred to skin cancer as a *problem* or a *disease*. However, neither word was likely to trigger the kind of emotional reaction that *epidemic* would. By using precise words, Cirucci communicates a feeling as well as a meaning about skin cancer, giving her audience a compelling reason to listen for more information.

DEVELOPING YOUR CREATIVITY

SPEECH WRITERS: SELDOM SEEN BUT OFTEN HEARD

President Ronald Reagan has delivered words written by Peggy Noonan; Lee Iacocca, former chairman of Chrysler, has delivered words written by Michael K. Morrison. Both Noonan and Morrison are speech writers, hired to draft speeches for government and business leaders. Although speech writers have been penning words for speakers since ancient times, their participation has traditionally been invisible. "Speech writers don't belong on the map," says one top writer. "The better you are, the more unnoticed you are."

These days, however, speech writers such as Noonan and Morrison are gaining recognition for their creativity with words. For example, Noonan wrote President Reagan's moving tribute to the astronauts who died aboard the space shuttle *Challenger*. She helped Reagan express the nation's sorrow and honor the astronauts' accomplishments with memorable lines such as: "The *Challenger* crew was pulling us into the future, and we'll continue to follow them."

Speech writers craft speeches for officials in state and federal government, such as President Bush, as well as for politicians seeking election. They also work in business, writing speeches for executives at corporations such as Citicorp, DuPont, Ford, and NYNEX. When Reginald Jones was chief executive of General Electric, he had such a busy speaking schedule that he kept six speech writers on staff.

If you're thinking of pursuing this aspect of public speaking, you'll need the creativity of a poet. Peggy Noonan knows this well. She sums up speech writing this way: "Poetry has everything to do with speeches—cadence, rhythm, imagery, sweep, a knowledge that words are magic, that words like children have the power to make dance the dullest beanbag of a heart."

President Bush, like other modern-day presidents, works with professional speech writers who can help translate ideas into skillful speeches for a variety of occasions.

Using Accurate Wording

Just as chefs are careful to choose the correct ingredients for each recipe, you'll want to choose the correct words for each speech and use them

If I reprehend anything in this world, it is the use of my oracular tongue, and a nice derangement of epitaphs!

EXHIBIT 12.5
Mrs. Malaprop's Malapropisms
Mrs. Malaprop, a character in Richard Sheridan's play *The Rivals*, inadvertently undercuts her credibility by misusing language, even though she is trying her best to impress.

estimate, dictionaries need updating every five to six years to keep pace with new or changed uses for words. As a speaker, you'll want to stay abreast of such changes so that you can express your ideas in ways that the audience can follow.[15]

You'll also want to watch out for **malapropisms**, mistakes in which you substitute a word that sounds similar but has an entirely different meaning from the word you actually need. Imagine your audience's confusion if you spoke of feeling *enmity* (hatred) instead of *amity* (friendship) for your closest friend, or if you said that someone was *extinguished* (wiped out) instead of *distinguished* (noted or famous). Such slips may sound funny, but they can undermine your credibility (see Exhibit 12.5). When in doubt, take a moment to recheck the accuracy of your words.

Also consider whether your wording is grammatically correct. This is important because your listeners may question the accuracy of your ideas if your speech is ungrammatical. For example, if you're planning a speech about the *media,* be sure your verbs agree with this plural noun. Many times, you can detect problems by trusting your ears: If a sentence sounds ungrammatical when you say it, it probably is. When you're unsure, the safest course of action is to check your grammar before you address your audience.

Using Unbiased Wording

In today's culturally diverse world, excellent public speakers show respect for their audiences by avoiding words that display bias on the basis of gender, race, ethnic group, age, or disability.

accurately. If a chef uses an incorrect spice or spices a dish too liberally, the meal won't taste the way it's supposed to. Similarly, if you choose the wrong word or use words incorrectly, your audience won't be able to grasp the meaning you intend. For this reason, excellent speakers are careful to use language accurately.

You can start by double-checking the accuracy of the words you use. Think about whether your words mean what you think they mean; if you're unsure, you can check the dictionary, especially for the meaning and usage of some technical words. For example, *data bank* has been replaced with *database* over the past few years. By one

Unbiased words can help bring audiences together and encourage open discussion of even the most controversial topics. At the same time, words that stereotype, demean, or insult can divide, annoy, or anger listeners, closing the door to meaningful communication.

Although you may be able to recognize blatantly biased phrases, be alert for more subtle references as well. Gender bias is a good example. You can quickly root out gender-biased terms such as *stewardess* (you can substitute flight attendant) and *fireman* (fire fighter), which reinforce stereotypical gender roles. And don't forget to change phrases such as *mankind; humanity,* is more inclusive. Here are four steps to help you accomplish gender-neutral public speaking:[16]

1. *Replace phrases that contain* man *or* woman *with gender-neutral terms.* For example:

INSTEAD OF	SUBSTITUTE
cleaning woman	office cleaner
foreman	supervisor
manpower	labor force

2. *Restructure sentences where necessary to eliminate sexist language.* For example:

INSTEAD OF	SUBSTITUTE
The Operations Department will select someone to be chairman of the new committee.	The Operations Department will select someone to chair the new committee.

3. *Use plurals to avoid pronouns that favor one gender.* For example:

INSTEAD OF	SUBSTITUTE
When a student requests a parking spot, he needs to allow three weeks for approval.	When students request parking spots, they need to allow three weeks for approval.

4. *Provide balance by alternating male and female examples, and mention women first some of the time.* For example:

INSTEAD OF	SUBSTITUTE
Managers are too quick to say, "He doesn't follow directions" or "He doesn't fit in with the group."	Managers are too quick to say, "She doesn't follow directions" or "He doesn't fit in with the group."

Bear in mind that doctors, politicians, astronauts, and executives can be either male or female, so avoid language that assumes a gender bias in any role. This is not always easy. Dr. Deborah Tannen, a specialist in women's and men's communication styles, points out that certain labels call to mind gender-based images. "All surgeons are presumed male, all nurses presumed female, unless proven otherwise," she says.[17] However, rather than refer to someone as a *woman doctor* or a *male nurse,* you can indicate gender—if it's relevant—by using a sentence structure that includes the pronoun *she* or *he.*

Of course, you can apply many of the ideas for avoiding gender bias to other types of bias, as well. Unless your audience needs to know the age, race, or ethnic background of someone you discuss in a speech, you'll want to omit such information. Likewise, leave out references to someone's disabilities, unless it's relevant to your topic or point. Your goal is to do away with biased phrases that categorize or patronize people.[18]

Using Concise Wording

In this era of sound bites, excellent speakers aim to get their messages across as concisely as possible. But the push for concise wording is hardly new. President Thomas Jefferson recognized it nearly two centuries ago when he observed, "The most valuable of all talents is never using two words when one will do."[19] Whether you have five minutes or thirty-five minutes in which to address your audience, you don't want to waste precious time on redundancies or excess wording. Such verbal clutter can keep listeners from understanding and remembering your intended message.

Compare the cluttered phrases that follow with their more concise equivalents:[20]

CLUTTERED PHRASE	CONCISE EQUIVALENT
full to capacity	full
at this point in time	now
a large number of	many
caused damage to	damaged
gave encouragement to	encouraged
subsequent to	after
hold a meeting	meet

Also watch out for the clutter of passive voice, which sounds wordy and dull. In contrast, active voice is more lively and direct. To see how this works, imagine President Lincoln's Gettysburg address written in passive voice: "It was four score and seven years ago that a government was established on this continent." Lincoln's actual words were powerful because his words reflected action: "Four score and seven years ago, our fathers brought forth upon this continent a new nation . . ."[21] Finally, be alert to extra words such as *very* and *really;* they clutter your speech and detract from the power of your words (see Exhibit 12.6). With practice, you'll be able to avoid clutter and use fewer words to get to the heart of the matter.

VIVID WORDING IN SPEECHES

When you use effective wording in a speech, you clarify your intended meaning. In addition, you want to attract and hold your audience's attention, so you'll choose words that are vivid. Lifeless words may be clear and accurate, but they won't help you touch the hearts and minds of your listeners. To bring your message to life, you can use vivid wording in four ways: metaphors, similes, imagery, and rhythm.

Using Metaphors

A **metaphor** is an implied comparison between seemingly dissimilar things. When you use a metaphor in your speech, you help your audience relate to something that's abstract and difficult to imagine by comparing it to something more concrete. This strengthens your point, heightens your audience's emotions, and increases the level of interest in your message.[22]

For example, Dr. Lonnie R. Bristow, head of the American Medical Association's Board of Trustees, wanted to stir up his student audience at Indiana University. Speaking against the efforts of the tobacco industry to promote smoking, he said in his conclusion:

> The tobacco industry is a mountainous boulder that will do everything it can to resist being moved. But we're beginning to see some strains, some cracks, some fissures in the rock.[23]

Bristow's metaphor casts tobacco manufacturers as a giant boulder that's not easily moved. Once he had fixed this similarity in his listeners' minds, Bristow's mention of strains, cracks, and fissures was both appropriate and vivid. In two brief sentences, his simple metaphor both reinforced his point and made it more interesting.

Checklist for Effective Wording in Speeches

1. Use familiar wording that listeners can understand and relate to.
2. Use concrete wording that explains specifically what you want to convey (avoid abstract wording that can leave room for misinterpretation).
3. Use precise wording so that your audience can understand the exact meaning you intend to convey.
4. Use wording that is both correct and accurate to effectively communicate your meaning.
5. Use unbiased wording when you refer to gender, race, ethnic group, age, or disability so that you can bring listeners together and facilitate open discussion.
6. Use concise wording to get your message across without redundancies or wordiness.

EXHIBIT 12.6

Pruning the Clutter of Powerless Words
Some of the clutter in speeches can actually undermine a speaker's credibility and authority. These powerless words include intensifiers, hedges, and hesitations. If you prune such cluttering forms from your speech, you'll sound more confident and authoritative.

Intensifiers   Words that are intended to strengthen a point but have the opposite effect (such as **so, very,** and **surely**)

Less powerful	**More powerful**
We really had a very, very informative meeting.	We had an informative meeting.

Hedges   Words that qualify or reduce the force of a statement by displaying lack of conviction (such as **I think** and **sort of**)

Less powerful	**More powerful**
I think utilities should be more careful with toxic waste.	Utilities should be more careful with toxic waste.

Hestitations   Distracting phrases used as placeholders while speakers get ready to say something (such as **you know** and **I mean**)

Less powerful	**More powerful**
I mean, the government should be more responsive, you know?	The government should be more responsive.

Metaphors are powerful devices to be used in moderation. You may want to extend a metaphor to reinforce a point or bridge two points effectively. However, if you endlessly repeat a metaphor or sprinkle variation on variation throughout your speech, you'll lose the novelty—and distract your audience from the real message. Instead of clichés (such as "fresh as a daisy"), look for fresh, memorable comparisons that will grab attention and help you make your point in an interesting way.

You'll also want to avoid *mixed metaphors,* comparisons that don't belong together. When you mix your metaphors, you can unintentionally confuse (and amuse) your listeners. For example, during a heated legislative debate, Silvio Conte, representing Massachusetts, once told the U.S. Congress, "This is no time to pull the rug out in the middle of the stream."[24] Either "pull the rug out" or "middle of the stream" would have been apt in a single metaphor; used together, they surely baffled Conte's listeners and detracted from his message. Therefore, to keep your audience focused on your message and your meaning, construct your metaphors with care.

Using Similes

A **simile** is an explicit comparison between two unlike things. Whereas a metaphor implies the comparison, a simile makes it directly through the words *like* and *as*. Like metaphors,

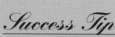

Success Tip

You can make abstract concepts more concrete through comparisons such as metaphors and similes. A few fresh, lively comparisons can add zing to your speech and give your audience new insights into your topic.

similes bring abstract things into focus by comparison with more concrete things. They can also help shape the beliefs of others by influencing feelings.

For example, Winston Churchill, Great Britain's prime minister during World War II, once used similes to illustrate three views of business:

Some people regard private enterprise as a predatory tiger to be shot. Others look on it as a cow they can milk. Not enough people see it as a healthy horse, pulling a sturdy wagon.[25]

Churchill's choice of similes communicated feelings as well as images. His third simile revealed his view of business ("as a healthy horse, pulling a sturdy wagon")—a view he hoped his audience would share. These similes were easily visualized and understood, and they were appropriate to the subject and occasion, which enhanced their strength.

As with metaphors, similes are powerful, and they're best used sparingly. Following one simile with another will dilute the effect, so carefully pace your similes. Also, weed out trite similes and seek fresh phrases that give your listeners new insights

SPEAKING ACROSS CULTURES

WHEN TO USE IDIOMS AND SLANG WITH CULTURALLY DIVERSE AUDIENCES

"It's raining cats and dogs." "The ball is in your court." "Eat your heart out." These everyday expressions are easily understood by U.S. listeners from Seattle, Washington, to Savannah, Georgia. However, the same phrases are sure to befuddle listeners in other nations. Although such expressions serve as shortcuts in the United States, they can become roadblocks with culturally diverse audiences.

When planning to speak in another country, think twice before using idioms and slang phrases that you would use with U.S. audiences. Avoiding idioms takes effort in extemporaneous speaking, because you're not reading your speech word for word. Even so, you can note more important phrases on your speaking outline. They'll be handy alternatives if you find yourself seeking a replacement for an idiom or a slang expression that you use often.

Of course, you may want to include one or two appropriate idiomatic expressions, as long as you're careful to explain their use. Giving listeners a sample of tasteful slang can add interest to your speech. To be safe, however, make sure in advance that the phrases aren't offensive to your audience.

Another approach would be to get help finding an equivalent expression in your listeners' native language. For example, if you want to say, "John is beating around the bush" to an audience in Italy, you might use the equivalent local idiom "*Giovanni sta menando il cane per l'aia*" (which means "John is leading his dog around the threshing floor"). Audience members will appreciate your thoughtfulness in learning a bit of their language. Moreover, you'll have a colorful new phrase to use later with other audiences.

Expressions that are common in one language may carry different meanings in other languages. This sign in a Paris airport says "To planes"; a corresponding sign in a U.S. airport might say "To gates."

senses. This creation of visual pictures and other sensory experiences through description is called *imagery*. When listeners can almost see, feel, taste, smell, or hear something, they're much more likely to understand and remember what you've said (see Exhibit 12.7).

Consider how Sheila W. Wellington uses imagery to support her view of working women past and present:

> When I was a child, my mother told me the story of the fire at the Triangle Shirtwaist Factory. It happened in 1911 in New York City, in the immigrant neighborhood where she grew up. A fire broke out in a factory where young women toiled in unimaginable conditions. Trapped in flames, 146 women died, piled against doors sealed tight to prevent their leaving before the day's work was over.[26]

Wellington's vivid imagery sticks with her listeners, and later in her speech, it makes a sharp contrast to working women today when she says: "We no longer see women literally locked into their workplaces."[27]

and perspectives. By using creative similes you can make your comparisons both vivid and memorable.

Using Imagery

You've seen how you can choose words that project a vivid mental image of your ideas, bringing your points alive by appealing to the

Using Rhythm

You can make your speeches more pleasing to the ear by using language patterns that create rhythm. This "ear appeal" can help you grab audience attention and make your words more memorable. Among the patterns you can use to create rhythm in a speech are parallelism, alliteration, antithesis, and repetition.

Parallelism

When you use **parallelism**, you arrange a series of words, phrases, or sentences into similar patterns. This repetition of pattern gives a unique, balanced structure to your words, which allows listeners to fit each word or phrase with the others. For example, when James B. Hayes, publisher emeritus of *Fortune* magazine, spoke about the state of children in the United States, he used parallelism to keep his audience's attention and to telegraph his message:

> I am speaking, of course, about the neglect of our children, about the neglect of our nation's greatest resource, about the careless neglect of our own future.[28]

This passage draws its rhythm from the phrase "about the neglect of . . ." Each time listeners hear that phrase, they're primed to link the words that follow with the other phrases that share the same structure. Hayes's use of parallelism enhances his message and emphasizes the last phrase by inserting the word *careless* to change the pattern just a little. Thanks to parallelism, Hayes's speech has ear appeal and is memorable.

Alliteration

Alliteration is the repetition of the same initial consonant sound in a series of words or phrases. This repetition draws attention to your words and gives listeners a handy device for remembering what you've said. As with any rhythmic pattern, overuse can turn your audience off and defuse the power of your words. When you use alliteration in moderation, however, the sounds add a subtle, memorable spice to your message.

For example, student Ruby Jones used alliteration in a classroom speech advocating the establishment of educational guidelines to better prepare graduates for the job market. An internal preview at the end of her introduction presented her three recommendations:

> As we leave our classrooms and enter the twenty-first century work force, we and millions of other students must graduate equipped with three skills. We need competencies, critical thinking, and creativity. Only

EXHIBIT 12.8
Using Antithesis Effectively
President Kennedy used antithesis skillfully to draw a dramatic contrast between opposing ideas mentioned in his speeches.

". . . we observe today not a victory of party, but a celebration of freedom . . ."

with these three skills—the three Cs—can we effectively compete in tomorrow's job market.

Notice how Jones repeated the *c* sound in all three phrases. Using alliteration drew attention to each of the recommendations in the sequence. In addition, presenting her ideas in terms of three Cs gave Jones's audience a handy way to remember the message.

Antithesis
Antithesis is contrasting two ideas within a parallel structure, sometimes suggesting a choice between the two. This device is both dramatic and rhythmic. It focuses your audience's attention on the disparity between the ideas. By accenting the contrast, you suggest a context in which two competing ideas can be considered.

President John F. Kennedy was a master at using antithesis effectively (see Exhibit 12.8). One of the most memorable presidential quotes of all time came from his 1962 inaugural address: "Ask not what your country can do for you—ask what you can do for your country." Notice the order of the ideas in this sentence. Kennedy first stated what he *didn't* want his audience to do before stating what he *did* want his audience to do. By positioning his suggested action in the second half of the sentence, the president left the audience with the idea of what they should do. If you follow

Kennedy's example when you use antithesis, you'll help your audience remember what you want rather than what you don't want.

Repetition
You can also create rhythm by repeating the same word or phrase several times in a section of your speech. This **repetition** can help you tie several ideas together so that your audience understands the connection. It also helps you reinforce your point and make it more memorable. For example, Reverend Martin Luther King, Jr., used skillful repetition in his famous 1963 speech, "I Have a Dream":

I have a dream that one day this nation will rise up and live out the true meaning of its creed, "We hold these truths to be self-evident, that all men are created equal." I have a dream that one day on the red hills of Georgia the sons of former slaves and the sons of former slave-owners will be able to sit down together at the table of brotherhood. I have a dream that one day even the state of Mississippi, a state swelling with the heat of injustice, sweltering with the heat of oppression, will be transformed into an oasis of freedom and justice. I have a dream that my four little children will one day live in a nation where they will not be judged by the color of their skin but by the

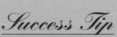

Success Tip
You can create rhythm by using parallelism, repetition, alliteration, and antithesis. These techniques add ear appeal to attract and keep your audience's attention and to make your points more memorable.

content of their character. I have a dream today.

King's repetition of "I have a dream" unified the various examples of equality that he cited. It also provided a strong sense of rhythm, which attracted and maintained the audience's attention. And in combination with the repeated imagery of heat ("the heat of injustice," "the heat of oppression") and the alliteration in the phrases about Mississippi ("swelling," "sweltering") the repetition further enhanced the emotional content of King's message.

APPROPRIATE WORDING IN SPEECHES

Could you use the wording from Reverend King's "I Have a Dream" speech in an entertaining after-dinner speech? Could you use the wording from President Kennedy's inaugural address in an informative classroom speech? Both speakers used effective, vivid wording to make their points; both speeches were well received—and long remembered—by their audiences. However, as powerful as those speakers' words were, they can't simply be dropped into other speeches.

Words and phrases that work in one public speaking situation may not be right in another. King and Kennedy knew this, and they adjusted their language for every speech they made. As you get ready to speak, you'll want to follow their lead and match your wording to your audience, your topic, your occasion, and yourself as the speaker.

Matching Wording to Your Audience

Keep your audience's needs and interests firmly in mind as you determine the appropriate wording for a particular speech. If you're thinking about using jargon, acronyms, or technical terms, consider the knowledge and background of your audience before you decide (see Exhibit 12.9). For example, when Raymond Chrétien, Canada's ambassador to the United States, spoke before the Association for Canadian Studies in

the United States, he didn't explain his use of the acronyms *NATO* and *IMF*.[29] His sophisticated audience understood that Chrétien was talking about the North Atlantic Treaty Organization and the International Monetary Fund.

In addition to avoid unnecessary jargon and terminology, you'll want to steer clear of obscene language and any words or phrases that could offend your listeners. Using profanity and abusive language runs counter to public speaking ethics because it shows disrespect for your audience. With just a word or two, you can destroy the rapport that you worked so hard to build. The stakes are high, so if you're not sure how listeners are likely to react to a word or phrase, simply leave it out.

Matching Wording to the Topic

You'll also want to carefully adjust your language to fit your topic. No matter what topic you choose, you'll want to use wording that is familiar, concrete, precise, accurate, unbiased, and concise. But what kind of vivid wording would you use to discuss a serious topic such as the history of the Vietnam War? An emotional topic such as euthanasia? A straightforward topic such as how to operate a wood chipper?

You might use metaphors, similes, imagery, or rhythm in a speech about Vietnam or euthanasia. These techniques of vivid wording are especially helpful when you want to influence your audience's attitudes, evoke a particular mood, and make your points more memorable. However, you'd probably use such techniques sparingly (if at all) in a speech about operating a wood chipper, because you're merely describing a procedure. In fact, you might use simpler and more direct language in the wood-chipper speech so that you can emphasize safety procedures. So before you choose your wording, think about the topic and what you want to communicate to your audience.

Matching Wording to the Occasion

As you know from personal experience, the language that you use on one occasion is often inappropriate for another occasion. Even though

EXHIBIT 12.9
Using Language That's Appropriate to the Audience

These two quotes from Supreme Court Justice Sandra Day O'Connor show how a speaker can match wording on the same topic to two distinct audiences.

American Bar Association Speech
Intentional discrimination on the basis of gender . . . violates the Equal Protection Clause, particularly where . . . the discrimination serves to ratify and perpetuate invidious, archaic, and overbroad stereotypes about the relative abilities of men and women.

New York University Speech
Do women judges decide cases differently by virtue of being women? I would echo the answer of my colleague, Justice Jeanne Coyne of the Supreme Court of Oklahoma, who responded that "a wise old man and a wise old woman reach the same conclusion."

speeches are more formal than conversations, you can vary the degree of formality depending on the occasion for your speech. For example, you'd use fairly informal language—sprinkled liberally with slang—in a speech during a party to celebrate your college basketball team's victory. In contrast, you'd avoid slang and stick to more formal language in a speech at a press conference to announce a medical breakthrough in treating cancer. By evaluating the formality of the occasion, you can gauge how formal the wording in your speech should be.

Matching Wording to the Speaker

In addition to being appropriate for the audience, topic, and occasion, your wording must be appropriate for you as a speaker. Of course, no two speakers use language in exactly the same way. President Kennedy's command of language enabled him to use antithesis to great effect; Reverend King's powerful delivery helped him hammer home important points using vivid imagery and rhythm. Even though you may not turn a phrase as elegantly as these speakers did, you can learn from their use of language. The key is to adapt wording and language patterns so that you can develop an effective speaking style that works for you.

Consider the wording that Emily Ann Ochoa used in a speech about her involvement with Junior Achievement programs. Ochoa, a ten-year-old student at Monte Vista Elementary School in Los Angeles, spoke to an audience of business leaders who support Junior Achievement:

> I live with my grandma Pat and my younger brother Daniel, and—may I add—"achievement" doesn't seem to be in my brother's vocabulary. But it is in mine. My mother takes drugs, doesn't have a job and lives on welfare. I do love my mom because she took care of us by herself when my father went to jail. It's very hard and lonely not to be able to have a normal life.[30]

Ochoa's simple and direct language was appropriate for her. As a fifth grader, she would have sounded pretentious and comical using fancy phrases or elaborate sentences. The wording she used was familiar, concrete, and unbiased; it conveyed her message in a straightforward and sincere way that suited her. Small wonder that the adult audience roared its approval after Ochoa finished speaking.

HUMOR IN SPEECHES

Did you hear the one about humor in speeches? Making an audience laugh is no laughing matter: Learning to use humor in a speech is, in reality, a serious business. Just ask Art Buchwald, an internationally known humor columnist who's been addressing audiences for more than 25 years. Buchwald is well aware that tickling an audience's funny bone can be ticklish.

"People won't laugh if they don't agree with you," he says. "You have to be on the same wavelength as the listener. If you're not, you won't be funny. My survival is based on the fact that I'm thinking with the audience. The greatest satisfaction a speaker gets is when the audience starts nodding while you're talking—not laughing but nodding. When I say that I've been afraid of computers ever since I tried to get out of the Book-of-the-Month Club, people start nodding."[31]

As Buchwald knows, humor means more than telling jokes. In fact, you don't have to be the class clown to use humor effectively in a speech. Rather, you're looking to inject a little humor that relates to your audience, to your topic, to your occasion, or to you as a speaker. You can add this humorous touch with an appropriate anecdote, a clever play on words, a funny quote, or a witty saying. Unlike stand-up comedians who try to induce side-splitting laughter, you want your listeners to nod and smile—and keep their attention on your message. If they're rolling in the aisles, they may lose your message among the belly laughs.

You can use humor in several ways in a speech. As you saw in Chapter 10, it's a good way to break the ice during your introduction, when you want to capture your listeners' attention and build interest in your speech. It's also useful for building rapport with your listeners. In addition, you can use humor to reinforce an important point. Of course, like any other element of public speaking, humor works best if it's not overdone or misused.

Using Humor to Capture Attention and Build Interest

One of the best places to insert humor is at the start of your speech, when you want to attract and maintain your audience's interest. At this point, your audience knows little about what you plan to say. By using humor early in your speech, you can introduce your topic and build interest in your viewpoint (see Exhibit 12.10). For example, Farah M. Walters, president of University Hospitals Health System in Cleveland, used a humorous quote early in her speech at a conference about cultural diversity. After she greeted her audience, she said:

Since the topic of today's meeting is *managing* diversity, I'm reminded of a comment once made by a truly great manager, Casey Stengel, when he was in his prime as manager of the Yankees. One day he was asked about the art of managing. "Managing," Casey replied, "is getting paid for home runs someone else hits." We're here today to discuss diversity. It's a difficult issue—an area where it's not always easy to hit home runs.[32]

Walters's humor was gentle and to the point. She carefully related Stengel's quote to her topic so her audience didn't have to wonder about its significance. In this way, Walters drew her listeners in and directed them toward the more complex issues she planned to address in the body of her speech.

Using Humor to Build Rapport

You can also use humor to establish a closer connection with your audience. Research confirms that apt humor often produces a more favorable audience reaction toward the speaker. Tasteful humor won't hurt your credibility; in fact, it can make you more human in the eyes of your audience.[33] Then, once you and your audience share a laugh, you're on your way to building a stronger rapport that will enhance your listeners' appreciation of your ideas.

However, you'll shatter this rapport if you target certain individuals or groups for your barbs. Not

Success Tip
Injecting some humor into your speech can help you capture attention and maintain your audience's interest, build rapport, and make an important point. Be sure that your humor is appropriate to the audience, the topic, and the occasion.

EXHIBIT 12.10
Using Humor to Lead into a Topic
Humor is often a good way to introduce a speech topic and build interest in the central idea. Here, comedian Bill Cosby uses light humor in a speech to the World Family Federation, a U.S.-based group that works worldwide to promote the value of intact families.

"No matter how calmly you try to referee, parenting will eventually produce bizarre behavior, and I'm not talking about the kids. *Their* behavior is always normal, a norm of acting incomprehensibly with sweetly blank looks."

only is this unethical, but you also run the risk of causing your listeners some discomfort. You may want to follow the lead of Malcolm Kushner, a humor consultant who advises, "Poke a little fun at yourself. Audiences love it and it immediately creates rapport." If you do this, be careful that you don't undermine the image of expertise and competency you need to give your words authority. Nonetheless, you can gain a reputation for a good sense of humor by offering personal anecdotes that are related to your topic or occasion.[34]

Using Humor to Make a Point

Humor is a good way to put across an important point. In fact, some studies suggest that listeners retain more information from speeches that contain humor.[35] To be effective, you'll want to draw your humor from your topic and your point. You'll also want to show your audience how your humor relates to your point.

For example, Ron Compton, chief executive of Aetna Life and Casualty, used humor when he spoke to a group of computer specialists. He attacked the myth that nontechnical people fear and avoid technology, using the rise of automated teller machines (ATMs) as an example. Noting that ATMs had become popular despite predic-

tions that customers would rebel against the loss of "personal service," Compton said:

Remember that "personal service"? Remember standing in those lines to cash a check for $50? And remember what that teller looked and acted like? Remember the stern look you'd get from the teller? Remember the suspicious look *your check* got—as if it were a holdup note in code? And then the teller would start slowly dialing one of those old rotary phones to see if you had enough money in your account to cover the check. And that's why people will stand out in the cold—even in the pouring rain—to use the automatic teller machines. They remember that "personal service" back in the bank, and they never want to confront that teller again.[36]

Compton's humor came from the vivid word picture he painted of experiencing old-fashioned, low-tech personal service. Listeners chuckled because they had shared the experience he was describing. By the end of this passage, Compton's audience was laughing and applauding loudly. The humor had really driven home the point and made it more memorable.

Ask an Expert

Michael Hackman
Associate Professor of Communication, University of Colorado—Colorado Springs

Q: I'm nervous about using humor in a speech. What if it flops? Are there any guidelines for using humor effectively in a public speech?

A: Everyone has had an attempt at humor fall flat at one time or another. And, yes, it can happen in front of an audience. Still, humor can be a very effective tool for managing communication apprehension and creating a connection between you and your audience. The realization that you can get an audience to respond favorably to your humorous message is often a great stress reliever. Further, audiences tend to find humorous presentations more interesting. So the bottom line is—humor is worth the risk, particularly if you follow a few simple suggestions.

The most effective humor in a public presentation involves personal examples and experiences. Let's face it—life is funny. Hardly a day goes by when most of us don't find something to laugh at. So when it's appropriate, share these stories with your audience.

All forms of ethnic, sexist, and sick humor are out. Research suggests that humor that attacks another person, or even yourself, can turn an audience off. Be sensitive with your humor. It's okay to gently poke fun, but don't attack. If you're looking for a model for your humor, consider Bill Cosby. His humor most often stems from his own experiences, and it rarely, if ever, offends or debases others.

Like anything else, too much humor can reduce your effectiveness. But, by following a few simple guidelines, you can greatly increase the likelihood that the next time you use humor in a public speech, you will achieve the results you desire.

1. Can humor be used with a culturally diverse audience? What guidelines would you suggest for helping speakers use humor effectively when their audiences come from a variety of cultural backgrounds?
2. Select a speech (from the appendix or from another source) and consider how the use of humor would make the topic or a particular part of the speech more interesting. Draft a letter to that speaker to explain your reasoning.

Using Humor Appropriately

Laugh and the world laughs with you—if your humor is appropriate. As already mentioned, be sure your humor has a real connection to your audience, your occasion, or your topic. Consider, too, how cultural differences might affect your audience's reaction: what elicits a laugh in one culture may well elicit a blank stare or a frown in another. And to avoid alienating your listeners, stay away from controversial topics. From an ethical perspective, humor that degrades is disrespectful and unsuitable. The same holds true for off-color humor, which is inappropriate in any public speaking situation.

If you decide to use humor, be sure to practice well in advance. You can't expect to simply drop in a humorous line and be rewarded with a laugh. You'll want to rehearse to get your timing right, and then ask several people for feedback before you use humor in front of an audience. If you find that you're uncomfortable using humor, eliminate it in favor of other techniques that can help you communicate. But even if you're able to use humor skillfully, remember that humor has its limits. It can enhance a good speech, but it won't save a poor one.

SUMMARY

Spoken words can touch your audience in three ways. First, they can help you create a powerful mental image that your audience will remember after your speech is over. Second, your words can influence your audience's feelings and attitudes. Third, they can inspire your listeners to take a specific action. To accomplish these three goals, you'll want to be aware of both the denotative or dictionary meaning and the connotative or emotional meaning of your words.

Spoken language differs from written language in several ways. Speeches use less formal language than written communication. In general, words and phrases in a speech are shorter, simpler, and more varied than those used in written communication. Unlike written messages, a speech may contain sentence fragments or slang. In addition, speeches contain more repetition than written communication. This helps listeners understand and remember what you've said. Also, spoken language allows for more personal interaction between speaker and audience. In this way, you can reveal your personality and interests and get immediate audience feedback about your ideas.

The wording of a speech has the potential to clarify or obscure your message. To communicate most effectively, choose words that are familiar, concrete, precise, accurate, unbiased, and concise. When you express yourself in familiar language, you define any unfamiliar terms and use simple words so that your listeners can understand and relate to your message. Use concrete wording that conveys specifically what you want to say and that leaves no room for misinterpretation. Also use wording that is precise so that your audience can understand the exact meaning you intend to convey. Moreover, be sure your wording is accurate. Show respect for your audience by avoiding words that display any type of bias. And finally, do everything you can to make your wording concise by avoiding clutter and using as few words as possible.

Vivid words bring your message to life. You can use vivid wording in four ways: metaphors, similes, imagery, and rhythm. A metaphor is an implied comparison between seemingly dissimilar things. In contrast, a simile uses the words *like* and *as* to make an explicit comparison between two unlike things. Both help bring abstract ideas into focus for your audience by drawing comparisons with something more concrete. Imagery is the use of words to create visual pictures and other sensory experiences for listeners.

Four techniques you can use to create rhythm in a speech are parallelism, alliteration, antithesis, and repetition. Parallelism is arranging a series of words, phrases, or sentences into similar patterns. Alliteration is the repetition of the same initial consonant sound in a series of words or phrases. Antithesis means contrasting two ideas within a parallel structure. Repetition creates rhythm by repeating the same word or phrase several times in a section of your speech.

Words and phrases that work in one public speaking situation may not be appropriate for another. Choosing appropriate words and phrases will strengthen your speech. It's important to match your wording to your audience's needs and interests, to the topic at hand, to the formality of the occasion, and to your personal speaking style.

You can use humor in a speech to serve three purposes. First, it can capture your listeners' attention and build interest in your speech. Second, it can help build rapport with your listeners. And third, it can reinforce an important point. Although humor can be effective in a speech, it can backfire if not used carefully.

KEY TERMS

alliteration (264)
antithesis (265)
connotative meaning (252)
denotative meaning (252)
malapropisms (259)
metaphor (261)
parallelism (264)
repetition (265)
simile (262)

APPLY CRITICAL THINKING

1. What speaker do you most admire for his or her ability to create mental images, influence feelings and attitudes, or inspire action? How does this speaker use language to accomplish these tasks? Cite one or two memorable examples, and indicate how you, as a listener, react to the words or phrases.

2. Why do speakers use clichés? List at least three clichés that your professors use during one day of classes. Suggest fresh wording for each cliché on your list.

3. In a speech about the need for donated blood, what type of imagery could you use to help a college audience envision the problems of insufficient blood supplies? Why would this imagery be effective?

4. In a speech about safe disposal of toxic wastes, what metaphor might you use to make the abstract dangers more concrete for an audience of state legislators? What simile might you use? Which do you think is more effective? Why?

5. In a speech about preventing teenage suicides, what concrete wording could you use to help an audience of high school students understand the finality of death?

6. Would you use humor in any of the speeches described in questions 3, 4, or 5? Explain why you think humor would or would not be appropriate in each case.

7. How can you test humor in a speech before you address your audience? If the humor in your speech doesn't seem to go over well, how can you determine whether the delivery or the wording is the problem?

SHARPEN YOUR SKILLS

Individual Exercises

1. Using the appendix and classroom speeches as sources, find one example each of metaphor and simile.

   a. What is the speaker trying to convey in each example?

   b. What can you suggest to convey the same meaning?

   c. Change the metaphor to a simile, and the simile to a metaphor. Do the changed phrases communicate as effectively as the original phrases? Why?

2. As you did in exercise 1, look for examples of vivid imagery and antithesis in a classroom speech or a speech in the appendix.

   a. What image is the speaker portraying? How is this image appropriate to the speech topic and the purpose?

   b. What other imagery can you suggest to express this idea?

   c. What makes the antithesis effective? Can you suggest a more powerful alternative?

3. Select and analyze the wording in a speech from the appendix.

   a. Identify any technical terms or jargon. Does the speaker define these terms? Do you think the audience would understand these terms without more explanation?

   b. Look for cluttered wording. What more concise alternatives can you suggest?

4. Assume that you're planning your next few classroom speeches. Arrange each of the following series of key words from the most abstract to the most concrete.

   a. newspaper, printed material, paper, *USA Today*

   b. beef, Big Mac, food, hamburger, meat

   c. mallard, animal, water fowl, bird

Group Exercises

5. Team with a classmate for this exercise. First, working separately, select a speech (from the appendix or from another source) that contains parallelism, repetition, alliteration, or antithesis.

   a. Read the passage aloud, and ask your classmate to identify the technique used to create rhythm. What effect does this passage have on the listener?

   b. Switch roles, and repeat the exercise as your classmate reads from the speech that he or she chose. How does this technique create rhythm? Is it effective?

6. With a classmate, listen to a speech on campus or on television.

   a. Note any biased phrases you hear during the speech. What assumptions are implicit in these phrases? What unbiased wording can you suggest in place of the speaker's phrases? Agree on the best way to word each idea.

   b. Note any gender-neutral phrases you hear during the speech. What gender-biased language are these phrases replacing? Do you both agree with the phrases this speaker used? What alternatives can you suggest?

   c. Does the speaker use any words that you consider biased on the basis of age or disability? Why do you think the speaker chose these words? Are they effective? Why?

Chapter Thirteen
USING VISUAL AIDS

LEARNING OBJECTIVES
After studying this chapter, you will be able to

1. Describe five ways that visual aids can strengthen your speech.

2. List and discuss the various types of visual aids.

3. Explain how the speaker serves as a visual aid.

4. Describe the various methods you can use to present visual aids.

5. Identify the questions you can ask at the start of the design process to determine the appropriate visual aids and presentation methods for your speech.

6. Explain how to apply the principles of simplicity, emphasis and balance, color, and visibility when designing visual aids.

7. Describe the actions you can take before and during your speech to use visual aids most effectively.

STRENGTHENING YOUR SPEECH WITH VISUAL AIDS

Professor Uwe Reinhardt of Princeton University knows that a picture can be worth a thousand words. During his speeches about the crisis in U.S. health care, Reinhardt shows two slides (see Exhibit 13.1). As he shows the first, a photograph of a steaming potato, he asks his listeners, "What is this?" Typically, a few people shout, "A hot potato." The next slide is of a cute child with a sad expression on her face. Reinhardt waits a moment before he tells his audience, "This also is a hot potato. It's a sick little girl nobody wants to insure."[1]

In a few moments, Reinhardt's photographs are able to accomplish what thousands of words and dozens of statistics cannot: they transform an abstract issue into a human concern. Photographs are **visual aids,** materials that you can use to supplement your speeches. You can also supplement your speech with nonvisual aids that communicate through the other four senses: letting your audience hear an audiotape or compact disc recording; letting your audience feel the thickness or roughness of a piece of cloth; or asking your audience to taste or smell a particular food. These are all supplementary aids that you can use together with your spoken words.

EXHIBIT 13.1
A Picture Is Worth a Thousand Words
Uwe Reinhardt, a professor at Princeton University, uses visual aids to contrast two images as he discusses the crisis in U.S. health care. The steaming hot potato in one image contrasted with the sad little girl in the second image helps Reinhardt make an important point about people who are not able to get health insurance.

EXHIBIT 13.2
How Much Do Visual Aids Improve Your Speech?
Visual aids definitely improve a speech's impact, according to research conducted by the University of Minnesota.

Audience Measure

Action	43.1%
Retention	10.1%
Agreement	5.5%
Comprehension	8.5%
Attention	7.5%
Perceptions	11%

Improvement

Visual aids are not only accepted, they're expected by today's audiences, who are accustomed to receiving information through multiple media. People watching television news shows get information from the images as well as from the sound effects and the commentators' words; people watching a music video get information about the song by observing the color and motion of the images as well as by listening to the words.[2] Providing information through both spoken words and visual aids can increase the audience's attention by more than 7 percent, increase the audience's comprehension by more than 8 percent, and improve the audience's retention of your ideas by more than 10 percent. Visual aids can also make a speech more than 43 percent more persuasive (see Exhibit 13.2).[3] Visual aids can strengthen your speech in five ways:

1. *Capturing and focusing audience interest.* By using visual aids during your speech, you can attract and hold your audience's attention.[4] Visual aids add variety to your presentation, keeping your audience tuned into what you're saying. They also focus your audience's attention on the points that you want to emphasize. Like Professor Reinhardt, you might show photographs (or use some other visual aid) to direct attention to a point you don't want your audience to miss.

2. *Clarifying your meaning.* You can use visual aids to clarify your intended message. Clarity is especially important when dealing with abstract ideas, which listeners may misinterpret unless you add charts, photographs, or other visual aids. The combination of words and visual aids can convey your meaning more effectively than words alone, enhancing the

audience's understanding of your message. For instance, if you show a North American map as you describe Henry Hudson's search for the Northwest Passage, your audience will quickly see why the explorer couldn't possibly succeed.

3. *Simplifying complex points.* When you want to explain something complicated, such as a series of steps or the inner workings of a machine, visual aids can help your listeners follow your explanation. In some cases, you may take your audience step by step through your explanation, using a model or a diagram. In other cases, you may actually give a hands-on demonstration of the steps in a process or a machine's operation, so that your audience can truly see your explanation in action.

4. *Reinforcing your ideas.* Listeners remember more when they're exposed to both spoken words and visual aids. Knowing this, you can use visual aids to reinforce your major points. For example, audience members who watched Professor Reinhardt's slides are more likely to remember his message about the human side of the health care crisis. The concrete images they saw may linger long after abstract words and statistics have faded.

5. *Building your credibility.* When you use visual aids skillfully, you can enhance your credibility and impress listeners with your professionalism. Having visual aids to supplement your words can also reduce your speech anxiety, giving you more control and helping you appear to be a more accomplished speaker.[5] On the other hand, if you don't use visual aids and other speakers do, your credibility may suffer by comparison. Moreover, you may seem less polished if your audience expects visual aids but you don't include any.

Visual aids can be effective in the classroom, in the boardroom, and in nearly any other public speaking situation. Despite the many reasons to use visual aids, bear in mind that they should supplement, not replace, your speech. In the

words of John W. Rowe, chief executive of New England Electric System, "Visual aids should be made to steer, not to row." So take care to choose visual aids that will enhance, not overwhelm, your message.

In the next section, you'll learn about choosing among the various types of visual aids and about the methods of presentation you can use. After that, you'll look at how to prepare visual aids, including design and production. In the final section, you'll see how to use visual aids in your speech effectively.

CHOOSING AND PRESENTING VISUAL AIDS

Your choice and presentation of visual aids is limited only by your imagination and creativity. Depending on your audience, your topic, the occasion, and the time allotted for your speech, you can choose one type or several types of visual aids. Once you've decided which types of visual aids to use, think about how to present them to your audience.

Types of Visual Aids

Visual aids come in all shapes and sizes. In fact, almost anything that relates to your speech can be a visual aid. The most commonly used types of visual aids are people, objects, models, drawings and diagrams, photographs, maps, charts and graphs, tables, and lists (see Exhibit 13.3)

People

"Start by thinking of yourself as a visual aid," advises communication consultant Geoff Bellman.[6] As the speaker, your body movements, facial expressions, voice qualities, and physical appearance all communicate information nonverbally. When you use these visual and vocal cues to reinforce your words, you will convey your message more effectively and leave less room for misinterpretation.

In addition, you may want to personally demonstrate or illustrate something related to

Success Tip

When you reinforce key points through visual aids as well as spoken words, your audience will remember more of your message.

EXHIBIT 13.3

Using the Nine Types of Visual Aids

Depending on the audience, the topic, and the purpose of the speech, a speaker can choose from a variety of visual aids.

Use yourself or other *people* to illustrate a point in your speech. You can do something, demonstrate something, or wear something.

Use an *object* to demonstrate how something looks or operates.

Use a *model* instead of an object if the object is too large, too small, too fragile, too expensive, or unavailable to show your audience.

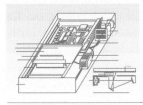

Use a *drawing* or *diagram* to explain and clarify how something looks or operates, to simplify details, or to clarify complex relationships.

Use a *photograph* to bring points to life and to present detailed, realistic portrayals of people, places, and things.

Use a *map* to pinpoint a location, highlight a geographic feature, or convey information about a location.

Use a *chart* or *graph* to support a point by presenting complex statistics or a series of numbers. Use charts to visually summarize steps in a process or the relationship among people and things.

Use a *table* to organize, summarize, and present detailed information in a clear, simple way.

Use a *list* to communicate a great deal of information in a simple way.

your topic during your speech (see Exhibit 13.4). For example, to support a speech on special sewing techniques, you might model an outfit embellished with smocking or embroidery. This makes a relatively abstract topic more concrete for your listeners. If your speech is about tap dancing, you can take your audience through a complex step by demonstrating each movement. And if you're a volunteer firefighter planning a speech about fire safety, you can build credibility by wearing an appropriate uniform or outfit.

You can also invite other people to serve as visual aids during your speech. For a speech about tennis, you might bring an experienced tennis player with you to demonstrate a proper serve. If you're speaking about fashion fads, you can ask one or two people to model clothing as you describe what made each style popular. Of course, your speech will go more smoothly if you practice with the people who are acting as your visual aids before you work together in front of an audience.

Objects

Objects can be useful visual aids when you want to show your audience how something looks or operates. A regulation baseball bat, a flowering fuchsia, and a hummingbird feeder are examples of objects that you might bring to supplement a speech on hitting home runs, cultivating flowers, or attracting hummingbirds. In fact, almost any object that helps you put a point across can serve as an interesting visual aid, as long as it's both safe and legal to bring to your speech.

Be sure that any object you use is large enough for all audience members to see. At the same time, your object should be small enough to conceal until you reach the appropriate part of your speech. To avoid distracting your audience, show the object only when you need it during your speech, and put it away after you're finished.

Models

In some cases, the object you'd like to use as a visual aid will be too large to bring with you, too small for your audience to see clearly, too fragile to handle, too expensive to use, or not available. Then you may want to show your audience a model instead of the actual object. When your speech calls for demonstrating an object's inner workings, you may want to use a cutaway or cross-section model. As long as everyone in the audience can see what you're referring to, your model may be smaller, larger, or the same size as the object it represents.

You can use a larger-than-life model to explain how tiny objects look or function. For example, you might hold up a large-scale model of a snowflake as you discuss its intricate design or a two-foot model of a human heart as you discuss bypass surgery. On the other hand, if the real object is quite large, you might substitute a smaller model, such as a scaled-down version of a locomotive or the solar system. If the dimensions of an object are important to your point, you may find that a life-size model works best. For a speech about first aid, for instance, your audience would get a more accurate idea of to use a tourniquet if you demonstrated on a full-size human dummy.

EXHIBIT 13.5

Using a Map to Support a Point
Commercially prepared maps can be visually attractive and useful if they can be projected large enough for the audience to see the important details to support a point. If they are too small, or contain irrelevant information for a speaker's purpose, then a simplified large-scale map should be prepared.

Drawings and Diagrams

You can use drawings and diagrams as visual aids to explain how something looks or operates. Both are fairly inexpensive, and they can be tailored to explain specific points in your speech. Drawings and diagrams are particularly useful for simplifying details and clarifying complex relationships.[7]

Imagine that you wanted to show your audience what the facade of a new school building would look like when completed. You couldn't show a photograph, but you could use a drawing. You might use a diagram to help listeners follow your explanation of the operation of a gasoline engine. Diagrams and drawings can help an audience quickly grasp ideas that words alone can't adequately describe.

Photographs

If you need realistic portrayals of people, places, and things, photographs are more detailed than drawings and diagrams. This realism can bring a point to life for your audience in a way that a drawing, an object, and a model cannot. That's why Professor Reinhardt used a photo of a child when he wanted to humanize the problems of the U.S. health care system. With a photograph, you can help your audience appreciate the rugged terrain of a mountain trail or the vivid colors of a Frank Stella painting.

Of course, your audience won't be able to see small photographs. You can have photos made into giant enlargements, slides, overhead transparencies, or handouts. If you can, crop photos to eliminate distracting details so that your audience can focus attention on what's important.

Maps

When you want to pinpoint a location or highlight a geographic feature, you can use a map as a visual aid. Maps can help you convey information such as concentrations of people or industry, weather patterns, landmarks, and transportation routes, among other details (see Exhibit 13.5). Unfortunately, most commercial maps contain too much detail and are drawn to a scale that's too tiny to be read by audience members. However, if you enlarge and simplify a map, you can show the important spatial relationships that support your ideas.

Robert A. Fildes, chief executive officer of the U.S. biotechnology company Cetus, used two simple maps to show a business audience why his company was expanding abroad. Fildes superimposed an outline of the United States, in one color, over an outline of Western Europe, shown in another color, and included population figures for both. Audience members could clearly see that the United States, with its 250 million people, is several times larger than Western Europe, with its 300 million people. The contrast between the two maps helped Fildes convey the importance—and the compactness—of the European market.[8]

Charts and Graphs

When you're planning to present statistics or any series of numbers as support material for a point, you'll want to use a visual aid that helps your audience digest the information. Early in this century, author H. G. Wells recognized the growing importance of understanding statistics when he observed, "Statistical thinking will one

EXHIBIT 13.6

Types of Charts and Graphs
Using charts and graphs as visual aids can help you clarify relationships among numbers and explain trends or patterns that are mentioned during a speech.

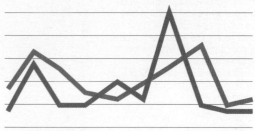

Line graph

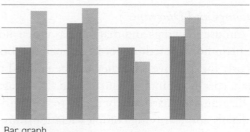

Bar graph

Pie chart

Pictogram

day be as necessary for efficient citizenship as the ability to read and write."[9] Putting your statistics into a chart or graph can clarify the relationships among the numbers and reveal any trends or patterns. You can use charts to visually summarize the steps in a process or the relationship among several people or things you're discussing. Among the most frequently used charts and graphs are line graphs, bar graphs, pictograms, pie charts, flow charts, and organizational charts (see Exhibit 13.6).

You can use a *line graph* to show changes over time or to show the relationship of two sets of numbers. Because line graphs are simple to read, you can show more than one number series without confusing your audience. In this way, you can visually compare two (and sometimes more) sets of numbers, such as the average wages of hourly workers and the average wages of salaried workers during the previous decade. By examining the direction and incline of these lines, audience members will quickly grasp the contrast between the two.

A *bar graph* portrays numbers as rectangular bars, making a series of numbers even easier to read and understand. You can use a bar graph to compare two or three sets of numbers or to show trends over time. Even though you'll discuss the numbers in your speech, bar graphs can help your audience develop a clear picture of what the numbers mean.

A *pictogram* is a graph in which the lines or bars are made up of symbols. By portraying numbers using symbols that relate to your topic or point, you add interest to the graph and reinforce what the numbers mean. Although pictograms are

visually striking, they can't portray specific amounts with the exactness of other graphs.

When you want to portray numbers as parts of a whole, you can use a *pie chart*. Each slice of the pie represents one part of the whole. Most of the time, you'll put the largest slice at the twelve o'clock position and arrange the other slices clockwise in descending order of size. In addition, you may want to use colors or patterns to call attention to a particular slice. Then, by comparing the size of the slices, your listeners can see how each relates to the others and to the whole.

A *flow chart* is effective for illustrating a sequence of steps. Each step is represented by a pictorial symbol or geometric shape so audience members can easily trace a path through the sequence. For example, Sandra Becker used the

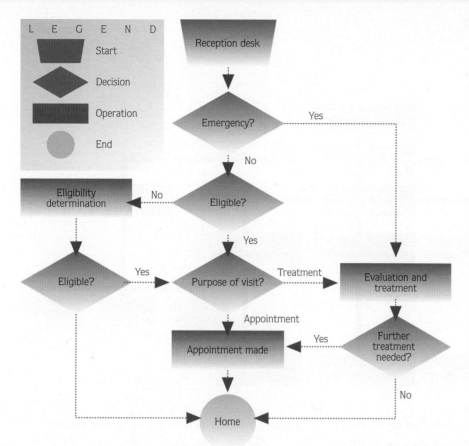

EXHIBIT 13.7
Using Flow Charts as Visual Aids
Using a flow chart can be helpful when you want to illustrate or explain a process or help your audience follow a particular sequence of events or activities.

By using short, descriptive phrases for headings and text entries, you can pack a lot of data into a small space. When you include numbers, remember to label the units so that your audience can tell whether you're talking about square feet, price per carton, millions of gallons used, and so on.

By using color in a table, you can focus your audience's attention on specific information and reinforce important points. For example, in a table summarizing a company's profits and losses for five years, you might show losses in red so that they're clearly distinguishable from profits. If you want your audience to examine the numbers for a certain year, you can call attention to them by using another color. However, avoid confusing your audience by using too many colors or packing too much detail into a chart.

flow chart in Exhibit 13.7 to supplement a student speech about independent medical treatment centers. By charting the flow of patients through one center, she helped her audience understand how patients and staff members interact.

In an *organization chart,* each box stands for a particular position in a company, and the lines indicate the relationship between positions (see Exhibit 13.8). Traditionally, the head of the organization is shown at the top of the chart, although not in every company. Explaining the reporting relationships among managers and employees would take a lot more words if you didn't use this type of visual aid.

Tables

When you want to organize, summarize, and present detailed information, you can use a table. Tables are all-text visual aids in which numbers or words are arranged in a grid of columns and rows.

Lists

Like tables, lists are all-text visuals that can communicate a great deal of information in a simple way. Think of how talk-show host David Letterman uses his "Top 10" lists. Each item is short and punchy so that audience members can immediately see the point. To add a touch of suspense, Letterman counts down his lists, holding item number one until last. Lists are

EXHIBIT 13.8

Using Organization Charts as Visual Aids

Organization charts are particularly useful for illustrating the reporting relationships among members of a company or other organization.

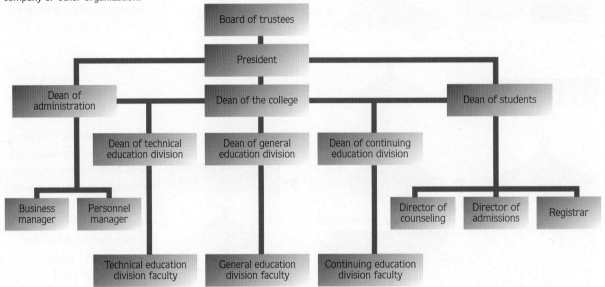

most effective when they're short and to the point. This way, your listeners won't spend a lot of time reading instead of listening to you.

You can use lists when you want to emphasize the connection between several items. For example, you can arrange the items on your list in ascending or descending order of importance. Then your audience can tell at a glance which is the most or least important. You can arrange the items in sequence to show what comes first, what comes second, and so on. As with tables, you'll want to keep list entries short and to the point to avoid confusing or overwhelming your audience.

Methods of Presentation

Once you've chosen the type of visual aid you want to use, your next step is to decide on the method you'll use to present it. You can choose among a wide variety of methods, including flip charts; overhead transparencies; slides; videotapes, films or DVDs; audio aids; multimedia and electronic presentations; chalkboards and whiteboards; and handouts. As you consider each option, take into account the facilities that are available where you'll be speaking, the size of your audience, how much money and time you want to spend on preparation, and your personal preferences.

Flip Charts

Many business speakers and professional trainers present their visuals on *flip charts*, large pads of paper mounted on easels. To use a flip chart, you reveal and discuss the information on the first page, then flip it over to reveal the next page, and so on. Flip charts are inexpensive and easy to prepare. Because of their size, they're most visible to relatively small audiences. As with any visual aid, however, you'll want to practice before the speech so you're comfortable working with the flip chart during your actual delivery.

You'll usually write information on your flip chart pages in advance; then you can reveal the information, page by page, as you talk about the corresponding point. Some speakers prefer to write on flip charts as they speak. John J. Byrne, chief executive officer of Fireman's Fund Insur-

TIPS FOR PREPARING VISUAL AIDS FOR INTERNATIONAL AUDIENCES

When you're planning a speech to an audience in another country, appropriate visual aids can be extremely helpful in getting your points across. However, what's appropriate in your country may not be appropriate in another country. Therefore, as you prepare visual aids for a speech outside your country, you'll want to pay extra attention to these details:

- Limit the number of words in your visual aids and, whenever possible, use your audience's language. Avoid slang, jargon, and technical terms that may not translate well.
- Think about how your audience is accustomed to seeing written material. Knowing that Arabs, for example, read from right to left, you would show your first point on the right of a transparency or handout and show your next point to the left.
- Avoid images that violate local customs. So that you don't offend your audience, find out in advance what is appropriate. For example, photographs of men and women touching are unacceptable in some countries. In addition, carefully research the portrayal of national and religious symbols if you plan to include any.
- Determine how colors are viewed. Colors have various meanings around the world. In the United States, green is associated with freshness, but it's linked with disease in some other countries. To avoid blunders, find out how local audiences think of a particular color before you use it in your visual aids.

Speakers preparing visual aids for audiences in Saudi Arabia would want to show women with their heads covered but should avoid showing woman driving, which violates a local custom.

Overhead Transparencies

Using overhead transparencies is a popular method of presenting visual aids to groups of almost any size. When you expect to use overhead transparencies, you'll prepare in advance by transferring your visuals to clear acetate sheets. During your speech, you lay one acetate at a time on the screen of the overhead projector, which projects the image onto a screen for everyone to see. With a bit of practice, you'll be able to do this without missing a beat in your speech.

One advantage of transparencies is relatively low cost. Another is flexibility: You can rearrange the order of your transparencies at any time, and you can write down additional points as you speak. Also, you can leave the lights on when you use overhead transparencies, which allows you to maintain eye contact with your listeners and check for feedback. In addition, transparencies are easy to store and transport.[11]

However, the advantage of flexibility can become a disadvantage if you inadvertently mix up the order of your transparencies. To avoid this problem, number your transparencies and check

ance, starts many speeches with a big, blank flip chart. As he talks, he writes points on the flip chart. This technique gives his speech a spontaneity that audiences enjoy.[10] Whichever method you choose, remember to practice before you use a flip chart. Also take care not to block the audience's view of the chart and not to lose eye contact with your listeners for long periods.

the order in advance. Unless you've practiced and become adept at writing on transparencies as you speak, use only prepared sheets.

Slides

Somewhat more sophisticated and more expensive than overhead transparencies are slides. Slides are fairly simple to use, once the slide tray and projector are set up. If you load your slides into a tray in advance, you'll have time to review both the order and the orientation of the slides to avoid mistakes. Also check that the projector is focused and working correctly before your audience arrives. Then, once you begin to speak, you can push the remote-control button to move from one slide to the next.

Showing vivid photographs or other colorful visual aids on slides can add a touch of professionalism to any speech. Well-designed slides can help you grab and hold an audience's attention throughout the speech. If you don't have to darken the room too much to make your slides visible, you'll still be able to watch your audience's reaction as you speak.

Videotapes, Films, and DVDs

Among the most attention-getting ways to present supplementary aids are videotapes, films, and DVDs. They can bring your points to life with moving images, color, and sound. To use these methods, you'll need to set up and check your equipment in advance. For large audiences, you'll need a projection screen or more than one monitor for viewing. You'll also want to have an extra extension cord on hand.

You can select from a wide range of prerecorded material, or make your own videotape or DVD to support a specific speech. Either way, be sure to check the quality and timing in advance. Cue up the tape or film, or jot down the DVD chapters you plan to use ahead of time. Check volume levels before your audience arrives. Then all you'll have to do is push a button or cue an assistant to play the material at the right time.

One caution: don't overuse video, film, or DVDs. You want your audience to concentrate on you and your message, not your presentation method.

Audio Recordings

At times, you'll want your audience to listen to support material during your speech. You can play an audiotape or CD of music, interviews, animal sounds, and so on. For a student speech about the Brazilian rainforest, for example, Hector Santiago played a recording of bird calls and animal sounds that gave his audience a taste of the exotic wildlife. You might choose to enhance a speech about the blitz of Britain during World War II with an excerpt from one of Winston Churchill's famous speeches from that time.

Audio recordings work well with audiences of any size. Just remember to test your equipment and check levels in advance, as you would for videotapes, films, and DVDs.

Multimedia and Electronic Presentations

One of the newest ways to impress audiences is by using a multimedia or electronic presentation of supplementary aids (see Exhibit 13.9). This presentation can simply be a computerized slide show or can be a sophisticated blend of sound, image, and animation. Affordable new technology and software have made electronic presentations common in business settings for both in-house and client presentations, but they can be set up in almost any environment with the proper equipment.

Using popular software such as Microsoft PowerPoint, Lotus Freelance Graphics, or Corel Draw, you can now easily blend photos, sound, graphics, video, and animation with conventionally designed slides for a high-impact presentation. With practice, you can even create and modify your electronic slides using your personal computer *during your speech*, much as you might jot information on a blank flip chart.

If you're addressing a small group, your personal computer monitor situated properly may be sufficient for display. For larger groups, LCD (liquid crystal display) projectors or display panels can lift the images from your personal computer

EXHIBIT 13.9

Making an Electronic Presentation

With an electronic presentation, you can show your audience a wide range of supplementary aids at the click of a mouse and use sound, motion, and color to add zing to your speech.

to display them on a projection screen similar to that used for overhead transparencies.

PowerPoint, included with current Microsoft Office software packages, provides templates and design wizards that make developing electronic presentations fairly simple. With a few clicks of your mouse, you can build high-contrast, highly readable slides, choose and change the order of presentation, select transitions such as dissolves or blackouts, and preview your presentation. Choosing the "manual timing" option, you can control the slide changes or pause the presentation during your speech using your mouse and keyboard.

After you've mastered the simple slide-show format, you can expand your electronic presentations to include as many multimedia features as your taste, schedule, creativity, and speech content suggest. The results can be dazzling. Dana R. Richardson, national director for technology for the accounting firm Ernst & Young, created an electronic multimedia presentation for a speech he gave to accountants. His audience was thrilled by the multimedia portion of his speech, which Richardson says "addresses all of the senses at the same time."[12]

Chalkboards and Whiteboards

Most classrooms—and many corporate meeting rooms—are equipped with chalkboards or

Success Tip

Keep your audience's attention on you, not your handouts. Unless your audience needs to follow along as you speak, wait to distribute your handouts until the end of your speech.

whiteboards that you can use to present information during any kind of speech. You can quickly and easily write a key point or draw a diagram on a board and, once you've finished discussing it, erase it and replace it with another visual aid. If you prefer, you can write your material on the board prior to the speech and keep it covered until you need it. All you need is a piece of chalk or, in the case of a whiteboard, an erasable marker and an eraser.

Despite these advantages, you'll want to steer clear of boards whenever possible. When you're writing on a board, your back is usually to the audience, so you can't maintain eye contact or check for feedback. Also, your listeners' attention may wander in the time it takes you to write a sentence or a few statistics on the board. Unless your words and numbers are extremely large and dark, not everyone in your audience may be able to make out what you've written. And if you put your visual aids on the board before your speech, your audience may read rather than listen to your introduction. You can head off these problems by using other presentation methods.

Handouts

When you want your audience to be able to consult a visual aid during or after your speech, you can provide copies of the information in the

Matching the Visual Aid to the Topic
Actor Robert Redford used a bronze plaque at Yosemite National Park as an outdoor visual aid when making a speech to mark the park's designation by the United Nations as a World Heritage Site.

form of handouts. For example, you might want to provide photocopies of a page of statistics, a chart, or a table that is too large or complex to be shown on an overhead transparency or a slide. Handouts can reinforce your major points and help listeners recall key points.

In most cases, you'll want to wait to distribute your handouts until the end of your speech. This way, audience members won't be distracted from your speech by reading or making notes on your handouts. When they're reading or writing, they aren't listening—and you won't be able to maintain eye contact or receive feedback, either. When museum director Francine Steffarelli passes out handouts during cultural events, she warns her audience, "Anyone I catch reading the handouts during my speech has to step up here and finish the presentation." When you address an international audience, however, you may want to bridge the language barrier by giving out copies of the most important visual aids so that listeners can follow along as you talk. And if any information is absolutely essential to understanding your ideas, you can distribute handouts ahead of time and call attention to them during your speech.

PREPARING VISUAL AIDS

Although you won't use your visual aids until you actually give your speech, you can start planning them well in advance. As you gather support materials and complete your research, keep your eyes open for important information that you can show your audience to prove your points. Then, as you develop your planning outline, look for the exact facts and figures that fit each major point. Once you've collected all the data you need for your visual aids, you're ready to work on designing each for maximum audience impact.

Designing Visual Aids

Start the design process by asking a series of questions about your audience, your topic, the speech location, and your personal skills and preferences. The answers to these four categories of questions can help you determine which type of visual aids and presentation methods are appropriate for your speech.

- *Audience.* What size audience will you be addressing? What supplementary aids will be able to be seen and heard by everyone in the audience? How will the ages and interests of audience members affect their reaction to certain supplementary aids and presentation methods?
- *Topic.* Does your topic lend itself to a particular visual aid or presentation method? Can you rule out one or more visual aids that don't make sense for your topic (such as using a map to dramatize regional taste differences in a speech about cooking chili)? (See Exhibit 13.10.)
- *Speech Location.* Are you going to speak in a large or small room? Indoors or outdoors? Can the lights be dimmed for certain presentation methods? Is electricity available? Is the right equipment available?
- *Personal skills and preferences.* What visual aids and presentation methods are you most skilled at using? Which do you prefer for particular

audiences, topics, or locations? Even if you have no experience with a specific type of visual aid or presentation method, you can still do a good job if you practice and gain proficiency before you face your audience.

In addition to answering these questions, be sure to consider which of your points need a visual aid. Not every point needs to be reinforced, clarified, or explained. By being selective, you can help your audience focus on the specific points you want to emphasize or explain. Too many visual aids can overpower a speech, so think about how many you really need and exactly where in your speech to use them. Then, as you plan your visual aids, you'll want to apply the design principles of simplicity, emphasis and balance, color, and visibility.

Simplicity

Keep your design as simple as possible. Experts point to too much information as the leading cause of ineffective visual aids.[13] If your visual aids are overloaded with detail, fancy typefaces, and frills, your audience won't know what to focus on. Busy-looking visual aids can be confusing and distracting. You don't want your visual aids to dominate your speech; instead, they should be designed as simply as possible so they complement your words.

As you design your visual aids, plan each to include only the facts or figures that relate to a single point. For example, use the key word

technique when drafting visuals, because complete sentences take up too much space and take longer to read and digest. As long as your visual aids contain the basic information, you can explain them to your audience when you present them during your speech. That way, your visual aids aren't taking the place of your speech.

Emphasis and Balance

Plan your design to emphasize what you want your audience to notice. You can make this emphasis clear by using size, color, or typeface, among other techniques. Not everything is equally important, of course, so choose only the one or two items that you want your audience to focus on. You might want your audience to compare two pieces of information on a single visual aid, for example, so you would plan your design to emphasize just those items.

However, even though you're emphasizing certain points, avoid throwing your visual aid out of balance. To maintain balance on a visual, allow sufficient space around and between items. Also plan on wide margins all around, keeping your margins equal on both sides for consistency. When you're including only a few words or numbers, you may want to position them in the center of your visual aid; as an alternative, you can set them off center with a graphic added for balance. When you're including more information, be sure to position your columns, rows, bullets, or other organizing features so that they look balanced and are easy to read.

Checklist for Designing Visual Aids

1. Consider your audience, your topic, the speech location, and your personal skills and preferences when you design your visual aids.
2. Consider which of your points, if any, would be enhanced by visual aids.
3. Keep the design of your visual aid as simple as possible.
4. Emphasize important information without throwing the visual aid out of balance.
5. Use color in visuals to attract the audience's attention, add excitement, highlight what the audience should notice, and point out the significance of certain information.

IMPROVING YOUR CRITICAL THINKING

DESIGNING VISUAL AIDS THAT DON'T LIE

Visual aids are supposed to enhance, not distort, information. Yet even the most solid statistics can take on unintended meaning when you design your visual aids improperly. Visual aids have to do more than simply present numbers: they also have to give an accurate impression of what the numbers mean.

One design decision is how to show scale in a graph. If you don't indicate the scale used in a bar graph, for example, your audience won't know how to interpret the length of the bars. If you exaggerate the scale you use in a line graph, your audience will get a distorted view of the graphed trend. To avoid such problems, choose realistic scales, and clearly mark them.

A second design decision is how to present a lot of information. Avoid the temptation to streamline your visual aid by omitting information here or there; you might give your audience a false impression. Instead of leaving data out, you may want to prepare two visual aids or group related details into broader categories for simplicity's sake.

A third design decision is how to choose the unit of measure for your numbers. When you're showing large numbers, you may want to scale down the units of measure. However, a number like 600,000 seems small if the scale is in billions; a number like 7 billion seems gigantic if the scale is in thousands. So think about how the scale makes the numbers appear before you make your decision. As you make all these design decisions, your goal is to prepare visual aids that communicate your information without distorting your audience's understanding.

Simply changing the scale can distort an audience's impression of a trend, as these two line graphs show. The graph on the left compresses the horizontal scale, while the graph on the right expands the vertical scale; each suggests a different view of the same data.

Color

No matter what kind of visual aid you use—and regardless of the presentation method you choose—you can add excitement and emphasis with color. Studies show that color is 32 percent more effective in attracting an audience's attention than black and white alone.[14] You can use color to highlight what you want your audience to notice. This may be a key word or number, a comparison between two items, a significant change, a solution, or a problem.

You can also subtly signal the significance of the highlighted item through your choice of color. For example, you might want to use green beverage cans in a pictogram indicating how many dozen cans were turned in during a recent recycling drive. Many people associate green with environmental concern, which reinforces the meaning of the figures in your pictogram.

To make information stand out, you'll want to choose colors that contrast with the color of the background. For example, dark colors such as

EXHIBIT 13.11
Color in Visual Aid Design

Here are "before" and "after" examples of the same table. Note the table on top is poorly designed. How would you improve it? The second example is an excellent design because of the use of color, clarity of information, and organization of data.

SPECIES DIVERSITY IN HAWAII

Group	Endemic	Non-native	Status Unknown	Total Species
Algae and other protists	4	5	1,724	1,733
Fungi and lichen	240	0	1,783	2,023
Flowering plants	850	861	183	1,894
Other plants	243	50	410	703
Mollusks	956	86	614	1656
Insects	5,188	2,543	175	7,906
Other anthropods	319	482	962	1,763
Other invertebrates	767	71	1,317	2,155
Fish	139	73	983	1,195
Amphibians	0	4	0	4
Reptiles	0	18	0	18
Birds	60	46	168	274
Mammals	1	19	24	44
Totals	**8,767**	**4,258**	**8,343**	**21,368**

H O W   M A N Y   S P E C I E S   A R E   T H E R E   I N   H A W A I I ?

Group	Native	Non-native	Unknown	Total
Algae, fungi, lichen	244	5	3,507	**3,756**
Flowers, shrubs, trees	1,093	911	593	**2,597**
Mollusks	956	86	614	**1,656**
Insects	5,188	2,543	175	**7,906**
Other invertebrates	1,086	553	2,279	**3,918**
Fish	139	73	983	**1,195**
Amphibians	0	4	0	**4**
Reptiles	0	18	0	**18**
Birds	60	46	168	**274**
Mammals	1	19	24	**44**
Totals	**8,767**	**4,258**	**8,343**	**21,368**

black and red are most visible on a light background; light colors such as white and yellow are most visible on a dark background. A little variety in color can add interest, but use a light touch (see Exhibit 13.11). The simplicity rule applies to color, too: so choose your colors carefully to avoid making your visual aids too busy.

Visibility

To be effective, visual aids must be visible to everyone in your audience. Just as most people in a giant audience won't be able to see a tiny object you hold up, they won't be able to read tiny print on a poster, an overhead transparency, or a slide. Therefore, you'll want to use lettering and graphics that can be seen by everyone, including the people sitting in the last row of your audience.

As a rule, make the main lettering on any slide at least 1/4 inch high, using larger type sizes for titles, if any. On the screen, this lettering will look much larger and will be visible to a crowd. You can use slightly larger type sizes on overhead transparencies. However, when you're hand-lettering posters or flip charts, you'll want to make your letters extremely large—2 inches high or larger—so that people in the back row can easily read the words and numbers. Thicker lettering is more visible than thinner lettering; upper- and lower-case letters are easier to read than all upper-case letters. Of course, you can use ordinary type sizes for any handouts.[15]

Producing Visual Aids

Whether you're preparing visual aids by yourself or with professional assistance, you'll want to start well in advance. Give yourself plenty of time to design and produce each visual aid. You may need extra time to finish hand lettering, to get slides made, or to create a realistic scale model. If you're using a videotape or audiotape, you'll need some time to edit your tape to fit your specific needs.

Computer-generated aids look more professional than those prepared by hand. If you're using a personal computer and graphics software to create charts, tables, graphs, diagrams, maps, or lists, allow time to experiment a little. Depending on the computer system you're using, you can turn out eye-catching overhead transparencies, slides, and handouts in relatively little time, once you know how. To produce a computerized presentation, you'll need time to prepare the visual aids, add a soundtrack, and put the entire multimedia show together.

USING VISUAL AIDS EFFECTIVELY

Now that your visual aids are completed, get ready to use them effectively. Before the day of your

speech, you'll want to practice using your visual aids. Also check in advance that your audience will be able to see and hear. During your speech, be sure to present each visual aid only when you discuss it. With a little practice, you'll be able to concentrate on your audience, not on your visual aids.

Practice with Your Visual Aids

You'll come off as more polished and more confident when you've practiced integrating your visual aids into the appropriate sections of your speech. Instead of forgetting to present a graph, fumbling for an object, or showing an overhead transparency upside down, you'll be ready to present the right visual aid at the right time. The more you rehearse, the smoother your actions and transitions will become—and the less nervous you'll feel. If you need help displaying a large object or handling some other supplementary aid, ask an assistant to practice with you until you both feel comfortable.

To remind yourself where each visual aid belongs in your speech, make notes directly on your speaking outline. Then as you're practicing, you'll know when to change slides or start a videotape. Only with practice can you figure out exactly how the equipment works or how to load a slide tray properly (see Exhibit 13.12). One run-through isn't usually enough, so plan to practice two or three times before the day of your speech.

Confirm That Your Audience Can See and Hear

Try your visual aids ahead of time to be sure that your audience will be able to see and hear from anywhere in the room. To do this, set up your visual aids, and then put yourself in your audience's place. Step to the back of the room or to the remotest location a listener might sit. Can you see? Can you hear? Now move from one side of the room to the other, checking that your supplementary aids can be seen and heard from every location.

Depending on the results of your test, you may decide to position a flip chart in a particular

Success Tip

You'll reduce your anxiety and gain confidence if you practice with your visual aids before you face your audience. As you rehearse, you'll become more proficient in operating any equipment, and your speech will go more smoothly.

EXHIBIT 13.12
Listen to Murphy
Murphy's law holds that "anything that can go wrong, will go wrong." Although nobody knows exactly who Murphy was, you can avoid falling victim to Murphy's law by planning ahead. As you practice with your visual aids, anticipate any problems you might face on the day of your speech, and plan accordingly.

For example, depending on your presentation method, you might take along an extra light bulb for the projector, an extra marker for the flip chart or whiteboard, or a spare extension cord for electrical equipment. For computerized presentations, you might bring an extra copy of your presentation on disk. Also, find out ahead of time whether the computer at the speech site is equipped for the kind of presentation you're planning.

You may not think of these potential problems until you actually start to rehearse. So be alert to these details as you practice your speech. Then, when you step in front your audience, you'll be glad that you listened to Murphy.

location, turn the volume controls higher, or make other adaptations. If you conduct this test before the day you're scheduled to speak, you'll have enough time to make any special arrangements necessary. You'll also find out, in advance, whether you have to replace any visual aids that don't pass the test.

Present Visual Aids When Discussing Them

Once you launch into your speech, you'll want to present each visual aid only when you're about to discuss it. If you reveal your visual aids too early or leave them in full view throughout your speech, some audience members may find their attention wandering from you to your visual aids. To avoid distracting your listeners, be sure to keep all visual aids out of sight until you're ready for each one. Once you've finished making your point about a visual aid, you can put it away.

If you're using an overhead projector, set up your first transparency ahead of time. Then you can switch the projector on when you reach the section in your speech where you need that transparency and switch the projector off after you've shown all the transparencies. Similarly, turn your slide projector on when you reach the section where you plan to show your first slide, then turn the projector off after you've shown all your slides. If you've placed lists, charts, or other visual aids on a flip chart, leave a blank page on top and turn it over to reveal the first visual aid

only when you're ready. You can turn the flip chart around or cover the page with a blank page when you're finished with it.

Also, avoid passing objects to audience members during your speech. People are likely to become so distracted looking at the object or waiting for their turn to examine it that they miss some of your points. So that you won't divert attention from your message, you can invite the audience to look at the object after your speech. As noted ealier, handouts can be distracting if distributed during a speech, so you may want to hold them until the end of your speech.

Concentrate on Your Audience

When you're showing a visual aid, be sure to keep your attention focused on your audience. You can't make a point effectively or maintain rapport with your audience if you talk to your visual aids. Of course, you may need to glance at a chart or another visual aid as you explain or describe it, but you don't want to read it word for word or deliver your speech to it.

By practicing ahead of time, you can learn how to present each visual aid and explain its significance without losing touch with your audience. You'll quickly learn how to peek at your visual aid and use your finger or a pointer to call attention to a particular item while keeping eye contact with your audience. This allows you to stay alert for feedback that lets you know whether your audience understands your visual aid and your explanation.

SUMMARY

Visual aids can strengthen your speech by capturing and focusing audience interest, clarifying your meaning, helping you explain complex points, reinforcing your ideas, and building your credibility. Use your imagination and your creativity when you plan your visual aids. Depending on your audience, your topic, the occasion, and the time allotted for your speech, you can choose one or several types of visual aids, including people, objects, models, drawings and diagrams, photographs, maps, charts and graphs, tables, and lists.

The speaker is an important visual aid. When you speak, your body movements, facial expressions, voice qualities, and physical appearance all communicate information nonverbally. By using visual and vocal cues to reinforce your words, you can convey your message more effectively and leave less room for misinterpretation. During your speech, you can also personally demonstrate or illustrate something related to your topic.

You can choose among a wide variety of methods to present your visual aids. Your choices include flip charts; overhead transparencies; slides; videotapes, films, and DVDs; audio aids; computerized graphics; chalkboards and whiteboards; and handouts. At the start of the design process, you can determine the appropriate visual aids and presentation methods by asking a series of questions about your audience, your topic, the speech location, and your personal skills and preferences.

When you're designing your visual aids, keep your design simple to complement your words. Avoid overloading your visuals with too much information, too many details, or too many frills. Plan a design that emphasizes what you want your audience to notice but doesn't throw the visual aid out of balance. Use color in your design to add excitement, provide emphasis, attract your audience's attention, and highlight something significant. Also, be sure that your visual aids are visible to your audience.

Four actions can help you use your visual aids more effectively. First, before the day of your speech, practice using your visual aids. Once you've practiced integrating them into your speech, your audience will see you as more polished and confident, and you'll feel less nervous. Second, confirm that your audience will be able to see and hear from anywhere in the room. Third, when you're speaking to your audience, present each visual aid only when you discuss it. Keep visual aids out of sight until needed, and put them away after you've made your point. Fourth, concentrate on your audience, not on your visual aids so that you can maintain eye contact and receive feedback.

APPLY CRITICAL THINKING

1. How can visual aids help you overcome interference that may prevent the successful transmission of your message?

2. Identify the type of visual aids best suited to explaining the following information, and discuss your reasoning:

    a. How a suspension bridge works

    b. The location of the three tallest Himalayan mountains

    c. Sources of information about studying abroad

    d. The number of new cars sold in the United States over the past three years

3. Identify the type of visual aids best suited to presenting the following information, and discuss your reasoning:

    a. The number of people employed by your college last year and this year

    b. The average temperature in January in four U.S. cities

    c. Wildflowers that grow in New Zealand

    d. Assembling a rocket from a kit

4. What are the advantages and disadvantages of inviting one or more members of the audience to help you with a visual aid during your speech?

5. Apart from color, what can you use to visually emphasize your major point in a line graph? A bar graph? A pie chart?

6. What are the advantages and disadvantages of using an animal as a visual aid during a speech about pet grooming?

7. How can you choose among presentation methods when you're unable to determine the size of your audience in advance?

SHARPEN YOUR SKILLS

Individual Exercises

1. Select a speech from the Appendix, and suggest the type(s) of visual aids that would be most appropriate.

a. Where in the speech would you use each visual aid?

b. What presentation method would you recommend for each, assuming a large audience? A small audience?

2. Observe an instructor who is using visual aids to explain a complicated process or concept.

a. Did the visual aids enhance or overwhelm the speech? Cite specifics to support your answer.

b. Would other visual aids or presentation methods have been more effective? Why?

c. Would fewer or more visual aids have been helpful? Why?

3. Look through books, newspapers, magazines, and other textbooks for one example each of a line graph, a table, and a diagram. Bring these examples to class and analyze how effectively each one communicates its point.

4. Plan how you'll use visual aids in an upcoming classroom speech.

a. What type of visual aid(s) best fit(s) your topic, audience, and speech location?

b. What point(s) can be explained or reinforced using visual aids?

c. Prepare a rough design of each visual aid you'll use in this speech. How can you use color and size most effectively?

Group Exercises

5. With a classmate, observe how a speaker (in person, on television, or on videotape) uses visual aids.

a. Separately, consider how the visual aids helped this speaker communicate with the audience. Were all the visual aids necessary?

b. Could any of the visual aids have been left out without impairing communication?

c. Compare answers with your classmate, and analyze any disagreements.

6. Working with another student, contact the local chamber of commerce and locate a businessperson who speaks to community groups, employees, or other audiences. Interview this speaker in person or by telephone, and be prepared to discuss the results in class.

a. Does the speaker regularly use visual aids? Why?

b. What types of visual aids does the speaker prefer? Why?

c. What types of presentation methods does the speaker prefer? Why?

d. Does the speaker's choice of visual aids or presentation methods vary by audience?

e. What advice about choosing and using visual aids can this speaker offer?

REHEARSING AND DELIVERING YOUR SPEECH

LEARNING OBJECTIVES

After studying this chapter, you will be able to

1. Explain the importance of an effective delivery.

2. Identify the elements of voice to focus on when rehearsing and delivering a speech.

3. Discuss the elements of body language to focus on when rehearsing and delivering a speech.

4. Describe how to use eye contact when you deliver your speech.

5. List the four methods of delivery.

6. Describe the steps in rehearsing for an extemporaneous speech.

7. Discuss how you can prepare for audience questions.

THE ART AND SCIENCE OF EFFECTIVE DELIVERY

*H*ow you say something is as important as what you say. Dave Thomas, the late founder of Wendy's hamburger chain, knew this well. When he appeared in television commercials, he spoke his scripted lines in a folksy, friendly style that made him seem approachable, even by complete strangers (see Exhibit 14.1). So when Catherine Phipps walked into a Wendy's outlet in Florida and spotted Thomas, she didn't hesitate to strike up a conversation. "I never met the man in my life," she said later. "But I felt like I knew him. The commercials, you know."[1]

Delivery makes all the difference in public speaking. The same words that make a friendly impression coming from Dave Thomas might sound distant and unconvincing when spoken by someone else. This is as true for classroom speeches as it is for television commercials, political debates, and any other public speaking situation.

Your delivery consists of the sound of your voice, the way you speak your words, your personal appearance, and all the nonverbal signals you send during your speech. As pointed out in Chapter 4, only part of a speaker's message is communicated verbally. The rest is communicated nonverbally, through body language and tone of voice.[2] This means that audience comprehension depends, in large part, on an effective delivery. It also means that your delivery will influence how

your listeners feel about you, about your message, and about your speech.

At the same time, you can't simply copy the way someone else delivers a speech. To be effective, you'll want to adapt your delivery to your audience, your topic, the occasion and setting for your speech, and your personal style. Delivery is so individual that yours is likely to vary even if you give the same speech two days in a row.

Good delivery is an art as well as a science: you can study and practice the basic skills, and then add your personal touch to come up with an approach that works well for you. What you're aiming for is a *transparent* delivery, one that doesn't call attention to itself but allows your audience to receive and understand your message. After you've finished your speech, you want your audience to remember your central idea, not the resonance of your voice or the elegance of your personal appearance.[3]

A good delivery is important for three reasons. First, it helps you build a relationship with your audience. Second, it allows you to share your attitudes and feelings. Third, it works with your words, not against them, to convey your intended meaning:

- *Building a relationship with your audience.* You can't depend on words alone to build a good relationship with your listeners. If you develop an enthusiastic and authoritative delivery, you'll demonstrate your interest in your audience and your topic. But stay away from a dramatic, oratorical delivery that sounds like you're talking *at* your audience. Instead, strengthen

your rapport with your audience by using a more natural delivery that sounds like you're talking *with* your audience. The best delivery is one that seems so natural that your audience doesn't notice it.

- *Sharing attitudes and feelings.* An effective delivery will show your audience how you feel about your topic, not just what you know about it. The way you deliver your speech helps your audience understand the attitudes and feelings behind your words. When your listeners sense that you care about the points you're making, they'll be inspired to care, too.[4]

- *Supporting your words to convey meaning.* Help your audience get every nuance of meaning from your words by using both your voice and your body language to communicate. Of course, this won't work if your nonverbal cues conflict with your verbal message. However, when your delivery integrates consistent nonverbal and verbal communication, you can effectively reinforce the meaning of your message and improve the impact of your speech.[5]

The next two sections examine the two components of delivery: voice and body language. The final section explores how to deliver your speech, how to rehearse your delivery, and how to prepare for audience questions.

EFFECTIVE USE OF VOICE

Your voice can make an immediate and lasting impression on your audience. Think about the voices of radio announcers, television performers, politicians, instructors, and other speakers you've heard. Do some voices make you want to hear more? Do others make you want to cover your ears? You may have heard speakers who drone listlessly on and speakers whose voices are lively and pleasant. How do you respond to their voices?

Just as you react to the voices of the speakers you hear, your listeners react to your voice and make judgments based on it. When listeners hear your voice, they decide whether to tune in or tune out. In addition, they listen for clues to your credibility and to your attitudes and feelings. So as you work on your voice when preparing to deliver your speech, pay attention to eight elements: pitch, rate, pauses, volume, variety, pronunciation, articulation, and dialect.

Pitch

Pitch is a measure of how high or how low your voice sounds. You can think of pitch in terms of the range of notes on a musical scale: a high-pitched voice sounds like the notes on the upper end of the scale; a low-pitched voice sounds like the notes on the lower end of the scale. Most people find a consistent pitch at which they're

EXHIBIT 14.2
Controlling Your Pitch
A person who speaks on "one note" is boring. A speaker who varies the pitch comes across as lively and interesting. How would you prefer to be perceived? This activity will demonstrate the flexibility of your own voice and show you how to use the lower range of your pitch. Repeat the following three sentences—each time at a deeper pitch:

"This is my normal pitch."
"Do, Re, Me, Fa, So, La, Ti, Do"
"This is my normal voice."

Now stop. Did you hear a difference between the first sentence and the last? Repeat the trio of sentences until you are in control of your pitch and can deepen it at will.

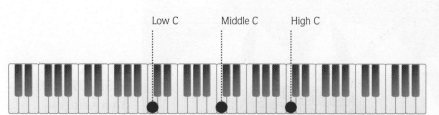

Low C   Middle C   High C

most comfortable speaking. For example, pop singer Michael Jackson has a high-pitched voice; newscaster Dan Rather and actress Lauren Bacall have low-pitched voices (see Exhibit 14.2).

Speakers who don't vary their pitch speak in a monotone. A monotone sounds boring and unemotional because it lacks **inflection**, variations in pitch (up or down) that convey meaning. When every word carries the same pitch, listeners quickly grow uninterested. They also have difficulty detecting the speaker's attitudes or feelings toward the ideas being expressed. In some cases, the intended meaning of a word is carried in the inflection; without inflection—or with the wrong inflection—that meaning will be lost.

Using inflection will help you maintain the interest of your audience and get your message across. As an exercise, say the following sentence out loud: "I don't believe you." The first time you read the sentence, raise your pitch on the first word; the second time you read it, raise your pitch on the second word; and the third time you read it, raise your pitch on the third word. By choosing the appropriate inflection, you can change the meaning, implication, and emphasis of your words. However, avoid upward shifts in pitch that are too dramatic; they can sound overly emotional to U.S. audiences.[6] Also avoid

an upward shift in pitch on the final word of a sentence unless you are asking a question. Otherwise your audience may misinterpret a statement of fact, for example, as a question.

Plan to use inflection to your advantage both as you rehearse and as you deliver your speech. First, be aware of the nuances of meaning that various inflections communicate. Second, decide on the inflections you prefer, and use those consistently when you rehearse. Third, mark your speaking outline to remind yourself of particularly important or unusual inflections. Then, as you address your audience, be alert for feedback that shows whether your listeners understand the meaning of your message.

Rate

Rate is the speed at which you speak. The average person speaks at a rate of 125 to 150 words per minute. Because most people can listen at a rate of 500 words per minute, slower speakers are likely to lose their audience's attention.[7] On the other hand, most audiences prefer listening to speakers who use a somewhat faster rate. President John F. Kennedy was a speedy speaker, delivering one speech at the rate of 327 words per minute.[8]

Speedier talkers may race through a speech so quickly that listeners don't have an opportunity

EXHIBIT 14.3

How to Change Your Speaking Rate
During a speech, you can change your speaking rate by varying the length of natural pauses between words and phrases, inserting new pauses, and changing the rate at which you speak some syllables and words.

New pauses are deliberately added for emphasis

The United Nations, PAUSE so much a dream PAUSE and creation PAUSE of the United States, is ready for use in a great common cause— PAUSE the cause of peace, development and democracy everywhere.

Natural pauses fall between words and phrases

Some syllables and words can be spoken more rapidly or more slowly to change rate

to absorb the ideas and make the connections between points. This is often the case with nervous speakers, who want to get through the ordeal more quickly. If you can't tell whether your rate is too speedy, you can videotape your rehearsal to check your rate.

Another way to detect excessive speed is to pay attention to your breathing as you rehearse. Feeling out of breath just a few minutes into your speech is a good indication that you're speaking too rapidly. You can slow yourself down—and reduce your anxiety—by using some of the breathing techniques discussed in Chapter 2. You can also slow down by speaking in shorter sentences, no longer than 18 words in length.[9]

Although you don't have to aim for a specific rate when you speak, you'll want to adjust your rate according to your topic, your audience, the occasion, and your personal preferences. For example, you can convey excitement, exhilaration, or urgency using a fast rate; in contrast, you can convey tranquillity, solemnity, or sadness using a slow rate. To vary your rate, you can change the length of pauses that fall naturally between words, phrases, or sentences; consciously add new pauses; and change the rate at which you speak syllables and words within phrases (see Exhibit 14.3).[10]

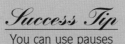
Success Tip
You can use pauses to give your audience time to absorb an idea, to signal a transition to a new idea or a new section, and to heighten audience anticipation for the next idea.

Pauses

A pause is more than just a way to vary your speaking rate. It's also an important way to add emphasis and meaning to selected phrases and sentences. You can insert a pause to allow the audience a moment to think about an idea, to indicate a shift to a new idea or to a new section of your speech, or to heighten audience anticipation of your next idea.

Excellent speakers are skilled at inserting and timing pauses. Reverend Martin Luther King used pauses to intensify the dramatic images in his "I Have a Dream" speech; President Kennedy used pauses to hammer home the statements of antithesis in his inaugural address. In fact, with planning and practice, every speaker can learn to use pauses effectively.

At first, you may feel slightly uncomfortable during the brief silence of each pause. Avoid the temptation to fill any silences with *verbal pauses,* sounds such as *um* and *ah.* Verbal pauses not only annoy listeners, they also hurt your credibility. If you tend to use verbal pauses, train yourself to take a quick breath instead.[11] Over time, you'll break the habit and become more confident as you improve your timing and observe how listeners react to your pauses.

Don Mell knows how pauses can enhance a speech if properly timed. When he was an Associated Press photographer in Beirut, he watched helplessly as his friend Terry Anderson was taken hostage at gunpoint. Later, as he planned a speech about the event, he worked with a speech coach who helped him add pauses for emphasis. Mell started each thought on a new line in his speech to remind himself to pause at the end of a line. He used indentation in the third, fourth, and fifth lines to indicate slightly shorter pauses. Here's how the second paragraph of his completed speech looked:

> The morning started like any other 'normal'
>   morning in Beirut.
> It was beautiful,
>   sunny,
>   crisp,
>   and uneventful.
> Terry and I had just finished a game of
>   tennis.
> He liked to play tennis to relax.
> He had things on his mind those days.
> He and his wife were expecting a new baby.
> He was worried about his dad's health.[12]

The pauses helped the audience feel the calm atmosphere of the morning of Anderson's abduction. They also served as stopping points to allow the audience to take in Mell's thoughts about Anderson's background and mood. These details were important, because Mell wanted his audience to understand the feelings of a man whose fate, at the time of the speech, was still uncertain. (Anderson was finally released 2,455 days after his abduction.)

Volume

Just as you can adjust the volume on your radio or television, you can adjust how loudly you speak, to overcome background noise and reach every listener in the room. You'll do best to aim for a volume that allows listeners in the back row to easily hear you and that doesn't overwhelm listeners who are close by. Remember that although your voice sounds loud to you, it's softer to people in the audience. So take your cues from audience feedback, and raise your volume if people in the back row appear to be straining to hear you or look puzzled.

To increase your volume without hurting your voice, open your mouth as you speak and use all of your breath to send your words out to the audience. To see how this works, put your hand on your diaphragm, inhale, and read this sentence so that you can be heard in the back of the room. The goal is to consistently project your voice and avoid running out of breath before you run out of words or strain your voice.

Consider using a microphone when you're going to address a large crowd, when you're speaking in a huge room or a room with poor acoustics, or when you're not able to project your voice to be heard by everyone (see Exhibit 14.4). Because the microphone will amplify your words, you don't have to raise the volume on your voice. If the amplification system is working properly, you'll be able to speak into the microphone in a normal, conversational tone and still be heard.

Variety

Spice up your speech by adding some variety to your voice. You can keep your audience interested throughout your speech by varying your pitch, rate, pauses, and volume. When your voice is pleasantly unpredictable, your audience won't know what's coming next, and they'll stay alert to find out. What's more, variety adds a personality and an immediacy to your words that can bring you closer to your audience by making your speech sound more like a spirited conversation.

In contrast, imagine what would happen if you spoke in a monotone and never varied your pitch, rate, pauses, or volume. To the audience, this lack of variety would be an indication that you're not interested in the topic or the audience. If you sound bored, why should your audience be interested?

EXHIBIT 14.4
Taking the Mike
The technique you use with a microphone depends on the type of microphone you use: hand-held, stationary, or clip-on. When you use a *hand-held microphone*, position it 6 to 12 inches from your mouth. If the microphone is attached to an electrical cord, beware of tangles.

A *stationary microphone* is attached to a floor stand or table, desk, or lectern. Generally, your mouth should be 8 to 10 inches away from a stationary microphone. You may be able to stand farther away if you're using a sensitive model.

A *clip-on microphone* attaches to the front of your clothing. If you're using a wireless model, you'll be able to move and gesture without worrying about the cord. Remember to avoid bumping this type of microphone once you're wearing it.

You can practice adding vocal variety by reading the following selection out loud. National Public Radio's Noah Adams included this paragraph as part of a speech he gave about the onset of winter near Lake Superior:

> The black bears up by the Canadian border went to sleep long ago. The snakes have found hiding places, the spiders are safe, wrapped in their own silk. The box elder bugs are tucked away in the bark of trees. And the leopard frogs have gone to the bottom of the lakes, before the ice comes. There are lots of woodchucks asleep in this part of the country. They would win a blue ribbon for hibernation, comfortable underground, breathing once in five minutes, their heart rate down to four beats a minute. It is said they sleep so deeply you could take one, curled up in a ball, and roll it across the floor without its waking up.[13]

Each time you read this selection, try changing your rate, the timing and placement of your pauses, and your volume. You may want to record one or two readings so that you can hear the effect of your changes. As you read, you can experiment with emphasizing different images, and find new ways to help the audience savor and remember the flavor of the countryside.

Pronunciation

All the variety in the world won't get your message across if listeners can't understand you due to poor pronunciation. **Pronunciation** is the ability to say each word correctly by making the proper sounds and accenting the correct syllable. Correct pronunciation is invisible, but incorrect pronunciation can damage your credibility. After all, if you mispronounce the name of the ebola virus as *E-bol-a* or *e-bol-A* rather than using the correct pronunciation, *e-BOL-a*, how can the audience believe that you're knowledgeable about this mysterious disease?

When you hear a word mispronounced over and over, you may, in time, forget its correct pronunciation and adopt the incorrect pronunciation. Also, you may not know how to pronounce some words that you've seen in print but never heard spoken. As a result, you may fall into the habit of mispronouncing certain words (see Exhibit 14.5).

If you're not sure how to pronounce a particular word, look it up in advance. Check not only the sounds to use but also the correct syllable to accent. Also check the pronunciation of any unfamiliar names or places. Then you'll be prepared to pronounce these words or names correctly as you rehearse, making the correct pronunciation a habit by the time you deliver your speech.

Articulation

Articulation is the ability to correctly form the sounds of each word. Whereas pronunciation refers to whether you say words correctly, articulation refers more specifically to making vowel and consonant sounds clearly and distinctly as you speak. If you substitute one consonant for another (saying *dese* for *these*), slush your *s*'s (saying

EXHIBIT 14.5

Test Your Pronunciation
How many of these words can you pronounce correctly?

WORD	CORRECT PRONUNCIATION	INCORRECT PRONUNCIATION
across	a **KROSS**	a **KROST**
comparable	**KOM** per able	kom **PARE** able
larynx	**LAR** inks	**LAR** niks
library	**LI** brer y	**LI** bery
mischievous	**MIS** che vous	mis **CHEE** vious
nuclear	**NEW** klee ur	**NEW** kew lur
perspiration	pers pir **A** shun	press pir **A** shun
picture	**PIK** tchure	**PIT** chure
recognize	**REK** og nize	**REK** a nize
strict	strikt	strik
surprise	sur **PRIZE**	sup **PRIZE**

shupport for *support*), or drop some vowels or consonants (such as the *g* in *-ing*), your audience may not be able to understand you.

Many people talk so quickly or say certain phrases so frequently that they don't bother to articulate the individual sounds in every word. This can confound U.S. and international audiences alike. For example, when a group of English-speaking Japanese employees transferred to Toyota's U.S. office, they needed a special language course to learn to decipher "Jeat yet?" as "Did you eat yet?" and "Cannahepya?" as "Can I help you?"[14]

You can work on specific articulation problems by making up practice sentences that include the sounds you want to learn to say more distinctly. For example, you might read aloud one or more of the tongue twisters below, picking up the pace on each successive try. Soon you'll be able to articulate each sentence clearly—and at your normal speaking rate.[15]

Peter Piper picked a peck of pickled peppers.
She sells seashells at the seashore.
Granny gray goose greedily gobbled golden grain in Graham's gabled granary.
The fish and chip shop's chips are soft chips.

In addition, you may want to record each speech as you rehearse. As you review the tape, listen for words that you're not articulating clearly and crisply. Practice saying each word slowly and distinctly, and then rehearse your speech again so that you'll be able to articulate each word at your normal speaking rate.

Dialect

A **dialect** is the pattern of vocabulary, grammar, and pronunciation that's used in a particular region or culture.[16] Nearly every region of the United States is associated with a specific dialect. If you were raised in the South, you may speak with a drawl; if you were raised in New York, you may "tawk about Noo Yawk." In addition, some U.S. subcultures have identifiable dialects. The same is true of people in other countries and cultures, who also develop unique and recognizable speech patterns.

No dialect is more or less acceptable than another. However, research shows that listeners form impressions based, in part, on their stereotyped

EXHIBIT 14.6
Using Body Language During Speech Delivery

Posture—leaning toward the audience adds to the speaker's emphasis

Eye contact—good eye contact shows this speaker's involvement with the audience

Facial expressions—an emphatic facial expression reinforces a key point

Personal appearance—this speaker's clothing indicates that he means business

Gestures—a hand gesture helps stress a particular idea

Movements—moving closer rivets the audience's attention

notions about people who speak with certain dialects. As a result, some audience members may believe that a speaker who uses a particular dialect is less intelligent or less capable.[17] This reaction has nothing to do with the content of the speaker's message; rather, it's based only on the sound of the speaker's voice.

Still, you don't have to do away with your dialect unless you're planning a career in television or a similar vocation where speaking without a dialect is a requirement. In general, speech coaches emphasize that their efforts are aimed at improving communication, not eliminating dialects.[18] In situations where your audience is familiar with your dialect, it probably won't be a barrier to understanding. However, if your audience can't understand your words because of your dialect, you may want to soften it so that you can get your message across.

EFFECTIVE USE OF BODY LANGUAGE

Body language is the second component of speech delivery that helps you communicate your message nonverbally. Just as they do with your voice, listeners look to your body language for clues about the meaning of your message and for clues to your credibility and competence. Body language can make a difference even when you're

delivering your speech to an audience that doesn't speak your language. "Your own facial gestures [expressions], your hand gestures, are very important in those situations," explains Paul E. Freiman, CEO of Syntex. "People who may not understand your language will assess you as a human being by what they see of you, as much as what they hear of you through a translator."[19]

As you rehearse and deliver your speech, you'll want to focus on six elements of body language. These include personal appearance, eye contact, facial expressions, gestures, movements, and posture (see Exhibit 14.6). When any or all of these six elements of body language conflict with your voice and spoken words, your audience is likely to be confused about what you stand for and what you want to convey. However, if the elements of your body language are in harmony with your voice and your words, you'll present your audience with a consistent, unambiguous message.

Personal Appearance

The first thing your audience notices about you is the way you look. Remember, you're not just a speaker, you're a visual aid. As a visual aid, you want your personal appearance to match the topic and the occasion as well as the audience's expectations. First impressions count. In fact, some studies indicate that people judge each other by what they see within the first few seconds of seeing or meeting each other.[20] So make your first impression as strong as possible.

You may distract your listeners from the meaning of your message if your clothing, hair style, jewelry, or any other aspect of your personal appearance seems out of place. Instead, plan to wear a tasteful outfit that is as formal or informal as the speaking occasion and topic demands. Also, choose jewelry and accessories that don't outshine you.

As you plan your appearance, remember the comment from the nineteenth-century London fashion plate, Beau Brummell. When told of a gentleman who was so well dressed that he turned heads, Brummell commented, "Then, in that case, he's *not* well-dressed."[21] The same holds true today: If your appearance draws attention, you're not going to be able to keep your listeners focused on your message.

Eye Contact

From the moment you step in front of your audience to the moment you leave the room, one of your top priorities as a speaker is to establish and maintain eye contact. Just as you would in any conversation, you'll want to make eye contact with the people you're addressing, one at a time. In this way, you'll be able to do several things:

- *Make a personal connection.* When you maintain eye contact with the people in your audience, you're reaching out to make a personal connection. This sends a nonverbal signal that you're interested in your listeners. In turn, they'll be more inclined to be interested in you and your message.
- *Build credibility.* Eye contact enhances your credibility as a speaker.[22] Listeners may think that you're being evasive, unfriendly, or dishonest if you don't look directly at them. In contrast, good eye contact goes a long way toward convincing an audience of your sincerity and competence.
- *Obtain feedback.* You can gauge reaction to your speech by looking directly at individuals in your audience. By observing their body language, you'll be able to determine whether your

listeners are puzzled, excited, uninterested, angry, or reacting in some other way to your ideas or your delivery. Knowing your audience's reaction, you can adjust your words or your delivery accordingly.

Although direct eye contact is not considered polite in some cultures, speakers in many Western cultures spend the majority of their time looking at their audiences. You can establish eye contact even before you begin your speech. Pick out a few friendly faces as you draw a breath and launch into your introduction. Look briefly into the eyes of one and then another as you start to speak. By focusing on a few listeners who are smiling, nodding, or giving other positive feedback, you can boost your confidence and reduce your speech anxiety.[23]

Once you're well into your introduction and you have your nerves under control, you'll want to widen your eye contact to include more people. Keep your eye contact friendly and interested, not glaring or challenging. Rather than mechanically scanning rows or repeatedly moving your gaze from front to rear, left to right, look randomly at audience members. This is more natural, and more personal, than any fixed or repetitive pattern of eye contact. As you make especially dramatic or crucial points, you'll want to be sure to have your eyes on your audience, not on your speaking outline, for maximum impact.

Facial Expressions

You can convey a wide range of emotions and attitudes through your facial expressions: surprise, sadness, happiness, and every feeling in between (see Exhibit 14.7). The range is so wide because, according to researcher Ray Birdwhistell, you can coordinate your facial features and muscles to create some 250,000 different expressions.[24] Of course, you don't have to be Jim Carrey to use facial expressions to convey meaning. In fact, you'll want to keep your facial expressions natural, unless you decide to exaggerate to drive home a particular point.

Consistency is the key: Match your facial expressions to what your words say. Start your

EXHIBIT 14.7

Some Facial Expressions Are Universal

According to research, six facial expressions used by speakers to convey emotion are interpreted the same way around the world: happiness, fear, surprise, disgust, anger, and sadness.

speech on a positive note by smiling at your audience. Unless you're talking on an extremely somber topic, a natural smile is a good way to break the ice and show that you're glad to be with your audience.

If you're nervous, you may not feel like smiling at first, but the physical action will help you dispel your tension and get in the mood to share your ideas with your audience. Once you're into your speech, you can change your facial expressions to correspond with the nuances of feeling you want to convey throughout your speech. In this way, you'll reinforce with your face what you're saying with your words. In addition, you can practice

SPEAKING ACROSS CULTURES

BODY LANGUAGE TABOOS: NONVERBAL GESTURES SOMETIMES SPEAK VOLUMES

Just as words don't always have exact equivalents in other languages, gestures and other elements of body language may not translate the way they are intended. Some time ago, during a speech to mark his arrival in the United States, Soviet President Brezhnev raised his arms with hands clasped in a show of friendship. Unfortunately, his gesture didn't translate the way he intended. Instead, the U.S. audience was offended by a gesture they took as a symbol of victory. To avoid such problems, you'll want to learn more about the meaning of body language before you deliver a speech in another country. Here are a few examples:

- *Translating hand gestures.* The "OK" gesture so common in the United States, made with the thumb and first finger forming a ring and the other fingers extended, is considered obscene in Brazil and Germany. In France, the gesture means that something is worthless; in Japan, the gesture refers to money. In the United States, another sign for "OK" is a thumbs-up gesture. The same gesture is rude in Nigeria; in Japan, it stands for the number five.
- *Translating eye contact.* In most Western cultures, eye contact is a sign of attention and respect. In contrast, lowered eyes indicate respect in some Asian, African, and Native American cultures.
- *Translating head movements.* U.S. speakers nod their heads up and down to indicate "yes" and shake their heads from side to side to indicate "no." The same head movements have the opposite meanings in Bulgaria.

Research the use of eye contact and other body language before you address an audience in another country.

musicians wouldn't be able to play the notes with the proper feeling. Similarly, in the course of your speech, you can use a gesture, like a flick of the baton, to more effectively express the meaning of your words.[25]

Many student speakers feel awkward about gesturing during their speeches. Some jam their hands in their pockets, lock them behind their backs, or grip one arm with the other as they speak, betraying their nervousness. Others gesture wildly or fidget continuously, distracting listeners. The result is a series of gestures that work against (rather than with) the words the speaker is using.

To be effective, your gestures should seem deliberate yet spontaneous and natural, just as they would during a personal conversation. As the playwright George Bernard Shaw once said, "I am the most spontaneous speaker in the world, because every word, every gesture, and every retort has been carefully rehearsed."[26] Like Shaw, you can plan your gestures as you rehearse. Consider which gestures will help you communicate the meaning of your words and the feelings you want to convey. Try various gestures in front of a mirror to see which ones make sense in context; if possible, plan to use a number of gestures during

reading the facial expressions of audience members so you'll understand how they are reacting to your speech.

Gestures

You can use hand and arm gestures to telegraph meaning to your listeners the way a conductor uses a baton to signal musicians as they play the notes in a musical score. Without the signals, the

your speech for the sake of variety.

Movements

Your movements before, during, and after your speech can be quite revealing. From the audience's perspective, the movements you make can indicate how close you feel to your listeners. President Bill Clinton knew this when he left his seat during a televised debate to move closer to a questioner in the audience. This movement communicated Clinton's interest in the questioner more effectively than words alone. Movements can also indicate how confident you are, and they can signal a transition from point to point or section to section in your speech.

Because movements do carry significance, you'll want to plan yours so that they create the effect you want. To give the impression of being comfortable and self-assured from the beginning of your speech, plan to walk purposefully and gracefully to face your audience. As you start your speech, stand firm, rather than shifting your weight or pacing as you speak. President Ronald Reagan used this technique, which nonverbally conveyed the message that he was comfortable and confident in front of any audience.[27]

During your speech, you can insert deliberate movements to signal changes in mood or content. However, to avoid distracting your audience, don't move as you explain a complex point or during an

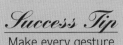

Success Tip

Make every gesture count. Identify gestures that will enhance the meaning you intend to convey in particular sections of your speech. Then rehearse the same gesture in the same way when you practice those sections.

emotional moment. At the end, move away from your audience at a controlled pace that's consistent with the impression of confidence that all your movements have conveyed throughout your speech.

Because movements always draw attention, don't move unless you have a good reason to do so (see Exhibit 14.8). When you do move, be deliberate, and know what you want to accomplish with each movement. For example, Tony Robbins, a California-based speaker, purposely bounds across the stage and even jumps in the air to grab the audience's attention when he's about to make a key point.[28] W. Mitchell moves his wheelchair to reinforce points during his motivational speeches about overcoming adversity. "My movements back and forth across the stage are just one more sign that helps convey that although I am disabled, I am not unable," he says.[29]

Posture

You can also communicate with your audience through your posture. If you slouch or slump, you risk giving the impression that you're not confident or, just as bad, that you don't care how your audience perceives you. On the other hand, if you stand tall, hold your head up, and keep your shoulders back, your posture will communicate self-assurance.

You'll want to aim for a natural posture that's not tense or stiff. Practice an open body stance that looks slightly relaxed rather than rigidly military. If you lean forward to make a point, avoid hunching over. When you hunch or slouch, you hurt your image and, at the same time, hurt your ability to project your voice. You can get the support you need to stand tall by planting your feet 12 to 18 inches apart (no wider than your shoulders) and balancing your weight evenly on both feet. This way, you won't divert the audience's attention by shifting from side to side or leaning to one side as you speak.

EFFECTIVE DELIVERY THROUGH REHEARSAL

All your planning, researching, and writing has been leading up to one special moment: the moment when you get up in front of your audience to deliver your speech. This is the moment when you actually share your ideas with your audience as you speak to inform, persuade, motivate, or entertain. And this is the moment when the two components of delivery, skillful use of voice and body language, come into play.

Famed Roman orator Cicero understood that successful public speaking depends on effective delivery. Writing in the second century B.C., he noted, "Without effective delivery, a speech of the highest mental capacity can be held in no esteem, while one of the moderate abilities, with this qualification, may surpass even those of the highest talent."[30] Cicero's observation is as true today as it was more than two thousand years ago: the most intelligent speech can't succeed without effective delivery—and good delivery can improve the audience's reception of a less-than-perfect speech. So you may have planned a powerful speech on prison reform, but you won't be able to touch your audience without an equally powerful delivery.

The best way to improve your delivery is by advance planning. First consider which delivery method you'll use. Then be sure to set aside time to rehearse your speech. Finally, as part of your planning, prepare for audience questions.

Consider the Methods of Delivery

You can deliver your speech in any of four ways: by reading from a manuscript, speaking from a memorized text, speaking impromptu, or speaking extemporaneously. Most of the time, you'll be speaking extemporaneously, although the other delivery methods are appropriate in certain situations.

Reading from a Manuscript

When you want to be sure that you present a speech exactly as planned, you can read from a manuscript. By reading word for word from a prepared script, you can avoid omitting important details or misstating points or evidence. Some politicians, government officials, corporate leaders, and other public speakers use this delivery method to ensure complete accuracy when they

---

Checklist for Effective Body Language

1. Dress neatly and appropriately for the audience, the topic, and the occasion.
2. Maintain eye contact with your audience throughout your speech to make a personal connection, build credibility, and obtain feedback.
3. Convey emotions and attitudes through natural facial expressions that match the meaning of your words.
4. Enhance your meaning by using a variety of natural arm and hand gestures that are consistent with your words and facial expressions.
5. Use movements that are purposeful and deliberate to show that you're comfortable and self-assured and to signal changes in mood or content.
6. Maintain good posture to communicate poise and confidence.

EXHIBIT 14.9
Teleprompters: Delivery Tools for Speakers in the Public Eye
When actor Christopher Reeve spoke at the 1996 Democratic National Convention he used a teleprompter as he delivered his speech.

know that every word they say will be reported and analyzed by the media. In addition, some speakers choose to read their speeches when they have an extremely limited time in which to cover all the points that must be made.

However, when you read from a manuscript, you distance yourself from your audience. You can't maintain good eye contact when you're looking down to read. Because you're not looking at your listeners, you'll miss the feedback that will tell you whether you're getting your points across. Just as bad, you risk boring your audience by reading every word, which sounds less dynamic and therefore less interesting than speaking. For these reasons, you'll want to avoid reading from a manuscript unless you're in a situation where you feel compelled to deliver your speech word for word.

If you must use a manuscript, you don't have to look or sound as though you're reading (see Exhibit 14.9). For example, John O'Brien, chief executive officer of Grumman, rehearses with his manuscript as many as 15 times before he delivers a speech. As he rehearses, he marks the manuscript with delivery tips. By the time he delivers the speech, the words are so familiar that he doesn't have to look down for long periods to read. Instead, he glances down quickly to pick up the next phrase, and then looks up to deliver it to the audience.[31] Using this method, O'Brien can make eye contact and check for audience feedback throughout his speech.

Speaking from a Memorized Text
Another way to deliver a speech exactly as written

is to speak from a memorized text. Speakers use this delivery method for many of the same reasons that they read from prepared manuscripts. Although few speakers today memorize complete speeches, in contrast to the nineteenth-century fashion for reciting classic speeches from memory, they sometimes memorize a section or two of a speech. For example, some speakers don't read from a manuscript or use a teleprompter. They prefer to memorize a few dramatic sections of a planned speech. Then they weave these sections together spontaneously as they deliver the speech.[32]

One danger of memorizing your speech is that you'll get so caught up in remembering what comes next that you don't actually see or interact with your audience. Your eyes may be open and facing the audience, but you're searching for your next words, not for audience feedback. What's more, you may lose credibility if you sound like you're mechanically reciting from memory.

Nonetheless, there are times when you may want to speak from memory. If you're giving a brief acceptance speech or offering a celebratory toast, you may want to memorize the few words you plan to say. Also, you may give your confidence a boost by memorizing the introduction or the conclusion of a longer speech. By committing those sections to memory, you won't be afraid of stumbling or stammering as you start or end your speech.

Speaking on the Spur of the Moment
Impromptu speaking is a method of delivering a speech with little if any preparation or rehearsal. Because you don't write or practice your words in advance, impromptu speeches are at the opposite

end of the delivery spectrum from reading a manuscript and memorizing text. You use impromptu speaking when you answer a question in class, dispute a point during a government or business meeting, or address any audience on the spur of the moment.

Although impromptu speeches can sound lively and spontaneous, they're often not as well organized, researched, or worded as a speech that has been planned and rehearsed ahead of time. However, a little planning for an "unplanned" speech can help you sidestep this problem. Here's how Paul E. Freiman, CEO of Neurobiological Techologies, Inc., approaches impromptu speaking. "I give all my speeches to our employees impromptu," he says. "But I never begin an impromptu speech without knowing what I am going to talk about."[33] Following Freiman's example, you can begin preparing for an unplanned speech by asking:

- What is my purpose in addressing this audience?
- What points do I want to make?
- What is the best order for my major points?
- What evidence can I offer to support my points?

If possible, jot down a few notes for guidance. Check the logic and organization of your points before you speak. In many cases, you can begin your introduction by restating the question, statement, or situation that prompted you to speak. Then move through each point, using transitions and signposts to help your audience follow your reasoning, and close with a clear and concise summary. If you're nervous about speaking without preparation, remember that your listeners don't expect perfection. They're waiting to hear your message, not to seize on any missteps. And every time you use impromptu speaking, it becomes a live rehearsal for the next time you use this delivery method.

Speaking Extemporaneously

Most contemporary public speakers use extemporaneous speaking: They plan and rehearse their speeches in advance, and then they choose their exact words during delivery. When you use this delivery method, you expand on the notes in your speaking outline as you address your audience. Your delivery sounds more spontaneous and natural than speaking from a memorized text or reading from a manuscript because you're putting the exact words and phrases together as you go along. You're not scrambling for something to say, as you might during an impromptu speech, because you planned your speech in advance. Just as important, you're able to maintain eye contact and search for feedback throughout your speech. More than any other delivery method, extemporaneous speaking allows you to concentrate on talking *with,* not *at,* your audience.

You've prepared by researching your purpose, your topic, your audience, your points, and your support material. Now, before you step in front of your audience, you'll want to rehearse so that you know not only what you're going to say but how you're going to say it. Then you'll be ready to face your audience, maintain eye contact, and communicate with confidence.

Rehearse for an Extemporaneous Speech

The better you know your speech, the more natural and convincing you'll sound when you deliver it. That's why one rehearsal isn't enough. Even though you'll choose the exact words as you address your audience, you'll want to practice a number of times until you're thoroughly familiar with your points, your speech organization, and your visual aids. Each time you rehearse is also an opportunity to test various elements of voice and body language so that you can determine which ones convey your meaning most effectively. Here are a few suggestions to help you plan your rehearsals:

1. *Read through the planning outline.* Go through your planning outline one more time to be sure you aren't trying to cram too many points into your speech. Also, make sure your points are in the correct order and that your support materials are appropriate and convincing. Read

EXHIBIT 14.10
Roll the Tape!
Videotaping your rehearsal is a good way to check the elements of voice and body language you will use when you deliver the speech in front of your audience.

through your introduction, conclusion, and transitions to make sure they're smooth and interesting.

2. *Prepare the speaking outline.* Next, condense the points in your planning outline to create a key word speaking outline. As discussed in Chapter 11, you may want to write out certain statistics, quotations, or other details, as well as a few critical points in your introduction or your conclusion. Add delivery cues where you want to enhance meaning. Also, add reminders where you plan to use visual aids. Be sure your speaking outline is both brief and easy to read.

3. *Practice from the speaking outline.* Now you're ready to practice your speech out loud, using the speaking outline to jog your memory. At first, you'll want to stand in place so that you can focus on wording your points as you rehearse your entire speech. As you get better at expanding the key words in your outline into full sentences, you can begin to practice with your visual aids.

4. *Practice in front of a mirror.* Once you feel comfortable speaking from your outline and using your visual aids, you can position yourself in front of a mirror as you practice. This allows you to check for distracting or inappropriate body language. It's also a good way to see how your posture and gestures appear to an audience.

5. *Time yourself.* To find out whether you'll finish

Success Tip

Make notes on your speaking outline as reminders to use effective voice and body language. Also note on your speaking outline where you plan to use visual aids so that you can practice your movements every time you rehearse.

within the time allotted—without rushing or padding—time your speech. If you're running short or long, think about which points can be expanded or condensed. Then time later rehearsals to be sure that you're completing your speech on schedule.

6. *Record your speech.* You may want to videotape your speech so that you can pinpoint areas for improvement (see Exhibit 14.10). Check for eye contact and for effective use of voice and body language, and then revise your speaking outline to reflect any changes or additions in delivery cues.

7. *Seek feedback.* Ask friends, classmates, relatives, or other willing volunteers to play the role of your audience as you rehearse. Let them know you're looking for constructive suggestions that will help you improve your public speaking skills. After you deliver your speech, ask for feedback about the content and organization of your points, the strength of your support material, the wording you used, the effectiveness of your visual aids, and the way you delivered your speech. These comments will help you further polish your delivery.

8. *Complete a final rehearsal.* If you can, arrange for a final run-through in the room where you'll speak (or a close substitute). Use the same visual aids and equipment that you'll use when you face your audience. This rehearsal

FIRE AWAY! HOW TO FIELD TOUGH QUESTIONS GRACEFULLY

It can happen to anyone: You're in the middle of a question-and-answer period when someone asks a question that's especially tough. Maybe you don't know the answer; maybe the question is hostile, or the answer would be embarrassing or revealing. What's the best way to handle such tough questions?

First, do your homework. As you plan your speech, compile a list of possible questions. By anticipating even the toughest questions, you can be prepared with logical, meaty answers and concrete examples to support your answers. This preparation will reduce your nervousness and boost your confidence.

Second, if you're asked an abrasive question, remain calm and composed. Your audience will find you more believable if you act confident and professional. Before you respond, you may want to disarm the question by rephrasing it more objectively. Then you can briefly present your point of view in unemotional language, instead of being drawn into a long or angry debate with your questioner.

Third, avoid giving the impression that you want to run away from a question. If you anticipate being asked questions that you're unqualified to answer, you might start the question period by saying, "Today I will answer questions only related to X, because that is my specialty." You might also refer specific questions to people who are better qualified to answer. Don't use lack of time as an excuse, because your audience will recognize that you're evading the question.

Fourth, be honest when you're asked a question you can't answer. Your audience will understand if you say "I don't know." Then, depending on whether the information is available, you can offer to get the answer later or talk with the questioner after the speech.

When handling audience questions, be prepared, remain calm, and be honest when you don't know the answer.

will give you a more realistic feel for the room and for where your audience will be seated. After this rehearsal, you can make any last-minute adjustments to your speaking outline so that you'll be ready to deliver your speech to your actual audience.

Prepare for Audience Questions

Depending on the type of speech you're delivering, the occasion, and the audience, you may face one more task before you face your audience: preparing for audience questions. Asking for questions can open the door to a dialogue with your listeners. Questions can also serve as feedback, letting you know which points were clear and convincing and which were not. This is your final chance to reinforce your ideas and your credibility, so you'll want to plan carefully.

Think about your audience's needs and interests, and consider what they might want to know that you haven't covered in your speech. In addition, think about questions that listeners might raise to challenge specific points or evidence that you've discussed. Also come up with questions that you want to answer so that you can expand on or emphasize a particular point.

Once you've listed all the questions that you anticipate, dread, or hope for, you'll be able to plan answers for each. If your topic is controversial or complex, you may want to prepare a sheet with specific details that you can consult as you answer. Then you can practice your answers until they're clear and to the point. You'll feel more relaxed and confident because you've done your homework, and your audience will see you as competent and professional. After you've delivered your speech and answered all questions, you'll leave your audience with a positive impression of your public speaking skills.

SUMMARY

Good speech delivery is important for three reasons. First, it helps you build a relationship with your audience. Second, it allows you to share attitudes and feelings. Third, it works with your words to convey your intended meaning. An effective delivery is transparent, not calling attention to itself but allowing the audience to focus on the message. Delivery consists of voice and body language.

When you rehearse and deliver a speech, you can use eight elements of voice: pitch (how high or low your voice sounds), rate (the speed at which you speak), pauses (which give your audience time to consider an idea, signal a shift to a new idea or a new section, and heighten audience anticipation of the next idea), volume (the loudness of your voice), variety (created by changing pitch, rate, pauses, and volume), pronunciation (the ability to say words correctly by making the proper sounds and accenting the correct syllables), articulation (the ability to form the sounds of each word correctly), and dialect (the pattern of vocabulary, grammar, and pronunciation used in a particular region or culture).

You can focus on six elements of body language as you rehearse and deliver your speech: personal appearance (the way you look and dress), eye contact, facial expressions (which help you convey a wide range of emotions and attitudes), gestures (using your hands and arms to enhance the meaning of your words), movements (before, during, and after your speech), and posture (the way you stand as you deliver your speech). You can use eye contact when you deliver your speech to help make a personal connection with your listeners, to build credibility, and to obtain audience feedback.

You can deliver a speech using any of four delivery methods: reading from a manuscript, speaking from a memorized text, using impromptu speaking, or speaking extemporaneously. When you rehearse an extemporaneous speech, you read through your planning outline and prepare the speaking outline. Then you start to practice from the speaking outline, timing yourself to see how your speech fits within the allotted time. After you record your speech and review the tape to pinpoint areas of improvement, you can ask friends or other volunteers to serve as an audience and give you feedback. Once you complete a final rehearsal, you're ready to deliver your speech.

If you'll be answering questions after your speech, you'll want to prepare by thinking about your audience's needs and interests. Also consider what your audience might want to know that you haven't discussed in your speech, and think about whether listeners might ask questions to challenge points or evidence that you've addressed. In addition, think about questions that you want to answer so that you can expand on or emphasize certain points. Then prepare answers for each question on your list, and make up a sheet with support material that you can consult to support your answers.

KEY TERMS

articulation (301)
dialect (302)
impromptu speaking (310)
inflection (298)
pitch (297)
pronunciation (301)
rate (298)

APPLY CRITICAL THINKING

1. Can good pronunciation make up for poor articulation? Can good articulation make up for poor pronunciation? Explain.
2. How might the discrepancy between speaking and listening rates affect listeners' reactions to a speaker's pauses?
3. What body language cues could you use to convey sadness during a speech about the aftermath of an earthquake?
4. What voice cues could you use to convey outrage during a speech about eliminating the death penalty?
5. Can you overuse eye contact? Explain.
6. Would you use the same gestures and movements in front of a small audience that you would in front of a huge crowd? Why?
7. Can you speak extemporaneously if you've memorized the introduction to your speech?

SHARPEN YOUR SKILLS

Individual Exercises

1. Select and analyze a speech from the appendix.

   a. Identify four specific words or phrases that could be enhanced through the effective use of voice. What techniques do you suggest in each case? Why?

   b. Identify four words or phrases that could be enhanced by the effective use of body language. What action do you suggest in each case? Why?

2. Using the speech you selected for exercise 1, prepare a list of five questions that the speaker might expect to be asked. What kind of supporting details should the speaker plan to have available to answer these questions?

3. Concentrate on the elements of voice as you rehearse your next classroom speech.

   a. Determine specific sections where you want to communicate emotion or stress an important point.

   b. Determine how to use your voice to convey meaning in each section, and then mark your speaking outline accordingly.

   c. Rehearse the speech and, if possible, videotape it. Then analyze your delivery to determine where changes are needed. Mark any changes on your speaking outline, and continue with your rehearsal schedule.

   d. After you've delivered the speech to your class, write a one- to two-page report discussing whether the techniques you used had the effect you expected. Suggest any changes that will make your delivery more effective.

4. Observe the body language used in a speech by a classmate or other speaker either in person, on television, or on videotape. Does the body language conflict with the meaning of the words? For any conflicts you identify, suggest how the speaker might change his or her body language to make the nonverbal message consistent with the verbal message.

Group Exercises

5. Team up with two classmates to observe a speaker's delivery and compare your observations.

   a. What method of delivery does the speaker use? Is the method effective?

   b. Note whether the speaker mispronounces any words, and then compare notes with your teammates. Do any words appear on more than one list? What is the correct pronunciation of each word?

   c. What does the speaker's body language suggest about his or her confidence or speech anxiety? Note specific clues that you observed in this speaker's body language. Do any clues appear on more than one list? What changes in body language can you suggest to convey confidence?

6. With another student, choose a speech from the appendix or another source. Take turns reading the speech out loud, first in a monotone with no variety, and then with variations in pitch, rate, pauses, and volume. Comment on how each delivery affects you as a listener and as a speaker. What suggestions can you offer to add variety to the other student's delivery?

Chapter Fifteen

SPEAKING TO INFORM

LEARNING OBJECTIVES

After studying this chapter, you will be able to

1. Explain why speaking to inform is actually teaching.

2. Identify the six major types of informative speaking.

3. Explain the difference between describing an event and describing a process.

4. Outline the challenges you'll face in speaking about concepts.

5. Describe the five most common ways to organize an informative speech.

6. List the two key reasons for using time as the organizing element in an informative speech.

7. List four guidelines for improving the effectiveness of your informative speeches.

UNDERSTANDING YOUR ROLE AS TEACHER

When you give an informative speech, your goal is to give your audience information they either didn't have or didn't fully understand before. The information may be as intangible as a philosophical principle or as practical as the steps needed to repair a bicycle gearshift, but in every informative speech, you plan to teach your audience something. Just as your teachers give you information, you give your audience information. With an informative speech, you can introduce a new topic, explain a difficult topic, intrigue your audience with interesting information, or summarize a large body of knowledge or information.

Informative speaking is one of the most important skills you can have, no matter what your career. Scientists and engineers need to communicate the results of their work to colleagues and managers. Teachers need to communicate information and concepts to their students. Salespeople need to explain products and their benefits. Accountants need to explain tax laws to their clients. The list goes on, and the message is clear: Learn how to inform effectively, and you'll increase your chances of being successful in life (see Exhibit 15.1).

The list of informative speaking subjects is practically endless, but not all subjects are approached in the same manner—and you might even approach the same subject in different ways for different speeches. As you explore the range of possibilities, it will become even more clear that various types of subjects need different approaches in informative speeches. Consider the subject of investing in a mutual fund (a diversified collection of company stocks that people buy shares in rather than buying the individual stocks themselves). Here are six ways you might approach this topic in an informative speech:

1. The risks of putting your faith in a single fund manager
2. What is a mutual fund?
3. The steps involved in investing in mutual funds
4. The day your mutual fund investments dropped 25 percent in value
5. The career of the legendary mutual fund manager Peter Lynch
6. Mutual funds are an investment in free enterprise

Each of these six approaches sounds quite different from the others. The first focuses on an *issue*, the second on an *object*, the third on a *process*, the fourth on an *event*, the fifth on a *person*, and the sixth on a *concept*. All six can be developed into effective speeches about mutual fund investing, but each represents a distinctly different type of informative speech. In some informative speeches, you'll need to use more than one approach. For the speech on investing in mutual funds, you might start with a description

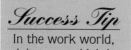

Success Tip
In the work world, doing a good job is only half the battle. You also need communication skills to share information effectively about the job you're doing. Informative speaking is essential.

EXHIBIT 15.1
Why Informative Speaking Is Important for Everyone
Informative speaking is one of the most important career skills you can develop. No matter how good your ideas are, you're not likely to impress colleagues and customers unless you can communicate clearly and concisely.

of mutual funds (an object) before moving on to the steps involved in actually investing (a process). The following sections provide some helpful examples and guidelines for the six types of informative speeches: objects, processes, events, people, and concepts.

Speaking About Issues

Much of the speaking you'll do in this class and in other public forums will be about **issues**, matters of discussion, debate, or dispute. You can get an idea of the range of possible issues to cover in informative speeches by watching or reading news reports. Here are some popular categories of issues for class speeches (for most of these, you'll want to focus your speech on a more specific issue, such as immigration's impact on higher education):

• Career and family conflicts
• Foreign policy
• Grading systems
• Gun control
• Home schooling
• Immigration
• Medical ethics
• Property rights
• Repressed memories
• School prayer
• Sexual harassment
• Unions and strike policies
• Violence in the media

If your assignment is to deliver an informative speech about an issue, make sure you don't slip into persuasive speaking—your job is to present the issue at hand, not to take one side or the other. For example, on the subject of states' rights, you could structure an informative speech to present the cases for and against the transfer of more authority from the federal government to individual state governments.

Specific Purpose
To inform my audience about the debate over states' rights
Central Idea
People in the United States disagree on the issue of governmental balance of power between the states and the federal government, and this debate affects many areas of contemporary public life.

Major Point 1: Opinions in the United States differ about the balance of power between the federal government and the various individual state governments.
Major Point 2: One major camp believes that the federal government has usurped powers belonging to the states and that, in many cases, states can manage government programs more efficiently.

Governor Involved in Scandal

Governor's Foes Launch Smear Campaign

Major Point 3: The major opposing camp believes that the federal government is the constitutionally designated authority in this country and is therefore in a better position to manage programs for the good of the entire country.

Major point 4: The implications of this debate are both profound and pervasive, covering virtually every aspect of public life, from religion to education to crime.

This brief example doesn't take sides or make judgments; that's the role of persuasive speaking, not informative speaking. In fact, maintaining your objectivity can be one of the biggest challenges when speaking about issues. By analyzing news reports about political events or social trends, you can see how difficult it is to maintain the line between reporting the news and sharing your opinion about the news. Compare the coverage of a news event by a conservative news source and a more liberal news source. Whether the difference is in the extent of the coverage or in subtle word choices, you will notice biases here and there (see Exhibit 15.2). The same thing can happen in your speeches.

Speaking About Objects

The next type of informative speaking involves objects. The usual definition of an **object** is something you can see, touch, or otherwise experience through your physical senses. Objects that might serve as topics for a speech include antique cars, artwork, plants, and sports memorabilia. However, some objects are intangible,

impossible to see in the usual sense, such as software (the actual bits and bytes themselves, not the displays you see on your computer), bank accounts, and databases. The techniques for describing these intangible objects are the same as for more tangible objects, so it's helpful to discuss them together. Here are a few questions to ask yourself as you plan speeches about objects:

- *What does your audience really need to know?* Deciding what to put in a speech and what to leave out can be a delicate balancing act when speaking about objects. For most objects, the list of points you could discuss is quite long, ranging from its history and development to the materials and techniques used to make it, to its applications and benefits. Chances are you'll have a more specific purpose in mind, so make sure you focus your information to meet that goal. For instance, a speech on the features to look for in a laptop computer must include a discussion of various types of screen displays available, but it probably doesn't need to include the technical details of each display.
- *How much knowledge can you assume your audience already has?* Of course, how much knowledge your audience needs depends on your audience and the topic you're planning to discuss. A group of experienced computer users will understand most of the basic ideas you'll need to discuss, but a group of computer novices won't. As always, careful audience analysis is a key to success.
- *How does your information relate to what the audience already knows?* By relating new information to something the audience already knows,

you can communicate both more efficiently and more effectively. You can draw these relationships either directly or through analogies. In the case of laptops, for instance, you could emphasize the importance of careful selection by drawing an analogy with selecting a traveling companion: "You wouldn't want a traveling companion who'll start driving you crazy after the first hour, and you won't want a laptop that drives you crazy, either."

- *Will it help to blend in some explanation of process?* Process descriptions are a type of informative speaking all their own, but you can often benefit by including some process description in a speech about an object. If describing a process related to the object will help the audience understand the object better, then by all means include the process.

Using the laptop example, the following brief outline illustrates most of these guidelines:

Specific Purpose
To inform my audience about the points they should look for when buying a laptop computer
Central Idea
The five most important points to consider when selecting a laptop computer are compatibility, memory, display quality, battery life, and weight.

Major Point 1: The need to be compatible with other computers or with networks and other equipment may exclude some choices, so consider this point early.

Major Point 2: Memory capacity (both RAM and disk) affects both what you can do and how quickly you can do it, so although more memory is almost always better, it costs more, too.

Major Point 3: Display quality in laptops varies much more than it does in desktop machines, including considerations such as clarity, update rate, and image size.

Major Point 4: Battery life determines how long you can work while disconnected from the wall outlet, so base your needs on how you'll use your laptop.

Major Point 5: Laptops vary considerably in terms of weight, and the difference of a few pounds is significant if you travel a lot.

This brief example covers quite a few major points, but you can see how all five are directed at the particular purpose established for this speech. The outline doesn't include information on the history or the future of portable computers, on the state of the computer industry, on the technologies behind the computer product itself, or on the advantages and disadvantages of owning a laptop. Those are perfectly acceptable topics for other informative speeches, but not this one.

Speaking About Processes

A **process** is a system or sequence of steps that transforms something into something else. It might be as dramatic as the process of human growth from birth to death, or it might be as straightforward as the business process that transforms a customer order into a shipped product. Processes you might cover in an informative speech can involve people, people interacting with machines, machines themselves, forces of nature, and so on. In some speeches, your goal is to help your audience understand processes that they'll never actually engage in themselves, such as the formation of hurricanes or perhaps the broadcast of wireless data transmissions. In others, your goal will be to help the audience get better at actually performing the process in question. Examples of this type of speech include raising money for a political campaign, preparing a house for painting, and writing a résumé. In other words, process speeches are "how-to" speeches.

Whether it's based on machinery, forces of nature, or actions of people, nearly every process involves five key elements: input, tools or forces, sequence of steps, output, and skills (see Exhibit 15.3). *Input* can range from physical materials to information. *Tools or forces* operate on those inputs in a *sequence of steps* from start to finish, at which point the *output* is produced. If a person is involved in the process, using the tools no doubt involves some *skills* as well.

A speech about process needs to describe these five elements. But because you're asking the audi-

EXHIBIT 15.3
Describing Processes
In a jet engine, fuel and air are converted into forward thrust. In a volcano, magma from the earth's core is converted into a mountain on the earth's surface.

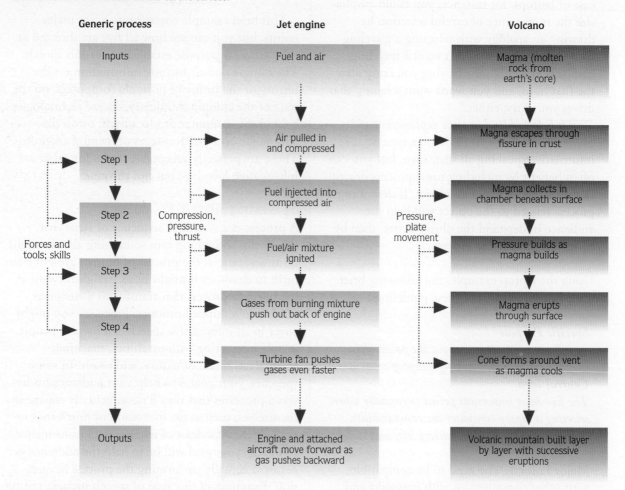

ence to follow a series of steps, make sure you balance details with the big picture. Too many steps, or too much detail in any particular step, can cause your audience to lose track of where they are in the process. You can use several techniques to help your audience follow along:

• *Provide an overview of the entire process first.* You're not plotting a mystery novel here; tell your audience where you're going and the major points along the way. This preview gives them a mental framework for organizing all the details as you present them.
• *If you have many individual steps to cover, group them into a few phases or stages.* Few people can

keep track of 10 or 15 steps, particularly when the steps cover unfamiliar territory. Of course, the phases should be logical, such as "preparation," "assembly," and "painting."
• *Review frequently.* After you've spent time explaining the details of a particular point or step, stand back and remind the audience of where you are in the overall process.
• *Summarize clearly.* Once you've covered the entire process, provide a quick, clear summary that covers just the major steps or high points.
• *Use visual aids.* Process speeches are natural candidates for flowcharts, demonstrations, and other supplementary aids.

The following brief example for a process speech demonstrates several of these guidelines:

Specific Purpose
To inform my audience about the major steps in writing a résumé.
Central Idea
A successful résumé is the result of thorough planning, careful drafting, and painstaking revision and polishing.

Major Point 1: Plan the contents of your résumé.

> **Subpoint A:** Identify the specific objectives for writing your résumé; decide how you want this piece of paper to represent you to potential employers.
> **Subpoint B:** Based on your research of potential employers, list the qualifications each is looking for.
> **Subpoint C:** List your own qualifications, including skills, experience, awards, education, and accomplishments.
> **Subpoint D:** Compare your qualifications with those that employers are looking for, and summarize your strengths and weaknesses.
> **Subpoint E:** Choose a résumé format based on your strengths (perhaps a format that emphasizes education or one that emphasizes practical job skills).

Major Point 2: Draft your résumé.

> **Subpoint A:** Start with the format you've chosen and write the headlines to identify the various sections.
> **Subpoint B:** Jot down the key points you want to cover in each section.
> **Subpoint C:** Draft each section according to those key points, always looking for ways to highlight your strengths.
> **Subpoint D:** Rewrite each section to ensure correct grammar, appropriate style, and clarity.

Major Point 3: Revise and polish your résumé.

> **Subpoint A:** Compare your draft with your objectives; does the résumé seem to accomplish what you want it to accomplish?

> **Subpoint B:** If possible, ask a person experienced in reading résumés to comment on your draft.
> **Subpoint C:** Make any changes required by A or B.
> **Subpoint D:** Ask another person to proofread your résumé.
> **Subpoint E:** Make any final changes required.

This example covers 14 steps in the process of writing a résumé, every one important for creating top-quality résumés. However, 14 steps is too much to cover without some additional organization, so the example groups the steps into three more manageable phases. This allows the audience to worry about steps in smaller groups of just four or five at a time.

Speaking About Events

Events are similar to processes in that both discuss things that happen, but with an event you're less interested in the steps in the process and more interested in the event itself. Of course, an event could be made up of a series of steps that occurred over time. In that case, you could describe the event chronologically, as a process. For example, an informative speech about a wedding could be described as it evolved through time, beginning with its preparation and planning, then how it occurred, and its aftermath. Sometimes it's useful to explore the causes and effects of an event, such as the reasons for massive flooding on the Red River or the effects of reduced government support for basic research (see Exhibit 15.4).

Some events occur over and over again (such as earthquakes, Chinese New Year, and solar eclipses). Other events occur just once, such as the Teapot Dome scandal or the Battle of Tippecanoe. You might also discuss one specific instance of a recurring event, such as the 1989 Loma Prieta earthquake in the San Francisco area. In addition, some events (such as earthquakes and elections) happen rather quickly, whereas others (such as the struggle for civil rights) are spread out over a longer period of time.

Take some time to ponder an event you might choose for a speech. What does it mean in the larger scheme of things? What caused it? If it was

EXHIBIT 15.4

Exploring Causes, Effects, and Meanings Associated with Events

When speaking about a specific event, such as the recent flooding along the Red River, you may want to organize your speech around causes or effects to help your audience understand the event's significance.

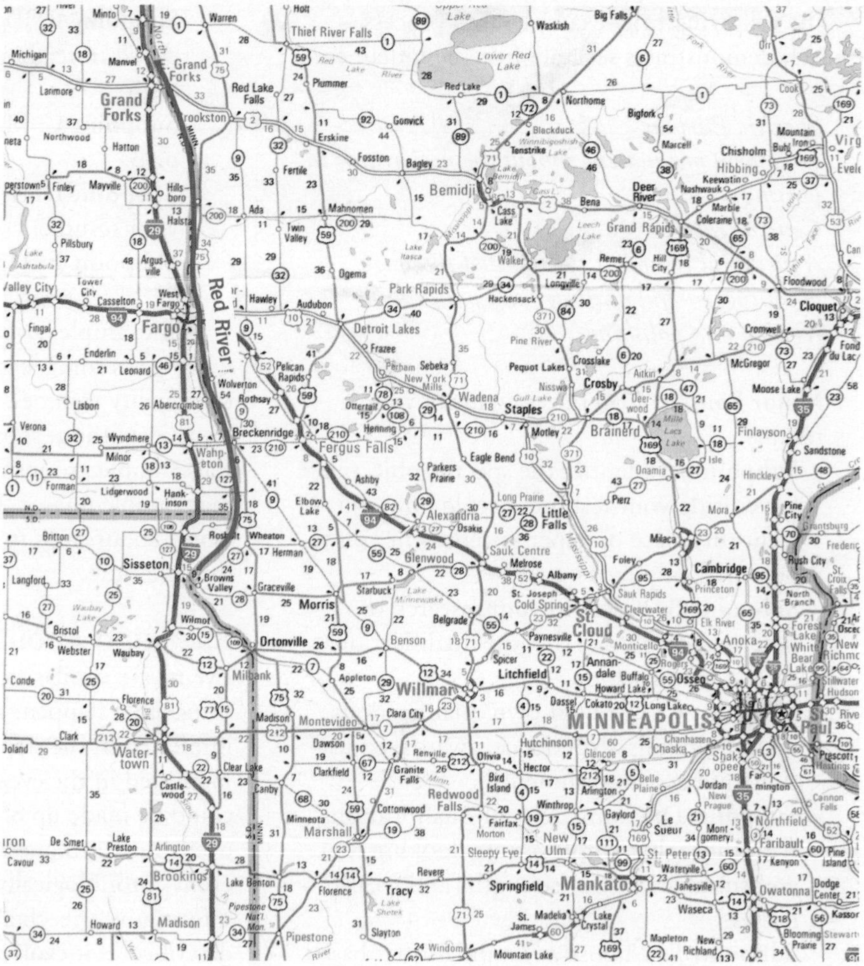

viewed as a negative event, could it have been prevented? You can often go beyond mere descriptions of an event to explore some fresh and interesting angles. For example, the Battle of Tippecanoe was fought in 1811 in Tippecanoe, Indiana, between a U.S. Army force led by future president William Henry Harrison and a group of Native Americans of the Shawnee tribe. What might at first seem like one more fight in a long list of U.S. wars actually has a number of interesting angles to pursue:[1]

- Tippecanoe helped spark a widespread rebellion by Native Americans against white settlers. This could lead to a discussion of the rights of Native Americans versus the rights of white settlers, either in the nineteenth century or today.
- The defeated Shawnee leader Tecumseh saw his plans for a confederation of Indian nations collapse after the battle. This could lead to discussions of how a fragmented Native American resistance couldn't match the larger integrated force of the U.S. Army, or of how,

even today, partnerships and coalitions are often vital for military success.

- Harrison's reputation got a big boost from the battle. In fact, his nickname became "Tippecanoe" and his public image as a man of the new American West played an important part in his successful election to the presidency in 1840. This could lead to a discussion of the role of heroes in our society, how heroes develop, or the role of military experience in shaping the careers of political leaders.

As you can see, it's possible to come up with some interesting approaches to what might otherwise be fairly dry material. Of course, you need to

Success Tip

Don't just describe or explain events and other subjects; ask what they might *mean* to audience members and look for interesting ways to relate those meanings to issues your audience cares about.

DEVELOPING YOUR CREATIVITY

HOW TO PAINT POWERFUL PICTURES THAT BRING YOUR SPEECHES VIVIDLY TO LIFE

It's a recipe for dullness. Take a dry, technical topic, use proper and expected language, and then wrap it all in a formal work environment, and you're almost guaranteed to have a dull informative speech. Those clunking sounds you hear are your listeners' heads hitting the table as you put them to sleep.

It doesn't have to be that way. Even the most technical topics can be spiced up with interesting language, colorful metaphors, and creative analogies. Consider this example:

> The compressor blade assembly maximizes incoming air pressure in order to maximize combustion energy, which in turn maximizes forward thrust.

Now, this may be accurate, and it may communicate exactly what the speaker wants to say, but an hour later the audience is likely to be dumb from all the formality. Try something like this instead:

> We pressurize the air to really fire things up in the combustion chamber and squeeze more power from the engine.

As long as the audience can follow what you're saying, this statement is both faster and more interesting. By eliminating words and phrases that the audience probably doesn't need, and by making the language more active and more colorful, you've made a fairly dull idea easier to listen to.

Of course, you don't want to insult the audience by making things too simple or too silly. You wouldn't say, "Mr. Jet Engine has a big appetite, so we feed him lots of fuel." Moreover, be sure your language doesn't get so colorful that it confuses or offends people. This is particularly important when addressing multicultural and multinational audiences who may not understand the slang or humor you're trying to use.

Even the most difficult technical topics can be discussed with interest and passion.

balance any discussion of the event with a fair discussion of its effects and implications.

Speaking About People

In a sense, people are another type of object when it comes to public speaking. You can describe what they look like, where they can be found, what they do, and so on. Speeches about people do present some special problems and opportunities, including the following:

- *People are best understood in the context of their own time.* You can pick almost any generation or period in history and find people who did something that seems ill-advised by contemporary standards but perhaps not by the standards of the time in which they lived.
- *Nobody's perfect.* This old cliché is important to remember when developing a speech about any human being. From the politician with a history of personal mistakes to the great musician with a history of drug abuse, many notable and important people have less-than-perfect lives. The

question for you as a speaker is to decide whether those imperfections are relevant to your speech. See the brief outline that follows for an example of how to handle this dilemma.

- *People can fill many varied roles.* People are fathers, mothers, sisters, brothers, friends, professionals, voters, and more. Best known for her 1852 novel *Uncle Tom's Cabin,* Harriet Beecher Stowe exposed many readers to the legal, moral, and social issues associated with slavery. However, she was also a wife, a mother, and the daughter of a noted minister whose religion she rejected after the death of her own son. Her other writings included a book that attacked the Calvinist religion and a book that helped fuel the Florida land boom in the late 1800s.[2] In other words, Stowe was much more than the one thing she was most noted for. In fact, some of the most interesting speeches about people concern the aspects of their lives that audiences haven't already heard about many times over.

A preliminary outline for a speech about the legendary jazz/blues singer Billie Holliday illustrates some of the problems and opportunities you encounter when speaking about people:[3]

> *Specific Purpose*
> *To inform my audience about the life and music of Billie Holliday.*
> *Central Idea*
> *Billie Holliday, one of the most famous singers in history, lived a life of both stunning accomplishment and personal tragedy.*

Major Point 1: Billie Holliday was born in Baltimore in 1915 and spent her early years in poverty.

Major Point 2: She moved to New York City in the 1920s and began singing in Harlem nightclubs.

Major Point 3: In 1935, Holliday gained widespread public recognition with her first recording.

Major Point 4: Through the 1940s and 1950s, she sang with a number of prominent orches-

tras and recorded with many famous musicians.

Major Point 5: She died in 1959 from the effects of years of heroin addiction and was in fact under arrest at the time.

What you see here is a life of some definite highs and some definite lows. What should you focus on? Her music? Her rise from poverty? Her trouble with drugs? Her achievements as a black woman in a society dominated at that time by white men? As with most people, Holliday presents many opportunities for a speaker. However, remember that an informative speech doesn't take a position on an issue or pass judgment on a person.

Speaking About Concepts

A **concept** is a general idea about something, usually abstract and intangible. We have a concept of democracy, of personal freedom, and of human rights. Values, theories, principles, and ideas are all kinds of concepts. Some examples include integrity, the theory of evolution, princples of communication, and ideas about alternative lifestyles. Concepts can be challenging to cover in an informative speech because they have no physical form; some aren't even consistently defined from one person to the next.

Concepts themselves exist only in our minds, although the results or ramifications of various concepts can be observed. For example, the physical *object* of a voting booth relates to the *process* of voting, which stems from our *concept* of democracy. You can't see democracy, but you can see its results (see Exhibit 15.5).

When planning a concept speech, you'll probably have to address this issue of intangibility. How can you help your audience visualize something in their minds that they can't see with their eyes? Consider how you might handle concepts such as friendship, the relationship of the individual to the state, the effect of interest-rate changes on the U.S. economy, or fuzzy logic.

The first step is to make sure your specific purpose and central idea statements are clear and precise. If you can narrow them down so that they point in a specific direction, you'll have a better

EXHIBIT 15.5

The Challenge of Speaking About Concepts
Concepts can be difficult to talk about because you don't have the luxury of a physical object to describe. Consider using tangible objects such as people to help illustrate intangible concepts such as democracy or justice.

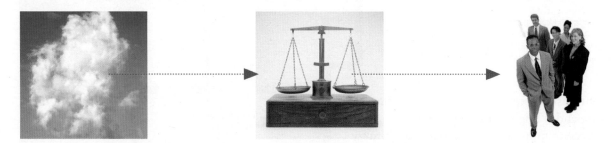

chance of presenting a concept speech your audience can follow. Say you're speaking on the topic of fuzzy logic, which is an alternative to the strictly black/white, yes/no method of logic that has dominated Western thought for centuries. In fuzzy logic, things don't have to be absolutely black or absolutely white; they have degrees of black and degrees of white. Things can be "more right" or "more wrong," not necessarily absolutely right or absolutely wrong.

In other words, fuzzy logic can be a difficult and highly abstract concept to talk about. If you were to plan a speech with the central idea of "informing my audience about the concept of fuzzy logic," you might run into trouble trying to explain something as abstract as a method of thinking. However, if you restricted your central idea to "informing my audience about the ways fuzzy logic is improving such everyday products as dishwashers and vacuum cleaners," you would have a goal that's narrower (and therefore easier to achieve) and that's tied to something your audience members already recognize (appliances).

Consider the fuzzy-logic vacuum cleaner. (Your audience may hate vacuum cleaners, but everybody knows what they are!) A traditional vacuum cleaner is either on or off; you turn it on when you think the carpet is dirty, and you turn it off when you think the carpet is clean. That's traditional yes-or-no logic at work. But what if the carpet in one room is cleaner than the carpet in another room? The standard power setting

Checklist for Selecting the Type of Informative Speech

1. Choose an *issues speech* to handle matters of discussion, debate, or dispute. Be sure to present the concept in a balanced, unbiased manner.

2. Choose an *objects speech* to talk about tangible (e.g., cars) or intangible (e.g., employment) subjects.

3. Choose a *process speech* to describe a system or sequence of steps that transform something into something else. Make sure your audience can keep track of the big picture while you're explaining the details of each step.

4. Choose an *events speech* to describe something that has happened; try to go beyond the event and address interesting implications of the event as well.

5. Choose a *people speech* to describe a person; as with an issues speech, keep your approach fair and unbiased.

6. Choose a *concepts speech* to cover abstract intangibles such as values, theories, principles, and ideas.

EXHIBIT 15.6
Illustrating Tough Concepts
You could explain the complex concept of fuzzy logic by using a simple vacuum cleaner example. Explain that the four rooms in this house need various levels of cleaning for various amounts of time. A traditional vacuum cleaner is either all the way on or all the way off, and it stays on until the operator has gone over the entire room, even if that's not the right amount of cleaning power or the right length of time. A fuzzy logic vacuum thinks in "degrees of clean" and "degrees of dirty" and adjusts itself for each floor condition.

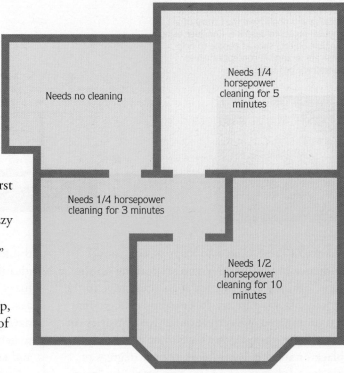

might waste energy by overvacuuming the first room, and it might do a poor job by undervacuuming the second room. With fuzzy logic and special sensors, the vacuum recognizes degrees of "clean" and degrees of "dirty" and adjusts suction power accordingly (see Exhibit 15.6)[4]. See how this process works? Using a common *object* that anyone can grasp, you've explained the exotic, abstract *concept* of fuzzy logic.

ORGANIZING YOUR INFORMATIVE SPEECH

Chapter 9 discusses speech organization in general. This chapter is concerned with choosing a specific structure for your informative speech. Some speeches, such as those dealing with processes, have a fairly obvious structure (sequential). Others have a wide array of structure options. When you choose a structure for an informative speech, you're looking for an organizing framework that will best support your informative goal (to convey information). A key question to ask yourself is "What will my audience find most difficult about this subject?" The answer to that question can help you identify the most effective organization.[5] The five most common informative structures are time, space, category, comparison and contrast, and cause and effect.

By Time

Whenever you need to discuss changes or developments, consider using a time structure.

Historical time structures can be linked to actual dates and times; **sequential time structures** involve a sequence of steps that happen one after another. If you're planning to describe the women's suffrage movement (which led to women in the United States gaining the right to vote), you'll want to anchor your talk with some specific dates. On the other hand, you probably won't need specific times and dates when describing the process involved in the formation of hurricanes. Of course, you may want to focus on the formation of a specific hurricane, in which case, the historical structure would make sense.

Compare the historical time structure used in the following brief sketch with the sequential time structure used in the sketch for the résumé-writing speech earlier in this chapter.[6]

Specific Purpose
To inform my audience about the major events in the history of organized labor in the United States.

Central Idea

Organized labor grew in both size and power from the late eighteenth century up through the 1940s and 1950s, but it has been in decline since then.

Major Point 1: From 1792 to 1929, labor unions grew to be a powerful element in the U.S. economy.

> **Subpoint A:** The first known union in the United States was formed in 1792 in Philadelphia.
>
> **Subpoint B:** Unions for craftworkers gained national status by the 1850s.
>
> **Subpoint C:** By 1880 the Knights of Labor had 700,000 members.
>
> **Subpoint D:** The 1886 Haymarket Riot in Chicago helped turn public opinion about Knights of Labor and labor in general.
>
> **Subpoint E:** By 1890 the new American Federation of Labor (AFL) had become the prominent national union.

Major Point 2: Union membership grew during the 1930s and 1940s but began to drop off during the 1950s.

> **Subpoint A:** The labor movement gained much help from laws passed during Franklin Delano Roosevelt's presidency from 1932 to 1945.
>
> **Subpoint B:** Industrial workers were increasingly organized by the Congress for Industrial Organizations (CIO) from the mid-1930s on.
>
> **Subpoint C:** AFL and CIO merged in 1955.
>
> **Subpoint D:** Disclosure of links to organized crime hurt labor's image in the late 1950s, leading to new regulations from Congress.
>
> **Subpoint E:** Union membership, which had been faltering since the mid-1940s, began to drop off dramatically in the late 1950s.

Major Point 3: Since 1960, membership has continued to decline, and unions are searching for a stronger position in our Information Age economy.

> **Subpoint A:** Although membership continued to decline, unions enjoyed strong political clout up through the 1970s.
>
> **Subpoint B:** Global competition, several presidential administrations less than friendly toward labor, and a rising service economy have continued to hurt industrial labor's position from 1980 on.
>
> **Subpoint C:** Today, labor is trying hard to gain a foothold in the new service- and information-oriented economy.

This sketch mixes some specific events, such as the founding of the first union in 1792 and the Haymarket Riot in 1886, with several trends or events that stretch over many years, such as the period of dominance enjoyed by the AFL from 1890 to 1930. Also, this sketch divides the 13 separate steps into three manageable phases to help the audience keep everything straight. Even with good organization, however, this speech presents quite a few dates for the audience to remember. Some visuals aids would be a big help.

By Space

Another common option for organizing your informative speech is by physical space and the relationships between locations, an approach known as the **space structure**. This technique is appropriate when you want the audience to visualize locations, distances, or arrangements of objects. All of the following topics can be handled nicely with a space structure:

- The battle lines held by both sides at various times during a Civil War battle
- The house design you are presenting in an architecture class
- The best places to visit in London
- The various regions in the human brain
- The design of a new truck

Organizing by space can feel a bit like organizing in sequence because you often step from room to room or place to place when describing something spatially. The key difference is the absence of any meaningful sequence. To build a house, you have to follow certain steps in a definite order (a sequential structure), but to describe a house, you can "move" through it in many different ways (see Exhibit 15.7).

By Category

If your subject matter lacks an obvious time or space dimension, consider a **category structure**, which divides the subject into logical classes or subgroups. This approach can work for a wide variety of informative speeches, although it should be accompanied by a warning label: You run the risk of boring your audience. Both historical and sequential structures, as well as space structures, entail some action. You move through time or space (even if that movement is only implied). With a category structure, however, you have no motion to help make your speech more interesting. You risk sounding like a dictionary, with one entry droning on after another.

Even with this potential drawback, the category structure is the best in many cases and the only choice in some cases. Say that you're developing an informative speech on do-it-yourself automotive maintenance. Your specific purpose is to explain the basic procedures that most drivers can perform on their own cars using simple tools. You might consider using a sequential structure, highlighting the maintenance to be performed at 5,000, 15,000, 25,000, and 50,000 miles. However, you'll probably keep repeating yourself because some of the tasks show up at every mileage interval. Using a space structure doesn't make sense either, because the size and shape of the various car parts aren't what's important. The best option is using a category structure. Here's one way to do it:

Specific Purpose
To inform my audience of the easy maintenance tasks they can perform on their own cars
Central Idea
Car owners with even modest skills and few tools can keep their cars running safer and longer by maintaining the cooling system, checking and changing engine oil, keeping an eye on tires, watching and listening for symptoms of trouble.

Major Point 1: Maintain your cooling system.
    Subpoint A: Check coolant level frequently.
    Subpoint B: Add coolant mix (antifreeze and water) according to owner's manual instructions.
    Subpoint C: Observe temperature light or gauge regularly.
Major Point 2: Check and replace engine oil at regular intervals.
    Subpoint A: Check oil level frequently.
    Subpoint B: Add oil whenever dipstick registers the minimum level.
    Subpoint C: Observe oil-pressure light or gauge regularly.
    Subpoint D: Change oil at manufacturer's recommended mileage interval (or have a professional do it for you).
Major Point 3: Make sure your tires are in good shape.
    Subpoint A: Maintain recommended level of air pressure at all times.
    Subpoint B: Check tires regularly for signs of damage or unusual wear (which can indicate improper air pressure or problems with the suspension system).
Major Point 4: Follow these general tips to save money and increase safety.
    Subpoint A: Look for leaks of any kind under the car.
    Subpoint B: Listen for unusual noises.
    Subpoint C: Look under the hood occasionally; even if you know nothing about the engine, you can still spot leaks, corrosion, loose parts, worn belts, and other potential problems.

You can see that the structure of this informative speech isn't very dynamic. It offers no movement or development for the audience to follow. However, this category structure is workable and logical, so it's the right choice. Remember that you can always spice things up with some interesting visuals.

Another way to keep a category speech interesting is to first talk about the overall significance or urgency of the topic being categorized. In a speech about aging, Katharine Graham, former publisher of the *Washington Post,* planned to talk about four categories of challenges that we all need to face in order to make old age as productive and enjoyable as possible. But rather than launching right into the four types of challenges, she spent the first third of her speech talking about the inevitability of aging and the personal struggles that some of her close friends experienced when trying to come to grips with getting older. (Her audience, the Jewish Council for the Aging, was made up of people who definitely cared about the subject of aging.) Here is an excerpt from her introduction:[7]

> Many years ago my friend Polly Fritchey and I took our sons to Switzerland to ski during spring break from school. We hiked on the mountains while the children schussed down the slopes.
>
> One day Polly and I were crossing a small glacier covered with about an inch of freshly fallen snow. Polly was walking ahead of me, crunching the surface as she went. I said: "Polly, I've been thinking about how to grow old gracefully. I've been studying Averell Harriman and Alice Longworth, who've done it beautifully, and I think I know the answer."
>
> "What is it?" Polly asked.
>
> "You have to read a lot," I replied, "and not drink."
>
> For a while all I heard was the crunch of Polly's steps. Finally she asked, "When do we have to start?"
>
> You can put it off, but eventually there comes a moment when you realize people think of you as old, even if you don't.

By offering this vivid and poignant personal story on the subject of aging, Graham built interest in her topic before discussing the four categories, thereby encouraging her audience to stay with her as she worked through the various points.

By Comparison and Contrast

If the subject of your speech can be related to something else (preferably something the audience already understands), consider using the **comparison-and-contrast structure.** *Comparison* means

EXHIBIT 15.8

Comparison and Contrast
This table concisely compares and contrasts the three types of memory discussed in the brief speech example.

Human Memory

Type	Input	Capacity	Duration
Sensory	Physical stimulation of eyes, ears, nose, and other sensory organs	As much as the sense receptors can hold at one instant	0–2 seconds
Short-term	Neural signals from the sense receptors	Around seven pieces of information	0–30 seconds
Long-term	Information from short-term memory	No known limit	From minutes to years

pointing out the similarities between two or more subjects; *contrast* means pointing out the differences. This structure usually has just two major points, one covering similarities and one covering differences. However, this is not always the best approach, particularly if you have three or more subjects, because it burdens the audience with keeping track of each subject's similarities and differences relative to each other subject's similarities and differences. In these cases, consider organizing by feature or issue, as this brief example does in comparing and contrasting human memory types:[8]

Specific Purpose
To inform my audience about the similarities and differences among the three major types of memory
Central Idea
We have three types of memory: sensory, short-term, and long-term, all of which are similar in some respects but quite different in others.

Major Point 1: The three types of memory differ in their primary function.

Subpoint A: Sensory memory holds data from the outside environment while the mind decides whether or not to act on them (e.g., reading a number from the phone book).

Subpoint B: Short-term memory lets a person work with data (e.g., remembering the number long enough to dial it).

Subpoint C: Long-term memory stores data for future use (e.g., memorizing the number to avoid having to look it up next time).

Major Point 2: The three memory types receive inputs from different sources.

Subpoint A: Sensory memory collects data from the five senses.

Subpoint B: Short-term memory automatically receives data whenever the brain decides to act on sensory input.

Subpoint C: Long-term memory receives information from short-term memory if you actively memorize it or if you are actively interested in it.

Major Point 3: Storage capacity differs among the three memory systems.

Subpoint A: Sensory memory can probably store as much as the senses can feed it, although data disappear from sensory memory instantly if they are not acted on and transferred to short-term memory.

Subpoint B: Short-term memory can store about seven separate pieces of data.

Subpoint C: Long-term memory is almost unlimited.

Major Point 4: Storage time also differs among memory types.

Subpoint A: Sensory memory lasts 0–2 seconds.

Subpoint B: Short-term memory lasts 2–30 seconds.

Subpoint C: Long-term memory can last years.

This speech emphasizes the contrast element of a comparison-and-contrast structure. Its informative goal is to help the audience see how the three types of memory differ in several important ways (see Exhibit 15.8). If the goal were to explain how the

IMPROVING YOUR CRITICAL THINKING

CAUSE AND EFFECT: CAN YOU SUPPORT YOUR CLAIMS?

Say you're preparing a speech on the effect that part-time employment has on a student's academic success. Furthermore, say your research shows that students who have jobs tend to have better grades. Is there a cause-and-effect relationship here? If so, what is it? Consider a few possibilities you could brainstorm from this information:

- Jobs give students better work habits, which lead to higher grades (cause and effect)
- Students with higher grades are more ambitious, so they also want to work while in school (correlation)
- Students who work to pay for tuition don't want to waste their own money, so they try harder in school (cause and effect)
- Students who get good grades need to spend less time on schoolwork so they have more time to pursue part-time jobs (correlation)

With just these four examples, you can see how easy it is to develop all kinds of theories about relationships between two factors (part-time employment and a student's academic success). The truth is, however, you simply cannot tell why students who work part-time get better grades without more information. You may think you have the right answer, or you may have identified a relationship that fits the way you feel about school and work, but you can't prove anything without further research (and you may not be able to prove anything conclusively even then).

Actually *proving* cause-and-effect relationships is difficult in most cases and downright impossible in many others. To prove that one thing causes another, you have to eliminate all other possible causes, and you have to eliminate mere coincidence. So before you start talking about causes and effects in your speeches, make sure you can truly make the claim.

human memory works overall, a sequential structure would probably be more appropriate.

By Cause and Effect

The **cause-and-effect structure** also involves relationships, but in this case you explore why something happens (its causes) and what happens as a result (its effects). You can also reverse the order to explore effects first, then their causes, depending on which side of the relationship you want to emphasize. Causal relationships are sometimes the best way to present informative topics (particularly issue and process topics) because they help the audience see important connections and understand consequences. For an informative speech on the dangers of smoking, for instance, a cause-and-effect structure is the obvious choice because you can use years of scientific research to illustrate the potential effects of smoking.

Proving cause-and-effect relationships to a jury—or dismissing them as coincidence, depending on which side you're on—is one of a trial lawyer's most important public speaking skills.

Chapter 7 discusses the three kinds of relationships that can exist between two factors or two sets of data. A quick review will help you avoid flawed reasoning when using the cause-and-effect structure. If two factors seem to be connected in some way (such as one changes right after the other one changes), you are witnessing either coincidence (no relationship at all), correlation (the two factors seem to move in similar ways but one doesn't cause the other to move), or cause and effect (one factor is driving the other). If you plan to use the cause-and-effect structure for your informative speech, it's your responsibility to make sure you really have a cause and effect relationship on your hands. Moreover, you have to make sure you have the cause and the effect correctly identified. Note how the presentation of ideas flows logically and convincingly in the following brief example:

Specific Purpose
To inform my audience about the cause of the decline of the Chesterton downtown district
Central Idea
The downtown district has been in dramatic decline ever since the new north-end freeway interchange was built three years ago.

Major Point 1: The interchange cut nearly 30 minutes off the drive to the two large malls out near St. Charles, encouraging shoppers to take their business out of the Chesterton city center.

Major Point 2: Downtown retail sales are down 40 percent from three years ago, which led to reduced employment downtown; sales at the two malls increased by a corresponding amount, and interviews with shoppers confirmed our suspicions about where the business went.

Major Point 3: As business dropped off, store owners contributed less to the performing arts center, causing it to cut budgets and eliminate a popular concert series.

Major Point 4: Other cultural attractions (such as art galleries) that rely on the performing arts center for support, promotion, or foot traffic went into economic decline as well.

Major Point 5: With fewer cultural events to attend downtown, fewer people visited restaurants and nightclubs in the area as well.

Major Point 6: The cycle of decline continues today, with declines in one aspect of downtown life triggering declines in another aspect and so on.

This example doesn't base its case on speculation or theory; it starts with solid evidence about driving times and retail sales, and then continues with a series of cause-and-effect relationships that add up to the overall effect of decline in the downtown area. Also, you probably noticed that this speech has a persuasive feel to it, in that it tries to convince the audience that the freeway interchange caused the decline of the downtown district. However, its primary purpose is still to

---

Checklist for Organizing Your Informative Speech

1. Use a *time structure* to organize information that is historical (linked to dates and times) or sequential (related to the order of a series of steps).
2. Use a *space structure* to organize information by physical space or by the relationship between locations.
3. Use a *category structure* to divide information into classes or subgroups.
4. Use a *comparison-and-contrast structure* to highlight similarities or differences.
5. Use a *cause-and-effect structure* to explore why something happens and what happens as a result.

EXHIBIT 15.9
Using Jargon
Jargon helps people in a particular profession communicate with one another efficiently, but it can be a mystery to outsiders.

Professional Jargon

Group	Term	Meaning
Dentists	gingiva	gums
	osseus	bony
	restoration	filling
	autoclave	steam sterilizer
Lawyers	replevins	repossession
	assumpsit	a promise
	curtilage	surrounding grounds and buildings
	panel	jury
	dissent	disagree
1930s Black Musicians	cat	swing player
	chick	girl
	jam	improvise
	riff	musical phrase
	hip	wise, sophisticated
	square	not hip
	too much	great, excellent

inform—to help the audience understand what happened and why.

DEVELOPING EFFECTIVE INFORMATIVE SPEECHES

The first two sections of this chapter described the various types of informative speeches and the choices you have for structuring them. This final section offers some useful advice that can apply to any kind of informative speaking. Follow these guidelines and you'll increase the effectiveness of your informative speeches, regardless of what topic you choose.

Don't Let Vocabulary Get in the Way

Human beings have developed an amazing array of highly specialized professions and other categories of knowledge and information. Next time you have the opportunity, stop and listen to people who work in a specialized field you know little about. Chances are you'll hear all kinds of acronyms, **jargon** (the specialized vocabulary of a particular field or profession), and references to unknown things, people, or principles. They talk that way because it's fast and efficient for them. To you and everyone else outside this field, however, their speech may be incomprehensible (see Exhibit 15.9).

Success Tip
Resist the temptation to show off when giving informative speeches. Your listeners came to fill in the gaps in their knowledge, not to be impressed by how much you know.

Many fields, from law and medicine to advertising and engineering, have vocabularies so specialized that outsiders get lost trying to follow along. It's not that outsiders couldn't learn the vocabulary, it's just that they haven't had the need or the opportunity to do so. Remember this whenever you plan a speech that involves a technical or complex subject. Even in the short amount of time you have to prepare your classroom speeches, you can adapt any unfamiliar vocabulary to your classmates. Choose your words carefully. Avoid unfamiliar terms if they aren't critical to your message. If you have to define and explain a large number of terms for your audience, your speech is probably too complicated.

Give People a Reason to Listen and Learn

Have you ever sat through a lecture that was clear, concise, and delivered with enthusiasm only to realize you haven't learned a thing because you don't care about the topic? The same unfortunate outcome can result from your informative speeches if your audience doesn't have a reason to care about your topic. So informative speeches often need a persuasive introduction. If your audience isn't already inclined to be interested (which is often the case, particularly in your classroom speeches), you need to "sell" your topic first. Tell listeners why the information you're about to convey will help them or at least entertain them in some way. The benefit to your listeners may be economic, spiritual, social, professional, or even merely practical. Carl Ledbetter, president of AT&T Consumer Products, followed this guideline in a speech about the Information Superhighway. In fact, the speech was subtitled "Unmasking the Jargon," and it included this promise within his opening remarks:[9]

> I'm going to try to help you in the next few minutes with some facts about just what this new Information Superhighway is, what it offers you as individuals and as civic and business leaders, and most important, why you should take an active interest in its development. I'll also do it in a way that seeks to unmask the jargon and hyperbole that surround most discussions of this topic.

This introduction appears to have been based on the very reasonable assumption that most everyone in the audience had heard lots of discussion about the Information Superhighway but didn't have a clear idea of its true meaning or benefits. Ledbetter sparked his listeners' interest by promising to help them understand what the Information Superhighway means and why they should care.

Approach Difficult Subjects from Multiple Angles

At one time or another, you've probably been confused by something a teacher said in class, only to have it make perfect sense when someone went over it for you after class. This sort of learning happens all the time when people get a second chance to understand something from another angle. An abstract principle might help one person understand a particular point, whereas a tangible example or different terminology will help another person understand it.

Keep this in mind whenever you need to convey a difficult idea. Don't hesitate to attack it more than once, using all the communication tools at your disposal. Try multiple examples and analogies. Don't be afraid of using simple, clear language, even if it doesn't sound as impressive. In his speech about the Information Superhighway, Ledbetter described "multimedia" as just a "fancy way to say movies with sound."[10] Not only do these everyday terms help communicate clearly, they can also help you build a bond with your audience by letting the air out of overblown language.

Lead People Down a Logical Path

Earlier in this chapter, the brief example about memory mentioned that short-term memory can hold a maximum of seven items for approximately 30 seconds. In other words, nobody will be able to remember all your speech, all at once. You have to take listeners step by step down a logical path so that each point builds on the previous one.

Think about the way you give directions to a couple of friends. You don't rattle off a bunch of random street names and expect them to piece everything together in the right order. You lead them in a logical way, from the first step to the last. The first step gets your friends to the second step, at which point they can forget about the first step—it has served its purpose. Then it's on to the third step, after which they can forget the second, and so on until they reach the final destination.

Good speeches work the same way. The speaker leads the audience, with each point serving the purpose of reaching the next point. This process leads up to the final "destination," which is the successful communication of your central idea.

SAMPLE INFORMATIVE SPEECH

Nikola Tesla: A Light Still Shining

(1) This morning when you flipped on the light, you probably didn't think much about how the electricity to power the bulb got into your room. As long as it works, who cares?

(2) But imagine that a hundred years ago a man told you he could broadcast electric power to you for free, from a single tower on Long Island, New York, *without wires*. In fact, he could send it anywhere in the world. Even today you'd think he was nuts, right? If it could be done, it would have been, wouldn't it? And free? We all know nothing comes free in this world—well, certainly not electricity, a luxury that you and I pretty much take for granted even though it's fairly expensive.

(3) Now suppose I tell you that this man, an inventor named Nikola Tesla, actually built his "free power" tower back around 1901, on 200 acres he bought on Long Island. As a brief look at his career will show, this is just one of the many fascinating accomplishments in the life of this fascinating man. And if you're curious, yes, the heavy metal band Tesla did name itself in the inventor's honor.

(4) Tesla's wooden tower was a 187-foot-tall octagonal pyramid, topped by a 55-ton metal dome almost half a football field in diameter. Below ground, sixteen iron shafts extended 420 feet straight down, where electric currents passing through them could "latch hold" of the earth, as Tesla explained. This arrangement set up the necessary vibration for wireless broadcasts of both information and energy. Nearby, a laboratory stood ready with special equipment designed by Mr. Tesla—some of it never seen before or since.

(5) J. Pierpont Morgan was one of Tesla's financial backers for the project. At first, he only agreed to give Tesla $150,000 in exchange for 50 percent of all of Tesla's patent royalties. That wasn't a bad deal. In 1900 Tesla was widely recognized as the electrical genius who discovered the scientific principles and invented all the mechanisms necessary to create the alternating current (AC) power-distribution system that literally lit up the world. He also invented radio two years before Marconi took the credit, and he invented radio-controlled boats and missiles—what we call robotics.

(6) In fact, over the course of Tesla's very productive life, he filed nearly a thousand patents—for transformers, oscillators, generators, AC motors for every application, x-ray machines, fluorescent light bulbs, solar energy equipment, and many inventions not built in his lifetime.

(7) So when J. P. Morgan saw Tesla's tower taking shape, he decided to invest in it more heavily. Some say he wanted the same kind of fame Tesla had brought to George Westinghouse, who bought Tesla's AC patents when the experts, particularly Edison, were telling the inventor to forget it because AC power would never work.

(8) Tesla promised Morgan that his tower would be able to send speeches, images, music, world news, or government documents to any location around the globe, whether on land or sea. The receivers would be inexpensive, pocket-sized devices, Tesla explained, and he predicted that the tower would generate income up to $25,000 per day. Around his tower, he intended to build a new World City—the locals called it Radio City, but Tesla preferred the name Wardenclyffe.

(9) Now remember—CNN was eight decades away. The greatest application of radio so far had been to send the letter S from England to Newfoundland. The first typewriter had just been invented, and George Eastman was still tinkering with the first cameras. The Daimler automobile was only three years old, and in Kitty Hawk, the Wright brothers had flown successfully for 59 seconds. World travel and long-distance communication were dreams of a future age.

Commentary

This informative speech exemplifies the combined use of a persuasive opening to gain audience attention and an historical time structure to aid comprehension.

(1) To gain attention and interest, the speaker opens with a reference to common experience.

(2) By planting a "what if" in the midst of this shared experience, the speaker hints at the possibility of something that could benefit her listeners personally (a persuasive technique).

(3) Now that the speaker has explained why her audience should care about her subject, she can introduce Tesla directly—a historical figure listeners might have shrugged off as irrelevant to their present lives. The speaker's persuasive introduction "sells" her topic. The speaker also provides a preview of the structure of the speech here (a brief historical look at Tesla's life), as well as an interesting anecdote that connects Tesla with contemporary listeners.

(4) The speaker continues her opening narrative, unfolding it along a chronological structure—and supplying information in a context that makes it interesting.

(5 & 6) When thrown in haphazardly, historical dates and facts can kill a speech, but here they've become part of the story. The speaker is putting Tesla in the context of his time, which is the best way to understand a historical figure, whether famous, infamous, or unknown.

(7) J. P. Morgan's actions are significant because they ultimately affected the potential audience benefit (free energy) that the speaker highlighted in the beginning of her speech.

(8) Having built interest, the speaker can creatively fill in what might have been "boring details," making Tesla and his plans more tangible.

(9) The speaker places her historical subject in perspective, comparing Tesla's vision with contemporary inventions to clarify the importance of Tesla's tower.

(10) But in 1903, Tesla said his World Telegraphy system would be operational within nine months. "I have no doubt that it will prove very efficient in enlightening the masses, particularly in still uncivilized countries," he told reporters. "The entire Earth will be converted into a huge brain, as it were."

(11) Tesla's communication system alone would have speeded up our society's development by almost a hundred years. But a world powered by free energy—that idea may have actually triggered the end of Tesla's financial support.

(12) Apparently Morgan didn't realize Tesla's full intent until just months before the tower's completion. The inventor was planning to send—not only information—but wireless power to factories, ships, planes, and cities, using inventions he had already tested at Colorado Springs with a smaller tower in 1899. Tesla claimed he could reach targets anywhere in the world with pinpoint accuracy, using his knowledge of the electromagnetic forces of the earth and the upper atmosphere to transmit the energy.

(13) To this day, no one fully understands Tesla's intended methodology; he kept many of his most important notes in his head. But physicist Andrea Puharich in 1976 postulated that it probably had more to do with contemporary high-energy physics than nineteenth-century electrical engineering.

(14) As for J. P. Morgan, legend has it that when he confronted Tesla and asked where the meters would be, Tesla replied, "Mr. Morgan, there will be no meters." And that was the end of Tesla's funding. But truly no one knows why the wealthy financier suddenly pulled out of the project. Even though Tesla showed Morgan dozens of designs for the aircraft, automobiles, and electronics his free energy could power—all inventions of the future that would have made Morgan very rich—Morgan refused to spend another cent.

(15) As Tesla's money gradually ran out, he could no longer pay his construction workers. Before the inventor packed up and returned to his lab in New York City, he managed just one demonstration for the local community: a shower of thunderbolts hundreds of feet long. However, Tesla's power tower never became fully operational.

(16) The inventor must have been frustrated, but he still had a wealth of ideas. Every year Tesla gave spectacular demonstrations and descriptions of what his inventions could do, but he was never again able to attract the investors he needed to pursue his most important ideas.

(17) In 1915 the Wardenclyffe property was deeded to the Waldorf-Astoria to pay off Tesla's hotel debts, and in 1917 the tower was torn down—some say for scrap; others say because it was a security threat during World War I. Tesla died a poor man in 1943, but he left the world much richer than it had been when he came into it in 1856, born to Serbian parents in a small Croatian village.

(18) As he wrote in a paper titled, "The Problem of Increasing Human Energy," "The scientific man does not aim at an immediate result. He does not expect that his advanced ideas will be readily taken up. His work is like that of the planter—for the future. His duty is to lay the foundation for those who are to come, and point the way."

(19) Point, he did. Physicist Niels Bohr said that "Tesla's ingenious invention of the (AC) polyphase system, as well as his exploration of the amazing phenomenon of high frequency oscillations, were the basis for developing completely new conditions for industry and radio communication, and had a profound influence upon the whole civilization."

(20) World War II radar inventions fulfilled a vision Tesla described decades before. Today, Japan's bullet trains borrow from Tesla's work with electromagnetism. And our stereos, televisions, and other electronic equipment would not work without his high-frequency transformer, known as the Tesla coil.

(21) But that's just the beginning. Every year the International Tesla Society in Colorado Springs holds a symposium at which inventors and research scientists from around the world compare notes about the latest developments of Tesla

(10) The quotation gives further insight into Tesla's character.

(11) By hinting at what's to come, the speaker plants a new reason to pay attention.

(12) Because of the scientific nature of Tesla's work, this speech could have easily bogged down in techno-speak; However, the speaker chose simple language and descriptions that any nonscientist can comprehend. (If she were speaking to a scientific symposium, she would have used more sophisticated terminology.)

(13) Again, a contemporary comparison adds perspective.

(14) The speaker maintains her informative purpose and sidesteps controversy by reporting both the common "legend" about Morgan's motives and the viewpoint that no one knows for sure what Morgan's motivations were.

(15 & 16) The speaker supplies additional facts about Tesla's accomplishments.

(17) Again, the speaker demonstrates how to handle the conflicting or controversial information that often turns up when researching a historical figure—that is, report differing perspectives fairly, and avoid taking sides. Also, the speaker has left the most common, "encyclopedia" information for last.

(18) This memorable quote adds another perspective from which to view Nikola Tesla.

(19) By quoting a credible, recognizable figure (Niels Bohr), the speaker supplies yet another perspective of Tesla, thus approaching a difficult subject from multiple angles.

(20) The speaker brings her subject into the lives of her listeners by reviewing the contemporary applications of Tesla's inventions.

(21) In preparation for the close, the speaker describes the current work that makes this historical figure important today.

technology. One hot topic is a joint project of the Navy, Air Force, University of Alaska, and ARCO oil company to build the equipment necessary to shoot radio-frequency energy into the upper atmosphere. ARCO's patents all refer back to Tesla's patent notes from the turn of the last century.

(22) Now, nearly a hundred years have passed since Tesla built his wireless power tower at Wardenclyffe. So far, no one has duplicated its design or fulfilled its purpose. We're still paying a premium for our gasoline, our electricity, our plane tickets, and the energy costs of manufactured goods.

(23) But imagine what could happen if we pursued Tesla's notion of a world where energy is freely extracted from natural sources and distributed without fees. What might we achieve with this freedom? Perhaps at the turn of *this* century, we'll be ready for Tesla's power tower.

(22 & 23) To close on a note of high interest, and to bring the speech full circle, she hints that Tesla's dream of supplying free energy to the world may yet come to pass.

Bibliography

Begich, Nick. "New Uses of Tesla Technologies for Global Control," *Extraordinary Science,* January/February/March 1995, 15–24.

D'Alto, Nick. "Edison, Tesla, and the Battle of the Currents," *Odyssey,* February 2002, 20.

D'Alto, Nick. "More Tesla/Edison Inventions That Changed the World," *Odyssey,* February 2002, 22.

Dommermuth-Costa, Carol. *Nikola Tesla: A Spark of Genius.* Minneapolis, Minn.: Lerner Publications Company, 1994.

Johnson, Jeff. "'Extraordinary Science' and the Strange Legacy of Nikola Tesla," *Skeptical Inquirer,* Summer 1994, 366–377.

Kline, Ronald. "Reconstructing Tesla," *Scientific American,* April 1997, 108.

Lake, Shawn. "Nikola Tesla, Inventor," *Cricket,* October 2002, 55.

Lange, Larry. "Tesla's Legacy Continues to Electrify Engineers," *Electronic Engineering Times,* July 13, 1998, p. 153.

Santo, Brian. "'Wizard' Traces Life and Times of Nikola Tesla," *Electronic Engineering Times,* April 17, 1997, 116.

"Tesla Was Right," *America's Network,* June 1, 2002, 184.

Tesla, Nikola. "The Problem of Increasing Human Energy," *The Century Illustrated Monthly Magazine,* June 1900, 175–211.

Tesla, Nikola, and David Hatcher Childress. *The Fantastic Inventions of Nikola Tesla.* Kempton, Ill.: Adventures Unlimited Press, 1993.

Tesla, Nikola. *My Inventions.* Williston, Vt.: Hart Brothers, 1982.

SUMMARY

Informative speaking is one of the most important personal and professional skills you can develop. Many careers, in fact, require effective informative presentations, and the better you are at presenting information, the better your chances of success. You'll probably have the opportunity to present a variety of subjects in many different forums, from schoolboard meetings to company training sessions.

After you've chosen (or been assigned) an informative speech topic, take a minute to analyze it. The nature of the topic can have a big impact on how you approach it. Informative topics break down into six basic speech types: issues, objects, processes, events, people, and concepts. First, identify which category your topic falls into, then study the particular nature of that category. With an informative speech about an issue, for instance, one of the most important things to keep in mind as you research and prepare is that you're making an informative speech, not a persuasive speech. Your job is to help the audience understand the two or more sides to the issue at hand, not to convince them that one side is right and the other is wrong. Here's how you can stay clear on the difference: If you're trying to change what people *know,* it's an informative speech; if you're trying to change how they *feel,* what they *believe,* or how they *behave,* it's a persuasive speech.

When you choose an organizational structure, you identify the strongest dimension or attribute in your topic, around which you'll build your message. Five of the most common informative structures are time, space, category, comparison and contrast, and cause and effect. Historical and sequential time structures work well for narratives and processes. Space structures work well when you want to relate things or locations by distance or direction. Category structures involve grouping subtopics according to some logical classification scheme other than time or space, such as color, age, price, importance, and so on. Comparison-and-contrast structures are good to use when you need to draw similarities and differences between two or more subjects, particularly when the audience is already familiar with one subject and you can introduce a new subject by comparing and contrasting it with the one they know. The cause-and-effect structure works in either direction, either starting with an effect and identifying its cause(s), or starting with a cause and showing the effects it's likely to have.

Four important guidelines can improve your informative speeches. First, make sure the words you choose work *for* you and not *against* you. Use clear, simple language that is colorful enough and interesting enough to keep the audience's attention. Second, make sure people care about the information you're about to give. You may have to engage in some persuasive speaking in your introduction to convince people that they'll benefit from paying attention to the informative part of your speech. Third, if you're trying to convey an unusual or complex subject, approach it from more than one angle using multiple examples, analogies, and explanations. Fourth, and perhaps most important, make sure your message is constructed in a logical manner that flows sensibly from one point to the next.

KEY TERMS

category structure (330)
cause-and-effect structure (333)
comparison-and-contrast structure (331)
concept (327)
events (323)
historical time structures (328)
issues (319)
jargon (335)
object (320)
process (321)
sequential time structures (328)
space structure (329)

APPLY CRITICAL THINKING

1. When you present an informative speech, you are, in a way, persuading the audience to listen to and accept your information. Is all informative speaking, therefore, persuasive? Explain your answer.

2. Would you agree with the claim that events are just "one-step processes"? Why or why not?

3. Why is a bank account considered an object?

4. What's wrong with an informative speech outline that has 12 major points?

5. How can hurricanes be considered processes?

6. Why are concepts usually harder to describe than objects?

7. Why are historical and sequential structures said to have a "plot"?

SHARPEN YOUR SKILLS

Individual Exercises

1. Assume you're writing an informative speech on the issue of ozone depletion in the atmosphere. Your central idea is this: "Most studies of ozone depletion have raised concerns about its effects on the Earth's atmosphere, although not everyone agrees it is a problem." Which organizational structure would you choose? Why?

2. Which of the six major types of informative speeches best fits each of the following topics?

    a. Credit card fraud

    b. Ways to clean up your credit record

    c. The role of private credit unions

    d. The risks of overextending yourself on credit card debt

3. For a historical process, such as the European colonization of North and South America, would you choose a historical time structure or a sequential time structure? Why?

4. Which of the following things do you think you know the cause(s) of? Could you prove your assertion?

    a. Gridlock in Congress

    b. Urban violence

    c. Illegal immigration

    d. Differences between the ethnic composition of the U.S. prison population and the composition of the overall population

Group Exercises

5. In a group of six students, divide into three pairs. You're going to "compete" to find the best way to organize a speech about the most recent presidential election. One team will create an outline using a time structure, another will outline using a comparison-and-contrast structure, and the third will use the cause-and-effect structure. The issue you're trying to inform an audience about is the low voter turnout. Which of the three outlines promises to deliver the most compelling and informative speech?

6. Competing with three or four other students, see who can create the most effective description of the process of hitting a tennis ball or a baseball. Why does the best description seem to outshine the others?

Chapter Sixteen

SPEAKING TO PERSUADE

LEARNING OBJECTIVES

After studying this chapter, you will be able to

1. Relate persuasive speaking to change.

2. List the three major types of persuasive messages.

3. Differentiate the four types of persuasive goals.

4. Discuss the importance of motivation in persuasive speaking.

5. Explain the difficulty in using public needs to motivate people.

6. Compare the uses of positive and negative motivation.

7. Describe the four negative reactions that audiences can have to persuasive speeches.

UNDERSTANDING THE CHALLENGE OF PERSUASION

How many times in an average week does somebody try to persuade you? Hundreds of advertising messages, from billboards to product placements in television shows and movies, try to convince you to buy something. Activists want you to attend rallies or write letters. Friends ask you for help or invite you to parties. Politicians on the nightly news want you to think or vote a certain way. Charities call on the phone for donations. Instructors encourage you to study. People ask you to dance or ask you for a date. The list is almost endless (see Exhibit 16.1).

Now, compare the number of persuasive appeals you receive with the number you actually respond to. Only a small fraction of the appeals you receive have any effect. You wouldn't have enough time or money to respond to all those appeals, even if you wanted to—and you don't want to respond to most of them. Disagreement and persuasion are two sides of the same coin; if there were no disagreements, there would be no need for persuasion.

Your own experience as a receiver of persuasive messages has prepared you for the most important lesson to learn about persuasive speaking: It is extremely difficult to persuade people to change. In fact, most of the time, persuasion simply doesn't work. People spend years developing and solidifying their values, beliefs, attitudes, and behaviors. Did you ever complain that your parents seemed set in their ways and didn't want to change or listen to new ideas? Well, it's not just your parents. *All* human beings are that way, to one degree or another. (This is not necessarily bad, either; think how crazy life would be if you did respond to every persuasive appeal you received!)

Given that persuasion is difficult and your chances of success rather low, the advice you've heard throughout this course about preparing thoroughly and understanding your audience is now more important than ever. The following section takes another look at audience analysis, exploring three factors about listeners that are particularly important to know before delivering a persuasive speech. After this discussion, you'll learn about the three types of persuasive claims and the four types of persuasive goals.

> *Success Tip*
>
> Remember that the purpose of persuasive speaking is to bring about change; focus all your efforts toward that goal.

Audience Analysis for Persuasive Speeches

Chapter 6 introduced you to the basics of audience analysis, covering age, attitudes, group affiliation, and other important factors. When you're preparing a persuasive speech, ask yourself three additional questions about your audience:

1. Are they friendly or hostile toward my position? (What's their general attitude toward my topic?)

EXHIBIT 16.1
Persuasive Communication Comes in Many Forms
These women are engaged in one of the most common forms of persuasive communication, personal selling.

2. How much do they know about the subject? (Are they well informed, vaguely informed, uninformed, or misinformed?)
3. How much do they care about it? (To what degree are they likely to have their egos and personal values tied up in the subject?)

The technique of decentering, described in Chapter 6 as the ability to put yourself in the place of your listeners, is an important tool to use here. If you want to persuade people to change, you have to understand where they are before they hear your speech.[1]

The third question concerns **ego involvement**, which is a measure of how closely an issue relates to a person's long-term values.[2] For example, someone who places a high value on individual freedom might be highly ego involved with such issues as gun ownership, censorship, and property rights. Of course, two people can have high ego involvement on the same issue—with totally opposite opinions or beliefs. Someone who has spent time and money to become a member of Handgun Control is probably ego involved on the issue of gun ownership, and so is the person who has spent time and money to join the National Rifle Association. The issue of gun ownership is tied closely to each person's values.

Whatever side they are on, ego-involved listeners are hard to persuade, and one of the reasons is that as soon as you begin to state your position, they start thinking up arguments against it. In fact, it's not uncommon for ego-involved listeners to end up even further away from your position as a result of your speech because they spend the time during your speech silently reinforcing their own positions.[3]

Looking at these three questions, people who are (1) hostile to your position, (2) well informed about the subject, and (3) highly ego involved are the most difficult to persuade.[4] The best you can hope for in most cases like this is to get people to stop and think about the issue. How much persuasion do you think occurs when two opposing groups of protesters meet in the street and start yelling at each other? Probably none at all; in fact, the confrontation probably *strengthens* each side's position. In contrast, a calm discussion might lead some people to at least consider the other side's position.

Speaking to an audience that is hostile, well informed, and ego involved calls for a particular kind of persuasive message. The **two-sided refutational message** considers both sides of an issue, then refutes the side the speaker doesn't agree with. The two-sided approach is the most effective way to persuade a hostile, well-informed, ego-involved listener. The **one-sided message**, in which you present only your side of the story, is less effective with such listeners. The **two-sided nonrefutational message**, in which you present both sides but don't refute the side you oppose, is the least effective of all.[5]

The Three Types of Persuasive Claims

When you deliver a persuasive speech, you are making a *claim* about something. You may be trying to convince people that you've discovered a new way to generate electricity, or you might be trying to convince people that skateboarding should be illegal on city sidewalks. Most of the claims you'll make fall into three categories: facts, values, and policies.[6]

Claims of Fact

When you try to convince an audience that something exists or that something is a certain way, you're making a **claim of fact**. In other words, you are trying to change what people believe to be true. Claims of fact can be the core of a persuasive message, but they are often used to support other claims as well. In the following speech about the potential dangers of milk fortified with additives, the student made a claim of fact about the danger of milk that contains too much vitamin D.[7]

> Let's examine the first possible problem with consuming fortified milk, that of overfortification with vitamin D, and let us consider the cases of three Massachusetts residents who were fooled by the information on the label. We could consider the case of a 72-year-old woman diagnosed by the Mayo Medical Center with anorexia and constipation in March of 1990. Or we could consider the case of a 15-month-old girl, diagnosed . . . with failure to thrive, anorexia, constipation, irritability, and vomiting. Or . . . the case of an 82-year-old man who was diagnosed with weakness, fatigue, a change in mental status, and weight loss. All three of these victims, according to the April 30, 1992 *Washington Post*, suffered from vitamin D intoxication. While this may sound frightening, the fact that they represent only 3 of the 12,000 households that were at risk of vitamin D intoxication due to a local dairy is shocking. . . . this dairy was found to contain vitamin D levels from near zero to 580 times the recommended amount.

In this instance, the speaker is asking you to believe several facts. She outlines the facts and cites credible sources. Most reasonable people would accept the claim of fact here, considering the prestige of both the *Washington Post* and the Mayo Medical Center.

When you're planning a speech that involves a claim of fact, make sure you distinguish facts from inferences. As you'll recall from Chapter 7, facts are pieces of data that you can prove directly, such as the hospital cases involving vitamin D intoxication cited above. Inferences, in contrast, are conclusions based on data. When making a claim of inference, you not only have to persuade the audience to believe your facts, you also have to convince them that you used acceptable reasoning to move from those facts to your conclusion. Trying to convince an audience that three people suffered from ill effects of vitamin D intoxication involves a claim of fact. Taking the next step and trying to convince listeners that vitamin D intoxication is a widespread problem involves a claim of inference. Are three cases in a country of 250 million people significant? Had the speaker wanted to make such a claim in this case, she would've needed more evidence.

Claims of Value

When you try to persuade an audience that something is good, bad, ugly, beautiful, right or wrong, you're making a **claim of value**. Claims of value range from lectures on art to sermons on morality. Although they may sound like personal opinions at times, effective claims of value are usually based on a set of underlying principles that can be examined and discussed. You may not get universal agreement, of course, but at least you can point to a system of values as the basis for your argument.

Say you're planning a speech to criticize contemporary urban architecture. One of your complaints is that too many high-rise buildings create palatial offices and apartments high above the city while leaving traffic jams, pedestrian hazards, and soulless concrete walls at the street level. You have more than a simple case of personal opinion here. You can argue that such buildings are benefiting a few people while alienating many people. A concern for the well-being of many, the common good, may be a principle the audience agrees with or will at least consider.

In a speech on transracial adoption, one student confronted the bias many adoption agencies and social workers have against placing a child of one race with adoptive parents of a different race. Rather than leaving the argument at the superficial level of personal opinion, she dug down to the values that do (or at least should, she argued) drive adoption decisions:[8]

> Contrary to these opinions, there are documented studies that prove transracial adoption to be beneficial. For example . . . a 20-year study done on black adoptees placed in white homes found that they "overwhelmingly reported that they love their white parents, have high self-esteem, and feel black." . . . The goal of transracial adoption is not to replace one culture with another, but to provide homes for children who do not have any.

By citing this and other studies, the speaker tried to convince the audience that transracial adoption is good for adopted children, and she made it clear that the overriding principle in these decisions should be what is best for the children. In other words, the speaker tried to move the argument from a question of race to a question of children's well-being, which is the value she holds to be more important in this issue. Prioritizing potentially competing values is an important part of defending a claim of value.[9]

Claims of Policy

With a **claim of policy**, you try to convince an audience of what should be. Many of your persuasive speeches, both during college and after, are going to fall in this category. Whether you're trying to convince the U.S. Congress to pass a landmark piece of legislation or just convince your local bicycling club to change its bylaws, you're advocating a change in policy. The following brief sketch outlines a speech to a campus ski club, pushing for a change in membership qualifications.

Specific Purpose
To convince club members that nonskiers should be allowed to join the Ski Club

Central Idea
Our restrictive membership requirements are illogical and financially unsound.

Major Point 1: Club membership has remained at the current level for the last five years.
Major Point 2: Most of the club's operating expenses come from members' dues.
Major Point 3: Expenses over the last five years have steadily increased.
  Subpoint A: Expenses are not proportional to membership count.
  Subpoint B: Most expenses are relatively fixed, or depend on things other than the number of members.
  Subpoint C: Increasing membership would increase income without an equivalent increase in expenses.
Major Point 4: Nonskiers can contribute to the club as well as learn from current members.
Major Point 5: A number of current members either do not ski or are very inexperienced.
  Subpoint A: They know how to ski but are not currently active.
  Subpoint B: How can we reject someone who wants to learn how to ski while we still maintain members who no longer ski?

The speaker in this case has laid out a logical argument for a change in policy. The presentation starts with an explanation of why the organization has a financial problem, then continues with a solution (allowing nonskiers to join). The last major point further emphasizes the insupportable nature of the status quo. You'll notice that this is a one-sided message. If the speaker knew the audience was hostile to the idea of extending membership to nonskiers, the persuasive appeal could be strengthened by considering, then refuting or disproving, the opposing viewpoints. You'll learn more about refutational speeches in Chapter 17.

The Four Types of Persuasive Goals
The three types of claims focus on the content of your message. To deliver those messages, you have

EXHIBIT 16.2
Claims vs. Goals
The three types of claims can be used to achieve four different types of persuasive goals. Here are some brief examples.

TYPE OF GOAL	TYPE OF MESSAGE		
	Claims of fact or inference ("What is")	Claims of value ("What is good/bad")	Claims of policy ("What should be")
To change or reinforce **values**	We are all influenced by the society in which we live.	Social responsibility is more important than individual freedoms.	We should respect others' rights to make their own choices in life.
To change or reinforce **belief**	Tobacco usage leads to numerous health problems.	People who care about themselves and others won't smoke.	Smoking should be banned in public buildings.
To change or reinforce **attitude**	Parents have a profound influence on the lives of children.	Children's moral and physical heath are important to society.	We should all take our parental responsibilities more seriously.
To change or reinforce **behavior**	If we don't increase tuition, we'll have to cut arts programs next year.	Premarital sex is immoral; therefore, you should wait until you're married.	We should pass a resolution requiring students to wear uniforms.

to change something in your listeners' heads or hearts. (Or, if your goal is to prevent change, you need to reinforce something in your listeners' heads or hearts.) The four attributes about your audience that you can attempt to change or reinforce through persuasion are their values, beliefs, attitudes, and behaviors. As with the various types of claims, you'll often attempt more than one persuasive goal in a single speech, as you build your case step by step. Exhibit 16.2 shows some examples of combining message-centered claims (facts, values, and policies) and audience-centered goals (values, beliefs, attitudes, and behaviors).

Changing or Reinforcing Values

As you read in Chapter 3, **values** are our ideas about what is right or wrong, important or unimportant. Values are more deeply seated and harder to change than attitudes or beliefs. Our values determine our positions on sensitive issues, such as gun control or states' rights versus federal jurisdiction. Many politicians claim to have "strong family values," hoping to appeal to voters. Values are debated often and at great length, but only rarely does a person change from one side to the other based on debates and speeches. Values bring our emotions into play because they involve

things we care about deeply. People often cannot discuss values rationally because of their emotional involvement. Consider the issue of abortion. We rarely hear calm, rational debate about it, but we often see clinics picketed by people on both sides of the issue who are screaming at each other.

Because values are so deep-seated and often difficult to change, it's important to set realistic goals for any persuasive speech that deals with values. On the more controversial religious, political, and social issues, you probably won't change an audience's values with a single speech. However, you can open the door to change by giving your audience things to think about. People may adopt or fail to adopt certain values because of their environment or because they haven't encountered any compelling evidence contrary to their own experiences. City dwellers may have a different view of gun ownership and gun-related crimes than someone from a rural environment who has grown up with longstanding traditions of gun ownership and hunting.

Changing or Reinforcing Beliefs

Beliefs are what we think is true or false, based on knowledge and experience. These beliefs might be the result of our own experience, or we might acquire them from other people (parents, friends, teachers, religious organizations). If you want to change someone's beliefs, you'll need compelling evidence to counteract your audience's previous experiences or teachings. You must convince audience members that what they thought was true really isn't and that what you're telling them is actually the truth. On the other hand, if you want your audience to continue believing what they now believe, you have to offer evidence that counters other attempts to change your listeners' minds. As you might expect, evidence that is backed up with a complete citation of the source is usually more persuasive than facts that you just present with no support.[10]

Because our beliefs are based on what we think are facts, it generally takes facts (or at least strong evidence) to make us change our beliefs. This reluctance to change is one reason attorneys screen jury candidates so thoroughly. When a juror has no strong beliefs about the crime or the case under consideration, attorneys can focus on persuading that juror to form an opinion. When a juror has strong beliefs, attorneys must first persuade the juror that those beliefs are wrong.

Changing or Reinforcing Attitudes

Attitudes are psychological responses we have after evaluating a person, object, concept, or other entity.[11] Attitudes are usually expressed by feelings, such as like or dislike, and can range from favorable to neutral to hostile. If you respect property and value honesty, your attitude toward a thief is likely to be hostile. If you also think it's good to help the unfortunate, your attitude toward a Robin Hood (who steals from the rich to give to the poor) is probably more ambiguous.

As you would expect, you should consider changing the content and flavor of your speech according to your analysis of the audience's attitude toward your topic. If you were addressing a group of political conservatives, for instance, your speech about censoring the Internet might be quite different from the speech you would give if you were addressing a group of liberals.

The first sketch is aimed at a conservative audience, who would probably like to minimize new government regulations. The second sketch is aimed at a more liberal audience, who would likely be more concerned with the loss of freedom of speech. The topic, general purpose, and specific purpose are the same, but different main points are used to focus audience attention on different parts of the problem. The idea is to get your audience to pay attention to the part of the problem about which they're most likely to agree with you. Also, listeners are more likely to remember information that support their own attitudes. By presenting content in a way that is compatible with their attitudes, you'll increase the amount of information they'll retain.[12] (Of course, it would be unethical to misrepresent your message just to accomplish this.)

Specific Purpose
Persuade the audience that access to the Internet, not the content of the Internet, should be regulated

Central Idea
We all want to limit children from having access to pornography and other adult information available on the Internet. Rather than pass new regulations, we should apply existing regulations (limiting minors' access to books and movies) to the Internet.

Major Point 1: All communication media can be used for pornography, libel, and fraud.
  Subpoint A: Regulations are already in place to cover other media, such as books and movies.
  Subpoint B: Rather than pass new legislation, just apply existing regulations to this new medium, controlling access rather than regulating content.

Major Point 2: No one wants children exposed to pornography.

Major Point 3: The Internet issue is not a new problem but rather a new technology; the solution should be technological.

Major Point 4: A technological solution exists.
  Subpoint A: Software could be modified to require a password for access.
  Subpoint B: Parents could have the option of completely blocking information *at the user level,* thus protecting the individual without limiting the content.

EXHIBIT 16.3
Choosing Facts or Emotions
Many topics can be addressed through both factual and emotional appeals; the specific purpose of your speech and your knowledge of the audience help determine the right choice.

Topic	Factual appeal	Emotional appeal
Education funding	Statistics on government loan programs	Story about person who dreamed of going to college but couldn't afford it
College drinking	Testimony from students about their consumption habits	Headline about death from alcohol poisoning during fraternity hazing
Responsible pet ownership	Facts about numbers and types of abandoned pets in the United States	Story about a particular mistreated animal, complete with the animal's name and lovable personality traits
Economics	Data on international trade balances	Soup lines in the Great Depression

Specific Purpose
Persuade the audience that access to the Internet, not the content of the Internet, should be regulated

Central Idea
We all want to limit children from having access to pornography and other adult information available on the Internet. Rather than pass new regulations, we should apply existing regulations (limiting minor's access to books and movies) to the Internet.

Major Point 1: One of the main attractions of the Internet is the free flow of ideas and information among individuals all over the world.
Major Point 2: Imposing any kind of censorship sets a dangerous precedent for other communication media.
Major Point 3: No one wants children exposed to pornography.
Major Point 4: This is a technology problem, for which there is a technological solution.
   Subpoint A: Online service providers should provide software that requires a password to completely block information at the user level.
   Subpoint B: This will limit access to the Internet where necessary or desired but won't restrict use for others.

Note the variety of claims employed in the two brief outlines. Claims of fact and claims of value are used to build up the speaker's ultimate message, which is a claim of policy.

Because attitudes are often based more on feelings than on facts, they might be more easily changed by appealing to your audience's emotions (see Exhibit 16.3). Anecdotes and stories about life experiences could be useful. The story of a single teenage mother struggling for an education so that she can support her family might change someone's negative attitude toward welfare recipients.

Changing or Reinforcing Behavior
Behavior is what people do, how they act. However, before people act, everything they see, read, or hear is filtered through a lifelong collection of beliefs, attitudes, and values. Often, behavior can be modified temporarily, but in order to make a lasting change in behavior, you usually have to change the audience's beliefs, attitudes, or values (see Exhibit 16.4). Of course, you aren't always concerned with long-term changes in behavior. One of the biggest arenas for public speaking in this country is political campaigning. Candidates are concerned primarily with how you'll act a few weeks from now on election day, not how you'll behave a year or five years from now.

Because most of us like to think that our behaviors reflect our beliefs and our values, an effective way to change people's behavior is to show that their current behavior does not support their beliefs or values. Show how a different behavior is more consistent with their beliefs and values, in other words. Clearly demonstrate how changing people's behavior will be a benefit to them, or how not changing the

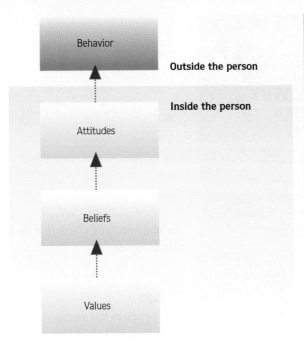

Outside the person

Inside the person

Major Point 4: Dental maintenance is relatively inexpensive compared with the cost of fixing problems later.
Major Point 5: A few minutes a day now spent on your teeth can save you hours in the dentist's chair later.

behavior will be harmful. (Positive versus negative motivation is discussed in more detail later in this chapter.)

The following brief sketch focuses on persuading college freshmen to change a behavior.

Specific Purpose
To convince the audience of college freshmen to take care of their teeth and see a dentist regularly.
Central idea
Regular maintenance now can prevent a lifetime of dental problems
Major Point 1: Your teeth are important not only to your health but to your looks as well.
Major Point 2: You will be more attractive to other people if you keep your teeth clean and healthy.
Major Point 3: If you do not take care of your teeth, you are setting yourself up for many problems in the future.
   Subpoint A: Cavities, fillings, crowns, and even loss of teeth
   Subpoint B: Gum problems, possibly requiring surgery or resulting in loss of teeth
   Subpoint C: False teeth (Do you want to be part of an ad for denture adhesives?)

In Chapter 3, you read about two unacceptable methods of changing behavior, manipulation and coercion. Either method can be effective, but the behavior change usually lasts only as long as the coercion or manipulation continues. Any changes you achieve will last longer if you use ethical techniques to motivate your audience. Think about your *ethic of persuasion* before giving a persuasive speech. Consider what information to present or not present when you try to change behaviors. Choose your content and delivery based not only on potential effectiveness but on ethical factors as well.[13]

ESTABLISHING MOTIVATION

Your listeners will change their minds or hearts only if they think changing is somehow more beneficial than not changing; they need a solid reason. Conversely, if you want people to maintain their existing values, beliefs, attitudes, or behaviors, you need to persuade them that not changing is preferable. In either case, your listeners need to be motivated, and it's your job to motivate them. When trying to motivate, it's essential that you understand their needs. They'll be in a better position to relate your persuasive message to those needs. Listeners' needs can be

SPEAKING ACROSS CULTURES

BELIEFS, ATTITUDES, AND VALUES: WHY YOU SHOULD ANALYZE THESE HIDDEN AUDIENCE ATTRIBUTES

Addressing audience members from another culture or from multiple cultures presents a special challenge in persuasive speaking. The three audience attributes that are hardest to observe—attitudes, beliefs, and values—are profoundly influenced by culture. Consider an important issue such as funding for health care. What may seem like an argument involving primarily medical and diagnostic issues can actually be laced with cultural issues as well. Consider these possibilities:

- People from various religious backgrounds might object to any kind of government funding for abortion or family planning.
- People from cultures that encourage multiple family generations to care for each other may wonder why the government would need to be so involved with child care or elder care.
- People from countries with socialized economies (such as Sweden) may automatically assume that it's the government's responsibility to provide health care for all citizens.
- People whose families have lived in this country for several generations may object to providing health care for recent immigrants, or at least for illegal immigrants.

Even from this short and incomplete list of issues, you can quickly get the idea that stumbling into such a topic without adequate preparation and audience analysis is a recipe for disaster. You can see how important it is to conduct research and prepare thoroughly. The biggest challenge is often identifying the point you might stumble over in the course of your speech. Surveying representative audience members can be a big help, even to the point of asking people how their cultures tend to view particular issues. Such research involves extra work, to be sure, but it can mean the difference between success and failure in persuasive speaking.

Cultural experiences can shape the attitudes, beliefs, and behaviors you are trying to influence through public speaking.

divided into both personal and public needs.

Personal or Public Needs

Every person has needs that must be fulfilled. If you can identify your audience's needs, you can develop more successful speeches by appealing to those needs. In a well-known model created by Abraham Maslow, needs can be grouped into five categories. These categories represent a hierarchy of needs that motivate all of us. Our most basic needs (food, water, shelter) fall in the first category at the bottom of the hierarchy and have to be satisfied first, according to Maslow. Then we can move up the hierarchy and consider satisfying higher needs.[14] To follow Maslow's model, organize and deliver your appeal based on where your audience stands relative to their needs.

1. *Physiological needs.* We need basics to survive, such as food, water, shelter, and air. These are our strongest needs, which must be filled

before we are really even aware of the higher needs. Several times a day we feel the need for food and water. People who have fasted or been without food know that the hungrier they get, the harder it is to think about anything else. Getting food becomes almost an obsession. For instance, if your audience members are hungry for lunch, they may be less inclined to pay attention to your speech.

2. *Security needs.* We need to feel safe, and security can take several forms. Home alarm systems allow us to feel safe in our homes. Having money in the bank allows us to feel secure that our families will not starve if we are temporarily unable to work. Adding earthquake coverage to our homeowner's insurance relieves our worry about being able to afford to rebuild the house in case of an earthquake. For example, in a speech about poorly trained and poorly supervised security guards who endanger the safety and property of people they were hired to protect, one student used an appeal for personal safety to encourage listeners to support legislation that would improve hiring and management practices.[15]

3. *Social needs.* We need to associate with and identify with friends and family. Some of us satisfy this need with very strong family ties. Others join clubs of people with similar interests. We socialize after work with our co-workers. Much of our socializing is done to fill our need to belong.

4. *Esteem needs.* We need to feel needed, loved, valued, or respected by those people important to us (family, friends, members of groups). We like knowing that our family understands and appreciates the things we do. Children are happy when they bring their artwork home from school and their mother praises it and posts it on the refrigerator. An employee feels good when her boss compliments her on a job well done. A tennis player is gratified when his doubles partner credits him with winning the match. All these seemingly little things add up to satisfying our need for esteem. Persuasive

speeches that try to elicit donations of time or money often appeal to our esteem needs. We all want to feel good about ourselves, and helping others is an important esteem factor for many people.

5. *Self-actualization needs.* We need to be the best we can, to achieve our full potential. A U.S. military advertising jingle tells us to "be all that you can be," implying that enlisting will help you achieve your best. The ad is appealing to our highest need. At this level, we are motivated to attain a high level of excellence, to somehow make a profound contribution to life in the broader scope of human affairs.[16]

You'll often want to appeal to multiple needs simultaneously. Suppose you want people to contribute money to a charity. The ability to deduct the contribution from income tax appeals to a financial security need, and the chance to do good for someone else appeals to the social need for belonging. For a speech advocating bicycling as a partial replacement for car use, one student mentioned benefits that included reduced wear and tear on cars (money is a security need), lower pollution (a physiological need for health), and reduced stress with improved quality of life (esteem and self-actualization needs).[17]

In addition to these personal needs, there are also public needs to consider. Many persuasive speeches address issues that require personal sacrifice for the greater good. Of course, sacrificing to serve the public good can help satisfy both personal self-esteem and actualization needs. By caring about the greater good and public needs, people can feel more valuable. Here are just a few examples of sacrifices for public needs:

- Asking people to cut down on their use of paper products to help preserve old-growth forests
- Suggesting that the audience skip one meal a week and donate the money to send food to a country suffering a famine

> ### Success Tip
> Your audience needs a compelling reason to change their attitudes, beliefs, or behavior.

- Encouraging people to give up the convenience of driving their own car and join a carpool to cut down on freeway congestion, air pollution, and gasoline consumption

The following speech addresses two prominent public issues, affirmative action and college education:

I can only suggest here the beginning of an answer that reflects a special concern. I believe any serious reformulation of approaches and strategies should make clear that special preferences and race-based numerical goals will not help dismantle the cycle of despair and destruction that produces an underclass in our society. The most promising hope lies in longer-term efforts—for example, in a fundamental rearrangement of expenditures (or even an increased expenditure) to improve on a vast scale the quality of education in our inner cities through early Head Start programs; financial incentives for students, teachers, and successful schools; and expanded apprentice programs that combine classroom instruction and on-the-job training. Through these and other programs, offered to all who are less privileged regardless of race or color, perhaps we can provide more promising grade school and high school students the kind of education that would make preferential admissions and reverse discrimination at the college level superfluous.

I am talking about real changes. Instead of adult remedies that are twenty or thirty years too late, we need strong and affirmative intervention at an earlier stage of a young person's development. This is not a new idea, but it remains a good idea (although insufficiently implemented) that deserves our strongest consideration. Yes, it will presumably cost more money, which means that charting a different course will not be easy. But I believe it will also do more good than harm, and it will certainly create less bitterness and division. The major problem

with affirmative action today is that instead of bringing us together as originally intended, it has pulled us apart. I know of no more important or urgent task facing all of us than trying to rebuild the national consensus on equal rights and equal justice so that we can move a step closer to fulfilling the promise made long ago of equal protection for all Americans.[18]

Note that the speaker isn't promising any immediate personal benefits for the members of the audience. It's a call for supporting a greater public good, at least as the speaker sees it. This speech highlights the challenge of speaking to public motivations. When you can't offer any personal benefits, you have to appeal to your listeners' civic pride, social responsibility, or some other public concern.

Positive Versus Negative Motivation

Achieving something positive and avoiding something negative can both be powerful motivators. The choice depends on the speaker's personal style, the audience, and the subject at hand.

Positive motivation is indicating the good results audience members can expect if they change. The value of their home will go up if they use your lawn-care products. The potholes will disappear from city streets if they vote for a bond issue. Their families will be safer if they participate in a Neighborhood Watch program.

Negative motivation is pointing out the bad things that could happen if audience members don't change. A speaker could point out that having unprotected sex might result in AIDS or other sexually transmitted diseases, that driving while intoxicated might result in an accident and perhaps death for the driver and others, or that children's education will suffer if an increase in the district's operating budget is not approved (see Exhibit 16.5).

Combining positive and negative motivation is sometimes effective. Speaking to a Weight Watchers meeting, you would point out both the benefits of losing weight and the dangers of not losing weight. The audience will feel better, look

EXHIBIT 16.5
Choosing Positive or Negative Motivation
In some cases, motivating an audience with a positive promise of change can be more effective. In others, a negative motivation may be more powerful. Some topics lend themselves to a combination of the two.

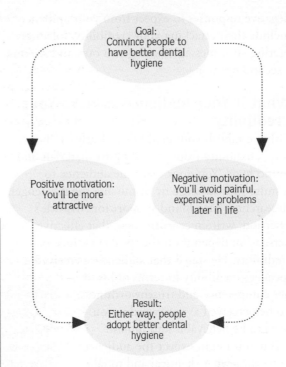

better, and be healthier if they *do* lose weight. And they face a higher risk of heart disease, high blood pressure, diabetes, and other problems if they *don't* lose weight.

Here's an example of how you could frame a speech to a homeowners' association, explaining a new curbside recycling program and persuading homeowners to use it:

> *Specific Purpose*
> *To convince homeowners that using the recycling program is to their advantage*
> *Central idea*
> *Solid waste disposal is a problem that affects everyone, and recycling is a good solution because it saves the consumer money, reduces the amount of garbage going into landfills, and helps conserve natural resources.*
>
> **Major Point 1:** Too much material is being deposited in landfills.
> **Subpoint A:** Landfills are filling up, and the city is running out of room for garbage.
> **Subpoint B:** Costs of garbage disposal are going up.
> **Major Point 2:** Much of what is being thrown away could be recycled and reused.
> **Major Point 3:** Recycling benefits everyone.
> **Subpoint A:** Individual consumers save money on garbage utility bills.
> **Subpoint B:** The city saves money on disposal costs.
> **Subpoint C:** Less land is needed for disposal sites.
> **Subpoint D:** Recycled materials reduce consumption of natural resources.

This example uses both negative and positive motivation. If the audience does not change, the city will run out of room for garbage and the cost of disposal will increase. If the audience does use recycling, there are benefits for all concerned.

ANTICIPATING AND MANAGING UNDESIRABLE RESPONSES

Anticipating the ways that audiences might respond when hearing your message can help you structure and present your argument more effectively. The three questions posed at the beginning of this chapter (Are they hostile or friendly? How much do they know? How much do they care?) are critical for persuasive speeches, but don't forget the other basics of audience analysis you learned about in Chapter 6.

Imagine yourself in the audience listening to your own speech. (To do this effectively, of course, you must know something about your audience.) Is there anything that might make your audience angry or bored? Anything that might make them doubt your message? If so, how can you change your speech to avoid these responses? Some negative responses to expect from your audience include their attacking your credibility, misinterpreting your message, tuning you out, and seeking a second opinion.

What If Your Audience Attacks Your Credibility

Either establish your credibility clearly or "borrow" credibility from your support materials and sound logic. You don't want the audience to dismiss your message by dismissing the messenger. Researchers have found support for Aristotle's assertion, written centuries ago, that effective persuasion depends on the speaker's ethos, or credibility. He stated that audiences perceived a speaker's credibility in terms of his or her competence and trustworthiness. To be perceived as trustworthy, you need to be believable and honest.

But you might expect the audience to be somewhat skeptical and to take a "show me" attitude.[19] We are bombarded with promises every day. If we use this brand of toothpaste or drink a certain brand of beer, our social life will improve. If we elect that candidate to the state legislature, violent crime will decrease. If we let our son stay up past his bedtime, he will be good the rest of the month. Some of the promises are valid, but many of them are misleading or even false. You

Success Tip

The more you know about your audience, the better you'll be able to anticipate— and prepare for— potentially negative reactions to your message.

must overcome the audience's natural skepticism by presenting yourself and your sources as honest, straightforward, informed, and reliable. If you stand to gain or lose by the results, be honest about it, but also point out the benefits to them.

Based on Aristotle's concepts, another key to building credibility is to know your material well and present it fluently. The audience will be more likely to believe you if you appear knowledgeable and comfortable with the information. If you appear hesitant, they may wonder whether you are trying to hide something. Speaker and author William Wettler says, "A persuasive speaker must convey a sense of knowing and speaking the truth."[20]

Your physical appearance is also important. A well-dressed, well-groomed speaker appears more credible than a sloppy one. On the other hand, don't overdress. People relate best to someone like themselves (see Exhibit 16.6). Again, it helps to know your audience. You would dress more casually to address a group of high school seniors than you would to address a gathering of college deans. But keep appropriateness in mind too. If you're 40 years old and speaking to a group of 16-year-old students, trying to imitate their casual style will probably look foolish. You can be casual, but in a way the audience expects of someone your age.

Here are some other techniques for establishing

Checklist for Countering Potential Negative Reactions

1. Make sure your audience is unable to attack your credibility. Pinpoint any weaknesses in your credibility, and find out whether you can boost your own credibility or borrow credibility from other sources.

2. Make sure your message allows no unintentional misinterpretation by people not yet leaning in your direction. If it does, discover where you can change your speech to clarify your message.

3. Make sure your message allows no intentional misinterpretation by people trying to avoid the action you're calling for. Leave no room for anyone to twist your evidence around to fit their existing attitudes, beliefs, values, or behaviors.

4. Make sure you can keep the audience from tuning you out.

5. Make sure you can point audience members toward second-opinion sources who will support your position.

EXHIBIT 16.6
Appropriate Appearances Build Credibility
This speaker's appearance fits the speaking situation; a formal business suit would not.

credibility.[21] Even though some of these are mentioned elsewhere, it's helpful to summarize.

- *Use straight talk.* Don't exaggerate or use overly emotional appeals. You don't want your listeners to think you're trying to put something over on them.
- *Be prepared to refute objections the audience might raise.* You might present some of the objections yourself to show that you're fair-minded.
- *Be specific.* Present figures and evidence that support your view. Do your homework.
- *Name your information sources.* Doing so is especially useful if your sources are known by the audience to be credible.

What If Your Audience Misinterprets Your Message

If people don't like what they hear, they may try to reinterpret what you've said until they create a more comforting message in their own minds. This tendency highlights the need to communicate your points clearly and concisely.

Be sure you're using language the audience understands. Avoid euphemisms, ambiguities, or anything that can be misinterpreted easily. Experienced speaker Tamra B. Orr suggests, "Use concrete, vivid language that paints a picture of what you are talking about."[22] This practice not only decreases the chance for misinterpretation

Success Tip
It certainly isn't fair, but it's true: Listening to two speakers who are equally competent and knowledgeable, audiences tend to view the man as more believable than the woman. In other words, women need to work harder at creating an air of credibility just to be perceived as being equal to their male counterparts.

but also helps hold audience members' attention so that they don't tune you out.

Be realistic, but at the same time make your message as appealing to audience members as possible so that it's easier for them to accept. Don't ignore the drawbacks, but help your audience see how the benefits outweigh the drawbacks.

On September 12, 2002, President George W. Bush addressed the United Nations General Assembly. Following Iraq's invasion of Kuwait in 1990, the U.N. Security Council had passed resolutions against Iraq that included mandatory weapons inspections. Twelve years later, those inspections had ended, and concern mounted that violations were being committed. President Bush sought to remind the Security Council of its obligations and to enlist their support in an enforcement campaign:

Iraq has answered a decade of U.N. demands with a decade of defiance. All the world now faces a test, and the United Nations a difficult and defining moment. Are Security Council resolutions to be honored and enforced, or cast aside without consequence? Will the United Nations serve the purpose of its founding, or will it be irrelevant?

The United States helped found the United Nations. We want the United Nations to be effective, and respectful, and successful. We want the resolutions of the world's most important unilateral body to be enforced.

To avoid misinterpretation, Bush clarified that, whatever the Security Council decided, the U.S. would enforce the resolutions:

> We will work with the U.N. Security Council for the necessary resolutions. But the purposes of the United States should not be doubted. The Security Council resolutions will be enforced—the just demands of peace and security will be met—or action will be unavoidable.

Less than two months later, the U.N. Security Council passed a new resolution supporting Bush's campaign against Iraq's military regime.

What If Your Audience Tunes You Out

Ignoring you is another likely response if people don't want to hear what you have to say. You need to make yourself and your message appealing to the listeners at a fundamental level.

Suppose you're asking audience members to support an increase in property taxes to keep the public library open. Many are likely to focus on "increased taxes" and tune out the reason for the increase. If you first set the stage by appealing to emotion and explaining that their children will benefit from the library, listeners may be more receptive to the solution they don't want to hear— increased taxes.

Emotional appeals help keep your audience from tuning you out. Consider the following student speech about proposed changes in a federally funded financial aid program for colleges:

> Little Johnny sits in class. Johnny works very hard, knowing that if he does well enough, one day he will be able to attend college. Johnny's dream is admirable, but it may not be as easy for Johnny to go to college when he grows up as it is for us here today. If Johnny is a minority, or if he is not good at taking tests, or if he wants to go to a small private university, he could be kept from his childhood dream.[24]

We all had dreams when we were younger, so this speech connects with audience members at a fundamental emotional level. As usual, it also helps to know your audience's needs so that you can focus on their needs rather than your own. Use examples that apply directly to listeners. As long as they feel you are talking about them (or people very much like them), they'll pay attention. Suppose you want to convince a group of college students to ask their legislators to oppose a spending bill. Maybe you could point out that the proposed budget contains no provision for federally insured student loans, for instance. If you were making the same appeal to a group of senior citizens, this example would be inappropriate. Instead, you might describe proposed cuts in Medicare. Most politicians are expert at this kind of adaptive persuasion.

What If Your Audience Seeks a Second Opinion

Using effective support materials is a good way to curb your listeners' natural reaction to seek a second opinion when they don't like what they hear from you. Let people know where they can find more information on the subject. When possible, use respected sources who have nothing to gain or lose by supporting your viewpoint.[25] Unbiased sources having no stake in the issue are more believable than those who would be affected either positively or negatively. If you are arguing against socialized medicine, the American Medical Association would not be an unbiased source. Under socialized medicine, the government would assume control of many things currently controlled by individual physicians, such as medical costs. Physicians' incomes would probably go down considerably.

Before you start your research, however, it's

HOW TO MINIMIZE THE AGONY OF NEGATIVE AUDIENCE REACTION

Few things are more stressful in public speaking than realizing that your audience is rejecting your message. The stress is compounded because you walked confidently into the speaking situation expecting people to listen to your arguments and reach the same conclusion you did. But now they're growing more and more negative before your very eyes.

The good news is that you can take steps to minimize these negative reactions. You can't always avoid them—there will be times when you simply can't convince everyone—but you can minimize them. In addition to doing extensive research on your topic and your audience, here are two creative strategies to help you deal with negative reactions.

First, pretend you're preparing a speech on the *opposite* side of the issue. If you plan to speak in favor of gun ownership, pretend you're preparing a speech against gun ownership. Then do some library research or conduct surveys to identify the points that you would make in such a speech. This will alert you to the beliefs, attitudes, and values that are likely to be held by listeners hostile to your real speech topic.

Second, ask someone to play devil's advocate for you. The best time to do this is after you've completed your planning outline so that you know what you'll say and in what order. Don't worry too much about getting the exact wording of your speech ready yet (you may have to change the outline after this exercise); the goal is to describe your central idea and major support points. The devil's advocate will then look for ways to "poke holes" in your argument and your evidence.

With either strategy, you'll identify key issues you're likely to run into when you actually give your speech. Moreover, knowing them ahead of time is the only way to prepare to meet them head on. Not only will you minimize those unsettling surprises during your speech, but you'll approach the speaking engagement with more confidence.

You can't always avoid negative reactions from your audience, but you can be prepared to handle them by understanding what your audience thinks and believes.

important to realize that you may not be able to find unbiased sources for many speeches. The very reason that many people write the books or magazine articles you're consulting is to make their case about a particular subject. So the next best choice is to find biased sources on both sides of an issue. This way, you can at least present and analyze opposing viewpoints.

Whether your sources are biased or not, make sure they will be perceived as relevant. For the socialized medicine topic, *Today's Health* would be relevant, but *Skydiver* magazine or *Truckdriver* magazine would not be perceived by most people as relevant sources.

The following excerpt from a speech on government regulations in higher education uses both relevant and respected sources, although they probably shouldn't be viewed as particularly unbiased:

Accrediting is a concern; we want to make sure that a degree ensures some level of consistency in degrees. James T. Rogers, Executive Director of the Southern Association of Colleges, points out that these regulations the government is suggesting,

"will have profound implications." The new plan will have too much control over what the schools can and cannot do. The fear of the government plan is widespread. In the December 1 issue of *The Chronicle of Higher Education,* Neil Rudenstine of Harvard and Nannerl O. Loehan of Duke explain that these regulations "threaten the very heart of what has made American Higher Education uniquely successful." These educators across the country realize that allowing government such strong holds over the schools will harm the education process.[26]

Even if the initial reaction to your speech doesn't seem favorable, don't assume all is lost. If you've communicated an idea that is meaningful and important to your listeners, they might need a little time to think it over before finally accepting or rejecting your position. Your speech may have a greater impact on the audience some time after you've finished speaking, a phenomenon known as the **sleeper effect.**[27]

Chapter 17 continues the subject of persuasive speaking, exploring more specific techniques you can use to accomplish your speaking goals.

SAMPLE PERSUASIVE SPEECH

Buy Organic

(1) Last weekend you may have settled down to a nice, piping hot pizza—the nation's second most popular food (after hamburgers). You can rationalize the calories—you'll cut back on the cookies next week. You can even reduce the fat. But have you considered the chemicals you're consuming?

(2) Today, although food labels aren't required to tell you, it's possible that the cheese on your pizza came from a cow whose milk production was stimulated by genetically engineered Bovine Growth Hormone (or BGH)—called "*crack* for cows" by some. But in addition to stimulating growth, BGH also increases a cow's susceptibility to infections. According to the Foundation on Economic Trends, "The Food and Drug Administration admits that the use of BGH in cows may lead to increased amounts of pus and bacteria in milk"—and increased amounts of antibiotics in your cheese.

(3) The tomatoes in your sauce may have been genetically bio-engineered with fish DNA to improve their shipping qualities. The pork sausage and pepperoni may have come from pigs bio-engineered with human DNA to improve their weight gain. And the herbs may have been irradiated to kill insects—whatever insects weren't killed in the fields by one of the 20,000 pesticides approved for use in the United States.

(4) The Environmental Protection Agency has released information indicating that 90 percent of the fungicides, 60 percent of the herbicides, and 30 percent of the insecticides now in common use are proven carcinogens. However, Al Heir of the EPA points out that "We have to weigh the benefits against the risks. Many of the fungicides, for example, are on the market because of their benefits to agriculture. We know they pose risks. Almost every one is carcinogenic. But their benefits to our food supply outweigh their risks." So carcinogenic chemicals are still being used to grow your pizza ingredients.

(5) Losing your appetite? I could spend all day telling you horror stories about the damage chemically intensive agriculture is doing to our food supply. But let me tell you just one. Then I'll explain what you and I can do right now—today.

(6) Because of all the dangers associated with DDT, this lethal pesticide was outlawed in 1972—more than twenty years ago. But today an undersea bed of DDT waste is still active near Catalina Island, a few miles off the Los Angeles coastline. The poisonous waste was washed into the Los Angeles sewer system by an agricultural company throughout the 1950s and 1960s. The sewer pipes carried the DDT a few miles out to sea, where scientists say the settled waste now covers an area "as large as the city of Pasadena and deep enough to fill 20 Rose Bowls."

(7) What does this have to do with your Friday night pizza? Did you order anchovies or shrimp on your pizza? Extensive research has revealed that the offshore DDT is still seeping up through the sediment and entering the food chain through small bottom feeders, which are eaten by larger fish, which are eaten in turn by eagles and other animals that are dying from DDT poisoning on Catalina Island. Dr. Andrew Weil, a medical doctor and author of the best-selling book *Spontaneous Healing,* is already advising his patients to avoid eating shellfish and other bottom feeders because of this threat of DDT contamination.

(8) Of course, no one foresaw this catastrophe when DDT was first hailed as a miracle pesticide shortly after World War II. But now the EPA says that trace amounts of deadly DDT are found in the fatty tissue of 99 percent of people in the United States. DDT is still being manufactured in the United States for sale and use outside U.S. borders. And what of the other 20,000 pesticides still being used in the United States? Will they wind up in our food chain too?

(9) There's yet another source of chemicals making an undesirable impact on your Friday-night pizza: food additives. The average food molecule now travels

Comments

This speech is intended to change listeners' beliefs and behavior, and it demonstrates the use of the five-step motivated sequence model of persuasion, which will be discussed in the next chapter. However, by reviewing these comments you can begin to see how it was used in this speech. Also, note that both positive and negative appeals are used to motivate change.

(1) To get the audience's attention (step 1), the speaker has chosen an example close to his classmates' hearts and experience: pizza. His speech will appeal to the basic physiological need for food and the security need for safety from harmful substances.

(2 & 3) The speaker explains the problem in terms that closely relate to his audience, and he uses arresting descriptions to keep interest high. Note how he "borrows" credibility from a respected government agency.

(4) To highlight the need (step 2), the speaker continues to amplify the nature of the problem. He airs an opposition argument (that the benefits of using chemicals outweigh the risks) and poses a counterargument he'll be emphasizing throughout the speech (that our food may be dangerously contaminated).

(5) In this transition, the speaker makes it clear he's leading up to a positive solution (the positive appeal). This promise alleviates the audience's natural tendency to tune out the negative information the speaker must present.

(6) The DDT narrative highlights the problem with more facts and statistics.

(7) Using a negative motivational appeal, the speaker connects the DDT problem directly to the foods his listeners are eating.

(8) The speaker emphasizes the dangers of chemicals in food by pointing out additional reasons for his audience members to be concerned.

(9) Note how the speaker continues to relate the problem back to the effect on listeners' basic needs for food and security.

about 1,300 miles to market, according to the Rocky Mountain Institute. During this journey, nutrients are lost. Nutrients are also lost when farmers continue to grow the same crops, year after year, on soils fertilized only by synthetic, petro-chemical fertilizers—a common practice today.

(10) So to improve nutrition, food processors have injected synthetic vitamins to "fortify" products made from crops grown on depleted soils, shipped over long distances, and stored for long periods. Synthetic preservatives give your pizza ingredients a long shelf life. Moreover, the flavor lost during all this shipping and handling is restored by additional food additives, such as the headache-causing MSG. According to the Center for Science in the Public Interest, the average person in the United States now consumes five pounds of food additives each year.

(10) The speaker's credibility is enhanced with relevant statistics from a reputable source.

(11) Now please don't despair. Agricultural researchers, govern-ment officials, and ordinary people like you and me are working on a solution. You've probably heard of "organic farming." The new term is *sustainable agriculture.* In 1990 Congress passed a Farm Bill that appropriated $6.7 million for research into sustainable agricul-ture. The bill also began the development of national standards for products labeled "organic."

(11) Now the speaker introduces a satisfying solution (step 3) and immediately supports the idea by pointing out that even Congress views it as a viable alternative.

(12) Sustainable agriculture, or organic farming, embraces chemical-free techniques (such as hand-picking pests, rotating crops, plowing under green crops to restore soil nutrients, and so on). In addition, with modern technology, organic farming is becoming feasible even on a large scale.

(12 & 13) The speaker describes how organic farming addresses the contamination problem the speech has defined.

(13) Organic farmers do use pesticides—as a last resort. But they choose botanically derived products such as rotenone or pyrethrum, which break down quickly into harmless by-products. Organic farmers fertilize with naturally occurring organic materials, such as bone meal or bat guano. Most important, organic methods preserve healthy soils, clean water, and pure air, while improving the taste and nutritional value of the crops being grown.

(14) Until recently, organically grown products were costly to produce and hard to find. That's changing rapidly. The Organic Farming Research Foundation says consumer demand pushed California's organic farm product exports from $200,000 a year to $10 million. Dr. Weil cites a statistic indicating that more than half of California's farms have turned to organic methods, and California supplies much of the country's produce year-round.

(14) Using positive appeals, the speaker helps his audience visualize the success of the proposed solution (step 4): Consumer demand has already caused changes, making organically grown foods more widely available.

(15) Organically nourished soils support vitamin-rich, healthy foods. Taste for yourself. Many say the carrots and potatoes taste sweeter, and the romaine is bushier and greener. Several wineries have switched to organic growing and processing techniques simply because the grapes taste better.

(15) The speaker describes benefits being reaped by other participants in the "buy organic" solution, but he still uses the "you" approach.

(16) Today, you can buy organically grown clothing—such as the organic cotton rugby shirts sold by trendy Patagonia. Or you can buy organic pretzels, thanks to Paul Newman's daughter Nell, who established the Newman's Own Organics division. You'll find organically grown produce and packaged products not only in health-food stores but also in many major supermarkets.

(16) As the speaker elaborates on the options and benefits, he makes participation sound easy.

(17) Moreover, the chemical-free philosophy is growing. Some retailers are reducing their in-store use of pesticides and waxes. And some food-processors are producing organically based breads, cookies, frozen entrees, and canned goods without chemical additives.

(18) In short, it's easier today for you and me to use our consumer muscle—our buying choices—to eat healthier now and to save our soil, water, and air for the future. We can send a strong message to growers like the lettuce producer quoted in Jerry Minnick's book *Gardening for Maximum Nutrition:* "I don't care what's on it, or what's in it, or what it tastes like, so long as it is the right shape, and the right number will pack into a box, and the box will pass the inspector."

(19) If you don't find organic choices, ask for them. And if the organically grown apple costs a few pennies more, think about what you're NOT getting. How much is it worth to keep the carcinogenic pesticide residues out of your pizza? To avoid the BGH, the antibiotics, the fish and human DNA? To avoid a tragedy like DDT contamination? How much is good health worth to you? Support the people giving you a choice, and buy the organic apple.

Bibliography

Boucher, Norman. "A Guide to Eating Organic," *Self* (May 1994): 210–212, 214.

Coco, Donna. "Dr. Weil's Cooking Dos and Don'ts," *Natural Health,* May/June 2002, 58.

Cone, Marla. "DDT Ills Still Haunt the Coast," *Los Angeles Times* (9 August 1995): A1, A12–A13.

Cone, Marla. "Sea Floor DDT Cleanup Would Pose Huge Problems." *Los Angeles Times* (10 August 1995): A1, A16.

Conover, Kirsten A. "Earth-Friendly Eating," *Christian Science Monitor* (15 April 1995): 12, 13.

"Consumer Tastes & Trends for 1994," *The Old Farmer's Almanac.* New York: Random House, 1994, p. 16.

Crinnion, Walter J. "Are Organic Foods Really Healthier for You?" *Llewellyn's 1995 Organic Gardening Almanac.* St. Paul, Minn.: Llewellyn's Publications, 1994, pp. 41–45.

Cunnington, Yvonne. "Grow Better Organically," *Chatelaine,* May 2001, 164.

Eller, Daryn. "20 Ways to Live Longer," *Women's Sports and Fitness* (January–February 1994): 70–75.

Frederick, Sue, and Whiteman-Jones, Michael. *Delicious!* Boulder, Colo.: New Hope Communications, 1994.

Joinson, Carla. "Who's Making the New Vegetables?" *Mother Earth News* (February–March 1995): 54–58, 96.

Marcus, Mary Brophy. "Organic Foods Offer Peace of Mine—At a Price," *U.S. News & World Report,* January 15, 2001, 48.

McFadden, Steven. "Cracks in the Foundation: Farms and Farmers in Transition," *Llewellyn's 1995 Organic Gardening Almanac.* St. Paul, Minn: Llewellyn's Publications, 1994, pp. 7–16.

Mendoza, Laura, and Duehring, Cindy. "What Does Organic Really Mean?" *Informed Consent* (November–December 1994): 52–56.

Minnich, Jerry. *Gardening for Maximum Nutrition.* Emmaus, Penn.: Rodale Press, 1983.

Ney, Tom. "Healthy Eating," *Organic Gardening,* May/June 2001, 20.

Rocky Mountain Institute. "Farm Subsidies: The 'Eyes to Acres' Ratio," *Rocky Mountain Institute Newsletter* 7, no. 2 (Summer 1991): 6.

Rocky Mountain Institute. "Lean Cuisine? Energy Use in Agriculture," *Rocky Mountain Institute Newsletter* 7, no. 2 (Summer 1991): 6.

Sauber, Colleen M. "The Meaning of the Word Organic," *Harvard Health Letter* (April 1994): 4–5.

(17) The speaker points out that the solution is a good idea and that others are embracing it—which boosts credibility and enhances the audience's visualization of the solution's success.

(18) This paragraph underlines how easily listeners can become part of the solution, and it stresses both the short- and long-term benefits listeners will reap. The speaker uses an emotion-stirring quote to prepare the way for his call to action.

(19) As the speaker prompts his audience to take action (step 5), he refutes a possible opposition argument (cost) by restating his basic appeal (to keep poison out of your food). Note how he keeps a tight focus on the issue, ensuring its relevance to his college audience.

Schwartz, George R. *In Bad Taste: The MSG. Syndrome.* New York: Penguin Books USA, 1990.

Seal, Mark. "Nell Newman's Organic Crusade," *New Age Journal* (April 1995): 72–77, 144–148.

"Study Confirms Organic Foods Have the Fewest Pesticides," *Environmental Nutrition,* July 2002, 7.

"Ten Reasons to Go Organic," *Llewellyn's 1994 Organic Gardening Almanac* (St. Paul, Minn.: Llewellyn's Publications, 1994), 147–150.

Tompkins, Peter, and Bird, Christopher. *The Secret Life of Plants.* New York: Harper & Row, New York, 1973.

Tregidgo, Richard. "Growing Organically," *American Nurseryman,* May 15, 2001, 51.

Ulick, Josh. "Eating Organic: What's in Your Cart," *Newsweek,* September 30, 2002, 52.

Weil, Andrew. *Spontaneous Healing.* New York: Knopf, 1995.

Williams, Florence. "Baa Baa 'Green' Sheep? Coyote Friendly Wool," *Los Angeles Times* (14 March 1995): A5.

SUMMARY

Attempts at persuasion take place all around us, all day long. Most of these attempts are unsuccessful, though, because getting people to change what they think, how they feel, and what they do is usually very difficult. People spend all their lives developing values, beliefs, attitudes, and behaviors, and you don't have much chance of changing those with a single speech. By setting realistic goals and understanding how much your audience knows and cares about your topic, as well as their attitude toward it, you can improve your chances of making small but successful changes.

No matter what your goal in a persuasive speech, you'll need to motivate the audience before you'll get them to change. The reason is that motivation is the driving force behind everything we human beings do. You're motivated to get out of bed and go to class every morning because you believe it'll help you succeed in some way. Similarly, your listeners need to sense some driving force before they'll make the effort to change.

Motivation is generated by needs, the gaps between where an audience is now and where it would like to be. You can classify audience needs as either personal or public. Personal needs include physiological, security, belonging, esteem, and self-actualization needs. Public needs, in contrast, concern a larger group, such as a school, a city, or an entire society. Note that in many appeals to public needs, you'll be asking people to make personal sacrifices for the greater good. For most persuasive speeches, you can choose positive motivation, negative motivation, or a combination of the two. To use positive motivation, you explain all the good things that will happen if the audience changes in the way you propose. Negative motivation involves the bad things that will happen (or continue to happen) if the audience doesn't change. Fear appeals, if used appropriately, are the most effective.

Remember that your audience is likely to resist the changes you're promoting. This resistance can show up as a variety of negative reactions, including attacking your credibility, misinterpreting your message (intentionally or unintentionally), tuning you out, and seeking a second opinion. The more you know about your audiences, the better you can prepare for these responses.

KEY TERMS

attitudes (349)
behavior (350)
beliefs (349)
claim of fact (346)
claim of policy (347)
claim of value (346)
ego involvement (345)
negative motivation (354)
one-sided message (345)
positive motivation (354)
sleeper effect (360)
two-sided nonrefutational message (345)
two-sided refutational message (345)
values (348)

APPLY CRITICAL THINKING

1. Explain the claim that persuasive speaking is by definition controversial.

2. Why is it important to use a two-sided message when addressing a potentially hostile audience?

3. Would a speech to city officials in which you try to persuade them to accept your population forecast be a claim of fact? Explain your answer.

4. If you were developing a speech for high school students on career choices, how would the audience's ego involvement affect your plans?

5. Do you think it's possible to persuade people to adopt behaviors that go against their values or beliefs? Why or why not?

6. When skeptical listeners seek a second opinion, are they trying to find someone to support your position or someone to refute it? Explain your answer.

7. When, if ever, is it ethical to use fear appeals or threats to persuade? Explain your answer.

SHARPEN YOUR SKILLS

Individual Exercises

1. What information would you consider giving your classmates in a speech designed to persuade them to pay back their student loans on time? Name three or four major points.

2. In a speech to convince an audience to stop believing in astrology, what information would you provide? Identify three or four major points.

3. Assume you've given a speech to your classmates on the need for better reporting of campus crime. Now you have the opportunity to give this speech to your school's administrative and security staffs. How might you adapt the speech to this new audience?

4. You're giving a speech, trying to convince classmates to write letters to the state legislature urging that the drinking age be lowered to 18. What are some possible negative reactions your classmates might have? List three.

Group Exercises

5. With three other students, refer to the brief example sketches provided in the chapter on the topic of regulating the Internet. Two of you take one side (that access, not content, should be regulated), and two of you take the other side. Conduct the research necessary to support the cases made by each speech proposal, and then compare notes. Which side came up with the most compelling evidence?

6. With a team of three or four students, pretend you are speech writers working for a U.S. senator. The senator wants to give a speech on the subject of immigration. Your team's first task is to identify all the attitudes, beliefs, and values that might affect voters' positions on this issue. Brainstorm all the possibilities you can think of, and then supplement your lists with library research. How many distinct attitudes, beliefs, and values can you identify?

Chapter Seventeen

DEVELOPING PERSUASIVE ARGUMENTS

LEARNING OBJECTIVES

After studying this chapter, you will be able to

1. List the three basic structures of persuasive speeches.

2. Describe the three common approaches to presenting solutions to problems.

3. List the steps in the motivated sequence method of persuasive speaking.

4. Contrast the three categories of persuasive appeals.

5. Compare deductive and inductive reasoning.

6. List the most common informal logical fallacies.

7. Enumerate the steps you can take to increase the effectiveness of emotional appeals.

ORGANIZING THE PERSUASIVE SPEECH

Chapter 16 explored the basic principles and issues in persuasive speaking. This chapter offers you some specific techniques to use in your persuasive speeches. In one of his most famous works, Aristotle talked about "discovering the available means of persuasion" in any situation. This chapter is about helping you discover the very best means for accomplishing your persuasive goals.[1]

As you probably know by now, effective persuasive speaking is more than simply pleading or ranting and raving. Persuasive speeches require careful planning and involve two important decisions: how to structure your speech and how to choose the type of appeal to use. First, consider three options for organizing a persuasive speech: proposing solutions to problems, comparing alternatives, and refuting an opponent.

Proposing Solutions to Problems

Many of the persuasive speeches you'll give, both in college and after, will propose solutions to some sort of problem. The specific approach you take in each case will depend on the subject, the audience, your relationship to the audience, and the speaking situation. This section presents three ways you can structure a problem-solving speech, starting with the most basic.

The Basic Problem-Solution Model

In the basic **problem-solution model**, you identify a problem and then propose a solution (see Exhibit 17.1). Note the two parts of this structure. You must first convince your audience that a problem exists, or they'll have little motivation to listen to your solution. After you've convinced listeners of a relevant problem, then you must provide a workable solution. Simply identifying a problem can be useful in some cases, such as when you want to solicit people's help in finding a solution. In most cases, though, you'll want the audience to endorse a particular solution, the one you're prepared to discuss.

Step 1: Convincing People That a Problem Exists
The task of convincing an audience that a problem exists ranges from simple to difficult, depending on the audience and the topic. Most people don't need much evidence to be convinced that drunk driving, teen pregnancy, and adult illiteracy are real problems. But other topics aren't so clearcut. In some cases, people don't understand the topic enough to see that a problem could exist. If you wanted to convince most people that large-scale computerized stock trading hurts individual investors by creating dramatic swings in stock prices, you'd first have to explain what computerized stock trading is and how it affects small investors. In other cases, the people in your audience might understand an issue perfectly but disagree on whether a problem actually exists. Property rights are a good example of this. Some people believe that government control over what they can and can't do with their real estate constitutes a big problem that hurts property values and limits personal freedoms. Other people believe that very same control is beneficial because it

EXHIBIT 17.1

Problem-Solution Models
Common approaches to delivering problem-solution speeches include the basic two-part approach, the motivated sequence method, and the AIDA model.

Basic two-part model

1. Convince audience that a problem exists

2. Present your solution

Motivated sequence method

1. Get the audience's attention

2. Highlight the need

3. Propose a satisfying solution

4. Help the audience visualize the solution

5. Prompt the audience to take action

AIDA model

1. Create *Awareness*

2. Build *Interest*

3. Foster *Desire*

4. Promote *Action*

---

protects the environment and neighboring properties.

Don't let your passion about a particular subject overshadow your need to analyze your audience thoroughly . Even though you may think an issue is the biggest and most important problem in the world, your audience may not know or care about it. Consider the content of most political speeches. Candidates usually stick to subjects that voters know about and care about. You hear plenty of speeches about violence on television, the state of education, or the role of the family in contemporary society. You hear far fewer speeches on international banking regulations or advanced scientific research, even though such topics may have equal or greater impact on the voting public. You must either choose a problem already familiar to your audience or take the time to educate your audience about the problem early in your speech. That education should alert your listeners to the existence of the problem, describe the problem, and explain why it's important to them.

Step 2: Convincing People That Your Solution Is Best

Moving past the problem to convincing people that you have the right solution is a critical transition in persuasive speeches because the solution will probably ask something of the audience. Whether or not your audience supports your solution depends on two questions: (1) Will they think your solution is

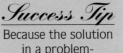

Success Tip
Because the solution in a problem-solution speech often calls for action from the audience, convince your audience that the benefit of solving the problem is greater than the cost (in time, money, energy, or whatever) of solving it.

worth the cost (or time or trouble or whatever it takes to implement it), and (2) will they believe your solution is the best alternative? Your solution might cost nothing and may be fairly simple for individual listeners to implement, such as voting for a particular candidate. On the other hand, you might be asking the audience for a huge commitment of time or money, or you might be asking people to change longstanding beliefs or values.

Say that you convince your audience that your city needs more foster homes, and then you present your solution: You ask everyone in the room to consider becoming a foster parent. At this point, more than a few people will probably decide that foster care really isn't such a big problem after all. Even though you changed the minds of your listeners in the problem part of your speech, those listeners changed their minds back when they learned that *they* were the solution. This doesn't make them bad people, of course. They would probably support some other solution to the problem. But such a reaction illustrates a key challenge in the problem-solution format: The solution sometimes requires a personal commitment of time or money from the audience, so you must convince audience members that your solution is worth the cost.

The second challenge related to problem-solution strategy is getting people to think you're presenting the best possible solution. That may not be as easy as it sounds. The solution you present, out of all the possible alternatives, needs to be perceived as right and important to the listeners. They need to think you've selected a novel approach to solving the problem, an approach that is also plausible and superior to the alternatives.[2] Would you be convinced if a classmate used the following approach in a persuasive speech?

Major Point 1: People tend to limit their job searches to those areas they can actually reach with available transportation.

    Subpoint A: Many jobs are located in suburban areas that aren't well served by public transportation.

    Subpoint B: In our city alone, thousands of people can't get to where the jobs are, and hundreds of employers outside the city limits can't get the workers they need.

Major Point 2: Therefore, the city should extend public transportation to every employer who promises to hire at least 50 additional people every year.

Something is missing in this speech, isn't it? The speaker guides you along a logical path in major point 1 that sounds like it might be a problem. Then all of a sudden, the speaker offers a specific solution in major point 2 without exploring any other alternatives. You may detect this shortcoming in speeches given by someone who has an interest (financial or otherwise) in convincing you that a particular solution is necessary. Most audiences want to know that you've explored the alternatives before choosing a specific solution. In this case, company-sponsored transportation, van pools, or loan guarantees to people who buy cars for commuting might be attractive alternatives as well.

Compare the previous approach with the following alternative:

Major Point 1: People tend to limit their job searches to those areas they can actually reach with available transportation.

    Subpoint A: Many jobs are located in suburban areas that aren't well served by public transportation.

    Subpoint B: In our city alone, thousands of people can't get to where the jobs are, and hundreds of employers outside the city limits can't get the workers they need.

Major Point 2: The city should extend public transportation to major employers outside the city limits.

    Subpoint A: Company-sponsored transportation might work for the biggest employers, but it places a heavy burden on smaller companies.

    Subpoint B: Van pools are an option, but they might leave the city open to lawsuits stemming from accidents, and the city's insurance company won't cover these situations.

    Subpoint C: Loan guarantees could work for people who want to buy cars in order to get to work but don't have sufficient credit to qualify on their own; however, such a plan is risky because it makes the city responsible for every loan that isn't repaid on time.

    Subpoint D: Extending bus and rail lines to major employment centers outside the city is a viable option that has the added advantage of providing easier access to downtown shopping, sports, and cultural events, so city merchants benefit as well.

    Subpoint E: After examining all four proposals, you'll agree that the city should extend public transportation to major employers outside the city limits.

The Motivated Sequence Method

The **motivated sequence method** was developed in the 1930s by Alan Monroe, a Purdue University speech professor. An enhancement of the basic problem-solution model, it combines motivation and problem solving in a sequence of five steps: attention, need, satisfaction, visualization, and action.[3] In general, you can plan to present the attention step in your introduction; the need, satisfaction, and visualization steps in the body of your speech; and the action step in your conclusion.

Step 1: Get the Audience's Attention

Your audience is full of busy people. Like you, they have many other things on their minds. You must

EXHIBIT 17.2

Catching Your Audience's Attention
This visual aid is perfect for a lecture on art because audiences will be attracted by its bold, dramatic appearance.

make them think that listening to you and what you have to say is important. Mystery writers know that the first couple of paragraphs in their books must grab the reader's attention, or no one will read their stories. Likewise, the first few sentences of your speech must make your audience want to hear the rest (Exhibit 17.2). Consider how a volunteer worker introduced a speech about helping deaf and blind people:[4]

> My friend Joan is deaf and blind. She could see and hear until she was in her early twenties. Then her hearing and vision started deteriorating. Today, at the age of 55, she lives in a world of total silence and darkness. She has not learned sign language. Instead she relies on her speech and a portable device called a Telebraille to communicate. The Telebraille consists of a typewriter keyboard on one side and a Braille pad on the other. As I type on the keyboard, the corresponding dots lift on the Braille pad. Joan holds her finger on the pad, reading letter by letter as I type. This is slow, but anyone who can read the keyboard and type, even with one finger, can communicate with Joan this way. I have learned to appreciate my vision and hearing, things I always took for granted.

Step 2: Highlight the Need

Explain the problem and persuade audience members that it needs to be solved. With every-

thing else that is going on in their lives, why should they devote time or attention to this problem? Depending on the nature of the problem, you can use facts or emotional appeals to convince the audience that the problem is real and must be solved. The example you've just read uses both, but it's mainly an emotional appeal:

> Joan still manages to be relatively independent. She lives alone, cooks her own meals, takes the bus to and from her job. There are a few things she cannot do, though. She needs help grocery shopping, running errands, and reading mail. That is where I come in. Once a week I drive her to the grocery store and guide her through the aisles. She gives me a typed copy of her shopping list, and she has a Braille version of the list. If she wants peanut butter, I tell her what brand is on sale and what size jars there are. She decides which size and brand she wants to buy. At the checkout stand, I fill in the date, payee name, and amount of her check. Joan uses a plastic template to show her where to sign the check.
>
> Joan and I were matched up by the Deaf/Blind Service Center (DBSC). There are many other clients who, like Joan, need some assistance with some parts of their daily lives.

The need step can involve as many as four substeps: stating the problem, illustrating the need, reinforcing the need through further evidence or examples, and relating the need to the audience.[5] In this example, the speaker used a very personal example to highlight the need for volunteer assistants. (The speech might've been made even stronger if the speaker had cited additional evidence regarding specific numbers of people who need assistance.)

Step 3: Propose a Satisfying Solution

How can the problem be solved? You can't just describe the problem and then leave the audience hanging there. It's up to you to propose a solution and use supporting evidence to convince audience members that your solution is a good one. Continuing with the same speech:

Some of the deaf/blind clients use sign language to communicate, but some of them, like Joan, use other methods, so you do not even need to be able to sign. Besides the regular job of shopping and helping read mail, there are one-time opportunities to help.

DBSC has a full-time coordinator to match up volunteers and clients. Volunteers must go through a screening process before being accepted. Then they are trained on how to work with deaf/blind people. The training includes guiding techniques, communication skills, and information on the various types and degrees of deafness and blindness. The emphasis is on doing things *with* the client, not *for* the client. The goal is for the deaf/blind person to maintain as much independence and control over his or her life as possible.

Like the need step, the solution step can involve a number of substeps, depending on the subject at hand. These include stating the proposed solution clearly, offering additional explanation as needed, demonstrating how the proposed solution will solve the problem (both theoretically and practically), and addressing any potential objections.[6]

You can see these elements at work in the example speech. For instance, a likely objection to an appeal such as this is that volunteers won't know how to help. The speaker clearly explains that the organization will teach them everything they need to know.

Step 4: Help the Audience Visualize the Solution

What will happen if audience members do follow your solution? What if they don't? How will changing benefit audience members personally? You must help them see both the positive and negative results of action and nonaction:

There are a lot of opportunities to help, and the work is rewarding. You get to meet some wonderful people. The DBSC staff is friendly and helpful. The clients, like any group of people, are varied and interesting. You might be asked to give a client a ride to or from the airport. This involves not only driving there, but also guiding the client to the gate and introducing him or her to the flight attendant.

Without the services provided by DBSC volunteers, many deaf/blind people would lose much of their independence. You can help prevent this from happening.

In this brief section, the speaker did a good job of describing (1) what might be expected of them if they volunteer and (2) the benefits that will result. The speaker makes it easy for her listeners to put themselves in a volunteer's shoes. The next step is to push the audience toward action.

Step 5: Prompt the Audience to Take Action

Tell the audience clearly what action you want them to take, how to achieve the solution you've helped them visualize. If they understand exactly what you want them to do, they are more likely to do it:

Please give DBSC a call. They are always looking for volunteers. If you cannot spare a couple of hours every week for a regular assignment, have them put you on their list for one-time opportunities. They will give you a call when something comes up, and you can decide each time if it is something you are willing and able to do.

In some speeches, you'll want to reiterate your main points in the conclusion and call to action. In this case, the speech is short enough that repeating the main points might sound too redundant.

The AIDA Model

The **AIDA model**, which stands for Awareness, Interest, Desire, and Action, is another variation on the basic problem-solution model. AIDA is similar to the motivated sequence method, but it was actually developed to help salespeople plan their presentations (which are, after all, persuasive speeches). You may find AIDA to be simpler to use because it requires only four steps instead of five.

Step 1: Create Awareness

Tell audience members about the situation and the need to change. Introduce them to the problem or idea in a way that makes them want to hear what you have to say—as this student did in a speech about false memory syndrome:

Connie Chung of the CBS Evening News stated, "(But) memories are far from perfect; there are some things that happen that we can't remember, then there are things we remember that never happened." Stephen Cook might finally agree. After his suit accusing Cardinal Bernardin of childhood sexual abuse was highly publicized, he has since dropped all charges, realizing his memories of abuse were purely fictitious. Stephen Cook's story embodies what the psychological community terms false memory syndrome. *Time* magazine describes false memory syndrome as "a troubling psychological phenomenon that

is harming patients, devastating families, influencing legislation, taking up courtroom time and stirring fierce controversy." The magnitude of this problem is highlighted by the fact that both *Time* and *U.S. News & World Report* featured false memory syndrome as their cover stories during one recent week.[7]

Step 2: Build Interest

People will engage their heads and hearts only after they've developed an interest in a problem or situation. Be sure to use language and situations that they can understand and relate to—as in the student's speech on false memory:

There is little question, given the number of cases throughout the country, that false memory syndrome both exists and is devastating individuals. The Gannett News Service reported that the False Memory Syndrome Foundation, headquartered in Philadelphia, fielded calls from over 11,000 individuals who were either therapy patients persuaded to believe they were victims of sexual abuse or individuals accused of abusing someone in the past. Through therapy, memories of abuse are "discovered," and given current legal trends, are then used to convict the accused. Juries today are finding people guilty with no evidence except therapist-induced memories.[8]

Step 3: Foster Desire

Make audience members want to change by explaining how changing will benefit them. This is the biggest part of your job. We are all resistant to change. You have to show your audience members what will happen if they change. It's easier to move them toward the known than toward the unknown, so try to think of questions your listeners might have, and answer them in

> *Success Tip*
>
> How you use the five steps in the motivated sequence model should vary depending on the listeners' attitude toward your topic. An audience that is hostile toward your subject will require a different speech than an audience already in favor of your message.

your speech. Continuing with the example of false memories:

> The result, as described by Dr. Richard Ofshe in *Society* magazine, is that "because the memories implicate family and community members of horrible crimes, the trauma of this therapy radiates outward to involve often dozens of innocent people. Thousands of families have already been shattered. The possibilities for fracturing family groups are all being realized: the accused spouse is divorced; siblings are forced to choose sides; grandparents are denied access to their grandchildren; grandchildren lose contact with their grandparents, and so on."[9]

Step 4: Promote Action

The point is whether or not people actually change. So it's important that you show them how to change, whether the focus is a belief, an attitude, or a behavior. Be sure you point out a desirable solution as well as the problem. You don't want to leave your audience feeling negative and helpless. Here's how the student speaking about false memory tried to move her audience to action:

> The first step to ending the injustice is through legislation. *The New York Times* reported that Illinois has recently introduced a bill "to protect people from lawsuits based on psychological quackery." This bill will reduce the statute of limitations for sexual abuse cases based on therapy induced memories. Furthermore, the 15 states that currently allow therapy-induced memories to serve as evidence need to rescind their laws. The remaining states that have no legislation dealing with these issues need to pass laws that do not allow therapy-induced memories in the courtroom. Therefore, the only way we can protect ourselves from being wrongly accused or even imprisoned is by insisting that these laws are changed in each of our own states.

> Second, the psychiatric community needs regulations regarding the use of hypnosis as a treatment for sexual abuse. As a model for our own personal advocacy, we can turn to the state of Ohio, where a citizen's group asked the State Board of Psychology to establish guidelines pertaining to therapy for patients who may have been abused or molested. We must confront our own State Boards of Psychology and demand that rigorous regulations be placed on counselors and therapists, declaring hypnosis and memory-induced therapies unethical.

> Third, and most important, we must be willing to take the time to protect ourselves. Before seeing a therapist of any kind for any reason, there are two things you need to ask your potential therapist. First, ask what percentage of the therapist's patients have been diagnosed as victims of childhood sexual abuse. If the number is unusually high and makes you uncomfortable, ask a second question. Find out what types of therapy the therapist tends to rely on. If the answer is hypnosis or suggestive therapy, seek out another therapist. Only by questioning our potential therapists can we ensure that our problems are accurately and fairly diagnosed.[10]

In addition to presenting problems and proposing solutions, you can pursue other options for organizing your persuasive speech, including the strategy of comparing alternatives.

Comparing Alternatives

In the **comparison-of-alternatives strategy**, you ask your audience to choose from two or more alternatives. With this format, you make an appeal for one particular alternative based on its relative advantages (see Exhibit 17.3). Say you're trying to convince a group of parents that it's better for their children to play on school sports teams, rather than on "select" teams, which have no school affiliation. You might structure your argument like this:

EXHIBIT 17.3
The Comparison-of-Alternatives Strategy
The comparison-of-alternatives strategy spends less time discussing the problem and more time discussing the available alternatives.

State the problem or decision at hand ····▶ List/explain the criteria for selecting the best alternative ····▶ Assess the alternatives you're not going to recommend ····▶ Conclude with an assessment of your recommended alternative

Specific Purpose
To persuade my audience that school teams are better for their children than the select teams made up of "star" athletes from more than one school.

Central Idea
School teams provide students with better facilities, proper supervision and training, and a chance to foster school spirit.

Major Point 1: The quality and availability of facilities affects both the safety and the enjoyment of athletics.

    Subpoint A: Select teams have to find whatever facilities they can, wherever they can, which can lead to safety concerns and scheduling problems.

    Subpoint B: School teams usually have their own facilities, which are managed and maintained by the school district, so you can count on safe facilities being available at reasonable times.

Major Point 2: Proper supervision and coaching are important for your children, not only to ensure their safety and well-being but also to give them the best chance to develop their skills.

    Subpoint A: Select team coaches may or may not have the necessary knowledge and skills to provide a safe learning environment.

    Subpoint B: School team coaches go through a careful screening and hiring process, and they have the chance to improve their knowledge and skills through continuing training.

Major Point 3: School spirit is an important part of student athletics.

    Subpoint A: Because select teams aren't connected to any particular school, they present no opportunity for fostering school spirit.

    Subpoint B: School teams give your children a chance to contribute to—and benefit from—school spirit.

This speech demonstrates the point-counterpoint nature of the comparison structure; it's almost like watching a tennis match. The order in which you make your points can influence your success. The **primacy and recency effect** is a concept that suggests people tend to remember the first thing they hear and the last thing they hear more than the points in between. Based on that idea, some experts say to use your best argument first and your second-best argument last.[11] Others say it doesn't matter which of the two is first, just use your best two arguments first and last. One author suggests that it depends on your audience: For an uninterested audience you should make the most important point first to get their attention; for a neutral or positive audience you should make the most important point last.[12]

When Ervin Douglas, president of the Public Broadcasting Service (PBS), was trying to persuade his audience that PBS should be the nationwide public "on-ramp" to the Information Superhighway, he first made the point that public broadcasting is already "a treasure of cutting-edge information technology" and that the country has already made significant investments in it. But he saved his most powerful point for last:

> The third major reason to make public broadcasting the national on-ramp is the most important: It is that we need to be concerned about ends, not just means; about mission, not just technology; about content, not just wires, waves, and fibers. The Information Superhighway, to do its job, must lead to decent destinations.
>
> Public broadcasting has that central meaning and purpose: It is *about* the interconnection between technology and content, technology and mission.[13]

By structuring his speech in this order, Douglas left the audience with his most significant point to ponder.

You've probably noticed that the comparison-of-alternatives strategy resembles the second half of a problem-solution strategy, in which you compare and dismiss a number of alternatives along the way to one preferred solution. That's a key point to remember when choosing your structure. If you have to "sell" people on a problem first, always go with one of the

FOCUSING ON ETHICS

TACTFUL WAYS TO GET TO THE POINT WITHOUT GETTING PERSONAL

The advice to attack an opponent's message and not his or her character may be easier said than done in many speaking situations. For one thing, the temptation to sweep aside the issues and jump right into character assassination grows with the intensity of the debate. Rivals can work themselves into such mutual dislike that the issues hardly seem to matter anymore. Also, an opponent's character or behavior may indeed be so questionable that it's hard not to consider it an issue for debate. Keeping to the issues can be particularly difficult when you're speaking in a debate or forum, or when you and an opponent respond to each other repeatedly through a series of public speeches. Whatever the situation, here are three guidelines to help you navigate these ethically murky waters:

- *Decide whether character is truly a relevant issue.* Does the fact that your opponent admits to being a poor parent have anything to do with his or her stand on a political issue? Probably not, although it might relate to issues such as child care or education. But if your opponent was once convicted of financial fraud, character might well be relevant to his or her opinions about banking regulations. If character is not relevant, however, keep it out of the discussion.
- *If you want to call the audience's attention to your opponent's character, try to use the issues as a mirror.* In other words, let the audience see the flaws in his or her message or methods, in the hope that these will reflect on your opponent's character. Don't call your opponent dishonest; show your evidence to the audience and let them decide your opponent isn't telling the truth.
- *If your character comes under attack, defend yourself with hard facts, and then get back to the issues.* If you counterattack with shots at his or her character, the discourse will most likely disintegrate into name calling and mudslinging that will rival the worst political debates. However, if you can demonstrate with convincing evidence that what the opponent says about you is wrong, you can blunt the attack before leading the discussion back to the issues. Most audiences will probably appreciate your efforts to get the discussion back on track.

Finally, consider the audience's potential reaction to character attacks. If you attack an opponent too harshly, you might call your own character into question.

Whether you're engaged in a formal debate or simply making a speech that refutes another person's ideas, you have an ethical obligation to focus on the issues and not on your opponent.

EXHIBIT 17.4
The Refutative Strategy
The refutative strategy comes right out and attacks another speaker's position or conclusions about a given topic.

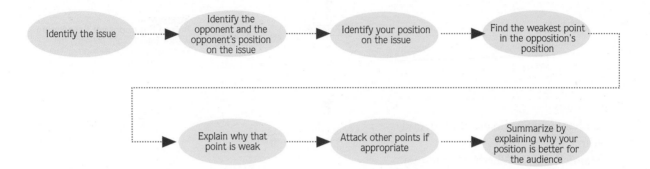

problem-solution formats (basic problem-solution, motivated sequence, or AIDA). You'll have little success in talking about solutions to a problem that people aren't aware of or don't think are important. On the other hand, if the audience is already familiar with the problem or issue at hand and is simply looking for the best solution, go with the comparison-of-alternatives strategy.

Refuting an Opponent

Persuasive speeches often involve the consideration of opposing sides to an issue. In the **refutative strategy,** you dismantle the other side's arguments to persuade people to accept your program for change (see Exhibit 17.4). If you're pushing for one particular solution, you can be sure that somebody, somewhere, is pushing for a different solution. The basic idea here is to convince the audience that the opposition's program is false, misguided, harmful, or negative in some other way. As discussed in Chapter 16, this two-sided refutational message is the best way to persuade audiences that are hostile to your position, well informed, and ego involved.

Depending on the strengths and weaknesses of the opposing position, you have a number of ways to refute. You must first decide whether you're going after something a speaker has said (or is likely to say) or whether you're simply

going after the speaker. Be careful to aim your objections at the opponent's program, not at your opponent. Do not get personal or attack your opponent's character, unless character is the central issue of your debate. We have all seen too many political campaigns start out dealing with issues and dissolve into mudslinging. Although mudslinging can be effective, to be sure, we must question the effect it has on politics and public speaking in general.

How will you convince the audience to accept your stance and reject your opponent's? This requires an understanding of both your audience and your opponent's message. You can choose from two basic strategies: convince the audience that your opponent's message itself is flawed, or convince the audience that the action recommended by your opponent will lead to undesirable consequences (see Exhibit 17.5). So you're attacking either your opponent's line of reasoning or the results that will occur. You may have the opportunity to combine the two strategies. Compare the two approaches in this example.

Your Opponent's Central Idea:
College scholarships should be awarded strictly on the basis of career potential.

Major Point 1: Scholarships are now awarded on a variety factors, including athletic talent,

EXHIBIT 17.5

Refutative Options
You have two options with the refutative strategy: Attack the message itself or attack the consequences of the message. Of course, you can attack both in some cases.

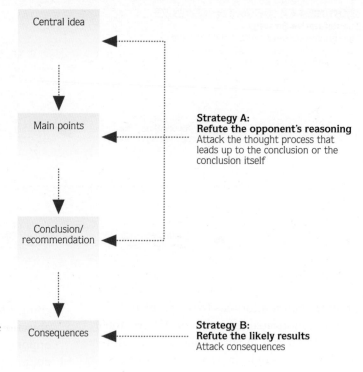

Central idea

Main points

Strategy A:
Refute the opponent's reasoning
Attack the thought process that leads up to the conclusion or the conclusion itself

Conclusion/
recommendation

Consequences

Strategy B:
Refute the likely results
Attack consequences

academic talent, financial need, and ethnic background.

Major Point 2: Whether the money behind these scholarships comes from public or private sources, we can say that overall, society is paying the bill.

Major Point 3: Scholarships should be viewed as financial investments, and the people who award scholarships should therefore try to get the highest return on their investments.

Major Point 4: The highest return to society will come from those students who go on to earn the most money, since they'll spend more as consumers, pay more taxes, and contribute more to charity.

Major Point 5: Therefore, scholarships should be awarded to those students who show the greatest promise for having successful careers.

Strategy A: Attacking the message itself: You've probably already identified several places to poke holes in this weak argument. The possibilities include the following:

- Lumping public and private scholarship funds together and treating them all as "society's" money is misleading. People and organizations who fund scholarships privately have every right to spend that money (or give authority to schools to spend that money) as they see fit. This is not society's money by any stretch of the imagination.
- The idea that scholarships are an investment

has an element of truth in it, but only in the broadest sense of the word "investment." Making the leap to a narrow financial interpretation, as this speaker did, excludes all other purposes for awarding scholarships, including citizenship, culture, opportunity, and so forth.

- Predicting a student's chances for financial success later in life is extremely difficult. For instance, traditional tests of aptitude can't measure ambition, luck, perseverance, changes in the economy, or personal connections—five factors that have helped many people achieve wealth.

Strategy B: Attacking the consequences of the recommended action: Just as there are several weak points in the message itself, there are several potential negative consequences of the recommended changes to scholarship criteria:

- It might transform the whole notion of higher education into simple career training; although this is a worthwhile and important goal, to be sure, there's much more to be learned in college than simply how to work at a career.

- It could deny higher education to people who make worthwhile (though nonfinancial) contributions to society, including teachers, artists, social workers, and researchers (among many others).
- It helps define success in strictly financial terms. This is an important measure for many people, of course, but it is not a universal measure of success, as evidenced by all the people who pursue potentially fulfilling but not terribly lucrative careers.

Even in this brief example, you probably noticed several types of weaknesses. To refute your opponent's message effectively, you need to identify its weaknesses and use any of the following methods to attack the weak areas:

- *Logic.* You'll read about the three primary methods of logical reasoning later in this chapter; for now, just remember that looking for logical flaws can help you unravel an opponent's argument. Follow the reasoning the opponent presents, and then look for holes (see the following section for more on logical appeals).
- *Emotion.* Just as emotion can be a powerful tool for promoting your message, it can be a powerful tool for refuting someone else's. If you can strike an emotional chord in your audience, you can help them feel the potential effects of your opponent's recommendation. Emotion can be enough to overcome clear logic in many cases, although you need to be careful not to manipulate peoples' emotions (discussed later in the chapter).
- *Morality and ethics.* It's entirely possible for a speaker's message to be logical, financially sound, safe, believable—and morally or ethically misguided. Knowing your audience well is vital here, since it's their definition of what's right and wrong that will be the deciding factor.
- *Risk.* You already know that your audiences may try to avoid the changes you call for in your own persuasive speeches, and you can some-

times use your audience's aversion to risk to your own advantage when refuting an opponent. What *might* happen if the audience accepts your opponent's position? Be aware that you can get into some murky ethical issues with such a tactic, however. You have a responsibility to your audience and to your opponent to avoid scare tactics that can't be reasonably substantiated.

- *Evidence.* What is your opponent using to support his or her position? If you think there isn't enough evidence to convince audience members—or if you think they shouldn't be convinced by the evidence they've heard— emphasize this shortcoming to your listeners. Depending on the evidence presented by the other side, you might be able to cite counterexamples, call into question whether the opposing evidence is sufficiently representative, question the credibility of authorities, minimize the importance of impact of the evidence, or question statistical interpretations.[14]
- *Credibility.* As Chapter 16 points out, audiences usually start out being skeptical. You can magnify this natural inclination by highlighting reasons for them to question your opponent's credibility. The potential for ethical mistakes and mudslinging is obvious, but when used properly, questioning your opponent's credibility is a perfectly acceptable and often very effective technique. If you can find a single significant weakness in your opponent's message or its consequences, emphasize it to your audience, and they may start to question other things your opponent says. If you can point out that a conclusion is flawed because the speaker overlooked some key evidence or misinterpreted some statistics, the audience will start to question other conclusions the speaker makes.

Chapter 16 introduced President Bush's successful speech to the United Nations regarding resolutions against Iraq. Bush's position was not uniformly supported in the United States. Some factions believed that current economic sanctions against Iraq were sufficient intervention. Others argued the sanctions were too extreme and they created economic hardship for Iraqi citizens. Bush refuted those competing images by redirecting the responsibility for Iraq's problems back to its leader, Saddam Hussein:

> In 1990, after Iraq's invasion of Kuwait, the world imposed economic sanctions on Iraq. Those sanctions were maintained after the war to compel the regime's compliance with Security Council resolutions. In time, Iraq was allowed to use oil revenues to buy food. Saddam Hussein has subverted this program, working around the sanctions to buy missile technology and military materials. He blames the suffering of Iraq's people on the United Nations, even as he uses his oil wealth to build lavish palaces for himself, and to buy arms for his country. By refusing to comply with his own agreements, he bears full guilt for the hunger and misery of innocent Iraqi citizens.

Bush delivered an emotional and ethical appeal in support of the people of Iraq by labeling the quest for their liberty as "a great moral cause." He relied primarily on logic and evidence, however, to support the contention that the earlier resolutions and sanctions (whatever your opinion of them) had not deterred Hussein. A majority of the speech lists infraction upon infraction, in parallel form, to demonstrate Hussein's contempt for the United Nations:

> In 1991, Security Council Resolution 688 demanded that the Iraqi regime cease at once the repression of its own people, including the systematic repression of minorities —which the Council said, threatened international peace and security in the region. This demand goes ignored.
>
> In 1991, the U.N. Security Council, through Resolutions 686 and 687, demanded that Iraq return all prisoners from Kuwait and other lands. Iraq's regime agreed. It broke its promise. Last year the

Secretary's General high-level coordinator for this issue reported that Kuwait, Saudi, Indian, Syrian, Lebanese, Iranian, Egyptian, Bahraini, and Omani nationals remain unaccounted for —more than 600 people. One American pilot is among them.
>
> In 1991, the U.N. Security Council, through Resolution 687, demanded that Iraq renounce all involvement with terrorism, and permit no terrorist organizations to operate in Iraq. Iraq's regime agreed. It broke this promise. In violation of Security Council Resolution 1373, Iraq continues to shelter and support terrorist organizations that direct violence against Iran, Israel, and Western governments.

More infractions are listed, including human rights violations, possession of restricted weapons, and the development of both biological and nuclear weapons of mass destruction. Drawing attention to his argument, Bush actually points out that his use of evidence supports his claim and counters potential refutation:

> We know that Saddam Hussein pursued weapons of mass murder even when inspectors were in his country. Are we to assume that he stopped when they left? The history, logic, and the facts lead to one conclusion: Saddam Hussein's regime is a grave and gathering danger. To suggest otherwise is to hope against the evidence. To assume this regime's good faith is to bet the lives of millions and the peace of the world in a reckless gamble. And this is a risk we must not take.

As this speech shows, it's important to think ahead, envision what your opponent might do in response to one of your moves, and then have a response ready.

Now that you have an understanding of several models for organizing a persuasive message, the following section addresses a pivotal question: What will make your message appealing to your listeners?

EXHIBIT 17.6
Deductive Reasoning
Deductive reasoning reaches conclusions in specific cases by referring to general principles.

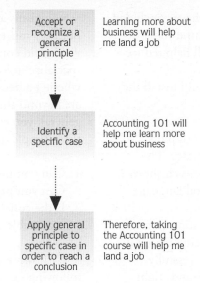

Accept or recognize a general principle → Learning more about business will help me land a job

Identify a specific case → Accounting 101 will help me learn more about business

Apply general principle to specific case in order to reach a conclusion → Therefore, taking the Accounting 101 course will help me land a job

CHOOSING THE APPEAL

After you've chosen the basic structure of your persuasive speech, your next major decision is the type of appeal to use. Persuasive appeals fall into three basic categories: logic, emotion, and character.[17] Most speeches include appeals from two or more categories. People usually respond first to how they feel about a topic, then they look for evidence to support their feelings,[18] so a combination of logical and emotional appeals can be very effective. Emotions by themselves can work as a powerful vehicle to change listeners' beliefs. They're most effective when you strengthen and support reason with passion.[19]

Logic

The **logical appeal**, also known as logos, deals with how people think. Rational people want to examine the evidence and make smart choices when they're called on to make decisions. For instance, we want to get the best product at the lowest price and the best results at school with the least amount of effort. Few people deliberately make decisions that they consider illogical, at least not as a matter of habit.

Although you've heard and said the word *logical* thousands of times in your life, the subject actually encompasses more than just

saying something is "logical" or "illogical." Logical arguments fall into two distinct categories of reasoning: deductive reasoning and inductive reasoning. You'll no doubt find appropriate opportunities for both approaches in your speaking career, and it's not uncommon to use both types in a single speech.

Deductive Reasoning

When you use **deductive reasoning,** you draw a specific conclusion by referring to general principles or ideas (see Exhibit 17.6). The foundation of deductive reasoning is the **syllogism**, which uses a series of premises to draw a conclusion. In the most basic form of syllogism, the **major premise** contains the general principle that applies to an overall group of people, objects, or other entities. The **minor premise** addresses the specific case about which you are arguing. Finally, the **conclusion** makes a logical claim based on the connection between the premises. Properly constructed syllogisms can be powerful persuasive tools because they leave rational listeners with no reasonable choice but to accept the conclusion as logical. See how the process works in this example:

> **Major premise:** Colleges and universities have a responsibility for the safety of students and staff on campus.

Minor premise: Safety experts have concluded that improving the lighting around the footpaths that cross the campus will help reduce personal assaults in those areas.
Conclusion: Therefore, we should install the additional lighting.

Naturally, you don't always want to phrase your argument in such mechanical language. The following excerpt from a student speech shows a syllogism put to use in more natural language:[20]

We as a society have an obligation to make sure these children aren't just being placed in homes, but are being placed successfully *[major premise]*. As the system stands right now, we are not giving these children a chance to enjoy a happy childhood or even to become productive members of society *[minor premise]*. Therefore, measures must be taken both by adoption agencies and by all of us to put the brakes to the 40 percent failure rate of these adoptions *[conclusion]*.

Reduced to its essential points, this paragraph fits the syllogism pattern like this:

Major premise: Society must place adopted children successfully.
Minor premise: The current system is not placing adopted children successfully.
Conclusion: Therefore, we should change the current system.

In many cases, stating both premises will make your speech sound tedious and overly obvious. You may not want to take the time to point out that colleges and universities are partly responsibly for student and staff safety, for instance. If so, you would construct your argument by stating the minor premise and conclusion but just implying the major premise: Safety experts have concluded that lighting will reduce personal assaults, so the college should install it. Syllogisms with unstated premises are called **enthymemes**, and they are quite common in both written and oral communication.[21]

Syllogisms and enthymemes are powerful tools, but they must be constructed properly in order to yield valid conclusions. Logicians (scholars who specialize in logic) apply a series of rules to test whether a deductive argument is valid. These tests are beyond the scope of this chapter, but in general, you can help ensure valid deduction with three simple questions:

1. Can you prove the major premise?
2. Can you prove the minor premise?
3. Is the conclusion reasonable—and is it the only reasonable conclusion, given the two premises?

With those questions in mind, consider the following example:

Major premise: Protein is an important element in a healthful diet
Minor premise: Cheeseburgers are high in protein
Conclusion: Therefore, cheeseburgers are healthful

Most of us would like for this conclusion to be true, but, sadly, it probably isn't. Even though both premises are provable, the conclusion is mistaken. The problem, of course, is that there is a lot more to "healthful" than just the presence of protein. You need the presence of other things and the *absence* of a lot of things, too—many of which show up in cheeseburgers. (Note that this must be considered an informal analysis of this syllogism; a formal logical test would involve some specific reasons why the syllogism is invalid.) Now consider this example:

Major premise: All athletes who promise to work hard in college, regardless of academic performance in high school or the results of entrance exams, should be considered for athletic scholarships.
Minor premise: Although she did poorly in high school, Darby has promised to work harder in college.
Conclusion: Therefore, Darby should be considered for an athletic scholarship.

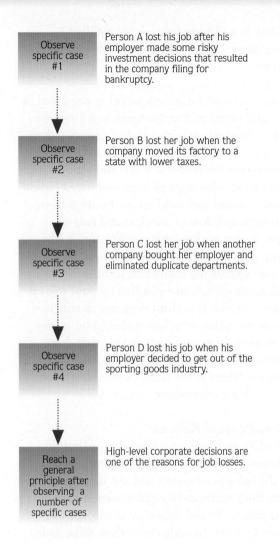

Person A lost his job after his employer made some risky investment decisions that resulted in the company filing for bankruptcy.

Person B lost her job when the company moved its factory to a state with lower taxes.

Person C lost her job when another company bought her employer and eliminated duplicate departments.

Person D lost his job when his employer decided to get out of the sporting goods industry.

High-level corporate decisions are one of the reasons for job losses.

EXHIBIT 17.7
Inductive Reasoning
Inductive reasoning reaches conclusions about general principles after observing many specific cases.

In this example, the conclusion is reasonable if the two premises are true—but what about that major premise? How many people are likely to agree with that statement? If either premise is not true or accepted by your audience, you can't use it to reach a valid and accepted conclusion. In this instance, you might have to spend the bulk of your speech proving the major premise, not the conclusion.

Inductive Reasoning
When you use **inductive reasoning**, you draw a general conclusion from specific cases (see Exhibit 17.7)—basically the opposite of deductive reasoning. If every professional basketball player you've ever seen is a great athlete, you could reasonably assume from these examples that all professional basketball players are great athletes—even though you haven't actually seen every one of them. If this way of thinking sounds familiar, it's because most of the things you believe resulted from piling up specific cases until you reached a general conclusion. Notice how different inductive reasoning is from deductive reasoning. With inductive reasoning, you don't assume a general principle is true until you've collected enough specific evidence to persuade yourself that it is probably true.

You can base inductive arguments on all kinds of evidence, including examples, statistics, expert testimony, and analogies. You learned about all four of these forms of support in Chapter 7, including what constitutes acceptable and unacceptable support. Here's a quick summary to help you evaluate your inductive persuasive arguments:

- *Induction based on examples.* For an example-based inductive argument to be valid, the examples must be both relevant and representative.
- *Induction based on statistics.* For a statistics-based inductive argument to be valid, the statistics must come from a reliable source, they must be current and representative, and the conclusions drawn from the statistics must follow logically.
- *Induction based on expert testimony.* For an inductive argument based on expert testimony to be valid, the testimony must be quoted accurately and used in proper context, the expert must truly be an expert (and as unbiased

as possible), and the testimony must be relevant to the subject at hand.

- *Induction based on analogy.* Analogy-based inductive arguments are useful and valid only if the analogy is being drawn between two things that are similar and if the audience is familiar with one of the two things.

Here's an example of inductive reasoning from a student who wanted to convince his audience that we are at risk from incompetent doctors who shouldn't be allowed to continue practicing medicine:[22]

> When Joyce Palso called the California State Medical Board to check on her plastic surgeon, Dr. Dean, she was relieved to hear that they had nothing on him. A week after her tummy tuck, though, Mrs. Palso's bandages were removed and two coal black patches of skin and an oozing red spot on top of an open wound were revealed. Dr. Dean assured her that was normal and sent her home. Actually, she had a post-operative infection of a heart valve because of her tummy tuck and required open heart surgery. Only after this operation was she told by the medical board that Dr. Dean had 11 malpractice suits filed against him and that the board had been trying to take his license away for over two years.

This is certainly an attention-grabbing introduction, but as induction-by-example, it isn't adequate by itself to prove the claim that dangerous doctors are a widespread problem. To accomplish this, the speaker continued with induction-by-statistics. The statistics made the case in a very powerful way:[23]

> It is hard to imagine that a doctor could injure, let alone kill, someone. After all doctors are supposed to save people's lives. And yet, according to the Institute of Medicine in a 2002 institute report, every year in the United States incompetent or impaired physicians kill 99,000 people.

> That means more people are killed by negligent doctors than die in traffic accidents.

This is a powerful technique often employed in successful problem-solution speaking: Grab the audience's attention with a strong example, then complete the inductive reasoning with statistics to prove that the problem is real and significant.

No matter what type of logic you use, a logical appeal is sound and valid when the steps from premise to conclusion are clear and easy to follow. Constructing logical arguments is like setting up a line of dominos and toppling the first one so that the entire line tumbles down in quick succession. Once you line up your logical "chain," step by step from evidence to conclusion, making that conclusion should be as easy and as obvious as tipping over that first domino. If you're having trouble explaining your line of reasoning, chances are there's something wrong with the logic somewhere.

Informal Logical Fallacies

Deductive and inductive reasoning are considered formal logic because you must follow specific rules to construct and test each argument. Both methods of argumentation are vulnerable to invalid reasoning if you don't follow the rules. In addition to these fallacies in formal logic, you need to watch out for *informal fallacies* as well, a category that covers just about every aspect of reasoning other than specific induction and deduction. Here are some of the most common informal fallacies:[24]

- *Ad hominem argument.* "Ad hominem" is Latin for "to the man." (Naturally, this problem applies "to the woman" as well!) An ad hominem argument is one that attacks the opponent and not his or her argument.
- *Ad populum argument.* "Ad populum" is Latin for "to the people," and it means trying to use the opinion or behavior of a majority of people to support a claim. An example of ad populum argumentation would be claiming that something must be right because most people

believe it.

- *Circular argument.* In a circular argument, the conclusion and the support are the same basic statement. Saying that the Bible is the word of God because the Bible says so is a classic example.
- *Distraction.* Diverting the audience's attention from the real issue or problem is another common fallacy. You've probably observed this one in operation in election year speeches. Often, a candidate responds to charges of corruption or incompetence by pointing out some flaw in his or her opponent.
- *Excluded middle.* The cable television program *Crossfire* is a prime example of the logical flaw of the excluded middle. On this show, two people who represent the left end of the political spectrum argue and issue with two people who represent the right end of the spectrum. Trouble is, most issues facing this country have a range of possibilities in the middle, which need to be considered when such issues are discussed. Failing to address those possibilities is an example of the excluded middle fallacy.
- *Confusing coincidence or correlation with causation.* You studied this issue back in Chapter 7, but it's important enough to repeat here: Just because B follows A, that doesn't mean B was *caused by* A.
- *Slippery slope.* In a slippery slope fallacy, you present only the first and last links in a chain of reasoning. You don't prove, through intermediate steps, that the links in between exist. Would it be logical to say that (A) you couldn't find a job upon graduation, so (B) your college must not have provided you with a good education? No, this is a slippery slope argument with many links missing in between A and B.
- *Straw man argument.* In a straw man argument, the speaker creates a position similar—but not identical—to the opponent's, then attacks that imaginary position, rather than the opponent's real position. This is, unfortunately, rather commonplace with political speeches. Say you're a U.S. senator, and that you want to restrict immigration in order to prevent foreign criminals from moving to the United States. Your

opponent appears on television and says what a bad idea it would be to close the border because it would prevent people from joining their families already living in the United States. Did you say that you wanted to prevent families from getting back together? Not at all, but your opponent created a straw man argument on the subject of immigration in order to cast doubt on your real argument.

- *Appeals to tradition.* When you use the **tradition appeal,** you point out the benefits of turning back to "traditional" values or to simpler times. With such an appeal, you try to paint a picture for your listeners of how things used to be better and have changed for the worse. You appeal to their nostalgia, pleasant memories of childhood, or ideas of how their childhood should have been. Next time an election rolls around, listen to how many candidates talk about returning to traditional values or generally getting back to the good old days. This can be a powerful emotional argument for listeners who are fed up with what they see on television or how scared they feel walking down city streets. However, there is no logical basis for the tradition appeal, in and of itself. Just because things have always been one way doesn't necessarily mean they should stay that way. Tradition appeals were used to block efforts to dismantle segregation and give women the right to vote. The good old days weren't always so good.

Even speakers with the best of intentions can commit logical fallacies if they don't pay close attention to their reasoning. As you develop every persuasive speech, double check both your formal and informal logic to make sure your conclusions are supportable and true.

Emotion

In contrast to a logical appeal, an **emotional appeal** speaks to the way people feel, a concept also known as **pathos.** People want to feel good about themselves and the world around them. To make them care about what you're saying, first convince them that you really care about your subject. Then convince them that they should care about your subject and that supporting your subject will make them feel good. An example of a speaker who appeals to audience emotions is Billy Graham. His sermons are more like stories, holding his listeners' rapt attention.[25]

Appeals for money for victims of an earthquake in Mexico City or a famine in northern Africa are almost always emotional. The speakers show pictures of the victims and ask for your help. You can appeal to a variety of emotions. Sympathy, guilt, pride, anger, love, and fear are all great motivators. No matter which emotion you target, the goal is to convince your audience that they will feel better if they do what you are suggesting. And don't exclude emotion from your logical appeals, either. Emotional appeals can put a human face on dry statistics and other forms or support.

Here are some useful guidelines for using emotional appeals effectively—and responsibly:

• *Appeal to positive audience values.* Because values

DEVELOPING YOUR CREATIVITY

SECRETS FOR DEVELOPING A PERSUASIVE PERSONA THAT WILL WIN OVER ANY AUDIENCE

Both research and a basic understanding of human nature tell us that speakers who are able to get the trust and respect of their audiences are more likely to be successful at persuasive speaking. Recognizing that is the easy part. How do you convince audiences that you are in fact worthy of their trust and respect?

Research into persuasive speaking turns up clues that you can use to refine your stage persona, the "character" you present when you step on stage. Of course, you have to be who you are; you can't slip into a false character, but there are things you can do to increase the audience's acceptance of you and your message:

• *Point out similarities between you and your audience.* Whether it's the same educational background, experience in the same industry, concern for the same social issues, or whatever, find something you have in common with the audience. People are more apt to trust people who are like themselves.
• *Treat your audience with courtesy and respect.* Even when you have a message the audience might not want to hear, you can still show respect for your listeners.
• *Prove that you know what you're talking about.* This might seem rather obvious, but it's easy to forget sometimes that the audience doesn't know you nearly as well as you know yourself. Demonstrating your expertise shouldn't be boastful and it doesn't have to be blatant. A phrase such as "When I was working on a similar project for IBM back in 1984" will convey your experience without boasting.
• *Criticize yourself and your message when such analysis is warranted.* If there is an obvious or significant weakness in your message, let the audience know that you know about it. When people learn that you're honest enough to criticize yourself, they'll be more inclined to believe the other things you have to say.

drive the way people think and act, using emotion to appeal to their values can be a very effective strategy. Of course, some people have values that mainstream society doesn't share,

EXHIBIT 17.8

Matching the Message, the Language, and the Delivery
These speakers demonstrate different emotional ranges,
adjusting their tone and style for the message and the audience.

and you have a responsibility to avoid appealing to negative values. Let's say you're developing a speech to protest free trade, and you build a case with examples and statistics of people who've lost their jobs as companies moved plants to low-wage countries. You appeal to the audience's positive sense of community and sympathy for these unemployed persons. However, a few of your white listeners with racist tendencies misinterpret your message as a supportable attack on the Mexican, Chinese, and other non-Caucasian workers in these low-wage countries. It's important to consider all the potential reactions your audience might have and to make sure your language is clear enough to avoid appealing to such negative values.

• *Use active, colorful language that stirs listeners' emotions.* Language is a wonderfully persuasive tool if you

use it creatively. To make an effective emotional appeal, use words that arouse passion.[26]

• *Match your language and your delivery to your message.* If you have a fiery message, choose fiery words and deliver them with passion (see Exhibit 17.8). If you have a gentle message, use nonthreatening language and a softer speaking style. In other words, make sure your message, the words you choose to convey it, and the style you use to deliver it are all part of an integrated package. Not only will you be less effective if there's some kind of mismatch, but audiences will think you're insincere.

• *Introduce and emphasize claims with emotionally charged examples.* One or two well-chosen and creatively presented examples can grab an audience's attention and engage the emotions you need to make your case. A student giving a speech about the danger of baby walkers didn't start off by stating that 42 percent of all head injuries occurring in children less than a year old are due to walker accidents. This is an appalling statistic, to be sure, but it doesn't have a specific, human face attached to it. The speaker started with a story about little Joey Staley, who fell down a flight of stairs in his walker. At the tender age of six months, Joey suffered a broken neck.[27] After hearing this heartbreaking example, the audience could more easily visualize all the statistics and medical information to follow; they knew about poor Joey.

- *Avoid being overly emotional.* You can lose credibility if the audience thinks you are so emotional that you can't see the facts in the situation. In addition, laying it on too heavy, particularly with negative emotions such as guilt or fear, can cause some people to do the exact opposite of what you're asking them to do. If you describe in graphic detail the horrendous conditions inside a famine-plagued refugee camp, some people may just stop listening because the reality is too hard to take.

- *Support emotion with facts, logic, narratives, and testimony whenever possible.* Supporting emotional appeals with logic is both a responsibility and an opportunity. The elaboration likelihood model (ELM) suggests there are two routes to persuasion, a central route that emphasizes logic and a peripheral route that emphasizes emotion. The central route requires more effort by your listeners because they have to think through the elements of your argument. You can use emotions on the peripheral route to keep the audience paying attention to your logical argument.[28]

Character

The final type of appeal involves how listeners perceive your ethos, or character. If listeners generally have a favorable attitude toward you as a person, you are more likely to be perceived as credible, as having good character.

Aristotle claimed that credibility is based on two factors: expertise and trustworthiness. You need to be perceived as well-informed or highly skilled relative to your topic, and your listeners need to believe that you're honest and sincere. A third factor is energy and charisma. A speaker who has charisma is perceived as engaging, likable, and attractive.

SAMPLE PERSUASIVE SPEECH

If It Doesn't Smell Nice—Don't Wear It!

(1) Have you ever settled down in a good spot at your local coffeehouse, spreading out your books and sipping your latté, only to have someone wearing heavy perfume settle in nearby? The smell clogs your senses and clouds your thinking. Or worse, if you're among the 83 million people in the United States who suffer from chronic sinus problems or allergies, the strong scent could even hamper your breathing, make you nauseous, or give you a migraine.

(2) The fragrance industry actually has a name for these perfumes. They're called "elevator gaggers." They gained popularity during the 1980s, and they seem to be lingering well into the 90s—perhaps because they're so hard to wash off!

(3) Actually, fragrance wearing and spraying is becoming an issue in some parts of the country, particularly among sufferers of MCS—multiple chemical sensitivity. The American Medical Association says there's no such ailment, but millions of people disagree—claiming symptoms of fatigue, fainting, dizziness, nausea, headaches, and respiratory difficulties. Medical experts do point out that perfumes can trigger migraine headaches. For the rest of us, heavy fragrances that overpower the smell of an expensive dinner are invading our personal space, at the least.

(4) Thousands of dollars are spent promoting the sex appeal and allure of costly perfumes, colognes, aftershaves, air fresheners, soaps, and other heavily scented products. The woman draped over the grand piano, promising some kind of forbidden pleasure, the youthful couple frolicking in the crashing surf, and the muscled arms of the man who wears a particular kind of aftershave—they're all chosen to convince you that *this* fragrance will make you appealing—particularly to the opposite sex. But what if you're turning off more people than you're turning on?

(5) Back in the 1920s, when Chanel No. 5 was introduced by fashion designer Coco Chanel, men and women wore fragrances lightly, if at all, for special evening occasions. According to veteran perfumer Maurice Raviol, the goal back then was to blend essential oils of flowers and spices to create "subtle, elusive whiffs of something beautiful."

(6) We can trace the history of fragrances back to the ancients who burned aromatic woods and resins in their temples to cover the smell of sacrifices. The Egyptians anointed each mummy with a unique scent so that if any part was separated in the afterworld, it could easily find its way back. Napoleon was still ordering perfumed gloves from Paris just a month before Waterloo, and his Josephine loved musk so much that her dressing rooms at Malmaison apparently still smell of it. But what's affecting you and I today dates back only a few decades.

(7) In 1953 Estee Lauder introduced Youth Dew, the first successful elevator gagger. Then in 1973, Charles Revson introduced Charlie—the perfume that changed the way women wore perfume. They called it a "lifestyle fragrance" and it was meant to be worn morning, noon, and night. Worse yet, it was cheap enough for everyone to afford.

(8) Charlie was quickly followed by Opium—the first of the heavy "oriental" scents of the 1980s. Giorgio came next—a sought-after status symbol and an unbelievable money-maker for its Beverly Hills creators. Giorgio was the elevator gagger of all time.

(9) The makers of Giorgio were the first to exploit the technology for putting scent strips in magazines and bills. Then, because they made bundles of money doing it, everyone else copied their strategy, as your nose can attest. Soon models were hired to spritz customers with Giorgio at Bloomingdales in New York. Eventually, the stuff was pumped out of atomizers over doorways, in elevators, and onto sidewalks. Still it sold in the millions. Farrah Fawcett, Jacqueline Bisset, and

Commentary

This persuasive speech not only exemplifies the use of the problem-solution structure but also demonstrates how to convince an audience to change their minds about a topic they may have trouble viewing as a serious problem. The speaker followed Monroe's motivated sequence model to build momentum, while taking care to use nonthreatening language and a softer style in keeping with the relative gentleness of the message.

(1–2) The first step in the motivated sequence model is to get the audience's attention, so the speaker grabs her listeners' attention by asking them to recall their own examples. For those who've never suffered from perfume pollution, she points to 83 million others who could be seriously affected.

(3) Now the speaker begins to highlight the need, widening her scope to include the perfume industry and consumer trends. This is step 2 in the motivated sequence.

(4) Two light emotional appeals are introduced with the inclusion of medical data (some people can be physically harmed by perfume scents) and common experience (none of us want our space invaded).

(5) The speaker continues to broaden the issue in listeners' minds by introducing the role advertising plays in the problem, followed by the logical appeal of the last sentence. Note how she forms this appeal as a question to keep her audience involved.

(6) Using facts and testimony, the speaker leads her audience into another perspective as she continues to amplify the problem.

(7) Through this historical angle, the speaker emphasizes that this problem is a relatively new issue, so some listeners may not have given it much thought. This understanding helps the audience members accept the change in viewpoint that the speaker wants them to make.

(8) The speaker continues to overcome audience resistance, building credibility by demonstrating how the use of some fragrances has evolved into something much more pervasive than a harmless personal enhancement.

(9) Giorgio is the final example of the ultimate "elevator gagger"—a vivid phrase used to remind the audience of the negative effects of strong, pervasive scents that pass the realm of "personal choice" and move into the public forum.

even Michael Jackson were said to wear Giorgio. Soon other manufacturers were spritzing too, and their perfumes got stronger to compete with Giorgio.

(10) Some industry experts theorize that these strong scents appealed to noses blitzed out by city bus and taxi fumes or dulled by the heavy smoking, drinking, and drug use of the postwar decades. Others think the strong perfumes epitomized an aggressive statement women wanted to make in the 1980s. Whatever the reason, by 1984 one Manhattan restaurant had banned Giorgio. And in April of that year, Bloomingdales spritzed the wrong woman.

(11) After spending 10 days in a New York hospital under treatment for serious respiratory distress, Deborah Martorano sued the department store for spraying her with an unknown fragrance without her permission. Ms. Martorano settled out of court for $75,000, but her lawsuit triggered new public debate over "perfume pollution": Your perfume could cause someone else discomfort or even serious physical harm, so whose rights prevail?

(12) Clerks started asking before they spritzed, and city governments and businesses started talking about "fragrance-free zones." Magazines like *The New Yorker* offered their subscribers scent-free issues. But as you can smell during any trek through the local shopping mall, the problem still lingers.

(13) Am I going to ask you to stop wearing perfume and to demand that others cease and desist? No, of course not. Although research into the olfactory senses is still in its infancy, scientific studies have already revealed that pleasant fragrances are soothing, relaxing, and inspiring; we couldn't and wouldn't want to live without them. And therein lies our dilemma: what to do when one man or woman's definition of "pleasant fragrance" overpowers and inhibits our own sense of smell.

(14) In response to public complaints, some cities and businesses are trying the "fragrance-free" solution, establishing areas or meeting places in which people are asked not to wear or spray personal or cleaning products with strong fragrances. A pastor in Boise, Idaho, holds a "fragrance-free" sermon every Sunday afternoon. The University of Minnesota's School of Social Work has banned students and faculty from using scented products that might trigger allergic reactions. Congress has even appropriated $250,000 to study the issue.

(15) Despite the fact that Solon of Athens set a precedent in the sixth century B.C. by prohibiting the sale of all perfumes in his cities, we can't really legislate good sense—or good smell. And the fragrance industry agrees. They've flown lobbyists out from the East Coast to any region that has considered adopting fragrance-free resolutions or laws.

(16) No, we can't actually outlaw the wearing or the manufacture of perfumes. Banning perfume use infringes on personal rights, and prohibiting its sale or manufacture puts government where we don't want it. Instead, by showing some personal good sense and restraint, we can solve this problem to everyone's satisfaction. We don't have to slather on the cologne like Napoleon did—at the rate of 50 bottles a month. And if we really want to be attractive to others, we can learn how to avoid the elevator gaggers. Here's the secret:

(17) All perfumes have a top note, which is the light, appealing scent you smell when you first sniff the bottle, a middle note, which is how the perfume smells a moment after it hits your skin, and a bottom note, which is the heaviest part of the scent, designed to linger all day, and in some cases, all week.

(18) Most fragrance purchasing decisions are triggered by the top note. But that lovely floral scent can turn sour on your skin twenty minutes after the cash register has closed on your $37-an-ounce purchase. So be kind to your friends, family, and classmates—try a perfume for an hour or two before you buy it.

(19) If it doesn't smell nice—don't wear it, don't praise it, and don't buy it for anyone else. You can contribute to the solution to a problem that affects millions of people, and you can make your own presence more enjoyable to people around you. They'll love you for it—and isn't that what we're all after, anyway?

(10) The speaker uses examples to show how the problem has mushroomed, with stronger perfumes, costlier promotions, and more public demand for these heavy, "status" fragrances.

(11) Note the use of logical and expertise appeals here and throughout the previous paragraphs.

(12) The narrative example brings the seriousness of the problem into clear focus. Through it, the speaker hopes to extinguish any lingering doubt that perfume pollution is a serious issue.

(13) The actions of reputable business and government leaders reinforce the speaker's argument that the problem exists.

(14) Now that the problem is clear, the speaker quickly defuses potential audience fears that her solution will place any unacceptable demands on them. Moreover, the speaker uses this opportunity to reinforce the rapport she's established, using a personal, friendly tone and appealing to both emotional and logical sensibilities.

(15) To convince her audience that her solution is best, the speaker has chosen to explore other options first. This approach also supports her argument that perfume pollution is serious—because others are already at work trying to solve the problem.

(16) The speaker is now ready to propose a satisfying solution. First, she lets her audience know what she's not proposing. She gains support for her solution by demonstrating that other options are not acceptable. She highlights the benefits of her solution by stating what it will NOT require listeners to give up—personal freedom.

(17–18) She introduces the idea of top and bottom notes to explain her proposed solution and to prompt the audience to take specific action.

(19) Note the tone of this paragraph as the speaker reiterates her call to action. It's personal, helpful, and informative, encouraging the audience to act out of good sense and a desire to feel good about their choices—again, using low-key appeals to both logic and emotion. The conclusion subtly twists the thousand-dollar love-appeal of traditional perfume ads into an appeal for the speaker's solution. Note also that the speaker is appealing to both public and private needs here.

Bibliography

Burt, Urin. "Point and Sniff," *Kiplinger's Personal Finance,* January 2001, 26.

Ebersole, Rene S., "Making Scents," *Current Science,* April 20, 2001, 8.

Hawn, Carleen, and Levine, Joshua. "The Sweet Smell of Excess," *Forbes,* October 11, 1999, 34.

James, Jennie. "Scents of Change," *Time,* April 10, 2000, 7.

Mogelonsky, Marcia. "Dollars and Scents," *American Demographics,* June 1997, 32.

Samuels, Allison. "Making Scents," *Newsweek,* September 30, 2002, 68.

Tant, Lisa. "Scents Appeal," *Chatelaine,* December 2001, 42.

Weiss, Giselle. "Scents and Sensibility," *Lancet,* August 31, 2002, 225.

Ying, Chu. "Scent Trip," *Flare,* November 2001, 72.

SUMMARY

The first step in developing a persuasive speech is to choose your structure. The three basic types are problem-solution, comparison-of-alternatives, and refutative. When you use the problem-solution structure, you can choose from the basic two-part problem-solution method, the five-step motivated sequence model (getting the audience's attention, highlighting a need that will create the motivation to change, proposing a solution that the audience will consider satisfactory, helping the audience visualize your proposed solution, and prompting the audience to take action), or the four-step AIDA model (attention, interest, desire, and action). Remember that it's important to convince people that a problem really exists. This may sound like an obvious point, but not everyone will perceive every issue in the same way you do. Some listeners may not be convinced that circumstances are as bad as you say they are; other listeners may think your so-called problem is actually a good thing. And if audience members don't accept your problem, they probably won't be interested in your solution.

Once you've decided on a structure, the next question is the best way to make your case. You can choose from three categories of persuasive appeals: logic, emotion, and character. Most persuasive speeches combine elements of both logic and emotion.

When you put together a logical appeal, make sure you're using the most appropriate type of logic. With deductive reasoning, you draw a specific conclusion by referring to general principles or ideas. With inductive reasoning, you work in the other direction, from a collection of specific points to a general conclusion.

You can base inductive reasoning on examples, statistics, expert testimony, or analogies.

Both deductive and inductive reasoning have some specific rules to follow to ensure valid logic. In addition to these two categories of formal logic, you have to watch out for a wide variety of informal logical fallacies, too. These range from ad hominem arguments (attacking an opponent instead of attacking his or her message) to straw man appeals (creating a fictitious position that is similar to your opponent's, then attacking that position instead of the opponent's real position).

Emotional appeals can be extremely persuasive, both on their own and in conjunction with logical appeals. To ensure effective and responsible use of emotional appeals, you should follow six guidelines: (1) appeal to positive values, (2) use active, colorful language that stirs listeners' emotions, (3) use emotional delivery to convey an emotional message, (4) use emotionally charged examples, (5) avoid being overly emotional since doing so runs the risk of losing credibility, and (6) back up your emotional appeals with facts and other forms of support. An appeal based on character depends on how your audience perceives your credibility, which is influenced by expertise, trustworthiness, and charisma.

KEY TERMS

AIDA model (373)
comparison-of-alternatives strategy (374)
conclusion (381)
deductive reasoning (381)
emotional appeal (385)
enthymemes (382)
inductive reasoning (383)
logical appeal (381)
major premise (381)
minor premise (381)
motivated sequence method (370)
pathos (385)
primacy and recency effect (375)
problem-solution model (368)
refutative strategy (377)
syllogism (381)
tradition appeal (385)

APPLY CRITICAL THINKING

1. Is what we call "common sense" a product of inductive or deductive logic? Explain your answer.

2. Does the opponent for a refutative speech have to be a specific person or group? Why or why not?

3. Would you say that deductive or inductive reasoning is more likely to lead to a provable conclusion? Why?

4. Could you have an effective emotional appeal without a logical appeal at all? Could you have an effective logical appeal without an emotional appeal? Why or why not?

5. Would a simple numerical statement about the number of children who starve to death every year be an effective persuasive appeal? Why or why not?

6. Why is a tradition appeal considered a logical fallacy?

7. Why is appealing to popular opinion a logical fallacy?

SHARPEN YOUR SKILLS

Individual Exercises

1. Would you use one of the problem-solution structures or the comparison-of-alternatives structure for a persuasive speech to your classmates on the subject of Reyes syndrome? Why? (Do some basic research into Reyes syndrome if necessary.)

2. Would you use a problem-solution structure or the comparison-of-alternatives structure for a persuasive speech to your classmates on the subject of financial aid for college students? Why?

3. What benefits could you promise an audience if they accept your solution of volunteering as tutors to help combat adult illiteracy?

4. What type of reasoning is at work in the following statement: "We've lost money on 48 of the 52 power plants we've constructed in South America in the last ten years. It's obvious that it's impossible to turn a profit in that market."

Group Exercises

5. With a team of three or four students, conduct the research necessary to put the following four points in most effective order:

   a. Without routine health-care options, many poor people are forced to wait until problems become so serious that they require emergency room care, which is much more expensive.

   b. Emergency rooms in many hospitals are already overcrowded with "traditional" emergency cases such as accidents and heart attacks.

   c. Children are suffering permanent damage from health problems that could have been prevented through adequate routine care.

   d. Many hospitals are forced to absorb the costs of emergency room visits by poor people with no health insurance coverage.

6. With a team of classmates, analyze three or four recent political speeches. (Check *Vital Speeches of the Day* for possibilities.) Identify as many logical flaws as you can find, including attacking an opponent's character instead of his or her ideas. Explain how you would fix each flaw while retaining the effectiveness of the original speech.

Chapter Eighteen

SPEAKING ON SPECIAL OCCASIONS

LEARNING OBJECTIVES
After studying this chapter, you will be able to
1. Identify the four major types of personal speaking you'll do on the job (other than traditional public speaking engagements).
2. Explain why presentation skills are so important to career success.
3. Describe the two major types of sales presentations and how they compare to traditional persuasive speaking.
4. List the key points to remember when introducing another speaker.
5. Explain why after-dinner speaking can be so difficult.
6. List the key points to remember when developing a eulogy speech.
7. Define a quick process for assembling impromptu speeches.

DEVELOPING SPEECHES FOR PROFESSIONAL AND SOCIAL SITUATIONS

*H*ave you ever been asked to make a toast at a wedding reception or to say a few words after receiving an athletic or academic award? These are just two of the many special-situation speeches that people are expected to make throughout their lives. This chapter will show you how to adapt the general principles you've learned in this course to a variety of professional and social situations that call for particular kinds of speeches.

In Chapter 6, the section on context mentioned the idea of rhetorical exigencies, or factors about the speaking situation that should influence what you say and how you say it. These rhetorical exigencies are what set special-situation speeches apart from your other speaking opportunities.[1] For instance, the toast you give at a wedding reception is influenced quite strongly by the situation. This is a time for joyful, sincere messages that focus on the newlywed couple. It's obviously not a time for sarcasm or messages that focus on the speaker. In other words, the situation more or less demands a certain kind of speech. This chapter covers speaking in three situations: speeches on the job, speeches at special events, and impromptu speeches.

SPEAKING ON THE JOB

Outside this class, most of your speaking opportunities will probably occur on the job. In fact, it's safe to assume that for every formal speaking engagement you might have, you'll probably have dozens of less formal opportunities to address colleagues, customers, and other audiences in meetings and other forums. You may be required to present information to individuals or groups, make recommendations on a course of action, sell goods or services, or provide training for other employees.

The style of these on-the-job speaking opportunities will vary greatly, depending on your audience. If you're presenting information to co-workers, the setting will probably be relatively unstructured. However, if you're making a recommendation to a group of high-level executives, a more structured setting is likely. The settings and styles for selling and training are also varied. For each occasion, you'll have to plan your speech, style, delivery, and even attire accordingly.

Although most of your on-the-job speaking will be either informative or persuasive, specific situations call for particular points of preparation and delivery. The following sections offer some guidance on presenting information, making recommendations, selling goods and services, and training.

Presenting Information

Employees and managers make a wide range of informational presentations, from informal status reports to formal research investigations. These presentations are informative speaking, to be sure, but the environment on the job often adds some special twists. Keep the following points in mind:

- *Your audience is likely to be keenly interested in your message.* Of course, your classmates may not always be perfectly attentive during your in-class speeches, but your future colleagues and managers usually have much greater interest in what you have to say, because your information can have a dramatic impact on your co-workers and the organization you all work in. Say that the company you work for is trying to decide whether to maintain its current markets and customers or actively seek new customers, and say that you're presenting the results of a marketing research project. Even if you're not recommending one course of action (which is often the case), the audience is likely to scrutinize every word you say because the information is so important. Making the wrong decision could lead to lost revenue, layoffs, and even bankruptcy in extreme cases. Expect to be questioned about where you got your data and how you analyzed it—particularly if your information points to a course of action that some audience members don't agree with.

- *Even simple presentations can serve as "snapshots" of your talent and performance.* Much of the impression you give executives and other key people in your organization is based on how well you make presentations. You may be a technical or creative genius, or the hardest worker in the company, but if you can't communicate those qualities during your presentations, your reputation and your career may suffer.
- *Many on-the-job presentations are highly technical or complex.* Clear descriptions, demonstrations, and explanations are a must in technical or complex presentations. Key people in your audience may need to make decisions on your information, even though they may not understand all the details. You have the responsibility of providing accurate summaries to help these people grasp important points and meanings. Remember, you may need to adjust the content and style of your delivery to reach various audiences, even within the same organization.
- *Most managers and executives are awash in data and information.* Imagine giving and listening to speeches for four or five hours a day, five days a week. The higher up the organizational ladder

people are, the more time they spend in meetings, talking and listening. In other words, these people receive a constant flow of data and information. As a result, they appreciate employees who can deliver concise, reliable summaries in as little time as possible. For example, if you are presenting the results of a research project, give them only the results and some basic information about the procedures. You can provide details in a written report. Limit your presentation to what they really need to know. If they want more information, they'll ask.

Because of these four points, be sure you know your audience and your material inside-out, backward, and forward. You're expected to be the expert on the subject, sharing what you know with your boss, your co-workers, or others who need the information. So prepare as thoroughly as possible. Careful preparation will help you head off any or all of the disasters that commonly strike on-the-job presentations (see Exhibit 18.1).

Making Recommendations

At some point you'll probably have to make recommendations on the job, ranging from minor issues such as a company function to major ones such as a companywide reorganization, a new product, or a merger. Remember, you'll be asked for a recommendation because you know something about the issue or because you're considered an authority on the subject. So before recommending anything, carefully weigh all the evidence yourself, and decide what course or option you believe is best.

Making recommendations is a form of persuasion, of course. Chapters 15 and 16 provide details about persuasive speeches, and "Structuring the Persuasive Speech" in Chapter 16 is especially helpful. In most cases, you'll want to convince your audience to accept one solution over others. You'll need to point out the advantages and disadvantages of your solution and the alternatives. Naturally, you'll want to emphasize the positive aspects of your solution and the

Potential problem	Why it's a problem
1. Failure to prepare people before the meeting	If people are hit with surprising information that they don't agree with, they'll start arguing with you (aloud or in their heads) while you're speaking; discuss with key audience members what you're going to talk about ahead of time.
2. Abstract, ill-defined purpose	Presentation will come across as half-baked mishmash; audience may assume your thinking is as weak as the presentation.
3. Lack of organization	People will struggle to follow your train of thought, which means they may get off the train before you reach your all-important conclusion or recommendation.
4. Distracting situation	Anything in the physical environment (e.g., too hot, too cold, squeaking chairs) can distract people from your message.
5. Relying on memory or a manuscript	Destroys your ability to be spontaneous, which can be particularly important if you expect any interaction with the audience.
6. Amateurish delivery	Poor delivery cripples even the best messages.
7. Poor or misused visual aids	They'll detract from your presentation instead of enhancing it as they're supposed to.
8. Microphone sabotage	If the room is big enough to require a microphone and you arrive at the last minute to discover the microphone doesn't work, many people will have to struggle to hear you and some won't hear you at all.
9. Terminal dullness	No matter how exciting your message is, a dull delivery will prevent people from paying attention to it.
10. Timing problems	Running over your allotted time annoys both the audience and speakers following you; you may be forced to skip key parts of your message.

EXHIBIT 18.1
What Can Go Wrong with Presentations: 10 Avoidable Disasters
All of these disasters are avoidable with careful preparation and practice.

negative aspects of others. As with many persuasive speeches, you may need to convey a considerable amount of information to support your position. Consider the following example:

The employee benefits committee has reviewed company vacation and sick leave policy, and we think the policy needs to be changed.

Currently, each employee earns from 10 to 25 days a year of vacation time, depending on length of service. In addition, each employee is allowed 10 days per year of sick leave. This sort of vacation and sick leave policy is fairly standard and has been unquestioned until recently. As part of our study to determine how to improve em-

ployee benefits, we analyzed data on how employees have used their sick leave over the last 15 years. We were rather surprised to learn that during this period, fewer than 10 percent of all company employees have used their full allotment of sick leave. In fact, 80 percent of employees used 5 days or fewer yearly.

In other words, it appears that we are rewarding employees who use a lot of sick leave and penalizing those with good attendance records. This doesn't seem fair to employees or good for the company. We therefore propose the following changes:

- Eliminate the annual 10-day sick-leave allotment.
- Change the term *vacation time* to *personal time off* or *PTO*.
- Increase each employee's annual PTO allotment by 5 days.
- Let employees use their days for whatever purpose they choose.

This new policy would benefit the 80 percent of employees who currently use 5 days or fewer a year of sick leave. Their

THREE QUESTIONS TO ASK YOURSELF BEFORE YOU RESPOND TO YOUR AUDIENCE

Whether you're delivering an informational presentation, a recommendation, a sales pitch, or a training program, you're going to get questions in nearly every case. The natural response to a question is to answer it immediately. However, jumping right into your answer might get you into trouble. Before answering, quickly ask yourself these three questions:

- *Why is this person asking this question?* People in the audience ask questions for three basic reasons: They really want more information, they actually just want an opportunity to demonstrate their own knowledge to the rest of the audience, and occasionally they just want to cause trouble for you. Take a second to analyze the question *and* the questioner before you respond.
- *Can I answer it?* You'll get questions you can't answer, whether because you really don't have the answer or you can't divulge it in front of the entire audience. In either case, don't ever try to fake it. You'll get more respect from the audience by being honest and admitting you don't know or can't give the answer. However, don't leave it hanging there. You can ask if anyone else in the audience can answer the question, you can offer to find the answer and get back to the person, or you can say that you can't answer the question publicly at this time.
- *Is now the best time to answer it?* Sometimes a question indicates that at least one person in the audience isn't getting your message (which means that others probably aren't, either). If you encounter such a question, it's best to answer it right away so that you can continue without losing more of your audience. However, if a question doesn't seem critical to your presentation's success and answering it will chew up valuable time or take the discussion off course, offer to answer the question at the end of your presentation or in private afterward.

With a little practice, you'll start to run through this list of questions automatically. You'll not only maintain better control of the situation as you learn to manage questions more effectively but also increase the success of your presentations by managing the flow of information according to plan.

---

available vacation time would increase. The 20 percent of employees who use more than 5 days' sick leave per year would have less available vacation. This seems more fair than the current policy, which penalizes employees with good attendance. Moreover, this change may encourage employees to adopt healthier lifestyles, since they'll benefit by having more healthy vacation days off. If such a shift does occur, the company might then save on its health-care costs as well.

If you have any questions or concerns, we'd be happy to discuss them now or after the meeting.

Notice how quickly the speaker gets through the information and makes the recommendation. This is classic problem-solution structure, with a reminder at the beginning regarding current policy. Notice the lack of detail in the presentation; the speaker gets to the point as quickly as possible, hitting only the high points. Most likely, one or more members of the audience would question the speaker about costs, administrative issues, possible effects on recruiting or employee morale, or other issues. The speaker doesn't try to cover every one of these issues but makes the case quickly and then invites questions.

Selling Goods and Services

Selling is an adaptation of persuasive speaking that can be divided into two categories: canned and interactive sales presentations. The **canned sales presentation** is like a traditional persuasive speech; you present your information and make your persuasive appeal using a carefully planned and highly structured approach. You've probably been the target of canned selling at one time or another. This method is particularly popular with telemarketers, who often begin their rehearsed pitch as soon as you pick up the phone. This canned method has two advantages: It makes it easier to be consistent from salesperson to salesperson and from customer to customer, and it requires less training to deliver. The main disadvantage of the canned approach is that it's largely one-way communication, based on the assumption that the seller knows what the potential buyer wants and needs. If the buyer has unique needs or lots of questions, the canned approach is usually not effective and can, in fact, turn people away.

The **interactive sales presentation** differs from traditional persuasive speaking and the canned approach because it's *interactive;* that is, the seller asks what the potential buyer needs and then adapts the sales presentation on the spot, based on what the buyer says. In this respect, the interactive presentation is more like person-to-person conversation than public speaking. However, interactive selling uses the same techniques you've learned for other persuasive speeches; you just don't have the luxury of planning out everything you're going to say and delivering those exact words as planned. Interac-

Success Tip

Just like traditional persuasive speeches, canned sales presentations must be shaped around carefully researched audience needs and perceptions because you usually don't have the opportunity to adapt once you've started.

tive selling requires more thinking on your feet as you ask questions and respond to verbal and nonverbal clues. In a sense, it's the standard problem-solution format with a twist: You're not always sure what the problem is when you start your presentation.

This doesn't mean that the interactive sales presentation is totally impromptu, even though experienced salespeople can make it seem that way. You can plan all the responses you're likely to need, based on how the listener might react during each stage of the presentation (see Exhibit 18.2). In fact, telemarketers who use the interactive approach often have these options programmed into a computer, and the presentation tracks the potential buyer's responses to each question.

One expert in selling divides the sales presentation into three time frames: credibility time, information time, and sales time. First, you establish credibility with the listener(s) so they know that you are knowledgeable enough and trustworthy enough to help them choose the right solution. Second, you ask questions and listen to what potential customers say they need. Third, based on what you've learned during the second phase, you then propose a solution that meets the customer's needs.[2]

Training

Training is one of the most common speaking tasks you face on the job. It's essentially informational speaking, with the added element of real-time audience feedback in most cases.

The purpose of training is to somehow change a work situation—to increase productivity, to improve employee morale, to prepare an employee for a promotion or job change, to meet the requirements of new legislation, and so on. Training can take many forms: You might present information to a group of people in a lecture-type setting. You might instruct a new employee one-on-one at a workstation. You might give a demonstration to a group of employees on how to use a

EXHIBIT 18.2

Planning an Interactive Presentation
When you plan an interactive presentation, try to anticipate likely responses, and try to have answers (or follow-up questions) ready for each one.

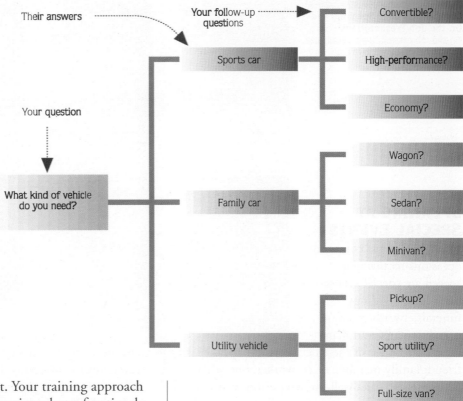

new piece of equipment. Your training approach will vary in different situations, but a few tips do apply to all training situations:

- *Be very familiar and comfortable with the material you are teaching.* Your audience is likely to have many questions, and you must be prepared to answer them knowledgeably and thoroughly.
- *Find out your audience's levels of skill or knowledge about your subject, and prepare your speech accordingly.* By focusing on your audience members, you won't be so far over their heads that they get lost and confused, and you won't be so simplistic that you insult their intelligence or bore them.
- *Encourage audience feedback.* Presenting the information is only half the challenge. The other half involves making sure the audience understands and can use the information on the job. Because of this, training sessions are usually much more interactive than traditional informative speaking.
- *Recognize that people have different learning styles.* Some prefer to learn by example, some

like to see the big picture first, and some like to see all the details laid out in a logical way. You won't always have the luxury of meeting every person's individual needs, but it's usually a good idea to cover difficult concepts in at least two styles to increase the chances that everyone in the audience grasps the message.
- *Understand that adults usually learn things so that they can solve real-life problems.* Most adults like to see a connection between what they're about to learn and some problem they face on the job or in their personal lives. (Learning just for the sake of learning still occurs, but less often in a work setting.) It's the desire to solve problems that creates the motivation to learn.[3]

By now, you've probably noticed some similarities and some differences between speaking on the job and speaking in public. Public speaking expert Frank Dance, who teaches both students and professionals, has developed a succinct summary of the differences—see Exhibit 18.3.

EXHIBIT 18.3

Comparing Public Speaking and On-the-Job Presentations
On-the-job presentations usually call for special preparation and delivery techniques.

Factor/circumstance	Public speaking	On-the-job presentations
Setting	People usually attend voluntarily	People are usually told to attend, so they may not be actively paying attention to you to start with
Audience participation	Usually passive	Often active; ability to think on your feet is important
Speaker's expected expertise	You've earned the right to speak	You're viewed as "first among equals," so credibility is important
Decentering	Somewhat important; depends on the situation	Very important
Use of visual aids	Sometimes	Usually; people in many organizations have access to sophisticated presentation equipment
Questions and answers	Sometimes	Usually, and often ongoing through the course of the presentation

SPEAKING AT SPECIAL EVENTS

Among the most common occasions requiring a speech are special events—birthdays, weddings, funerals, awards ceremonies, banquets, and many others. For most of these occasions the speaker is a friend, family member, or co-worker, but other occasions call for a well-known person who is often well paid for speaking. Leading commencement speakers (athletes and political leaders) can be paid at least as much for one speech as college graduates can expect to make in their first year on the job.[4] Good after-dinner speakers are always in demand.

Speeches for special events are usually more personal and can be less formal than other types of public speeches. The subject of the speech is often a person or group being honored, welcomed, or introduced. Here are several points that apply to all kinds of special event speeches:

• *As a rule, special event speeches should be brief.* Even old-time jugglers, comedians, and other vaudeville performers limited their acts to 12 minutes or less.[5] Err on the side of brevity. No one will complain if your speech is shorter than they expect.

• *Preparation is crucial.* In most cases, you are not the center of attention for the event, and you don't want to become the center of attention by stumbling or forgetting what you had to say. No matter how short your speech will be, plan it in advance, organize it well, and practice until you can deliver it smoothly. If you need notes or other materials, have them well organized and accessible. You don't want to waste time and look foolish fumbling for note cards or props. The better prepared you are, the more you'll be able to relax and present a good speech.

• *Special events are usually emotional occasions.* Consequently, your speech should also arouse emotions in your audience. The audience might be feeling nostalgic, for instance, and a good commemorative speech will expand on the nostalgia. One good way to do this is to use memories that fit the occasion.[6] These might be memories of incidents involving the person or event being commemorated or memories of other incidents that evoke similar feelings. Tell a story about the incident, the impressions it made, and what was learned from the experience.

• *People are likely to remember special events for years to come, so be careful.* You don't want to be caught forever on somebody's wedding videotape making a crude remark or insulting someone with inappropriate humor. On the positive side, these speeches can be great opportunities to say something meaningful and memorable, so plan carefully and rise to the occasion.

Keep these general points in mind whether you're introducing other speakers, presenting or accepting honors and awards, welcoming attendees and guests, entertaining dinner audiences, or celebrating accomplishments and milestones.

Introducing Other Speakers

The purpose of a speech of introduction is not only to introduce another speaker, not only to let the audience know something about the speaker, but also to build interest in the speaker and help form a bond between the speaker and the audience. Toward that end, whenever you're introducing others, plan to tell your audience the following:[7]

- What the topic is
- Why the topic is important to the audience
- Why the speaker is qualified to address them on this subject
- Who the speaker is

As this list implies, consider announcing the speaker's name last, especially if the speaker is well known to the audience. If you announce the name earlier, the audience will applaud, interrupting your introduction.

One good way to gather information for your introduction is to talk to the speaker in advance. Think of yourself as a newspaper reporter; ask what the speaker wants you to say, what the topic or title of the speech is, and how long the speech will be. If you have information about the speaker from other sources, verify it with the speaker. You certainly don't want to say anything false or misleading in your introduction.

Some other things to remember: Keep your introduction very short (one to two minutes), pronounce the speaker's name correctly, focus on the speaker rather than on yourself, don't give too much information about the speaker's speech, don't be overly lavish with praise that the speaker can't live up to, and avoid trite, overused phrases. Here's a good example:

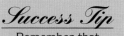

Success Tip

Remember that when speaking at special events, you are rarely the main focus. Unless you're the recipient of an award or other honor, don't outshine the star.

Our speaker today claims that fourteen years ago she was terrified of public speaking, just like most Americans. But after seeing herself on videotape, she decided that it was time to conquer her fears.

Since that time she has founded several successful Toastmasters clubs, has been named "Toastmaster of the Year" twelve times, and has won more than 75 awards for speaking, training, sales, and leadership. While working for Bristol Myers' U.S. Pharmaceutical Division, she was named "Sales Representative of the Year" for being the number-one representative in the number-one district in the country.

For the next thirty minutes, our speaker will demonstrate how to turn your fear of public speaking into excitement. Her program is entitled "Getting Your Butterflies to Fly in Formation." Please join me in giving a warm welcome to our speaker, Mary-Ellen Drummond.[8]

Note how this introduction builds interest in Drummond's speech while describing her qualifications. By the time the audience hears her name, there should be no doubt that she is the right person to be delivering this speech. Also, note that the speaker in this introduction focuses entirely on the audience and on Drummond. You can see how the introductory speaker functions as a matchmaker in a sense, coupling the needs of the audience with the promised benefits of the speaker.

In some cases, your job of introducing the speaker may include moderating a question-and-answer session after the speech.[9] Repeat each question to make sure the whole audience has heard it, then let the speaker answer. Cut off questions after the designated amount of time, thank the speaker again, thank the audience for attending, and lead the applause for the speaker.

The speaker presenting Vaclav Havel in the following speech had the advantage of introducing someone with a worldwide reputation for heroic leadership, so there was little need to build up the audience's interest. However, she took care to remind the audience of Havel's courage, accomplishments, and commitment to freedom as a way to help set the stage for his speech:

INTRODUCTION SPEECH
Linda Darby Stellens

Our speaker today has been called the "king of the dissidents," "a European Ghandi," and "one of the most beloved heads of state in the world" by *Vanity Fair* magazine. The *Utne Reader* has described him as "a visionary politician who doesn't have time to be full of himself." The world knows him as the playwright who became president—a man who spent five years in prison for writing and speaking out against the totalitarian regime that was holding his country in chains, and who emerged to engineer its rebirth as a free nation. He is rightly credited with keeping alive the political resistance that triumphed in the "Velvet Revolution" of 1989—the peaceful overthrow of 41 years of communist rule over Czechoslovakia.

Back in 1979, when this man was offered the choice of imprisonment or a passport to the United States, he refused the passport. Today he is known throughout the world for his uncompromising values, his passionate essays and speeches, his courageous leadership, and his selfless commitment to the improvement of our global society. I am sure his remarks today will have great meaning to us all. Please welcome with me the honorable President of the Czech Republic, Mr. Vaclav Havel (VAHTS-lahv HAH-vel).[10]

Presenting Honors and Awards

Many of the guidelines for presenting honors and awards are like those for introducing other speakers. In a presentation speech, you want to tell the audience what the award means, who is getting the award, and what the recipient has done to deserve the award. If the recipient is one of several people considered for the honor or award, you may want to acknowledge the people who weren't chosen, particularly if they are in the audience. And if there is an interesting fact about the award itself, include that information as well. For instance, the prepared speech used to present awards to students in the Lambda Pi Eta Honors Society points out that these Greek letters stand for logos, pathos, and ethos—key elements of public speaking. Including facts such as these can make the award presentation more meaningful and interesting to people in the audience.

An award presentation speech can be longer than introducing a speaker, depending on the situation. The emphasis is on the recipient's past actions, not what the recipient will say when accepting the award. Here's a classic example—a speech by then Vice President Lyndon Johnson honoring astronaut John Glenn on his historic orbital flight.[11]

My fellow Americans.

It is a high privilege to welcome one of the great pioneers of all history, Colonel John Glenn.

He is one of the best-known men in all the world, and it pleases all of us so much to see this wonderful American family reunited again here in the sunshine of Florida.

Four years ago President Eisenhower urged before the United Nations that all nations explore space together for peaceful purposes. President Kennedy in his first State of the Union Message again urged all nations to explore space together for peaceful purposes.

But it remained for this stalwart marine, John Glenn, and his achievement, to bring forth from Premier Khrushchev a proposal that we attempt to work together in space.

So, Colonel, you must feel that you have been able to do something that two presidents have not been able to do. And while we do not know what is in the offing, we know the prayers that are in our hearts, and I know that you join with me in the happiness that we all feel in seeing this great man reunited with his lovely wife, his two typically American children, his mother and father, and his mother-in-law and father-in-law.

Colonel Glenn, it's wonderful to have you aboard.

The style may not fit every presentation occasion, to be sure, but it fit the context of that historic moment back in 1962.

Another important point to consider is the mechanics of actually handing an award to a recipient. Being careful not to drop the award, pass it from your left hand to the recipient's left hand, leaving your right hand free. Shake hands, congratulate the recipient, step back and applaud (if appropriate), and yield the floor to the recipient.

When the mayor of Coronado, California presented a local couple with an award for their private garden, she placed the accomplishment in the context of the city's reputation with visitors from around the world. She then went on to detail why the judges chose the couple's garden, while giving a kind nod to the citizens who were considered but not given the award:

PRESENTATION SPEECH
Mayor Mary Herron—
Coronado Beautification Award

As Mayor of Coronado, California, I am frequently called on to present awards and commendations, but this particular award has great meaning for our community. We have inaugurated the Coronado Beautification Award to recognize the outstanding efforts of our citizens who provide this island community with its memorable elegance, its visual refreshment—in short, some of the most beautiful gardens we've seen anywhere in the world!

As you all know, Coronado frequently plays host to presidents and dignitaries, and not a few celebrities, officials, men and women of the Armed Forces, America's Cup racers, and other fascinating people from around the world. As they travel our small-town streets, gazing at the mansions, the

Victorians, and the cozy cottages, one of the most commonly heard remarks is, "Oh, look at that beautiful garden!" The world has come to our doorstep and appreciates what it sees. We felt it was time to honor our next-door neighbors for the hours, thought, expense, and good old-fashioned toil they've invested to make our island community a blooming paradise.

This choice was not an easy one for our judges to make, as they'll be glad to tell you, but after much study and consideration, our judges have named Brian and Andrea Applegate of 555 "B" Avenue as our first recipients of the Coronado Beautification Award. If you've driven or walked by the Applegates' home, you know that they have not been content to keep their roses, wisteria vines, flowering plums, and exotic annuals well-tended inside the walls of their classic cottage garden. For the passersby who might feel shy about peeking through the arched trellis for a glimpse, the Applegates have extended this floral profusion outside their garden walls. They've planted a colorful abundance of roses, shrubs, annuals, and perennials along the sidewalks of their corner lot, where everyone can enjoy them.

Mr. and Mrs. Applegate, if you'll step up here please . . . I am honored to present you with this plaque which pays tribute to your selfless toil and investment. You have truly beautified our community, and you richly deserve the first Coronado Beautification Award!

(She presents the plaque, steps aside, and joins the applause for the beaming couple.)

Accepting Honors and Awards

The key to a successful acceptance speech is to be brief, especially if other people are receiving awards or honors after you. The dancer Mikhail Baryshnikov once accepted an award for actress Marlene Dietrich. When he asked her what he should say, she told him, "Take the thing, look at it, thank them, and go. That's it! They don't have time to listen anyway."[12] This is extreme—but good—advice. You want to let the audience know that you sincerely appreciate the honor without wasting too much of their time.

Be sure to credit other people who helped you achieve what you are being honored for, but keep the list short and meaningful. The help might have been direct (such as co-workers contributing to a project) or indirect (such as your family not complaining about the extra time you spent on the project rather than with them).

Avoid being overly effusive. You'll usually want to avoid phrases like "greatest day of my life" or "best thing that has ever happened to me." These tend to sound insincere. Express sincerely what the honor means to you, limiting the use of superlatives. Temper your enthusiasm with humility.[13]

Elie Wiesel spent most of his adult life tracking down Nazi war criminals, and when he was awarded the Nobel Peace Prize, he began his acceptance speech with the following paragraphs:[14]

It is with a profound sense of humility that I accept the honor you have chosen to bestow upon me. I know your choice transcends me. This both frightens and pleases me. It frightens me because I wonder: Do I have the right to represent the multitudes who have perished? Do I have the right to accept this great honor on their behalf? I do not. That would be presumptuous. No one may speak for the dead, no one may interpret their mutilated dreams and visions.

It pleases me because I may say that this honor belongs to all the survivors and their children, and through us, to the Jewish people with whose destiny I have always identified.

This introduction by Wiesel to his acceptance speech is so effective that he almost could have stopped right there.

The acceptance speech given by the couple who won the garden contest is a model of graciousness. Notice how they thank people who've helped them along the way and share the joy they experience as gardeners, rather than focusing on their own talents or accomplishments.

ACCEPTANCE SPEECH
Mr. Brian Applegate

Thank you, Mayor Herron, friends, judges of the committee. My wife and I are quite touched by this honor, considering the many beautiful homes and gardens that cover this island. It has always been our joy to fill our garden with new plants, and things just kept expanding, until I believe we have finally run out of room for more. If our joy brings pleasure to others, then so much the better. Andrea, would you like to add a word?

Mrs. Andrea Applegate:

I would just like to thank our many friends who have given us cuttings from their own gardens; our children, who have endured our passion for pulling weeds and digging in the manure every spring; my mother, who taught me how to prune a rose; and the committee for bestowing this honor upon us. We've just been doing what we love to do, and we're glad you've enjoyed it, too. Thank you all.

Welcoming Attendees and Guests

The welcoming speech is intended to make participants feel comfortable with the group or at the event they are attending. As the presenter of the welcoming speech, you represent the people who organized the event. What you say helps set the tone for the entire event.

While limiting your speech to between three and five minutes, be sure to include vital information, such as information about the organiza-

> *Success Tip*
>
> Award shows on television are good opportunities to learn about acceptance speeches—both good and bad.

tion or event, about the people being welcomed, about the location of important facilities (if needed), and about what the audience can expect from the rest of the event.[15] If you think your audience has other pressing questions or concerns that may keep them from paying attention to or enjoying the programs that follow, it's a good idea to address these points at the beginning. On the other hand, you don't want to spend five minutes pointing out the location of the restrooms and the procedure for getting a lunch ticket.

In the following welcoming speech, the speaker starts on a high note: pointing out the growth and importance of telecommuting, which is the subject of the conference. The welcome goes on to describe some highlights of the conference and the organization behind it. Notice how the speaker refers listeners to an information packet that contains all the details they'll need without spending any valuable time going over the details.

WELCOMING SPEECH
Laine Downs—National Conference of the
Telecommuting Advisory Council

Good morning and welcome to the tenth National Conference of the Telecommuting Advisory Council. We are glad to see so many of you here today, proving what we have known since our inception in 1987: that telecommuting is a viable and important work style which has grown tremendously in recent years, largely due to your efforts. Many of you are responsible for implementing telecommuting programs at your companies; others among you are responsible for the government programs that are funding community telecenters throughout the nation; and still others among you are businesspeople who recognize the economic bonus telecommuting can offer, not only to the telecommunications industry, but to community businesses that benefit as workers stay closer to home.

Our purpose this weekend is to provide you with the most current information available about advances in the U.S.

telecommuting sector. We have scheduled important forums throughout the conference covering the economic, environmental, social, technological, and legislative issues related to the telecommuting workforce. On Saturday morning, we're offering a special workshop on "How to Implement a Pilot Telecommuting Program" and I'm told that there are a few spaces left, so if you're interested, please head over to the registration table in the lobby as soon as we're finished here.

When you came in you received a packet of information about the conference; inside you'll find a complete schedule of conference events and a detailed map of the hotel, which will show you where every event is being held. If you need more information or if you wish to change or add to your workshop registrations, our staff will be glad to help you after this morning's session.

As you know, the Telecommuting Advisory Council began as a grass-roots organization and we have grown phenomenally, gaining our nonprofit status in 1993 and expanding to encompass regional chapters in Arizona, Texas, Colorado, New Jersey, and Oregon, with city chapters in San Diego, Los Angeles and Orange County, Sacramento, Atlanta, Seattle, San Francisco, Chicago, and of course, our national headquarters in Washington, D.C. We're proud to announce the formation of our International/ European Community Telework/Telematics Forum or ECTF, which you'll be hearing more about later.

The Telecommuting Advisory Council has also established a presence on the World Wide Web, our newsletter is growing every month, and our quarterly audioconferences have met with enthusiastic approval from our membership. We expect more of the same in the next ten years as larger numbers of the working population discover the benefits of telecommuting and as employers and

EXHIBIT 18.4
The Challenge of After-Dinner Speaking
After-dinner speaking challenges the most experienced communicators. Audience members are likely to be distracted by dessert, coffee, and conversations taking place around the table.

community governments discover the economic, qualitative, and environmental benefits of allowing workers to telecommute.

We're very excited about being at the forefront of this new development, and we know that by the end of this weekend, you will leave our conference not only with new friends and associates who can support your efforts in the telecommuting field but also with new information, ideas, and skills gained from the distinguished faculty and panel representatives we've been able to assemble. So, again, I welcome you, and look forward to seeing all of you at our breakfast forum on Sunday.[16]

Entertaining Dinner Audiences

An audience listening to an after-dinner speech wants to be entertained.[17] They've probably worked all day, eaten a large meal, and more than likely had a few drinks. They do not want to sit through a deadly serious speech—they want something light and humorous. Consequently, after-dinner speeches are some of the most difficult speeches to plan and deliver successfully. Entertaining people is a unique skill.

Chances are the audience didn't come to hear you at all—they came for the dinner.[18] You'll have to win them over and convince them that they'll enjoy listening to you more than conversing with their neighbors (see Exhibit 18.4).

Because some people in the audience have probably been drinking, the after-dinner audience can be one of the most difficult. Alcohol loosens people's inhibitions, and you might get more response from your audience than you want. You may have trouble with hecklers. Examine your speech closely and remove any material that might raise objections from the audience. You might also lose people's interest because they are drowsy, or they may be more interested in getting the waiter's attention or talking to a tablemate. One Xerox Corporation senior executive has a policy never to speak after alcohol is served. He suggests giving before-dinner speeches (or even before the cocktail hour) rather than after-dinner speeches whenever possible.[19] This approach can also help a speaker relax and enjoy the meal, without worrying about the speech while trying to eat and carry on conversations.

Celebrating Accomplishments and Milestones

Accomplishments and milestones speeches can range from toasts (see Exhibit 18.5) to commencement addresses to funeral eulogies. They're usually very personal and delivered by someone who knows the subject or person well. These commemorative speeches convey information, to be sure, but they're much more than simple informative speeches. They aim to inspire the audience, to celebrate the human spirit, to help an audience cherish a special event or a special person. When she spoke at the 50th anniversary celebration of the D-Day invasion in World War II, England's Queen Elizabeth recounted the profound importance of the invasion and the role of Allied troops. She concluded by thanking the soldiers and inspiring the audience with this

EXHIBIT 18.5

Chinese Toasts: The Meaning Behind the Rituals

Most American businesspeople who travel to China are struck both by the number of banquets they are required to attend and by the number of toasts raised at these affairs. Despite differences in locale, in the kind of occasion being marked, and in the status and number of guests, the toasts frequently include exactly the same wording. This lack of variation has led many Western entrepreneurs to dismiss Chinese toasts as little more than a quaint foreign ritual.

Charles Needham knows otherwise. As chief executive officer of the San Diego–based telemarketing firm WorldSHOP, Needham recently negotiated a joint venture with China Central Television to broadcast his firm's home-shopping program on Chinese television. Although many observers hailed the contract as a triumph of salesmanship and negotiating expertise, Needham attributed his success to having done his homework beforehand. "To operate successfully in China," he explained, "you have to understand the subtleties of Chinese life—especially those surrounding eating and drinking."

Needham knew that in China, there is a centuries-old tradition of using toasts and wine with food to accomplish diplomatic ends. Banquets were held to give warring parties a protected, ritualized opportunity to negotiate their differences. The toasts raised were the first move, the opening bid for the terms of peace. This long tradition continues to resonate with Chinese businesspeople today. The welcoming banquet toast is understood as the occasion for revealing one's opening position in a coming business transaction.

When Needham heard his host propose that they become "business associates and newfound friends . . . (and) clasp hands with united hearts and concerns and walk together toward future success," he understood that he was being invited to take on

obligations, not rights. His host also noted that doing business with China Central Television would involve "mutual respect and trust," a shorthand reminder that Chinese business transactions go much more slowly than Western ones do. When his host called for a commitment from both sides to "compensate for each other's weaknesses," Needham knew that the road ahead was likely to be bumpy, but if he was willing to "move forward with relentless effort," he could expect to join China Central Television on "the bridge of success."

Needham knew the background of the Chinese custom of toasting. He says, "I knew I had a fighting chance as I listened to my host give the first toast at the welcoming banquet." Because he paid careful attention to the specific wording of his host's opening remarks, he was able to decode the toast and approach his Chinese colleagues with knowledge and understanding.

closing sentence: "May we, your fellow countrymen be worthy of what you did for us."[20] Such a statement goes far beyond simply thanking the soldiers and commemorating the occasion. It speaks to everyone who benefited as a result of the Allied victory (and their children and grandchildren). It inspires people to live quality lives that justify the tremendous casualties suffered in the war.

Many of the commemorative speeches you'll be asked to give will celebrate the lives or events in the lives of people you know. A successful tribute focuses on biographical information. You should emphasize the person's positive aspects and accomplishments, but don't exaggerate. Be sincere; say nice things, but don't overdo it. Be realistic. Mention your connection with the person, but keep the stuff about you short, focusing on the person being honored.

One milestone at which you may be asked to speak is a funeral. Here are a few things to remember if you are asked to give a **eulogy**, a tribute delivered at a funeral service:[21]

- Talk to other friends and family; find out what they think is important to say.
- Emphasize the positive aspects of the deceased's life, but again, be realistic.
- Keep it short. Avoid using poems or long quotes, unless requested by the family. The audience wants to hear about the person being eulogized, not the wisdom of somebody else.

Senator Edward M. Kennedy delivered a eulogy at the funeral of his brother, Senator Robert F. Kennedy. He ended with the following words:[22]

My brother need not be idealized or enlarged in death beyond what he was in life. He should be remembered simply as a good and decent man who saw wrong and tried to right it, saw suffering and tried to heal it, saw war and tried to stop it.

Those of us who loved him and who take him to his rest today pray that what he was to us, and what he wished for others, will some day come to pass for all the world.

As he said many times, in many parts of this nation, to those he touched and who sought to touch him: "Some men see things as they are and say why. I dream things that never were and say, why not."

Obviously, words of eulogy as fitting as these were no doubt prepared with great care before the speech.

Another milestone often celebrated is marriage. Obviously the stars of a wedding celebration are the bride and groom. If you're asked to make a toast or be master of ceremonies, keep the focus on the newlyweds, not on yourself. Keep your remarks short and in good taste. Prepare your words ahead of time and memorize them. If you can't memorize the toast, it's probably too long.[23]

Graduation is another milestone marked with speeches. The commencement address usually contains advice to the graduating class. It also usually contains anecdotes or bits of the speaker's personal history that support the message. Here again, limit the length of your speech. Ten to fifteen minutes is safe. Caps and gowns are hot, folding chairs get uncomfortable, and the audience may be restless.[24] The graduates have spent years sitting through long lectures—they'll probably appreciate your not making them sit through one more.

Brief stories, amusing quotes, touching memories, and hard-won bits of advice are all good material for commencement speeches. Most speakers combine material that's available to anyone (such as famous quotations) with personal insights and experiences. Anyone can quote

Shakespeare; you were invited to speak because of the particular insight you can add to standard graduation fare. When former Vice President Al Gore delivered a commencement address at Harvard, he drew parallels between his own temporary disillusionment with public service as a young man and a trend he sensed in the country today:[25]

> I left Harvard in 1969 disillusioned by what I saw happening in our country and certain of only one thing about my future: I would never, ever go into politics.
>
> After returning from Vietnam and after seven years as a journalist, I rekindled my interest in public service. Yet I believe the same disillusioning forces that for a time drove me away from politics have continued for the country as a whole.

His speech wasn't really about his own experiences; it was a call for renewed faith in democracy among the graduates present. However, by demonstrating that he had been in those cynical shoes before, he was able to show a way back to faith in the democratic process. By weaving his own story through the speech, he was able to make his message much more interesting and compelling.

THINKING ON YOUR FEET: THE IMPROMPTU SPEECH

Perhaps the most important tip for giving impromptu speeches is to be prepared.[26] You can

WHEN EVERYTHING GOES BLANK: IMPROMPTU SPEAKING SECRETS YOU CAN USE AT A MOMENT'S NOTICE

It'll happen sooner or later in life, so you might as well get ready for it. Sometime, somewhere, a finger will point your way, and you'll be asked to get up and say a few words. Here are some dos and don'ts to help turn these potentially embarrassing situations into positive opportunities to strut your stuff:

- *See whether you can gracefully get a few minutes to prepare.* If the boss turns to you without warning and asks you to talk, maybe you can suggest that the group take a five-minute break before moving into the topic you're supposed to talk about. This will give you plenty of time.
- *Don't apologize for not being better prepared.* The audience will either realize what's going on (in which case they'll probably have some sympathy for you) or they won't know that you just got tapped on the shoulder five seconds ago (in which case apologizing for not being better prepared will just make you look even more ill-prepared).
- *Pause for a moment to collect yourself before you start.* It may seem like an eternity to you, but a reasonable audience won't mind a few seconds of silence.
- *Don't start out with a formal introductory sentence.* Even if you're quick enough to compose one on the spot, a formal introductory sentence is probably a mistake. If you try it, you'll raise your audience's expectation that you're ready to provide an entire speech that's well developed and formal, which is definitely not the case.

Above all, remember that these surprise minispeeches must be kept simple and short. It's far better to make one important point successfully than to try to slog through several half-baked ideas. If the situation really calls for a more involved analysis or presentation, try to use your moment at the microphone to arrange another meeting for covering the topic adequately.

Don't be afraid to take a second to collect your thoughts if you need to; the audience probably won't even notice a brief pause, but they will notice if you stumble ahead unprepared.

often predict when you might be asked to say a few words. Chances are small that you'll be asked to speak on a topic you know nothing about. However, if you're going to a meeting and you're an expert on the subject under discussion, you'll probably be asked to say a few words.

The next most important tip is to take a few seconds to organize your thoughts before you begin speaking—*don't* start speaking without some idea of what you'll say, only to stop and struggle for words. Experienced speakers use a variety of techniques to help them quickly organize what they plan to say. Here's one good approach adapted from the critical thinking skills that debaters develop. It takes only a few seconds in most cases:[27]

1. Identify the single most important idea you plan to communicate.
2. Identify two or three support points for that single idea.
3. Piece together an opening sentence, preferably one that ties what has just gone on in

EXHIBIT 18.5
Literally Thinking on Your Feet
Here's an example of how a speaker can formulate a quick, impromptu speech while walking from his or her chair to the front of the room.

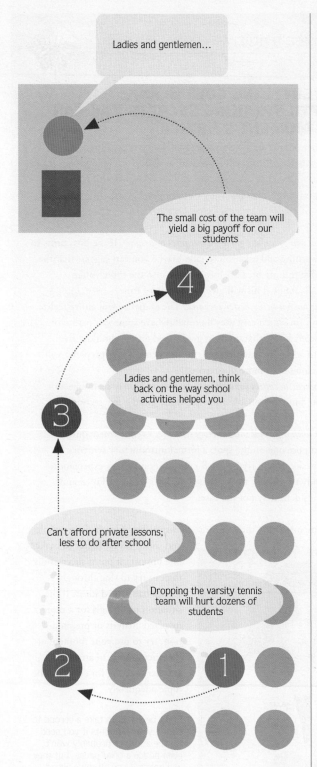

Ladies and gentlemen...

The small cost of the team will yield a big payoff for our students

4

Ladies and gentlemen, think back on the way school activities helped you

3

Can't afford private lessons; less to do after school

Dropping the varsity tennis team will hurt dozens of students

2   1

the room with what you're going to say.

4. Come up with a solid closing sentence that repeats your central idea.

Of course, this isn't the order in which you'll cover points when you speak, but it's a good sequence for *planning* what you'll say because it focuses your attention on the key point. You can even work through this process while you're walking toward the front of the room, if need be (see Exhibit 18.6). For this process to work, you must already have supporting points in mind. You obviously don't have time to do any research, but as mentioned earlier, you're normally asked to speak on subjects you already know something about, so you should have a ready supply of support points stored in your memory. The critical thinking skills that debaters use can be successfully incorporated into any impromptu speaking situation.

SUMMARY

Chances are, the skills and concepts you learn in this class will be applied most often in situations other than traditional public speaking. You'll have all kinds of opportunities to speak on the job, from informal employee gatherings to formal presentations before top executives and important customers. These on-the-job situations fall into four basic categories: presenting information, making recommendations, selling goods and services, and training.

In many respects, presenting information on the job is a lot like the informative speeches you already know about. One reason informative presentations are so important is that people in positions of power often judge employees to a large degree on what they see in presentations. In other words, if you can communicate well during these presentations, you and your work will make a good impression on key people.

Making a recommendation is quite similar to making a persuasive speech, and you would usually follow the strategy of problem-solution or comparison of alternatives. In most cases, you'll want to minimize detail and get right to the point. You can offer more supporting evidence and other details in a written report if people are truly interested. Also, keep in mind that on-the-job presentations are typically much more interactive, so expect your audience to ask questions.

Selling is also a form of persuasive speaking. Salespeople can choose from the canned approach, in which a fixed, rehearsed presentation is delivered to the customer from beginning to end, or the interactive approach, in which the seller asks questions and adjusts the presentation as the potential buyer provides answers and makes decisions.

If you have the opportunity to train other people, you'll see how training is similar to informative speaking, only with more extensive audience interaction. In addition, on-the-job learning is usually motivated by on-the-job problems. If people don't think they need your information to solve a pressing problem, they won't be motivated to learn from you.

Outside of day-to-day work activities, people may be asked to deliver a variety of special-event speeches at weddings, funerals, graduations, awards ceremonies, and other events, including the introduction of other speakers. You'll want to keep these speeches short and concise, since you're usually not the center of attention on these occasions. Also, these events tend to be rather emotional, and people often remember them for years, so be sure to take extra care to craft your words and delivery so that they're appropriate.

For most of these special-event speeches, you'll have plenty of time to prepare as you would normally for any public speech. However, there will be times when you're unexpectedly asked to step up to the microphone and "say a few words" about some topic or other. Fortunately, it's usually a topic you already know something about. Just take a few seconds before you start to speak. Identify the single key point you want to make, two or three supporting points, an introduction that ties into whatever came right before your speech, and a conclusion that will emphasize your key point all over again.

KEY TERMS

canned sales presentations (400)
eulogy (409)
interactive sales presentations (400)

413

APPLY CRITICAL THINKING

1. As an applicant on a job interview, would you be speaking informatively or persuasively? Explain your answer.

2. Would an audience of your corporate colleagues be likely to have a highly emotional reaction to a logical, informative presentation? Why or why not?

3. What feature of the canned sales presentation can make it backfire?

4. Are you learning about public speaking in the same way someone would learn about it on the job? Explain your answer.

5. Why is it safe to assume that most special-event speeches should take audience emotions into account?

6. Why is it important not to give away too much information when you're introducing another speaker?

7. What does it mean to be "prepared" for impromptu speaking?

SHARPEN YOUR SKILLS

Individual Exercises

1. Pretend you're a tour guide at a nearby historical site (pick a real site). Draft a three-minute introductory speech that you could give to tourists, explaining the significance of the site. Be sure to take your audience and the speaking situation into account.

2. Pretend that you're a sales representative for your college or university and that it's your job to recruit high school students. Study Exhibit 18.2 as an example, and then draw a diagram that includes the key parts of your message and the most likely questions that high school seniors and their families will have when choosing a school.

3. How might you approach a training situation in which employees are resisting the change that created a need for training in the first place (such as installation of a new computer system)?

4. Assume that you've been asked to introduce the president of your college or university at a local social event. List the points you need to know about the president in order to make an effective speech of introduction.

Group Exercises

5. In groups of four or six students, practice making speeches of introduction. Pair up and tell your partner about each other's next speech. Then prepare a 1–2 minute introduction for the speech. All students in the group should present their introductions to the group, after which the group provides feedback. If your instructor chooses, you can also give these introductions to the entire class before each student gives a speech.

6. A moderator will pick a controversial topic and point to one student in the class. This student will have 10 seconds to frame an argument on one side or the other of the issue and must then stand and talk for 60 seconds. The moderator will then point to another student, who also has 10 seconds to prepare, and who must then get up and refute what the first student said.

Chapter Nineteen

SPEAKING IN SMALL GROUPS

LEARNING OBJECTIVES

After studying this chapter, you will be able to

1. Identify the three major types of groups.

2. Describe the three categories of roles people play in group communication.

3. Explain why group norms can be an advantage in some cases and a disadvantage in others.

4. Discuss the difference between a group leader and a facilitator.

5. List the five steps in the group decision-making and problem-solving process.

6. Explain why communication technology requires new and different communication skills.

7. Enumerate the key issues in planning and leading a successful meeting.

EXHIBIT 19.1
The Complexity of Group Communication
As the size of a group increases, the number of communication links within the group increases dramatically.

UNDERSTANDING GROUP DYNAMICS

Next time you're working with several classmates on a team project, sit back and observe the group for a few moments. Listen to what various individuals say and how they say it. People use speech in groups to accomplish many goals: to help others, to gain attention, to take control, to impress others, and to put others down, to name just a few. Some people ask questions to advance the group's goals, some to advance their own goals, and some to demonstrate how much they know. **Group communication** is a complex process in which people communicate face to face, have a common purpose or goal, feel a sense of belonging to a group, and influence one another.[1]

When groups communicate successfully, the result is higher performance and better success toward reaching established goals.[2] In order to communicate successfully in a group, you'll need to understand how groups function, make decisions, and solve problems. Working in a group is much more complicated than speaking in front of an audience. For starters, people working in groups have much more interaction with each other (see Exhibit 19.1). Your listening and observation skills will be called into play. Individual personalities become more apparent, both enhancing and interfering with the decision-making process. This section gives you an overview of group dynamics by describing the various types of groups, the roles people play in groups, the norms and expectations that influence behavior, and the notion of group leadership.

Types of Groups

In both your career and your personal pursuits, you'll have the chance to participate in many kinds of groups. The type of group you participate in often affects the type of speaking and communication you're expected to engage in. Here are the most common types of groups:[3]

- *Formal groups.* Organizations and individuals with common goals and interests create **formal groups** to pursue their various objectives. These can be permanent, such as the admissions department at your college, or temporary, such as a politician's reelection committee.
- *Teams.* Teams are an increasingly popular alternative or supplement to formal groups.[4] Many companies and government agencies are setting up teams of people to solve problems, develop new businesses, and perform other important tasks. A team can involve people from a number of formal groups, which can create a unique set of communication chal-

EXHIBIT 19.2

The Diversity of Group Communication

The nature of group communication can vary widely, depending on the people in the group, their relationship with one another, and the group's purpose.

lenges. For instance, a team made up of people from the finance, personnel, and engineering departments of a company may find themselves stumbling over diverse vocabulary and different approaches to interpersonal communication.

- *Informal groups.* **Informal groups** are set up by their members, rather than by an official organization of some kind. These groups cover every conceivable interest and activity, from bird watching to backyard barbecuing. Business executives may form an informal group to walk or work out while talking over business decisions. Even friends who get together to party or attend baseball games constitute an informal group. As you probably know from personal experience, communication in these informal groups can range from wonderful to dreadful—and success or failure often hinges on the communication skills of the people in a group.

Groups can differ widely in terms of how they communicate, and not everyone in the group communicates in exactly the same way (see Exhibit 19.2). Various individuals tend to take on different communication roles within the group. Plus, some groups expect people to play well-defined and formal roles, whereas others let people behave and speak as they see fit. The next section explores these various roles in more detail.

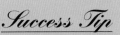

Success Tip

Use humor in meetings if it's appropriate and if you're good at it. Humor at the wrong times or humor that offends people in the group or people they care about will slow the group's progress.

Roles in Groups

To a large extent, a person's communication tasks and opportunities are defined by his or her role in a group. Even in very informal groups, people tend to play particular roles, from followers to leaders to planners. Sometimes these roles are well defined, much like the various positions on a sports team. Other times the roles are ambiguous and changeable.

Some people seem to be born leaders, tending to take control of any group they are members of. For other people it comes more naturally to sit back and let someone else run the show. A given person may have different roles in different groups, leading in one but following and supporting in another. Researchers have identified dozens of specific group roles, but it's possible to simplify this by putting the roles into three basic groups:[5]

- *Working toward the group's goals.* Helping the group accomplish whatever it is trying to accomplish is a positive role. While playing such roles, people engage in communication such as offering helpful information, asking questions that prompt others to consider important issues, and nudging the group back to productive discussion if the conversation strays or bogs down. Of course, calling a role "positive" doesn't mean that everybody smiles and agrees with everybody else. You can play a positive role by disagreeing with the entire group if you think the group is headed in the wrong direction. Your contribution is positive because you're helping the group get back on track.

- *Keeping the group functioning smoothly.* Focusing on the group's communication process is also a positive role. People in such roles encourage others, search for compromises, and make sure everyone has the opportunity to contribute. By keeping the group functioning smoothly, people indirectly support the group's ultimate goals, but they are more concerned with maintaining positive working relationships and clear communication among group members.

- *Working toward individual goals.* Seeking to satisfy personal needs rather than the group's needs is a negative role. While playing such roles, people may continually whine, no matter what the group proposes, or they may try to dominate every discussion, particularly as a way to control others or to show off. People who like to entertain and tell jokes all the time can have a negative influence as well, since they tend to distract the group from productive work. However, in the right situations, some humor and kidding around can be helpful, such as when discussions and debates grow tense or tedious. The important thing is to use humor to move the group forward, not simply to entertain. Also, in helping move the group toward its goal, keep in mind that it's acceptable to have some concern for your own goals. Just don't let your individual goals overshadow the group's goals.

Follow the conversation in this hypothetical meeting and notice how various people seem to follow roles that help or hurt the group's progress. The group is a five-person committee of students appointed by the student body president to choose a location for the campus's end-of-year picnic. The group does not have a formally appointed leader; the students represent five different academic and athletic departments.

Lars: Well, great. Another time-wasting task from our fearless leader.

Kimiko: I know, I know. But how about we rip through the possibilities quickly so we can get back to more important work.

Alayne: Yeah, like lunch.

Anil: Actually, I'd say this task is rather important. The students want this to be an enjoyable time, so we should pick a place with nice facilities.

Kimiko: I think you have a good point there.

Lars: If we wanted to give the students a good time we'd just give them the day off from class.

Alayne: Now, now, Lars. Did you wake up on the wrong side of the cave this morning?

Kimiko: How about we go around the room and let each person suggest a favorite place? I liked last year's site a lot. What was the name of that park? Evergreen Ridge, I think it was.

Anil: That was a good place. But you know, I drove by it a few weeks ago and saw that the parking lot has been torn up for some kind of construction. It's really a mess. You have a second choice?

Kimiko: Well, in that case, I'd suggest the country club in Mill Creek.

Anil: Yeah, that's a great place. I think that's my vote, too.

Lars: Oh me too, I love hanging out with overpaid lawyers and doctors.

Alayne: Maybe you could find a shrink there, Lars. Oh, just kidding. How about that new virtual reality place down by the harbor?

Lars: OK, I guess I could vote for that one. We could all use an escape from reality.

Kimiko: You've been rather quiet, Chris. Which place do you prefer?

Chris: I don't really have a preference. Wherever you guys decide I'm sure will be fine.

You may even know someone who fits each of these roles. Lars was negative from the word go and seems more interested in complaining than in

EXHIBIT 19.3
Group Norms Influence Communication

Norms and expectations can differ widely between formal and informal groups. Language and behavior that would be perfectly acceptable in an informal group might be inappropriate in a formal group setting. Conversely, formal behavior would be out of place in an informal group.

actually getting any work done. Anil provided good information and careful thought, while not actually pushing the other members to decide. Alayne proved to be a bit of a jokester, although her humor did help the group move toward a solution by keeping Lars's negativity in check. Chris barely communicated at all, sitting back while the rest of the group did the talking. It's Kimiko who emerged as the leader, pushing the group to find a solution.

Of course, people aren't restricted to one role forever or even for the duration of one meeting. You might generally be a leader who moves the group toward a solution, but at times work at building group harmony or helping reluctant members share their opinions.

Norms and Expectations

You've probably had that awkward feeling of watching someone in a group behave or speak in a way that just doesn't "fit" the group's style. It might be someone who's overly casual in a fairly formal group, or someone who's argumentative in a group that's supposed to be friendly and laid back. As groups evolve over time, they develop a set of expectations that strongly influence how people behave, including how they are expected to speak. For example, it may be perfectly fine to use slang and humor when speaking in one group but not in another.

These behavior expectations are called **group norms** because they represent what the group considers "normal." Every group has its own set of norms. Some are formal and explicit (such as bylaws and procedures for speaking); others are more informal and less explicit. The less explicit norms are harder for members to learn—each member must often figure them out by observing the behavior of group members and the response of other group members to determine what is acceptable and expected behavior.

Norms create pressures to conform (see Exhibit 19.3). This peer pressure is a powerful influence in any group. In many respects, such pressure to conform is helpful because it encourages people to work together. For instance, if a group expects its members to treat each other with respect, individual members will be discouraged from disrespectful behavior that could divert the entire group's attention from the goals to be accomplished.

In other cases, though, the pressure to conform to norms is counterproductive. The pressure to cooperate and to avoid conflict can be so strong that people don't ask questions; they set aside any personal concerns for the sake of conforming to the group, which can lead the group in directions it really shouldn't go. When the pressure to conform has more influence than the merits of an

FIVE GUARANTEED WAYS TO LIGHT A CREATIVE FIRE IN YOUR GROUP

Many people think creativity is a trait or a talent enjoyed by a few specialists—musicians, painters, writers, and so on. But everybody can learn to think creatively, and leaders skilled in group communication can help those around them think more creatively, too. Here are five steps leaders can take to fire up the creative spark in any group:

1. *Set high goals.* Challenge people to reach higher than they've ever reached before, and they'll be forced to think of new ways to meet those goals.
2. *Recognize and reward creativity and innovation.* Looking for new and better ways to do things can bring out the creative best in everybody.
3. *Don't let policies and procedures get in the way.* If rules are keeping people from thinking and communicating creatively, change the rules.
4. *Make sure people have the training and tools they need.* Creative thinking works best when people aren't distracted by their equipment and when they have enough training to understand their work.
5. *Look for ideas anywhere and everywhere.* Most people who are considered creative always have their eyes and ears open for fresh ideas. Many "new" ideas are really just old ideas recombined in new ways.

Perhaps most important, convey the message that the same old ways of thinking aren't going to cut it anymore. Nudge people out of their ruts and challenge them to look for new and different solutions.

Challenging groups to solve tough problems together is a common way to foster both creativity and cooperation.

idea or plan under discussion, people are suffering from **groupthink;** they go along with the rest of the group not because they truly agree but because they are trying to conform.[6] Groupthink can lead to unfortunate and even tragic consequences. One example would be people going along with a group decision to drive home after drinking, even though individuals in the group know that it's a stupid thing to do. Gang activity is another example of conformity that leads to negative consequences. Watch for these symptoms of groupthink:[7]

- Disagreement with the group's plans and decisions is discouraged, even if the disagreement is calm and well-intentioned.
- The group avoids obvious problems and points of conflicts.
- The group puts pressure on nonconformists to adopt the majority opinion.
- Information that challenges the group consensus is ignored or discounted.
- The group and its leader(s) feel invulnerable and infallible.

Group Leadership

Every group has a leader or leaders, either officially or unofficially. The leadership role may be official, such as the head of a department or the president of the student council, or it may be an informal role that someone assumes to help the group move toward its goals. Even something as

EXHIBIT 19.4
Facilitating Versus Leading
Facilitators interact with group members
and help the group move toward its
goal; this is a more complex role than
simply lecturing to the group.

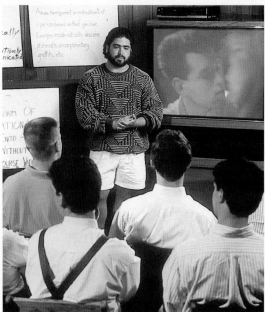

simple as getting a group of friends to agree on
where to go for dinner calls for leadership.

Leaders have a wide range of communication
styles—depending on their personal preferences,
the degree of formal authority they have over
members of the group, and the goals the group is
expected to accomplish. Compare the following
statements that a group leader might make to
move a group toward action:

1. "C'mon you bums. Shut off the PlayStation
   and let's go shoot some hoops."
2. "I think it might be a good idea for Sherri and
   Sebastian to work on the conference site
   selection while the rest of us figure out which
   state officials should be invited. Sound like a
   good plan to you guys?"
3. "OK, let's break into teams of five and brainstorm ways to increase volunteer activity next
   year."
4. "Johnson! Take Hatch and Pollard and cover
   the alley. Move it, now! I don't want to lose
   him this time!"

In the first example, a casual insult is acceptable
speech because the informal leader is clearly
among friends. The speaker in the second example
is casual but much more respectful, as you would

expect in a professional meeting. Compare this
with the third example, where the leader simply
commands the group to do something. Although
it is a direct command, it's not rude or condescending. It's simply a fast, efficient way to move
the meeting along. The fourth example might be
from a police captain who is commanding officers
to move into position to prevent someone from
escaping. The language is abrupt and conveys a
strong sense of urgency. It's what you might
expect in a tense, dangerous situation. This kind
of language would cause great offense in a business or faculty meeting, but it fits other situations
well enough (a zookeeper supervising the release
of an animal into a new exhibit, or a supervisor
handling a sudden problem on an assembly line).

Leaders have varying degrees of control, which
influences how they can and should communicate. If you're asked to chair a meeting of colleagues, none of whom officially report to you,
you don't have any formal authority over these
people. Any attempt to control them or "boss
them around" will probably lead to frustration
and resentment. You're playing the important role
of **facilitator** in this case, which means it's your
job to move the group toward its goal without
commanding anyone (see Exhibit 19.4). A good
facilitator may take on many roles in addition to

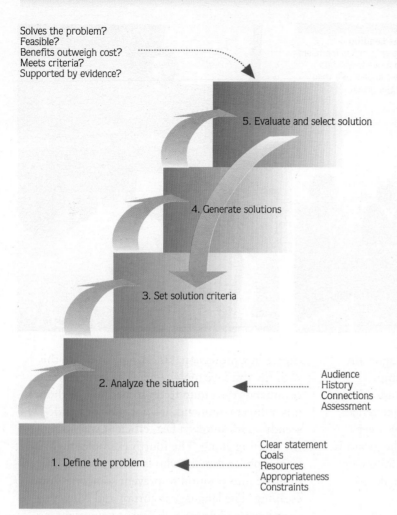

Solves the problem?
Feasible?
Benefits outweigh cost?
Meets criteria?
Supported by evidence?

5. Evaluate and select solution

4. Generate solutions

3. Set solution criteria

2. Analyze the situation

Audience
History
Connections
Assessment

1. Define the problem

Clear statement
Goals
Resources
Appropriateness
Constraints

EXHIBIT 19.5
The Group Problem-Solving Process
Groups can follow these five steps to solve problems and reach decisions. Remember, you may have to back up to the solution criteria if you can't find an acceptable answer the first time around.

job done while still letting people communicate is as much an art as a science, and the people who do it well have usually practiced the skill over the course of many meetings and group functions. More than anything else, a leader's use of task-relevant communication helps a group meet its goals.[9]

MAKING DECISIONS AND SOLVING PROBLEMS IN GROUPS

Most groups don't just sit around and talk, of course. They get together for a reason, and the two most important reasons are to make decisions and to solve problems. Making decisions simply involves making choices between options or alternatives. Problem solving is a bit more complex because the group can generate new options or alternatives from which to choose. Formal groups often engage in well-defined problem-solving processes, but even informal groups usually follow certain steps to solve problems and make decisions. This section presents a five-step process that all types of groups can use effectively (see Exhibit 19.5). If the problem or situation is relatively simple, the whole process may be completed in one session. For more difficult or complex situations, several sessions may be necessary. As you read through the steps, think back on meetings or other gatherings you've participated in where the group

managing a team or meeting: role model, catalyst, trainer, guide and goad (gentle motivation), peacemaker, and coach or mentor.[8]

The leader's communication style helps set the norms for the group, and one of the responsibilities of leadership is ensuring effective communication, so leaders need to watch their own communication carefully. As leader, if you shut down discussions of alternatives and are abrupt or unfriendly, the group will follow your lead and communicate less. (Such behavior may be the best approach for a police captain directing officers at a crime scene, but it's generally not productive in most other situations.) At the other extreme, if you sit back and let people talk as much as they want about whatever they want, the group will get frustrated with the lack of progress. Leading a group in a way that gets the

EXHIBIT 19.6
The Importance of Defining the Problem
Suppose you're a member of a civic organization that's trying to raise voter turnout in the presidential elections. This simple diagram shows how important it is to define the problem before jumping into solutions; the possible solutions are very different (and very difficult in this case), so you need to make sure you're solving the real problem.

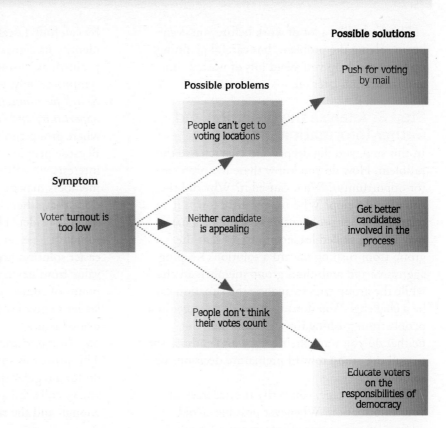

could have benefited from a structured problem-solving process. How many times did people hash and rehash the same problem? The point of this process is to produce better solutions in less time.[10]

Step 1: Define the Problem or Opportunity

Defining the problem you're trying to solve or the opportunity you want to address is an important first step. This advice might sound obvious, but it's easy for a group to run into communication trouble if people aren't clear about what they're supposed to do. Say you're a member of the local school board. Volunteer activity has dropped off in the last year, and some people on the board think it's because parents feel out of touch with school administrators. Should you jump right in to solve this problem? No, because there are really several potential problems: Are parents taking the time to find out what's happening in the schools? Are administrators communicating effectively with the parents? Is being out of touch the real reason for volunteer activity dropping off?

If you tried to solve this "problem" without defining it first, people in the group would likely seek a solution by going in different directions, preventing the group from making much progress (see Exhibit 19.6). The key to success is defining the problem first and then tackling this one problem in a coordinated fashion. Moreover,

something that the group initially identifies as a problem may really just be a symptom of some other problems, requiring more research to uncover the fundamental issues involved. In this case, you might want to state your problem as "We need to find out why volunteer activity has dropped off." Here are five guidelines for getting off to a good start in problem solving or decision making:[11]

1. Define the problem or opportunity in specific terms so that everyone knows where you're starting from.
2. Discuss what the group's goals are so that everyone knows where you're going.
3. Identify resources within the group (or the group's control) that could be applied to the problem or opportunity.
4. Make sure the problem is important enough to solve and that this group is the right group to do it.
5. Identify all the constraints you're working under, including schedules and budgets.

This looks like a lot of work before you even begin solving the problem, but careful planning up front can help you avoid lots of wasted time and frustration later on.

Step 2: Analyze the Situation and Gather Information

In this step, you dig deeper and characterize the problem. How do you know there is a problem (or opportunity)? What caused it? Why did the situation develop? Who is affected? How is it related to other problems or issues? This phase may require skilled leadership to prevent the group from rushing toward a solution. Keeping aggressive and ambitious group members in check while the group tries to analyze the situation can be a challenge. You don't want to discourage these people from pushing toward a solution, but neither do you want their energy and enthusiasm to pull the group toward premature decisions or solutions.

Also at this stage, you verify the accuracy of your information. Whenever possible, avoid relying on one source of information. People involved in the issue will have their own opinions about what is happening and possibly their own agendas. Be sure to get a broad and balanced picture of the situation. Carefully examine all the information you get to make sure it's valid and relevant to the issue at hand. Here are some helpful guidelines for this step:[12]

1. *Identify your audience.* In many cases, your group or its leader will need to report the results of your activities to somebody. Knowing who your audience is from the beginning will help you craft an acceptable solution and help make sure you collect the right supporting information. For instance, there's a big difference between reporting back to top managers in a company and reporting back to the general public, to Congress, or to a campus organization.
2. *Understand the history of the situation and its causes.* One of the dangers of rushing toward a solution is that you may end up treating the symptoms of the problem and not the causes.

By carefully researching a problem, you can identify its causes and work to eliminate the problem at its source. If you eliminate the symptoms only, you leave the problem intact.

3. *Search for connections between this problem or opportunity and other issues.* This is one area where group communication is most valuable. Because people with different experiences and interests view things differently, some group members may be able to point out connections that others in the group may otherwise never consider. These connections may sometimes reveal more problems to solve or easier solution possibilities. To get the most value from having the group together at this point, of course, it's important for the group leader to give everyone a chance to bring up related issues.
4. *Step back and assess the information you have.* This process is similar to the assessment you do for a regular speech. You look at everything you've collected and decide whether you have enough and the right kind of information.

How do you know when you've analyzed the problem or opportunity sufficiently? That depends on the situation. In some cases, the group leader will conclude that the group has enough information to move on toward a solution, or the members may decide they're comfortable enough to press ahead. In other cases, the group might simply run out of time and be forced to choose a solution based on whatever information is available.

Step 3: Establish Solution Criteria

Once the group has enough information to move ahead, the next step is to decide what will constitute a good choice when it's time to make that choice. In other words, what are the criteria for selecting the best possible option, and which criteria are the most important? Is saving money important? Satisfying the audience? Having fun? Sticking to a particular set of moral or legal principles?

Say you're leading a group that's trying to identify potential sites for a foster home for troubled teenagers. Before you can pick the best site, you need to define what "best" means. The group might come up with a list of criteria like this:

- *Size:* The facility should accommodate at least ten teens and three resident counselors; with two teens to a bedroom and private bedrooms for each counselor, we'll need a house with at least eight bedrooms.
- *Location:* The home should be located away from seedier parts of the city and still be close enough to a high school, a shopping area, a teen center, and public recreation. We also need to check zoning rules for each potential site to make sure group homes like this are allowed.
- *Facilities:* We need some place for people to hang out and get some exercise, such as a yard or a basketball hoop.
- *Quality:* We don't need a luxurious house, but we want one that's in good enough shape that we won't be forced to repair it constantly.
- *Cost:* We have $25,000 for a down payment, and we figure we can handle monthly mortgage payments of $1,500. At 6 percent for 30 years, this works out to about $275,000. Of course, we'd like to spend less if we can.

Now, if you've ever searched for a house or an apartment, you know that you rarely find that ideal place—which leads to the next key decision: Which criteria are most important, and which are you willing to let slip, at least a little? Could you accept fewer bedrooms or a house that needs some repair? Of course you'd like to get the ideal house, but it's helpful to define both *ideal* and *acceptable* so that everyone agrees on how far from the ideal the group is willing to go.

Step 4: Generate Potential Solutions

With a list of ideal and acceptable criteria in your hands, you're ready to identify possible solutions. In the case of the foster home, for instance, your list of possible solutions would be a list of large houses that fit the criteria (or that come close, anyway).

The techniques you use to generate a list of potential solutions depend on the problem or opportunity. For the foster home, you'd probably ask a real estate agent to help you find houses that fit your criteria. In many other cases, you'll want to brainstorm as a group. Finding analogies in the solutions chosen by other groups can be helpful as well. State governments, for example, often compare notes on programs that worked and those that didn't.

Remember that this stage is not about choosing solutions. It's about finding or creating as many possible solutions as you can. Don't dismiss any possibilities at this point (unless they're totally unworkable, such as a home that costs a million dollars). Even solutions that sound crazy might work out, with a few modifications. Also, in the creative environment of a brainstorming session, a wild idea might trigger a more practical idea from another group member. You'll have a chance to weed out the truly wild ideas in the next step. For now, just let the ideas flow.

Step 5: Evaluate the Possibilities and Select the Best Solution

Now it's time to compare the possible solutions you've identified to the decision-making criteria you developed in Step 3 (see Exhibit 19.7). In many cases, you'll now have a long list of possibilities and perhaps more than one "right" answer. On the other hand, some possibilities will be obviously unsatisfactory and can be eliminated quickly. Compare the remaining suggestions to determine which is best. Some issues to consider during this process:[13]

- Does the solution actually solve the problem?
- Can it be done? If so, can it be done economically?
- Do the advantages outweigh the disadvantages? Will the solution cause new problems?
- Does the solution meet the established decision-making criteria?
- Does the information gathered support this solution?

Keep in mind that even though you're comparing a list of possibilities with a list of decision

EXHIBIT 19.7
Choosing the Best Solution
To choose the best solution, compare
each alternative to the decision criteria
you established earlier in the problem-
solving process.

How to Choose a Pack Animal

Animal	Heat tolerance	Load capacity	Docility	Food	Initial cost
Ideal	120Y	400 lb	High	Natural veg	$50
Camel	140Y	300 lb	Low	Natural veg	$1,000
Mule	110Y	200 lb	Medium	Oats	$25
Horse	90Y	200 lb	High	Oats	$500
Ox	120Y	500 lb	High	Special fodder	$1,000
Elephant	130Y	1000 lb	High	Natural veg	$20,000

criteria, other factors can creep into the decision at this point. Regarding the foster home location, for example, one of the committee members may be required to work at the home but not live there, so this person might push for a particular location because it means an easier commute. One of the biggest challenges for the group and the leader in particular is to make sure people judge the possibilities according to the agreed-on criteria. Of course, you may find that the process of comparing possibilities uncovers a new criterion that needs to be considered. It may be that commute time is an important issue for the group. If so, you'll need to go back to Step 3 and adjust your list of criteria before reexamining your options.

FOSTERING EFFECTIVE GROUP COMMUNICATION

Group communication requires all the skills you're developing for regular public speaking—and then some. Talking and listening in meetings and other group gatherings is more complex and more personal than standing behind a lectern and delivering a one-way speech. This section offers some guidelines for successful group communication, whether you're leading a business meeting or working with your roommates to solve a housing dilemma.[14]

Stay Focused on the Group's Goals

After the goals for the group have been defined, it's important to keep the focus of discussion and activity on those goals. When things get rough or boring, it's all too easy to get sidetracked onto simpler issues. Maintaining focus is the responsibility not only of the group leader but also of each group member.

A written agenda and a clear definition of the group's purpose will let everyone know what the topic for discussion will be—and what the group needs to accomplish. In some cases, it may even be worthwhile to apply the formal rules of parliamentary procedure to make sure the group stays focused.[15] However, even these precautions don't automatically guarantee that the group will stay on track—which is one reason that group norms are so important. If some people in the group expect everyone to get the job done correctly and efficiently, others who might tend to stray from the task will feel the pressure to stay on course.

Be Patient While the Group Develops

A new group needs time to get on its feet and become effective. Members need time to get to know one another and to recognize each other's styles. This might seem like a waste of time, but it's an important part of the group communication process. It takes time to choose a leader, either formally or informally, and for other roles to be assigned or assumed. As group members become better acquainted and more comfortable with one another, the work process can become more efficient. A small amount of time spent on group development can have a large payoff in group rapport and the ability to work together.

Recognize and Manage Interpersonal Conflicts

You may have had the unfortunate experience of watching a group self-destruct because of interpersonal conflicts. It might have been two roommates who couldn't get along, lab partners who didn't think someone was pulling his or her own weight, or a colleague who was mad at the company and

Success Tip

By all means, try to give a new group time to bond and develop. If you don't have time, though, take special measures, such as telling people that the group needs to get to work right away, apologizing in advance for any misunderstanding, and encouraging people to speak up immediately if things aren't working.

refused to help the group do its job. Total group breakdowns may be infrequent, but the problems that lead to collapse can also hamper a group's effectiveness, even if the group stays together. Rooting out these problems and addressing them is vital.

In one sense, interpersonal conflicts that spill into public view are easier to deal with because they are so recognizable. If people start yelling at each other in a meeting, you have a good idea of where the problem lies. However, the submerged conflicts are hard to pin down. You may notice that someone never seems to agree with another group member or support that person's proposals. You may find people trying to introduce or avoid certain topics, with no apparent reason or logic. You may just sense that something is wrong and be unable to put your finger on it (see Exhibit 19.8). If you can't figure out the problem by observing the group in action, pull one or two people aside and ask them what's going on.

Encourage Full Participation

Every group is likely to have people with vastly different personality types. Some people will sit back and let others monopolize the discussion, rarely if ever speaking. Others will seem to talk incessantly, using as many words as possible to say very little. Group success often depends on encouraging quiet people to contribute more and talkative people to listen more.

If you're a group leader, it becomes your responsibility to encourage all members to participate. One effective way to do this is to talk to members individually outside the meeting, letting each one know they have your support. This can give shy people the confidence to speak up in the meeting and let talkative people know that their contribution is appreciated and that they don't need to justify every statement or opinion.[16] Besides encouraging

EXHIBIT 19.8
Recognizing Conflict Signals
This man appears to be intently interested in the speaker's message, but his facial expression and body language suggest that he may not be in complete agreement with the speaker.

participation, this one-on-one communication allows you to become better acquainted with team members, to better understand their personality styles, and to learn what unique contributions they can make to the group.

In addition to talking with members outside the meeting, a group leader can also give positive feedback during the meeting. Let the speaker know that you heard what was said and thank the speaker for contributing. Keep criticism constructive.

If more subtle means of controlling talkative members are not effective, you may need to resort to some sort of time limit. One corporate executive distributes an agenda with time limits clearly specified. When a speaker is nearing the end of his or her allotted time, the facilitator voices a reminder. If the speaker continues to talk, a loud alarm clock goes off.[17] Another executive takes a tennis ball to each meeting. Only the person holding the ball is allowed to speak. This discourages more aggressive group members from cutting in on others. These two techniques may seem extreme or contrived, but they emphasize the importance of encouraging full participation from all group members. Another suggested technique is to appoint the talkative member to take notes, thus restraining that member from speaking.[18]

Be Supportive of Others

Make your criticism constructive. It is okay (even desirable at times) to disagree with someone else in the group, but direct your comments to the issue, not to the person

voicing an opinion. Avoid phrases like "stupid idea" or "ridiculous notion." Instead, say something like "I don't think that will work because . . ." and present your reason.

An important part of being supportive is the ability to truly listen to what the other person is saying. Listening in small groups may be difficult, but all group members need to share this responsibility.[19] Concentrate on what is being said by other group members rather than on what you want to say next. Ask questions to clarify anything you don't understand. Realize that your solution is only one possible solution, and be willing to consider other ideas. Finally, be sure to participate fully yourself. Be willing to do your fair share of the work—before, during, and after the meeting.

Use Technology Wisely and Appropriately

In many cases, technology has changed the nature of meetings by helping to free people from the limitations of distance and time. To conquer distance, people in far-flung locations no longer have to travel to one site in order to have a meeting. They can meet via videoconferencing, which allows live interaction over television or computer screens. An alternative to videoconferencing is using computerized online "chat" sessions, where the participants communicate by typing what they have to say and reading what others have to say. Some systems let people work simultaneously on the same document (or illustration) by displaying it on everyone's computer screen.

Computer technology can also help people address the problem of differing time zones, which prevent people from being available at the same time. Electronic mail lets people stretch a "meeting" over many hours or days, as people read and reply to messages sent by others in the group. Although these e-mail sessions aren't meetings in the usual sense, they are often used to replace regular meetings.

Such technologies provide some clear benefits, but they can also require some new communication skills. In an online chat session, for instance, you lose all of the nuances of nonverbal communication. The words you type have to convey all of the meaning you intend to communicate. When talking to someone in person, you can use facial gestures and body language to add meaning to what you say—and to gauge the responses of others in the meeting. If people roll their eyes to express disbelief when you say something, you can immediately back up your

---

Ask An Expert

Adelina M. Gomez, Ph.D.
Communication Department, University of Colorado, Colorado Springs

Q: During group discussions, what specific signals might indicate submerged conflict? What can I do about those signals?

A: Conflict in any context can be potentially damaging unless the individuals concerned have some knowledge of their own conflict management styles. Since most people have little knowledge of the role of conflict in the communication process, they may try to avoid it and refuse to acknowledge that conflict exists. As an oral process, group discussion is a breeding ground for conflict avoidance. But when someone in the group believes in confronting conflict, the environment can become stressful for everyone.

Submerged conflict can be a "feeling" that something is wrong but no one is willing to discuss it. Some signals of submerged conflict are found in the nonverbal behaviors of group members. For example, some members may tend not to look at someone with whom they have conflictive feelings about an issue, goal, or problem. Or some may adopt a defensive style of communication, which usually suggests that a person believes he or she is being personally attacked for an idea, suggestion, or recommendation.

What can we do about these signals? Be aware and observant of our personal style of verbal and nonverbal behavior. We need to ask, "What messages do I send to others when I sense conflict?" "What can I change about me that will send the message that it's okay for others to disagree with my ideas and that conflict is okay because it's part of the communication process?" Finally, "How can I convince myself and others that each person is unique as an individual and as a member of a particular culture?"

1. As a speaker leading a group discussion following a presentation, what can you do to identify and manage conflicts that arise from differences in culture rather than differences in ideas?
2. During the next class discussion about a particular student speech or a specific ethical issue, watch your classmates for nonverbal signals of submerged conflict. If you were leading the discussion, what would you do to manage the conflict while encouraging full participation and keeping all participants focused on the group's goals?

---

statement with another statement. You don't get this kind of feedback in an online session. And even though videoconferencing provides a visual link, it's not always as effective as interacting in person. You only see as much as the video cameras see, and you might not be able to scan the entire audience quickly, as you can during an in-person speech. Technology will continue to change the way we communicate, and it's important to recognize the strengths and limitations of each tool you use. Despite some preliminary findings suggesting that computer technology can improve group decision making and group effectiveness, there is still no substitute for face-to-face contact.[20] Even in companies and groups that use communication technology extensively, people still come together occasionally to establish the bonds that help teams and other groups succeed (see Exhibit 19.9).

PLANNING AND LEADING MEETINGS

Much of the group communication you'll participate in will take place in organized meetings. These meetings will range from the rigidly structured and formal to the casual and relaxed, but the factors that make them successful are similar in any case. Here are the general steps to follow in planning and leading a meeting. Keep in mind that the way you plan and conduct meetings makes a tremendous impression on others in your group, so be sure it's a positive impression.

• *Define the purpose—and agree on it.* Even meetings with a seemingly obvious purpose, such as "reviewing next year's budget proposals," can mean different things to different people. One person might show up at such a meeting to find out why his department isn't getting as much money as it got last year. Another might show up to propose a new idea for which he or she needs additional money. To avoid misunderstandings, write a clear statement of the meeting's purpose, distribute it ahead of time if possible to the people who will attend, and make sure they agree before you move ahead.

• *Invite the right people.* It's frustrating to realize halfway through a meeting that someone with vital information or decision-making authority isn't present so the meeting can't continue. On the other hand, as a participant, it's frustrating to sit all the way through a meeting and realize you had no purpose and nothing to contribute. One of the leader's chief responsibilities in planning a meeting is to make sure the right people show up.

• *Set the agenda and give people a chance to review it.* Except for wide-open brainstorming sessions and other creative activities, meetings should operate according to an agenda defined before the meeting starts. Let people know in advance what you plan to cover and how long you'll spend on each topic. This way they can plan their time better and make sure they're prepared to participate.

• *Verify that the location is adequate and available.* Make sure the room or other facility will help your meeting, not hurt it. This involves everything from having enough chairs to making sure that the overhead projector has a good light bulb.

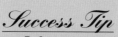

Success Tip

Before every meeting, try to estimate how much each attendee's time is worth. Add that up, and then multiply by the amount of time you plan to spend in the meeting. Share that number with your audience, if appropriate. Most people will be amazed how much meetings cost.

Time is both irreplaceable and expensive; don't waste the group's time trying to find more chairs or a piece of equipment after the meeting has started.

- *Start—and end—on time.* Once people get the impression that your meetings don't start on time, they'll show up later and later. Starting a meeting of 20 people just 15 minutes late adds up to *five hours* of wasted time. Also, end on time so that people can fulfill other commitments without leaving your meeting's issues unresolved.

- *On the other hand, don't be a slave to the agenda or the clock.* Sticking to the agenda and the schedule are good advice in most cases, but doing so can sometimes be counter-productive. If a new and important issue arises during the meeting, it might be necessary to address it before moving on. Similarly, if you're working on an important problem or opportunity, you may not want to end

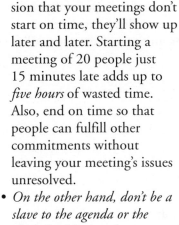

IMPROVING YOUR CRITICAL THINKING

OPEN-MINDED MEETINGS: THE ULTIMATE IDEA GENERATOR!

The process for planning and conducting meetings involves some fairly rigid rules: set an agenda, start on time, and so on. But some people are discovering another way that seems to be more effective in the right situations. Called "open-space meetings," these get-togethers are as loose and unstructured as the traditional meeting is fixed and formalized.

Organizational consultant Harrison Owen devised the idea after various meeting participants told him the best thing about meetings they attended was the coffee breaks. During these unstructured periods, people could discuss problems, look for similarities in different parts of the organization, and generally talk and listen freely. Owen's response was to design a meeting format that is, in his words, "one long coffee break."

The first big difference is the agenda. Open-space meetings don't have one. The participants decide what they should talk about in order to solve whatever problem or address whatever situation they're facing. The purpose of avoiding a fixed agenda is to let the people who know how to solve the problem decide what's most important to discuss.

The second big difference is the invitation list. Owen figures that the people most appropriate for a meeting will decide to attend. The logic seems sound; People who are forced to attend a meeting but who don't really want to be there probably won't make much of a contribution.

Supporters of the open-space concept, which include such well-known organizations as Reebok, the World Bank, and the U.S. Forest Service, say it brings up issues and solutions that would have been buried in a structured, agenda-driven meeting. On the other hand, even Owen acknowledges that open-space meetings aren't the best solution for every situation. They're probably best when the problem or situation is loosely structured and many people in the organization might have something to contribute. Perhaps the biggest advantage of open-space meetings is their ability to tap into the talents, ideas, and energies of people throughout the organization.

Unstructured discussion time is often the most productive part of a meeting because it helps people exchange information freely and build on each other's ideas.

the meeting at the designated time. Whether to end or not depends on both the subject and the audience, naturally.

- *Follow up and make sure others do, too.* Get a reputation as someone who does what he or she commits to doing. Moreover, if you're in a leadership position, see to it that others follow up on their commitments, too.

While the meeting is under way, you can employ all of the suggestions to foster good group communication. And as mentioned earlier, meetings (and all other forms of group get-togethers) are a complex communication process. They don't succeed automatically, but they do present an opportunity for bringing groups of people together both to solve problems and to grow closer as a team. And not least important, small group meetings give the individuals who plan, lead, and present them a chance to shine in front of their peers, managers, and in some cases, the public. So make the most of these great opportunities to show your skills.

SUMMARY

Most people will spend far more time speaking (and listening) in small groups than they'll spend delivering traditional speeches. Even if you haven't yet joined the workforce full time, you've probably been in dozens of groups already, from sports teams to religious organizations. And if you do have some years of on-the-job experience, you know all about the importance of group communication. Groups present many opportunities for both persuasive and informative speaking.

Groups come in three basic types: formal groups, informal groups, and teams. Although the group types vary widely, all share some basic functions and features that are important to their success. In any kind of group, the individual members tend to play certain roles (although not the same role all the time in every case). Some of these roles help the group reach its goals, and some help the group work together productively and peacefully. On the other hand, not all roles people play help the group. People who complain constantly, distract others with jokes, or try to pursue personal agendas are negative influences in any group. At best, these people don't contribute to the group's success, and at worst, they slow the group down and even lead to its failure or collapse.

Fortunately, groups do have some methods for keeping people in line. Group norms are standards of expected behavior. Norms develop over time, and new members are expected to follow along. These expectations can help a group by encouraging people to work together productively. They can also hurt a group by discouraging honest and well-intentioned dissent. In the worst cases, this conformity leads to

groupthink, in which people go along with the group not because they think the group is right but because they've surrendered the responsibility of thinking for themselves.

Leadership is also key to group success, even in groups that don't have an official, designated leader. The leader's communication skills and style are important because they contribute directly to the group's success and because they set the tone for other group members. A leader who is sensitive and supportive will encourage others to speak in the same way.

Most of the group situations you'll find yourself in will revolve around making decisions or solving problems. An efficient five-step process for this includes defining the problem or opportunity, analyzing the situation and gathering the information you'll need, establishing the criteria you'll use to select the best solution, generating a list of possible solutions, and then analyzing your possibilities and selecting the best one.

No matter what the group's purpose, you can take several steps to improve communication among all the members: Stay focused on the goal you want to reach, give the group enough time to grow together, take care of interpersonal conflicts between group members to keep these issues from hurting the group as a whole, push for full participation by encouraging quieter members to speak up and domineering members to hold back, support others, and use technological tools wisely and efficiently.

You have a great opportunity to demonstrate your communication skills whenever you plan or lead a meeting. Steps in planning include getting agreement on the purpose and the agenda, making sure you get the right

people involved, and efficiently handling logistical issues such as location, timing and meeting follow-up.

KEY TERMS

facilitator (421)
formal groups (416)
group communication (416)
group norms (419)
groupthink (420)
informal groups (417)

APPLY CRITICAL THINKING

1. Does your public speaking class qualify as a group in the sense discussed in this chapter? Why or why not?

2. Could a group norm of open, honest communication ever hurt a group's progress?

3. Are group norms the same as the cultural norms discussed in Chapter 5? Explain your answer.

4. Is there a "right" amount of time to allow for brainstorming and other idea-generation techniques? Explain your answer.

5. Do groups always go through the five decision-making/problem-solving steps listed in the chapter? Think carefully, then explain your answer.

6. Do you agree that every member of a group should have equal time when it comes to participating in meetings? Why or why not?

7. What are some potential risks of the open-space meeting concept?

SHARPEN YOUR SKILLS

Individual Exercises

1. You're a shift manager at a local restaurant, and every time you call an employee meeting, the staff complains about rude customers. How should you handle the situation?

2. Review the example of the five managers meeting to find a company picnic site (in the section "Roles in Groups"). Explain why Kimiko should be considered the group's leader, even though she has no formal authority over the other members.

3. List five nonverbal cues that could indicate some kind of interpersonal conflict involving two or more members of a group.

4. Although it's generally good advice to give a group time to develop before expecting too much from it, you don't always have that luxury. In terms of communication, what advice would you give to leaders who have to pull groups together quickly and produce results almost immediately?

Group Exercises

5. With three or four other students, solve a crossword puzzle together as a group (most daily newspapers offer one). When you're finished, see whether you can identify who emerged as a leader in the group, if anyone did.

6. In a group with three or four other students, have each student assess his or her group communication behaviors. In the group, discuss everyone's strengths and what ideas the group has for improvement.

Appendix A
Suggested Speech Topics

I. GET-ACQUAINTED SPEECHES

The following topics are fairly lighthearted and can sometimes be funny or poignant. They make good icebreakers or first-day speeches. They can be assigned so that you have time to prepare, or they can be assigned as impromptu speeches so that you can practice thinking on your feet: Shake them up in a bag, pull one out, plan for a couple of minutes, and then go ahead and speak.

Personalized Topics and Personal Opinion

1. What I expect to learn in this course
2. My public speaking goals
3. Past public speaking experiences: the good, the bad, and the ugly
4. The best (or worst) speech (or speaker) I have ever seen and heard
5. How I *should* prepare a speech and how I *really* do it
6. How I *should* practice a speech and how I *really* do it
7. How I *should* deliver a speech and how I *really* do it
8. The greatest (worst) speech of all time
9. The greatest (worst) speaker of all time
10. The best (worst) communication experience of my life

Sentence Completions

1. I often wonder why I _____.
2. I would be good at teaching _____.
3. I am afraid of _____.
4. I used to be _____ but now I'm _____.
5. It's easy for me to _____.
6. I feel best when I _____.
7. Something I consider to be truly beautiful is _____.
8. Something I consider to be truly ugly is _____.
9. People would be surprised if they knew I _____.
10. I am sorry that I didn't _____.
11. I get angry when _____.
12. Some of the most important advice I've ever been given is _____.
13. What I remember most about junior high is _____.
14. Something I consider important in a friendship is _____.
15. Something I want to accomplish in the next year is _____.
16. Three things I would change about my hometown are _____.
17. If I could take three things to a desert island, they would be _____.
18. The novel that I'm going to write (and that will make me famous) will be _____.
19. The part of my life that feels the longest so far is _____.
20. If I could give an unlimited gift to anyone, I would give _____ to _____.
21. One piece of advice I'd give to a younger sibling would be _____.
22. One talent I've always wanted but don't seem to have is _____.
23. The leadership quality I admire most is _____.

24. If I were born the opposite sex, I would be different than I am now in the following ways: _____.

25. The best thing about good friends is that they always _____.

My Favorite

1. My favorite holiday
2. My favorite older person
3. My favorite charity
4. My favorite place
5. My favorite type of book
6. My favorite sport
7. My favorite terrain
8. My favorite "pet peeve"
9. My favorite store
10. My favorite street
11. My favorite person in history
12. My favorite animal
13. My favorite famous person
14. My favorite flower
15. My favorite childhood game
16. My favorite television show
17. My favorite place to dance
18. My favorite magazine
l9. My favorite hi-tech item
20. My favorite radio station
21. My favorite leisure activity
22. My favorite movie (type of movie)
23. My favorite place to go skiing (if you don't ski, discuss what it is about skiing that you do or do not like)
24. My favorite thing to do on the weekend

Grab Bag

1. What I'll never do again
2. The most important thing I've learned in college
3. Why it pays to be honest
4. Where I would like to go for my "ideal" vacation
5. My feeling about New Year's resolutions
6. Three of the most important things I've learned about people
7. The joy of having lots of (or few) relatives
8. Why every man or woman should (should not) get married

9. Why I like (don't like) living in my hometown
10. The richest gift my parents gave me
11. Why patience is a virtue
12. My mother's best cooking
13. An instance when I knew better
14. Why everyone should have a pet
15. To drink or not to drink
16. My most embarrassing moment
17. Three ways to relax
18. The trials of a father (mother)
19. The best novel I've ever read and why
20. The best movie I ever saw
21. The best teacher I ever had
22. How to (not to) get a job
23. The thing (things) I am afraid of
24. The role of youth in society
25. I love (or hate) television because
26. What I like most (or least) about football
27. The funniest person I've ever met (or seen)
28. The value of a college education today
29. My life after college will be

II. IMPROMPTU SITUATIONAL SPEECHES

The following topics are fairly serious, and they're about hypothetical situations. They can be used to practice your ability to think on your feet and to structure a persuasive speech quickly. You need to imagine the situation described and how you would speak in that situation.

1. You are speaking to a group of students on your campus. Encourage them to accept an increase in tuition this coming fall.
2. The town you live in suffers from a great deal of juvenile vandalism. Explain to a group of community members why juvenile recreational facilities should be built instead of a juvenile detention complex.
3. You are speaking to the Humane Society. Support or oppose the use of animals for medical research purposes.
4. You are talking to civic leaders of your community. Try to convince them to build an art gallery.
5. You are speaking to the Chamber of Com-

merce. Speak for or against raising the drinking age to 21 for all alcoholic beverages.

6. You are speaking to a group of university students. Support or oppose the draft for women.

7. You are speaking to a group of adults who don't know how to swim. Encourage them to enroll in a beginner's swimming class.

8. You are speaking to the faculty senate at your campus regarding the grading policy. Agree or disagree with abolishing letter grades and instituting a new pass/fail policy.

9. You are speaking to a group of parents regarding pets. Support or oppose the idea that all children should have a pet.

10. You are speaking to a group of high school seniors. Support or oppose the idea of attending a community college before enrolling at a four-year school.

11. You are speaking to a group of incoming freshmen at your school. Tell them what is special about this school and why you think they should attend it.

12. You are speaking to a group of overweight people. Convince them that they should lose weight, and describe a program for them to follow.

13. You are speaking to a first-grade class at an elementary school. Explain why they should brush their teeth after meals.

14. You are speaking to a group of traveling salespeople. Convince them that they should wear their seatbelts while driving.

15. You are speaking to the scheduling committee of your school. Support or oppose the scheduling of evening classes.

16. You are speaking to a group of cigarette smokers. Convince them to stop and outline ways to quit.

17. You are speaking to a group of new drivers. Support or oppose the signing of the organ donation card on the back of driver's licenses.

18. You are speaking to a group of parents. Speak for or against television viewing by their children.

19. You are speaking to a group of people who drive to campus. Convince them to take the bus.

20. You are speaking to a group of elderly people. Convince them to adopt an exercise program.

21. You are speaking to a group of instructors. Convince them to dismiss class on Groundhog Day.

22. You are speaking to a group of vegetarians. Convince them to eat meat.

23. You are speaking to a group of alcoholics. Convince them to join Alcoholics Anonymous.

24. You are speaking to a group of mature adults. Convince them that body piercing has a legitimate place in society.

III. CRITICAL ISSUES SPEECHES

The following subjects are matters of concern to many people. Most of them can be approached either informatively or persuasively. This list contains general subjects that need to be narrowed to a more specific topic. Following each general entry are some suggestions for a more narrow topic. Of course, you will also need to develop a specific purpose. For example, under environmental concerns, if you focus on energy conservation, your specific purpose might read like this: to convince the audience that each one of us has a responsibility to participate in conserving our scarce energy resources.

Another way to locate critical issues would be to "surf" any CD-ROM program such as Microsoft's *Encarta*. The broad categories and their subcategories contained in the *Encarta* directory might suggest an interesting critical issue topic.

1. Abuse (alcohol, drugs, emotional, physical, rehabilitation)
2. Crime (capital punishment, delinquency, gun control, poverty, prison reform, terrorism, vandalism)
3. Education (support, quality, standards)
4. Environmental concerns (energy conservation, global warming, pollution, population control, rare species and wildlife extinction, world hunger)

5. Financial issues (banking, investing, the challenges faced by two-income families)
6. Gerontology (aging, health care for elderly people, hospice care)
7. Government (domestic policy, foreign policy, social security taxes, welfare)
8. Health care (AIDS, eating disorders, euthanasia, gene therapy, nationalization, organ donors)
9. Human rights and concerns (homelessness, minority rights, religious freedom)
10. Information age and computers (electronic mail, Internet, technophobes, voice mail)
11. International concerns (nuclear power and weapons, terrorism, world peace)
12. Legal issues (the courts, justice and the judiciary, lawyers, wills)
13. Liberal arts (architecture, fine art, history, literature, music, pop culture)
14. Media (advertising, censorship, governmental control, violence)
15. Philosophy and religion (types, belief systems, practices)
16. Politics (Democrats and Republicans, elections, legislative bodies and legislation, the presidency)
17. Sports (amateur and professional, baseball, football, golf, hang gliding, hockey, rappelling and rock climbing, spectator and participant sports, tennis)

IV. COMMUNICATION TOPICS

The following subjects are related to communication in general and can be approached lightheartedly or more seriously. Most of them would fit either an informative or a persuasive speech assignment, depending on what position you take.

These subjects are general and need to be narrowed. Following each general subject are some suggestions for a more narrow topic. Of course, you will also need to develop a specific purpose. For example, you might choose to talk about interpersonal communication, and you might narrow the focus to a purpose like this: to explain what goes wrong with interpersonal communication and how to improve these interactions.

Foundations of Communication

1. Rhetoric (what rhetoric is and why it's important to public speaking, Greek tradition, Roman tradition)
2. Purposes of communication (why we communicate, the benefits of communicating)
3. Types of communication (intrapersonal, interpersonal, small groups, public speaking, speaking in organizations)
4. Importance of communication (in your life, in society, in the workplace)
5. Quality of communication (what it means to communicate appropriately or effectively, how we form impressions of other people as communicators)
6. Nonverbal communication (the barriers or problems involved, what you can do to improve how you communicate nonverbally)
7. Verbal communication (the barriers or problems involved, what you can do to improve how you communicate verbally)
8. Nonverbal and verbal communication (how these two ways of communicating are alike or different, how they can work together most effectively)

Other Communication Topics

1. Animal communication (whether some animals use a form of communication that is similar to that used by humans; how human communication is different; whether chimps, dolphins, or gorillas communicate symbolically in the same way humans do)
2. Bias and communication (biased language, gender, profanity, racism, sexism)
3. Children and communication (development of language in children, developing self-concept and self-esteem, communicating with children who have autism, communicating with children who have hearing disabilities)
4. Conflict and communication (arbitration, mediation, problem solving, strategies for managing conflict, conflict styles)

5. Culture and communication (how culture influences communication, what you can do to improve how you communicate with people unlike you, intercultural public speaking, traveling)

6. Deception and communication (why we deceive, how we can detect deceptive communication, whether it's okay to lie, whether animals can lie)

7. Education and communication (censoring student newspapers, communication behaviors of students and of teachers, communication in the classroom)

8. Ethics and communication (what ethical communication is; whether it's ever ethical to gossip, lie, distort the truth; whether it's ever ethical to withhold information and thus limit another person's informed decision making)

9. Humor and communication (appropriate and effective use of humor, how to tell a joke or funny story)

10. Intimacy and communication (relationship development and deterioration, communicating in families and with significant others, flirting and intimacy, relationships in the 1990s)

11. Law and communication (courtroom communication, lawyers and judges, expert witnesses, jury selection, the power of persuasive lawyers, videotaping and broadcasting trials)

12. Listening and communication (the barriers or problems that have an impact on how well we listen, what we can do to improve how well we listen, listening to public speakers, providing feedback)

13. Mass media and communication (advertising, photojournalism, propaganda, public service campaigns, sensationalism, social effects of mass communication, speeches on radio and TV, violence on TV)

14. Medicine, health and communication (doctor/patient communication, faith healing, placebos, terminally ill people)

15. Organizations and communication (interviewing, technical presentations and briefings, leadership, work groups and teams)

16. Perception and communication (how your world perception influences the way you communicate; what you can or should do about it; what you need to know about perception, differences in perceptions)

17. Persuasion and communication (credibility, ethics, audience analysis and perspective-taking)

18. Politics and communication (censorship, freedom of speech, presidential addresses, public speaking and public policy, world relations)

19. Religion and communication (evangelists, homiletics, motivation and persuasion)

20. Self and communication (how your self-perception influences the way you communicate, what you can or should do about it, what you need to know about self-disclosure)

21. Sports and communication (communication between coaches and teams, motivating athletes, sports broadcasting, team building)

22. Technology and communication (information as power, technology and power, transmission of information today, new methods and speed as factors)

23. Written and spoken communication (whether one has more power, which one has played a more important role in history, the differences between cultures having written languages and cultures having only oral communication)

Appendix B
Speeches for Analysis

A COMMEMORATIVE SPEECH

The following commemorative speech was delivered to the people of South Africa on May 10, 1994. Nelson Mandela was celebrating the hard-won liberty and equality for all South Africans. The noble rhetoric and lofty language are appropriate for this auspicious occasion. In fact, this speech is a good example of how the needs of the speaking situation dictate what is said and how the speaker says it. In addition to well-chosen and inspiring words, President Mandela uses repetition and alliteration to build momentum throughout the speech. With repeated references to *We,* he attempts, rhetorically, to unite the people of South Africa and heal the wounds that have divided his country. This speech proudly marches to conclusion and ends on a high note. Readers today can almost see the sun streaming down on South Africa as freedom begins its reign.

GLORY AND HOPE: LET THERE BE
WORK, BREAD, WATER, AND SALT
FOR ALL
By Nelson Mandela, President of South Africa
*Delivered to the People of South Africa, Pretoria,
South Africa, May 10, 1994*

Your majesties, your royal highnesses, distinguished guests, comrades and friends: Today, all of us do, by our presence here, and by our celebrations in other parts of our country and the world, confer glory and hope to newborn liberty.

Out of the experience of an extraordinary human disaster that lasted too long must be born a society of which all humanity will be proud.

Our daily deeds as ordinary South Africans must produce an actual South African reality that will reinforce humanity's belief in justice, strengthen its confidence in the nobility of the human soul and sustain all our hopes for a glorious life for all.

All this we owe both to ourselves and to the peoples of the world who are so well represented here today.

To my compatriots, I have no hesitation in saying that each one of us is as intimately attached to the soil of this beautiful country as are the famous jacaranda trees of Pretoria and the mimosa trees of the bushveld.

Each time one of us touches the soil of this land, we feel a sense of personal renewal. The national mood changes as the seasons change.

We are moved by a sense of joy and exhilaration when the grass turns green and the flowers bloom.

That spiritual and physical oneness we all share with this common homeland explains the depth of the pain we all carried in our hearts as we saw our country tear itself apart in terrible conflict, and as we saw it spurned, outlawed and isolated by the peoples of the world, precisely because it has become the universal base of the pernicious ideology and practice of racism and racial oppression.

We, the people of South Africa, feel fulfilled that humanity has taken us back into its bosom, that we, who were outlaws not so long ago, have today been given the rare privilege to be host to the nations of the world on our own soil.

We thank all our distinguished international guests for having come to take possession with the people of our country of what is, after all, a common victory for justice, for peace, for human dignity.

We trust that you will continue to stand by us as we tackle the challenges of building peace, prosperity, nonsexism, nonracialism and democracy.

We deeply appreciate the role that the masses of our people and their democratic, religious, women, youth, business, traditional and other leaders have played to bring about this conclusion. Not least among them is my Second Deputy President, the Honorable F. W. de Klerk.

We would also like to pay tribute to our security forces, in all their ranks, for the distinguished role they have played in securing our first democratic elections and the transition to democracy, from bloodthirsty forces which still refuse to see the light.

The time for the healing of the wounds has come.

The moment to bridge the chasms that divide us has come.

The time to build is upon us.

We have, at last, achieved our political emancipation. We pledge ourselves to liberate all our people from the continuing bondage of poverty, deprivation, suffering, gender and other discrimination.

We succeeded to take our last steps to freedom in conditions of relative peace. We commit ourselves to the construction of a complete, just and lasting peace.

We have triumphed in the effort to implant hope in the breasts of the millions of our people. We enter into a covenant that we shall build the society in which all South Africans, both black and white, will be able to walk tall, without any fear in their hearts, assured of their inalienable right to human dignity—a rainbow nation at peace with itself and the world.

As a token of its commitment to the renewal of our country, the new Interim Government of National Unity will, as a matter of urgency, address the issue of amnesty for various categories of our people who are currently serving terms of imprisonment.

We dedicate this day to all the heroes and heroines in this country and the rest of the world who sacrificed in many ways and surrendered their lives so that we could be free.

Their dreams have become reality. Freedom is their reward.

We are both humbled and elevated by the honor and privilege that you, the people of South Africa, have bestowed on us, as the first President of a united, democratic, nonracial and nonsexist South Africa, to lead our country out of the valley of darkness.

We understand it still that there is no easy road to freedom.

We know it well that none of us acting alone can achieve success.

We must therefore act together as a united people, for national reconciliation, for nation building, for the birth of a new world.

Let there be justice for all.

Let there be peace for all.

Let there be work, bread, water and salt for all.

Let each know that for each the body, the mind and the soul have been freed to fulfill themselves.

Never, never and never again shall it be that this beautiful land will again experience the oppression of one by another and suffer the indignity of being the skunk of the world.

The sun shall never set on so glorious a human achievement!

Let freedom reign. God bless Africa!

A COMMEMORATIVE SPEECH

The following commemorative speech was presented at the 1995 Catalyst Awards Dinner in New York on March 22, 1995. The topic of women in the workforce is obviously important, but the speaker's approach makes the speech memorable. This speech is a pointed and informative discussion of gender roles in the workplace, and it's based on history and interesting facts, not just emotion. The speaker draws clear pictures of women and their changing roles in society over the last century. Vivid images of women bring the speech to life: women dying in the flames of a burning factory they can't escape, women enduring intolerable working conditions, and more. Note how Wellington lauds the progress that has occurred and then, in the same breath, calls our attention to the need for continued commitment to change.

WOMEN WORKING, A CENTURY OF CHANGE

By Sheila W. Wellington, President, Catalyst
Delivered as the 1995 Catalyst Awards Dinner Speech, New York, New York, March 22, 1995

Nineteen hundred and ninety-five begins the last half of the last decade of the 20th century. It is a time of extraordinary challenge and change for American society. What do these challenges, these changes mean for women? Will progress be halted? Will the benefits we have brought to the nation's economy be lost?

The answer is clear from the merest backward glance. It is appropriate that on this—Catalyst's 20th annual awards dinner—we take that glance.

One hundred years ago, at the dawn of the last millennium, our bustled Victorian great-grand-mothers could not run for a bus, let alone for Congress. If the race—as the Victorian poet claimed—went to the swift, women lost.

Girdled, corseted, enveloped in yards of gingham and lace, women were balanced precariously on their pedestals.

The average woman was married with 3.56 children—down from 7 the century before. High infant mortality meant 122 infants were lost out of 1000 live births. Lacking both birth control and anesthesia, we lived an average of 51 years—three years longer than men.

If not a woman with means and therefore with servants, she labored hard, in a home where one in seven had a bathtub, and none had electricity to power yet-to-be invented vacuum cleaners, or irons, or washing machines.

Still poorer women worked for wages outside the home. Seventeen percent of Caucasian women, chiefly immigrants, were employed, mainly in textile and garment factories. Forty-one percent of black women were employed, mainly as agricultural laborers or as servants. Needless to say, women's wages were pitifully low.

Things have changed. Women now choose when and if to marry. Some keep their own names. Infant mortality has dropped to 9 per 1000. Projected female life expectancy for the turn of the next century is 80—seven years greater than men.

Forty-seven percent of women work outside the home. By the year 2000, it is projected that 60 percent of women will be in the workforce.

The all-American family—the family I grew up in—with a father who works, a stay at-home mom, and two kids—can be found in only 4 percent of households.

The end of the 20th century finds a woman up on a telephone pole or down in a Navy submarine, running a company or driving a big rig cross-country. Women still serve coffee, but we also serve in the president's cabinet. Nearly 350 female presidents run U.S. colleges and universities. Eight women hold Senate seats, and 47 women currently sit in the House.

Has such enormous change made women happier? Certainly, though sometimes we need the long view to see it clearly.

When I was a child, my mother told me the story of the fire at the Triangle Shirtwaist Factory. It happened in 1911 in New York City, in the immigrant neighborhood where she grew up. A fire broke out in a factory where young women toiled in unimaginable conditions. Trapped in flames, 146 women died piled against doors sealed tight to prevent their leaving before the day's work was over. That image—of all those women bolted into their jobs so they couldn't save themselves—seared into my imagination.

Many factors have led to the improved status of women, but the single most important was a national event that is now taken so for granted that few of us recognize its newness and its potency. Seventy-five years ago, on August 26,

1920, with Tennessee's ratification of the 19th Amendment, women gained the right to vote.

Women couldn't vote when my mother was born. Every time I think about it, it startles me, even as Edith Wharton wrote her novels, as Helen Keller graduated from Radcliffe with honors, even as women manufactured the arms that led to victory in WWI and the nation's move to global primacy, women still could not vote. To make the ballot a reality, women and men of vision and guts, with many different goals and aims and views, came together. Recognized as having ideas, women would become individuals, would enter true adulthood.

Progress continues. For thousands of years of human evolution, the critical factor distinguishing men and women's work was physical strength. Men slaughtered the beast and dragged it home. Now, in the Information Age, what predominates is what Peter Drucker calls "knowledge work." Knowledge and ideas are the great equalizers. In intellectual labor, women can compete as equals. Women's brains go to work. And the smartest, ablest, most foresighted of both genders know this.

You—in this room—know this.

The three companies we honor tonight—Deloitte And Touche, Dow Chemical Company, and JC Penney—know this.

We no longer see women literally locked into their workplaces. But, we do find women struggling in outmoded workplace structures to balance their personal, family, and work lives. We find women struggling to have their voices, their ideas, heard in the ranks of senior management and in the Board room.

There is work still to be done.

Yet every day, more and more women and men recognize the imperative of changing to meet the changes brought about in this century.

Women have always worked, in the home or out of it. We always will. As the century closes, more and more women work for a paycheck, while others find their own ways to contribute to society.

But whatever American women do as the millennium draws to a close, we do it recognizing ourselves, and being recognized as rational beings, as free citizens. This is the challenge of change the 20th century has wrought.

At bottom, it is the reason Catalyst, building on the firm foundation established by Felice Schwartz, retains optimism and its vibrancy.

What we at Catalyst do, what you in this room do in collaboration with us, serves the national purpose.

The clock will not turn back.

The clock moves inexorably forward.

A PERSUASIVE SPEECH

The following persuasive speech was delivered before the U. S. Treasury Executive Institute in Washington, D.C., on November 12, 1992. The topic is one that anyone now living and working in the United States can easily relate to. Davidson describes five factors, or "mega-realities," that are contributing to the erosion of leisure time in the United States. He provides solid evidence for the existence of each factor and gives some instructional advice for what to do about it. Despite the fact that this is a rather long speech, it contains intriguing information that's well organized and easy to follow. Davidson structures his remarks around the five mega-realities: Each factor is presented and described, and then followed by a solution. The speech concludes with the ultimate solution: advice on achieving a complete self in the 1990s, despite the proliferation of mega-realities.

OVERWORKED AMERICANS OR OVERWHELMED AMERICANS? YOU CANNOT HANDLE EVERYTHING
By Jeff Davidson, Author and Management Consultant
Delivered before the U.S. Treasury Executive Institute, Washington, D.C., November 12, 1992

Here is a multiple-choice quiz question. Which word best describes the typical working American today: A) Overworked, B) Underworked, C) Energetic, D) Lazy.

While much has been written of late as to whether A, B, C, or D, is correct, the most appropriate answer may well be: "None of the above." Powerful social forces have the potential to turn each of us into human whirlwinds charging about in "fast forward." Work, time *away from work,* and *everything in between* appear as if they are all part of a never-ending, ever-lengthening to-do list, to be handled during days that race by.

To say that Americans work too many hours, and that too much work is at the root of the time-pressure we feel and the leisure we lack, is to miss the convergence of larger, more fundamental issues. We could handle the longer hours (actually less than 79 minutes more per day) that we work compared to the Europeans. It's everything else competing for our attention that leaves us feeling overwhelmed. Once overwhelmed, the feeling of overworked quickly follows.

Nearly every aspect of American society has become more complex even since the mid-1980s. Traveling is becoming more cumbersome. Learning new ways of managing, and new ways to increase productivity takes its toll. *Merely living* in America today and participating as a functioning member of society guarantees that your day, week, month, year and life, and your physical, emotional, and spiritual energy will easily be depleted without the proper vantage point from which to approach each day and conduct your life.

Do you personally know *anyone* who works for a living who consistently has unscheduled, free stretches? Five factors, or "mega-realities," are simultaneously contributing to the perceptual and actual erosion of leisure time among Americans, including:

—Population growth;
—An expanding volume of knowledge;
—Mass media growth and electronic addiction;
—The paper trail culture; and
—An overabundance of choices.

Population

From the beginning of creation to 1850, world population grew to one billion. It grew to two billion by 1930, three billion by 1960, four billion by 1979, and five billion by 1987, with six billion en route. Every 33 months, the current population of America, 257 million people, is added to the planet.

The world of your childhood is gone, forever. The present is crowded and becoming more so. Each day, world population (births minus deaths) increases by *more than ,260,000 people.* Regardless of your political, religious, or economic views, the fact remains that geometric growth in human population permeates and dominates every aspect of the planet and its resources, the environment and all living things. This is the most compelling aspect of our existence, and will be linked momentarily to the four other mega-realities.

When JFK was elected president, domestic population was 180 million. It grew by 70 million in one generation. Our growing population has *not* dispersed over the nation's 5.4 million square miles. About 97 percent of the U.S. population resides on 3 percent of the land mass. Half of our population resides within 50 miles of the Atlantic or the Pacific Ocean, and 75 percent of the U.S. population live in urban areas, with 80 percent predicted by the end of the nineties.

More densely packed urban areas have resulted predictably in a gridlock of the nation's transportation systems. It *is* taking you longer merely to drive a few blocks; it's not your imagination, it's not the day of the week or the season, and it's not going to subside soon. Our population and road use grow faster than our ability to repair highways, bridges and arteries. In fact, vehicles (primarily cars) are multiplying twice as fast as people, currently approaching 400 million vehicles, compared to 165 million registered motorists.

Some 86 percent of American commuters still get to work by automobile, and 84 percent of inner city travel is by automobile. The average American now commutes 157,600 miles to work during his working life, equal to six times around the earth. Commuting snarls are increasing.

City planners report there will be no clear solution to gridlock for decades, and all population studies reveal that our nation's metropolitan areas will become home *to an even greater percentage of the population.* Even less populated urban areas will face unending traffic dilemmas. If only the gridlock were confined to commuter arteries.

However, shoppers, air travelers, vacationers, even campers—everyone in motion is or will be feeling its effects.

Knowledge

Everybody in America fears that he/she is under-informed. This moment, you, and everyone you know, are being bombarded on all sides. *Over-information* wreaks havoc on the receptive capacities of the unwary. The volume of new knowledge broadcast and published in every field is enormous and exceeds anyone's ability to keep pace. All told, more words are published or broadcast *in a day* than you could comfortably ingest in the rest of your life. By far, America leads the world in the sheer volume of information generated and disseminated.

Increasingly, there is no body of knowledge that everyone can be expected to know. In its 140th year, for example, the Smithsonian Museum in Washington D.C. added 942,000 items to its collections. Even our language keeps expanding. Since 1966, more than 60,000 words have been added to the English language—equal to half or more of the words in some languages. Harvard Library subscribes to 160,000 journals and periodicals.

With more information comes more misinformation. Annually, more than 40,000 scientific journals publish over one million new articles. "The number of scientific articles and journals published worldwide is starting to confuse research, overwhelm the quality-control systems of science, encourage fraud, and distort the dissemination of important findings," says N*ew York Times* science journalist William J. Broad.

In America, too many legislators, regulators and others *entrusted* to devise the rules which guide the course of society *take shelter in the information overglut by intentionally adding to it.* We are saddled with 26-page laws that could be stated in two pages, and regulations that contradict themselves every fourth page. And, this phenomenon is not confined to Capital Hill. Impossible VCR manuals, insurance policies, sweepstakes instructions, and frequent flyer bonus plans all contribute to our immobility.

Media Growth

The effect of the mass media on our lives continues unchecked. Worldwide media coverage certainly yields benefits. Democracy springs forth when oppressed people have a chance to see or learn about how other people in free societies live. As we spend more hours tuned to electronic media, we are exposed to tens of thousands of messages and images.

In America, more than three out of five television households own VCRs, while the number of movie tickets sold and videos rented in the U.S. each exceeded one billion annually starting in 1988. More than 575 motion pictures are produced each year compared to an average of 175 twelve years ago. In 1972, three major television networks dominated television—ABC, NBC and CBS. There are now 339 full-power independent television stations and many cable TV subscribers receive up to 140 channels offering more than 72,000 shows per month.

All told, the average American spends more than eight solid years watching electronically how other people supposedly live.

To capture overstimulated, distracted viewers, American television and other news media increasingly rely on sensationalism. Like too much food at once, too much data, in any form, isn't easily ingested. You can't afford to pay homage to everyone else's 15 minutes of fame. As Neil Postman observed, in *Amusing Ourselves to Death: Public Discourse in the Age of Television,* with the three words, "and now this . . ." television news anchors are able to hold your attention while shifting gears 180 degrees.

Radio Power

Radio listenership does not lag either. From 5 A.M. to 5 P.M. each weekday in America, listenership far surpasses that of television viewership. Unknown to most people, since television was first introduced, the number of radio stations has increased tenfold, and 97 percent of all households own an average of five radios, not counting their car radios. On weekdays, 95.2 percent of Americans listen to radio for three hours and fourteen minutes. Shock-talk disc jockeys make $300,000 to $600,000 per year and more, plus bonuses.

With a planet of more than five billion people, American media are easily furnished with an endless supply of turmoil for mass transmission. At any given moment somebody is fomenting revolution somewhere. Such turmoil is packaged daily for the evening news, whose credo has become, "If it bleeds, it leads." We are lured with images of crashes, hostages, and natural disasters. We offer our time and rapt attention to each new hostility, scandal or disaster. Far more people die annually from choking on food than in plane crashes or by guns, but crashes and shootings make for great footage, and play into people's fears.

With its sensationalized trivia, the mass medias overglut obscures fundamental issues that *do* merit concern, such as preserving the environment.

Meanwhile, broadcasts themselves regularly imply that it is uncivil or immoral not to tune into the daily news—"all the news you need to know," and "we won't keep you waiting for the latest. . . ." It is *not* immoral to not "keep up" with the news that is offered. However to "tune out"—turn your back on the world—is not appropriate either. Being more selective in what you give your attention to, and to how long you give it, makes more sense.

Tomorrow, while dressing, rather than plugging in to the mass media, quietly envision how you would like your day to be. Include everything that's important to you. Envision talking with others, making major decisions, having lunch, attending meetings, finishing projects, and walking out in the evening. You'll experience a greater sense of control over aspects of your position that you may have considered uncontrollable.

There is only one party who controls the volume and frequency of information that you're exposed to. That person is you. As yet, few people are wise information consumers. Each of us needs to vigilantly guard against being deluded with excess data. The notion of "keeping up" with everything is illusory, frustrating, and self-defeating. The sooner you give it up the better you'll feel and function.

Keen focus on a handful of priorities has never been more important. Yes, some compelling issues must be given short shrift. Otherwise you run the risk of being overwhelmed by more demanding issues, and *feeling overwhelmed always exacerbates feeling overworked.*

Paper Trails

Paper, paper everywhere but not a thought to think. Imagine staring out the window from the fifth floor of a building and seeing a stack of reports from the ground up to your eye level. This 55-foot-high stack would weigh some 659 pounds. *Pulp & Paper* reports that Americans annually consume 659 pounds of paper per person. In Japan, it's only 400 pounds per person; in Europe, Russia, Africa, Australia, and South America, far less.

Similar to too much information, or too many eyewitness reports, having too much paper to deal with is going to make you feel overwhelmed and overworked. Americans today are consuming at least three times as much paper as ten years ago. The long-held prediction of paperless offices, for now, is a laugher.

There are two basic reasons why our society spews so much paper:

—We have the lowest postal rates in the world, and

—We have the broadest distribution of paper-generating technology.

Last year, Congress received more than 300 million pieces of mail, up from 15 million in 1970. Nationwide more than 55 million printers are plugged into at least 55 million computers, and annually kick out billions of reams. Are 18,000 sheets enough? Your four-drawer file cabinet, when full, holds 18,000 pages.

The Thoreau Society reports that last year, Henry David Thoreau, who personally has been unable to make any purchases since 1862, received 90 direct mail solicitations at Walden Pond. Under our existing postal rates, catalog publishers and junk mail producers can miss the target 90 percent of the attempts and still make a profit—*only 2 percent of recipients* need to place an order for a direct mailer to score big.

Direct mailers, attempting to sell more, send you record amounts of unsolicited mail. In 1988, 12 billion catalogs were mailed in the U.S., up from 5 billion in 1980—equal to 50 catalogs for every man, woman, and child in America. In the last decade, growth in the total volume of regular, third-class bulk mail (junk mail) was 13 times faster than growth in the population. The typical (overworked? or overwhelmed?) executive receives more than 225 pieces of unsolicited mail each month, or about 12 pieces daily. Even Greenpeace, stalwart protector of the environment, annually sends out 25 million pieces of direct mail.

Attempting to contain what seems unmanageable, our institutions create paper accounting systems which provide temporary relief and some sense of order, while usually becoming ingrained and immovable, and creating more muddle. Certainly accounting is necessary, but why so complicated? Because in our overinformation society reams of data are regarded as a form of protection.

Why is documentation, such as circulating a copy to your boss, so critical to this culture? Because everyone is afraid of getting his derriere roasted! We live in a culture of fear, not like a marshal law dictatorship, but a form of fear nonetheless. "If I cannot document or account, I cannot prove, or defend myself." Attempting to contain what seems unmanageable, organizations and institutions, public and private, create paper accounting systems. These systems provide temporary relief and some sense of order. Usually they become ingrained and immovable, while creating more muddle. These accounting systems go by names such as federal income taxes, deed of trust, car loan, etc. Sure, accounting is necessary, but why so complicated? Because in the era of overinformation, overinformation is used as a form of protection.

Of the five mega-realities, only paper flow promises to diminish some day as virtual reality, the electronic book, and the gigabyte highway are perfected. For the foreseeable future, you're likely to be up to your eyeballs in paper. *Start where you are*—it is essential to clear the in-bins of your mind and your desk. Regard each piece of paper entering your personal domain as a potential mutineer or rebel. Each sheet has to earn its keep and remain worthy of your retention.

An Overabundance of Choices

In 1969, Alvin Toffler predicted that we would be overwhelmed by too many choices. He said that this would inhibit action, result in greater anxiety, and trigger the perception of less freedom and less time. Having choices is a blessing of a free-market economy. Like too much of everything else, however, having too many choices leaves the feeling of being overwhelmed and results not only in increased time expenditure but also in a mounting form of exhaustion.

Consider the supermarket glut: Gorman's *New Product News* reports that in 1978 the typical supermarket carried 11,767 items. By 1987, that figure had risen to an astounding 24,531 items—more than double in nine years. More than 45,000 other products were introduced during those years, but failed. Elsewhere in the supermarket, Hallmark Cards now offers cards for *105* familial relationships. Currently more than 1260 varieties of shampoo are on the market. More than 2000 skin care products are currently selling. Seventy-five different types of exercise shoes are now available, each with scores of variations in style, and features. A *New York Times* article reported that even buying leisure time goods has become a stressful, overwhelming experience.

Periodically, the sweetest choice is choosing from what you already have, choosing to actually have what you've already chosen. More important is to avoid engaging in low level decisions. If a tennis racquet comes with either a black or brown handle, and it's no concern to you, take the one the clerk hands you.

Whenever you catch yourself about to make a low-level decision, consider: does this really make a difference? Get in the habit of making *fewer* decisions each day—the ones that count.

A Combined Effect

In a *Time* magazine cover story entitled, "Drowsy America," the director of Stanford University's sleep center concluded that "Most Americans no longer know what it feels like to be fully alert." Lacking a balance between work and play, responsibility and respite, "getting things done" can become an end-all. We function like human doings instead of human beings. We begin to link executing the items on our growing "to do" lists with feelings of self-worth. As the list keeps growing longer, the lingering sense of more to do infiltrates our sense of self-acceptance. What's worse, our entire society seems to be irrevocably headed toward a new epoch of human existence. Is frantic, however, any way to exist as a nation? Is it any way to run your life?

John Kenneth Galbraith studied poverty-stricken societies on four continents. In *The Nature of Mass Poverty,* he concluded that some societies remain poor (often for centuries) because they *accommodate* poverty. Although it's difficult to live in abject poverty, Galbraith found that many poor societies are not willing to accept the difficulty of making things better.

As Americans, we appear poised to accommodate a frenzied, time-pressured existence, as if this is the way it has to be and always has been. *This is not how it has to be.* As an author, I have a vision. I see Americans leading balanced lives, with rewarding careers, happy home lives, and the ability to enjoy themselves. Our ticket to living and working at a comfortable pace is to not accommodate a way of being that doesn't support us, and addressing the true nature of the problem head-on.

The combined effect of the five mega-realities will continue to accelerate the feeling of pressure. Meanwhile, there will continue to be well-intentioned but misdirected voices who choose to condemn "employers" or "Washington D.C." or what have you for the lack of true leisure in our lives.

A Complete Self

We are, however, forging our own frenetic society. Nevertheless, the very good news is that the key to forging a more palatable existence can occur one by one. *You,* for example, are whole and complete right now, and you can achieve balance in your life. You *are not* your position. You are not your tasks; they don't define you and they don't constrain you. You have the capacity to acknowledge that your life is finite; you cannot indiscriminately take in the daily deluge that our culture heaps on each of us and expect to feel anything but overwhelmed.

Viewed from 2002, 1992 will appear as a period of relative calm and stability when life moved at a manageable pace. When your days on earth are over and the big auditor in the sky examines the ledger of your life, she'll be upset if you *didn't* take enough breaks, and if you don't enjoy yourself.

On a deeply felt personal level, recognize that from now on, you will face an *ever-increasing* array of items competing for your attention. Each of the five mega-realities will proliferate in the '90's. You *cannot handle everything,* nor is making the attempt desirable. It is time to make compassionate though difficult choices about what is best ignored, versus what does merits your attention and action.

A COMMEMORATIVE SPEECH

The following commencement address was presented at the University of West Florida on October 28, 1993. The speech is lighthearted, it's easy to read (and listen to), and most important, it's short. The brevity would certainly be appreciated by anyone who has suffered through lengthy graduation speeches full of rambling platitudes about the graduates' brilliant future. Instead, Martha Sanders uses a simple theme of three-word phrases to provide some homespun advice to the graduates seated before her. She uses examples and stories to illustrate each of the three-word phrases and to make them memorable.

LEARN TO LISTEN WITH YOUR HEART
FAREWELL TO GRADUATES
By Martha Saunders, Assistant Professor of
Public Relations
*Delivered at the University of West Florida,
October 28, 1993*

In the Department of Communication Arts we spend a great deal of time thinking and talking about words—the meaning of words, the persuasive value of words, the ethical implications of words and, generally, the impact of words as they are delivered in messages among people. Because of this, I was especially captured by a magazine article a few months ago which discussed how words influence people.

The article suggested that the most important messages that humans deliver to one another are usually expressed in very simple terms. I hope that doesn't shock you now that you've spent these past few years having your minds crammed with complicated thoughts. The article went on to suggest that the *most influential messages* in our language most often come in three-word phrases.

I had to agree that three-word phrases such as "I love you," or "There's no charge," or "And in conclusion" certainly were capable of prompting a strong reaction in me, and as I had hoped to impress you with profound thought today, I decided to share with you *three* three-word phrases that I have found useful as I have moved along in my life.

The first three-word phrase I've found useful in life is this: *I'll be there.* Have you ever thought about what a balm those three words can create?

I'll be there. If you've ever had to call for a plumber over a weekend you know how really good these words can feel. Or if you've been stranded on the road with car trouble and used your last quarter to call a friend, you know how good those words can be. Think about them:

"Grandma, I'm graduating in August!" *I'll be there.*

"Roommate, I'm stuck at the office and can't get to the airport to meet my sister!" *I'll be there.*

"Mom, the baby cries all night and if I don't get some sleep I'll perish!" *I'll be there.*

Recently I was talking with a local business person who is occasionally in a position to hire UWF graduates, and she told me the single most impressive thing a job candidate can do is to demonstrate a real interest in the well-being of that business. Someone who will help further the objectives of that organization, whether or not he or she is "on the clock" is going to be a valuable person. In other words, *be somebody who will be there.*

One of my favorite stories about someone who knew how to "be there" is told of Elizabeth, the Queen Mother of England, who was asked whether the little princesses (Elizabeth and Margaret Rose) would leave England after the Blitz of 1940. the queen replied:

> "The children will not leave England unless I do. I shall not leave unless their father does, and the king will not leave the country in any circumstances whatever." *I'll be there.*

The second three-word phrase I want to present to you is perhaps the hardest to learn to say—I know it was for me and sometimes still is. That is, *maybe you're right.* Think about it. If more people were to learn to say *maybe you're right* the marriage counselors would be out of business and, with a little luck, the gun shops. I know from experience it can have a disarming effect on an opponent in an argument. In fact, one of my lawyer friends uses it often in his closing remarks—and he is a *very* successful lawyer. *Maybe you're right.*

It has been my experience that when we get so hung up on getting our own way that we will not concede on *any* point, we are doing ourselves a real disservice. Make life a little easier on yourself. Remember the old saying: "There are a hundred ways to skin a cat—and every single one of them is right." *Maybe you're right.*

The third phrase I want to introduce to you I must have heard a thousand times when I was a little girl. Whenever I was faced with a hard decision I would turn to my caregiver and ask what I should do. Her response was always the same three-letter phrase— *"Your heart knows"*— then she would go on about what she was doing.

"My heart knows?" I would think to myself. "What's that supposed to mean? I need advice here. I need for you to tell me what to do."

She would just smile and say, *"Your heart knows, honey, your heart knows."*

But as I was an imperious child, I would throw

my hand on my hip and say, "Maybe so, but my heart isn't talking!"

To this she would respond— *"Learn to listen."*

This brings me to the point of my speech. You know, life doesn't come in the form of a degree plan. There's no Great Advisor out there who will give you a checklist and say, "Do these things and you'll earn your degree in 'life.'"

To some extent, the page is blank now. You may have a rough outline of where you're headed, but I can assure you, you won't get there without having to make some tough decisions—and decision making is never easy.

You may be able to find people to suggest what you should do, but for the most part, no one will be willing to accept the responsibility for your mistakes. You'll have to make your own choices.

My advice to you today is to learn to listen to your heart. The psychologists call this "tuning in to our subconscious." Spiritual leaders call it "turning to a higher power." Whatever you call it, there is an ability in each of you to find the right answers for your life. It's there and it's a powerful gift that all the education or degrees in the world can't acquire for you. You've had it all along— now, you're going to have to use it.

In "The Bending of the Bough," George Moore wrote: "The difficulty in life is the choice." Choose well, Graduates.

AN INFORMATIVE SPEECH

The topic of the following speech draws anyone who is interested in public speaking. Whether or not you agree with Willich's thesis, you'll be intrigued by his discussion of what makes persuasion effective. Willich presents an argument for the lost art of traditional oratory. By that, he means persuasive speaking in a grand or ornamental style, using the rhetoric of emotion or pathos. He observes that today's persuasive speaking is dominated by the presentation of a well-reasoned argument, using the rhetoric of logic or logos. Note the ways Willich makes his own argument persuasive. For example, he uses metaphor, referring to traditional oratory as the thoroughbred champion of persuasion. He also provides both familiar and unfamiliar examples that support his case. And in the final analysis, he never asks us to discard logical rhetoric but merely to revive traditional oratory.

TRADITIONAL ORATORY: THOROUGH-BRED OF PERSUASIVE SPEAKING
Dean Willich, Wittenberg University, Ohio

Think for a moment, how many persuasive speeches have you as a competitor or judge had to sit through in the past year? Probably a great deal. Out of those speeches, how many of the subject matters do you recall? Probably a great deal fewer. Of that still smaller subgroup, how many persuasive speeches in the past year have actually moved you to act? My guess is few, if any at all. In the last 25 years, persuasive speaking in forensic competitions has evolved into the domination of first affirmative style speech patterns much like that of debate. While this style has a valid place in persuasive speaking, its exclusivity in speech competitions is a travesty. For persuasive speaking is far more diverse than this. The National Forensics Association defines persuasive speaking as "a speech given to convince, to move to action, or inspire on a significant issue." This definition is inclusive to a wide variety of styles. So, let us look at another style of persuasive speaking. One rarely seen in the past two decades is traditional oratory or persuasive speaking in a grand or ornamental style. I would like to introduce you to the tradition of oratory, then look at the contemporary state of persuasive speaking, and finally, show you how a synthesis between the two will help us grow to be more effective persuasive speakers.

As I was composing my speech, I found several different definitions of oratory, many differing descriptions of oratory, but none were able to capture the essence of oratory. So rather than fallaciously attempting an analytical description of oratory, I would like to, for the next few moments, afford you the opportunity to experience oratory, the thoroughbred of persuasive speaking. Upon inquiry, one will find the lineage of this thoroughbred to be most pristine, for it was conceived in the ebb and flow of Eastern and

Western Culture, born to the Greek Tradition, reared by the great minds of Plato and Aristotle, trained through the teachings of Cicero, Quintilian and St. Augustine. As noted by Halford Ryan in *Classical Communication for the Contemporary Communicator,* 1992, the strength of this equine has been used to shape history from the Funeral Oration of Pericles in the Fifth Century, B.C., to the orations of Winston Churchill calling Britains to "never surrender." Its beauty has been glorified from the poetics of Homer to the Rainbow Coalition of Jesse Jackson. *Traditional oratory is the thoroughbred champion of persuasion.*

According to Harold Lentz in *A History of Wittenberg College,* 1946, my own state of Ohio once reveled in the glory of oratory. In the almost 100 years between the Civil and World Wars, Ohio sponsored collegiate oratory competitions. These competitions traveled from city to city, college to college, year after year. The hosting city would celebrate with week-long festivals in speech climaxing in one single event. People came from miles around, dressed in their Sunday best to witness this one single event. Choirs would be called out and orchestras set the stage for this one single event. And competitors . . . foregoing all other ambitions, would rigorously train the entire year, for this one single event. And this one single event had splendor more grandiose that any sporting event could ever hope to have. This one single event was the competition for the crown of Ohio's greatest orator.

Where is that glory today? As we look around our forensic competitions we find *an exclusivity of first affirmative style speaking in which we present a very well-reasoned, clear and concise argument for others to critique.* This is not a speech to refute such a style, for we cannot argue the well established effectiveness of *logical rhetoric.* But imagine for a moment, if the greatest oration of modern history were delivered in a first affirmative style.

> "I have a dream.
> Today I'd like to introduce you to this dream.
> This dream has 3 parts . . ."

Would we have listened to Martin Luther King that day in Washington, D.C.? Would we have heard that message that was to shake our nation? Would we have been moved? . . . I think not. But because of his majestic oration that fateful day as he stood at the foot of the Lincoln Memorial, the tremors of his speech are still being felt almost 25 years after the last syllable was uttered.

We cannot ignore the well-established effectiveness of logical rhetoric, but nor can we ignore the total majesty of our thoroughbred. Think of the great leaders of our nation, such as Abraham Lincoln, who moved a war-torn nation engulfed in bitter strife, and preserved a union.

We cannot ignore well-established effectiveness of logical rhetoric, we need the full strength and beauty of our steed, traditional oratory. There are masses which need to be moved. The masses to be moved are not always the multitude, however. There are masses in your community, masses on your campuses, masses right here at this oratorical event. How many times have we heard first affirmative style argument for recycling? Yet, when we walk out the door, we find trash cans steeped with recyclable wastes. And that's because it's one thing to convince an audience, and wholly another to move them to act.

So how do we move people to act? By synthesizing the best of the present with the tradition of the past. Edwin Dubois Shurter suggests in his book, *The Rhetoric of Oratory,* that we look at oratory as having a two-fold objective. First, we must present very clear, concise, rational arguments; herein lies the strength of oratory. The other objective is to present this argument in a way in which it will move the audience to act upon that argument. This requires the beauty of traditional oratory. We have become experts in regard to the element Shurter calls "conviction." But we must find ways in which to engage our audiences. This is what Shurter calls "the elements of persuasion." These "elements" are not unknown to us. We need only look back to the tradition of oratory, searching its history to find the paradigms which can still teach us today. Aristotle, for example, over 2500 years ago, set forth the canons of rhetoric which were later defined and canonized by the Romans. The "elements of persuasion" are found in all canons of rhetoric. We must heed all canons of rhetoric, varying those we currently use and expanding upon those we tend to overlook.

While we cannot ignore the well-established effectiveness of logical rhetoric, nor can we afford to put our thoroughbred out to pasture. As Thomas Biddington Maculay states, "A speaker who exhausts the whole philosophy of a question, who displays ever grace of diction, yet produces no effect on his audience, may be a great essayist, a great statesman, a great master of composition, but he is not a great persuader."

Therefore, I implore you to consider revivification of traditional oratory. Judges, acknowledge its place and allow it in your rounds. Coaches, enhance it on your teams and encourage it among your members. Competitors, find and nurture it in yourselves. And together we can revive the full strength and beauty of our thoroughbred. For as Collette Winfield reminds us in *Original Oratory* 1988, "Oratory peaks to the mind; it touches and moves the heart; and it sings in the soul." Heart . . . Mind . . . Soul . . . All that is the essence of humanity. Oratory is all that is the essence of Persuasion.

A PERSUASIVE SPEECH

It's difficult to refute the premise that placing money-making potential over saving lives is wrong. Thus, the one-sided message presented here is the best choice. This problem-solution persuasive speech is effective because the language is well tailored to a college audience; potentially complex medical and legal concepts are explained in a detailed yet easy-to-understand way. The pathos, or emotional appeal, is strong because of such persuasive word choices as *shameful* and *ludicrous,* and irony is used in examples such as the Salk Foundation. Still, the emotional appeal is not overdone. Most of the power of the speech comes from its logic. The evidence is well cited and the solution flows deductively from the problem. Additionally, the solution is multifac-

eted and includes both personal and institutional actions.

GENETIC PATENTS: THE DEADLY POTENTIAL OF RESEARCH EXCLUSIVITY
Elizabeth Storey
Eastern Michigan University
Coached by Ray Quiel and Brendan Kelly

One in forty Americans of Jewish descent carries the gene for Canavan's disease—a degenerative brain disorder that causes the children who have it to die by the age of fifteen. In 1981, Dan and Debbie Greenburg were approached by researchers at Miami's Children's Hospital and asked them to donate the blood and tissue of their two children who were dying of Canavan's. Mr. Greenburg told CBS News on July 29, 2001 that he and his wife were so eager to find the gene that caused their children's suffering that after the death of their children, they donated the brains of both Jonathan and Amy to the hospital.

What the Greenburgs didn't know was that their generous gift of life would become a deadly bottom line. Years later when Children's Hospital isolated the Canavan's gene and received its patent, the hospital ordered an international ban on all genetic research and testing for Canavan's disease. The March 7, 2001 *Journal of the National Cancer Institute* explained that identical bans have been imposed by the companies that hold the patents for the genes which cause breast cancer, prostate cancer, cystic fibrosis, ovarian cancer, and countless others.

Patents were meant to reward ingenuity with profit by providing exclusive rights to their holders. However, genetic patents are prompting medical researchers to stop their race for the cure at the patent office. Sadly, innocent lives are being lost in this battle for research exclusivity. According to the August 23, 2001 *Deseret Sun News* 20,000 international genetic patents have already been issued and 25,000 more are in the application stage. It is critical that we take control of genetic patenting. Today we first outline the problems of patenting human

DNA, next we will examine what has allowed patents to play such a powerful role in medicine, and finally produce solutions that will put patent practices back in their place and put health care back in the hands of doctors. Jonas Salk recognized that patents have little to do with medicine when he refused to patent his polio vaccine. However, according to the April 2001 *Journal of the American Bar Association,* decades later the Salk Foundation holds over 400 medical patents.

There are two clear harms rooted in genetic patenting; first, bans on research are stifling lifesaving medical progress, and second, the lack of competition is causing genetic screening to be unaffordable. First, companies holding patents can prohibit all research relating to their particular gene. The University of Pennsylvania was conducting a multigenerational study on breast cancer when Myriad Genetics was awarded the patent for the breast cancer gene. CBS News reported on July 29, 2001 that the university received a letter stating that they were in violation of Myriad Genetics's exclusive rights, and the university's lawyer terminated the study immediately. The February 2002 *Utne Reader* stated that many years of research on breast cancer was lost. Additionally, St. Mary's Hospital in Manchester was conducting promising research on the treatment and cure of cystic fibrosis, the single greatest killer of Caucasian children. According to the May 20, 2000 *New Scientist,* they were ordered to not only stop their study, but also mail their findings to the company which holds the cystic fibrosis gene patent.

The April 1, 2001 *Washington Monthly* reported that one in four laboratory physicians have abandoned a clinical test because of gene patents. In the article, Stanford bioethicist Dr. Mildred Cho went on to explain, that nearly 50% reported "they had not designed new tests for fear that the minute they cleaned their test tubes a patent lawyer would come knocking." Second, companies holding patents can charge a king's ransom for access to their particular gene, placing genetic screening out of the price range for may people. The August 11, 2001 *Toronto Star* explained that the Canadian government recognized that 87% of women who carry the mutated breast cancer gene will develop cancer, and so, offered the genetic screening test for this gene to all women free of charge. However, now that Myriad Genetics has exclusive rights to the breast cancer gene, this same test costs the Canadian government $3,850 each. Due to its astronomical cost, the September 20, 2001 *Ottawa Citizen* reported that the government has been forced to stop offering the test. Without affordable genetic screening, thousands will get cancer and thousands will die. And what is the good of genetic testing if people can't afford to use it?

There is no guarantee that with modifications to patent law we will find cures for these genetic conditions. Medical researchers have made advancements over the last few decades that hold the promise for such cures. It is our duty to keep searching. It is shameful not to give people a chance.

The causes of this abhorrent practice are clear and simple. The harms of gene patenting are rooted in two inherent flaws; first that patents and profits are inextricably linked, and second the U.S. patent code cannot handle the ethical implications of human DNA. Abraham Lincoln, president, lawyer, and patent holder, explained that patents should "add the fuel of interest to the fire of genius" and that is precisely what patent law does. As the 2000 *Journal of Clinical Genetics* explained, patents guarantee the development of new technology by providing the incentives of profit and exclusive rights, so companies can legally reap rewards while medical progress is commanded to halt until their patent runs out. Second, patent laws cannot handle the ethical implications that occur when human DNA is the "patentable" product. When the original patent code was presented to Congress for approval in 1790, there was no way to foresee this problem. According to the August 30, 2001 *Seattle Post Intelligence,* there has never been a ruling on how the laws apply when human DNA is the subject of the patent.

That is how the company that has held the Alzheimer's gene patent for only three years has made enough profit off that patent alone to literally buy the Palace of Versailles. Dr. Eric Johnson, a Phoenix geneticist, told the November 1, 2002 *Mother Jones* that he works for a Catholic charity hospital that, quite simply, cannot afford to fight companies with those kind of resources. A middle ground, under which patent holders have both an economic incentive to invest and motivation to protect patients, must be reached. It is critical that the U.S. patent laws hold higher ethical standards for the patenting of human DNA. It is ludicrous to think that the same ethical standards that were designed to protect such inventions as cotton gins and Kool-Aid can defend human life. A reasonable solution, suggested by the previously cited *Journal of Clinical Genetics,* called for Congress to revise the U.S. patent laws so that inventors could patent the processes they create for genetic research, but wouldn't allow patents on the products of that research. That way, a company could profit from a test it develops regarding a particular gene, but could not prevent other researchers from developing other tests regarding the same gene. Once multiple tests are developed, the resulting competition would lower prices to an affordable level.

Thankfully, the previously cited *Journal of the American Bar Association* explained that Congress made very similar changes before. In 1996, the patent laws were modified so that surgical patents could not infringe on a patient's care. Senator Debbie Stabenaw is dedicated to ensuring that similar legislation is passed again. In a personal e-mail with Senator Stabenaw's office, she urged me to ask that you voice your support for House Bill 3967 that will provide this change and was introduced on Capitol Hill on March 14, 2002. I have provided a handout with contact information for a variety of organizations and people who are asking citizens to become involved. I will make this handout available at the round's end. The March 25, 2002 *San Francisco Chronicle* explained the ability of this piece of legislation to create expedient political change is directly related to the support received from constituents. However, until this legislation is passed, make a difference on a personal level by making a tax-free donation to your local hospital to fund genetic screening to those who cannot afford it.

Today, we have identified the clear harms of genetic patenting. We have identified what causes gene patents to play such a powerful role in medicine, and thankfully produced solutions that will give integrity back to the U.S. patent laws and protect human life.

Dan and Debbie Greenburg made a donation, like so many others, to help scientists find the genetic source for human suffering. However, the patent for this discovery is impeding its ability to help the children who suffer from Canavan's disease. It is ridiculous that organizations designed to heal are able to prevent so many from being healed, in the name of profit.

A PERSUASIVE SPEECH

The following persuasive speech argues on behalf of participation in the arts by persons with disabilities. Erik Anderson uses a problem-solution structure, first outlining the importance of artistic expression for special populations and emphasizing that such expression may even be more important for disabled persons. Then Anderson suggests how audience members can become involved in the arts for special populations and why they should. Within the problem-solution structure, Anderson persuades effectively, using both logic and emotion.

A PLEA FOR THE ARTS
by Erik Anderson, Grand View College, Iowa
Coached by Douglas Larche

Let's say that you have a dream. That dream is to be a professional performing or visual artist. Perhaps you want to be a singer or a dancer, or maybe you might want to be a painter or a sculptor. Some people would tell you that this is an unrealistic dream, and that you should concern yourself with more important things. Now, let's also say, for the sake of argument, that you have a physical or mental disability. Should that dream be any less realistic or any less attainable? It certainly would not be any less important to you.

I would like to look at the issue of arts for the disabled. I would like to show you that the arts are vitally important to special populations and that the disabled are capable of a wide range of creative expression. More than just the "arts and crafts" that are sometimes associated with them. Finally, I would like to show you not only how to be involved with arts for special populations, but also why you should.

> There's something locked up deep inside.
> Won't you help me find the key
> That opens doorways where I hide,
> And treasurechests of me.

Artistic expression is important for everyone. It provides us with a way to feed our need for self-improvement and self-esteem, and some-times even peer approval. For the disabled, however, it can be even more important because other avenues of expression are sometimes limited.

Artistic creativity and disability have long been tied together. After all we have all heard that you must, as the cliché says, "suffer for your art."

Dr. Phillip Sandblom, in his book *Creativity and Disease,* maintains that "because disease (in this case, disability) limits other activity, it figures heavily into artistic creativity." For the disabled, the arts provide a vital means of expression and achievement. Sandblom also suggests that persons with disabilities have a great need to excel. Often this is to compensate for things they feel that they lack. Lord Byron, who had a club foot, put it this way: "Defor-mity is daring. It is its essence to o'ertake mankind by heart and soul and make itself equal—aye, the superior to the rest. There is a spur in its halt movements to become all that the others cannot, in such things as still are free to both." I can attest to this myself. You cannot know what it means to me to be able to stand here today and compete on an absolutely equal footing.

Because the arts are such an accessible means for the disabled to build their self-esteem, they are often used as a tool in therapy. Availability of arts experiences for special populations is vital.

Homer's *Iliad* and *Odyssey,* Da Vinci's *Mona Lisa,* the famous *Fifth Symphony* by Beethoven—what do these great works have in common? Handel's *Messiah,* Milton's *Paradise Lost*—certainly they are all classics. Each one of them is a masterwork, a testament to their creator's timeless artistic skills. But what else do they have in common? *The Telltale Heart* by Edgar Allen Poe, *Tartuffe* by Molière, *Robinson Crusoe* by Robert Louis Stevenson, even Stevie Wonder singing "Ebony and Ivory"—what do they have in common? These are the works of disabled artists.

As with any group, disabled artists display a wide range of creative capabilities. Our culture has benefited greatly from the works of these disabled artists, and we are proud to list them among our number. But these are only a few. The number of disabled artists is staggering.

Whistler	Monet
Renoir	Chopin
Vivaldi	Paganini
Byron	Mattisse
Van Gogh	Schumann
Sir Walter Scott	Emily Dickinson
D. H. Lawrence	Chekhov
Mozart	Sarah Bernhardt
Toulouse-Lautrec	Helen Keller
Lionel Barrymore	Ronnie Milsap
Ray Charles	Stevie Wonder
José Feliciano	Billy Barty
Itzhak Perelman	

And these are still only a few! Disabled artists are capable of truly great things. Availability of arts experiences for special populations is vital.

> With paint and crayons I will draw
> A world of beauty, strength and awe.
> With costumes, makeup, words to say,
> I'll be an actor in a play.
> With just one lesson, just one chance,
> I'll twirl and swirl in wondrous dance.
> With instruments and with my voice,

I'll make the music of my choice.
With just a little of your time,
I'll be a silent, perfect mime.
The arts will let the whole world see,
Beyond the "dis" is "ability"!

Fortunately, there are things that we can do to ensure that the arts continue to be available to special populations. There are a number of organizations whose purpose is to provide services for the disabled. Monies for these organizations are always less than what is needed. And if you cannot make a financial contribution to help provide arts opportunities to the handicapped or if you wish to help further, they always need volunteers. It isn't difficult to become involved. All you have to do is say "How can I help?" I have been involved for the past ten years with an organization called Very Special Arts. It is an international organization that exists specifically to provide arts experiences to the handicapped.

Another thing that we can do is support legislation designed to provide equal opportunities for the disabled. This may not have a direct effect on arts opportunities, but it will affect our society's perception of special populations over time. As our society comes to see the disabled, not as people who lack ability, but people, who like everyone else, are simply doing the best they can with what they have; then art will, as it often does, imitate life.

The question then becomes "Why should I become involved if I don't have a disability?" Maybe you will become involved because you know someone with a disability whose quality of life could be improved through exposure to the arts. Maybe you will become involved because it will nurture your own sense of achievement and self-esteem. Or maybe you will become involved because you, or someone you know, may become disabled, and you will realize then what an important role the arts play for the disabled. Whatever the reason, become involved. Availability of arts experiences for special populations is vital.

I cannot hear, I cannot talk, I cannot even see.
I cannot run, I cannot walk, but look inside of me!
For though I think uniquely, and I travel in a chair,
My journey's filled with passion and with bold artistic flair.

I long to leap, unfettered, on flights of fancy free,
To mold the lifeless clay to visions only I can see.
To paint with strokes of wisdom, to pen the purest page,
To play the ageless actor on the timeless human stage.

To sing and play and juggle!
To dance and shout and mime!
To share my spirit's struggle
In my very special rhyme!

I am the Child Disabled, I am your brother-son:
I am your sister-daughter, the world's forgotten one.
So bring the arts unto me! The barriers destroy!
The handicap of yesterday is Tomorrow's Child of Joy.

So, upon examination of the issue, there is no argument that the arts are vitally important to special populations. And certainly our culture has benefited a great deal from the contributions of disabled artists. Their work establishes beyond question that the disabled are capable of great things. And considering how important it is to support arts for the disabled, I urge you to *BE* involved.

In closing, I would like to again quote Father Gander whose poetry I have been using as illustration. He said, "Perhaps, armed with the knowledge that our culture has benefited immeasurably from these special people, we will nurture the opportunities of their artistic heirs of tomorrow . . . perhaps we will be their patrons . . . their audiences . . . their advocates . . . their fellow artists . . . their friends."

AN INFORMATIVE SPEECH

Not only is this speech on a fascinating topic, it is a good example of how textbook definitions sometimes blur in actual practice. Though this is essentially a speech about an object presented "by category," there is a hint of "by time" as the points indirectly reference past, present, and future. Sometimes background history can be summarized in opening statements; in this case it is deserving of an entire main point. Through all the points, the nostalgic reference to the children's classic *Charlotte 's Web* is well maintained. Not only is this a good strategy for engaging the audience, it has a direct connection to the actual device—the charlotte—explained in the speech. In this way, technical elements are explained clearly and without excessive jargon.

BIOSTEEL
Eileen Monaghan
Saint Joseph's University
Coached by Todd Anten and Danielle Rogowski

The barn was dark and quiet. Wilbur's life was in danger. His only chance of survival: To get his friend Charlotte to write a note, any note, that would save his life. And Charlotte did, printing out in bold letters "some pig." This is, of course, the plot of E. B. White's classic tale *Charlotte's Web*, where Wilbur the pig was saved from becoming a side order of bacon thanks to a spider named Charlotte, who had a talent for writing words such as "radiant" and "terrific" in her webs. While this unlikely friendship between a spider and a pig has touched the hearts of children worldwide, it's another recent animal friendship, that between a spider and a goat, that has scientists shouting out "terrific."

For years, scientists have known that spider silk is one of the strongest materials in nature. *Business 2.O Magazine* of April 2002 says that it's "stronger than steel, lighter than cotton, and harder to tear than Kevlar." However, reproducing spider silk in a way that makes it useful to humans has been impossible. Until now. The *Ottawa Citizen* of 1/18/02 reports that scientists recently discovered that by implanting certain spider genes in goats—

yes, goats—they could create BioSteel, an artificial spider-silk strong enough to hold the weight of a jumbo jet. These "spider-goats" mark the first time that scientists have been able to produce large quantities of spider silk on demand. Considering that BioSteel can revolutionize the way we make thousands of goods, from stockings to bndges, all while improving the Earth's air quality, it would behoove us all to learn more about this real-life odd couple. So let's FIRST: learn about past attempts to replicate spider silk, SECOND: discover how a few goats saved the day, so that we may FINALLY: reveal how BioSteel may find its way into our lives.

Wilbur certainly understood the value of spider silk. After all, he was some pig. The web said so! But why are we humans so enamored with the substance? Well, the quest to create synthetic spider silk is considered to be the Holy Grail of materials science because it is an amazingly strong, flexible and durable building material. ABCnews.com of 1/13/02 explains that scientists are particularly interested in replicating a special kind of spider silk called "dragline silk," the silk that spiders use to make the spokes in their webs, which make them stand up to wind, rain, and various disgusting bugs. *The New York Times* of 1/18/02 goes on to explain that dragline silk is not just strong, but light, elastic, and easily recyclable.

Scientists' first instinct was to farm spiders and harvest their silk, the same way that the Chinese have farmed silkworms for thousands of years. However, this plan proved to be fruitless—and silkless. Why? Because as Russ Smith, curator of the reptile house at the Los Angeles Zoo told *The Christian Science Monitor* on 2/21/02, "Spiders eat other spiders." Given that a workforce of spiders would constantly snack on each other, scientists decided to fall back on a more creative option: Freako genetic experiments.

See, spider silk is mostly made up of protein, so scientists tried to create spider silk the same way they've replicated other proteins: By injecting silk genes into bacteria. Unfortunately,

National Geographic Today of 1/17/02 reports that scientists couldn't implant spiders' genes into bacteria because the silk proteins are just too large. But then they considered: Why not try implanting the genes in something bigger, like animals? That's when scientists at the Nexia Corporation discovered that the mammary glands of goats are anatomically similar to a spider's silk glands, and scientists knew that they had finally had a chance to produce large quantities of spider silk. In 2000, Webster and Peter, the first two goats to carry the spider silk gene, were born.

When researchers at Nexia and U.S. Army scientists played matchmaker, they discovered that spiders and goats could produce something even more amazing than Charlotte's talking webs. To appreciate how they pulled it off, let's weave through the process of how Peter and Webster make spider silk.

The 1/18/02 issue of the journal *Science* explains that researchers at Nexia injected a spider's silk gene into a goat's one-celled egg before it was fertilized. This spider silk gene becomes only one of 70,000 genes in a goat's body. Don't worry, this doesn't mean that horrific spider-goat creatures will take over the Earth—yet—since the gene is only active in the goat's body when she's lactating. Otherwise, the gene lies dormant.

Sciencenet.com, accessed on 2/19/02, reports that the spider silk gene becomes one of the goat's chromosomes only about 5% of the time. However, once the gene is part of the goat's DNA code, it will pass the gene to its offspring. Both male and female goats can carry the gene, but since only female goats are able to lactate, only the female goats can produce BioSteel. When goats with the spider gene are milked, instead of milk they produce a serum about the thickness of maple syrup.

The next step was for Nexia to figure out a way to extract the silk from this goat goo. And for guidance, they turned right to the pages of Charlotte's Web. *The Baltimore Sun* of 1/18/02 says that Nexia used a tube that they appropriately dubbed a "charlotte" to mimic the actions of a spider's spinneret. A syringe is filled with the goat's serum, and the serum is squeezed through

the charlotte. Out the other end comes a thin filament, which is then stretched in the same way that spiders normally stretch their silk with their legs. This action pulls the silk tighter so that the molecules line up, providing maximal strength. Finally, *NY Newsday* of 2/12/02 explains that the newly stretched fibers are passed through a bath of alcohol that quickly extracts the excess water. In the end, you're left with 100% goat silk, which Nexia calls "BioSteel."

Now the process has not yet been perfected. On 1/18/02, the NPR segment "All Things Considered" questioned the likelihood of creating enough BioSteel to replace regular steel. However, Peter and Webster already have 48 brothers and sisters that possess the spider silk gene, which are being kept at a military base in New York. These goats have all demonstrated the ability to produce up to a liter and a half of serum per day each—thousands of times greater than the amount of silk a whole ranch of spiders could produce on their own. Just as we have enough cows to provide milk for people, scientists have faith that in the years to come they will be able to produce the massive quantities of BioSteel necessary.

Perhaps we shouldn't be so surprised at Charlotte's ability to write words in her webs. After all, she was a very anal speller. But the production of BioSteel has shown that spider silk can be used for more than just writing creepy messages; it can positively impact almost every aspect of our lives.

Because the U.S. army assisted in creating BioSteel, it's no surprise that they're getting the first shot at putting it to use, specifically to make improved armor for soldiers. The 1/18/02 Glasgow Herald explains that the Pentagon is already in talks with Nexia to create a new line of soft yet virtually impenetrable body armor composed of BioSteel, and they expect it to be in use within four years. And just to be safe, many clothing designers are lobbying for BioSteel filaments to be included in all clothing, from jackets to pants, to my personal favorite, panty-hose.

And it doesn't stop at clothes. The *Times-Picayune* of 2/2/02 predicts that sutures used for medical procedures will soon be made of BioSteel, allowing for the stronger closure of wounds. Because

BioSteel is 100% natural, when the wound closes, the sutures dissolve harmlessly into the body. *The Economist* of 3/16/02 states that BioSteel sutures could be particularly helpful for opthalmological, vascular, or neurological surgeries, since they have more strength than nylon, and none of its difficulties in holding knots. Doctors also hope to use BioSteel to make artificial limbs, tendons, and muscles that will never suffer from the wear and tear of general use. And this is just the beginning. From fishing line, to space equipment, to suspension bridges, to skyscrapers that can withstand an earthquake of any size, BioSteel's uses stretch as far as our imaginations. Anything that currently uses steel may eventually be replaced with BioSteel.

BioSteel isn't only being lauded for what it will do, but also for what it won't do: pollute the atmosphere. The Nexia Corporation's press release on 1/18/02 explains that the manufacturing of steel releases millions of tons of toxic chemicals into the atmosphere every day, but the production of spider silk in goats is completely natural.

Perhaps Charlotte should change her message from "some pig" to "some goat." Today, we learned how those pesky spider webs are actually of use. Then we discovered how a partnership between goats and spiders could unlock the power of spider silk. And after we caught a glimpse of the potential uses for BioSteel in the near and distant future, we discovered that we truly are closer to creating a world wide web. And as for BioSteel's possibilities, we only have to turn back to Charlotte and reread the simple message she left in her web: Terrific.

AN INFORMATIVE SPEECH

Although the use of fish metaphors in the preview may be heavy-handed, the light humor and vivid language of this informative speech are maintained throughout. The text recommends looking at difficult subjects through multiple angles. In this speech, an interesting but virtually unknown scientific phenomenon is explained through audience-centered analogies such as cooking chicken and basic car maintenance. The explanation of the freezing and thawing process, in

particular, is clearly written. This speech also represents a clear standard for informative speeches—they can show both pros and cons of the topic. In this case, not only are the benefits and varied uses of the discovery detailed, the ethical and financial complications are also addressed.

AFGPS: THE FISH ANTIFREEZE
Eric Long
Bradley University
Coached by Dan Smith

For years, scuba divers and fortune hunters have been scouring the ocean floor looking for treasure. Recently, scientists took up the hobby. Equipped with black plastic-coated goggles, waterproof pen protectors, and hush puppy flippers, scientists decided to investigate water near the polar icecaps, because near-freezing water must be more "intellectually stimulating" than the plush Caribbean. However, these scientists discovered two things: not many pirate ships sunk off the coast of Antarctica, and the polar icecaps have some fish that are . . . pretty cool. Literally. These fish, including icefish and Antarctic cod, have yet to be "yuppyized" by the technological advancements of protective latex. In order to survive in these frigid environments, fish biologically produce antifreeze glycoproteins, or AFGPs, that keep them alive by preventing them from freezing. According to *Scientific American*, on August 21, 2001, the discovery of AFGPs will change the way we freeze everything, with applications ranging from organ preservation to eliminating that annoying layer of freezer burn on your favorite ice cream. In order to further understand the "coolness" of this new scientific advancement, we must first dive into the scientific and chemical basis of AFCPs, view the lifeboat of practical applications, and finally swim through the implications of this new product to see how 'fishy' it really is.

Understanding how AFGPs will be incorporated into our everyday lives requires that we first understand normal cell freezing, and then observe how this fish antifreeze prevents such freezing. A normal living or formerly living tissue such as a chicken breast is primarily made of water. When temperature drops, the water begins to freeze. As the water begins to freeze, ice and/or ice crystals are brought to the surface for the same reasons that ice cubes float at the top of water. As these ice crystals come to the surface, they begin to bond with other water molecules, the same way frost accumulates in your freezer or water beads on your car: water has a strong molecular attraction to other water molecules. Therefore, when tissue thaws, the surface ice crystals melt and drain away, as they are now attached to outside water molecules. This leaves the tissue stripped of many of its cells, changing the molecular make-up. In simple terms, this is why that chicken breast left in your freezer too long cooks to be very dry and chewy: the amount of water lost has changed its molecular make-up, unless you'r ejust a terrible cook.

Antifreeze glycoproteins (AFGPs) naturally found in fish of polar regions, prevent this phenomenon. As stated by an American Chemical Society press release on August 18, 2001, AFGPs act like a shield, keeping water in, keeping ice crystals out, as ice cannot bond with and is repelled by this unique protein molecule. Fish in the arctic regions are coated inside and out with this type of antifreeze. On the outside, AFGPs are bonded directly to their tissues, and ice crystals cannot attach which could eventually damage the tissue. Inside, these fish have AFGPs in their bloodstream. AFGPs used internally act similar to the antifreeze in your car, but instead of using an oil-based additive to lower the freezing point, AFGPs prevent ice crystals from forming at all by covering all of the molecules in the bloodstream with its unique protein cover, but in a safe biological manner.

The applications of AFGPs lie primarily in the medical and food industries. The medical uses of AFGP technology reside in organ preservation and blood enhancement. According to the September 2001 issue of *Washingtonian,* 77,000 Americans await organ transplants, which is double the amount of 1993. However, as the waiting list grows, the supply remains constant, meaning there is a need to use all potential organs wisely. Transferring organs requires freezing, and if frozen too long, ice crystals will emerge that can damage the tissue of the organ. However, if an organ is coated with AFGPs , ice crystals can not attach and the organ can remain frozen indefinitely. This ends all fears within the transportation process, as the organ has more than enough time to get to its next owner.

AFGP technology also improves the blood supply. AFCPs placed in human blood work much like AFGPs in fish blood; by covering all of the molecules in a unit of blood, ice crystals cannot form and blood can remain frozen without harm. This is important because the blood supply is used in streaks, especially during the summer months or in the wake of a tragedy. Remember, blood only has a six week shelflife. In fact, the February 21, 2002 *Boston Herald* reports that September 11 produced a large blood supply, but nearly 20% had to be discarded because of age. AFGPs placed in blood guarantees that we have an adequate supply on hand for when we need it most.

AFGPs also have a more practical side within the food industry by enhancing crop production and food storage. As *Science Daily* states on August 20, 2001, AFGPs can be used to spray crops to prevent frostbite or can be directly placed into a plant's genetic code to make it frost resistant. This is great news for Farmer Brown, as it increases the number of growing months each year. It especially aids the fruit industry as it prevents annual loss to frostbite and paves the way for fruit to be produced in more northern regions.

After food is produced, AFGP's can aid storage. According to *New Scientist* of August 25, 2001, AFGP's unique way of preventing ice crystal formation means food can be kept in the freezer for a longer period of time, as the taste or texture will not be affected by freezer burn. In the future, if food contains this natural anti-freeze, you can pull grandma's ten-year-old meatloaf out of the freezer and enjoy, or send it home with a poor hungry college kid.

Additional uses for AFGPs will lie wherever ice-crystals pose a threat. For example, the

December 17, 2001 Pittsburgh *Post Gazette* reveals that scientists are investigating the potential of AFGPs to be sprayed on roads to prevent ice, eliminating the corrosive side effects of salt.

After understanding the chemistry behind AFGPs and their applications, we must understand the scientific and social implications. Scientific implications include medical safety and risk. From a health perspective, AFGPs are found in nature, meaning there is no scientific cause for alarm as this product is 100% safe. Whether this fish antifreeze is used to preserve a liver for your body or the liver in your freezer, the medical and nutrition worlds have a safe, new preservation technology. However, such technology also poses risks to today's consumer-driven market, of which medicine and organ transplants are no strangers. The possibility of freezing organs indefinitely has the potential to create bidding wars for life-saving transplants. AFGP technology must be used in a combination with objective medical ethics.

Social implications include time and potential backlash. According to the September 4, 2001 *Washington Post,* AFGP technology does not have a specific date for an open market launch, but should be widespread in the near future for the following reasons. First, the September/October 2001 *Journal of Bioconjugate Chemistry* states that AFGPs can now be synthetically produced in large quantities at a very low cost, which is the first step. Also, a company known as A/F Protein has just received patents for AFGP use in organs and ice cream.

However, such technology also faces agricultural backlash as it enhances our reliance on genetically enhanced crops, which the United States has had trouble exporting in recent months. Also, if food prices drop, more pressure will be put on the government to provide adequate farm subsidies. In short, AFGPs may be a breakthrough technology with break-even financial consequences.

Today we have explained how AFGPs work, their applications, and implications. With this understanding we see that there is the possibility, with the help of our fishy friends and scuba diving scientists, to radically change our preservation tactics from the ER to your freezer and every-

where in-between. While we wait for AFGPs to become the best freezer friend since the Zip-Lock bag, we can relax knowing that a permanent relationship between fish technology and human survival is definitely in the cards . . . so, Go Fish!

A COMMEMORATIVE SPEECH

The following commemorative speech was presented by Dr. Martin Luther King, Jr. in Washington, D.C. on August 28, 1963. Dr. King's powerful message about continuing the struggle for civil rights is one of the most famous speeches of the twentieth century. King was speaking to a crowd of 200,000 supporters who had gathered at the Lincoln Memorial to demonstrate their support for a civil rights bill that was stalled in Congress. King's concrete, compelling language portrays the consequences of racial discrimination in human terms rather than as vague conceptual issues. Using vivid imagery, metaphor, and rhythm, King speaks eloquently of his dream of freedom for all. The phrase "I have a dream" echoes throughout the second half of the speech and is answered by the phrase "let freedom ring" as it's repeated throughout the conclusion. These recurring phrases reinforce the mental images created by King's words, and they help motivate listeners to take action. King's dramatic delivery was so effective that by his closing words, listeners were rising to their feet and applauding thunderously in acclamation.

I HAVE A DREAM
Martin Luther King, Jr.

I am happy to join with you today in what will go down in history as the greatest demonstration for freedom in the history of our nation.

Five score years ago, a great American, in whose symbolic shadow we stand today, signed the Emancipation Proclamation. This momentous decree came as a great beacon light of hope to millions of Negro slaves, who had been seared in the flames of withering injustice. It came as a joyous daybreak to end the long night of their captivity.

But one hundred years later, the Negro still is not free. One hundred years later, the life of the Negro is still sadly crippled by the manacles of segregation and the chains of discrimination. One hundred years later, the Negro lives on a lonely island of poverty in the midst of a vast ocean of material prosperity. One hundred years later, the Negro is still languished in the corners of American society and finds himself an exile in his own land. And so we've come here today to dramatize a shameful condition.

In a sense we've come to our nation's Capitol to cash a check. When the architects of our republic wrote the magnificent words of the Constitution and the Declaration of Independence, they were signing a promissory note to which every American was to fall heir. This note was a promise that all men—yes, black men as well as white men—would be guaranteed the unalienable rights of life, liberty, and the pursuit of happiness.

It is obvious today that America has defaulted on this promissory note insofar as her citizens of color are concerned. Instead of honoring this sacred obligation, America has given the Negro people a bad check—a check which has come back marked "insufficient funds."

But we refuse to believe that the bank of justice is bankrupt. We refuse to believe that there are insufficient funds in the great vaults of opportunity of this nation. And so we've come to cash this check—a check that will give us upon demand the riches of freedom and the security of justice.

We have also come to this hallowed spot to remind America of the fierce urgency of now. This is no time to engage in the luxury of cooling off or to take the tranquilizing drug of gradualism. Now is the time to make real the promises of democracy. Now is the time to rise from the dark and desolate valley of segregation to the sunlit path of racial justice. Now is the time to lift our nation from the quicksands of racial injustice to the solid rock of brotherhood. Now is the time to make justice a reality for all of God's children.

It would be fatal for the nation to overlook the urgency of the moment. This sweltering summer of the Negro's legitimate discontent will not pass until there is an invigorating autumn of freedom and equality. Nineteen sixty-three is not an end, but a beginning. Those who hope that the Negro needed to blow off steam and will now be content will have a rude awakening if the nation returns to business as usual. There will be neither rest nor tranquillity in America until the Negro is granted his citizenship rights. The whirlwinds of revolt will continue to shake the foundations of our nation until the bright day of justice emerges.

But there is something that I must say to my people, who stand on the warm threshold which leads into the palace of justice. In the process of gaining our rightful place, we must not be guilty of wrongful deeds. Let us not seek to satisfy our thirst for freedom by drinking from the cup of bitterness and hatred.

We must forever conduct our struggle on the high plane of dignity and discipline. We must not allow our creative protest to degenerate into physical violence. Again and again we must rise to the majestic heights of meeting physical force with soul force.

The marvelous new militancy which has engulfed the Negro community must not lead us to a distrust of all white people. For many of our white brothers, as evidenced by their presence here today, have come to realize that their destiny is tied up with our destiny. They have come to realize that their freedom is inextricably bound to our freedom. We cannot walk alone.

As we walk, we must make the pledge that we shall always march ahead. We cannot turn back. There are those who are asking the devotees of civil rights, "When will you be satisfied?" We can never be satisfied as long as the Negro is the victim of the unspeakable horrors of police brutality. We can never be satisfied as long as our bodies, heavy with the fatigue of travel, cannot gain lodging in the motels of the highways and the hotels of the cities. We cannot be satisfied as long as the Negro's basic mobility is from a smaller ghetto to a larger one. We can never be satisfied as long as our children are stripped of their selfhood and robbed of their dignity by signs stating "For Whites Only." We cannot be satisfied as long as a Negro in Mississippi cannot vote and a Negro in New York believes he has nothing for which to vote. No, no, we are not satisfied, and we will not be satisfied until justice rolls down like waters, and righteousness like a mighty stream.

I am not unmindful that some of you have come here out of great trials and tribulations. Some of you have come fresh from narrow jail cells. Some of you have come from areas where your quest for freedom left you battered by the storms of persecution and staggered by the winds of police brutality. You have been the veterans of creative suffering. Continue to work with the faith that unearned suffering is re-demptive.

Go back to Mississippi, go back to Alabama, go back to South Carolina, go back to Georgia, go back to Louisiana, go back to the slums and ghettos of our Northern cities, knowing that somehow this situation can and will be changed. Let us not wallow in the valley of despair.

I say to you today, my friends, so even though we face the difficulties of today and tomorrow, I still have a dream. It is a dream deeply rooted in the American dream.

I have a dream that one day this nation will rise up and live out the true meaning of its creed, "We hold these truths to be self-evident, that all men are created equal."

I have a dream that one day on the red hills of Georgia the sons of former slaves and the sons of former slaveowners will be able to sit down together at the table of brotherhood.

I have a dream that one day even the state of Mississippi, a state sweltering with the heat of injustice, sweltering with the heat of oppression, will be transformed into an oasis of freedom and justice.

I have a dream that my four little children will one day live in a nation where they will not be judged by the color of their skin but by the content of their character. I have a dream today.

I have a dream that one day, down in Ala-bama, with its vicious racists, with its governor having his lips dripping with the words of interposition and nullification, one day right there in Alabama little black boys and black girls will be able to join hands with little white boys and white girls as sisters and brothers. I have a dream today.

I have a dream that one day every valley shall be exalted, every hill and mountain shall be made low, the rough places will be made plane and the crooked places will be made straight, and the glory of the Lord shall be revealed, and all flesh shall see it together.

This is our hope. This is the faith that I go back to the South with. With this faith we will be able to hew out of the mountain of despair a stone of hope. With this faith we will be able to transform the jangling discords of our nation into a beautiful symphony of brotherhood. With this faith we will be able to work together, to pray together, to struggle together, to go to jail together, to stand up for freedom together, knowing that we will be free one day.

This will be the day—this will be the day when all of God's children will be able to sing with new meaning, "My country 'tis of thee, sweet land of liberty, of thee I sing. Land where my fathers died, land of the pilgrim's pride, from every mountainside, let freedom ring." And if America is to be a great nation, this must become true.

So let freedom ring from the prodigious hilltops of New Hampshire. Let freedom ring from the mighty mountains of New York. Let freedom ring from the heightening Alleghenies of Pennsylvania!

Let freedom ring from the snowcapped Rockies of Colorado! Let freedom ring from the curvaceous slopes of California!

But not only that. Let freedom ring from Stone Mountain of Georgia!

Let freedom ring from Lookout Mountain of Tennessee!

Let freedom ring from every hill and molehill of Mississippi. From every mountainside, let freedom ring.

And when this happens, when we allow freedom to ring—when we let it ring from every village and every hamlet, from every state and every city—we will be able to speed up that day when all of God's children, black men and white men, Jews and Gentiles, Protestants and Catholics, will be able to join hands and sing in the words of the old Negro spiritual, "Free at last! Free at last! Thank God almighty, we are free at last!"

A COMMEMORATIVE SPEECH

The following eulogy was presented by President Ronald Reagan on the evening of January 28, 1986. That morning, the space shuttle *Challenger* exploded barely a minute after liftoff, killing all seven astronauts aboard. Because one of the astronauts was a schoolteacher, millions of schoolchildren and families across the country had been watching as the spacecraft exploded during live television coverage. Of course, it became the responsibility of the president to eulogize and honor the memory of the Americans who had just lost their lives. President Reagan had been scheduled to present a State of the Union address, but he postponed it and instead presented this eulogy for the astronauts. Even as Reagan offers comfort in a time of mourning, he pledges commitment to the space program and emphasizes the great sacrifice that may be necessary to pioneer and explore space. Then never losing sight of the everyone's loss, President Reagan concludes by recalling the honor of *Challenger's* crew members and the country's last sight of them waving good-bye.

EULOGY FOR THE CHALLENGER ASTRONAUTS
President Ronald Reagan

We come together today to mourn the loss of seven brave Americans, to share the grief that we all feel and perhaps in that sharing, to find the strength to bear our sorrow and the courage to look for the seeds of hope.

Our nation's loss is first a profound personal loss to the family, and the friends and loved ones of our shuttle astronauts. To those they have left behind—the mothers. the fathers, the husbands and wives, brothers and sisters—yes and especially the children—all of America stands beside you in your time of sorrow.

What we say today is only an inadequate expression of what we carry in our hearts.. Words pale in the shadow of grief; they seem insufficient even to measure the brave sacrifice of those you loved and we so admired. Their truest testimony will not be in the words we speak but in the way they led their lives and In the way they lost their lives—with dedication, honor and an unquenchable desire to explore this mysterious and beautiful universe.

The best we can do is remember our seven astronauts—Our Challenger Seven—remember them as they lived, bringing life and love and joy to those who knew them and pride to a nation.

They came from all parts of this great country—from South Carolina to Washington State: Ohio to Mohawk. New York; Hawaii to North Carolina to Concord, New Hampshire. They were so different, yet in their mission, their quest, they held so much in common.

A Nation Remembers

We remember Dick Scobee, the commander who spoke the test words we heard from the space shuttle *Challenger*. He served as a fighter pilot in Vietnam, earning many medals for bravery; later as a test pilot of advanced aircraft, before joining the space program. Danger was a familiar companion to Commander Scobee.

We remember Michael Smith, who earned enough medals as a combat pilot to cover his chest, including the Navy Distinguished Flying Cross, three Air Medals and the Vietnamese Cross of Gallantry with Silver Star, in gratitude from a nation he fought to keep free.

We remember Judith Resnik, known as J. R. to her friends, always smiling, always eager to make a contribution, finding beauty in the music she played on her piano in her off hours.

We remember Ellison Onizuka, who, as a child running barefoot through the coffee fields and macadamia groves of Hawaii, dreamed of someday traveling to the moon. Being an Eagle Scout, he said, had helped him soar to the impressive achievements of his career.

We remember Ronald McNair. who said that he learned perseverance in the cotton fields of South Carolina. His dream was to live aboard the space station, performing experiments and playing his saxophone in the weightlessness of space. Well, Ron, we will miss your saxophone; and we will build your space station.

We remember Gregory Jarvis. On that ill-fated flight he was carrying with him a flag of his university in Buffalo, New York—a small token, he said, to the people who unlocked his future.

We remember Christa McAuliffe, who captured the imagination of the entire nation, inspiring us with her pluck, her restless spirit of discovery; a teacher, not just to her students but to an entire people, instilling us all with the excitement of this journey we ride into the future.

We will always remember them, these skilled professionals, scientists and adventurers, these artists and teachers and family men and women, and we will cherish each of their stories—stories of triumph and bravery, stories of true American heroes.

Sadness and Pride

On the day of the disaster, our nation held a vigil by our television sets. In one cruel moment, our exhilaration turned to horror; we waited and watched and tried to make sense of what we had seen. That night, I listened to a call-in program on the radio. People of every age spoke of their sadness and the pride they felt in "our astronauts." Across America, we are reaching out, holding hands and finding comfort in one another.

The sacrifice of your loved ones has stirred the soul of our nation and, through the pain, our hearts have been opened to a profound truth: the future is not free, the story of all human progress is one of a struggle against all odds. We learned again that this America, which Abraham Lincoln called the last best hope of man on Earth, was built on heroism and noble sacrifice. It was built

by men and women like our seven star voyagers, who answered a call beyond duty, who gave more than was expected or required, and who gave it with little thought to worldly reward.

We think back to the pioneers of an earlier century, the sturdy souls who took their families and their belongings and set out into the frontier of the American West. Often, they met with terrible hardship. Along the Oregon Trail you can still see the grave markers of those who fell on the way. But grief only steeled them to the journey ahead.

Today, the frontier is space and the boundaries of human knowledge. Sometimes, when we reach for the stars, we fall short. But we must pick ourselves up again and press on despite the pain. Our nation is indeed fortunate that we can still draw on immense reservoirs of courage, character and fortitude—that we are still blessed with heroes like those of the space shuttle *Challenger.*

Program Will Go On

Dick Scobee knew that every launching of a space shuttle is a technological miracle. And he said if something ever does go wrong, I hope that doesn't mean the end to the space shuttle program. Every family member I talked to asked specifically that we continue the program, that that is what their departed loved one would want above all else. We will not disappoint them.

Today, we promise Dick Scobee and his crew that their dream lives on; that the future they worked so hard to build will become reality. The dedicated men and women of NASA have lost seven members of their family. Still, they, too, must forge ahead with a space program that is effective, safe and efficient but bold and committed.

Man will continue his conquest of space, to reach out for new goals and ever greater achievements. That is the way we shall commemorate our seven *Challenger* heroes.

Dick, Mike, Judy, El, Ron, Greg and Christa, your families and your country mourn your passing. We bid you good-bye. We will never forget you. For those who knew you well and loved you, the pain will be deep and enduring. The nation, too, will long feel the loss of her seven sons and daughters, her seven good friends. We can find consolation only in faith, for we know in our hearts that you who flew so high and so proud now make your home beyond the stars, safe in God's promise of eternal life.

May God bless you all and give you comfort in this difficult time.

Endnotes

Chapter 1

1. Dawn-Marie Streeter, "Watchdog Group Presses for a Better Metro-North Commute," *New York Times*, 19 June 1994, sec. 14, 5.

2. Adapted from Patti Reid, "Student Takes His Recycling Drive Straight to the Top," *New York Times*, 1 March 1992, sec. 12, 1, 6.

3. Sherwyn P. Morreale, Michael Z. Hackman, and Michael R. Neer, "Predictors of Behavioral Competence and Self-Esteem: A Study Assessing Impact in a Basic Public Speaking Course," *Basic Communication Course Annual* 7 (November 1995): 125–141.

4. Dan B. Curtis, Jerry L. Winsor, and Ronald D. Stephens, "National Preferences in Business and Communication Education," *Communication Education* 38 (January 1989): 6–14; Kathleen Edgerton Kendall, "Do Real People Ever Give Speeches?" paper presented at the 76th Annual Meeting of the Eastern Communication Association, 2–5 May 1985, Providence, Rhode Island.

5. L. Keith Williamson, "The Origins of Rhetoric: Corax and Tisias Reconsidered," paper presented at the 73rd Annual Meeting of the Speech Communication Association, 5–8 November 1987, Boston; George P. Rice, "Classical Theories of Communication," *Vital Speeches of the Day*, 1 October 1986, 763–765.

6. Richard A. Katula, "The Role of Communication and Argument in Citizenship Education," paper presented at the Institute for Writing, Thinking, and Citizenship Education, July 1987, Cambridge, Massachusetts.

7. Gregory T. Lyons, "Gorgias' Rhetoric: Epistemology, Doxa, and Style," paper presented at the 39th Annual Meeting of the Conference on College Composition and Communication, 17–19 March 1988, St. Louis; La Rue Van Hook, *Greek Life and Thought: A Portrayal of Greek Civilization*, revised edition (New York: Columbia University Press, 1930), 160–163.

8. William L. Benoit, "Isocrates on Rhetorical Education," *Communication Education*, April 1984, 109–119; Debra Mazloff, "Isocrates' Philosophy of Education," paper presented at the Annual Meeting of the Central States Communication Association, 11–14 April 1991, Chicago.

9. Van Hook, *Greek Life and Thought*, 142–145.

10. Roland Hall, "Dialectic," in *The Encyclopedia of Philosophy*, vols. 1 and 2, edited by Paul Edwards (New York: Macmillan, 1967), 385–386; Gilbert Ryle, "Plato," in *The Encyclopedia of Philosophy*, vols. 5 and 6, edited by Paul Edwards (New York: Macmillan, 1967), 314–333; Van Hook, *Greek Life and Thought*, 234–244; Patricia Palmerton, "The Legitimization of Dialectic: Socratic Strategy in the 'Gorgias,'" paper presented at the Annual Meeting of the Central States Speech Association, April 1983, Lincoln, Nebraska.

11. G. B. Kerferd, "Aristotle," in *The Encyclopedia of Philosophy*, vols. 1 and 2, 151–162; Hall, "Dialectic," 385–386; Jane Sutton, "Aristotle, Motion, and Rhetoric," paper presented at the 77th Annual Meeting of the Eastern Communication Association, 30 April–3 May 1986, Atlantic City, New Jersey.

12. P. H. DeLacy, "Marcus Tullius Cicero," in *The Encyclopedia of Philosophy*, vols. 1 and 2, 113–114; Michael Grant, *The Classical Greeks* (New York: Scribners, 1989), 248; Michael Volpe, "The Persuasive Force of Humor: Cicero's Defense of Caelius," *Quarterly Journal of Speech* 63, no. 3 (October 1977): 311–323.

13. *Quintilian on the Teaching of Speaking and Writing*, edited by James J. Murphy (Carbondale and Edwardville: Southern Illinois University Press, 1987), xiv–xxxiii; Fritz Graf, "Gestures and Conventions: The Gestures of Roman Actors and Orators," in *A Cultural History of Gesture* (Ithaca, N.Y.: Cornell University

Press, 1991), 36–58; Steven L. Reagles, "Insights from Past Inventional Theory for Present Critical Thinking and Writing," paper presented at the Annual Meeting of the Midwest Regional Conference on English in the Two Year College, 7–9 October 1993, Madison, Wisconsin.

14. Jim Bennet, "The Gettysburg Address óPerfection in Three Paragraphs," *IABC Communication World,* October 1991, 19.

15. Durthy A. Washington, "'I Have a Dream': A Rhetorical Analysis," *The Black Scholar* 23, no. 2 (Summer, 1993): 16–19.

16. Carl Wayne Hensley, "What You Share Is What You Get," *Vital Speeches of the Day,* 1 December 1992, 115–117.

17. Wolvin and Coakley, *Listening,* 62–64; Michael Z. Hackman and Craig E. Johnson, *Leadership: A Communication Perspective* (Prospect Heights, Ill.: Waveland Press, 1991), 8–10.

18. John R. Johnson, "Understanding Misunderstanding: A Key to Effective Communication," *Training and Development Journal,* August 1983, 62, 64–67.

19. Pamela Shockley-Zabalak, *Fundamentals of Organizational Communication* (New York: Longman, 1991), 54.

20. Otto Johnson, ed., *1996 Information Please World Almanac* (Boston: Houghton Mifflin, 1996), 398.

21. Frederick Gilbert, *Power Speaking* (Redwood City, Calif.: Frederick Gilbert Associates, 1994), 195–196.

22. Michael Mandel and Christopher Farrell, "The Immigrants," *Business Week,* 13 July 1992, 114–120, 122; "Less Yiddish, More Tagalog," *U.S. News & World Report,* 10 May 1993, 16.

23. Yitzhak Rabin, "The Signing of the Peace Treaty Between Israel and Jordan," *Vital Speeches of the Day,* 15 November 1994, 66–67.

24. Matthew Lipman, "Critical Thinking—What Can It Be?" *Educational Leadership,* September 1988, 38–43; Ernest T. Pascarella, "The Development of Critical Thinking: Does College Make a Difference?" *Journal of College Student Development,* January 1989, 19–26; Robert S. Feldman and Steven S. Schwartzberg, *Thinking Critically: A Psychology Student's Guide* (New York: McGraw-Hill, 1990), 13–31.

25. Nancy Kober, "What Critical Thinking Approach Is Best?" *The School Administrator,* January 1991, 14–17.

26. Rod Plotnik, *Introduction to Psychology,* 3d ed. (Pacific Grove, Calif.: Brooks/Cole Publishing, 1993), 298.

27. Glen Martin, "Tragic Trilogy," *Winning Orations of the Interstate Oratorical Association* (Mankato, Minn.: Interstate Oratorical Association, 1994), 74–77.

28. Ronald B. Adler and George Rodman, *Understanding Human Communication,* 5th ed. (Fort Worth, Texas: Harcourt Brace, 1994), 121.

29. "Clark: Enlivening History Through Veterans of World War II," *New York Times,* 10 December 1989, 67–68.

30. "Training 101: Abe Lincoln, Presentations, and Bunnies," *Training & Development,* January 1994, 17–19.

31. Filson, *Executive Speeches,* 25.

32. Kent E. Menzel and Lori J. Carrell, "The Relationship Between Preparation and Performance in Public Speaking," *Communication Education* 43, no. 1 (January 1994): 17–26.

33. "Speaking Tips from the Experts," *The Toastmaster,* December 1993, 22.

Chapter 2

1. Thomas Leech, *How to Prepare, Stage, and Deliver Winning Presentations,* new and updated edition (New York: Amacom, 1993), 21–22.

2. Heidi M. Rose, Andrew S. Rancer, and Kenneth C. Crannell, "The Impact of Basic Courses in Oral Interpretation and Public Speaking on Communication Apprehension," *Communication Reports* 6, no. 1 (Winter 1993): 54–60.

3. Larry W. Carlile, Ralph R. Behnke, and James T. Kitchens, "A Psychological Pattern of Anxiety in Public Speaking," *Communication Quarterly* 25, no. 4 (Fall 1977): 44–46.

4. David Sharp, "Send in the Crowds," *Health,* April 1992, 66–70.

5. Ralph R. Behnke, Chris R. Sawyer, and Paul E. King, "The Communication of Public Speaking Anxiety," *Communication Anxiety* 36 (April 1987): 138–141.

6. J. M. May, *Trials of Character: The Eloquence of Ciceronian Ethos* (Chapel Hill: University of North Carolina Press, 1988), 42–43.

7. Arden K. Watson, "Helping Developmental Students Overcome Communication Apprehension," *Journal of Developmental Education* 14, no. 1 (1990): 10–17; J. C. McCroskey, "Oral Communication Apprehension: A Reconceptualization," in M. Burgoon (ed.), *Communication Yearbook* 6 (1982): 136–170.

8. Robert Brody, "Podium Power," *Executive Female,* July–August 1989, 22–24.

9. John A. Daly, Anita L. Vangelisti, Heather L. Neel, and P. Daniel Cavanaugh, "Pre-Performance Concerns Associated with Public Speaking," *Communication Quarterly* 37, no. 1 (Winter 1989): 39–53.

...

10. Joe Ayres, "Coping with Speech Anxiety: The Power of Positive Thinking," *Communication Education* 37 (October 1988): 289–296.

11. Watson, "Helping Developmental Students Overcome Communication Apprehension," 10–17.

12. Tim Hopf and Joe Ayres, "Coping with Public Speaking Anxiety: An Examination of Various Combinations of Systematic Desensitization, Skills Training, and Visualization," *Journal of Applied Communication Research,* May 1992, 183–198.

13. Sharp, "Send in the Crowds," 67–70.

14. Charles Osgood, "Speaking Easy," *Reader's Digest,* January 1990, 145–146, 148.

15. Mary Rowland, "Shedding the Fear of Speaking," *New York Times,* 17 May 1992, 17.

16. Wanda Vassallo, *Speak with Confidence* (Cincinnati: Betterway Books, 1990), 21.

17. D. Stanley Eitzen, "Ethical Dilemmas in American Sport," in *Vital Speeches of the Day,* 1 January 1996, 182–185.

18. Andy Wood, "Superbugs: Scourge of the Post-Antibiotic Era," *Winning Orations of the Interstate Oratorical Association* (Mankato, Minn.: Interstate Oratorical Association, 1994), 23–25.

19. Robert E. McAffee, "The Road Less Traveled," *Vital Speeches of the Day,* 15 August 1994, 652–655.

20. Nancy Letourneau, "Faulty Credit Reports," *Winning Orations of the Interstate Oratorical Association* (Mankato, Minn.: Interstate Oratorical Association, 1992), 43–46.

21. Robert D. Haas, "Ethics—A Global Business Challenge," *Vital Speeches of the Day,* 1 June 1994, 506–509.

22. Wood, "Superbugs," 23–25.

23. Robert A. Plane, "The Quest for Shared Values," *Vital Speeches of the Day,* 1 February 1995, 250–251.

24. Plane, "The Quest for Shared Values," 250–251.

25. Randall L. Tobias, "In Today Walks Tomorrow: Shaping the Future of Telecommunication," *Vital Speeches of the Day,* 15 February 1993, 273–276.

26. Donald McPartland, "Faceless Enemies," *Winning Orations of the Interstate Oratorical Association* (Mankato, Minn.: Interstate Oratorical Association, 1994), 58–61.

27. Heather Larson, "Stemming the Tide," *Winning Orations of the Interstate Oratorical Association* (Mankato, Minn.: Interstate Oratorical Association, 1994), 116–118.

28. William Safire, "Secrets of Great Speeches," *Current Books,* Summer 1993, 78–81.

29. Nelson Mandela, "Glory and Hope," *Vital Speeches of the Day,* 1 June 1994, 486.

30. Brody, "Podium Power," 22–24.

31. Kent E. Menzel and Lori J. Carrell, "The Relationship Between Preparation and Performance in Public Speaking," *Communication Education* 43 (January 1994): 17–26.

Chapter 3

1. Colman McCarthy, "How About A Little Civility, By George?" *Washington Post,* 13 May 1995, sec. a, 15.

2. Frank E. X. Dance and Carol C. Zak-Dance, *Speaking Your Mind: Private Thinking and Public Speaking* (Dubuque, Iowa: Kendall/Hunt, 1994), 30.

3. "Free Speech in the United States," *Academic American Encyclopedia,* accessed online, 28 January 1996.

4. "Free Speech in the United States," 28 January 1996.

5. "Free Speech in the United States," 28 January 1996.

6. "Free Speech in the United States," 28 January 1996.

7. Mark M. Miller, et al. "How Gender and Select Demographics Relate to Support for Expressive Rights," presented at the 75th Annual Meeting of the Association for Education in Journalism and Mass Communication, August, 1992, Montreal, Quebec, Canada.

8. Courtland L. Bovée and John V. Thill, *Business Communication Today,* 3d ed. (New York: McGraw-Hill, 1992), 222.

9. McCarthy, "How About a Little Civility, By George?"

10. Trudy Lieberman, "Plagiarize, Plagiarize, Plagiarize, Only Be Sure to Always Call It Research," *Columbia Journalism Review* 34, no. 2 (17 July 1995): 21.

11. Daphne A. Jameson, "The Ethics of Plagiarism: How Genre Affects Writers' Use of Source Materials," *Journal of the Association for Business Communication,* 56, no 2, (1993), 18–28.

12. R. P. Hart, R. Carlson, and W. Eadie, "Attitudes Toward Communication and the Assessment of Rhetorical Sensitivity," *Communication Monographs* 47 (1980): 1–22; Stephen W. Littlejohn and David M. Jabusch, "Communication Competence: Model and Application," *Journal of Applied Communication Research,* 10, no. 1 (Spring 1982): 31.

13. Sharon L. Bracci, "Shaping the Contours of a Postmodern Communication Ethic: A Roundtable Discussion," a panel presented at the 81st Annual Meeting of the Speech Communication Association, November, 1995, San Antonio, Texas.

14. Pamela Shockley-Zalabak, *Ethics in Public Speaking,* videotape of lecture in Communication 210, Relationship of the Speech and Thought Curriculum, Fall Semester 1990, University of Colorado, Colorado Springs.

15. Courtland L. Bovée, Michael J. Houston, and John V. Thill, *Marketing,* 2d ed. (New York: McGraw-Hill, 1995), 128.

16. Tom Pelton, "'Things Haven't Changed a Bit: Klan Rallies Stir Fights, Memories of Tragic Era," *Chicago Tribune,* 20 August 1995, 3.

17. Marvin Karlins and Herbert I. Abelson, *Persuasion,* 2d ed. (New York: Springer Publishing, 1970), 128.

18. Bovée and Thill, *Business Communication Today,* 444.

19. Richard J. Maturi, *Stock Picking* (New York: McGraw-Hill, 1993), 4.

20. Robert G. Hagstrom, *The Warren Buffett Way* (New York: Wiley, 1995), 36.

21. Interview conducted and translated by Josip Novakovich, "Split Personality," *Tennis,* December 1995, 51–54.

22. Karl R. Wallace, "An Ethical Basis of Communication," *The Speech Teacher,* January 1955, 1–9.

23. Shockley-Zalabak, *Ethics in Public Speaking;* Aristotle, *The Rhetoric,* translated by W. Rhys Roberts (New York: The Modern Library, 1954), 56–57.

24. Shockley-Zalabak, *Ethics in Public Speaking.*

25. Myles Martel, *Fire Away! Fielding Tough Questions with Finesse* (Burr Ridge, Ill.: Irwin Professional Publishing, 1994), 267.

26. Madelyn Burley-Allen, *Listening: The Forgotten Skill* (New York: Wiley, 1982), 31–32.

Chapter 4

1. Susan Faludi, "Speak for Yourself," *New York Times Magazine,* 26 January 1992, 10, 29.

2. Donald Walton, *Are You Communicating?* (New York: McGraw-Hill, 1989), 36.

3. L. Barker, R. Edwards, C. Gaines, K. Gladney, and F. Holley, "An Investigation of Proportional Time Spent in Various Communication Activities by College Students," *Journal of Applied Communication Research* 8 (1980): 101–109; Richard A. Hunsaker, "Critical Listening—A Neglected Skill," presentation to the 77th Annual Meeting of the Speech Communication Association, Atlanta, Georgia, 31 October to 3 November 1991.

4. Andrew D. Wolvin and Carolyn Gwynn Coakley, "A Survey of the Status of Listening Training in Some Fortune 500 Corporations," *Communication Education* 40 (April 1991): 152–164; Charles R. Day, Jr., "How Do You Rate as a Listener?" *Industry Week,* 28 April 1980, 30, 32, 35.

5. Carl R. Rogers and F. J. Roethlisberger, "Barriers and Gateways to Communication," *Harvard Business Review,* November–December 1991, 105–109.

6. Brenda Ueland, "Tell Me More," *Utne Reader,* November–December 1992, 104–109.

7. Ward, "Now Hear This," 20–22.

8. Rogers and Roethlisberger, "Barriers and Gateways to Communication," 105–109.

9. C. Glenn Pearce, "Learning How to Listen Empathically," *Supervisory Management,* September 1991, 11.

10. Andrew Wolvin and Carolyn Gwynn Coakley, *Listening,* 4th ed. (Dubuque, Iowa: Brown, 1992), 300.

11. Wolvin and Coakley, *Listening,* 380–381.

12. Kittie Watson and Larry Barker, "Seven Dangerous Assumptions Speakers Make About Listeners," *Communications Briefings,* June 1994, 8a–8b.

Chapter 5

1. Dorothy Leads, "People Shouldn't Wonder, 'What Was That About?" *National Underwriter,* 99, 14, April 1996, 12–13.

2. *Winning Orations 1994* (Mankato, Minn.: Interstate Oratorical Association, 1994).

3. Ronald B. Adler and George Rodman, *Understanding Human Communication,* 5th ed. (Ft. Worth, Texas: Harcourt Brace, 1994), 376.

4. Hanley Norins, *The Young & Rubicam Traveling Creative Workshop* (Englewood Cliffs, N.J.: Prentice-Hall, 1990), 47.

5. Wayne Weiten, *Psychology Applied to Modern Life,* 2d ed. (Belmont, Calif.: Wadsworth, 1986), 484.

6. Weiten, *Psychology Applied to Modern Life,* 176.

7. Based on Rebecca McDaniel, *Scared Speechless: Public Speaking Step by Step* (Thousand Oaks, Calif.: Sage Publications, 1994), 146.

8. Joe Holmes, "That's Incredible," *The Toastmaster,* August 1993, 8, 10.

9. "Central Intelligence Agency," Microsoft Encarta. Copyright © 1994 Microsoft Corporation. Copyright © 1994 Funk & Wagnall's Corporation.

10. Marvin R. Lamb, *Journal of Experimental Psychology Animal Behavior Processes,* 17, 1991, 45–54.

11. Roger E. Axtell, *Do's and Taboos of Public Speaking* (New York: Wiley, 1992), 50; Ralph G. Nichols and Leonard A. Stevens, *Are You Listening?* (New York: McGraw-Hill, 1957).

12. Ron Suskind and Joann S. Lublin, "Critics Are Succinct: Long Speeches Tend to Get Short Interest," *Wall Street Journal,* 26 January 1995, A1–A8.

13. Larry L. Barker and Deborah A. Barker, *Communication,* 6th ed. (Englewood Cliffs, N.J.: Prentice-Hall, 1993), 325.

14. Ed Wohlmuth, *The Overnight Guide to Public Speaking* (New York: Penguin, 1990), 39; McDaniel, *Scared Speechless: Public Speaking Step by Step,* 43.

15. Jaime Jose Serra Puche, "The North American Free Trade Agreement," *Vital Speeches of the Day,* 15 April 1993, 395–398.

16. Adapted from Molly A. Lovell, "Hotel Security: The Hidden Crisis," *Winning Orations 1994* (Mankato, Minn.: Interstate Oratorical Association, 1994), 18–20.

17. Adapted from Linda A. Long, "I'll Be Watching You," *Winning Orations 1994* (Mankato, Minn.: Interstate Oratorical Association), 97–99.

Chapter 6

1. Barbara Langham, "Speaking with Style," *Successful Meetings,* 7 June 1994, 84–86; Susan St. John, "Get Your Act Together," *Presentations,* 8 August 1995, 26–33.

2. Laurie Schloff and Marcia Yudkin, *Smart Speaking* (New York: Penguin Books, 1992), 101–102.

3. Ron Hoff, *I Can See You Naked* (Kansas City: Andrews and McMeel, 1992), 194–195.

4. Bob Boylan, *What's Your Point?* (New York: Warner Books, 1988), 21.

5. Frank E. X. Dance and Carol C. Zak-Dance, *Speaking Your Mind: Private Think and Public Speaking,* 2d ed. (Dubuque, Iowa: Kendall/Hunt, 1994), 106–107.

6. Margaret Ambry and Cheryl Russell, *The Official Guide to the American Marketplace* (Ithaca, N.Y.: New Strategist Publications, 1992), 433.

7. Ambry and Russell, *The Official Guide to the American Marketplace,* 436.

8. Ambry and Russell, *The Official Guide to the American Marketplace,* 439, 441.

9. William J. McGuire, "Attitudes and Attitude Change," in *The Handbook of Social Psychology,* 2d ed., edited by Gardner Lindzey and Elliot Aronson (New York: Random House, 1985), 287–288.

10. M. M. Ferree and B. B. Hess, *Analyzing Gender: A Handbook of Social Science Research* (Beverly Hills, Calif.: Sage Publications, 1987) 9–31.

11. Rod Plotnik, *Introduction to Psychology,* 3d ed. (Belmont, Calif.: Wadsworth, 1993), 388.

12. *Daily Policy Digest,* 28 June, 2002, 1.

13. Douglas Hurd, "Britain's Strengths and Influence in the World," *Vital Speeches of the Day,* 15 March 1995, 337–338.

14. Herbert L. Petri, *Motivation,* 3d ed. (Belmont, Calif.: Wadsworth, 1990), 326.

15. Bovée, Houston, and Thill, *Marketing,* 121.

16. Myron W. Lustig and Jolene Koester, *Intercultural Competence* (New York: HarperCollins, 1993), 41.

17. Debra A. Dovel, instructor (English as a second language), Everett Community College (Everett, Washington), personal communication, 14 April 1995.

18. Sandy Linver, *Speak and Get Results* (New York: Simon & Schuster, 1994), 209–212.

19. Ed Wohlmuth, *The Overnight Guide to Public Speaking* (New York: Penguin, 1993), 84–90.

20. Lloyd F. Bitzer, "The Rhetorical Situation," *Philosophy and Rhetoric,* 1, 1–14, 1968.

21. Jan Broenink, personal communication, 27 February 1995.

22. Wanda Vassallo, *Speaking with Confidence: A Guide for Public Speakers* (Cincinnati: Betterway Publications, 1990), 57.

23. Kittie Watson and Larry Barker, "Seven Dangerous Assumptions Speakers Make About Audiences," *Communication Briefings,* June 1994, 8a–8b.

24. Ambry and Russell, *The Official Guide to the American Marketplace,* 254.

25. Thomas P. Loughman, "The Role-Playing Journal," *Bulletin of the Association for Business Communication,* 57 (March 1994): 35–36.

Chapter 7

1. Don Colburn, "The Cutting Edge—Drunken Driving Dips, But Young Still Dying," *Washington Post,* 20 December 1994, sec. z, 5.

2. Frank E. X. Dance, "Researching the Speech," a lecture presented in the Speech and Thought Curriculum at the University of Denver, 1988.

3. Stella Vosniadou and Andrew Ortony, "The Influence of Analogy in Children's Acquisition of New Information," *Text: An Exploratory Study,* Technical Report No. 281 (Cambridge, Mass.: Bolt, Beranek and Newman, 1983).

4. Lani Arrendondo, *The McGraw-Hill 36-Hour Course: Business Presentations* (New York: McGraw-Hill, 1994), 118–119.

5. Jill Catherine Dineen, "The Fiasco of Financial Aid Fraud," *Winning Orations 1994* (Mankato, Minn.: Interstate Oratorical Association, 1994), 12–15.

6. Yitzhak Rabin, "Israel and Jordan: Peace Is Our Goal," *Vital Speeches,* 15 August 1994, 644–645.

7. Leanne O. Wolff, "Family Narrative: How Our Stories Shape Us," a paper presented at the 79th Annual Meeting of the Speech Communication Association, 1993, Miami Beach, Florida; Elayne Snyder, *Persuasive Business Speaking* (New York: Amacom, 1990), 61; William G. Kirkwood, "Parables as Metaphors and Examples," *Quarterly Journal of Speech* 71 (1985): 422–440.

8. Kenneth Wydro, *Think on Your Feet* (Englewood Cliffs, N.J.: Prentice-Hall, 1981), 110.

9. David E. Weber, "Applied Storytelling: Narrative Skills for Communicators," a short course presented at the 81st Annual Meeting of the Speech Communication Association, 1995, San Antonio, Texas.

10. Wydro, *Think on Your Feet,* 110.

11. Andy Wood, "The Dangers of Deceptive Drugs," *Winning Orations 1993* (Mankato, Minn.: Interstate Oratorical Association, 1993), 17–20.

12. Jerri Gillean, "The Unfinished War," *Winning Orations 1994* (Mankato, Minn.: Interstate Oratorical Association, 1994), 1–3.

13. Joan Detz, *How to Write and Give a Speech* (New York: St. Martin's, 1992), 26–27.

14. Arrendondo, *The McGraw-Hill 36-Hour Course: Business Presentations,* 20.

15. Detz, *How to Write and Give a Speech,* 24–25.

16. Margaret Ambry, *Consumer Power: How Americans Spend Their Money,* 418.

17. Amy Sjolander, "The Disintegration of the American Jury System," *Winning Orations 1994* (Mankato, Minn.: Interstate Oratorical Association, 1994), 138–140.

18. Rebecca White, "America's Youth in Crisis," *Winning Orations 1994* (Mankato, Minn.: Interstate Oratorical Association, 1994), 77–79.

19. Robert Rosenfeld, *The McGraw-Hill 36-Hour Business Statistics* (New York: McGraw-Hill, 1992), 111–112. Note that these error margins are based on a 95 percent confidence interval using the formula $n = 1/e^2$.

20. White, "America's Youth in Crisis," 77–79; U.S. Bureau of the Census, *Statistical Abstract of the United States: 1993* (Washington, D.C.: GPO, 1993), 16, 99.

21. Robert B. Rackleff, "Using Statistics Effectively," *Public Relations Journal,* September 1990, 31–32.

22. *Statistical Abstract of the United States: 1993,* 120.

23. *Statistical Abstract of the United States: 1993,* 454.

Chapter 8

1. Leon Fletcher, *How to Speak Like a Pro* (New York: Ballantine Books, 1983), 60.

2. Michael M. Klepper, *I'd Rather Die Than Give a Speech* (Burr Ridge, Ill.: Irwin, 1994), 99–100.

3. Sandy Whitely, ed., *The American Library Association Guide to Information Access* (New York: Random House, 1994), 4.

4. Whitely, *American Library Association Guide,* 21–68.

5. This section adapted from Whitely, *American Library Association Guide,* 99–114.

6. Whitely, *American Library Association Guide,* 107–109.

7 Whitely, *American Library Association Guide,* 111–113.

8. Ross and Kathryn Petras, *The 776 Stupidest Things Ever Said* (New York: Doubleday, 1993), 1.

9. Henry Ehrlich, *Writing Effective Speeches* (New York: Paragon House, 1992), 55–56.

10. Whitely, *American Library Association Guide,* 79–82.

11 Whitely, *American Library Association Guide,* 114–116.

12. Whitely, *American Library Association Guide,* 91.

13. Whitely, *American Library Association Guide,* 84.

14. Whitely, *American Library Association Guide,* 88–89.

15. University of Washington Home Page, online search, 6 April 1995.

16. Charles J. Stewart, "Teaching Interviewing for Career Preparation," Bloomington, Ind.: ERIC Clearinghouse on Reading and Communication Skills, 1991, ED 3334 627.

17. Shirley Yaskin, "Interviews: Are You Prepared?" *School Press Review,* 66, 1, (Summer–Fall 1990): 10–l6.

18. Steven Ross, "Accommodative Questions in Oral Proficiency Interview," 1992 *Language Testing,* 9, 2, 173–186; Felix T. Chu, "Interviewing in Educational Research: A Bibliographic Essay," ERIC Clearinghouse. 1993, ED 360 664.

19. Steve Stecklow, "Cheat Sheet: Colleges Inflate SATs and Graduation Rates in Popular Guidebooks," *Wall Street Journal,* 5 April 1995, Al, A6.

20. Joan C. Roderick, "Interviewing: Don't Underestimate Its Importance," *Business Education Forum,* 39, (1985): 7-8.

21. Terrence D. Wells, "Be Ready for the Unexpected," *School Press Review,* 66, 1, Summer–Fall, 1990,14–15.

22. Frankie Clemons, "Proceedings: International Technical Communication Conference," 1983, ERIC Clearinghouse, ED 239 272.

23. Peter Jones and John Polak, "Computer-Based Personal Interviewing: State-of-the-Art and Future Prospects," *Journal of the Market Research Society,* 35, 3, (July 1993): 221–233.

Chapter 9

1. Christopher Spicer and Ronald E. Bassett, "The Effect of Organization on Learning from an Informative Message," *The Southern Speech Communication Journal* 41 (Spring 1976): 290–299.

2. John O. Greene, "Speech Preparation Processes and Verbal Fluency," *Human Communication Research* 11, no. 1 (Fall 1984): 61–84.

3. Jennifer Travis, "The World Through a Child's Eyes," *Winning Orations of the Interstate Oratorical Association* (Mankato, Minn.: Interstate Oratorical Association, 1994), 103–105.

4. Leon Fletcher, *How to Speak Like a Pro* (New York: Ballantine Books, 1983), 62.

5. Sherwyn Morreale, Adelina Gomez, and Pamela Shockley-Zalabak, "Oral Communication Competency Assessment and Cultural Diversity," in S. G. Amin, P. B. Barr, and D. L. Moore, eds., *World Business Trends* (London: Proceedings of the 1994 International Conference of the Academy of Business Administration, 1994), 126–140.

6. Shelly Schwab, "Television in the Nineties: Revolution or Confusion?" *Vital Speeches of the Day*, 15 October 1994, 21–24.

7. Based on Sonya Dehn, "An Ounce of Prevention," *Winning Orations of the Interstate Oratorical Association* (Mankato, Minn.: Interstate Oratorical Association, 1994), 119–121.

8. Based on Amy Sjolander, "The Disintegration of the American Jury System," *Winning Orations of the Interstate Oratorical Association* (Mankato, Minn.: Interstate Oratorical Association, 1994), 138–141.

9. Stephen R. Maloney, *Talk Your Way to the Top* (Englewood Cliffs, N.J.: Prentice-Hall, 1992), 58–59.

10. Based on Patricia Braus, "Will Boomers Give Generously?" *American Demographics,* July 1994, 48–52, 57; "LifeLines," *Modern Maturity,* November–December 1995, 72.

11. Winston Lord, "Changing Our Ways," *Winning Orations of the Interstate Oratorical Association* (Mankato, Minn.: Interstate Oratorical Association, 1994), 177–179.

12. Merie Witt, "Outpatient Surgery Centers," *Winning Orations of the Interstate Oratorical Association* (Mankato, Minn.: Interstate Oratorical Association, 1994), 130–133.

13. Jeffrey D. Greene, "The Poisoned Fields," *Winning Orations of the Interstate Oratorical Association* (Mankato, Minn.: Interstate Oratorical Association, 1994), 124–127.

14. Based on Alfred Mutua, "The Roles and Functions of Amnesty International," *Winning Orations of the Interstate Oratorical Association* (Mankato, Minn.: Interstate Oratorical Association, 1994), 136–137.

15. Based on Witt, "Outpatient Surgery Centers," 130–133.

16. Steve Sax, "Turning the Corner on Crime," *Vital Speeches of the Day*, 15 April 1995, 402–403.

17. Philip M. Burgess, "Making It in America's New Economy: Part Time or Leased Employees," *Vital Speeches of the Day*, 15 September 1994, 716–719.

18. Sue Weber, "Title Unknown," *Winning Orations of the Interstate Oratorical Association* (Mankato, Minn.: Interstate Oratorical Association, 1992), 66–69.

19. Ed Wohlmuth, *The Overnight Guide to Public Speaking* (New York: Signet, 1993), 60–61.

20. Carol J. Walker, "Zoos and Aquariums: Are They an Endangered Specie?" *Winning Orations of the Interstate Oratorical Association* (Mankato, Minn.: Interstate Oratorical Association, 1994), 9–12.

21. Walker, "Zoos and Aquariums: Are They Endangered?" 9–12.

22. Edward E. Crutchfield, Jr., "Managing in a Changing Environment," *Vital Speeches of the Day*, 1 August 1994, 625–628.

23. Deval L. Patrick, "Struggling for Civil Rights Now," *Vital Speeches of the Day*, 15 November 1994, 91–94.

24. Walker, "Zoos and Aquariums: Are They Endangered?" 9–12.

25. Walker, "Zoos and Aquariums: Are They Endangered?" 9–12.

Chapter 10

1. Bob Boylan, *What's Your Point?* (New York: Warner Books, 1988), 117.

2. L. S. Harms, "Listener Judgments of Status Cues in Speech," *Quarterly Journal of Speech* 47 (1961): 164–168.

3. Rebecca Witte, "America's Youth in Crisis," *Winning Orations of the Interstate Oratorical Association* (Mankato, Minn.: Interstate Oratorical Association, 1994), 77–79.

4. Witte, "America's Youth in Crisis," 77–79.

5. John F. Ferguson, "Vietnam Veterans," *Vital Speeches of the Day*, 1 February 1995, 242–243.

6. Murray Weidenbaum, "A New Look at Health Care Reform," *Vital Speeches of the Day*, 1 April 1995, 381–384.

7. Merie Witt, "Outpatient Surgery Centers," *Winning Orations of the Interstate Oratorical Association* (Mankato, Minn.: Interstate Oratorical Association, 1994), 130–133.

8. Heather Larson, "Stemming the Tide," *Winning Orations of the Interstate Oratorical Association* (Mankato, Minn.: Interstate Oratorical Association, 1994), 116–118.

9. Dorothy Sarnoff, *Speech Can Change Your Life* (Garden City, N.Y.: Doubleday, 1970), 180.

10. Heidi L. Wadeson, "Huffing: The Drugs of Choice?" *Winning Orations of the Interstate Oratorical Association* (Mankato, Minn.: Interstate Oratorical Association, 1994), 91–94.

11. Gretchen Richter, "Health Care Combat Zones," *Winning Orations of the Interstate Oratorical Association* (Mankato, Minn.: Interstate Oratorical Association, 1994), 34–37.

12. John J. McGrath, "Sell Your CEO! Winning the Corporate-Image Battle in the '90s," *Vital Speeches of the*

Day, 1 May 1995, 444–447.

13. Jenean Johnson, "Post-Antibiotic Era: Is This Our Future?" *Winning Orations of the Interstate Oratorical Association* (Mankato, Minn.: Interstate Oratorical Association, 1994), 144–147.

14. Chris Fleming, "Title Unknown," *Winning Orations of the Interstate Oratorical Association* (Mankato, Minn.: Interstate Oratorical Association, 1994), 50–52.

15. Marlene Dolitsky, "Aspects of the Unsaid in Humor," *International Journal of Humor Research* 5 (1992): 33–43.

16. Warren E. Leary, "Apollo Team Celebrates Anniversary with Clinton," *New York Times*, 21 July 1994, sec. c, 18.

17. Tom Ealey, "Let's Improve Our Speech Writing!" *The Toastmaster*, May 1994, 24–27; Stephen R. Maloney, *Talk Your Way to the Top* (Englewood Cliffs, N.J.: Prentice Hall, 1992), 122–123.

18. John E. Baird, Jr., "The Effects of Speech Summaries upon Audience Comprehension of Expository Speeches of Varying Quality and Complexity," *Central States Speech Journal* (Summer 1974): 119–127.

19. Witt, "Outpatient Surgery Centers," 130–133.

20. Ferguson, "Vietnam Veterans," 242–243.

21. Michael Tanner, "Patient Power," *Vital Speeches of the Day*, 1 October 1994, 752–756.

22. Andrea Owens, "Title Unknown," *Winning Orations of the Interstate Oratorical Association* (Mankato, Minn.: Interstate Oratorical Association, 1992), 26–28.

23. Philip M. Burgess, "Making It in America's New Economy," *Vital Speeches of the Day*, 15 September 1994, 716–719.

24. James B. Hayes, "The New American Revolution," *Vital Speeches of the Day*, 15 April 1995, 399–401.

25. Meryl Irwin, "Title Unknown," *Winning Orations of the Interstate Oratorical Association* (Mankato, Minn.: Interstate Oratorical Association, 1993), 56–59.

26. Richter, "Health Care Combat Zones," 34–37.

27. Norm Bertasavage, "Remember This," *Vital Speeches of the Day*, 1 July 1994, 555–556.

28. Maria Lucia R. Anton, "Sexual Assault Policy a Must," *Winning Orations of the Interstate Oratorical Association* (Mankato, Minn.: Interstate Oratorical Association, 1994), 26–28.

Chapter 11

1. Brent Filson, *Executive Speeches* (Williamstown, Mass.: Williamstown Publishing, 1991), 144.

2. Filson, *Executive Speeches,* 105.

3. Lilly Walters, *Secrets of Successful Speakers* (New York: McGraw-Hill, 1993), 121.

4. Adapted from Jimmy Rubio, "A Cure for AIDS," *Winning Orations of the Interstate Oratorical Association* (Mankato, Minn.: Interstate Oratorical Association, 1994), 55–58; Diane Bennett, "From the Lone Ranger to Power Rangers," *Vital Speeches of the Day*, 1 February 1995, 251–254; Laial Dahr, "Schools: Learning Zone or Battle Zone?" *Winning Orations of the Interstate Oratorical Association* (Mankato, Minn.: Interstate Oratorical Association, 1994), 61–64.

5. Thomas Leech, *How to Prepare, Stage, and Deliver Winning Presentations,* new and updated edition (New York: Amacom, 1993), 102.

6. Filson, *Executive Speeches,* 158.

7. Kent E. Menzel and Lori J. Carrell, "The Relationship Between Preparation and Performance in Public Speaking," *Communication Education*, January 1994, 17–26.

Chapter 12

1. C. Ray Penn, "A Choice of Words Is a Choice of Worlds," *Vital Speeches of the Day*, 1 December 1990, 116–117.

2. Frederick Gilbert, *Power Speaking* (Redwood City, Calif.: Frederick Gilbert Associates, 1994), 21–22.

3. Ryan Ries, "An Ominous Warning," *Winning Orations of the Interstate Oratorical Association* (Mankato, Minn.: Interstate Oratorical Association, 1992), 89–91.

4. Ben Smith, "Daytime Dilemma Dismays Drivers," *Winning Orations of the Interstate Oratorical Association* (Mankato, Minn.: Interstate Oratorical Association, 1991), 87–89.

5. Milton W. Horowitz and John B. Newman, "Spoken and Written Expression: An Experimental Analysis," *Journal of Abnormal and Social Psychology*, 68, no. 6 (1964): 640–647.

6. Judith Humphrey, "Writing Professional Speeches," *Vital Speeches of the Day*, 15 March 1988, 343–345.

7. Dorothy Sarnoff, *Speech Can Change Your Life* (Garden City, N.Y.: Doubleday, 1970), 182.

8. Roger E. Axtell, *Do's and Taboos of Public Speaking* (New York: John Wiley, 1992), 48–50.

9. Pamela Kay Epp, "Convenience Food Packaging," *Winning Orations of the Interstate Oratorical Association* (Mankato, Minn.: Interstate Oratorical Association, 1991), 66–69.

10. Quoted in Thomas Leech, *How to Prepare, Stage, and Deliver Winning Presentations,* new and updated edition (New York: Amacom, 1993), 237.

11. Passage and translation from Donald Walton, *Are You*

Communicating? (New York: McGraw-Hill, 1989), 174.

12. Michael Riley, "There's No Place Like Home," *Winning Orations of the Interstate Oratorical Association* (Mankato, Minn.: Interstate Oratorical Association, 1992), 74–77.

13. Darwin R. Peterson, "National Health Care in the United States," *Winning Orations of the Interstate Oratorical Association* (Mankato, Minn.: Interstate Oratorical Association, 1992), 1–3.

14. Patricia A. Cirucci, "S.P.F.S.: Stay Protected From the Sun," *Winning Orations of the Interstate Oratorical Association* (Mankato, Minn.: Interstate Oratorical Association, 1992), 111–113.

15. Lani Arrendondo, *The McGraw-Hill 36-Hour Course: Business Presentations* (New York: McGraw-Hill, 1993), 151–152.

16. Based on information from Joan Detz, *How to Write and Give a Speech* (New York: St. Martin's Press, 1992), 60–61.

17. Deborah Tannen, *Talking from 9 to 5* (New York: William Morrow, 1994), 116–117.

18. Courtland L. Bovée and John V. Thill, *Business Communication Today,* 4th ed. (New York: McGraw-Hill, 1995), 167–168.

19. Quoted in Walton, *Are You Communicating?* 187.

20. Adapted from Leech, *How to Prepare, Stage, and Deliver Winning Presentations,* 237; Detz, How to Write and Give a Speech, 62–64.

21. James C. Humes, *Standing Ovation* (New York: Harper & Row, 1988), 17–18.

22. J. Vernon Jensen, "British Voices on the Eve of the American Revolution: Trapped by the Family Metaphor," *Quarterly Journal of Speech* 63 (February 1977): 43–50.

23. Lonnie R. Bristow, "Protecting Youth from the Tobacco Industry," *Vital Speeches of the Day,* 15 March 1994, 333–336.

24. Morris K. Udall, "Stalking the Elusive Malaprop," *The Saturday Evening Post,* October 1988, 38, 40, 91–92.

25. Quoted in Elayne Snyder, *Persuasive Business Speaking* (New York: Amacom, 1990), 149.

26. Sheila W. Wellington, "Women Working: A Century of Change," *Vital Speeches of the Day,* 15 June 1995, 516–517.

27. Wellington, "Women Working," 516–517.

28. Raymond Chrétien, "The United States and a United Canada," *Vital Speeches of the Day,* 1 January 1996, 189–192.

29. "Tomorrow's Entrepreneurs: A Star Speaker Is Born," advertisement, Junior Achievement, 1994.

30. Kate Rounds, "Art Buchwald Talks About Humor,"

Meetings & Conventions, February 1988, 54–59.

31. Farah M. Walters, "Successfully Managing Diversity," *Vital Speeches of the Day,* 1 June 1995, 496–500.

32. Charles R. Gruner, "Advice to the Beginning Speaker on Using Humor—What the Research Tells Us," *Communication Education* 34 (April 1985): 142–147.

33. Mei-Jung Chang and Charles R. Gruner, "Audience Reaction to Self-Disparaging Humor," *The Southern Speech Communication Journal* 46 (Summer 1981): 419–426; "The Humor Advantage," *D & B Reports,* September–October 1988, 62–63.

34. Ron Zemke, "Humor in Training," *Training,* August 1991, 26–29.

35. Maloney, *Talk Your Way to the Top,* 132–133.

Chapter 13

1. Stephen R. Maloney, *Talk Your Way to the Top* (Englewood Cliffs, N.J.: Prentice Hall, 1992), 117.

2. Robert W. Pittman, "We're Talking the Wrong Language to 'TV Babies,'" *New York Times,* 24 January 1990, A23.

3. Virginia Johnson, "Picture-Perfect Presentations," *Training & Development Journal,* May 1989, 45–47.

4. Emil Bohn and David Jabusch, "The Effect of Four Methods of Instruction on the Use of Visual Aids," *Western Journal of Speech Communication* 46 (Summer 1982): 253–265.

5. Joe Ayres, "Using Visual Aids to Reduce Speech Anxiety," *Communication Research Reports* 8 (June 1991): 73–79.

6. "You're a Visual, Too," *Presentation Technologies,* November 1992, 12.

7. Mary S. Auvil and Kenneth W. Auvil, *Introduction to Business Graphics: Concepts and Applications* (Cincinnati: South-Western, 1992), 83.

8. Brent Filson, *Executive Speeches* (Williamstown, Mass.: Williamstown Publishing, 1991), 204–205.

9. Quoted in Darrell Huff, *How to Lie with Statistics* (New York: Norton, 1954), overleaf.

10. Filson, *Executive Speeches,* 156–157.

11. Karen Wormald, "Use Transparencies to Enhance Presentations," *The Office,* July 1991, 58–59.

12. Ripley Hotch, "Making the Best of Presentations," *Nation's Business,* August 1992, 37–38.

13. "How Not to Design Your Presentation Graphics," *Managing Office Technology,* November 1993, 39.

14. Michael Wayne, "Color's Ability to Excite and Influence," *The Office,* July 1990, 34.

15. James F. Carey, "Make Visual Aids Pull Their Weight," *Journal of Management Consulting,* 5, no. 3 (1989): 25–31; David Nadziejka, "Can They Read When You

Speak?" *Bulletin of the American Society for Information Science,* April–May 1987, 22–23; Edgar B. Wycoff, "You Just Can't Be Enough with a Visual Aid," *Manage* (Winter 1986): 3–5.

Chapter 14

1. Liz Doup, "Wendy's Big Cheese," *The News Times* (Danbury, Conn.), 5 March 1995, D1–D2.
2. Carley H. Dodd, *Dynamics of Intercultural Communication,* 3d ed. (Dubuque, Iowa: Brown, 1991), 199; Albert Mehrabian, *Silent Messages: Implicit Communication of Emotions and Attitudes,* 2d ed. (Belmont, Calif.: Wadsworth, 1981), 33.
3. Frank E. X. Dance and Carol C. Zak-Dance, *Speaking Your Mind: Private Thinking and Public Speaking* (Dubuque, Iowa: Kendall-Hunt Publishing, 1994), 158.
4. Kenneth Wydro, *Think on Your Feet* (Englewood Cliffs, N.J.: Prentice-Hall, 1981), 90–92.
5. Diane Arthur, "The Importance of Body Language," *HR Focus,* June 1995, 22–23.
6. Laurie Schloff and Marcia Yudkin, *Smart Speaking* (New York: Plume, 1992), 20.
7. Steven Grubaugh, "Public Speaking: Reducing Student Apprehension and Improving Oral Skills," *Clearing House,* February 1990, 255–258.
8. Mary-Ellen Drummond, *Fearless and Flawless Public Speaking: With Power, Polish, and Pizazz* (San Diego, Calif.: Pfeiffer, 1993), 32.
9. Jack Franchetti and George McCartney, "How to Wow 'Em When You Speak," *Changing Times,* August 1988, 29+.
10. Charles F. Diehl, Richard C. White, and Kenneth W. Burk, "Rate and Communication," *Speech Monographs* 26 (1959): 229–232.
11. Lawrence A. Hosman, "The Evaluative Consequences of Hedges, Hesitations, and Intensifiers: Powerful and Powerless Speech Styles," *Human Communication Research* 15, no. 3 (Spring 1989): 383–406; Lillian Glass, *Talk to Win* (New York: Perigee Books, 1987), 144.
12. Stephen C. Rafe, *How to Be Prepared to Think on Your Feet* (New York: HarperBusiness, 1990), 96–97.
13. Noah Adams, *Saint Croix Notes* (Boston: Houghton Mifflin, 1990), 62.
14. Courtland L. Bovée and John V. Thill, *Business Communication Today,* 4th ed. (New York: McGraw-Hill, 1995), 64.
15. Drummond, *Fearless and Flawless Public Speaking,* 38–40.
16. Myron W. Lustig and Jolene Koester, *Intercultural*

Competence (New York: HarperCollins College, 1993), 177.
17. Lustig and Koester, *Intercultural Competence,* 177–178.
18. Rochelle Shoretz, "A Von-Vay Ticket for Accents," *Business Week,* 20 September 1993, 110.
19. Brent Filson, *Executive Speeches* (Williamstown, Mass.: Williamstown Publishing, 1991), 238–239.
20. Ken Jurek, "Presenting . . . You," *Presentations,* September 1994, 10–14.
21. Filson, *Executive Speeches,* 197.
22. Steven A. Beebe, "Eye Contact: A Nonverbal Determinant of Speaker Credibility," *Speech Teacher* 23 (1974): 21–25.
23. Sprague and Stuart, *The Speaker's Handbook,* 342.
24. Roger E. Axtell, *Gestures: The Do's and Taboos of Body Language Around the World* (New York: Wiley, 1991), 10.
25. Philip N. Douglis, "Compare and Contrast Gestures to Express Meaning," *Communication World,* May 1995, 35.
26. Elayne Snyder, *Persuasive Business Speaking* (New York: Amacom, 1990), 121.
27. Paul Waldie, "The $100,000 Seminar: Now That's Motivation," *The Financial Post,* 20 March 1993, S14–S15.
28. Lilly Walters, *Secrets of Successful Speakers* (New York: McGraw-Hill, 1993), 119.
29. Quoted in Dorothy Sarnoff, *Speech Can Change Your Life* (New York: Dell, 1970), 211.
30. Filson, *Executive Speeches,* 176–177.
31. Peggy Noonan, "Behind Enemy Lines," *Newsweek,* 27 July 1992, 32–33.
32. Filson, *Executive Speeches,* 180.

Chapter 15

1. Microsoft Encarta, "Tippecanoe," Microsoft, 1995; Eric Foner and John A. Garraty, eds., *The Reader's Companion to American History* (Boston, Houghton Mifflin, 1991), 491.
2. Foner and Garraty, *The Reader's Companion to American History,* 1035–1036.
3. Microsoft Encarta, "Billie Holliday," Microsoft, 1995.
4. Bart Kosko, *Fuzzy Thinking* (New York: Hyperion, 1993), 187.
5. Katherine E. Rowan, "A New Pedagogy for Explanatory Public Speaking: Why Arrangement Should Not Substitute for Invention," *Communication Education,* 44, 2, July 1995, 236–250.
6. David J. Rachman, Michael H. Mescon, Courtland L. Bovée, and John V. Thill, *Business Today,* 7th ed. (New York: McGraw-Hill, 1993), 296–299.

7. Katharine Graham, "Aging," *Vital Speeches of the Day*, 1 August 1995, 639–640.

8. Rod Plotnik, *Introduction to Psychology*, 3rd ed. (Pacific Grove, Calif: Brooks/Cole, 1993), 238.

9. Carl S. Ledbetter, Jr., "Take a Test Drive on the Information Superhighway: Unmasking the Jargon," *Vital Speeches of the Day*, 1 July 1995, 565–569.

10. Ledbetter, "Take a Test Drive," 566.

Chapter 16

1. Frank E. X. Dance and Carol C. Zak-Dance, *Speaking Your Mind: Private Thinking and Public Speaking* (Dubuque, Iowa: Kendall/Hunt, 1994).

2. Alice H. Eagly and Shelly Chaiken, *The Psychology of Attitudes* (Orlando: Harcourt Brace Jovanovich, 1993), 148.

3. Carl Larson, *Persuasion: Theory and Research*. Videotape of Lecture in Communication 210, The Speech and Thought Curriculum, Fall Semester, 1990. University of Colorado, Colorado Springs.

4. Larson, *Persuasion: Theory and Research*.

5. Mike Allen, "Meta-Analysis Comparing the Research of One-Sided and Two-Sided Messages," *Western Journal of Speech Communication*, 55 (Fall 1991): 390–404; Jerold L. Hale, Paul A. Mongeau, and Randi M. Thomas, "Cognitive Processing of One- and Two-Sided Persuasive Messages," *Western Journal of Speech Communication*, 55 (Fall 1991): 380–389; Mike Allen, Jerold Hale, Paul Mongeau, Sandra Berkowitz-Stafford, Shane Stafford, William Shanahan, Philip Agee, Kelly Dillon, Robert Jackson, and Cynthia Ray, "Testing a Model of Message Sidedness: Three Replications," *Communication Monographs*, 57 (December 1990): 275–291.

6. Annette T. Rottenberg, *The Structure of Argument* (Boston: St. Martin's, 1994), 23.

7. Tina Bracewell, "Milk—Does It Do the Body Good?" *Winning Orations 1993* (Mankato, Minn.: Interstate Oratorical Association, 1993), 14–17.

8. Sara Hessenflow, "Transracial Adoption," *Winning Orations 1993* (Mankato, Minn.: Interstate Oratorical Association, 1993), 34–37.

9. Rottenberg, *The Structure of Argument*, 33.

10. John C. Reinard, "The Empircal Study of the Persuasive Effects of Evidence," *Human Communication Research*, 15, 1 (Fall 1988): 3–59.

11. Eagly and Chaiken, *The Psychology of Attitudes*, 1.

12. Adrian Furnham and Eddie Procter, "Memory for Information About Nuclear Power: A Test of the Selective Recall Hypothesis," *Current Psychology Research and Reviews* 8, no. 4 (Winter 1989–1990): 287–297.

13. Ralph Barney and Jay Black, "Ethics and Professional Persuasive Communications," *Public Relations Review:* 20, 3 (Fall 1994): 233–248.

14. Abraham H. Maslow, *Motivation and Personality* (New York: Harper & Row, 1970), 46–47.

15. Aimee Glover, "Security Guards: Thugs in Uniform?" *Winning Orations 1993* (Mankato, Minn.: Interstate Oratorical Association, 1993), 105–108.

16. Ernest Becker, *The Birth and Death of Meaning: A Perspective in Psychiatry and Anthropology* (New York: Free Press, 1962),

17. Laura Surella, "Pedal Power," *Winning Orations 1993* (Mankato, Minn.: Interstate Oratorical Association, 1993), 78–81.

18. John H. Bunzel, "The California Civil Rights Initiative," *Vital Speeches of the Day*, 15 June 1995, 530–534.

19. Lani Arrendondo, "Knock 'em Dead," *Success,* July–August 1994, 28.

20. William Wettler, "The Persuasive Power of Clearly Reasoned Conviction," *The Toastmaster,* January 1994, 19.

21. William Friend, "Winning Techniques of Great Persuaders," *Association Management,* February 1985, 82.

22. Orr, "Persuasion Without Pressure," 21.

23. William Perry, "Bosnia: We Must Stay the Course," *Vital Speeches of the Day*, 15 April 1995, 386.

24. Dawna King, "Restrictive Government Regulations in Higher Education," *Winning Orations 1994* (Mankato, Minn.: Interstate Oratorical Association, 1994), 100.

25. John C. Reinard, "The Empirical Study of the Persuasive Effects of Evidence: The Status After Fifty Years of Research," *Human Communication Research,* Fall 1988, 34.

26. King, "Restrictive Government Regulations in Higher Education," 102.

27. Mike Allen and James B. Stiff, "Testing Three Models for the Sleeper Effect," *Western Journal of Speech Communication,* 53 (1989): 411–426.

Chapter 17

1. Aristotle, *The Rhetoric,* translated by W. Rhys Roberts (New York: Modern Library, 1954), 27–55.

2. Donald D. Morley, "Subjective Message Constructs: A Theory of Persuasion," *Communication Monographs* 54, no. 2 (1987): 183–203.

3. Tamra B. Orr, "Persuasion Without Pressure," *The Toastmaster,* January 1994, 21.

4. Speech prepared by Sue Bye, June 1995.

5. Raymond S. Ross, *Understanding Persuasion,* 4th ed. (Englewood Cliffs, N.J.: Prentice-Hall, 1994), 180–181.

6. Ross, *Understanding Persuasion*, 181–182.

7. Adapted from Cindy Weiseneck, "False Memory Syndrome," *Winning Orations 1994* (Mankato, Minn.: Interstate Oratorical Association, 1994), 141.

8. Weiseneck, "False Memory Syndrome," 142.

9. Weiseneck, "False Memory Syndrome," 142–143.

10. Weiseneck, "False Memory Syndrome," 143.

11. Jeff Scott Cook, *The Elements of Speechwriting and Public Speaking* (New York: Collier Books, 1989), 203–204.

12. Frank K. Sonnenberg, "Presentations That Persuade" *The Journal of Business Strategy*, September–October 1988, 55.

13. Ervin S. Duggan, "Which Ramp onto the Information Superhighway?" *Vital Speeches of the Day*, 1 July 1995, 574–576.

14. John D. Ramage and John C. Bean, *Writing Arguments*, 3d ed. (Boston: Allyn & Bacon, 1995), 176–177.

15. William Perry, "Bosnia: We Must Stay the Course," *Vital Speeches of the Day*, 15 April 1995, 387–388.

16. Perry, "Bosnia: We Must Stay," 387–88.

17. Ingrid Abramovitch, "How to Persuade," *Success*, December 1994, 16.

18. Lani Arrendondo, "Knock 'em Dead: Command Attention with Persuasive Presentation Techniques," *Success*, July–August 1994, 28.

19. Andy Roob, "Vehicles to Belief: Aristotle's Enthymeme and George Campbell's Vivacity Compared," a paper presented at the Annual Meeting of the Central States Communication Association, April 1991, Chicago.

20. Kristie Probst, "Special Needs Adoptions," *Winning Orations 1993* (Mankato, Minn.: Interstate Oratorical Association, 1993), 59–62.

21. Katherine J. Mayberry and Robert E. Golden, *For Argument's Sake,* 2d ed. (New York: HarperCollins, 1996), 61.

22. Rodd A. Prins, "Dangerous Doctors," *Winning Orations 1993* (Mankato, Minn.: Interstate Oratorical Association, 1993), 31–34.

23. Libertarian Pary press release, November 2002.

24. Mayberry and Golden, *For Argument's Sake,* 64–67.

25. Stephen R. Maloney, *Talk Your Way to the Top* (Englewood Cliffs, N.J.: Prentice-Hall, 1992), 57.

26. Roob, "Vehicles to Belief: Aristotle's Enthymeme and George Campbell's Vivacity Compared."

27. David ElíHatton, "The Walk of Death," *Winning Orations 1993* (Mankato, Minn.: Interstate Oratorical Association, 1993), 76–78.

28. Richard E. Petty and John T. Cacioppo, *Attitudes and Persuasion: Classic and Contemporary Approaches,* (Dubuque, Iowa: Wm. C Brown, 1981): 255–267;

"Source Factors and the Elaboration Likelihood Model of Persuasion," *Advances in Consumer Research,* 11 (1984): 668–672.

Chapter 18

1. Lloyd F. Bitzer, "The Rhetorical Situation," *Philosophy and Rhetoric,* 1, 1–14.

2. Mike Jones, "Understanding Sales Time Frames," *American Agent & Broker,* October 1994, 16–17.

3. Ron Zemke and Susan Zemke, "Adult Learning: What Do We Know for Sure?" *Training,* July 1995, 31–40.

4. Anne R. Carey and Julie Stacey, "Commencement Cash" *USA Today,* 20–22 May l994, A1.

5. Charles Osgood, *Osgood on Speaking: How to Think on Your Feet Without Falling on Your Face* (New York: Morrow, 1988), 41.

6. James C. Humes, *Standing Ovation: How to Be an Effective Speaker and Communicator* (New York: Harper & Row, 1988), 173.

7. Jerry L. Tarver and Sara Means Geigel, "It Is with Great Pleasure That I Introduce . . . ," *IABC Communication World,* June 1988, 30.

8. Mary-Ellen Drummond, *Fearless and Flawless Public Speaking with Power, Polish, and Pizzazz* (San Diego, Calif.: Pfeiffer, 1993), 143.

9. Tarver and Geigel, "It Is with Great Pleasure," 30.

10. Lyndon Johnson, "Transcripts of Ceremonies in Florida Honoring Colonel Glenn," *New York Times,* 24 February 1962, 16.

11. Osgood, *Osgood on Speaking,* 39.

12. Elayne Snyder, *Persuasive Business Speaking* (New York: American Management Association, 1990), 195.

13. Elie Wiesel, "Nobel Peace Prize Acceptance Speech," *New York Times,* 11 December 1986, A1, A12.

14. Wanda Vassallo, *Speaking with Confidence: A Guide for Public Speakers* (Cincinnati: Betterway Books, 1990), 119.

15. Ed Wohlmuth, *The Overnight Guide to Public Speaking* (New York: Penguin, 1990), 91.

16. Art Buchwald, "Art Buchwald Talks About Humor," *Meetings & Conventions,* February 1988, 57.

17. Matthew Budman, "Manager's Tool Kit: Speech Then Cocktail Reception," *Across the Board,* June 1994, 62.

18. Queen Elizabeth, "50th Anniversary of D-Day," *Vital Speeches of the Day,* 1 July 1994, 547–548.

19. Don Aslett, *Is There a Speech Inside You?* (Cincinnati: Writer's Digest Books, 1989), 106.

20. Edward M. Kennedy, "Eulogy to Robert F. Kennedy," *New York Times,* 9 June 1968, 56.

21. Owen Edwards, "What Every Man Should Know: How to Make a Toast," *Esquire,* January 1984, 37.

22. Joan Detz, *How to Write and Give a Speech* (New York: St. Martin's Press, 1992), 87.

23. Al Gore, "Cynicism or Faith: The Future of a Democratic Society," *Vital Speeches of the Day*, 15 August 1994, 645–649.

24. Leon Fletcher, *How to Speak Like a Pro* (New York: Ballantine Books, 1983), 138.

25. Stephen C. Rafe, *How to Be Prepared to Think on Your Feet* (New York: Harper, 1990), 116; Matthew D. Davis and Scott G. Dickmeyer, "Critical Thinking Pedagogy: Opportunities to Take Limited Preparation Beyond the Realm of Competition," paper presented at the 79th Annual Meeting of the Speech Communication Association, November 1993, Miami.

Chapter 19

1. Steven A. Beebe and John T. Masterson, *Communicating in Small Groups: Principles and Practices*, 3d ed. (Glenview, Ill.: Scott Foresman/Little, Brown, 1990), 5.

2. Abran J. Salazar, et al., "In Search of True Causes: Examination of the Effect of Group Potential and Group Interaction on Decision Performance," *Human Communication Research*, 20, no. 4 (June 1994): 529–559.

3. Courtland L. Bovée, John V. Thill, Marian G. Wood, and George P. Dovel, *Management* (New York: McGraw-Hill, 1993), 503–505.

4. Carl E. Larson and Frank M. LaFasto, *Teamwork: What Must Go Right, What Can Go Wrong* (Thousand Oaks, Calif: Sage, 1989), 13–26.

5. B. Aubrey Fisher and Donald G. Ellis, *Small Group Decision Making: Communication and the Group Process*, 3d ed. (New York: McGraw Hill, 1990), 211–212.

6. Fisher and Ellis, *Small Group Decision Making*, 218.

7. Fisher and Ellis, *Small Group Decision Making*, 40, 218–220.

8. Margaret Kaeter, "Facilitators More Than Meeting Leaders," *Training*, July 1995, 60–64.

9. Katherine W. Hawkins, "Effects of Gender and Communication Content on Leadership Emergence in Small Task-Oriented Groups," paper presented at the 78th Annual meeting of the Speech Communication Association, 1992, Chicago.

10. Mike Robson, *Problem Solving in Groups*, 2d ed. (Brookfield, Vermont: Gower, 1993), 23.

11. Fisher and Ellis, *Small Group Decision Making*, 144.

12. Fisher and Ellis, *Small Group Decision Making*, 145.

13. Fisher and Ellis, *Small Group Decision Making*, 146.

14. Adapted in part from Steven A. Beebe, J. Kevin Barge, and Colleen McCormick, "The Competent Group Communicator: Assessing Essential Competencies of Small Group Problem Solving," presented at the Speech Communication Association, November 1995, San Antonio, Texas.

15. Richard Fiordo, "Parliamentary Lessons: Applying Parliamentary Principles to Small Group Communication," paper presented at the 77th Annual Meeting of the Speech Communication Association, November 1991, Atlanta.

16. George Milite, "Communicating One-on-One with Members" *Supervisory Management*, May 1992, 11.

17. Barbara Hetzer Wagner, "Executive File: Meetings," *Business Month*, March 1990, 27.

18. "Making Meetings Work" *Supervisory Management*, January 1995, 7.

19. George E. Tuttle, "Listening Strategies and Behavior for Participants in Small Group Processes: A Need-Based Prescription," paper presented at the 13th Annual Meeting of the International Listening Association, March 1991, Seattle.

20. Craig R. Scott, "Using Group Decision Support Systems in Teaching the Small Group Communication Course," paper presented at the 63rd Annual Meeting of the Western States Communication Association, February 1992, Boise, Idaho.

Literary Copyrights and Acknowledgments

Publications, Inc. For material adapted from Frank E. X. Dance, "What Do You Mean Presentational Speaking?" *Management Communication Quarterly*, 1 (1987): 260–271. Copyright © 1987 and adapted by permission of Sage Publications, Inc.

Martha Sanders. For reprint of "Learn to Listen With Your Heart: Farewell to Graduates." Reprinted by permission.

Paula Shockley-Zalabak. For material adapted from a lecture, "Ethics in Public Speaking." Copyright © 1990 and adapted by permission of author.

Sheila Wellington. For reprint of "Women Working: A Century of Change." Reprinted by permission.

Tom Willett. For reprint of "It's as Simple as Color, Cut, and Paste." Reprinted by permission.

Dean Willich. For reprint of "Traditional Oratory: Thoroughbred of Persuasive Speaking." Reprinted by permission.

Winning Orations for the speech "Genetic Patents: The Deadly Potential of Research Exclusivity" by Elizabeth Storey, Eastern Michigan University. Permission granted by Winning Orations (Mankato, MN: Interstate Oratorical Association, 2002).

Source Notes

7: Adapted from Leon Fletcher, "A Remedy for Stage Fright," *The Toastmaster,* June 1994, 8–10; Greg Dahl, "Fear of Fear," *The Toastmaster,* June 1994, 10–11; "A Survival Guide to Public Speaking," *Training & Development Journal,* September 1990, 15–16, 18–25.

19: Adapted from Walter Shapiro, "Biden's Familiar Quotations," *Time,* 28 September 1987, 17; Michael T. O'Neill, "Plagiarism: (I) Writing Responsibly," *The ABCA Bulletin,* June 1980, 34–36; John L. Waltman, "Plagiarism: (II) Preventing It in Formal Research Reports," *The ABCA Bulletin,* June 1980, 37–38.

28: Adapted from Laurie Schloff and Marcia Yudkin, *Smart Speaking* (New York: Plume, 1992), 25–26.

29: Based on Laurie Schloff and Marcia Yudkin, *Smart Speaking* (New York: Plume, 1992), 25–26; Mary-Ellen Drummond, *Fearless and Flawless Public Speaking* (San Diego: Pfeiffer, 1993), 15–18; 30–31.

32: Based on Robert Fearon, *Advertising That Works* (Chicago: Probus, 1991), 59; Roger von Oech, *A Whack on the Side of the Head* (New York: Warner Books, 1983), 24–25, 108–109.

54: Pamela Shockley-Zalabak, "Ethics in Public Speaking," videotape of lecture in Communication 210, Relationship of the Speech and Thought Curriculum, Fall Semester 1990, University of Colorado, Colorado Springs; Dag Hammarskjold, *Markings* (New York: Knopf, 1964), 112 (**Note:** this quote was modified to make it gender-neutral)

60: Frank O'Hare and Edward A. Kline, *The Modern Writer's Handbook* (New York: Macmillan, 1993), 469–473; Christine Kinealy, "How Politics Fed the Famine," *Natural History,* January 1996, 33–35.

62: Adapted from Pam Shockley-Zalabak, "Ethics in Public Speaking," videotape of lecture in Communication 210, Relationship of the Speech and Thought Curriculum, Fall Semester, 1990, University of Colorado, Colorado Springs.

74: Laurie Schloff and Marcia Yudkin, *Smart Speaking* (New York: Plume, 1991), 197, 232–234; Courtland L. Bovée and John V. Thill, *Business Communication Today,* 4th ed. (New York: McGraw-Hill, 1995), 67–71.

70: Adapted from F. I. Wolff, N. C. Marsnik, W. S. Tacey, and R. G. Nichols, *Perceptive Listening* (New York: Holt, Rinehart and Winston, 1983): 70–71.

77: Based on Frank K. Sonnenberg, "Barriers to Communication," *Journal of Business Strategy,* July–August 1990, 56–59; Brank McKinsey, "What Successful Speakers Can Teach Us About Communicating," *Public Relations Quarterly,* Fall 1990, 14–16; Cynthia Hamilton and Brian H. Kleiner, "Communication: Steps to Better Listening," *Personnel Journal,* February 1987, 20–21.

80: Based on Lyman K. Steil, Larry L. Barker, and Kittie W. Watson, *Effective Listening: Key to Your Success* (Reading, Mass.: Addison-Wesley, 1983), 114–115; James J. Floyd, *Listening: A Practical Approach* (Glenview, Ill.: Scott, Foresman, 1985), 85–87; Robert L. Montgomery, *Listening Made Easy* (New York: Amacom, 1981), 23; Florence I. Wolff and Nadine C. Marsnik, *Perceptive Listening,* 2d ed. (Fort Worth: Harcourt Brace Jovanovich, 1992), 132.

89: The central idea in the example is based on Molly A. Lovell, "Hotel Security: The Hidden Crisis," *Winning Orations 1994* (Mankato, Minn.: Interstate Oratorical Association, 1994), 18–20.

92: Ray Harlan, *The Confident Speaker* (Bradenton, Fla.: McGuinn & McGuire, 1993), 36–39; J. D. Novak, D. B. Gowin, and G. T. Johansen, "The Use of Concept Mapping and Knowledge Vee Mapping with Junior-High School Science Students," *Science Education,* 67, no. 5 (1983): 625–645.

93: Adapted from Paulette Dale and James C. Wolf, *Speech Communication for International Students* (Englewood Cliffs, N.J.: Prentice-Hall, 1988), 11.

94: Leslie Wayne, "The Race to the Lectern," *New York Times,* 8 September 1995, C1; Dottie Waters and Lilly Waters, *Speak and Grow Rich* (Englewood Cliffs, N.J.: Prentice-Hall, 1989), 25.

96: Based on Roger E. Axtell, *Do's and Taboos of Public Speaking* (New York: Wiley, 1992), 50; Ralph G. Nichols and Leonard A. Stevens, *Are You Listening?* (New York: McGraw-Hill, 1957).

100: Larry L. Barker and Deborah A. Barker, *Communication,* 6th ed. (Englewood Cliffs, N.J.: Prentice-Hall, 1993), 261; John Hasling, *The Audience, the Message, the Speaker* (New York: McGraw-Hill, 1993), 206.

113: Dorothy Leeds, "Tuning in to Your Audience," *Executive Female,* July/August 1989, 32; Lilly Waters, *Secrets of Succesful Speakers* (New York: McGraw-Hill, 1993). 29.

113: Lilly Walters, *Secrets of Successful Speakers* (New York: McGraw-Hill, 1993), 29.

115: Lorraine Glennon, ed., *Our Times* (Atlanta: Turner Publishing, 1995), 206, 337, 405, 569, 572, 592, 650; U.S. Bureau of the Census, *Statistical Abstract of the United States: 1993* (Washington, D.C.: GPO, 1993), 359.

116: Adapted in part from Marjorie Brody and Shawn Kent, *Power Presentations* (New York: Wiley, 1993), 78.

118: Adapted from A. H. Maslow, "A Theory of Human Motivation," in *Readings in Managerial Psychology,* 3d ed., edited by Harold J. Leavitt, Louis R. Pondy, and David M. Boje (Chicago: University of Chicago Press, 1980), 522.

119: Thomas Leech, *How to Prepare, Stage, and Deliver Winning Presentations* (New York: Amacom, 1993), 67.

120: Rebecca Piirto, *Beyond Mind Games: The Marketing Power of Psychographics* (New York: American Demographics Books, 1991), 127–128.

121: Robert T. Moran, "Tips on Making Speeches to International Audiences," *International Management,* April 1989, 59.

124: Adapted in part from James W. Robinson, *Better Speeches in Ten Simple Steps* (Rocklin, Calif.: Prima Publishing, 1989), 20.

137: Based in part on *Mayo Clinic Family Health Book* (CD-ROM version) (Eagan, Minn.: IVI Publishing, 1993).

145: Joan Detz, *How to Write and Give a Speech* (New York: St. Martin's, 1992), 26–27.

152: Statistics taken from U.S. Bureau of the Census, *Statistical Abstract of the United States: 1993* (Washington, D.C.: GPO, 1993), 405.

153: Based in part on Robert B. Rackleff, "Using Statistics Effectively," *Public Relations Journal,* September 1990, 31–32.

164: Lani Arredondo, *The McGraw-Hill 36-Hour Course: Business Presentations* (New York: McGraw-Hill, 1994), 136.

164: "Fatal Pursuit," *People,* 15 July 1996, 154; Orville Schell, "In the Land of the Dear Leader: North Korea's Grand Illusion Begins to Unravel," *Harper's,* July 1996, 58; Puangpen Intaraprawat and Margaret S. Steffensen, "The Use of Metadiscourse in Good and Poor ESL Essays," *Journal of Second Language Writing,* 4, no. 3 (1995): 253–272.

167: Donald Walton, *Are You Communicating?* (New York: McGraw-Hill, 1989), 191.

170: Ron Hoff, *I Can See You Naked* (Kansas City: Andrews and McMeel, 1992), 70.

184: Lani Arredondo, *The McGraw-Hill 36-Hour Course: Business Presentations* (New York: McGraw-Hill, 1994, 136–138.

191: Adapted from Leon Fletcher, *How to Speak Like a Pro* (New York: Ballantine Books, 1983), 62–63.

192: Based on Myron W. Lustig and Jolene Koester, *Intercultural Competence: Interpersonal Communication Across Cultures* (New York: HarperCollins, 1993), 217–221.

201: Based on William J. Madia, "Making the Right Choices," *Vital Speeches of the Day,* 15 May 1993, 459–463.

205: Adapted from Rebecca McDaniel, *Scared Speechless: Public Speaking Step by Step* (Thousand Oaks, Calif.: Sage Publications, 1994), 86–87.

211: Based on Rebecca McDaniel, *Scared Speechless: Public Speaking Step by Step* (Thousand Oaks, Calif.: Sage Publications, 1994), 99–102; Dorothy Sarnoff, *Speech Can Change Your Life* (Garden City, N.Y.: Doubleday, 1970), 203.

215: James W. Robinson, *Better Speeches in Ten Simple Steps* (Rocklin, Calif.: Prima Publishing and Communications, 1989), 117.

217: Based on John Kinde, "Using Spontaneous Humor," *The Toastmaster,* February 1994, 14–15; Brent Filson, *Executive Speeches* (Williamstown, Mass.: Williamstown Publishing, 1991), 138–141.

221: Based on Ron Suskind and Joann S. Lublin, "Critics Are Succinct: Long Speeches Tend to Get Short Interest," *Wall*

Street Journal, 26 January 1995, A1, A8; Sylvia Simmons, *How to Be the Life of the Podium* (New York: Amacom, 1991), 220–221; Bob Boylan, *What's Your Point?* (New York: Warner Books, 1988), 119.

240: Lilly Walters, *Secrets of Successful Speakers* (New York: McGraw-Hill, 1993), 122–123.

246: Based on Niki Flacks and Robert W. Rasberry, *Power Talk* (New York: Free Press, 1982), 124; "Oceans and Seas," *The 1994 Information Please Almanac* (Boston: Houghton Mifflin, 1993), 485.

255: Adapted from Joan Detz, *How to Write and Give a Speech* (New York: St. Martin's Press, 1992), 54–55; Dorothy Sarnoff, *Speech Can Change Your Life* (Garden City, N.Y.: Doubleday, 1970), 67.

258: Based on information from Terry Eastland, "Speech! Speech!" *The Washingtonian,* November 1988, 117–120, 122, 124–126, 128; Hugh Sidey, "Of Poets and Word Processors," *Time,* 2 May 1988; John A. Byrne, "Nobody Ever Throws Fruit at the Speechwriter," *Business Week,* 12 October 1987, 112–113, 116.

259: Based on information from William M. O'Barr, *Linguistic Evidence: Language, Power, and Strategy in the Courtroom* (San Diego: Academic Press, 1982), 61–75; John W. Wright, III, and Lawrence A. Hosman, "Language Style and Sex Bias in the Courtroom: The Effects of Male and Female Use of Hedges and Intensifiers on Impression Information," *Southern Speech Communication Journal* 48 (Winter, 1983): 137–152; Bonnie Erickson, E. Allan Lind, Bruce C. Johnson, and William M. O'Barr, "Speech Style and Impression Formation in a Court Setting: The Effects of 'Powerful' and 'Powerless' Speech," *Journal of Experimental Social Psychology* 14 (1978): 266–279.

262: Based on information from Myron W. Lustig and Jolene Koester, *Intercultural Competence* (New York: HarperCollins, 1993), 216–217; Roger E. Axtell, *Do's and Taboos of Public Speaking* (New York: Wiley, 1992), 160.

275: Virginia Johnson, "Picture-Perfect Presentations," *Training & Development,* May 1989, 45.

283: Based on information from Courtland L. Bovée and John V. Thill, *Business Communication Today,* 7th ed. (Upper Saddle River, NJ: Prentis-Hall, 2003).

288: Based on information from A. K. Dewdney, *200% of Nothing* (New York: Wiley, 1993), 17–21; Mary S. Auvil and Kenneth W. Auvil, *Introduction to Business Graphics: Concepts and Applications* (Cincinnati: South-Western, 1992), 40, 192–193; Darrell Huff, *How to Lie with Statistics* (New York: Norton, 1954), 60–64.

298: Marjorie Brody and Shawn Kent, *Power Presentations: How to Connect with Your Audience and Sell Your Ideas* (New York: Wiley, 1993), 29.

299: Speech excerpt from "The United Nations Today," Boutros Boutros-Ghali, *Vital Speeches of the Day,* 15 July 1995, 581–583.

301: Based on information from Frederick Gilbert, *PowerSpeaking* (Redwood City, Calif.: Frederick Gilbert Associates, 1994), 174; Elayne Snyder, *Persuasive Business Speaking* (New York: Amacom, 1990), 130–132.

302: Adapted from Jo Sprague and Douglas Stuart, *The Speaker's Handbook,* 3d ed. (Fort Worth: Harcourt Brace Jovanovich, 1992), 334–335.

306: Based on information from Myles Martel, *Fire Away! Fielding Tough Questions with Finesse* (Burr Ridge, Ill.: Irwin, 1994), 181–183; Roger E. Axtell, *Gestures: The Do's and Taboos of Body Language Around the World* (New York: Wiley, 1991), 62–63; Loretta A. Malandro, Larry L. Barker, and Deborah Ann Barker, *Nonverbal Communication,* 2d ed. (New York: McGraw-Hill, 1989), 308.

309: Based on information from Matthew Parris, "Is the Teleprompter Wrecking the Art of Public Speaking?" *The Times* (London), 6 October 1993, 16; Ty Ford, "Software Drive Teleprompters . . . Some Are More Equal than Others," *Audio Visual Communications,* April 1991, 17–19; Carolyn Dickson, "Lights . . . Camera . . . Action!" *Training & Development Journal,* October 1990, 48–52.

312: Based on information from Myles Martel, *Fire Away! Fielding Tough Questions with Finesse* (Burr Ridge, Ill.: Irwin, 1994), 115–117; Susan G. Thomas, "Dealing Successfully with Hecklers and Snipers," *Business Horizons,* September–October 1991, 64–67.

357: Sherron B. Kenton, "Speaker Credibility in Persuasive Business Communication," *Journal of Business Communication* 26, no. 2 (Spring 1989): 143–157.

386: Larry Beason, "Strategies for Establishing an Effective Persona: An Analysis of Appeals to Ethos in Business Speeches," *Journal of Business Communication* 28, no. 4 (Fall 1991): 326–346.

387: Lawrence L. Tracy, "Taming the Hostile Audience," *Training & Development Journal,* February 1990, 33–36.

398: William S. Howell and Ernest G. Bormann, *The Process of Presentational Speaking,* 2d ed. (New York: Harper & Row), 1987, 12–16.

399: Adapted in part from Marjorie Brody and Shawn Kent, *Power Presentations* (New York: Wiley, 1993), 116–124.

402: Adapted from Frank E. X. Dance, "What Do You Mean Presentational Speaking?" *Management Communication Quarterly*, 1, 1987, 260–271.

420: Hanley Norins, *The Young & Rubicam Traveling Creative Workshop* (Englewood Cliffs, N.J.: Prentice-Hall, 1990), 1–19.

431: Claudia H. Deutsch, "Round-Table Meetings with No Agenda, No Tables," *New York Times*, 5 June 1994, sec. f, 5; Minda Zetlin, "Open-Space Meetings Widen Corporate Horizons," *Management Review*, October 1994, 5.

Photo Credits

Chapter 11
232: Jonathan Nourok/PhotoEdit
241: John Elk/Stock, Boston

Chapter 12
253: AP/Wide World
254: Bob Daemmrich/Stock, Boston
258: Reuters NewMedia Inc./Corbis
259: Robert Burroughs and courtesy the Old Globe Theatre and Katherine McGrath
263: Tom Craig/FPG
264: Tate Gallery/Art Resource, New York
265: UPI/Corbis-Bettmann
267: AP/Wide World
269: John Harrington/Black Star

Chapter 13
274 top: Myrleen Ferguson/PhotoEdit
274 bottom: Martin Rogers/FPG
278: Jonathan Nourok/PhotoEdit
279: Reprinted by permission of Reed International Books, Ltd. and the Penguin Group
285: Larry Lawfer/Picture Cube
286: Phil Bard/Sygma

Chapter 14
297: Courtesy Wendy's International
301: Tony Freeman/PhotoEdit
303: Dan Bosler/Tony Stone
305 top left: Ron Chapple/FPG
305 top middle: Robert Brenner/PhotoEdit
305 top right: Pedro Coll/Stock Market
305 bottom left: R. Lord/Image Works
305 bottom middle: Arthur Tilley/FPG
305 bottom right: Penny Tweedie/Tony Stone
306: Spencer Grant/PhotoEdit
307: AP/Wide World
309: Porter Gifford/Gamma Liaison
310: Loren Santow/Tony Stone
312: Rob Crandall/Stock, Boston

Chapter 15
319: Johnny Stockshooter/International Stock
325: Tim Jewett/Zuma Press
327: Handmade Graphics
330: Handmade Graphics
334: Bob Daemmrich/Tony Stone
339: Corbis-Bettmann

Chapter 16
345: Bob Daemmrich/Stock, Boston
352: Bob Daemmrich/Image Works
357: Bob Daemmrich/Image Works
359: A. Ramey/Stock, Boston
363: Eric Millette/Picture Cube

Chapter 17
371: David Shopper/Stock, Boston
376: Michelle Bridwell/PhotoEdit
386: Ricke Browne/Stock, Boston
387: Spencer Grant/PhotoEdit
391: Dan Lecca/FPG

Chapter 18
407: AP/Wide World
408: Spencer Grant/Picture Cube
410: David Young-Wolff/PhotoEdit

Chapter 19
417: Walter Hodges/Tony Stone
419 left: Bob Daemmrich/Stock, Boston
419 right: International Stock
420: Ed Lallo/Gamma Liaison
421 left: Michael Krasowitz/FPG
421 right: B. Mahoney/Image Works
428: Michael Krasowitz/FPG
430: Charles Gupton/Stock, Boston
431: Ron Chapple/FPG

Index